Resource Units in
HAWAIIAN CULTURE
REVISED EDITION

Donald D. Kilolani Mitchell, Ed.D.

Nancy Middlesworth
Book Design and Illustrations

KAMEHAMEHA SCHOOLS PRESS
Honolulu

KAMEHAMEHA SCHOOLS®

The paper used in this publication meeting the minimum
requirements of the American National Standard for Library
Sciences—Permanence of Paper for Printed Library Materials,
ANSI Z39.48 1992

Printed in the United States of America

ISBN: 978-0-87336-016-6

Library of Congress Catalog Number: 82-83353

19 18 17 16 15 14   (rev.) 4 5 6 7 8

CONTENTS
Papa Hō'ike

FOREWORD
'Ōlelo Ha'i Mua

In the Kamehameha 'ohana, there are few individuals as beloved and honored as Dr. Donald Kilolani Mitchell (1906–1989), author of *Resource Units in Hawaiian Culture.*

He joined the Kamehameha Schools faculty in 1930 and a year later founded Hui 'Ōiwi, a Hawaiian culture club for boys that engaged in and studied Hawaiian traditions. Such opportunities in schools were rare for Hawaiians at the time. He was a leader at Kamehameha Schools, establishing Hawaiian studies in the curriculum and encouraging its application in daily settings outside the classroom. During his tenure at Kamehameha he inspired generations of Hawaiians, conducted hundreds of workshops for teachers, lectured to thousands of individuals, and served as a guiding force in the Hawaiian studies community.

By the 1960s he began writing *Resource Units in Hawaiian Culture,* which brought together his research of over three decades. Since its first publication in 1969, it has become a staple reference for Hawaiian studies educators. It represents a classic ethnographic study of Hawaiian material and ideological culture reflective of the era in which Dr. Mitchell conducted his studies. His detailed narratives portray a rich landscape of Hawaiian culture organized in units focusing on various activities in traditional Hawaiian society. Mitchell's descriptions form an album of snapshots of Hawaiian society. Dr. Mitchell concludes each unit with a postscript that explains developments in the topic area up through the time of his writing. To encourage further study, he also offers resources that he found useful in his many years of research and teaching.

Dr. Mitchell's other publications include *Hawaiian Games* (1975), *Hawaiian Treasures* (1978), *Kū Kilakila* (1993) as well as numerous articles contributed to magazines, journals, and newspapers.

His scholarship and lifetime commitment to Hawaiian studies brought Dr. Mitchell many honors: The Ke Ali'i Pauahi Award in 1975 from the Kamehameha Schools, the Living Treasure of Hawai'i Award in 1980 from the Honpa Hongwanji Mission, the Outstanding Non-Hawaiian Award from the Association of Hawaiian Civic Clubs, and the Nā Maka Mahalo 'Ia Award in 1989 from Brigham Young University–Hawai'i.

Yet for all of his honors and academic contributions, Dr. Mitchell is still better remembered for his warm and passionate embracing of Hawai'i, Hawaiians, and Hawaiian culture. His dedication to keeping Hawaiian traditions alive and sharing them with others has paved the way for many to follow in making Hawaiian culture a living part of our world. In this way, Dr. Mitchell will always be lovingly remembered as a true *kupuna* of our Kamehameha 'ohana.

■ **About the Illustrator/Designer**
Nancy Middlesworth was born in Wahiawā, O'ahu. She attended Texas Academy of Art in Houston for her graphics training, and studied fine arts in Mexico and Thailand.

Ms. Middlesworth has worked in the graphics field for many years. She began working for Kamehameha Schools in 1974 as a graphic artist, specializing in illustrating Hawaiiana. Presently she lives and works in Portland, Oregon and continues to draw for her own pleasure.

PREFACE
'Ōlelo Hoʻākaka Mua

Many of the praiseworthy cultural accomplishments of the Hawaiian people are examined and discussed in these units. Described here are the unusual as well as the everyday features of this remarkable civilization that flourished with vigor and efficiency in the days before the life-style was changed by the introduction of foreign ways.

Centuries ago seafaring adventurers from the Marquesas and Society Islands brought with them a functioning Polynesian culture when they settled in Hawaiʻi. The voyages to and from these southern islands ceased, perhaps some 700 years ago.

During the five centuries of isolation from all outside contact, the Hawaiian people, by their ingenuity and resourcefulness, improved nearly every phase of their culture. They developed useful materials not known to their ancestors. In addition, the people adapted and upgraded many of the time-tested articles and ideas which they had brought with them from their former homeland.

When we review these creative attainments in the field of early Hawaiian arts and crafts we learn with great pleasure that the artisans and craftsmen, when compared to those of other Pacific cultures, excelled in many laudable ways.

A study of these accomplishments, which are explained in detail in the units, shows that the following are "peaks" which the Hawaiian people attained in their culture:

■ Canoes which were the most functional, streamlined, expertly hewn and assembled.

■ Feather work, the greatest number of brilliant, artistically designed and intricately fashioned symbols of royalty.

■ Wooden bowls, considered the most beautiful for their simple, uncluttered designs and expert workmanship.

■ Gourd bowls and bottles. Gourds were grown in greater numbers and of a greater variety of shapes and sizes. Some were artistically decorated.

■ Twined baskets, in a variety of sizes, shapes and designs. Plaited from smooth vine rootlets with skill and good taste.

■ Sleeping mats, plaited in large numbers from small, sturdy fibers in intricate designs.

■ Bark cloth superior to all others in fineness of texture, variety of designs and colors and with the greatest selection of tools employed.

■ Musical instruments of considerable variety and tone quality, half of which were invented in Hawaiʻi.

■ Chants of many types, the unwritten literature of great poetic quality.

■ Dances honoring the gods, the nobility and nature. They also provided lively entertainment. The *hula* attained a high degree of artistic quality and perfection.

■ Agriculture flourished under the resourcefulness and diligence of the planters who served as engineers and as skilled plant breeders.

■ Ingenious fishermen used expertly made hooks, lines and nets. Here were the only shoreline fishponds in the Pacific.

■ A hundred sports and pastimes provided vigorous competition for the energetic and quiet relaxation for others. Many games were locally conceived.

■ The people practiced a religion of respect for nature and their ancestors which permeated and gave meaning to all human activities. When it was abolished by royal decree the entire social structure crumbled and the craftsmen ceased their most creative works.

In 1931 the late Dr. E.S.C. Handy, Bishop Museum ethnologist, wrote the following for a booklet entitled, "Cultural Revolution in Hawaii." His highly respected opinions are included here since the out-of-print booklet is rarely seen today:

If a culture may be judged by its fruits, it is evident that on the whole, for the native people in the Hawaiian environment, the old Hawaiian civilization had much to its credit. An inferior and ill adapted civilization does not produce superior physical and cultural fruits. The fruits of the old Hawaiian system appear on the whole to have been good, if we may judge by the physical perfection and health of the race; their genial, generous, wholesome and happy nature, which has survived all vicissitudes; the high development of agriculture by means of intensive irrigation, which made a relatively large population possible; a similarly intensive and skillful fishing industry with great development of artificial fish preserves where the nature of coasts and inlets made these practicable; technical perfection of crafts such as canoe-making and other woodwork, and feather imbrication which excited the admiration of early visitors and produced the capes today so highly prized in museum collections; and finally, the subtile and complex social and ceremonial life, poetry, dancing, lore and mythology whose intricacies ethnologists are today striving to draw out of the oblivion to which they were in the nineteenth century consigned. These and many other phases and details of the old Hawaiian life attest superior racial inheritance and cultural heritage, intelligently and naturally adapted to a unique and on the whole beneficent, although in many ways difficult and exacting environment.

Hawai'i's residents of all ethnic groups and our many visitors should find it interesting to learn about the creditable accomplishments of our early Hawaiian settlers. Those persons of Hawaiian ancestry should take special pride in learning more of the noteworthy achievements of their forebears.

Hawaiian culture is studied today, in most instances, through the medium of the English language. However, all of the objects, materials, processes and places have Hawaiian names. One understands the culture more intimately if he learns the derivation and the meaning of these Hawaiian words. Some authorities believe that it is necessary to understand the language in order to really comprehend the deeper meanings of Hawaiian culture.

■ Hawaiian words used in these Units

The authority for the spelling and diacritical marks of most of the Hawaiian words used here is the Pukui-Elbert *Hawaiian Dictionary,* 1971 edition. The few exceptions *(kahi* not *kāhi)* are based on changes appearing in the more recently published Pukui-Elbert-Mookini *The Pocket Hawaiian Dictionary,* 1975, and the manuscript, now at the University Press of Hawaii, for the revised edition of the Pukui-Elbert *Hawaiian Dictionary. Place Names of Hawaii* by Pukui-Elbert-Mookini is the authority for geographical names appearing in these Units.

The 'Ahahui 'Ōlelo Hawai'i, the association of Hawaiian language teachers, recommended a uniform spelling system in 1978. Among their suggestions, which are observed in these pages, is one to delete the dashes or hyphens that have been used to separate the syllables in proper names and common nouns. They urge the use of the *'okina* (glottal stop [']) and the *kahakō* (macron [¯]) in writing all words which should have these diacritical marks.

This writer has attempted, with considerable help from the language specialists, to place the diacritical marks where needed on all Hawaiian words (See Unit 4 for an explanation of these).

A number of Hawaiian words have been anglicized and appear in the English dictionaries. The plural of these words may be written with an "s," such as "two leis." An "s" is not used for other plurals but the reader will become accustomed to "two *kāhuna*" and "three *heiau."*

Lāhainā refers to the Maui town and district many years ago. Lahaina is the accepted spelling and pronunciation now. The spelling of the healing *heiau* on 'Aiea Heights is now Keaīwa.

The numerous quotations in this book from Capt. James Cook and his officers are printed with the spelling, capitalization and punctuation used by these writers of 1778 and 1779.

THE ACKNOWLEDGEMENTS
Nā ʻŌlelo Hoʻomaikaʻi

The author wishes to express a sincere *mahalo* to Mary Kawena Pukui, my Hawaiian culture teacher for many years. The results of her delightful sharing form a very special part of the units in this book.

Those generous people from local educational and governmental institutions who were both helpful and inspirational are Rhonda Teʻo Annesley, Dr. Richard Kekuni Blaisdell, Pat Edmondson, Dr. Kenneth P. Emory, Dr. Dorothy Hazama, Homer ʻAhuʻula Hayes, Violet Kuʻulei Ihara, Marion Kelly, Beatrice Krauss, Col. David M. Peters, Leilani Pyle, Wesley Sen, R.M. Lokomaikaʻiokalani Snakenberg, Puanani Van Dorp and Eleanor Williamson.

My co-workers and dear friends at The Kamehameha Schools, always willing to support me in my endeavors as they did in this volume, are Neil Kahoʻokele Hannahs, Gordon Keaweāheulu Piʻianaia, Lesley Agard, Nuʻulani Atkins, Marsha Bolson, Mandy Bowers, Lahapa Burke, Hoʻoulu Cambra, Kaiponohea Hale, Noelani Kamekona, Leimomi Nahinu, Sarah ʻIlialoha Quick, Māhela Rosehill, Sigrid Southworth, Ramsey Taum, Grady Wells, Audrey Wong and Joanne Yamasaki (graduate). A sincere *mahalo* to these talented helpers.

My very special thanks to Nancy Middlesworth for designing and illustrating this book. And to Ruth Thomas and Stella Hanohano Judd for typing the manuscript.

The maps, prepared by Manoa Mapworks for the Center for Pacific Islands Studies, University of Hawaiʻi, and by the Pacific Scientific Information Center, Bishop Museum, are used with their permission.

I wish to dedicate this volume to the memory of my late wife, Winifred, who contributed her special expertise in Hawaiian culture and English expression to the earlier editions and urged me to revise and expand them and publish this one.

D.D.K.M.

THE INTRODUCTION
Ka ʻŌlelo Mua

Captain James Cook Visited Hawaiʻi, 1778-79

A scholar specializing in Polynesian life wrote, "The traditional Hawaiian culture vanished before it could be properly recorded."

Captain Cook and his officers recorded for us the only glimpses that we have of Hawaiʻi before the culture was changed by influences from the outside world. A number of their written accounts are included in these units. These quotations reveal the style of late 18th century English writing by retaining the spelling, capitalization and punctuation as published in Cook's Journal and reprinted with comments by J.C. Beaglehole.

In order that we learn the names of these men and the circumstances under which they wrote, we are including a brief account of Cook's third and last voyage.

This expedition of over four years' duration began with the sailing of Cook's ship, the Resolution (462 tons with a complement of 112 men), from Plymouth, England, in July of 1776. Cook, commander of the expedition and the Resolution, had as 1st Lieut. John Gore and as 2nd Lieut. James King.

The second ship, the Discovery (298 tons, manned by a complement of 70), was under the command of Capt. Charles Clerke. John Webber was the artist and David Nelson the botanical collector. The principal surgeons were William Anderson, William Ellis, and David Samwell.

John Ledyard, an American and Sgt. of the Marines on the Resolution, published his own account of this voyage.

The expedition visited Capetown, Tasmania, New Zealand, Tonga, and the Society Islands.

Cook sailed north from the Society Islands toward the Arctic in an attempt to find a passage by sea from the Pacific to the Atlantic Ocean north of the American continent. He reached, by chance, the uncharted Hawaiian Islands. His is the first visit by Europeans to these islands that is recognized by present-day historians.

On January 18, 1778, members of Cook's party sighted Oʻahu, then Kauaʻi and Niʻihau. They found suitable anchorage at Waimea, on leeward Kauaʻi. Cook went ashore on three different days on Kauaʻi and once on Niʻihau. He and his officers, Anderson, Clerke, and King, while ashore observed the people and conversed with them. They secured artifacts as gifts and by barter. They took on board water and a variety of foods from these two islands. Their journals contain a great deal of interesting information about the area and the people as the result of this first, brief contact.

The expedition left Niʻihau February 2 for the Pacific Northwest, where the ships cruised along the coasts of lands now called Oregon, Canada, and Alaska. After an unsuccessful search for the Northwest Passage, they returned to Hawaiʻi for repairs to the sloops, and food and refreshment for the crews.

The island of Maui was sighted on November 26, but adverse winds and currents kept the ships from anchoring for seven weeks. During this time, they received visitors and provisions from canoes that came to them from Maui and Hawaiʻi.

On January 17, 1779, the ships anchored in Kealakekua Bay on the west coast of Hawaiʻi. Here the visitors established friendly relations with the people, accepted a vast amount of provisions as gifts and by barter, collected culture materials of great interest, and wrote at length in their journals about Hawaiian life.

After obtaining sufficient provisions and repairing the vessels, the ships departed on February 4, but returned on February 11 to repair a damaged mast on the Resolution. The reception by the people was not as friendly this time, since the visitors had depleted the food supplies in this area.

Marion Kelly, Bishop Museum Anthropologist, has totaled the figures from Cook's Journal on the food supplies furnished by the Hawaiians at Kealakekua Bay. Lt. James King wrote that the ship's crews consumed at least 16.8 tons of food. He added, "Besides this, the incredible waste which, in the midst of such plenty, was not to be guarded against, . . ."

Hogs, totaling 16.8 tons, were salted and placed in casks. Hawaiian salt of excellent quality was used. The unused casks were opened when the expedition returned to England a year and a half later and the pork was edible. This was an important experiment for the late 19th century of successfully preserving fresh meat by salting. The visitors were also provided many casks of fresh water and considerable fire wood.

Students of Hawaiian culture today are amazed at the ability of the people of the Kealakekua region to produce and part with such tremendous amounts of food. The people admitted suffering considerable hardship in doing so.

Capt. Cook was killed in an unfortunate encounter with the people on the morning of February 14. Friendly relations were restored after a time, the repaired mast put in place, and the expedition sailed from Kealakekua Bay on February 22 with Capt. Clerke in command.

The vessels skirted the islands of Maui, Lāna'i, and Moloka'i, then anchored off Waimea Bay, O'ahu, for water. More provisions were secured on Kaua'i and Ni'ihau before the ships sailed for Northwest America on March 15.

Again the search for the Northwest Passage was unsuccessful, although the members of the expedition made valuable scientific observations. After Capt. Clerke's death in August, Capt. Gore became commander of the expedition, and King was made captain of the Discovery.

The expedition left these waters on October 9, sailed along the coast of Japan, stopped at Macao and the Cape of Good Hope, and reached England on October 4, 1780, after a voyage of four years, two months, and 22 days.

UNIT 1:
Brief Study
of the Pacific

BRIEF STUDY OF THE PACIFIC

The magnitude of the scope of this unit can be shown by calling to mind these geographical facts about the Pacific:

■ It is the world's largest ocean, estimated at 63 to 70 million square miles.

■ It covers one-third of the world's surface and contains half of the world's water, totaling some 165 million cubic miles.

■ It contains deeper parts than any other ocean. The average depth is about 14,000 feet, around Hawai'i it is 18,000 feet, and a "deep" near Guam reaches 35,800 feet.

■ It has innumerable islands—at least 7,500 is the estimate of Mr. E. H. Bryan, Jr., of Bishop Museum. (See Fosberg, p. 38)

The climate in each area of the Pacific is influenced by the nature of the ocean currents and the prevailing winds. These have more effect than latitude upon the temperatures and other weather conditions of an island or coastline. As the elevation of the land rises, the temperature decreases. It usually drops about three to four degrees Fahrenheit for each 1,000 feet in altitude on the earth's surface.

The living conditions and the economy of the people are directly related to their climate.

■ The winds in the Pacific affect man and his environment. The northeast and southeast trade winds bring cooler air toward the regions near the equator. The westerly winds which blow across areas both north and south of the trades are caused by the rotation of the earth. Wet and dry monsoons blow according to the season in the western Pacific. Hurricanes may cause damage to shipping and to land areas in the western Pacific, as the winds can reach forces of 150 miles an hour. While these violent storms can pose a danger to Hawai'i, their strength is generally dissipated before they reach the islands.

The northeast trade winds, blowing as they do over the cool ocean waters, help give Hawai'i its delightful climate. They may blow for long periods of time, especially during the summer when they are most appreciated.

The disagreeable southwesterly winds are known as *kona* winds or storms. *Kona* in Hawaiian is leeward, in contrast to *ko'olau* which is windward. *Kona* winds, most often between October and April, blow onto the islands from the southwest and are warmer and more humid since warm air can carry more moisture.

When the winds are light a condition of land and sea breezes occur, especially on the larger islands. During the day the sun warms the land which causes the air to become heated and rise. This brings the sea breeze to replace it. At night the earth cools faster than the sea so the cool air moves out to sea to replace the rising warm air.

■ A map giving the ocean currents shows two clockwise currents in the North Pacific and two counterclockwise currents in the South Pacific. Other currents, though smaller or more restricted, greatly influence the regions which they touch. See a chart of the ocean currents in the Pacific in Freeman, p. 20 and Lindo, p. 111 (from Freeman).

■ The ocean surrounding the Hawaiian Islands has a great tempering effect upon the land temperatures. The ocean temperature ranges from 74 to

75 degrees F. in March and 79 to 80 degrees in September. Coasts on the windward side which are exposed to the tradewinds have the least variation in temperature between day and night. At Kāneʻohe, Oʻahu the temperature may vary 8 degrees; at Lihuʻe, Kauaʻi, 11.5 degrees and at Kahuku, Oʻahu 12 degrees.

On the leeward side and at elevations above 6,000 feet the daily range increases such as at ʻEwa, Oʻahu, 19 degrees; at Kāʻanapali, Maui, 20 degrees and at the summit of Haleakalā, 17 degrees.

Although the sun is highest at noon, the day's highest temperatures occur about two hours after noon. The lowest temperatures are near sunrise since the earth and the air have been cooling longest.

■ Earthquakes are frequent in the Pacific. Volcanic eruptions may be expected occasionally from certain of the 300 volcanoes which are more or less active. See Armstrong, pp. 36-37, for a discussion and photographs on volcanism.

■ Tsunami or tidal waves cause destruction from time to time. See Unit 2 on this subject for Hawaiʻi.

■ The daily rise and fall of the tides may be many feet on some of the shores of the continents bordering the Pacific, but usually ranges from one to two feet around most of the Hawaiian Islands.

■ Geographers have divided the main groups of islands within the Pacific into three areas:

1. **Polynesia,** the many islands. Examples: Hawaiʻi, Samoa, Tahiti, and the Marquesas.

2. **Micronesia,** the small islands. Examples: Marshalls, Carolines, and Marianas. These are a part of the Trust Territory of the United States, but their present political status is under discussion. The Gilbert Islands, once a British Crown Colony, became the commonwealth nation of Kiribati on July 12, 1979. The Phoenix, Line, and other small islands became part of Kiribati.

3. **Melanesia,** the islands of the blacks. Examples: Fiji, Solomons. The names of these island groups are not words native to the Pacific. They were taken from the Greek and applied to them by geographers.

■ The Pacific became known to the European world through:

1. Marco Polo who first saw it while in China in the late 1200s.

2. Balboa who saw the eastern shores from Panama in 1513.

3. Ferdinand Magellan, who commanded the first expedition to sail around the world, 1519-1521. Magellan was killed on the Philippine island of Mactan in 1521.

4. Captain James Cook who in three long voyages, 1768-1779, explored more of the Pacific than any other man.

5. George Vancouver who sailed with Cook, then commanded his own voyage of discovery 1790-1795.

6. See Buck, 1953, for many more explorers of the Pacific.

■ The Pacific islands may be classified geologically into four main types:

1. **Volcanic islands** which have been built up from the ocean floor by successive volcanic eruptions. Examples: Hawaiʻi, Tahiti, Samoa.

2. **Sea-level coral reefs** which form atolls or low sandy islets, are built on submerged volcanic islands. Some near Hawaiʻi are Palmyra, Jarvis, and Howland. Others are the Tuamotus, and many of the islands in the Marshall and Caroline Islands.

3. **Islands of elevated reef rock** are larger than the low islets. Examples are Makatea in the Tuamotus and Nauru Island. Parts of many other islands, including Oʻahu, contain some elevated reef rock.

4. **Continental islands** are the remnants or the mountain tops of an ancient continent that extended from Southeast Asia as far as Fiji. These are large islands with rich soil and some with valuable minerals and oil. Examples: Fiji, New Guinea, New Caledonia.

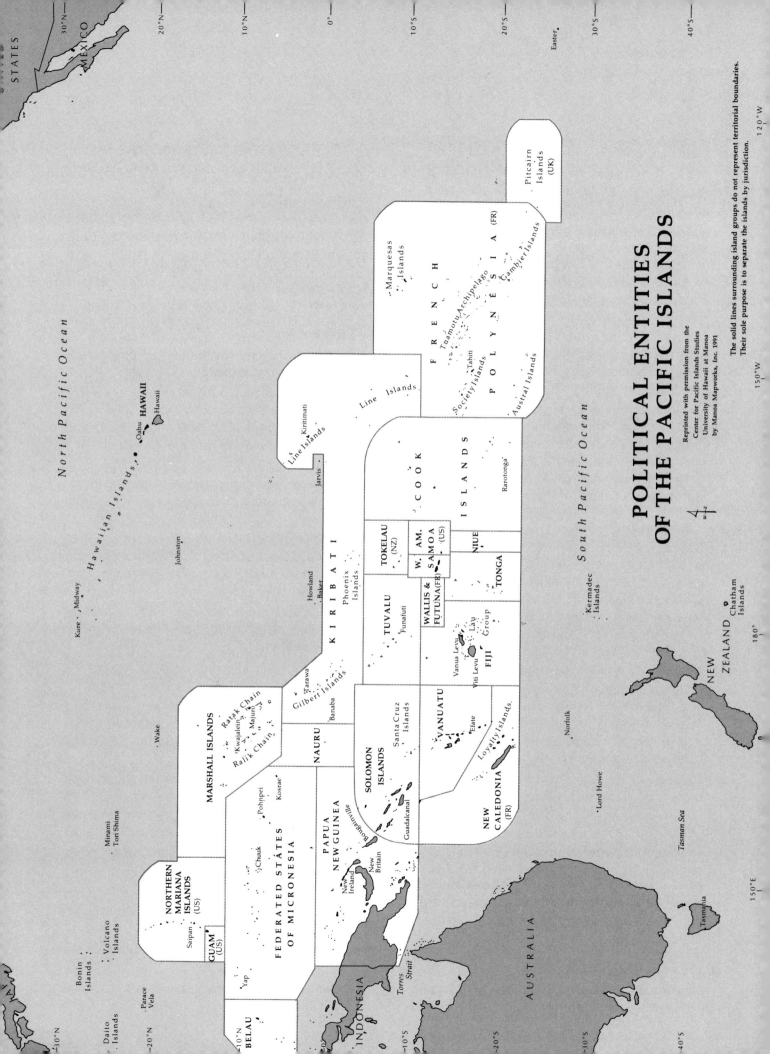

POLITICAL ENTITIES OF THE PACIFIC ISLANDS

Reprinted with permission from the
Center for Pacific Islands Studies
University of Hawaii at Manoa
by Manoa Mapworks, Inc. 1991

The solid lines surrounding island groups do not represent territorial boundaries. Their sole purpose is to separate the islands by jurisdiction.

North Pacific Ocean

South Pacific Ocean

UNITED STATES

MEXICO

30°N
20°N
10°N
0°
10°S
20°S
30°S
40°S

120°W
150°W
180°
150°E

Pitcairn Islands (UK)

Easter

FRENCH POLYNESIA (FR)

Marquesas Islands

Tuamotu Archipelago

Gambier Islands

Tahiti
Society Islands

Austral Islands

Line Islands

Kiritimati

Line Islands

Jarvis

HAWAII
Oahu
Hawaii
Hawaiian Islands

Johnston

Kure
Midway

COOK ISLANDS

Rarotonga

TOKELAU (NZ)

W. AM. SAMOA (US)

NIUE

Howland
Baker

Phoenix Islands

KIRIBATI

TUVALU
Funafuti

WALLIS & FUTUNA (FR)

TONGA

Kermadec Islands

Tarawa

Gilbert Islands

Banaba

NAURU

Lau Group

Vanua Levu

Viti Levu

FIJI

Santa Cruz Islands

VANUATU

Efate

New Caledonia (FR)

Loyalty Islands

Norfolk

Lord Howe

MARSHALL ISLANDS

Ratak Chain

Kwajalein
Majuro

Ralik Chain

Wake

Kosrae

Pohnpei

Chuuk

SOLOMON ISLANDS

Bougainville

Guadalcanal

NEW ZEALAND

Chatham Islands

Tasman Sea

Minami Tori Shima

Bonin Islands

Volcano Islands

Daito Islands

Parace Vela

NORTHERN MARIANA ISLANDS (US)

Saipan

GUAM (US)

Yap

FEDERATED STATES OF MICRONESIA

PAPUA NEW GUINEA

New Ireland

New Britain

BELAU

INDONESIA

Torres Strait

AUSTRALIA

Tasmania

30°N
20°N
10°N

■ Understanding and Appreciations

1. Review briefly the effects on man of the earth's rotation, revolution, and its inclination on its axis.

2. Check your ability at map reading and your knowledge of latitude and longitude by noting on a map of the Pacific the equator, the Tropics of Cancer and Capricorn, the International Date Line, and your home, if you live in the Pacific.

3. Contrast the navigation problems of the crew of a voyaging canoe with those who are navigating a jet plane. Discuss the concept of the "shrinking world."

4. Give reasons why most of the Pacific island groups became dependencies of larger world powers during the 19th century. Why did the people of Western Samoa want to become an independent nation? (They became independent of New Zealand on January 1, 1962.)

■ Student Activities

1. **Geology.** Prepare a report on the formation of an atoll. Read and tell something about Palmyra, the atoll closest to Hawai'i. Collect and display specimens of geologic interest such as types of lava, reef rock, and sandstone. Read and report on the "ring of fire," the name given to the belt of volcanoes that surround the Pacific.

2. **Geography.** Sketch a map of the Pacific. By dividing lines indicate Polynesia, Micronesia, and Melanesia. Select one or more of the following topics for added information to be placed on your map: Temperature, Rainfall, Ocean Currents, or Winds.

3. **Biology.** Read what is known and report on the coming of plants and animals to the islands of volcanic origin such as Hawai'i. (Zimmerman, Vol. 1)

4. **Politics and Population.** Select certain islands and learn their political status and the size of their population. List the Pacific islands or island groups under the American flag. Hawai'i is a state, but what is the political status of Guam and American Samoa?

■ Audio-Visual Aids

Consult the available lists of movie films and slides for subjects of interest to the class. Movies of the travel type are available for Hawai'i, Samoa, Tahiti, Fiji, New Zealand, and some of the islands of Micronesia.

Read about tidal waves in *Pacific Science,* Vol. I, No. 1, January 1947, pp. 31-37, "The Tsunami of April 1, 1946, in the Hawaiian Islands," by G.A. MacDonald and others. Keep up to date through newspaper articles on actual tsunami or waves that threaten Hawai'i.

■ Evaluation

1. The vocabulary for this unit will provide a test for certain word meanings.

2. Use a wall map or a large globe, preferably both, for an oral test of the students' knowledge of latitude, longitude, time belts, and such geographical features as continents and islands.

3. Prepare several examination questions of the essay type that concern larger concepts of the Pacific.
   Suggestions:
   a. Discuss the formation of volcanic and continental islands in the Pacific. See Armstrong, p. 32.
   b. Show how the prevailing winds and ocean currents affect the climate of islands and of coastal areas.
   c. Tell how the life and work of the Pacific peoples are influenced by their climate.
   d. What do some of our political scientists mean when they say that in the future more world history will be made in the Pacific than in the Atlantic?

4. Mimeograph outline maps of the Pacific rim and its islands, and, according to the emphasis placed on the following subjects, ask the students to:
   a. Name the continents and main islands.
   b. Sketch in the chief ocean currents and prevailing winds.
   c. Outline the areas of Polynesia, Micronesia, and Melanesia.
   d. Name the chief economic products of the main islands.
   e. Designate the volcanic, low, and continental islands.

■ Reading List

Anderson, Bern. *Surveyor of the Sea.* The life and voyages of Capt. George Vancouver. Seattle: University of Washington Press, 1960.

Armstrong, R. Warwick, ed. *Atlas of Hawaii.* 2nd ed. Developed and compiled by the Department of Geography, University of Hawaii. Honolulu: University Press of Hawaii, 1983.

Beaglehole, J.C., ed. *The Journals of Captain James Cook.* 3 vols. and atlas. Cambridge, UK: Hakluyt Society, Cambridge University Press, 1955-67.

Bishop Museum. Consult the *Publication List* for titles on geology and volcanology, and for listings of the separate islands being studied.

Bryan, E.H. Jr. *American Polynesia.* Coral Islands of the Central Pacific. Honolulu: Tongg Publishing Company, 1941. (The best publication with maps and descriptions of these islands.)

———. *Guide to Islands in the Tropical Pacific.* Honolulu: Bishop Museum Press, 1972.

———. *Guide to Place Names in the Trust Territory of the Pacific Islands* (the Marshall, Caroline, and Mariana Islands). Honolulu: Bishop Museum Press, 1971.

———. *Land in Micronesia and Its Resources.* An annotated bibliography. Honolulu: Bishop Museum Press, 1970.

———. *Panala'au Memoirs.* Honolulu: Bishop Museum Press, 1974. (The experiences of colonists on the islands of Jarvis, Baker, Howland, Canton, and Enderbury during the years 1935-1941.)

Buck, Peter H. *Explorers of the Pacific.* Honolulu: Bishop Museum Special Publication No. 43, 1953.

———. *Vikings of the Pacific.* Chicago: University of Chicago Press, 1959. First published in 1938 as *Vikings of the Sunrise,* New York: Frederick A. Stokes. (A classic on Pacific navigation and customs.)

Cameron, Roderick. *The Golden Haze.* With Captain Cook in the South Pacific. Cleveland: World Publishing Company, 1964.

Campbell, Archibald. *A Voyage Round the World.* Honolulu: University of Hawaii Press, 1968.

Feher, Joseph. *Hawaii: A Pictorial History.* Honolulu: Bishop Museum Special Publication No. 58, 1969.

Fosberg, F.R., ed. *Man's Place in the Island Ecosystem.* A Tenth Pacific Science Congress symposium. 1963. Honolulu: Bishop Museum Press, 1970.

Freeman, Otis W., ed. *Geography of the Pacific.* New York: John Wiley & Sons, 1951.

Golson, Jack, ed. *Polynesian Navigation.* A symposium on Andrew Sharp's theory of Accidental Voyages. Wellington, N.Z.: The Polynesian Society Memoir No. 34, 1963.

Lindo, Cecilia K., and Nancy A. Mower, eds. *Polynesian Seafaring Heritage.* Honolulu: Kamehameha Schools and The Polynesian Voyaging Society, 1980.

MacLean, Alistair. *Captain Cook.* Garden City, NY: Doubleday & Company, 1972.

Mitchell, Donald D. Kilolani. *Hawaiian Treasures.* Honolulu: Kamehameha Schools Press, 1978. (A map inside the front cover shows the extent of Captain Cook's third voyage in the Pacific during which he visited Hawai'i.)

Motteler, Lee S. *Pacific Island Names; A Map and Name Guide to the New Pacific.* Honolulu: Bishop Museum Press, 1986.

Oliver, Douglas L. *The Pacific Islands.* 1951. Honolulu: University of Hawaii Press, 1989 (rev. ed.).

Price, A. Grenfell, ed. *The Explorations of Captain James Cook in the Pacific.* As told by selections from his own journals, 1768-1779. Melbourne, Aus.: Georgian House, 1958.

Rienits, Rex, and Thea Rienits. *The Voyages of Captain Cook.* London and New York: Paul Hamlyn, 1968.

Sharp, Andrew. *The Discovery of the Pacific Islands.* Oxford: Oxford University Press, 1962.

Vaughn, Thomas. *Captain Cook, R.N. The Resolute Mariner.* Portland: Oregon Historical Society, 1974.

Wiens, Herold J. *Pacific Island Bastions of the United States.* Princeton, NJ: Van Nostrand Searchlight Book No. 4, 1962.

World Book Encyclopedia. Chicago: World Book, Inc., 1988. See Pacific Islands, Pacific Ocean, and articles concerning specific islands.

Zimmerman, Elwood C. *Insects of Hawaii.* Vol. I. Introduction. Honolulu: University of Hawaii Press, 1948.

UNIT 2:
Origins
and
Migrations

ORIGINS AND MIGRATIONS

Scientists at Bishop Museum in Honolulu and authorities working in other museums and universities in the field of Polynesian origins have collected data which they consider to be conclusive evidence to substantiate their theory of the origin of the Polynesian peoples.

From the many facts available at this time, they believe that groups of people from southeast Asia, people who have been called Indo-Malaysians or Island Asians, sailed into what we now call western Polynesia in canoes about 1500 B.C. These Caucasoid-Mongoloid people settled in Tonga and became the ancestors of the Polynesians.

Scientists are continuing to search for more definite information about the origin and movements of these people through all available records left by them over the 3500 year period. Clues are sought in the Polynesian chants and stories. The archaeologists are digging for buried records in the form of artifacts and other traces of their culture. Biologists are studying the plants and animals that were carried along the migratory routes.

There is evidence that the Polynesian ancestors visited some of the islands in Melanesia where they secured the jungle fowl (moa), the sugar cane (kō) and other plants believed to be native to these areas.

■ The theory that the Polynesians first settled in Tonga and Samoa, then migrated to the Marquesas and Society Islands from which they later dispersed to the other Polynesian islands such as Hawai'i and New Zealand is being checked by three methods:

1. Radio-carbon dating, using charcoal from the earliest imu or cooking sites. The amount of radio activity left in the charcoal, due to the presence of carbon 14, is measured by experts to determine the age of the specimen. Dates for samples taken in Hawai'i go back more than 1000 years. (See Emory, Bonk and Sinoto, *Fishhooks*, page x.)

2. Language change, by means of which linguists have estimated, for instance, that the Hawaiians have been separated from the Tahitians for nearly a 1000 years. This conclusion was reached after a comparative study of a long list of words from the two languages.

3. Genealogies, by which Hawaiian chiefs are able to trace their ancestors back about 40 generations to the Tahitian chiefs of nearly a thousand years ago. The Maoris of New Zealand also are able to recite elaborate genealogical records.

Questions concerning the origin of the Hawaiian people are among those most frequently asked by visitors to Bishop Museum. Students living in Hawai'i should learn not only what is now known but keep alert to new discoveries in Polynesian origins and migrations. These stories are carried in the local newspapers and, in due time, in Bishop Museum publications.

■ In the late fall of 1963, Dr. Kenneth Emory and Dr. Y. Sinoto discovered evidence that the earliest settlers to Hawai'i came from the Marquesas and that the Tahitian chiefs and settlers came at a somewhat later date.

■ Read the account of Heyerdahl's voyage on the raft Kon Tiki (*The Kon Tiki Expedition*) in 1947 from Peru to the Tuamotu Islands. Point out the fallacies in his theory of the South American origin of the Polynesians. Secure help from the writings of the Bishop Museum scientists.

Read Andrew Sharp's *Ancient Voyagers in the Pacific*, then *Polynesian Navigation*, edited by Jack Golson, a symposium which assessed Sharp's theories.

Study the accompanying map, "Polynesian

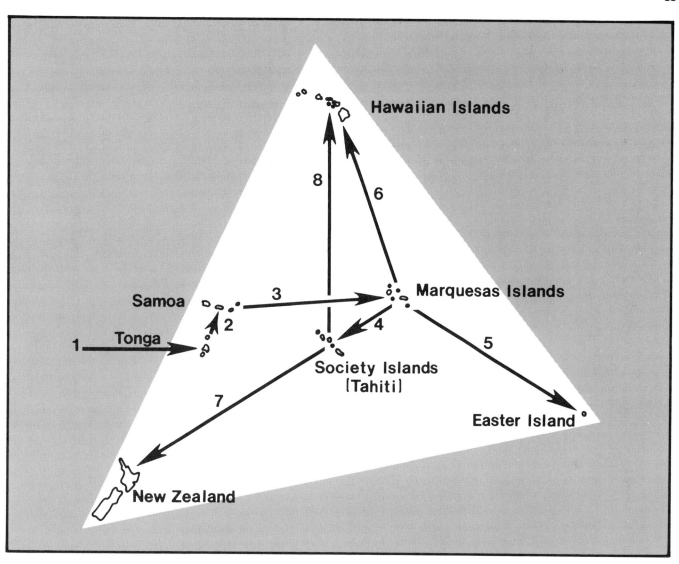

Settlement Pattern." This updated adaptation was approved by Dr. Kenneth Emory in 1981.

Polynesian Settlement Pattern

Probable order of settlement and approximate dates:

1. Indo-Malay or Island Asian people arrived in Tonga from the west about 1,500 B.C. or possibly earlier.

2. Some of these settlers, now to be called Polynesians, migrated from Tonga to nearby Samoa.

3. Some left Samoa, western Polynesia, about the first century A.D. and settled in the Marquesas Islands.

4. Islands in the Society Group were settled a little later from the Marquesas.

5. Marquesas islanders sailed to Easter Island, Rapa Nui, and settled there about 500 A.D.

6. Marquesan voyagers sailed to Hawai'i, probably between 500 and 750 A.D. In Hawai'i as well as the previous landings, we believe that the settlers found the islands uninhabited.

7. Emigrants from Tahiti sailed to New Zealand, perhaps after 750 A.D., and became the Maori people.

8. Society islanders from Raiatea (Hava'iki) came to Hawai'i, probably between 1,000 and 1,250 A.D. By this time all of the larger islands in Polynesia had been discovered and colonized. Some of the smaller islands supported settlements, others were used as "stepping stone" islands which provided places for rest and refreshment on the long voyages to and from the large island groups. See *Polynesian Seafaring Heritage* 1980, pp. 19, 20.

■ **Understandings and Appreciations**

1. Suggest possible motives that might have caused the Polynesian ancestors to leave the Asian region and sail into the unknown islands of the Pacific. Why did their descendants continue to sail on and on until they had discovered and settled all of the important islands of Polynesia?

2. Using the scale on a map or a chart of distances furnished by a steamship or airline, check the distances in miles between selected islands. (The captain and a crew member from the Hōkūleʻa gave us the nautical miles listed below.)

>   Tonga to Samoa 515
>   Samoa to the Marquesas 1,890
>   The Marquesas to Tahiti 880
>   The Marquesas to Easter Island . . . 1,940
>   The Marquesas to Hawaiʻi 1,885
>   Tahiti to New Zealand 2,210
>   Tahiti to Hawaiʻi 2,370

   These figures will give a person an appreciation of the long voyages of the early Polynesians, especially the Hawaiians. (Golson in *Polynesian Navigation* gives Distance Tables, pp. 9-10, covering some but not all of the Polynesian islands.)

   How many miles would a double canoe average in a day on its voyage of one month from Tahiti to Hawaiʻi? Compare the Polynesian navigators to the European ones at the time of Columbus.

3. Who were the real *menehune* and the Tahitian *manahune*? Account for the mythical *menehune now discussed in Hawaiʻi. (Read Menehune of Polynesia* by Luomala, Bishop Museum Bulletin 203.)

4. Describe a large ocean-going double canoe loaded with settlers, their provisions, and their domestic animals and plants ready for the journey from Tahiti to Hawaiʻi. (Read Titcomb's *The Voyage of the Flying Bird* ; Michener's *Hawaii*, Chapters I and II; Finney's *Hōkūleʻa*; and Lindo's *Polynesian Seafaring Heritage*.)

5. Read in the *Pacific Islands Yearbook* and in other sources about the atolls and small islands populated by Polynesian people who migrated to the west. Some of these are Kapingamarangi, Nukuoro, Tikopia, Sikaiana, Ontong Java, Rennell, and Bellona.

■ **Student Activities**

1. Read in King Kalākaua's *Legends and Myths of Hawaii*, page 31, the impressive list of 32 chiefs and kings who have ruled Hawaiʻi in succession since 1095 A.D. See also "Some Alii of the Migratory Period," by Cartwright, Bishop Museum Occasional Paper, Vol. X, No. 7, 1933. Show how such lists help the genealogists decide how long the chiefs have ruled in Hawaiʻi.

2. Consult the encyclopedia for the information needed to make a report to the class on determining the age of a piece of charcoal from an *imu* by the carbon-14 method. Quote several carbon dates from Emory and others (*Fishhooks*, page x).

3. Attempt to find persons who speak Samoan, Tahitian, and Hawaiian. If personal informants are not available, then consult dictionaries in the library. Make a list of ten or more common words in three Polynesian languages. Write them in parallel columns and note their similarities and differences. For example:

English	Hawaiian	Tahitian	Samoan
woman	wahine	vahine	fafine
house	hale	fare	fale
man	kāne	tāne	tāne

4. Sketch a map of the Pacific and plot the probable migratory routes of the Polynesian peoples. (See the wall map in Bishop Museum.)

5. Make a model or a sketch of the ocean-going canoe typical of one of the Polynesian cultures. See the model canoes in Bishop Museum, illustrations in Sharp's *Ancient Voyagers in the Pacific*, the cover design on Titcomb's *Voyage of the Flying Bird*, and numerous illustrations in Haddon and Hornell's *Canoes of Oceania*, Vol. I, Bishop Museum Special Publication No. 27. Reprinted 1975. There are sketches and photos of the Hōkūleʻa in Lindo's *Polynesian Seafaring Heritage*.

6. Learn the first seven lines of the chant credited to Kamahuʻalele which he spoke when he first saw Hawaiʻi on his voyage from Tahiti. (For the entire 31 line chant in Hawaiian and English see the Fornander Collection of Hawaiian Antiquities and Folk-lore, Vol. IV, Part I, Chapter IV, pp. 20-21.)

Eia Hawai'i, he moku, he kanaka,	Behold Hawai'i, an island, a man,
He kanaka Hawai'i ē!	Hawai'i is a man indeed!
He kama nā Tahiti;	A child of Tahiti;
Iā Papa i hānau.	Papa begat him.
'O Mo'ikeha ka lani nāna e noho	Mo'ikeha is the chief who shall dwell
Noho ku'u lani iā Hawai'i,	My chief shall dwell in Hawai'i,
Noho iā Hawai'i a lūlāna.	Dwell in Hawai'i and be at peace.

7. Was Hawai'i Loa a real or mythical navigator? See Barrere, Bishop Museum Anthropological Records, No. 3, 1969. In this volume also read about the *menehune*. How real are they?

■ **Audio-Visual Aids**

All islands: Hōkūle'a - at times this Polynesian double canoe is berthed at a port on O'ahu or one of the neighbor islands. Visitors are welcome. Short cruises may be scheduled.

O'ahu: Falls of Clyde - Pier 5, Honolulu Harbor. Restored sailing vessel with interpretive displays.

Maui: Carthaginian II - Lahaina small boat harbor. Whaling ship with displays.

The following plants are believed to have been introduced into Hawai'i by the ancestors who came in the voyaging canoes. The list is alphabetical and not in order of importance in Hawaiian life.

'ape, large taro-like plant	mai'a, banana
'auhuhu, fish poison	milo, wood for food dishes
'awa, tranquilizing drink	niu, coconut
'awapuhi kuahiwi, ginger	noni, Indian mulberry
hala, pandanus	'ohe, bamboo
hau, tree, hibiscus family	'ōhi'a 'ai, mountain apple
hoi, bitter yam	'ōlena, turmeric
ipu, gourd	pā'ihi, nasturtium family
kalo, taro	pia, arrowroot
kamani, wood for food dishes	pi'a, a yam
kī or lā'ī, ti	'uala, sweet potato
kō, sugar cane	uhi, most important yam
kou, wood for food dishes	'ulu, breadfruit
kukui, candlenut	wauke, paper mulberry

See chart giving the scientific names, origin, growing methods and uses of the above-named plants in *Polynesian Seafaring Heritage,* pp. 122-23.

The animals brought by the settlers were the: pua'a, pig   moa, chicken   'īlio, dog   'iole, rat

■ **Vocabulary** Hawaiian words concerning migrations and origins:

wa'a	canoe	Kahiki	Tahiti
kālai	to hew	Polapola	Borabora
hōkū	star	Hawaiki	traditional homeland

■ **Current Happenings or Trends of Significance to This Unit**

1. At the present time, an unusual amount of research is being conducted to learn more about the origin and migrations of the Polynesian peoples. Read about the discoveries in the local newspapers.

2. Make a study of the migrations of Polynesians, particularly the Samoans, to Hawai'i since World War II. Consult the entertainment pages of the daily papers for the names of the Samoan, Tahitian, Tuamotuan and other Polynesian entertainers at Waikīkī.

3. Visit the villages at the Polynesian Cultural Center at Lā'ie, O'ahu. Ask the informants at each of the villages to give you an estimate of the number of people from their particular island group now living in Hawai'i. Ask also how many might be living on the mainland. These would be guesses in most cases, but would show that a surprising number of Polynesians are away from their home islands. Why?

4. Read the accounts in the local papers or consult Dr. Sinoto at Bishop Museum regarding his archaeological work conducted since 1963 in the islands to the south. According to evidence discovered by Dr. Sinoto and Dr. Emory, the earliest migrants to Hawai'i came from the Marquesas, followed by settlers from Tahiti.

■ **Evaluation**

1. Use the words listed as a check on spelling and word meanings.

2. Trace an outline map of the Pacific rim and the important islands or island groups. Ask the pupils to trace the probable migration route of the Hawaiian people.

3. Recite Kamahu'alele's chant if it was assigned for memory work.

4. Carry out the following suggestions in the form of essays:

   a. Write a paragraph describing radio-carbon analysis, genealogies, or language change as a method of dating the length of time that the Hawaiian people have lived in Hawai'i.

   b. Compare the first Polynesians in Hawai'i to the Pilgrims of the Plymouth Colony during the first year that each group adapted to new situations and waited for the food crops to mature.

   c. Explain the uses that the Hawaiian people made of the four land animals which they brought with them from the south.

■ **Reading List**

Armstrong, R. Warwick, ed. *Atlas of Hawaii.* 2nd ed. Developed and compiled by the Department of Geography, University of Hawaii. Honolulu: University Press of Hawaii, 1983.

Barrau, Jacques, ed. *Plants and the Migrations of the Pacific Peoples.* A Tenth Pacific Science Congress symposium. Honolulu: Bishop Museum Press, 1963.

Barrère, Dorothy B. *The Kumuhonua Legends.* A study of late 19th century Hawaiian stories of creation and origins. Pacific Anthropological Records No. 3. Honolulu: Bishop Museum Press, 1969.

Blackman, Maralyn. *Hōkūle'a.* Honolulu: Polynesian Voyaging Society, 1976. (Book 4 in a series for children on sea voyaging.)

Bryan, E.H. Jr. Ch. 1, "The Hawaiians and the Polynesian Race." Ch. 2, "Whence the Polynesians?" In *Ancient Hawaiian Life.* 1938. Honolulu: Books About Hawaii, 1950.

Buck, Peter H. *Vikings of the Pacific.* Chicago: University of Chicago Press, 1959. (First published in 1938 as *Vikings of the Sunrise.* New York: Frederick A. Stokes.)

Cartwright, Bruce. *Some Aliis of the Migratory Period.* Honolulu: Bishop Museum Occasional Paper No. 7 (Vol. 10), 1933.

Ellis, William. *Journal of William Ellis. A Narrative of a Tour of Hawaii....* 1826. Rutland, VT and Japan: C.E. Tuttle, 1979.

Emerson, Nathaniel B. *Long Voyages of the Ancient Hawaiians.* Honolulu: Hawaiian Historical Society Paper No. 5, 1893.

Emory, Kenneth P. "Coming of the Polynesians." *National Geographic,* Dec. 1974. 146:732-745. (Illustrations by Herbert Kane.)

Emory, Kenneth P., and Yosohiko H. Sinoto. *Oahu Excavations.* Honolulu: Bishop Museum Special Publication No. 49, 1961.

Emory, Kenneth P., William J. Bonk, and Yosihiko H. Sinoto. *Fishhooks.* 1959. Honolulu: Bishop Museum Special Publication No. 47, 1968.

Feher, Joseph. *Hawaii: A Pictorial History.* Honolulu: Bishop Museum Special Publication No. 58, 1969.

Finney, Ben R. *Hōkūle'a: The Way to Tahiti.* New York: Dodd, Mead & Company, 1979.

———, comp. *Pacific Navigation and Voyaging.* Wellington, N.Z.: Polynesian Society Memoir No. 39, 1976.

Golson, Jack, ed. *Polynesian Navigation.* A symposium on Andrew Sharp's theory of Accidental Voyages. Wellington, N.Z.: Polynesian Society Memoir No. 34, 1963.

Haraguchi, Paul. *Weather in Hawaiian Waters.* Honolulu: Pacific Weather Inc., 1979.

Haddon, A.C., and James Hornell. *Canoes of Oceania.* 3 vols. 1936, 1937, 1938. Honolulu: Bishop Museum Special Publications No. 27, 28, 29; reprinted in one volume 1975.

Handy, E.S.C. *The Problems of Polynesian Origins.* Honolulu: Bishop Museum Occasional Paper No. 8 (Vol. 9), 1930.

Heyerdahl, Thor. *American Indians in the Pacific.* London: George Allen & Unwin, 1952.

———. *The Kon Tiki Expedition.* London: George Allen & Unwin, 1950.

Johnson, Rubellite K., and John K. Mahelona. *Na Inoa Hōkū.* A catalog of Hawaiian and Pacific star names. Honolulu: Topgallant Publishing Company, 1975.

Kane, Herbert K. *Voyage: The Discovery of Hawaii.* Norfolk Island, Aus.: Island Heritage, 1976.

Kapepa, Stanley. *A Canoe for Uncle Kila.* Honolulu: Polynesian Voyaging Society, 1976. (Book 2 in a series for children on sea voyaging.)

Kyselka, Will. *An Ocean in Mind.* Honolulu: University of Hawaii Press, 1987.

Kyselka, Will, and George Bunton. *Polynesian Stars and Men.* The puzzle of the ancient navigation of the Polynesians. Honolulu: Bishop Museum Press, 1969.

Kyselka, Will, and Ray Lanterman. *North Star to Southern Cross*. Honolulu: University Press of Hawaii, 1976.

Lewis, David. *We, the Navigators*. The ancient art of land finding in the Pacific. Honolulu: University Press of Hawaii, 1975.

———. *The Voyaging Stars*. Secrets of the Pacific Island navigators. New York: W.W. Norton & Company, 1978.

———. "Wind, Wave, Star and Bird." *National Geographic*, Dec. 1974. 146:747-54, 771-811.

Lindo, Cecilia K., and Nancy A. Mower, eds. *Polynesian Seafaring Heritage*. Honolulu: Kamehameha Schools and The Polynesian Voyaging Society, 1980.

Luomala, Katharine. *Menehune of Polynesia*. Honolulu: Bishop Museum Bulletin No. 203, 1951.

Makemson, Maude W. *The Morning Star Rises*. New Haven: Yale University Press, 1941. (Polynesian astronomy.)

Malo, David. Ch. 3, "The Origin of the Primitive Inhabitants of Hawaii Nei." Ch. 4, "Of the Generations Descended from Wakea." In *Hawaiian Antiquities*. 1898. Honolulu: Bishop Museum Special Publication No. 2, 1976.

Michener, James A. Ch. 1, "From the Boundless Deep." Ch. 2, "From the Sun-Swept Lagoon." *Hawaii* (A novel). New York: Random House, 1959.

Mower, Nancy A. *The Vision of Mo'ikeha*. Honolulu: Polynesian Voyaging Society, 1976. (Book 1 in a series for children on sea voyaging.)

———. *The Voyage to Tahiti*. Honolulu: Polynesian Voyaging Society, 1976. (Book 3 in a series for children on sea voyaging.)

Sharp, Andrew. *Ancient Voyagers in the Pacific*. Wellington, N.Z.: Polynesian Society Memoir No. 32, 1956.

Sneider, Cary, and Will Kyselka, eds. *The Wayfinding Art, Ocean Voyaging in Polynesia*. A collection of essays. Berkeley: University of California, 1986.

Stokes, John F.G. "Whence Pa'ao?" Honolulu: Hawaiian Historical Society Paper No. 19, 1928.

Suggs, Robert C. *The Island Civilizations of Polynesia*. New York: The New American Library, 1960.

Titcomb, Margaret. *The Voyage of the Flying Bird*. New York: Dodd, Mead & Company, 1963.

———. *The Voyage of the Manu Lele*. Honolulu: Aloha Books, 1956.

Zimmerman, Elwood C. *Insects of Hawaii*. Vol. I. Honolulu: University of Hawaii Press, 1948.

See also Reading List for Unit 12.

UNIT 3:
Geology
and Geography

GEOLOGY AND GEOGRAPHY

The Hawaiian Chain is the name some geographers use for the range of mountain-top islands, 1,523 miles in length, which make up the state of Hawai'i. The two islets which form Midway are the only islands in the chain or archipelago not included in the state. They are a National Defense Area under the control of the U.S. Navy Department.

Geographers list 132 islands, exposed reefs, and shoals as making up the state's total area of 6,425 square miles. The eight largest islands which account for 99 per cent of the land are in the southeastern 400 miles of the chain.

The Leeward Islands, or officially the North-western Hawaiian Islands, are the tops of huge volcanic mountains which rise 15,000 feet from their bases on the ocean floor. These rocky or sandy islets, most of which lie but a few feet above sea level, were probably reduced from their former size by the forces of erosion over several million years.

Hawai'i is the southernmost state in the United States, and only Alaska projects farther west. Honolulu, the capitol, is 4,830 miles from the nation's capitol, Washington, D.C. It is six hours away by standard time.

In latitude or distance above the equator, the Hawaiian archipelago extends from 18 degrees, 54 minutes to 28 degrees, 15 minutes north. Most of the Leeward Islands are above the Tropic of Cancer.

In longitude Hawai'i lies between 154 degrees 40 minutes to 178 degrees 75 minutes west. The most distant of the Leeward Islands are less than 2 degrees from the 180th meridian which is the International Date Line.

■ Forming the Hawaiian Islands

For years our scientists have explained the formation of the Hawaiian Islands in the light of what was then known about volcanism and the earth's movements. They believed that a huge crack or fissure opened in the floor of the ocean, beginning in the area of Kure and Midway islands. Lava was forced out from this crack and by successive eruptions through the ages formed Kure, the first of the islands in the Hawaiian Chain.

New vents opened to the southwest, and the older ones closed. Eventually Ni'ihau, Kaua'i, and the rest of the islands were formed. Now the only active vents are under the Big Island.

Interestingly enough this is the story that the Hawaiian people told of Pele moving her fires from island to island in a southeasterly direction until she finally made her home in Kīlauea Crater.

■ Since the early 1960s geophysicists have proposed a new explanation for the formation of the Hawaiian Islands based on the continental drift theory.

The rigid upper layer of the earth, some 60 miles thick, is called the lithosphere from the Greek word *lithos* meaning "stone." Beneath it is a plastic-like layer, as deep and sometimes deeper than the lithosphere. It is called the asthenosphere from the Greek word *asthene* for "weak."

The continents and the plates on the sea floor move on this plastic asthenosphere. Throughout great periods of time these masses have drifted

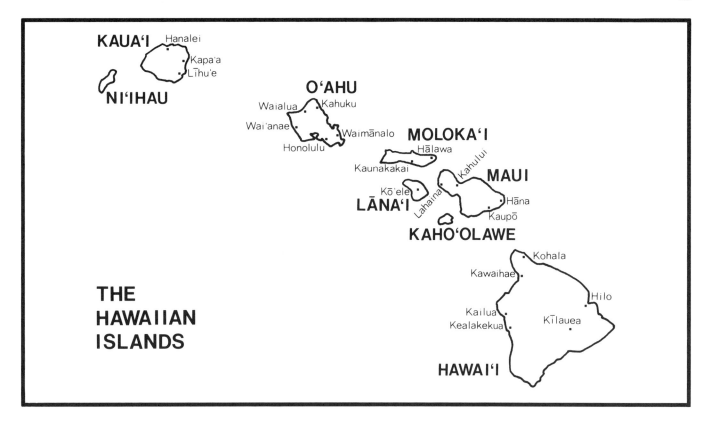

THE
HAWAIIAN
ISLANDS

slowly away from and then into one another. At the margins of the plates they grind past one another.

The Hawaiian Islands lie someplace near the middle of the Pacific plate which, according to this theory, is moving in a northwesterly direction at the rate of some four inches a year.

Vents, also called hot spots or flumes, occur in various places in the mantle of the earth, and through these flow magma or molten rock. Magma is called lava when it reaches the earth's surface.

Along or near the shores of the continents or other land masses bordering the Pacific are a series of these vents which form a circle, though not an unbroken one. These are more or less active volcanoes and form what is called the "Ring of Fire."

To explain the formation of the Hawaiian Islands by this theory one must visualize a vent or flume (also called a plume) of quite a permanent nature emanating from the depths and piercing the asthenosphere and the lithosphere. The magma rises through this vent and pours out on the ocean floor. By successive flows through long periods of time a mountain is formed which eventually rises above the surface of the ocean, as did Kure Island, the first in the chain.

It is not possible to tell after the passing of such long periods of time the height that this island reached. Today it is an islet a few feet above sea level, but it must have been much higher when it was formed 25 million years ago.

Since the Pacific plate on which Kure rests is moving to the northwest at the rate of some four inches a year, the island moved away from the vent which formed it. This building process began again and in due time Midway Island was formed.

The northwest drift of the Pacific plate continued until a chain of islands was formed. Among the larger and better known are Pearl and Hermes Atolls, Lisianski Island, Laysan Island, French Frigate Shoals, Necker Island, and Nihoa Island.

Our inhabited islands from Ni'ihau to Hawai'i were formed in this way. Ni'ihau rose above the sea some five million years ago. The forces of erosion are at work as is plainly evident on Kaua'i, the next island in the chain.

The Big Island has been in contact with this lava-flowing vent for a million years or so. The mass which we call the Kohala mountains was formed and slowly moved on northwest. Mauna Kea, the next huge mountain to be formed, may have reached its maximum height some half million years ago. Mauna Loa, the largest in volume of

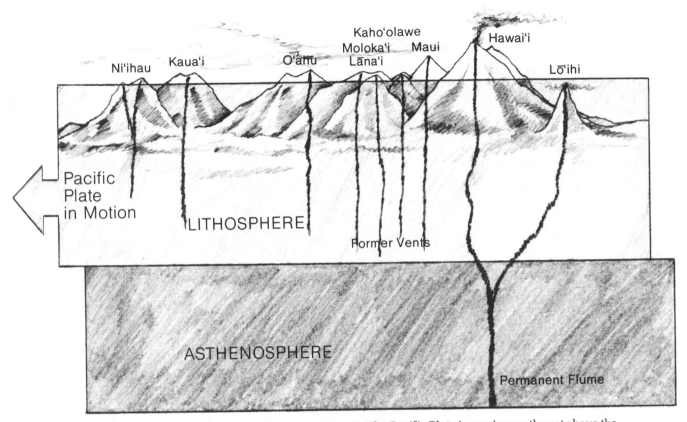

Ni'ihau Kaua'i O'ahu Kaho'olawe Moloka'i Lāna'i Maui Hawai'i Lō'ihi

Pacific Plate in Motion

LITHOSPHERE

Former Vents

ASTHENOSPHERE

Permanent Flume

The Drift Theory of the Formation of Volcanic Islands: The Pacific Plate is moving northwest above the asthenosphere at the rate of some four inches a year. Magma moving up the flume has formed the older Hawaiian Islands and is continuing to add to the Big Island and the underwater islet Lō'ihi.

Hawaiian mountains, continues to grow through lava poured from its summit crater, Moku'āweoweo, from Kīlauea and Maunaulu craters on its lower flanks and from rifts below these craters.

This slow, northwest drift continues. Soundings and pictures taken by a deep-tow camera called Angus show that a volcano is forming a new island 18 miles southeast of the Big Island. The name Lō'ihi (tall) has been suggested for this 8,800 foot mountain which is still three-quarters of a mile below the ocean's surface.

The Hawaiian Islands are one of seven chains of islands or sea mounts in the Pacific which were formed by the southeast to northwest movement of the Pacific plate over vents which have been termed "island-making machines." Other writers use the term "production line" to visualize this process of island building through the upwelling of molten magma beneath a moving crusted plate.

Read more about this theory of the formation of Hawai'i in Decker's *Volcano Watching,* and Sullivan's *Continents in Motion.*

■ **The Age of the Islands**

Residents and visitors ask questions about the age of the islands, the age of certain craters which are landmarks, and also—will Diamond Head or Punchbowl erupt again?

Only recently have methods been devised to determine with accuracy the age of the rocks, or the minerals within the rocks of Hawai'i. The preferred method now is by radiogenic measurements. Potassium 40 within the rocks breaks down very slowly into argon 40 gas. By laboratory methods too involved to explain here the scientist determines the amounts of potassium and argon 40 still in the rock. The age is calculated from these figures.

Ian McDougall, an Australian geologist, measured the ages of Hawaiian rocks in 1964. More can be read on this subject in Decker, 1980, p. 40; Stearns, 1966, pp. 74-78; and McDonald and Abbott, 1970, pp. 263-69.

Ages of Hawaiian Volcanic Rocks
Based on the Potassium-Argon Method

Island	Age in Millions of Years
Necker	11.3
Nihoa	7.5
Kaua'i	3.8 - 5.6
O'ahu: Wai'anae	2.7 - 3.4
Ko'olau	2.2 - 2.5
Moloka'i: West	1.8
East	1.3 - 1.5
Maui: West	1.3 - 1.15
East	0.8
Hawai'i: Kohala	Less than 1.0
Mauna Kea	0.6
Mauna Loa	less than 0.5

■ Diamond Head and Punchbowl

Long after O'ahu had been formed and considerable erosion had taken place there were volcanic revivals. Many cinder cones or tuff cones were formed during this period. One explanation of this activity is that great quantities of sea water flowed into the magma deep under the island which formed steam. Ash and lava were thrown out in explosive eruptions. Two of the best known of the craters formed at this time are Diamond Head (Lē'ahi or Lae'ahi) and Punchbowl (Pūowaina).

Diamond Head received its English name from calcite crystals in the rocks that resembled diamonds from a distance. The secondary eruption which formed this crater occurred some 100,000 to 150,000 years ago. Subsequent activity as late as 5,000 years ago in this area formed Black Point and the Kaimukī dome.

Punchbowl crater of ash and lava dates to about the same time as Diamond Head. Tantalus and Round Top craters erupted as late as 5,000 years ago and ash from them fell into Punchbowl.

Volcanologists will not assure us that these craters will not erupt again.

■ Earthquakes and Tsunami

The swelling of the masses of magma deep in the earth and the shifting of nearby rocks causes vibrations and trembling of the earth. These are earthquake tremors. Vibrations also come from breaking of rocks under stress. These are measured by an instrument called a seismograph.

Of the several methods of measuring earthquake vibrations, the best known uses the Richter scale which determines the magnitude. This measures the actual amount of energy released during an earthquake on an open-ended scale beginning with one. There is no upper limit given on this scale, but 7 is very destructive. The highest recorded has been 8.5 to 9.

The increase in number and severity of earthquakes is one of the sources of information used in predicting a volcanic eruption. The tiltmeter supplies additional evidence by telling if ground swelling is taking place.

Tsunami is a Japanese word meaning a "long wave in a harbor." It is not a tidal wave or an ordinary ocean wave, but a seismic sea wave.

Tsunami are usually associated with severe earthquakes. The quakes themselves do not cause the tsunami. They are caused by severe faulting, sudden displacement of layers of rock in the ocean floor, submarine volcanic activity, or landslides above or below sea level.

Seismic waves generated by sudden earth movements may travel at speeds up to 500 miles an hour across the open ocean.

Most tsunami that have reached Hawai'i in the past were generated on shores far from these islands. These huge waves have, however, occasionally resulted from local conditions.

At least a half-dozen severe tsunami have caused damage along Hawai'i's shores since 1837.

■ Earthquake, Tsunami, and Mud Flow

1868 During late March heavy rains in the hills back of Wai'ōhinu, Ka'ū, at an elevation of 3,500 feet, soaked the soil and ash. On April 2 a severe quake, estimated at 8 or more in intensity agitated the soil and ash into a fluid mud. One mud flow a mile long, and a second two miles long and a half-mile wide, swept down hill. The second flow is said to have buried 500 domestic animals and a village with 31 persons. What were then called tidal waves swept in over the tops of coconut trees destroying nearly everything along the coast. The quakes leveled all European-type buildings in the area. This is considered the greatest Hawaiian earthquake of historic times.

1946 An earthquake in the Aleutian Islands generated destructive waves on April 1. According to Stearns (1966) the waves traveled 2,240 statute miles in 4.57 hours, a speed of 490 miles an hour. The first waves were at 15-minute intervals, and at most places the third and fourth waves did the greatest damage. Hilo, Hawai'i, was hit hardest causing the death of 159 persons and 25 million dollars in damage. The waves reached a height of 55 feet on the island of Hawai'i and 45 feet at Hā'ena, Kaua'i.

1960 A quake on Chile shores generated a tsunami that traveled to Hilo, 6,600 miles away, in 14 hours and 56 minutes. The speed of the seismic wave was 442 miles per hour. The third wave rose to 35 feet and struck Hilo Bay at 40 miles per hour. The damage was estimated at 20 million dollars and 61 people lost their lives.

A tsunami warning system is proving to be helpful. Not all quakes generate tsunami. Gauges to measure wave heights are placed on various Pacific islands. If a wave approaches Hawai'i from an area, South America for instance, where it passes no intervening islands, no warning can be given.

■ Heat of Molten Lava

Most scientists use the Centigrade or Celsius scale which measures the boiling point of water at 100 degrees and the freezing point at zero. Americans, however, seem to cling to the use of the Fahrenheit scale which measures boiling water at 212 degrees and freezing at 32 degrees.

The hottest lavas from Kīlauea volcano measure 2,200 degrees Fahrenheit or 1,200 degrees Centigrade. This is 12 times hotter than boiling water and three times hotter than molten lead. The melting temperature of iron is 1,535 degrees Centigrade, a little higher than the hottest lava.

The temperature and the color of erupting lava change, or cool, together. An instrument called an optical pyrometer allows the operator to compare the color of the glowing lava to the color of an electric bulb.

Color estimates on the Centigrade scale are:

	degrees
White hot lava	1,200
Yellow	1,100
Orange	900
Bright red	700
Dull red	500

Volcanologists may determine the temperature of lava more accurately by using a ceramic rod with two wires of different metals twisted together at the end. The wires generate a small electric voltage when subjected to the intense heat of the lava. The instrument is called a thermocouple. The lava temperature, determined by measuring the voltage, is more accurate than by the optical method.

■ Rocks, Minerals, and Semiprecious Stones

Most people are surprised at the large number of different kinds of minerals and stones found in and among Hawai'i's lava rocks.

Manhoff and Uyehara in their book *Rockhounding in Hawai'i* describe 62 different materials that are classed under this heading. Their book is unique in that they tell the collector where he may find these stones on each of the five larger islands.

Unfortunately there are no precious gems in Hawai'i, and the few semiprecious ones are usually small and not always easy to find. However, the members of the Rock and Mineral Society of Hawai'i as well as individual collectors have fun "rockhounding." Read the Manhoff and Uyehara book for information, photographs, and maps on this subject.

Seven stones or minerals are listed here alphabetically as ones most often seen and sought after:

Calcite. Milky white calcium carbonate crystals of calcite gave Diamond Head its name. Calcite forms stalactites in caves and may be banded white, yellow, or brown. As a rock it is known as travertine or Mexican onyx.

Chalcedony. This cryptocrystalline quartz may be white, blue, lavendar, green, red, and brown. When banded it is known as agate. Non-banded brown or red stones are jasper. White or light colored specimens are chalcedony. The agate called Hawaiian moonstone is the hardest stone found here. Bishop Museum has an excellent collection of jaspers cut and polished by Mr. A.H. Cornelison.

Feldspar. This complex silicate is called Hawaiian sunstone or topaz. Some stones are found of the size and quality of gems. They are clear yellow to white and too soft for stones in finger rings.

Obsidian. Some pieces of this volcanic glass have been cut into gems. During an eruption both filaments and droplets of volcanic glass cool and drift away. The drop-shaped pellets are called Pele's tears. Imported, not local, ones are sold in gift shops. Pele's hair, the glass filiaments in green, gold, brown, or black, resemble glass wool.

Olivine. Small, green olivine crystals are found in many places in the islands. The sand on some beaches is tinged in green from countless numbers of these tiny stones. Rarely are they large and clear enough for gem stones. The olivine settings in the jewelry in local gift shops are all from the southwestern states or Mexico. The gems may be tagged as of volcanic origin but they are not from Pele's volcanoes.

Quartz. These crystals are formed in cavities by gases and hot water solutions rising through the lava in the crater of a volcano. Crystals, colorless or yellow, have been found from two or three inches in length and a half-inch in diameter. The crystals are hexagonal prisms with a six-sided pyramid at one or both ends. When cut into gems they are called rock crystal or Hawaiian diamonds.

Zeolite. Very common whitish or yellowish minerals of a complex and variable composition, often consisting of seven or more minerals. They have been deposited in cavities of many basaltic rocks by gases or hot-water solutions.

Commercial use of rocks and minerals:

Building materials:
Basaltic lava rock, limestone, and sandstone for walls or buildings.
Fieldstone or moss rock for garden walls.
Volcanic cinders for roads and as a concrete aggregate.
Pumice for insulation and as a concrete aggregate.
Lime for mortar and converted into cement.
Clay to line seashore salt-evaporating pans.
Sand: coral beach sand, or black sand for concrete.
Ceramic clay for pottery.
Salt by solar evaporation, once a thriving industry.
Cinders for orchid and other gardens.

■ Regrowth of Plants after a Volcanic Eruption

A volcanic eruption may cover an area of land, once verdant and productive, and leave it barren of plant life.

Some flows leave large or small areas, called *kīpuka*, untouched although they are surrounded by lava.

Plants, in time, always grow back on the devastated places. Studies have been made which show that a growth of algae comes first, then lichens, and next mosses and ferns. The first of the native woody plants is usually the *'ōhi'a lehua*.

See the reading list to learn more about invasion

Regrowth of Vegetation: After a volcanic eruption the order in which plants establish themselves on recent flows is; algae, lichens, mosses, ferns and then the woody plants such as *'ōhi'a lehua*.

and recovery of vegetation in booklets by Decker and by Smathers and Mueller-Dombois.

■ Submergence and Emergence

The shorelines of our islands have submerged and emerged many times during their geologic lifetime. These changes of great significance are caused by the uplifting and lowering of the island land masses due to great movements in the earth's crust or by the increase and decrease in the volume of water in the ocean.

During the periods of glaciation great quantities of water evaporated from the oceans. It condensed and fell in the cold regions where it froze into great ice caps over the poles and in the northern areas of the continents. With climatic changes some of the ice melted and the water flowed into the oceans causing the level to rise again.

During the third glacial epoch about three times as much water was trapped in the polar ice as is the case at the present time. If the present ice caps should melt, Honolulu and all other coastal cities would be submerged more than 200 feet.

Most geologists agree that the sea level around the Hawaiian islands during the past million or more years has been at least 450 feet lower and as much as 250 feet higher than it is today. Figures for much greater submergence and emergence are given in the literature. (Stearns, 1966, pp. 15-24. McDonald, 1970, pp. 204-213)

When the shores were submerged for long periods of time, broad coral reefs formed. Since these have emerged, extensive plains of coral limestone are visible as on Oʻahu's flat lands at ʻEwa, Waimānalo, and Kahuku.

When the seas were high the waves lapped at the bases of certain mountains. This caused erosion as can be seen by the vertical cliffs on windward Oʻahu, the Nā Pali coast of Kauaʻi, and Molokaʻi's sea cliffs.

■ Geothermal Power

There is a great amount of energy in the form of heat in the earth's interior. When we are able to harness it economically, this heat could supply the needs of the people for years to come. There are several theories explaining the source of the earth's internal heat:

1. This might be the original heat trapped at the time of the formation of the earth 4.5 billion years ago.

2. Heat is generated at the disintegration of natural radioactive elements.

3. Heat results from friction such as rock masses moving against one another. Energy is not created or destroyed, the physicists tell us. It is transferred from one kind of energy to another. The internal heat may be responsible for moving the plates on which the land masses move. The friction from this movement could in turn generate heat.

Power, measured in watts, is the unit or rate at which energy is used. Power is used in household appliances and in the engines that do our work. We have a power crisis, not an energy crisis today.

In volcanic areas such as Hawaiʻi, the ideal, in securing geothermal powers, is to be able to drill into shallow reservoirs which have a continuous supply of steam and hot water.

In 1973 a deep hole was drilled near the summit of Kīlauea crater for research purposes, not for geothermal power. The drill reached its limit at 1,262 meters and encountered water at a temperature of 137° C. Among the facts learned at this drilling was that wells in lower rift zones, not volcanic summits, should reach the proper temperature more readily.

In 1976, in a zone between Pāhoa and Pohoiki, a deep well was drilled. At 1,950 meters, the bottom of this hole, the temperature of the water and steam was 340° C. More wells are being drilled to learn if this area will produce power to generate electricity as is being done so successfully in The

Geysers field in California, in Iceland, and in New Zealand. One of the problems not yet solved is the control of the noise and of the odor of the steam at a geothermal plant. The drillers have met some resistance from Hawaiian families who say that we have no right to invade Pele's domain.

■ Summary

A summary of the geological features shows that Hawaiʻi is a chain of subtropical islands, cooled by northeast trade winds and ocean currents, with large acreages weathered into fertile lands for plantations and ranches, and with sufficient rain to provide water for agriculture and for the needs of nearly a million people. Harbors, natural or improved by man, furnish anchorage for ships from many ports. Rivers and lakes are few but mountains, valleys, and beaches create a landscape of such beauty that visitors are attracted to Hawaiʻi in ever increasing numbers.

■ Understandings and Appreciations

1. Study the globe, then explain the significance of the statement that "Hawaiʻi is farther from every place than any other place on earth." What effect did this have on the coming of living things to Hawaiʻi - (a) by natural means? (b) by man?

2. Compare the productivity of the soil on the geologically "old" island of Kauaʻi with that of the recent lava flows on the island of Hawaiʻi. Can man speed up the process of changing rock to soil? (Note the experiment in Puna of crushing and packing the ʻaʻā lava with heavy bulldozers.)

3. Study Oʻahu's geological formations which, by trapping and holding water, produce an artesian condition. Why is the water which is pumped from among the lava rocks nearly free from minerals? Read about the "hard" water from the limestone areas in other states or countries. Consult publications from the Honolulu Board of Water Supply to learn the danger of pumping too much fresh water from Oʻahu's wells. What is the source of water for the towns and plantations on the neighbor islands?

4. Show that the geological formations which produced vast areas suitable for agriculture affected the economic and human development of Hawai'i. In contrast to American Samoa and other Pacific Islands with no extensive cultivable land, Hawai'i's broad acres attracted foreigners who developed plantations with imported labor.

5. When magma, the molten rock in the interior of the earth, is forced out and flows on the surface it is called lava. Hawaiian words are used to describe the two principal types of lava. These words have been adopted by volcanologists and are in use wherever lava is studied. They are:

'A'ā - the lava with rough, chunky surface. It may be slow-moving with a dark exterior and difficult to walk over when cool.

Pāhoehoe - lava with a smooth, ropy-appearing surface. It is much more liquid in texture than 'a'ā and may move more swiftly down hill. When cool it is easier to walk over, except for the danger of stepping into lava bubbles.

Also of interest is that volcanic eruptions are usually divided into two types:

The Vesuvius or explosive type.
The Hawaiian or quiet type.

■ **Student Activities**

1. Sketch a profile of the Hawaiian Chain to show the large proportion that is under water (See Bryan, *Hawaiian Chain,* p. 2). Show that Mauna Kea rises nearly 32,000 feet above its base on the sea bottom.

2. Sketch in color or make a three-dimensional model of the eight principal Hawaiian islands. Show the comparative size, the topography, and other features of geographical interest.

3. We learn that water pressure amounts to one ton per square inch for every vertical mile in actual depth. The ocean around Hawai'i is about 18,000 feet deep. What water pressure per square inch had the lava to overcome to force its way through the first feet of water above the ocean floor as it moved upward to build the islands? (Answer - 3½ tons. Note that we are accustomed to about 15 pounds per square inch of air pressure on our bodies at sea level.)

4. Read and tell one of the stories of the mythical volcano goddess Pele and of her deeds as she formed the islands from Kaua'i to Hawai'i. (W.D. Westervelt, *Hawaiian Legends of Volcanoes*)

5. Name the highest mountains on each of the six large islands and give their approximate heights. Quote figures for O'ahu or Kaua'i to show how the mountains affect the rainfall on the leeward side.

6. The Wailua on the island of Kaua'i is called the only navigable river in Hawai'i. What vessels sail on its waters? Name two streams on O'ahu and two on Hawai'i. Why are there so few on the Big Island? Study the growth habits of coral, then show how the streams were responsible for the entrances through the reef to Honolulu and Pearl Harbor.

7. Review the well-known geographical features by locating on one or more of the islands: an isthmus, a peninsula, a lake, a canyon, a large bay, an active volcano, and a swamp.

8. Locate Hawai'i on the globe or a map of the Pacific. Note that the figures 20-20 (spoken by your oculist) help keep the approximate location of the islands in mind. Hawai'i is about 20 degrees north of the equator and 20 degrees from the international date line or 180th meridian. The exact location of Kilolani Planetarium on the Bishop Museum grounds is:

21° 20' 9" north latitude
157° 52' 21" west longitude

This may be read twenty-one degrees, twenty minutes, and nine seconds north latitude and one hundred fifty-seven degrees, fifty-two minutes, and twenty-one seconds west longitude.

9. Visit buildings that are constructed or faced with local building stones or materials:

Adobe - adobe school house, Mission Lane.
Coral blocks - Kawaiaha'o Church.
Basaltic lava - Bishop Museum.
Sandstone - older part of St. Andrew's Cathedral.
Limestone - facings on several of the new Mormon churches and on Texaco filling stations.

10. List and try to visit some of the stones that are considered to be of special interest on your

island. These stones are special because they are associated with religious, cultural, or historical events and not because of the composition or nature of the stones.

Oʻahu:

So-called "sacrificial stone" at Kolekole Pass. (See Stearns, 1966, pp. 81-92.)

Healing stones at Wahiawā.

Kukaniloko stones near Wahiawā.

Bishop Museum Courtyard - Kapaʻaheo Shark God, other stones.

Moanalua Valley - Petroglyph stone.

Crouching Lion - Makaua at Kahana Bay.

And many, many more.

Hawaiʻi:

Naha stone, in front of Library in Hilo.

Pinao stone, in front of Library in Hilo.

■ Audio-Visual Aids

Movies:

Consult the film listings for movies of the Mauna Loa, Kīlauea, and Puna eruptions. Many local families have taken interesting movies and color slides of recent eruptions. Some of these amateur photographers might be asked to project their pictures for school classes. Certain of the "travel" movies of Hawaiʻi show colorful views of geographical features which may be shown to a class with the idea of identifying these.

Field Trips:

A field trip should help the pupils learn to see the features that are being discussed. A short walk in the area of the school may be sufficient to note both geological and geographic features. An extensive drive with someone trained in this field should be a revealing experience. Classes should take Stearn's *Road Guide to Points of Geologic Interest* on a trip around the island to study the formations discussed in the book.

■ Vocabulary

Explain the following words in relation to Hawaiʻi:

ʻaʻā	basalt	limestone
pāhoehoe	igneous rocks	reef rock
kīpuka	sedimentary rocks	olivines

■ Current Happenings or Trends of Significance to this Unit

Current events for this unit might show how nature and men are changing the geographical features of the Islands.

1. If an eruption has occurred recently tell of its effect, if any, upon the region it invaded.

2. Have the local newspapers carried accounts of earthquakes, tsunami, or seismic waves or severe storms?

3. Has dredging altered any shorelines as was done in the construction of Magic Island along Ala Moana Park?

4. Has the Board of Water Supply dug wells or tunnels into the water-bearing strata?

5. Were any swamps or ponds drained or filled to reclaim land for house sites or other purposes? How was Kuapā Pond on Oʻahu changed by the Hawaiʻi Kai developers? Salt Lake?

■ Evaluation

Prepare an essay type exam to test for the broad concepts that were presented in the geography and geology of Hawaiʻi. In testing, use some of the questions and vocabulary words given in this unit. Give credit for the student projects such as maps, models, and collections of specimens.

■ Reading List

Armstrong, R. Warwick, ed. *Atlas of Hawaii.* 2nd ed. Developed and compiled by the Department of Geography, University of Hawaii. Honolulu: University Press of Hawaii, 1983.

Ashdown, Inez M. *Ke Alaloa o Maui.* The broad highway of Maui. Wailuku, Maui: Ace Printing Company, 1971.

———. *Recollections of Kahoolawe.* Honolulu: Topgallant Publishing Company, 1979.

Bier, James A. *Reference Maps of the Islands of Hawaiʻi.* Hawaiʻi and Maui, 1988 (4th ed.); Oʻahu, 1987 (3rd ed.); Kauaʻi, 1986 (3rd ed.); Molokaʻi and Lanaʻi, 1982 (rev. ed.). Honolulu: University of Hawaii Press.

Bryan, E.H. Jr. *American Polynesia and the Hawaiian Chain.* Honolulu: Tongg Publishing Company, 1942. (Contains maps, illustrations and information concerning the chain to the northwest of Kaua'i as well as similar data on many of the little-known islands which have some significance to the people of Hawai'i.)

———. "Geographical Background of the Pacific." In *Aspects of Hawaiian Life and Environment.* Honolulu: Kamehameha Schools Press, 1965.

———. *The Hawaiian Chain.* Honolulu: Bishop Museum Press, 1954. (The most popular single reference on the geology and geography of the entire Hawaiian Group.)

Bunton, George W. *The Tides.* Honolulu: Bishop Museum Special Publication No. 54, 1966.

Carlquist, Sherwin J. *Hawaii: A Natural History.* 1970. 2nd ed. Lawa'i, Kaua'i: Pacific Tropical Botanical Society, 1981.

Coulter, John W. *A Gazetteer of the Territory of Hawaii.* Honolulu: University Press of Hawaii, 1935. (Helpful maps showing the islands divided into districts.)

Daws, Alan G. *The Illustrated Atlas of Hawaii.* Norfolk Island, Aus.: Island Heritage, 1970.

Decker, Barbara. *Road Guide to Hawai'i Volcanoes National Park.* Mariposa, CA: Double Decker Press, 1986.

Decker, Robert, and Barbara Decker. *Volcano Watching.* Hawaii Volcanoes National Park, Hawai'i: Hawaii Natural History Association, 1980. (Excellent reference.)

———. *Volcanoes.* San Francisco: W.H. Freeman and Company, 1981.

Dudley, Walter C., and Min Lee. *Tsunami!* Honolulu: University of Hawaii Press, 1988. (Describes the great tsunami of 1946 and other major waves in Hawai'i.)

Dunmire, W. *Birds of the National Parks in Hawaii.* Hilo: Natural History Association, 1961.

Feher, Joseph. *Hawaii: A Pictorial History.* Honolulu: Bishop Museum Special Publication No. 58, 1969.

Foster, H.L. *Relief and Outline Maps of Hawaii.* Honolulu: Hawaii State Department of Education, Office of Social Studies, 1966.

Grigg, Richard W. *Hawaii's Precious Corals.* Norfolk Island, Aus.: Island Heritage, 1977.

"Hawaii." In *World Book Encyclopedia.* Chicago: World Book, Inc., 1988. (A study of all of the available encyclopedias shows that this would be the most helpful to teachers and students for this unit.)

Kay, E. Alison, ed. *The Natural History of the Hawaiian Islands.* 1972. Honolulu: University Press of Hawaii, 1976. (Articles on geology, volcanology, reef building, climate, soil and many other subjects.)

Kaye, Robin. *Lanai Folks.* Honolulu: University of Hawaii Press, 1982.

Kyselka, Will, and Ray Lanterman. *Maui—How It Came to Be.* Honolulu: University Press of Hawaii, 1980.

Lindo, Cecilia K., and Nancy A. Mower, eds. *Polynesian Seafaring Heritage.* Honolulu: Kamehameha Schools and The Polynesian Voyaging Society, 1980.

Macdonald, Gordon A., and Agatin T. Abbott. *Volcanoes in the Sea.* 1970. Honolulu: University Press of Hawaii, 1983.

Macdonald, Gordon A., and Douglass H. Hubbard. *Volcanoes of the National Parks of Hawaii.* Hawaii Volcanoes National Park and the Hawaii Natural History Association, 1978.

Macdonald, Gordon A., and Will Kyselka. *Anatomy of an Island.* A geological history of O'ahu. Honolulu: Bishop Museum Special Publication No. 55, 1967.

Macdonald, Gordon A., et al. *Geology and Groundwater Resources of the Island of Kauai.* Honolulu: State Department of Public Lands, 1960.

Manhoff, Milton, and Mitsuo Uyehara. *Rockhounding in Hawai'i.* Our rocks, minerals, and semiprecious stones. Honolulu: Hawaiiana Almanac Publishing Company, 1976.

McBride, Leslie R. *About Hawaii's Volcanoes.* 1977. Hilo: Petroglyph Press, 1984 (rev. ed.).

Rublowsky, John R. *Born in Fire.* A geological history of Hawaii. New York: Harper & Row, 1981 (juvenile).

Smathers, Garrett, and Dieter Mueller-Dombois. *Invasion and Recovery of Vegetation after a Volcanic Eruption in Hawaii.* Washington, D.C.: National Park Service Monograph No. 5, 1974.

Stearns, Harold T. *Geology of the State of Hawaii.* Palo Alto, CA: Pacific Books, 1966. (Generously illustrated with maps, photographs and drawings.)

———. *Road Guide to Points of Geologic Interest in the Hawaiian Islands.* 2nd ed. Palo Alto, CA: Pacific Books, 1978.

Stearns, Harold T., and Gordon A. Macdonald. *Hawaii.* Washington, D.C.: U.S. Geological Survey Bulletin No. 9, 1946.

———. *Lanai and Kahoolawe.* Washington, D.C.: U.S. Geological Survey Bulletin No. 6, 1940.

———. *Maui.* Washington, D.C.: U.S. Geological Survey Bulletin No. 7, 1942.

———. *Molokai.* Washington, D.C.: U.S. Geological Survey Bulletin No. 11, 1947.

———. *Niihau.* Washington, D.C.: U.S. Geological Survey Bulletin No. 12, 1947.

Stearns, Norah D. *An Island is Born.* Honolulu: Honolulu Star-Bulletin Ltd., 1935. (A description of the geologic birth of O'ahu.)

Sterling, Elspeth, and Catherine C. Summers. *Sites of Oahu.* Honolulu: Department of Anthropology, Bishop Museum, 1978.

Sullivan, Walter. *Continents in Motion. The New Earth debate.* New York: McGraw-Hill Book Company, 1974.

Summers, Catherine C. *Molokai: A Site Survey.* Pacific Anthropological Records No. 14. Honolulu: Department of Anthropology, Bishop Museum, 1971.

Tilling, Robert I., et al. *Eruptions of Hawaiian Volcanoes: Past, Present and Future.* Washington, D.C.: U.S. Geological Survey, 1987.

United States. *Hawaiian Islands, Gazetteer No. 34.* Washington, D.C.: U.S. Government Printing Office, 1956. (Contains 7,250 standard names for Hawai'i, Midway, and Johnston Island.)

Zimmerman, Elwood C. Vol. I, Introduction, Ch. 1, "Geological History of Hawaii." In *Insects of Hawaii.* Honolulu: University of Hawaii Press, 1948.

UNIT 4:
Communication,
with Special
Reference to
the Hawaiian Language

COMMUNICATION
With *Special Reference*
to the Hawaiian Language

For many centuries the chief medium of communication in Hawai'i was the spoken word. Hawaiian is a poetic, expressive language with a vocabulary of some 25,000 words. Its appeal to the listener may be attributed to the frequency of vowel sounds and the absence of clusters of consonants. The grammar, with complicated pronouns, demonstratives, possessives, and particles, should not be compared to the Latin or English. It should be studied as the framework for a language that expresses the philosophy of the Hawaiian people.

■ The Hawaiian alphabet *(pī'āpā)* consists of five vowels and seven consonants plus the hamzah or glottal stop *('okina* or *'u'ina)*. This mark is usually typed as an apostrophe and printed as an inverted comma or a single initial quotation mark. It is also essential to add the macron *(kahakō* or *mekona),* a straight, horizontal line over certain vowels where needed to denote the proper pronunciation and meaning of the words. The macron over a vowel causes it to be lengthened or stressed. This changes the meaning of the word as well as its pronunciation. Today a word is considered to be misspelled if the *'u'ina* or *kahakō* is omitted. Examples:

malama - light	Nana - name of a star
mālama - to care for	nanā - to strut
	nānā - to observe
poi - food	kai - sea
po'i - lid, cover	ka'i - to lead

The alphabet, written with a macron over each vowel for purposes of pronunciation, is recited:

'ā, 'ē, 'ī, 'ō, 'ū,

hē, kē, lā, mū, nū, pī, wē

Early dictionaries were alphabetized in this fashion, but the word order in recent dictionaries follows the English alphabet.

■ The Hawaiian language is rich in words describing nature and family relationships. Place names numbered many thousands in pre-European times. The Puku'i-Elbert *English-Hawaiian Dictionary* gives many insights into Hawaiian thinking as expressed in the language. For the word *palapala* (document) there are 63 entries of Hawaiian words, for *aha'aina* (feast) 23 entrees, *hale* (house) 133 and for *ua* (rain) 64 entries.

■ Hawaiian belongs to the family of languages which includes the Indonesian, Melanesian, and Polynesian. This family covers more of the earth's surface than the home area of any other language family, but much of this huge region is water. Over a hundred million people in Indonesia use some form of this language as a native or a second language. In Polynesia, some 300,000 people speak one of the Polynesian "dialects." The Western Polynesian languages spoken in Tonga, Samoa, and nearby islands are older and more complex than the Eastern Polynesian languages spoken in the Society Islands, Marquesas, New Zealand, Hawai'i and the small islands in this area.

Dr. Samuel H. Elbert, Professor Emeritus of Hawaiian Language and Linguistics at the University of Hawaii, wrote that "Hawaiian has the simplest sound system of any Malayo-Polynesian language, and perhaps of any language in the world. . . . A famous linguist suggested that, because of its simple sound system, its simple grammar, its rich vocabulary, and its receptivity to incorporation of loan words, Hawaiian would be preferable to Esperanto or English as a world language." (Unpublished manuscript, "Hawaiian and its Many Kin," in the files of the Hawaiian Studies Institute of The Kamehameha Schools.)

■ **Early Messages**

The chiefs sent messages by swift runners *(kūkini)* who followed the trails between villages and districts. They are credited with great speed as they carried messages orally or sometimes by means of symbolic objects. (Read Kahekili's answer to Kamehameha's messenger Kikāne who threw down before him a white *'ulu maika* stone signifying life and a black one denoting war.) (Kamakau, *Ruling Chiefs of Hawaii,* p. 150)

Messengers used canoes between the islands and between districts on any of the islands when it was more expedient to go by water. (In July, 1782, the chief Kekūhaupi'o went by canoe to Kohala with the message that the youthful Kamehameha should return to Kona. Soon after his return, Kamehameha began his conquest of the islands. (Kamakau, *Ruling Chiefs of Hawaii,* p. 117)

As the women pounded tapa with wooden mallets *(hohoa)* on a log *(kua kuku)* they were able to send messages a distance of several miles, or around an island by frequent relays. The code which they used was not recorded. (Brigham, *Ka Hana Kapa,* p. 78)

The temple drum *(pahu heiau)*, with sharkskin head stretched over a section of coconut trunk, produced several different sound effects according to the manner in which it was struck *(pa'i)* with the hands. Its sounds were said to have informed the listeners about the temple activities. The conch shell *(pū)* was blown to announce the arrival of visitors by land or in canoes.

■ **Bell Stones** *(Pōhaku Kīkēkē)*

Certain close-grained lava stones are resonant when struck with other stones. Those observed at the Cave of the Adzes on Mauna Kea, Hawai'i, and at Poli'ahu *heiau,* Kaua'i, seem to be in their original location and not transported to the spot for the purposes of communication. The sign placed near the bell stone at Poli'ahu *heiau* by the Division of State Parks reads:

> This stone played an important part in the communication system of this sacred Wailua area. According to tradition it was used by the Poli'ahu heiau to signal to its companion heiau, Malae. It was also used to announce the approach of expectant mothers to the birth-stone at Holo-holo-kū. When struck with another stone it gives off a loud ringing sound.

■ **Petroglyphs** *(Ki'i Pōhaku)*

Figures or symbols incised into stone in pre- and post- European times suggest attempts to convey messages or to record events. Hundreds of petroglyphs have been photographed, sketched and studied by Bishop Museum ethnologists and by professors in the Art Department of the University of Hawai'i. Read the interpretation of the meaning of some of the early petroglyphs given by William Ellis in *A Narrative of a Tour Through Hawaii,* 1917 edition, p. 346, or page 334 in the 1963 edition. See the index to *Thrum's Annual* for references to petroglyph studies and sketches. Also see Reading List, books by Cox and by McBride.

■ **Communicating by Tattooing or Burning the Skin**

David Malo wrote that certain *kauwā* were tattooed on the forehead so that all who saw them might know of their low social status. Those tattooed were called *"kauwā lae-puni,"* slaves with bound foreheads; or *"kauwā kikoni,"* the pricked slave. (Malo, 1976, pp. 70-72)

As a mourning rite for a beloved chief, some of his friends would heat the bottom of a small wooden calabash and apply this heated surface to their cheeks or bodies. These disc-shaped burns were interpreted as expressions of love for their departed chief.

Other persons burned irregular marks on their skin with sticks heated over a bonfire or an *imu* fire.

■ **Communication by Bonfires or Signal Fires**

At Ahipu'u (hill of fire) high in Nu'uanu Valley stood a beacon fortress called Haipu. Wood was stacked on it ready to light at a moment's notice. A guard was maintained at all times at war strength. In case of a raid by warriors coming through the pass at Nu'uanu Pali the bonfire was lighted. Thus Honolulu chiefs and their forces were alerted. (See *Sites of Oahu,* 1978, p. 300)

The lowest portion of the rim of Ulupa'u Crater on Mōkapu Peninsula faces the island of Moloka'i. In planning to invade and conquer O'ahu, Kahekili, ruler of Maui and Moloka'i, sent spies to gather information on the strength of the O'ahu forces. The spies relayed their messages to lookouts on Moloka'i by signal fires within Ulupa'u Crater which were not visible to the people of O'ahu.

■ **Non-verbal Communication**

The first accounts we have of communication in Hawai'i by gestures rather than words were recorded by two of Captain Cook's officers in 1779. These men were Surgeon's Mate David

Samwell and James King.

The following quotes retain their spelling and capitalization. Concerning non-verbal communication Samwell wrote:

> ... when a question is put to them that they mean to answer in the negative, instead of speaking they will just shew the tip of the Tongue between their Teeth which signifies a-ouree ['a'ole] or no! They have another Method of denying which is by giving their right hands a little turn & sometimes they use the Tongue & hand together but either of itself will do, & in this way they give negative answers as often as by speaking. (Beaglehole, pp. 1187-88)

While ashore after Cook's death, a friendly chief came to King with a message from Kalani-'ōpu'u. He informed the King that Cook's body would be brought back the next morning. King wrote:

> There appeard a great deal of sincerity in his Manner, & being asked if he did not tell lies he made the signs of truth amongst them which is by hooking the two forefingers together, & they were seldom found to fail when this was done. (Beaglehole, p. 554)

■ Some of the following forms of communication may be observed today. Most of them may be considered Hawaiian, but a few are more widely used:

When a head is tilted backwards the person assumes a manner of superiority or of self-importance.

A head tilted forward suggests humility.

A delicate lifting of the eyebrows (eyebrow flash) means yes.

One indicates a direction by a gesture from the head, never by pointing a finger.

Arms folded across the chest or folded and clasping the shoulders seem to say "kapu" or stay away. (Ho'ope'a nā lima.)

Hands swinging freely at the sides are ready to be extended to greet, clasp, and embrace an approaching friend.

Arms akimbo, that is hands on the hips with elbows pointed outward, suggest the threatening posture of an overlord who is eager to give commands to others.

Crossing the hands behind the back (Ho'ope'a kua) is considered insulting to others as it is thought to be a way of wishing bad luck.

Palms upward, toward the gods, receive emi-nations from above. Palms turned downward receive vibrations from the earth. Following is another interpretation of this statement:

> Kau ka lima iluna, pōloli ka 'ōpū;
> Kau ka lima ilalo, piha ka 'ōpū.
> Meaning
> If the hand turns upward, idle hands, you will hunger;
> If the hand turns down, working hands, you will be filled.

To call by beckoning, hold the extended hand sideways, the palm facing the body, and beckon in that position.

When seated on the floor with legs outstretched, it is insulting to point one's toes at another.

■ **Introduction of the English Language**

English was the commonest of the several foreign languages heard in Hawai'i during the period of Pacific exploration. Captain James Cook, 1778-79, and Captain George Vancouver, 1792-94, each remained some weeks in Hawai'i with their English-speaking crews. Although the missionaries taught and preached in Hawaiian during the early years, they emphasized the use of English, at the request of the rulers, in the Chiefs' Children's School, 1839-49.

The Hawaiian Constitution of 1840 provided for a public school system with English as the medium of instruction (Wist, pp. 46-48). "By 1850 English had become the language of business, diplomacy, and to a considerable extent, of government itself" (Wist, p. 70). At the end of the monarchy in 1893 the Hawaiian language common school was almost a thing of the past (Wist, p. 73).

Until the provision was repealed by the 1965 Legislature through Act 175, the Revised Laws of Hawai'i (40.3) stated that "the Hawaiian language shall be taught . . . in all high schools of the State; and that daily instruction . . . shall be given in every public school conducted in any (Hawaiian Homes Commission) settlement . . ." (Simpson, Robt. J. *The Educator and the Law in Hawaii.* 1964, p. 66). The respect for Hawaiian continues to the present time as is shown in the mandate of the 1978 Constitutional Amendment, Article X, Section 4 requiring the State to "promote the study of Hawaiian culture, history and language."

■ **Printing in Hawaiian and English**

The youthful Hawaiian student Henry 'Ōpū-kaha'ia (Obookiah), while studying in Goshen, Connecticut, in 1814-16, prepared a simple dictionary, grammar and spelling book in Hawaiian. He translated the book of Genesis and some of the Psalms into Hawaiian from English and Hebrew texts. It was his fervent desire to return to his islands and to teach the Christian gospel.

Unfortunately Henry died of typhus fever on February 17, 1818 at the age of 26, before the first missionary party left for Hawai'i in 1819. Four of his Hawaiian classmates who had been educated in the Foreign Mission School, Cornwall, Connecticut, accompanied the missionaries to Hawai'i on the brig Thaddeus. They were Thomas Hopu, William Kainui, John Honolii and George Kaumualii. These young men gave the missionaries lessons in Hawaiian conversation during the five month's voyage.

Attempts to express Hawaiian in writing became a challenge to the missionaries as they became more familiar with the language. The ordained ministers, Hiram Bingham and Asa Thurston, had studied Latin, Greek and Hebrew. As linguists they sought to use the simplest alphabet possible in writing Hawaiian.

The vowels were not a problem if given the "continental sound." But the consonants were numerous and unclear to both the Hawaiians and the missionary teachers. The *k* and *t* sounds seemed to be interchangeable and *t* at times was pronounced like *d*. To use *l* or *r* and *w* or *v* was also a puzzle.

The alphabet must be clear enough to convert oral Hawaiian into sounds that would be understood by all listeners and also to transform some English and many Biblical words into Hawaiian.

■ **Spelling Book, Lesson I**

Although the orthography was still in question, printer Elisha Loomis set up the type for page 1, Lesson I of the first spelling book. On the afternoon of July 7, 1822, a crowd gathered before the Ramage Press in the thatched structure on Missionary Row. Governor Ke'eaumoku of Maui (brother of Ka'ahumanu) visiting on O'ahu with his aides, was asked by Mr. Loomis to pull the lever of the press which struck off the first impression of the printed word in the Hawaiian Islands. Also present on this important occasion were Hiram Bingham, ship captains and interested Hawaiians.

This first spelling book used the five vowels

and seven consonants which eventually became the standard alphabet. This was determined by the Committee on Language made up of Hiram Bingham, Charles S. Stewart, Levi Chamberlain and their Hawaiian informants. After some six years of study, the letters of the alphabet were decided upon by voting and the decision was announced on July 14, 1826.

The early spelling books and primers, however, used as many as a dozen additional consonants which the writers thought were necessary to spell some English words but primarily to print Biblical names, places and the names of religious articles.

Some of these consonants in the spelling books and primers were:

B, *Baibala* (Bible)	R, *Ruta* (Ruth)
D, *Daniela* (Daniel)	S, *Setepano* (Stephen)
F, *Felika* (Felix)	T, *Timoteo* (Timothy)
G, *Golia* (Goliath)	Z, *Zakio* (Zacchaeus)

One hundred and thirty years were to pass before the diacritical marks were added to Hawaiian words to help insure their proper pronunciation and meaning. Today the glottal stop ('okina) and the macron (kahakō) are used consistently in the Pukui-Elbert dictionaries and books of place names. Most instructors of the Hawaiian language consider words misspelled if these marks are omitted.

The New Testament was translated into Hawaiian and printed by 1832 and the Old Testament was completed in 1839. The complete Bible, 2,335 pages, was available to the people by May 10, 1839. The American Bible Society (ABS) took over the printing responsibilities in the 1850s and the latest edition of 1544 pages was run in 1966. The Hawaiian Bible (Baibala Hemolele) is out of print as of this writing.

■ The first newpaper or periodical in Hawai'i was *Ka Lama Hawaii*, a four-page weekly which was written and printed in Hawaiian at Lahainaluna, Maui, from February 14 to December 26, 1834. A dozen different Hawaiian newspapers were published through the century that followed. The last was *Ka Hoku o Hawaii*, Hilo, 1906-1948. (See Mookini, Esther T. *The Hawaiian Newspapers*, 1974)

The first English newspaper was the *Sandwich Island Gazette and Journal of Commerce*, Honolulu, July 30, 1836, to July 27, 1839.

Of the six daily newspapers published in Honolulu at this time (early 1982) two are in English, two in Japanese and English, one in Chinese and English and one in Korean.

A number of weeklies are published for and distributed to local communities. Weekly or monthly papers or magazines are printed for church, ethnic, labor, military and business organizations and also by those interested in natural history, the arts, and local history. Many public and private schools write of their activities in their newspapers.

Books and pamphlets were printed by the mission presses on a variety of subjects. The Bible, catechisms, and hymns received early attention. For the mission schools, books were written and printed on geography, arithmetic, physiology, astronomy, and higher mathematics. Works printed in Hawaiian from 1822 to 1843 are listed in Dibble, *History,* pp. 416-419. Dibble notes that over 113 million pages were printed during the first ten years. Larry Windley, in *Hawaii Historical Review,* lists 118 works printed at Lahainaluna from 1834 to 1846.

Hawaiian culture and history in their many phases continue to furnish subject matter for a multitude of writers. One of the most serious collectors of Hawaiian books reported that these islands outrank almost any other subdivision of the United States in the number and quality of volumes produced, a figure out of all proportion to its geographical size and literate history. (*Sales Builder,* June 1941, p. 2)

■ **Mail and Stamps**

In 1850 Mr. H.M. Whitney received royal permission to receive and deliver mail in the publication room of his print shop. This ended the haphazard "help yourself" system previously carried on by the captains of transpacific and inter-island ships. In December 1850 Kamehameha IV asked the customs collectors in the port towns to serve as postmasters and thus inaugurated a postal system in Hawai'i. Whitney was appointed postmaster general and served until 1856, then again from 1883 to 1886.

The first Hawaiian stamps were issued October 1, 1851, in two-cent, five-cent, and 13-cent denominations, printed in Honolulu. The Hawaiian kingdom was one of the first governments to issue postage stamps. The world's first was Great Britain's penny black issued in 1840. The United States printed its first stamps in 1847. Because of their rarity Hawai'i's earliest stamps are among the most valuable in the world. In 1963 the two-cent, 1851 issue sold for $41,000, the largest amount ever paid for a single stamp. Another two-cent stamp sold for $30,000 in 1966. A 13-cent stamp brought $21,000 in 1952. (See the index to *Thrum's Annual* for many references to stamps.)

The first inter-island airmail was inaugurated October 8, 1934. Overseas airmail began November 23, 1935.

■ **Telegraphic Cable**

The completion of the Commercial Pacific Cable from San Francisco to Honolulu was celebrated on January 2, 1903, with telegraphic messages sent to and received from prominent persons on the mainland, among them President Theodore Roosevelt. On July 4, 1903, the cable was completed to Midway, Guam, and Manila. From the Philippines messages could be sent to Hong Kong and Yokohama by cables installed earlier.

■ **Wireless Telegraph**

Wireless telegraphy between the islands began on November 13, 1900, when the first messages (in code) were sent and received between O'ahu and Moloka'i. Communication was extended to Lāna'i, Maui, and Hawai'i and by March 2, 1901, the Inter-Island Telegraph Company was opened for business. In 1906, after Kaua'i was added to the system, the Mutual Telephone Company acquired and improved this form of communication.

See *Thrum's Annual,* 1929, pages 66-69, for the story of the installation of the Naval Radio Station in 1906, radio communication with the mainland in 1914, and with the Orient in 1916. Early radio amateurs of Hawai'i are featured in the *Sales Builder* for April, 1940.

■ **Radio**

Broadcasting by commercial radio stations began in Honolulu on May 11, 1922. The managers of KGU, owned at that time by the Honolulu Advertiser and KDYX (later KGMB and now KSSK or KISS), a Honolulu Star-Bulletin station, were engaged in heated competition, each seeking to be first on the air.

Marion Mulrony spoke a few words into the KGU microphone at 10:57 a.m. which were heard by interested listeners.

It was at noon on May 11, 1922, that the voice of Marion Mulrony went out over KGU's air waves introducing Governor Farrington. Then at 7:30 that evening there was a one-and-a-half-hour program. . . .

Excerpt from a letter to this writer from KGU's operations manager dated February 10, 1967.

Among the features on the evening program was Johnny Noble's Moana Orchestra which closed the broadcast with "Aloha 'Oe."

At 11:12 a.m. just fifteen minutes after KGU's opening remarks, KDYX began broadcasting a program consisting of greetings by Governor Farrington, talks and musical selections.

Radios for use in automobiles became available in Hawai'i in April, 1930.

Mainland sports events began to be received direct to Hawai'i by 1930 with KGU's broadcast of football games.

The first direct transmission of a Hawaiian musical program was on Christmas morning, 1930, by KGMB to the National Broadcasting Company.

In 1989 there were eighteen AM and eight FM commercial radio stations on O'ahu (including one commercial AM station with a studio on O'ahu but a transmitter on Moloka'i). The island of Hawai'i had five AM and four FM stations in 1989, and Maui had three AM and six FM stations. Kaua'i had two AM and one FM stations.

These statistics are taken from the 1989 *State of Hawaii Data Book*. (The call numbers and frequencies for O'ahu stations are printed weekly in the *Sunday Star-Bulletin and Advertiser's* "TV Week" insert.)

■ Telephone Communication

In 1878 Mr. Charles H. Dickey installed Hawai'i's first telephones, one in his home and the other in his store three miles away at Ha'ikū, Maui. This was two years after Alexander Graham Bell had invented the telephone.

Rival telephone companies were chartered in Honolulu in 1880 and 1883 but merged in 1894 as the Mutual Telephone Company, which in 1954 changed its name to the Hawaiian Telephone Company.

Independent companies were organized on the neighbor islands between 1880 and 1895 but they were purchased in 1928 by O'ahu's Mutual Telephone.

Honolulu's all-dial system, started in 1910, finally included all of the islands by 1957. Radiotelephone service between the islands and to the main-

land began in 1931 and was extended to Japan in 1938. In 1962 the more efficient and economical point-to-point microwave radio system was installed.

In 1959 the telephone company realized its goal of establishing toll-free calling on each of the islands. The island of Hawai'i is now the largest toll-free dialing area in the world. There continues to be a charge for telephoning between the islands, but direct-dialing reduces the toll.

The first pay phones, with rates at five cents a call, were installed in Honolulu in July, 1935.

■ Underseas Cables

Transpacific radiotelephone service ended in 1957 when Hawaiian Telephone laid the first submarine telephone cable in the Pacific. This 4,800-mile cable costing $37 million was the longest to be attempted at that time and over the roughest undersea terrain. The first call was placed during inaugural ceremonies on October 8, 1957.

A second Hawai'i-mainland cable was laid in 1964, to meet an increasing need for this service. A cable was also laid to Japan and the Philippines by way of Wake, Midway, and Guam.

A third Hawai'i-mainland cable was laid in 1974 and a second to the Orient in 1975.

■ Communication in the Space Age

The first live television program was beamed to Hawai'i from the mainland in 1966 via the "Lani Bird" communications satellite. In 1967 satellite circuits were placed in full-time service carrying telephone, television, and data transmission. Most calls between Hawai'i and the mainland today are by satellite. Our voice travels 22,300 miles to an orbiting communications satellite, then back down an equal distance to the person being called. The one-way trip through the satellite takes about 3/10ths of a second.

Most of the O'ahu residents have seen the two huge dish antennae, looking like white discs at the Pupukea earth station on a 400-foot cliff over looking the North Shore. These are each about ten stories high and weigh 300 tons. They are used to transmit and receive long distance calls to and from the mainland. Nine out of ten calls are routed this way by satellite.

The state-wide microwave radio network completed in 1980 now links the six major islands. The network includes 56 radio stations and 14 passive repeaters.

From some areas in Hawai'i one can direct-dial between the islands, to most of North America, and to 131 foreign countries.

"Pay your bills by telephone" is now a common occurrence with the electronic fund transfer system.

■ Television

Two commercial television stations began broadcasting in Honolulu in 1952. On December 1, at 5:05 p.m. KGMB-TV first broadcast live programs and televised motion pictures. KONA-TV (now KHON-TV) began its regular programing on December 16 but it had broadcast a few local shows earlier.

On May 5, 1957 at 6:30 p.m. KHVH-TV was first to transmit color slides and movies. The first programs sent live to and from the mainland via the Lani Bird satellite were on November 19, 1966.

The state had 19 television stations—17 commercial and two public—in 1989, including satellites but excluding translators and cable television. Eight cable TV companies served 307,000 subscribers. Most programs are in color and received live from the mainland. Antenna and receivers have been placed on locations on Hawai'i, Maui and Kaua'i that can properly receive and retransmit the programs. In this process the transmitted material is converted to a different frequency.

The installation of cables to carry programs to areas on O'ahu where reception was poor or unavailable began in April, 1961.

■ Communicating with Pictures

Photography as a form of communication adds another topic of interest to this unit. For more than a century Hawai'i's natural scenery and varied ethnic groups with their colorful customs have made these islands a "photographer's paradise."

A Frenchman, "Senor" L. Le Bleu arrived in Honolulu on December 22, 1846, with the equipment for taking daguerreotypes and soon enjoyed a thriving business. Thus, Honolulu had a photographer just eight years after the science of making stable images was perfected by Daguerre in Paris. (*Paradise of the Pacific,* January 1946, pp. 21-22)

Dr. Hugo Stangewald is credited with introducing the first camera into Hawai'i in 1857. "It was a cumbersome apparatus using wet plates which required three-minutes exposure in bright sunlight." (*Sales Builder,* December 1938, p. 7)

For stories and photos of 13 of Hawai'i's leading professional photographers and examples of their art, see the *Paradise of the Pacific* for June 1960, *Photographers of Old Hawaii,* by Joan Abramson and *Na Pa'i Ki'i* by Lynn Davis.

■ Understanding and Appreciating This Unit

Although Hawaiian has now fallen into disuse as a medium of communication by the majority of the Hawaiian people (an estimated 20,000 may continue to use it) the language continues to function as:

1. Occasional colorful and expressive words and phrases in the active vocabularies of island residents.

2. The majority of geographical and street names.

3. The lyrics for the most beloved of the older Hawaiian songs.

4. The family names of many families and the given name of a large number of girls and of boys in both Hawaiian and non-Hawaiian families.

5. The names for estates, homes, boats, and pets.

6. The place names needed to determine boundaries in land holdings.

Young people of Hawaiian ancestry who can do so are encouraged to learn the language in order to gain a deeper insight into their culture, for the pleasure of conversing with their elders, and to be able to share their knowledge of the culture with others. With some individuals this could develop into an enjoyable or profitable hobby. For a number of students a knowledge of the language and culture along with skill in some of the arts and crafts should develop into full-time employment in the interpretation of Hawaiian culture.

7. The following institutions, departments, or agencies on O'ahu need one or more persons in their organization who speak Hawaiian and have a knowledge of local customs: Bishop Museum, Queen Emma Museum, 'Iolani Palace, Royal Mausoleum, Hawaiian Historical Society, Archives of Hawaii, the State Surveyor's Office, the Land Office, the Hawaiiana Room of the main library and the University of Hawai'i Library. The neighbor island museums and libraries also need staff members skilled in Hawaiian language and

culture.

A knowledge of Hawaiian would be helpful to all instructors of Hawaiian culture and Hawaiian history. For Hawai'i this would include the fourth, seventh grade and high school teachers of Hawaiian studies in the State Department of Education and in most of the private schools. At the present time Hawaiian language teachers are in demand for evening classes for adults as well as full-time teachers in the high schools and colleges.

Persons engaged in the visitors industry, especially the tour drivers, airport greeters, and hotel clerks, have many opportunities to use Hawaiian. Radio and television announcers are confronted with Hawaiian names of places and persons. Many of them would profit by more knowledge of the language and its pronunciation.

■ Student Activities

For students in Hawaiian Culture classes who have a sincere interest in learning something about the language in a limited time the following activities are suggested:

1. Learn the Hawaiian alphabet. (See page 1 of this unit)

2. Learn to count to ten. Say: 'ekahi, 'elua, 'ekolu, 'ehā, 'elima, 'eono, 'ehiku, 'ewalu, 'eiwa, 'umi.

3. Learn to say the motto of Hawai'i and tell what it means. (See it later in this unit)

4. Sing *Hawai'i Pono'ī,* the State Song handed down from the Monarchy, and interpret its meaning. King Kalākaua wrote the words in 1874. Bandmaster Henry Berger adapted them to music.

HAWAI'I PONO'Ī

Hawai'i pono'ī	Hawai'i's own
Nānā i kou mō'ī	Look to your King
Kalani ali'i	The royal chief
Ke ali'i	The chief
Chorus	
Makua lani e	Chiefly parent
Kamehameha e	Kamehameha
Na kāua e pale	We will defend
Me ka ihe.	With the spear.

See Elbert and Mahoe, 1970, for stanzas 2 and 3.

5. List the following place names of concern to each student and, if in Hawaiian, learn to pronounce them correctly and know what they mean: The pupil's home island, his district, his town and street.

6. Each student who has a Hawaiian name should know what it means. Those who haven't should select an appropriate one to use in his Hawaiian Culture class.

7. *'Ōlelo no'eau,* sayings of wisdom, give an insight into the way people think and believe. Students should be encouraged to learn a number of these sayings from the following. (Some teachers require the students to learn one proverb a week.) A larger selection may be read in Handy and Pukui, *The Polynesian Family System in Ka'u, Hawaii* and in Judd's, *Hawaiian Proverbs and Riddles,* Bishop Museum Bulletin No. 77.

    a. *Ua mau ke ea o ka 'āina i ka pono.* The life of the land is perpetuated in righteousness.

    The motto of the Monarchy and the State of Hawai'i is one line selected from an address given by Kamehameha III in 1843 at the celebration of the restoration of the Kingdom. Lord Paulet of Great Britain had taken possession of the government. The King and people offered only "passive resistance," a policy that they believed to be "righteous" *(pono).* In time the "life of the land" was restored.

    The full text of the address of Kamehameha III at Kawaiaha'o Church has not come down to us as far as we know. The following four lines from the speech were given to this writer by the Hawaiian scholar Simeon Nawaa. We believe that our State Motto will mean more to us if we know the historical background that caused its pronouncement.

    He aupuni palapala ko'u;
    Aia i ka lani ke Akua;
    O ke kanaka pono 'oia ko'u kanaka.
    Ua mau ke ea o ka 'āina i ka pono.

    My kingdom is a kingdom of knowledge;
    Its God is in heaven;
    The righteous man is my man.
    The life of the land is perpetuated
    in righteousness.

    b. *E mālama 'ia nā pono o ka 'āina e nā 'ōpio.* The traditions of the land are perpetuated by its youth.

c. *E aloha kekahi i kekahi.*
Love one another.

d. *E hana kaulike.*
Play fair.

e. *Kūlia i ka nuʻu*
Strive to reach the summit.
(Queen Kapiʻolani's motto)

f. *Kūlia e loaʻa ka naʻauao.*
Strive to obtain wisdom.

g. *Imua. Imu ā lanakila.*
Forward. Forward to victory.

h. *ʻOnipaʻa*
Be steadfast. (Motto of Kamehameha V and
of Liliʻuokalani)

i. *E makaʻala kākou.*
We are alert.

j. *Ka ikaika o ka manaʻo me ke kino.*
Be strong in mind and body.

k. *Mai makaʻu i ka hana.   Makaʻu i ka moloā.*
Do not fear work.   Fear laziness.

l. *Uwē ka lani, ola ka honua.*
When the heaven weeps, the land lives.

m. *Hoe aku i kou waʻa.*
Paddle your canoe ahead.

n. *Kau ka lima iluna, pōloli ka ʻōpū.*
If the hand turns upward, idle hands, you
will hunger.

o. *Kau ka lima ilalo, piha ka ʻōpū.*
If the hand turns down, working hands, you
will be filled.

8. Sketch one or several petroglyphs at the top of
a page and write your interpretation or story
about the figure or figures.

9. In the newspaper for May 11 and 12, 1922,
there is a story of a race between the two radio
stations to be first to broadcast. KGU began
broadcasting at noon on May 11, 15 minutes
before its rival KDYX (now KGMB).

10. For a comparison of the Polynesian dialects
see Dibble, *History*, pages 409-410. The Lord's
Prayer is given in seven of the dialects.

11. Conduct a survey to learn the number of
students that are enrolled in classes in Hawaiian at the University of Hawaii and in public
and private day and night schools. How many
are in second or third year Hawaiian?

12. Contact the University Press of Hawaii to find
out how many Hawaiian language texts and
dictionaries were sold during the past year or
two.

13. Select a radio or TV program and list the
number of Hawaiian words that are used in a
given period of time. How many words were
mispronounced? Listen for such common names
as Kalākaua, Kapiʻolani, and Kauaʻi. Learn
how these should be pronounced before judging
others.

14. Survey the popular bookshops for the number
of publications related to learning Hawaiian.
What phrase books can you find that are
published for the visitors?

15. Discuss the language with older persons who
use it. Note that Hawaiian, in common with all
languages, continues to change with use and
time. Ask your informant about such pairs of
words, old and new: ʻaʻole - ʻaʻale, maʻona -
maʻana, puaʻa - puʻa. Some of these changes
are heard only when the words are spoken
rapidly.

16. Try to verify the statement that since the early
1960s there has been an upsurge of interest by
the local public in the Hawaiian language.
Although good instructors are scarce there are
increasing numbers of excellent language texts
and dictionaries.

17. Read about and discuss the communication
possibilities of satellites in receiving live TV
programs in Hawaiʻi and in sending programs
from Hawaiʻi to the Mainland and the Orient.

■ **Audio-Visual Aids**

Opportunities for listening to people speak in
Hawaiian will be easy for some persons and
difficult for others. In nearly every community in
Hawaiʻi there are informants who will come to the
classroom occasionally to speak with the pupils.
Language records and tape recordings may be used
to supplement the "native speakers." *Kūpuna*
(persons of the grandparent generation) are now
compensated for teaching Hawaiian in a number
of the public schools.

Flash cards printed for use in language study
with a picture on one side and the identification on
the reverse side are helpful in vocabulary building
and in review. Create your own set for Hawaiian
words.

The students may prepare colorful posters for

the bulletin boards by using their own sketches or pictures from magazines to illustrate sentences in Hawaiian describing or explaining the pictures.

The students may listen to recordings of the older Hawaiian songs and attempt to understand the words, the phrases, and to grasp the meanings.

Attend services at Kawaiahaʻo, Kaumakapili, or any church in which part of the service is in Hawaiian.

Early communication aids referred to in this unit and on display at Bishop Museum are: drums, conch shells, the kapa log and beater, and petroglyphs.

Bishop Museum has the pair of telephones that King Kalākaua used between his boathouse and the Palace. Also in storage is an exhibit showing a portion of the first underseas cable in cross section. These might be shown on request.

■ Vocabulary

No vocabulary review is given here for the Hawaiian words. Check your understanding of these words:

communication	Esperanto
alphabet	code
petroglyph	daguerreotype
dialect	satellite

■ Evaluation

Check to ascertain that the students feel the drama of man's long search for more dependable, more accurate, and faster methods of communication.

Where emphasis was given to learning Hawaiian words and sentences, test the students' accuracy in these. Conduct as much of this as possible in an oral manner.

■ Reading List

Abrahamson, Joan, ed. *Photographers of Old Hawaii.* Island Heritage Bicentennial Library. Norfolk Island, Aus.: Island Heritage, 1975.

Brigham, William T. *Ka Hana Kapa: The making of bark cloth in Hawaii.* Honolulu: Bishop Museum Press, 1911.

Cox, J. Halley. *Hawaiian Petroglyphs.* Honolulu: Bishop Museum Special Publication No. 60, 1970.

Davis, Lynn. *Na Paʻi Kiʻi.* The photographers of the Hawaiian Islands, 1845-1900. Honolulu: Bishop Museum Press, 1980.

Day, A. Grove. "How to Talk in Hawaii." In *The Hawaii Book.* Chicago: J.G. Ferguson Publishing Company, 1961. 128-133.

Day, A. Grove, and Albertine Loomis. *Ka Paʻi Palapala.* Early printing in Hawaii. Honolulu: Printing Industries, 1973.

Dibble, Sheldon. *History of the Sandwich Islands.* 1843. Honolulu: Thrum, 1909.

Dutton, Meiric K. *Henry M. Whitney.* Pioneer printer-publisher and Hawaii's first postmaster. Honolulu: Loomis House Press, 1955.

Elbert, Samuel H. "The Hawaiian Dictionaries Past and Future." *Hawaiian Historical Society Report for 1953.* Honolulu: Hawaiian Historical Society, 1954. 5-8.

———, ed. *Selections from Fornander's Hawaiian Antiquities and Folk-Lore.* Honolulu: University Press of Hawaii, 1959. (The most popular of Fornander's stories reprinted in Hawaiian and English. This follows the original text with no macrons and few hamzahs.)

———. *Spoken Hawaiian.* Honolulu: University Press of Hawaii, 1970. (A language text widely used by college and adult classes. Revised periodically.)

Elbert, Samuel H., and Noelani K. Mahoe. *Nā Mele o Hawaiʻi Nei.* 101 Hawaiian songs, Hawaiian and English. 1970. Honolulu: University of Hawaii Press, 1978.

Elbert, Samuel H., and Mary K. Pukui. *Hawaiian Grammar.* Honolulu: University Press of Hawaii, 1979.

Ellis, William. *Journal of William Ellis. Narrative of a Tour in Hawaii. . . .* 1826. Rutland, VT and Japan: C.E. Tuttle, 1979.

Feher, Joseph. *Hawaii: A Pictorial History.* Honolulu: Bishop Museum Special Publication No. 58, 1969.

Grace, George W. *The Position of the Polynesian Language within the Austronesian (Malayo-Polynesian) Language Family.* Honolulu: Bishop Museum Special Publication 46, 1959.

Hadley, Joe. *Hawaiian Stories.* An introduction to Hawaiʻi's pidgin English. Kapaʻa, Kauaʻi: Valley House, 1974.

Handy, E.S.C., and Mary K. Pukui. *The Polynesian*

Family System in Ka'u, Hawai'i. 1958. Rutland, VT and Japan: C.E. Tuttle, 1972. (Numerous proverbial sayings in Chapter VII.)

Hogan, Pat. *A History of Stamps of Hawaii, 1851-1900*. Honolulu: Stamps of Old Hawaii, 1980.

Johnson, Rubellite K., ed. and trans. *Ka Nupepa Ku'oko'a*. A chronicle of entries, October 1861-September 1862. Honolulu: Topgallant Publishing Company, 1975.

Johnson, Rubellite K. *Kukini'aha'ilono*. Carry on the news. Native life and thought from the newspapers of 1834-1948. Honolulu: Topgallant Publishing Company, 1976.

Judd, Bernice, Janet E. Bell, and Clare G. Murdoch. *Hawaiian Language Imprints, 1822-1899*. A bibliography. Honolulu: Hawaiian Mission Children's Society and the University Press of Hawaii, 1978.

Judd, Henry P. *The Hawaiian Language*. Honolulu: Honolulu Star-Bulletin Ltd., 1939.

Judd, Henry P., Mary K. Pukui and John F.G. Stokes. *Introduction to the Hawaiian Language*. Honolulu: Tongg Publishing Company, 1945. (A popular dictionary giving 4,500 words in English with their Hawaiian equivalents and 6,000 Hawaiian words with English meanings.)

Kahananui, Dorothy M. *E Pāpā'ōlelo Kākou*. 1969. Third edition updated by Sarah Quick and illustrated by Robin Burningham. Honolulu: Kamehameha Schools Press, 1986. (Considered the best text written for high school students. Equally useful for adult beginners in Hawaiian.)

Kahananui, Dorothy M., and Alberta P. Anthony. *E Kama'ilio Hawai'i Kākou*. Let's speak Hawaiian. 1970. Honolulu: University Press of Hawaii, 1974. (Tapes to accompany the above title are available through National Center for Audio Tapes, University of Colorado, Boulder, CO 80302. Phone: 303-492-7341.)

Kamakau, Samuel M. *Ruling Chiefs of Hawaii*. Honolulu: Kamehameha Schools Press, 1961. (See also *Index to Ruling Chiefs of Hawaii* by Elspeth P. Sterling, Bishop Museum, 1974.)

Loomis, Albertine. *Grapes of Canaan*. Hawaii 1820. The true story of Hawaii's missionaries. 1951. Honolulu: Hawaiian Mission Children's Society, 1966 (paperback).

———. *The Best of Friends*. The story of Hawaii's libraries and their friends, 1879-1979. Honolulu: Press Pacifica, 1979.

McBride, Leslie R. *Petroglyphs of Hawaii*. Hilo: The Petroglyph Press, 1969.

Mellen, George, ed. *The Sales Builder*. Issues from 1932 to 1941.

Mookini, Esther T. *The Hawaiian Newspapers*. Honolulu: Topgallant Publishing Company, 1974.

Pogue, John F. *Moolelo of Ancient Hawaii*. Trans. Charles W. Kenn. Honolulu: Topgallant Publishing Company, 1978. (Contains original Hawaiian text.)

Porter, John R. *Hawaiian Names for Vascular Plants*. Honolulu: University of Hawaii College of Tropical Agriculture, 1972.

Pukui, Mary K., and Samuel H. Elbert. *Hawaiian Dictionary*. Hawaiian-English, English-Hawaiian. Revised and enlarged edition. 1971. Honolulu: University of Hawaii Press, 1986.

Pukui, Mary K., Samuel H. Elbert, and Esther T. Mookini. *Place Names of Hawaii*. Revised and expanded edition. Honolulu: University Press of Hawaii, 1974. (Paperback edition 1976; *Pocket Place Names of Hawaii*, 1989.)

———. *The Pocket Hawaiian Dictionary*. Honolulu: University Press of Hawaii, 1975.

Sherwood, Zelie D. *Beginner's Hawaiian I*. Honolulu: Topgallant Publishing Company, 1981.

Simonds, W.A. *The Hawaiian Telephone Story*. Honolulu: Hawaiian Telephone Company, 1958.

Snakenberg, Robert L. *Hawaiian Language Program Guide*. Honolulu: State of Hawaii Department of Education, Office of Instructional Services, 1979.

Williams, Edith B. (Kulamanu). *Ka 'Ōlelo Hawaii no na Keiki*. The Hawaiian language for children. Honolulu: Edith B. Williams, 1962.

Windley, Larry. "Lahainaluna Printing." *Hawaii Historical Review*, Jan. 1966. II(2):275-289.

Winne, Jane L., and Mary K. Pukui. *'Olelo No'eau a ka Hawaii*. Folk sayings from the Hawaiian. Honolulu: Privately printed, 1961.

Wist, Benjamin O. *A Century of Public Education in Hawaii (1840-1940)*. Honolulu: Hawaii Educational Review, 1940.

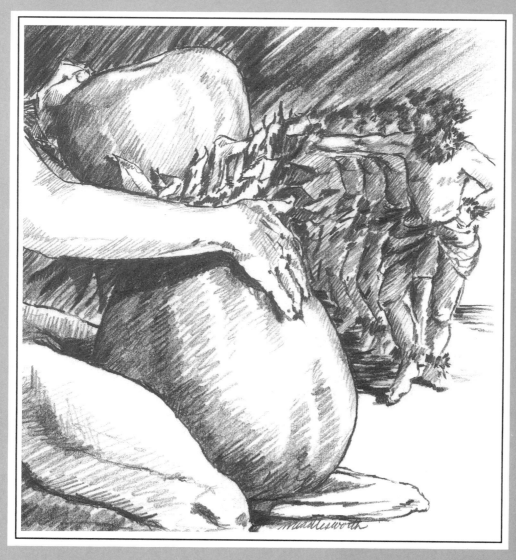

UNIT 5:
Chants,
Musical Instruments
and the Hula

CHANTS, MUSICAL INSTRUMENTS AND THE HULA

■ Chants and Chant Styles

In pre-European music the words and their meanings were more important than the vocal forms of expression. This resulted in the development of several chant forms or styles without true melody or harmony as these musical terms are used today.

The two major divisions of chants, according to most authorities, are:

1. The *oli*, usually unaccompanied solos employing but two or three tones. The *oli* include all of the *mele* or chants not composed for dancing.
2. The *hula* chants, *mele hula*, with marked rhythm to accompany the dancer, usually with a range of four or five tones. Instruments were used in most performances to carry the rhythm.

The chants were divided by subject matter into nine classes of poetry by Edith Rice Plews (pp. 177-193). Also read Helen Roberts (pp. 57-69) and Jane Winne (p. 200). These will be discussed in detail in Unit 6, "The Poetry and Prose of Hawai'i." Examples are prayers, songs of praise, prophecies, name chants, love songs, genealogies and dirges.

One or more persons (*haku mele*) might compose a chant. If it was composed for a person it became the property of that individual. (For details of composing, see Kahananui, 1962, p. 7; Tatar, 1979, pp. 53-68.)

The principal styles of chanting are usually recognized as the:

1. *Oli*, characterized by long sustained phrases.
2. *Kepakepa*, a rhythmic recitation with clear diction and no prolonged vowels. Also called *ko'i honua*, used for reciting genealogies with the words and names pronounced clearly.
3. *Ho'āeāe*, love poems with short phrases and prolonged vowels.

4. *Ho'ouwēuwē*, tearful lamentations for the deceased or expressions of grief for a friend who is departing on a journey.
5. *'Ai ha'a*, called emphatic chanting with fast tempo. Used in vigorous forms of the standing *hula* such as *hula ku'i Moloka'i*.

■ Musical Instruments

Some of the instruments accompanied the hula, others were played for the enjoyment of the player and his listeners. Some served both purposes. A number were genuinely musical in nature, some produced musical sounds for special purposes, and others seem to some persons today as musical sound-producing toys.

■ Stringed Instrument:

'Ūkēkē - a mouth bow or musical bow. Usually three strings of finely twisted sennit (*'aha*) were stretched the full length (17 to 24 inches) of the bow of *kauila* or *'ulei* wood. Today nylon or gut strings and any available hard wood are used. The strings are secured to notches in one end and wound around a "fish tail" projection at the other. The width of the bow is one to one and two-fifths inches in the center and thin or pliable enough to be bent or bowed slightly as it is strung. This elastic force keeps the strings taut. If the strings lie too close to the bow to vibrate properly, small wooden bridges or wedges are placed under them

Ūkēkē. The mouth bow is played by strumming the strings with the right fingers while holding the wooden back against the parted lips. The soft sounds conveyed messages of love.

at each end.

In playing the instrument the convex side of the wooden back is held against the parted lips with the left hand. The "fish tail" end extends to the left. The strings are plucked or brushed with the right thumb or a fiber held by the thumb and finger of the right hand.

The mouth serves as a resonator for the words which are chanted in the throat. The chant is usually of a very personal nature and meant to be understood only by the person to whom it is directed.

The Marquesan 'utete, three feet long and with one string, may be the "ancestor" of the 'ūkēkē.

The tones of the 'ūkēkē and the accompanying chant can be heard but a short distance. In demonstrations today they are amplified in order to be heard by an audience of any size.

Read Buck, pp. 388-390; Tatar, pp. 392-94; Emerson, pp. 147-49.

Listen to Palani Vaughn's recording *Ia Oe E Ka Lā* Vol. I, the title song, for 'ūkēkē music reminiscent of the era of Kalākaua's coronation in 1883.

■ Wind Instruments:

1. *'Ohe hano ihu* - nose flute. (*'ohe* - bamboo, *hano* - sound, *ihu* - nose). The nose flute is made from a section or internode of bamboo 10 to 20 inches long and an inch or so in diameter. The native *'ohe* has much thinner walls than the introduced varieties and makes flutes with better tone quality and much easier to blow.

'Ohe hano ihu. The bamboo nose flute produces pleasant tones when the player blows across the hole at the end and stops one or both holes with his fingers. The sounds carry messages of love.

In making a flute, retain the node at one end of the length of bamboo and saw the other off. Drill the hole for the nose close to the node. then drill two additional holes along the length of the flute. Space these holes after examining existing flutes or by referring to directions or photos.

To play the flute, grasp it with the fingers of your left hand, place your right nostril over the hole near the node, and close your left nostril with your left index finger or left thumb. Blow across, not into, the hole at the node end. To produce the different tones, close and open the holes with the fingers of your right hand while supporting the instrument in a horizontal position with your right thumb.

There is a revival of interest in making and using nose flutes. Entertainers are playing these instruments on the stage and in recordings. In earlier days they were used to accompany chants but most often they carried sentiments between lovers.

Read Buck, pp. 390-391; Tatar, pp. 270-272; Emerson, pp. 145-46.

Listen to Tom Hiona (FW8750) Band 14; Palani Vaughn, *Ia 'Oe E Ka Lā,* Vol. 3, *"Nalohia Ka Makua."*

2. *Pū* - shell trumpet or conch shell (*pū* - to blow or to sound). These large shells are converted into trumpets by sawing off the small end or apex of a triton (*Charonia tritonis*) or drilling a hole in the flattened apex of the helmet shell (*Cassis cornuta*). The holes vary from the size of a nickel to a quarter. When blown the resulting sound may carry as far as two miles. The *pū* was not used as a musical instrument in old Hawai'i, but to announce the arrival of personages or to summon people for special events. Today one or several "trumpeters" may announce the opening of pageants. The tone is deep in large shells and shrill in small ones. The *pū* is capable of being used musically as has been done in Hawai'i and in Florida. (Kanahele, pp. 307-08.)

Captain James King, on board a ship anchored in Kealakekua Bay in February 1779 gave us our first record of conch shells. King refers to them twice in his journal. He spells the plural of conch "knocks and concks." The sounds of the conch shells were heard on shore during the troubled days before Cook's body had been returned and peace had been made between the Hawaiians and the Englishmen.

Vast Crouds of people were on the side where the Captn was kill'd, Knocks blowing & every appearance of hostility. (Beaglehole, p. 559)

The Concks in the morning blew which we were told by the priests last Night was a sign of Defiance, many of the Canoes went out of the bay, & great bodies of People marching off, satisfied I suppose with their own Courage. (Beaglehole, p. 561)

A large white Cassis on display in Bishop Museum attracts the visiting children who have been told that it is the *kihapū* which the magic dog *Puapualenalena* took from the *menehune* (or the gods) and carried it to Chief Kiha, (or Chief Liloa), in Waipi'o Valley back in legendary or early historic times. (Pukui and Curtis, 1949)

(The *pū* is an ideal means of calling children home from play.)

Read Buck, pp. 393-94; Tatar pp. 306-08; Emerson, pp. 130-31.

3. *Ipu hōkiokio* - gourd nose whistle. The Hawaian planters grew the greatest number and variety of gourds to be found anywhere in the Pacific. Small oval or pear-shaped gourds were available for making these whistles, which are known only in Hawai'i.

The gourd whistles, along with the nose flute (*'ohe hano ihu*) and the musical bow (*'ūkēkē*) were known to have been used by lovers to serenade or entertain each other in the evening or at night. These soft, sweet-voiced instruments were called *nā mea ho'oipoipo*, or things for making love.

This whistle is played by blowing across a hole bored into the stem end or on one side of the gourd. The player closes one nostril with a finger or his thumb in order to direct all of the air from his other nostril across the hole. Different sounds are produced by stopping one, two, or three of the finger holes drilled into the gourd.

The 20 gourd whistles in Bishop Museum range from one and three-fourths to three inches high, and one and one-half to two and three-quarters inches in diameter. The holes measure one-half inch in diameter or slightly less. A few have burnt-in decorations in the form of triangles.

Occasionally *hōkiokio* were made from small coconut shells or hollowed-out *kamani* seeds. This

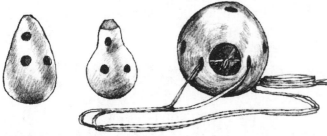

Instruments to Convey Messages of Love: Hōkiokio. The gourd nose whistle is played by blowing across one hole while stopping one or more of the remaining holes with the fingers. A lovers' whistle.

Oeoe. Roarers are made by piercing holes in small gourds, coconuts or *kamani* nuts. When whirled by a cord they emit a whistling sound.

whistle is used today largely in demonstrations.

Read Buck pp. 391-93; Tatar pp. 176-77; Emerson, pp. 146-47.

4. *Oeoe* - roarer, bull roarer (*oe* - whistle). Small gourds, coconuts, or *kamani* nuts are pierced with two holes through which a string is passed. The wind whistles through several other drilled holes as the instrument is whirled in circles by the string.

Small coconuts are made into roarers by filing a small opening at the stem end that provides an aperture which causes a whistling sound as the *oeoe* is whirled around.

Oeoe are classed as sound makers or toys, not true musical instruments. The name "bull roarer," hardly appropriate for the small Hawaiian instrument with a shrill, piping voice, derives from a variety of Appalachian and East Coast toys that when swung have a voice rising from bass to low tenor.

Read Buck, p. 394; Tatar, p. 270.

5. *Pū lā'ī* - Ti leaf whistle (*pū* - trumpet, *lā'ī* - ti leaf). A strip of green ti leaf an inch or more in width is folded and rolled into a spiral, cone-shaped tube. The large end may be pierced with a *nī'au*, coconut-leaf midrib or tied with a cord to prevent it from unrolling. The small end is flattened and serves as the mouthpiece. The blower may vary the sound quality by pinching his lips against the reed-like mouthpiece or by covering the whistle with both hands and opening or closing the palms. This whistle is a toy or soundmaker, not a true musical instrument.

Read "The Ti-leaf Trumpet" (Pukui and Curtis, 1949). Also Buck, p. 393; Tatar, p. 316; Emerson, p. 147.

6. a. *Nī'au kani* - singing splinter (*nī'au* - coconut leaflet mid-rib, *kani* - to sound).

b. *'Ohe kani* - (*'Ohe* - bamboo, *kani* - to sound). This is not an ancient instrument but an adaptation of the jew's (jaw's) harp. It was featured in Kamehameha's court as early as 1811. It is played somewhat like the *'ūkēkē*. The base of the instrument is a flat strip of wood or bamboo four to eight inches long. It may or may not have a slit cut into one end. Lashed to this in two places is the *nī'au* or *'ohe* splinter extending one or two inches beyond the end of the base. If the base has been split, the splinter vibrates in this opening. With his left hand the player holds the base of the instrument between his lips and against his teeth. With the index finger of his right hand he strikes the splinter back and forth causing it to vibrate. By changing the contours of his mouth cavity and expelling air over the splinter, he creates changing sounds. He can also chant a love song, a *mele ho'oipoipo*. Emerson wrote that this instrument is of Hawaiian invention. One hears it today only in demonstrations.

Read Buck, pp. 394-95; Tatar, pp. 265-66; Emerson, p. 147.

Pahu hula

■ **Percussion Instruments:**

1. *Pahu hula* - *hula* drum or shark skin drum (*pahu* - drum). The *pahu* is one of the most important instruments used to accompany the *hula*. Its deep solemn tones inspire the dancers and stir the emotions of the spectators.

La'a-mai-Kahiki (La'a from Tahiti), an adventurous navigator of the migratory period of six or more centuries ago, according to legend, brought the *pahu* to Hawai'i. A patron of the *hula*, he instructed teachers in the use of the *pahu* and of the bamboo pipes *(kā'eke'eke)*, which he introduced at the same time. La'a is a form of the name Laka, now credited with both male and female forms. Each is considered god or goddess of forest growth and patron or patroness of the *hula*.

The *pahu* is hewn from a section of a mature, seasoned coconut tree trunk some 15 to 25 inches long. The bark is removed and the log hollowed from both ends, leaving a septum about one-third the distance from the bottom. This lower portion is decorated by cutting openwork patterns in the shape of triangles, crescents, and arches. The upper opening is covered with shark skin, stretched taut and lashed to the openwork below with sennit cords *('aha)*.

The drummer sits before the *pahu* and may strike *(pa'i)* the drum head with both hands using the fingers and heel of the hand. By striking different parts of the drum head he produces a variety of sounds. The drummer may use the left hand only on the *pahu* and hold the fiber *(kā)* in his right hand to strike the *pūniu* which may be tied to his right leg above the knee.

Though difficult and time consuming to fashion, *pahu hula* are being made and used in rather large numbers today.

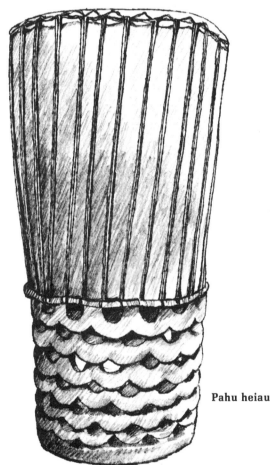

Pahu heiau

Pahu hula. A *hula* drum was made from a coconut tree log hollowed at both ends. The drum head of sharkskin is held taut by sennit cords. The base consists of studs, a continuation of the body of the drum. The use of studs is known in only three *pahu*.

Pahu heiau. A temple drum, 46 inches high, was used in ceremonies in the temple. This *pahu*, the only one of its kind known, is from Papa'ena'ena heiau on the slopes of Diamond Head.

The *pahu heiau* is a drum the same general construction as the *pahu hula* only much larger. The only known example is the one in Bishop Museum, said to have come from Papaʻenaʻena *heiau* on Diamond Head. It is 46 inches high. Such drums were kept in the *hale pahu*, a special drum house within the walls of the *heiau*.

Drums, mentioned but a few times in Cook's journals, were observed as being used in accompanying the dance, as a part of *hoʻokupu* or gift giving, and in ceremonies respecting the dead.

Read Buck, pp. 396-401; Tatar, pp. 288-90; Emerson, pp. 140-41.

Listen to Tom Hiona (FW 8750) Band 2, 8 and 13; Kaupena Wong (Poki SP 9003) Band I-1.

2. *Pūniu* - coconut knee drum. (*pū* - container, *niu* - coconut). Also called *kilu*. The top, or upper fourth, is removed from a large, polished coconut shell to form the resonance chamber of this drum. A ring-shaped cushion (*pōʻaha*) of *kapa* or a ring of sennit or other cordage, is placed on the base of the shell. The drum head, which tightly covers the opening, is traditionally from the durable skin of the *kala*, a scaleless fish. The skin from the right side of this flat fish was preferred by some *kumu hula* (Emerson, 1976, p. 141).

Cords pass from the edges of the drum head to the ring-shaped cushion to hold the skin taut. Tying cords, 12 to 22 inches long, attached to each side of the base allow the drum to be tied securely to the right thigh of the player. He strikes the drum head with a thong (*kā*) of braided or twisted sennit, which he holds in his right hand. His left hand is free to strike the *pahu* at his left side.

Pūniu or *Kilu*. The cords of this coconut shell drum were tied to the seated drummer's right thigh above the knee. He struck the fish-skin head with a fiber *kā* held in his right hand. This drum is usually used with the *pahu hula*.

The drummer produces light, high-pitched sounds while striking the *pūniu*, which are a pleasing contrast to the deep, noble vibrations caused by striking the *pahu* with his fingers and the heel of his left hand.

The six-inch fiber thong (*kā*) used with the *pūniu* was originally braided or twisted from sennit (*ʻaha*) and knotted at the striking end. Today the *kā* is often made by braiding ti leaves into a suitable size.

Traditionally the *pūniu* was played with the *pahu* to accompany the *hula*. Recently it has been played alone, also to accompany the *hula*.

In earlier times some pūniu were lashed to an attractively carved wooden base. Bishop Museum has such a base, bearing carved human figures. One in a Glasgow museum has the coconut shell lashed to a simple wooden base which is four and one-half inches tall.

Bishop Museum has a rare type of *pūniu* which might be called a *pūipu* since the resonance chamber is a gourd about the size of a coconut shell.

Read Buck, p. 401-05; Tatar, pp. 316-17; Emerson, pp. 141-43.

Listen to Tom Hiona (FW 8750) Band 1 and 13.

3. *Ipu hula, ipu heke, pā ipu* - gourd *hula* drum (*ipu* - gourd, *heke* - head, *pā* - to strike). This drum-like instrument (not a true drum, as it has no membrane for a drum head) consists of two gourds glued together. The stem end is removed from a long, globular gourd (*ʻolo*) which may be from 12 to 22 inches long and eight to 16 inches in diameter. A squat gourd (*heke*), seven to 11 inches high and about the same diameter, has both ends cut away. (These measurements are from gourds, some old, in Bishop Museum.) The *heke* or top gourd is fitted closely into the long one and securely fastened with breadfruit gum. During construction a ring or collar, several inches wide, cut from another gourd is, in some cases, fastened between the top and bottom gourds to give added strength.

The resulting instrument, shaped like a figure 8, is easy to carry because of its light weight. A wrist loop of twisted *kapa* is fastened to the lower gourd or to the collar by passing the ends through two small holes and knotting them.

The *ipu* is sounded by striking it (*paʻi*) with the fingers and the palm of the right hand and by thumping (*kū*) the bottom against the matted floor

Ipu Heke: These drum-like instruments consist of two gourds glued together. The one on the right has a collar cut from another gourd to give it added strength. The drummer, while seated, supports the gourd with the wrist loop and his left hand while he thumps the bottom against the matted floor. He strikes the side or bottom of the lower gourd with his right fingers and palm.

or a folded piece of *kapa*.

The *ipu,* one of the most important instruments in marking time and emphasizing the rhythm of the chant and the hula, is of local invention.

Samwell wrote on January 25, 1779, that he and his companions were entertained by an elderly woman wearing dog tooth leglets *(kūpeʻe niho ʻīlio)* and dancing within a small circle or ring to the sound of the drum.

> On one side of the Ring sat the Drummer, his Drum was made of three Gourd Shells inserted into each other, he beat the bottom of it against the Ground & sung a Song in slow time. (Beaglehole, p. 1168)

The three gourd shells mentioned here must refer to an *ipu hula* with a collar, described earlier, cut from a third gourd and fitted between the two which form the actual drum.

There are 13 *ipu hula* in the Bishop Museum collection. All are made from two gourds, but some are fitted with a collar three inches or more in width.

For some years now, single gourds *(ipu heke ʻole)* have been used by each dancer in addition to

the double gourd in the hands of the chanter.

Since insect pests have stopped gourd growing in Hawaiʻi, large numbers are shipped in from California and Mexico to satisfy the needs of the *hula* teachers and students.

Read Buck, pp. 405-07; Tatar, pp. 173-76; Emerson, 142-43.

Listen to Tom Hiona (FW 8750) Band 3 and 9; Kaupena Wong (Poki SP 9003) I-3, 5. II-1, 7.

4. *ʻUlīʻulī* - gourd rattle (*ʻulī* - to rattle). Shot-like seeds of the canna *(aliʻipoe)* are placed in a small gourd or, in recent years, a tree gourd *(laʻamia)* or a coconut. A fiber handle, tipped with a disc of feathers, is attached to the gourd. In earlier times some of these instruments were without the decorative feather disc. The dancer traditionally holds one *ʻulīʻulī* in the right hand and shakes it to produce the rattling sound. The left hand is free to carry out the graceful interpretive motions of the *hula.* In present day programs the *ʻulīʻulī* is a common and colorful instrument. Some dancers use one in each hand, a modern innovation, called the *haole hula* or *hula ʻauana.*

John Webber, draughtsman with Captain Cook, sketched three views of a man dancing with an *ʻulīʻulī* which was capped with a large disc *(heke)* of cock feathers. The dancer is wearing a brief *malo* and a dog tooth leglet or *kūpeʻe niho ʻīlio* on each leg.

Dr. Buck wrote of this instrument, which was developed in Hawaiʻi, that it "is a tribute to the artistic taste and inventive genius of the early Hawaiian craftsmen." (Buck, 1957, p. 414)

Read Buck, pp. 411-14; Tatar, p. 408; Emerson, p. 144.

Listen to Tom Hiona (FW 8750) Band 5; Pele Pukui (Poki SP 9003) I-6.

5. *ʻŪlili* - triple gourd rattle (*ʻūlili* - wandering tattler bird which makes a whirring cry). Three gourds are slipped on a rod slightly smaller in diameter than a broom handle. The outer gourds are fixed to the rod, but the center one rotates freely. A cord is secured to the rod and issues from a hole in the center gourd. When the cord is wound and unwound by the player, who holds the center gourd and pulls and releases the string, a whirring sound is produced. This seemed to suggest the sound made by the tattler bird which is called the *ʻūlili.* Modern instruments are made from the more durable and readily available coconuts and the tree gourds (la'a mia). The two end coconuts or gourds hold a few seeds of the canna (ali'ipoe) or small pebbles. When whirled these produce staccato sounds. In the standing hula the dancers are able to pull the full length of the string to cause a prolonged whirring sound. Or they pull out a short length to cause a brief whirr. A combination of long and short sounds provides a varied rhythm for the hula 'ūlili.

Read Buck, pp. 414-15; Tatar, pp. 407-08.
Listen to Tom Hiona (FW 8750) Band 12.

6. Pū'ili - split bamboo rattle (pū - to sound, 'ili - bark or skin). A piece of bamboo some 20 inches long and one and one-half to two inches in diameter is split into narrow strips or strands except for a section of about five inches at one end which serves as a handle. Bamboo is cut away to leave spaces between the strands. The player or dancer produces a rustling sound when he taps the pū'ili against his or his partner's body, the floor mat, or another pū'ili.

Dancers usually sit on the floor in two rows facing each other when doing a hula with the pū'ili. However, they may stand and face the audience or each other. Dancers may exchange the pū'ili in mid-air.

The sound of the pū'ili may remind the listener of the wind rustling the coconut leaflets.

Traditionally but one pū'ili was used by each dancer. When held in the right hand, the left hand was used to gesture and to receive the gentle tap of the tip of the pū'ili. Today dancers frequently use two instruments, often with vigor and loud rustling.

Read Buck, pp. 415-16; Tatar, pp. 311-12; Emerson, p. 144.

Listen to Tom Hiona (FW 8750) Band 6; Pele Pukui (Poki SP 9003) II-6.

7. Kāla'au - hula rhythm sticks (kā - to strike, la'au - wood). Traditionally a kauila rod a yard or more in length was held in the left hand close to the body and struck with a short rod of the same wood but usually less than a foot long. Modern dancers most often use two identical kāla'au, usually a foot or less in length.

Several kumu hula, however, are reviving the use of a long and a short resonant stick. Some troupes are using one stick as tall as the dancers. In the hula they stomp one end of the longer stick on the floor and then against the stick held by the next dancer closeby. When struck together, the sticks must be held lightly in order to vibrate and give off a resonant sound.

The kāla'au was frequently used with the papa hehi, the next instrument to be discussed.

Read Buck, pp. 408-10; Tatar, pp. 199-200; Emerson, 144-45;

Listen to Tom Hiona (FW 8750) Band II - Kāla'au and papa hehi; Pele Pukui (Poki SP 9003) II-2, kāla'au only.

8. Papa hehi - treadle board or footboard (papa - flat, hehi - to tread, stamp). Foot boards, about an inch thick and somewhat larger than the dancer's foot, are fashioned with the upper surface concave and the lower surface flat. A small cross piece of wood is centered under the board so that it can be tipped and tapped in treadle fashion by the dancer's foot. A flat stone was used in this fashion in years past. This instrument is primarily to keep time and is always used with the kāla'au which gives a brilliant resonance in contrast to the thud of the foot board. The papa hehi is associated with Kaua'i and Ni'ihau, where it is supposed to have originated. A few dancers continue to use the papa hehi today.

On his brief visit to Kaua'i in 1778, Cook recorded in his journal that one of his gentlemen saw the papa hehi and kāla'au. He wrote:

> We had no oppertunity to see any of their amusements and the only musical instruments that was seen among them was a hollow vessel of wood like a platter and two sticks, on these one of our gentlemen saw a man play: one of the sticks he held as we do a fiddle and struck it with the other, which was smaller and something like a drum stick and at the same time beat with his foot upon the hollow Vessel and produced a tune that was by no means disagreeable. This Musick was accompaned with a song, sung by some woman and had a pleasing and tender effect. (Beaglehole, p. 1186)

According to the entries in their journals, Cook's party saw seven of the instruments described in this unit, and they brought away two more instruments not recorded in their writings. The latter two were the pūniu and the hōkiokio.

Read Buck, p. 410; Tatar, p. 294.
Listen to Tom Hiona (FW 8750) Band 11, Kāla'au and Papa Hehi.

9. 'Ili'ili - stone castanets ('ili'ili - pebble). Two water-worn pebbles of close grained lava are held in each hand and clicked together to mark the time in a sitting or standing hula. The stones may be

found in wet or dry stream beds and along beaches. Very smooth, bubble-free stones that fit the dancer's hands are preferred. Dull looking stones may be brightened and darkened by rubbing them with oil from roasted *kukui* nuts.

Most programs featuring a variety of dances will include one or more *mele hula* accompanied by the *'ili'ili*. "Pu'uonioni," is one of the most popular *hula* with the *'ili'ili*.

Read Buck, p. 410; Tatar, p. 164; Emerson, p. 120.

Listen to Tom Hiona (FW 8750) Band 10; Pele Pukui, (Poki SP 9003) I-2.

10. *Kā'eke'eke, pahūpahū,* or *'ohe kā'eke* - bamboo pipes or bamboo stamping tubes (*kā* - to strike, *'eke* - a container, *pahū* - booming sound, *'ohe* - bamboo).

Bamboo pipes of varying lengths, with one end closed by a node, are held, one in each hand, and struck against the ground or against a stone padded by a mat or a fold of tapa. A chanter may pitch his voice to the tone produced by one of the pipes. More than a century ago as many as six performers were reported using two pipes each to accompany a *hula*. In the revival of this instrument in recent years, as many as two dozen players have been trained to accompany Hawaiian songs with tuned pipes to secure delightful harmonic and rythmic effects.

Pipes should be made from the thin-wall, long-jointed native bamboo. The length of the tube, not its diameter, determines the pitch. For instance, a 26-inch tube is middle C, a 52 inch tube is C below middle C. Hopkins gives the lengths of each tube needed to make an "orchestra" of 11 different bamboo tubes. Timothy and Lokalia Montgomery should be given credit for making and calibrating some of the first tuned sets consisting of 24 tubes or so. They trained children from a number of schools to play them as an accompaniment to Hawaiian songs.

Read Buck, p. 407-08; Tatar, pp. 195-96; Emerson, pp. 143-44.

Listen to Tom Hiona (FW 8750) Band 4; Kaupena Wong, (Poki SP 9003) I-7.

11.   a. *Kūpe'e niho 'īlio* - (*kūpe'e* - leglet, *niho* - teeth, *'īlio* - dog).

b. *Kupe'e pūpū* - (*pūpū* - shell). Dance leglets of dog teeth, of shells, and of shells and seeds and also wristlets of boar tusks were once worn by *hula*

dancers. The leglets added something to the sound effects during the more active movements of the dance.

The leglets consist of a four-sided piece of netting strung closely with dogs' teeth, shells, or seeds. Of the 13 complete ones in Bishop Museum, ornamented with dogs' teeth, a typical one has an upper border nine and one-half inches wide, a lower border 14 and three-fourths inches wide, and a depth in the middle of eight and one-fourth inches. Lacing cords and loops are provided on the sides to fasten the instrument to the leg below the knee. The outer surface is closely covered with rows of dogs' teeth which overlap. A leglet with 20 rows of teeth would have 41 teeth on the narrow edge and 56 teeth on the wide edge. This gives a total of 995 canine teeth, contributed by 249 dogs. The total number of teeth in the 13 leglets in Bishop Museum is 11,218 teeth, coming from 2,805 dogs. Dogs were an important flesh food in Hawai'i and were bred in large numbers. The canine teeth (each dog has but four) were removed from the dogs' jaws after they had been cooked in the *imu* and served at a meal.

In 1779, Captain King, of Cook's expedition, in describing an entertainment given by a man on the beach at Kealakekua Bay, Hawai'i, states that the entertainer held an instrument (*'uli'uli*) in one hand, had some pieces of seaweed tied round his neck, wore a *malo*,

> . . . and round each leg, a piece of strong netting, about nine inches deep, on which a great number of dog's teeth were loosely fastened, in rows. . . . Mr. Webber thought it worth his while to make a drawing of this person, as exhibiting a tolerable specimen of the natives; the manner in which the maro [*malo*] is tied; the figure of the instrument before mentioned, and the ornaments round the legs, which at other times, we also saw used by their dancers. (Buck, 1957, p. 533)

> . . . round the small of her Legs were tyed some Matting with Dogs Teeth stuck in it in rows which they called Coobe [*kūpe'e*], from the lowest Row the Teeth increased in bigness to the upper, & being loose on shaking her leg they made a rattling Noise. (Beaglehole, p. 1168)

Bishop Museum has strings of dog's teeth previously labeled necklaces, but now known to be teeth collected, pierced with a pump drill, (*nao wili*) and strung until enough were available for a leglet.

Bishop Museum has recently acquired, from

the Hooper Collection, a leglet containing 525 strombus shells fastened in 18 rows to the background netting. Only eight of these *kūpe'e pūpū* are known to exist.

A leglet in the Vienna Museum, from the Cook Expedition, contains horizontal bands of white shells and black seeds in pleasing contrast. The shells are strombus and the seeds, from the native *wiliwili (Erythrina sandwiciensis)*, have turned black with age.

Both John Webber and Louis Choris sketched men dancing with the dog tooth leglets. David Samwell saw a woman wearing them while dancing.

Men wore bracelets of boar tusks (Buck, p. 555) while dancing, but they are largely ornamental. (Feher, 1969, p. 124)

Today the leglets are made from macrame or burlap as a base. Shells, seeds or ceramic teeth are pierced and sewn securely to the base. This writer has observed that dark colored shells or seeds, especially when widely spaced on the fabric, are not attractive on the legs of women *hula* dancers.

Read Buck, pp. 553-561; Tatar, pp. 220-21.

12. *Umauma* - the human chest. Kaupena Wong, in his notes for the album *Mele Inoa* (Poki SP 9003), reminds us "Sometimes the human body served as a musical instrument as in the *pa'i umauma*, chest-slapping *hula*." (Emerson, p. 153)

Listen to Kaupena Wong (Poki SP 9003) II-3. In the *pa'i umauma* two sounds are heard in addition to the chanting. The striking of the chest is a low, hollow sound, and the striking of the thighs is a sharper sound.

■ The Hula

The *hula* is the folkdance of the Hawaiian people which interprets the words and meanings of the rythmic dance chants called the *mele hula*. In the commonest form of the *hula*, the dancer's body remains relatively stable, his feet mark the time, and his arms and hands describe or interpret the meanings of the words in the *mele hula*. In the more exuberant forms the dancers move about entertainingly using the body as well as the feet and hands. Facial expressions vary according to the type of *hula* being danced.

The *hula* dates back to the early days of Hawaiian experiences. Legends vary as to its origin. Kapo might have been the first dancer; if so, this gives her the honor of being the first

goddess of the *hula*. In one legend she is a sister of the volcano goddess Pele. Both Laka and Hōpoe are credited with teaching Hi'iaka to dance and to chant.

La'amaikahiki (La'a from Tahiti) on his first trip to Hawai'i brought the *pahu* drum. On his second trip he again brought a *pahu* and, according to the legend, the bamboo stamping tubes (*kā 'eke*) and the nose flute. It seems that *kā'eke* at that time referred to the *pahu* drum also. As a patron of the *hula*, La'a traveled throughout the islands teaching the dance, the *mele hula*, and the use of the *pahu* drum.

The *hula* honored the gods, the *ali'i*, and exalted many forms of nature. It provided delightful entertainment.

The *hula* was placed under the watchful eyes of the gods. *Kapu* were pronounced which affected the teachers and students. Ceremonies of a very exacting nature were developed and observed.

Both young men and women learned to dance. Candidates were carefully screened, kept secluded, and trained under strict discipline.

The dances and chants were taught by a *kumu hula*, a skilled man or woman of great dedication, Most often the "school" was a large thatched structure, the *hālau hula*, spacious and airy and closed on all sides against the spying eyes of the villagers. The *hula* may have first been taught in the *hālau wa'a*, a similar but more open structure used for the final construction and storing of canoes (*wa'a*). Later *hālau hula* were built.

The most important furnishing in the *hālau hula* was the *kuahu* or altar. A block of *lama* wood covered with yellow *kapa* stood upon the altar. As a part of their training, the student dancers brought and placed upon the *kuahu* greens which they had ceremonially gathered in the mountains. Some of the following were considered necessary for all *kuahu*: maile, 'ōhi'a lehua, halapepe, 'ie'ie, 'ōhi'a 'ai, koki'o, hau, 'ulu, mai'a, kī, 'ilima and such ferns as *palapalai, pala'ā, hohiu, ēkaha* and '*iwa*. (Emerson, p. 19-20, and others)

After long and arduous training, the students were ready to graduate with a ritual called the *'ūniki*. After a ceremonial bath in the sea, they sat down to the feast of *ai-lolo* where they ate the pig which was prepared especially for them. Songs and chants lifted the *kapu*, relatives and friends came to congratulate the graduates, who performed the dances and chants which they had learned.

The Altar to Laka: Our artist's conception of the *kuahu* or altar which stood in every *hālau* as the abode of Laka, the *hula* goddess. In some *hālau* it was a shelf or frame built against the wall of the structure. Greenery, sacred to Laka, was gathered ceremonially in the mountains and was used to decorate the *kuahu*. At appropriate times the dancers approached the *kuahu* and placed their head and neck *lei* on the altar.

Laka was represented on the *kuahu* by a block of *lama* wood wrapped in yellow *kapa*.

Only then were they ready to leave the *hālau*. (Emerson, pp. 32-35)

Some trained dancers were invited to the courts of the *ali'i* where they entertained the members of the chief's family and his visitors. Other dancers traveled from place to place dancing in return for sustenance and gifts. A few became *kumu hula* (teachers).

The young, agile dancers were called the *'ōlapa*. (*'Ōlapa* means to flash. It is also the name of a native forest tree with leaflets that dance in the slightest breeze.)

The *ho'opa'a* are the older men and women, once dancers, but now those who chant for the dancers and accompany themselves on the *pahu, ipu,* or other instruments (*ho'opa'a* is to learn, to memorize). Their name credits them with learning and remembering the many chants and dances.

The best known and perhaps the only remaining *heiau* dedicated to the *hula* is Kē'ē, at Hā'ena on Kaua'i. This does not mean that the *hula* was a religious dance as is often erroneously stated.

There is a *makai* terraced stone area at Kē'ē and a *mauka* unpaved platform. The entire complex consists of man-made structures, now in disrepair, and large natural stones bearing names.

It is said that the *hula* was taught at this *heiau*, and that such personages as Laka and Lohi'au danced here. (M. Kelly, pp. 95-121)

■ **The Hula Kahiko** - (*kahiko* - ancient).

The missionaries, early in their labors of teaching and preaching, attempted to stamp out the *hula*, which they found most objectionable. In 1830, Kuhina-nui Ka'ahumanu, by then a convert to Christianity, forbade public *hula* performances. The fun-loving young Kamehameha III, after Ka'ahumanu's death, relaxed this edict and other strict practices. But by 1835 he followed the wishes of his missionary advisors and again barred the *hula*.

During these years knowledgable elders in the country districts, away from the mission stations, taught the *hula*. People of influence in these areas invited the dancers into their homes to entertain. In this way the *hula* traditions were kept alive.

Kalākaua is credited with the revival of the *hula*, the recitation of the *mele hula*, and the use of the instruments associated with the dance. These performances were a colorful part of the entertainment at his court and at his coronation in 1883. Again at the King's 50th birthday jubilee in 1886, he was honored with many public performances of the *hula*. These dances revived at Kalākaua's time and those remembered from still earlier days are called today the *hula kahiko* - the ancient dances.

■ **The Hula 'Auana** - (*'auana* - to wander, drift, stray, or go from place to place).

The modern *hula* is usually danced to songs with melodies, not the chanted *mele hula*. The lyrics are in Hawaiian, English, or Hawaiian interspersed with English words. Its devotees claim that this form of the *hula* was developed to please the visitors to Hawai'i and the young people, most of whom do not understand the Hawaiian language or appreciate the old ways.

Sometimes called the Waikīkī hula, these performances are presented with greater emphasis on the motions than on the words, although the motions do interpret the word meanings to some extent. These were the dominant dances from sometime around the 1930s to the late 1960s, especially at shows frequented by visitors.

The current heightened interest in most phases of Hawaiian culture has been termed the Hawaiian Renaissance. This rather gradual awakening began in the 1970s, and one of the noticeable features was the revival of many of the so-called old hula. Even the younger kumu hula are teaching these as well as creating original texts and dances in the spirit of the hula kahiko.

■ The Hula in 1779

There are numerous references to dances in Cook's journals. It is surprising that more dances were not seen and mentioned during this Makahiki season. The word hula (or hura) was not recorded.

In the following quotations two men dancers are mentioned while 21 women are noted by count, and many more are referred to as members of dancing groups, the sizes of which are not given. Is it possible that Cook's men preferred to watch the hula girls and to write about them, not the men dancers?

Webber sketched a man in a spirited dance with the 'ulī'ulī. He made no drawings of women dancers, but artists to follow him did so.

The dancers mentioned here describe the participants as standing, sitting, and half-kneeling.

King described dances honoring the memory of a chief who had died. They were held in front of the house where the body lay.

> . . . a Mat was spread upon the Area, & two men & 13 women came & sat themselves down, in three unequal rows; the two men in front, with three of the Women, their Necks & heads were decorat'd with Featherd ruffs, broad green leaves variously scollopd were thrown with a good deal of taste about the Shoulders, & both Men & Women had a greater quantity of their Cloth wrapt round them, than on Ordinary occasions. . . .
>
> The Company seatd on the Mat began by moving their Arms with little inflexion of the body, in a very slow but graceful manner, & which was accompanied with a melancholy tune, they after-

wards kneeld, or rather half kneeling & sitting began to move their Arms to a much quicker tune.

> . . . At intervals a single man & woman would repeat something in recitative with motions, & at other times their Motions & tunes were so quick & lively, as to destroy its being entirely a grave ceremony. This Performance last'd an hour. . . . (Beaglehole, p. 822)

Samwell, in February 1779, wrote about the ceremony described above but gives a more dramatic conclusion:

> We saw none of their Chiefs buryed but some of our Gentlemen strolling about one of the Towns happened to see a short Ceremony preparatory to the burial of one of the Indians. Before the House in which the dead body lay the Court was covered with Matts, two young Girls stood holding a large bunch of feathers, black on one side and white on the other, ten Women dressed on the occasion with two Men performed a solemn kind of a dance during which time the place is sacred or Taboo, no one daring to profane it with their presence; when the Dance is over the Women sit down in a Circle put their faces to the Earth all together and give a howl, which concludes the Ceremony. (Beaglehole, pp. 1184-85)

Samwell wrote of the costume and dance of an elderly woman and of her dog tooth leglets. He mentions a drum or ipu hula made from three gourds:

> January 25, 1779. Two or three of us near the Dusk of the Evening returning from a short walk met on our Way with an Entertainment different from any we had yet seen among these people; it was a woman dancing to the Sound of a Drum. As it was begun just as we arrived on the Spot, & the Scene of it in a place by which they knew we were to return from our Excursion, we concluded that it was prepared for our Entertainment, especially as the Indians behave to us wherever we go with the greatest kindness and good nature & strive to do every thing in their power to oblige us.
>
> Within a small Circle sat a pretty little Girl upon a Matt by herself, she seemed of some Consequence & she invited us to sit down by her. An elderly woman advanced into the Ring dressed upon the Occasion, She had a feathered Ruff called Herei [a lei] on her Head, a large Piece of Cloth was rolled round her waist with part of it hanging below her Knees, round the small of her Legs were tyed some Matting with Dogs Teeth stuck in it in rows which they call Coobe [kūpe'e], from the lowest Row the Teeth increased in bigness to the upper, & being loose on shaking her leg they made a rattling Noise.

On one side of the Ring sat the Drummer, his Drum was made of three Gourd Shells inserted into each other, he beat the bottom of it against the Ground and sung a Song in slow time. The Dancer threw her arms about & put her body into varous Postures, sometime looking stedfastly toward the sky. Her Step was slow & not unlike a Country man's Hornpipe Step, in this manner she moved about sometimes making a Circle round the ring & every now & then repeating a song in concert with the Drummer. She continued dancing about a quarter of an hour & we thought much superior to any dances we had seen among Indians before. (Beaglehole, p. 1167)

Samwell described a dance performed on board the Discovery while the ships were cruising off Hawai'i, January 10, 1779:

Sunday Jan 10th. The ships continue far from the shore, two or 3 Canoes came off to us, many Girls on board. In the afternoon they all assembled upon deck and formed a dance; they strike their Hands on the pit of their Stomach smartly & jump up all together, at the same time repeating the words of a song in responses, their Manner was upon the whole more like that of the New Zealanders than that of the Otaheiteans. (Beaglehole, p. 1157)

The following are from Samwell's summary of his observations: "... the Young women spend most of their time singing and dancing of which they are very fond." (Beaglehole, p. 1181)

In the Evenings They sit before their Houses or under the Shade of the Cocoa nut trees, diverting themselves by looking at the young women or Children dancing. . . . (Beaglehole, p. 1187)

Samwell described a *hula* performed by seven girls who had sailed on the Discovery from Hawai'i to Waimea Bay on O'ahu. The date was February 27, 1779.

... soon after our coming to an anchor they performed a dance on the Quarter deck which we had not seen before; it might be perhaps to express their Joy on their safe arrival at this place, it was performed by two at a time—they did not jump up as in the common dance but used a kind of regular Step & moved their Arms up and down, repeated a Song together, changed their places often, wriggled their backsides and used many lascivious Gestures. Upon the Whole we thought it much more agreeable than their common Dance. (Beaglehole, p.1222)

■ **Hawaiian Singing in 1778-79**

There are many references to singing and to songs in Cook's journals. The word "chant" is used

once. The reader wonders if the Englishmen were recording the fact that the Hawaiian people were singing melodic songs and that they were able to sing in parts.

Dr. N.B. Emerson, in writing on music and the *hula,* quotes James King's journal. He speaks of King as being a "man of distinquished learning" who wrote:

... their songs, which they sing in parts, and accompany with a gentle motion of the arms, in the same manner as the Friendly Islanders, had a very pleasing effect.

King recorded the opinion of two of Cook's officers who, in this instance, were discussing both Tongan and Hawaiian music:

Captain Burney and Captain Phillips of the Marines, who have both a tolerable knowledge of music, have given it as their opinion [that] they did sing in parts; that is to say, that they sang together in different notes, which formed a pleasing harmony. (Emerson, 1976, p. 150)

A few comments and quotations are given here to show the nature of the occasions during which the people sang.

Singing was a part of the ceremony which honored Cook and gave him the "Title and Dignity of Lono." This ceremony was conducted by the priests in front of the sacred house Hale o Lono near Hikiau Heiau. This scene was sketched by Webber and entitled "An Offering Before Capt. Cook, in the Sandwich Islands." It appears as a hand colored engraving (Plate 129) on p. 139 in *Captain Cook's Artists in the Pacific,* compiled by Murray-Oliver in 1969. A black and white version entitled "Ceremonial Presentation of a Pig to Cook" is printed in Beaglehole, Plate 55, opposite p. 528.

As Cook walked to a second ceremony, a herald sang to announce the *kapu moe,* or prostrating *kapu.*

Samwell wrote on January 19, 1779:

As an introduction he who appeared to be the Chief Priest took a small Pig by the hinder legs and struck it's head against the Ground, after which he held it over a blaze without the Circle till it expired. He then laid it at Captn Cook's feet and put his own foot upon it, singing a Song in which he was accompanyed by all except the Servants who were carving the barbequed Hog. The song was all this while kept up, interrupted now and then by short Speeches made by the Priest, which were sometimes repeated after him, at other times assented to by short responses from the Under Priests and Servants.

After this the Priests dined on the barbequed Hog; when they had done the Company dispersed except two of the Priests that took Captain Cook to another part of the Island about 5 Miles off, where much such another Ceremony was gone through. In their Way thither a Herald went before them singing, and thousands of people prostrate themselves as they passed along and put their Hands before their Faces as if it was deem'd Vilation or Sacrilege to look at them. (Beaglehole, p. 1162)

Samwell wrote on January 26, 1779:

It is customary with the 2nd Priest of this place, whose name is Kaireekea & whom we call the Curate, to bring every day a barbequed Hog to the Tents in Procession with a number of Priests singing in concert with him. The Ceremony lasts about half an hour, they sing sometimes all together, at other times in responses till near the Conclusion, which is wound up entirely by Kaireekea; his song lasts about 10 minutes, after which they fall to & eat the Hog. (Beaglehole, p. 1169)

Two boys swam from Hikiau Heiau to the stern of the ship Discovery and sang together in a solemn manner a dirge about the death of Captain Cook. They remained in the water ten or 15 minutes singing the entire time until they were invited on board and accepted as friends. (Beaglehole, p. 1210)

_____

■ **Understandings and Appreciations**

1. Discuss the statement "Hawaiian people of old were more interested in the meanings of words of the songs than in the vocal forms of expression." What influence did this have on the type of music that developed?

2. Read thoughtfully the English translations of several chants. Note that they are poems, often showing love of nature, of places and of people. When the meaning is clear, and when the emotional tone is conveyed by the chanter, do they seem monotonous as young people sometimes claim?

3. Listen carefully to the recorded chants by Tom Hiona, Pele Pukui, and Kaupena Wong as suggested in this unit.

4. Scan the Founder's Day Book of The Kamehameha Schools for songs that have developed from old chants or from chant forms. Examples: *He Inoa No Pauahi,* and *Pauahi O Kalani.*

5. Review the list of Hawaiian instruments and also those in a modern band or orchestra. Note that the Hawaiian craftsman, lacking metals and steel tools, was quite resourceful in developing the instruments that he did.

■ **Student Activities**

1. Make and learn to play several of the simple musical instruments such as the nose flute, *kāʻekeʻeke, oeoe* or ti-leaf whistle. Photographs or sketches of the instruments may be found in several of the books in the Reading List. Most of the materials can be secured without cost. The booklet edited by Jerry Hopkins gives simple directions for making each of the Hawaiian instruments.

2. Learn a chant! Not all voices are right for the classical chant styles, but anyone should be able to "recite" a chant. A simple one is the Tree Shell Song, *"Kāhuli Aku."* See Emerson, pag 121. The fourth grade pupils at The Kamehameha Schools Elementary Division learn the game chant for *palaʻie,* the loop and ball game. For other game chants, such as those used with string figures, see Dickey, "String Figures from Hawaii." The *palaʻie* chant and one for a string figure were recorded at Kamehameha by Hoʻoulu Cambra. A cassette containing these may be purchased at The Kamehameha School Store or at the Bishop Museum shop.

3. Listen to and learn the "farewell songs" of Polynesia and the Pacific:

Hawaiʻi — *Aloha ʻOe.*   Maori — *Po Ata Rau*
Tahiti — *Maruru a Vau* Fiji — *Isa Lei*
Samoa — *Tofa mai Feline*

■ **Audio-Visual Aids**

1. Project the color movie "Hoʻolauleʻa" produced by Francis Haar for the Honolulu Academy of Arts. Iolani Luahine dances to chants by the expert, the late Tom Hiona, who uses several of the instruments described in this unit.

2. An exhibit of choice specimens of all the important musical instruments may be seen in the Hawaiian Hall, Bishop Museum. Additional instruments in the study collections may be

examined by appointment.

■ **Vocabulary**

1. oli   'ūkēkē   'ulī'ulī
   mele   pahu   'ūlili
   haku mele pūniu   pū'ili
   hīmeni   ipu   kā'eke'eke

2. Discuss and try to develop a definition of *music* that satisfies the members of the class.

3. Attempt to define Hawaiian music. Do you agree with the definition on pages xxiii and xxiv in the illustrated history entitled *Hawaiian Music and Musicians*, edited by George S. Kanahele?

4. Distinguish between the words "recite" and "chant." Define the musical terms - melody, harmony, and rhythm.

■ **Current Happenings or Trends of Significance to this Unit**

1. Read about the development of the *hīmeni,* an adaptation of the word hymn. (Kahananui, "Influences on Hawaiian Music.") Who were Laiana and Hualālai? What is a *hō'ike?*

2. Make a brief study of the instruments now associated with Hawaiian music that have been introduced since Capt. Cook's time.

   George Kaumuali'i played the bass viol on the brig Thaddeus while off the coast of Kailua, Kona, and later in Honolulu on April 23, 1820.

   The guitar, believed to have been brought by the Mexican and Spanish cowboys *(paniolo)* about 1832. The slack key *(kī hō'alu)* form of playing developed locally.

   In 1878 the Portuguese brought a small guitar-like instrument called the braguinha. It became the 'ukulele. Joseph Kekuku, while a student at The Kamehameha Schools in 1893-94, made his own steel bar and developed the sliding technique for playing his guitar. Thus the steel guitar or *kīkā kila* was born. Read about these instrument and more in *Hawaiian Music and Musicians.*

3. The four musically talented members of the Kalākaua family influenced the Hawaiian music of their period by composing countless songs, a number of which are popular today. These composers are sometimes called "Nā Lani 'Ehā," the four chiefs.

4. Captain Henry Berger, German-trained director of the Royal Hawaiian Band, enriched Hawaiian music through his teaching, musical arrangements, and compositions over a period of forty-three years.

5. Charles E. King, graduate of The Kamehameha School for Boys, class of 1891, collected traditional songs and composed many more. He is credited with publishing more than 200 songs, most of them in his *"Hawaiian Melodies"* and *"Songs of Hawaii."*

6. In addition to the six composers named above, there are many more whose songs are dear to the hearts of those who have known them over a period of years. The following composers, no longer living, wrote in the style of their period in music history. Most, but not all, wrote the lyrics in Hawaiian. Some added English words or phrases to their Hawaiian songs. Read more about these musicians in *Hawaiian Music and Musicians,* and in *The Golden Years of Hawaiian Entertainment.*

Almeida, Johnny K.	Lyons, Lorenzo
Beamer, Helen Desha	Machado, Lena
Cunha, Sonny	McIntire, Lani
Everett, Alice	Mossman, Bina
Iona, Andy	Namakelua, Alice
Isaacs, Alvin	Nape, David
Kaai, Ernest	Noble, Johnny
Kane, Matthew	Owens, Harry
Noble, Johnny	Prendergast, Ellen W.
Kealakai, Mekia	Pukui, Mary Kawena
Lam, Maddy	Taylor, Emily K.
Lee, Ku'i	Todaro, Tony
Lincoln, Bill Aliiloa	

7. Only a few of today's composers are listed below. Most of these have written more of their lyrics in Hawaiian than in English. Others, however, have maintained the Hawaiian feeling in their music even though the words are in English.

   Read more about them, and others not listed here, in the books named above.

Aluli, Irmgard	deMello, Jack
Anderson, Alex	Hale, Kaipo
Beamer Family	Kamae, Eddie
Bekeart, Edna	Kimura, Larry K.
Byrd, Jerry	Vaughn, Palani
Cummings, Andy	Wong, Kaupena

■ **Evaluation**

1. If emphasis was placed upon a study of the musical instruments, the students should be judged on their understanding of the use of the more important instruments in the dance and with the chants. Credit should be given to those who make and learn to play some of the instruments. A valuable experience would be for a student to give an oral report to the class on the making of an instrument and a demonstration of the music or sound.

2. If Hawaiian chants were learned they may be recited by individuals or in groups and a check made of their excellence. If the chants accompanied games or dances, these activities can be evaluated too.

3. The vocabulary offers a list of words for spelling, for definitions, and as topics for talks or essays.

4. Questions of the essay type may be asked over the development of Hawaiian music from the hīmeni to the present-day forms.

■ **Reading List**

Barrère, Dorothy B., Mary K. Pukui, and Marion Kelly. *Hula.* Historical perspectives. Pacific Anthropological Records No. 30. Honolulu: Bishop Museum Press, 1980.

Beaglehole, J.C., ed. *The Journals of Captain James Cook.* Vol. III, Parts 1 and 2. Cambridge, UK: Hakluyt Society, Cambridge University Press, 1967.

Beamer, Winona. *Nā Hula o Hawai'i.* Songs and dances of five generations of the Beamer family. Island Heritage Bicentennial Library. Norfolk Island, Aus.: Island Heritage, 1976.

———, collector and annotator. *Nā Mele Hula.* A collection of 33 Hawaiian hula chants. Vol. I. La'ie, Hawai'i: Institute for Polynesian Studies, 1987.

Bryan, E.H. Jr. "Poetry, Music and the Hula." Ch. 15 in *Ancient Hawaiian Life.* 1938. Honolulu: Books About Hawaii, 1950. (Informative chapter with illustrations of the instruments and a bibliography.)

Buck, Peter H. *Arts and Crafts of Hawaii.* Honolulu: Bishop Museum Special Publication No. 45, 1957. (Illustrations and descriptions of the old instruments.)

Burlingame, Burl, and Robert K. Kasher. *Da Kine Sound.* Conversations with people who create Hawaiian music. Vol. I. Kailua: Press Pacifica, 1973.

Cambra, Zaneta H. "Polynesia: A Region Within the Pacific Islands. 5, Hawaii." In *New Grove Dictionary of Music and Musicians.* 20 vols. London: Macmillan, 1980 (rev. ed.). (A discussion on vocal music includes *mele hula* vocal performance characteristics. Ten *hula* instruments and their use are described.)

Charlot, John. "The Hula in Hawaiian Life and Thought." *Honolulu* magazine, Holiday Annual, November 1979.

Damon, Ethel M. *Na Hīmeni Hawaii.* A record of hymns in the Hawaiian language. Honolulu: The Friend, Honolulu Star-Bulletin Press, 1935.

Dickey, Lyle A. *String Figures From Hawaii.* Honolulu: Bishop Museum Bulletin No. 54, 1928. (Chants to accompany the string figures.)

Dodge, Ernest S. *Hawaiian and Other Polynesian Gourds.* Honolulu: Topgallant Publishing Company, 1978.

Elbert, Samuel H., and Noelani K. Mahoe. *Nā Mele o Hawai'i Nei.* 101 Hawaiian songs, Hawaiian and English. 1970. Honolulu: University Press of Hawaii, 1978.

Feher, Joseph. "Music and Dance." In *Hawaii: A Pictorial History.* Honolulu: Bishop Museum Special Publication No. 58, 1969. 122-125.

Felix, John H., Leslie Nunes, and Peter Senecal. *The 'Ukulele, a Portuguese Gift to Hawaii.* Published by the authors. Printed in Hawaii by Offset House, 1980.

Hausman, Ruth L. *Hawaii: Music in Its History.* Rutland, VT: C.E. Tuttle, 1968.

Hess, Harvey. "Kepā Maly is Living Symbol of Renaissance." *Ha'ilono Mele,* Vol. VI, No. 9, Sept. 1980. Honolulu: The Hawaiian Music Foundation.

Hohu, Martha P., Chairman, Revision Committee. *Leo Hoonani Hou.* Honolulu: Fisher Corporation, 1953. (Book of hymns in Hawaiian for use in the Congregational [United Church of Christ] churches.)

Hopkins, Jerry. *The Hula.* Hong Kong: APA Productions, 1982. Distributed by Press Pacifica.

Kaeppler, Adrienne L. *Pahu and Pūniu.* An exhibition of Hawaiian drums. Honolulu: Bishop Museum Press, 1980.

Kahananui, Dorothy M. *Music of Ancient Hawaii.* Honolulu: Privately printed, 1962. (Excellent exposition on the subject by a music instructor of long experience. Illustrated.)

———. "Influences on Hawaiian Music." In *Aspects of Hawaiian Life and Environment.* Honolulu: Kamehameha Schools Press, 1965.

Kanahele, George S., ed. *Hawaiian Music and Musicians.* An illustrated history. Honolulu: University Press of Hawaii, 1979.

———. *Kī Hōʻalu.* The story of slack key. Honolulu: The Hawaiian Music Foundation, 1973.

Kelly, John M., Jr. *Folk Songs Hawaii Sings.* Rutland, VT: C.E. Tuttle, 1962. (Music and words to folk songs of the various ethnic groups living in Hawaiʻi.)

Kelly, Marion. "Hālau Hula and Adjacent Sites at Keʻe, Kauaʻi." In *Hula.* Historical perspectives. Pacific Anthropological Records No. 30. Honolulu: Bishop Museum Press, 1980.

———. *Pele and Hiʻiaka Visit the Sites at Kēʻē, Hāʻena, Island of Kauaʻi.* Honolulu: Bishop Museum Press, 1984.

King, Charles E. *Book of Hawaiian Melodies.* 1920. Honolulu: Charles E. King, 1950.

———. *Songs of Hawaii.* Many printings to 1950. Miami Beach, Florida: Hansen House.

Luomala, Katharine. *Hula Kiʻi, Hawaiian Puppetry.* Honolulu: University of Hawaii Press, 1984.

Mackenzie, Jean. *Tandy.* Biography of a Hawaiian singer who attained fame in Grand Opera. Island Heritage Bicentennial Library. Norfolk Island, Aus.: Island Heritage, 1975. (The 12-inch recording which accompanies the book features operatic arias and beloved Hawaiian songs.)

Mahoe, Noelani K., comp. and soloist. *E Hīmeni Hawaiʻi Kākou.* Let's sing Hawaiian songs. Honolulu: Governor's Committee on Hawaiian Text Materials, 1973.

Malo, David. *Hawaiian Antiquities.* 1898. Honolulu: Bishop Museum Special Publication No. 2, 1976. (See index for chants and musical instruments.)

Mellon, George. "Kani Ka Pila." *The Sales Builder,* December 1940. 13(12):2-14. (Highly readable article on the development of music in Hawaiʻi. Illustrated.)

Mitchell, Donald D. Kilolani. *Hawaiian Games for Today.* 1975. Honolulu: Kamehameha Schools Press, 1980. (Gives the Hawaiian words and English translations for two game chants. They are recorded on cassettes which may be purchased.)

———. *Hawaiian Treasures.* Music, 111-124; Hula, 125-128. Honolulu: Kamehameha Schools Press, 1978.

———. *Kīkā Kila.* The story of the Hawaiian steel guitar. Honolulu: The Hawaiian Music Foundation, 1973.

Noble, Gurre P. *Hula Blues.* The story of Johnny Noble, Hawaiʻi, its music and musicians. Honolulu: Tongg Publishing Company, 1948.

Peters, Robert E. *Leo Kiʻekiʻe.* The story of falsetto singing in Hawaii. Honolulu: The Hawaiian Music Foundation, 1973.

Plews, Edith R. "Poetry." Ch. 17 in *Ancient Hawaiian Civilization.* A series of lectures delivered at the Kamehameha Schools by E.S.C. Handy [and others]. 1933. Rutland, VT and Japan: C.E. Tuttle, 1965 (rev. ed.).

Pukui, Mary K., and Caroline Curtis. *Pikoi.* 1949. Honolulu: Kamehameha Schools Press, 1983.

Pukui, Mary K., and Alfons L. Korn. *The Echo of Our Song.* Chants and poems of the Hawaiians. Honolulu: University Press of Hawaii, 1973.

Roberts, Helen. *Ancient Hawaiian Music.* 1926. Bishop Museum Bulletin No. 29. Reprinted by Dover Publications, 1967. (An informative study of 400 pages, 15 illustrations and 151 musical selections.)

Silva, Wendall, and Alan Suemori, eds. *Nana I Na Loea Hula.* Look to the Hula Resources. Honolulu: Kalihi-Palama Culture and Arts Society, 1984. (Contains 140 biographies and photos of hula resource experts.)

Smith, Emerson. "Hawaii's Royal Composers." In *The Hawaii Book.* Chicago: J.G. Ferguson, 1961. 301-303.

———. "The History of Musical Development in Hawaii." *Hawaiian Historical Society Annual Report for 1955.* Honolulu: Hawaiian Historical Society. 5-13.

———. A series of articles on Hawaiian music in *Paradise of the Pacific:* September-December 1954; January-June and August-December, 1955.

Stoneburner, Bryan C. *Hawaiian Music: An Annotated Bibliography.* New York: Greenwood, 1986.

Tatar, Elizabeth. *Nineteenth Century Hawaiian Chant.* Pacific Anthropological Records No. 33. Honolulu: Bishop Museum Press, 1982. (Includes a recording of chant-types and styles.)

———. *Strains of Change: The Impact of Tourism on Hawaiian Music.* Honolulu: Bishop Museum Special Publication No. 78, 1987.

———. Articles on most of the musical instruments are placed alphabetically in *Hawaiian Music and Musicians.* Ed. George S. Kanahele. Honolulu: University Press of Hawaii, 1979.

Todaro, Tony. *The Golden Years of Hawaiian Entertainment, 1874-1974.* Honolulu: Tony Todaro Publishing Company, 1974. (Photos and biographical sketches of over 300 entertainers and composers, a list of songs and their composers, and a discography of Hawaiian albums.)

Topolinski, John. "Hula." In *Hawaiian Music and Musicians.* Ed. George S. Kanahele. Honolulu: University Press of Hawaii, 1979.

Winne, Jane L. "Music." Ch. 18 in *Ancient Hawaiian Civilization.* A series of lectures delivered at the Kamehameha Schools by E.S.C. Handy [and others]. 1933. Rutland, VT and Japan: C.E. Tuttle, 1965 (rev. ed.).

Wong, Kaupena. "Ancient Hawaiian Music." In *Aspects of Hawaiian Life and Environment.* Honolulu: Kamehameha Schools Press, 1965.

UNIT 6:
Poetry
and Prose

POETRY AND PROSE

The *oli* and *hula* chants *(mele hula)* may be studied as poetry because of the beauty and melodious rhythm of the words and phrases. Hawaiian spoken literature is without the rhyme which characterizes some forms of English poetry and verse.

The stories of old were most often told in a conversational manner, partly because chanting them required special talent and training. However, some of the stories which are recorded in informal prose are interspersed with brief chants.

The literature is somewhat indefinitely classed by Martha Beckwith (1970) into two groups:

a. *Ka'ao,* the legends or tales of a fictional nature. Beckwith, p. 2, writes that these were "composed to tickle the fancy rather than to inform the mind as to supposed events."

b. *Mo'olelo,* the historical tales and the traditions concerning the gods, heroes, local happenings, and family events. This was by far the larger group since the people of old thought of the exploits of their gods and heroes as basically historical.

Edward Joesting, writing in *Hawaii: A Pictorial History,* p. 126, divides the spoken literature into three classes:

a. Stories of gods and ghosts.
b. A recitation of ancestors as they appear in genealogies of chiefs, and
c. Stories of fiction in the form of legends and romances.

In the chief's households, skilled story-tellers entertained the members of the court and the visitors. Here the genealogies were perpetuated. "Even in the humblest family, story-telling furnished entertainment for long evenings." (Beckwith, 1970, pp. 5-6)

A study of the literature of old Hawai'i reveals much about the activities and the thoughts of the people, such as their love of the beauties of nature, respect for or awe of the natural forces, and an interest in the gods, heroes, and the chiefs. The stories show an understanding of human emotions and a love for the physical pleasures found in games, music, and the dance. Everyday life was colored by philosophic and religious convictions.

A comparative study of the legends of Polynesia and other Pacific islands gives clues to the relationships and migrations of the peoples. For instance, the chief exploits of the hero Māui must have been told by the earliest Polynesians and carried by them to all of the islands upon which they eventually settled. Some other tales originated locally after the migrations had ceased.

Without a manuscript to refresh his memory, the story-teller relied upon his highly developed faculty of being able to repeat a long legend or chant without error after hearing it once. This was termed *'apo,* or "catching" (memorizing) instantly the exact words of the story. (Rice, 1923, pp. 4-5; 1977, p. xiv) Through the years, variations or changes were purposely introduced to please certain listeners. Variations have been introduced to adapt stories to certain localities or to honor new heroes by substituting their names for the traditional ones.

■ The chants are divided, by subject matter, into nine classes of poetry by Edith Rice Plews (1965, pp. 181-197). Other discussions and explanations of chants are by Helen Roberts (1926, pp. 57-69), Samuel Elbert (1979, pp. 298-305) and Jane Winne (1961, p. 200). The classification by Edith Plews is used here to name the types of chants and to give illustrations in Hawaiian and English of all but one. The examples are taken from her lecture in *Ancient Hawaiian Civilization,* printed in 1933 and reprinted with different pagination in 1965. Page numbers are given in the pages to follow for both the 1933 and 1965 editions.

1. *Mele kaua,* the war chants. The chant of the hero Kawelo with a literal translation by William Hyde Rice (1933, pp. 177-179; 1965, pp. 181-83):

KAWELO

Pehu kaha ka limu o Hanalei
Pehu ka luna i ka maka o ka ʻōpua
Haʻi hewa ka lima i ke kaua kamaliʻi
E i aku ke kaua i ka hope
Me he ku la na ke kai hohonu
Me ka hiwahiwa a Kauakahi
Heōpuʻu ʻoe, he kākala kēlā
Na ka ʻole ka huʻe a ke ʻaki ē
ʻEa Kauahoa ka uʻi o Hanalei
Ala ʻo Kamalama ka uʻi o Kualoa
Ala ʻo Kawelo ka uʻi o Waikīkī
Ala ʻo Kaelehapuna ka uʻi o ʻEwa
Ala ʻo Kalaumeki ka uʻi o Waiʻanae
Huhue aku kāua moe i ke awakea.
Kāpae ke kaua e ka hoahānau.
E waiho iaʻu i kou hoahānau.
ʻAʻole hoʻinā lā o kuʻu hōʻike
Kuʻu hoa hele o ka wā kamaliʻi
Hoa kui lehua o Waikaeʻē
A kāua e kui kāne ai
I lei no ke kaikuaʻana haku o kāua.
E ala e Hanalei
Hanalei ʻāina anuanu
ʻĀina koʻekoʻe
ʻĀina a ka peʻa i noho ai
ʻEa Kauahoa
Ka meʻe uʻi o Hanalei ā

(translation)

Swelled now is the limu of Hanalei.
Swelled above the eyes is the cloud of morning.
In vain is the battle at the hands of children.
The great battle will follow
As the deep sea follows the shallow water.
In vain are the clouds dispersed.
O Kauahoa, the strong one of Hanalei!
Awake, O Kamalama, the strong one of Kualoa!
Awake, Kawelo, the strong one of Waikīkī!
Awake, Kaelehapuna, the strong one of ʻEwa!
Awake, Kalaumeki, the strong one of Waiʻanae.
We will all gather together at noonday.
Postpone the battle, my brother. Leave me.
This is not the day for us to give a mock battle.

Friend of my boyhood days, with whom I made *lehua* leis
At Waikaeʻē for our lord and older brothers.
Awake, O Hanalei, the land of chill and rain,
The land where the bat stayed
Awake O Kauahoa, the handsome one of Hanalei!

2. *Mele koʻihonua,* the genealogies and exploits of chiefs and legendary heroes. The example is from the poem Haui ka lani, Fallen is the Chief, composed about the year 1772. The first eleven lines only are given here. The English translation is by Judge Lorrin Andrews. (Plews, 1933, pp. 179-83; 1965, pp. 183-87)

HAUI KA LANI

Haui ka lani, ka mauliauhonua,
He mauli haulani, mālolo ʻauheʻe—
He mālolo ʻauheʻe hulimoku kēia;
He ana hanu kēia no ke ʻauheʻe lā!
Ke haʻi mai nei ka pō i ka heʻe,
Ua kā i laila kuʻu pō ʻauheʻe—
Kuʻu pō maoli, mākole, ka ala,
Hina wale i ke ala kāpapa, ke one;
Ke au me ka honua,
Ua lilo, eia la ia Kalani,
Ua hele kino aliʻi, ka hanohano.

(translation)

Fallen is the Chief; overthrown is the kingdom,
Gasping in death, scattered in flight;
An overthrow throughout the land;—
A hard panting from the rapid flight;
Countless the numbers from the universal rout.
The night declares the slaughter.
There extended lay my conquering night.—
Mine own night, dark and blinded,
Falling on the road, falling on the sand;
The sovereignty and the land
United in the Chief, are passed away.

3. *Mele kūō,* chants of praise. The example is the beginning of "Maikaʻi Kauaʻi." English translation by Mrs. Plews. (1933, pp. 184-86. 1965, pp. 188-190)

MAIKAʻI KAUAʻI

Maikaʻi Kauaʻi hemolele i ka mālie.
Kupu kelakela ke poʻo o Waiʻaleʻale,
Kela i ka lani kilakila Kawaikini,
Ka no ka helekua linohau Alakaʻi,
Māloʻeloʻe ka lāʻau huli ʻe mai ka pua,
Ke ʻike iho iā Maunahina.

(translation)

Beautiful is Kauaʻi beyond compare.
She sends forth a bud in the summit of
    Waiʻaleʻale,
She flowers in the heights of Kawaikini,
Her strength radiates in awful splendor from
    Alakaʻi;
Though I weary, though I faint, she renews my
    strength in her soft petals:
I have myself beheld Maunahina!

4. *Mele ʻoliʻoli,* lyrics and odes. A lyric from Kawelo, translated by William Hyde Rice, follows: (Plews, 1933, p. 186; 1965, p. 190)

ʻO Hanalei ʻāina ua
ʻĀina anuanu
ʻĀina koʻekoʻe
ʻĀina a ka peʻa i noho ai
Noho ana ka ʻūkiukiu o Hanakoa
I ka pali o Kalehuawehe
Pua ke lama me ka wiliwili.
ʻO ka ua lele ma waho o Mamalahoa
ʻO Kauahoa ka Meʻe uʻi o Hanalei
ʻO ke kanaka a Kamalama i hopu ai ʻo Kauahoa
He mea ʻe ka nui—e—a
Eia ka hoʻi ua kanaka nui o Kauaʻi ʻo Kauahoa.

(translation)

Hanalei, the land of cold and wet.
Hanalei, the land where the clouds hover!
The ukiukiu, the northerly storm, of Hanakoa,
The cliffs of Kalehuawehe are in vain.
The *lama* and *wiliwili* are in flower.
The rain that flies beyond Māmalahoa
Is like Kauahoa, the man that Kamalama will
    defeat.

5. *Mele paeāea,* provocative songs. Defined as a chant of supplication, perhaps as a means of fishing for something. Classed as vulgar so no example is given. This seems to be the type that Winne calls *Mele hakukole,* a chant in derogation of an individual. (Plews, 1933, p. 200; 1965, p. 204)

6. *Mele inoa,* name songs. These are songs in praise of a person, usually a chief or chiefess. They are composed and "presented" to the person in chant form and then become the possession of the person named.

The Kamehameha *mele inoa* given here was chanted by Kaupena Wong during the ceremony dedicating the statue of the King in Washington, D.C. April 15, 1969. Taken from Senate Document

Number 91-54, U.S. Government Printing Office, Washington, D.C. 1970, p. 13.

KAMEHAMEHA

ʻO Kamehameha lani kāʻeu ke ano kapu,
ʻO ka haku manawa kapu aliʻi kēnā
He aliʻi no ka muʻo lani kapu o Lono,
Nona ke kapu, ka wela,
Ka hahana i holo i luna o ka wēkiu
Lū ka ōlaʻi, nāue ka honua,
ʻOni ke kai, nāueue ka moku,
ʻIke i ka lepa koa a kalani,
Hāʻawi wale mai ʻo Kahekili
Ua lilo iā kalani nui Kekuʻiʻapoiwa i ke kapu,
ʻAnapu wela ma ka honua mea,
He inoa
He inoa no kalani Kamehameha kapu aliʻi, he inoa
He inoa no Kamehameha.

(translation)

Kamehameha is Chief, for him the profound *kapu,*
A lord indeed, a sacred chief is he,
A chief from the highest and most sacred realm of
    Lono.
His is the *kapu,* the fiery *kapu,*
The burning *kapu* that reaches the very heavens,
The earth quakes, it is set a-tremble.
The sea is disturbed, the land is moved,
And these are the signs of a mighty warrior.
A gift was given by the Chief, Kahekili.
It was carried away by the high chiefess
Kekuʻiʻapoiwa, the sacred one.
A flash of hot light over the earth is he.
We chant his praise.
We praise the king, Kamehameha, a noble chief,
    we praise him.
We honor the name Kamehameha.

7. *Mele ipo,* love songs. (Also called *Mele kūpeʻe*). The following, chanted as the dancer binds on anklets *(kūpeʻe)* before the performance, and calls his or her sweetheart a *lei.* Translation by Mrs. Plews. (1933, p. 189; 1965, p. 193)

MELE KŪPEʻE

ʻAʻala kupukupu ka uka o Kānehoa
E ho-a!
Hoa nā lima o ka makani, he Waikaloa.
He Waikaloa ka makani anu Līhuʻe.
ʻĀlina lehua i Kaukaʻōpua
Kuʻu pua,
Kuʻu pua ʻiʻini e kui a lei.
Inā iā ʻoe ke lei ʻā maila.

(translation)

Fragrant is the grass of upland Kānehoa,
Bind on the anklets, bind!

Bind with the hand of the soughing wind,
    Waikaloa.
Balmy Waikaloa, wind cooling Līhuʻe,
Blemished is the *lehua* before my cloud from the
    sea,
My loved one, my flower—
Flower I yearn to bind in my *lei*,
O, that you were as near as my *lei*—be my *lei!*

8. *Mele kanikau*, dirges or laments. These were composed and chanted at the death of a person. Such a dirge was not chanted again although it was remembered by members of the family. Most skilled chanters today will not recite a *kanikau* as a demonstration for fear that it might be instrumental in causing someone's death.

The following lament was chanted by Kamāmalu, consort of Kamehameha II, as they were leaving Hawaiʻi for England in 1823. She seemed to sense that she would never return to her native soil. From Kamakau, 1961, pp. 256-57. "Father" and "you" refer to Kamehameha the Great.

KAMĀMALU'S LAMENT
E ka lani e, e ka honua e,
E ka mauna e, e ka moana e,
E ka hū e, e ka makaʻāinana e,
Aloha ʻoukou.
E ka lepo, aloha ʻoe,
E ka mea a kuʻu makua kāne i ʻeha ai e,
Aloha ʻoe.
E ka luhi a kuʻu makua kāne i ʻimi ai e.
Ke haʻalele nei maua i ko luhi,
Ke hele nei no au mamuli o ko kauoha,
ʻAʻole au e haʻalele i kou leo.
Ke hele nei no au ma ko kauoha i ʻolelo mai ai iaʻu.
    (translation)
O heaven, O earth,
O mountains and sea,
O commoners and people,
Farewell to you all.
O soil farewell,
O land for which my father suffered,
Farewell.
O burden that my father strived for.
We two are leaving your labors.
I go in obedience to your command,
I will not desert your voice.
I go in accordance with the words you spoke
    to me.

9. *Mele pule*, prayers. Many prayers were composed and chanted to help in the activities of individuals, of families, and of larger communities. Some of these were invocations to family gods or other gods, requests to free people or places from *kapu*, prayers for protection from evil, and offerings of thanks for favors received.

The example here is the prayer used by a *kahuna ʻanāʻanā* who can pray to death and can also defend from death. His words are to ward off the evil that is keeping the patient ill.

These are the closing lines of the chant with English translation by William Hyde Rice. (Plews, 1933. pp. 191-93; 1965, pp. 195-97)

Pale ka pō, puka i ke ao, iaʻu nei lā
Inoa o ke kahuna
E nānā ʻia mai ka maʻi a kākou
Inā he make i ka ʻai i ka lā
I ke kapa, i ka ʻōlelo, i ka leʻaleʻa ʻe,
I ke kaha ma nā alanui lā
I ka hele ʻana, i ka noho ʻana,
I ka maunu lilo, hakina mea ʻai lā,
Ka ʻōhumu, ke keʻemoa, ka nonohua,
I nā make nō apau, e ʻueke, e kala ʻia.
Lawe ʻia aku nā hala nui, nā hala liʻiliʻi
A kiola, hoʻolei loa i Moana-nui-kai-oʻo.
Inā i laila ʻo Kū, me Hina, paʻa ʻia ka make
Kuʻu ʻia mai ke ola nui, ke ola iki,
Ke ola loa nō, i ka puaneane,
Ke ola ka hoʻi ia a ke akua,
ʻEliʻeli kapu, ʻeliʻeli noa, noa loa nō.

    (translation)

Let the Night pass, and Daylight come to me, the
    Kahuna.
Look at our sick one; if he be dying from food
    eaten in the day,
Or from tapa, or from what he has said,
Or from pleasures he has had a part in,
Or from walking on the highway,
From walking, or from sitting down,
Or from the bait that has been taken,
Or from parts of food that he has left,
Or from his evil thoughts of others,
Or from finding fault, or from evils within,
From all deaths: Deliver and forgive!
Take away all great faults, and all small faults,
Throw them all into Moana-nui-kai-oʻo, the
    great ocean!
If Kū is there, or Hina: Hold back death!
Let out the big life, the small life,
Let out the long life, for all time:
That is the life from the gods.

This is the ending of my prayer
It is finished; 'Āmama ua noa.

■   Elizabeth Tatar, author of the article on the chant in *Hawaiian Music and Musicians,* adds several more chant types:

Mele kānaenae, prayers of supplication and praise to dieties and high chiefs. Before a *hula,* these chants may be given for Laka, Kapo, Pele, and Hi'iaka.

Mele ma'i, in praise of the genitals, usually of a chief or a first-born child.

Mele he'e nalu, a person's own surfing chant.

Mele ho'āla, chanted to awaken a person. (If the spirit wandered during sleep, as if in a dream, the person must be awakened cautiously.)

Mele ahi, the fire *kapu* of a chief's name.

In addition to these, there were many simple chants used in games *(mele paha),* in occupations, and professions. When the mission schools opened, chants were composed to help in learning and memorizing school subjects.

■   Hawaiian literature in prose form includes the many folk tales concerning the origin of stones, springs, plants and certain animals. Here are told the exploits of certain gods, of the culture heroes, and the *menehune* and *'e'epa.* The hero stories are usually known by the name of their chief character, such as the well-known Māui exploits. (See Luomala)

Padraic Colum describes Māui's minor accomplishments and his seven famous deeds, in which Māui:

1. Won a Place for Himself in the House.
2. Lifted up the Sky.
3. Fished up the Great Island.
4. Snared the Sun and Made Him go More Slowly.
5. Won Fire for Men.
6. Overcame the Long Eel.
7. Strove to Win Immortality for Men.

Among the other heroes and heroines are Pele, Kamapua'a, Hina, and Pikoi. Animal stories often personify the sharks, lizards, eels, owls, dogs, and other creatures. Most of these animals could change at will from their animal to a human form. Kamapua'a could be a man, a pig, or the fish called *humuhumu-nukunuku-apua'a.* These people with supernatural powers were known as *kupua.*

Hawaiian poetry has an obvious meaning to the reader, or it may present a series of ideas or word pictures that may not be closely connected. Many poems are said to have a deeply hidden meaning known as the *kaona.* Only those skilled in the language and traditions are able to understand and reveal these. Other meanings that may be found in some poetry are given by Plews (1933, pp. 174-75; 1965, pp. 178-79) and Bryan (p. 53).

_____

■   **Understanding and Appreciations**

1. Name several traits of the early Hawaiian people that are revealed to the present day readers through the folk-lore. How do the stories help us picture life and thought of long ago?

2. People of Hawaiian ancestry have said that they have gained an added pride in their early culture as they became more familiar with the literature of their forebears.

   Kama'āina residents of the 50th State are proud to know that Hawaiian lore, like the music, is considered a colorful addition to the folk tales of America. Compare one or more specific legends or the general theme of a Hawaiian legend to American Indian stories known to you or that you may read for this special purpose. (Example, snaring the sun, see Luomala, Bishop Museum Bulletin 168.)

3. Can you account for stories which seem to be Hawaiian but closely resemble Bible stories? See Reading List for the *Kumuhonua Legends,* by Dorothy B. Barrere, 1969.

4. What type of introduced stories may have been responsible for reducing the Hawaiian *menehune* to dwarf-like size? See *Kumuhonua Legends.*

■   **Student Activities**

1. Students should learn one or more legends in which the scene is laid in their home section of the island. Perhaps this story will explain the origin of some feature or some early happening in their neighborhood. From Reading List see: Ashdown, Bennett, Sterling, and Summers.

2. Students will find it interesting to learn the stories of the Seven Deeds of Māui. Several

stories about Pele and the members of her family should be in the repertoire of tellers of Hawaiian tales.

3. Students with an interest in the language will find a challenge in learning a stanza or more of the chant, *Water of Kāne* in Hawaiian and English. (Emerson, 1965 pp. 257-259) (English only—Colum, *Legends,* pp. 218-219)

4. Read about the skills and the activities of the bards or professional story-tellers in pre-European times. Compare them to those in the same profession who entertained the titled families in old England.

5. List the animals found in the Hawaiian tales familiar to you. Did these animals talk or communicate with man in some way? What other forms did some of the animals take?

6. List the plants and flowers found in the poetry and chants. Some say that the *lehua* is mentioned most often. What do you find?

7. How do you account for the popularity of the *menehune* stories? (See Luomala, *Menehune of Polynesia,* and Rice, *Hawaiian Legends.*)

8. Are all legends products of the distant past or are storytellers creating new ones at this time?

9. Select an appropriate legend and dramatize it for a school drama club or for a puppet show.

10. Could you portray two or more of the important incidents from a legend as scenes for a float in the Aloha Week parade? Excellent examples: Legend of the Naupaka; The Goddess Hina and La'a-mai-kahiki.

11. Why were the tales of gods and ghosts told only during the daytime?

■ **Audio-Visual Aids**

1. The Bishop Museum's Department of Hawaiian Linguistics has collected an extensive library of tapes of chants and of legends, both old and recent. By appointment, an instructor or a very small group may listen to these, and in some cases copies may be purchased.

2. Kamokila Campbell, *Legends of Hawaii,* long-play recordings:
   a, Vol. 1 RLP 100
      (1) Legend of Pele
      (2) Legend of Mānoa
      (3) Legend of the Salty Sea

b. Vol. 2 K 100
   (1) Hina, Woman of the Moon
   (2) Legend of Rainbow Goddess
   (3) Legend of the Singing Stick

3. Folkways Record F.W. 8750, *Hawaiian Chant, Hula, and Music* contains two *oli* chants and 12 *hula* chants, classed as poetry.

4. *Keoni's Poi Pounder,* a movie available locally, portrays a modern story which does not, as the film implies, explain the true source of the name of Mokoli'i islet, known to some as the Poi Pounder. Some of the sequences in the movie are "un-Hawaiian."

■ **Vocabulary**

ka'ao	fictional	mo'olelo
historical	*kaona*	genealogy
'apo	derogation	*mele inoa*
migrations	Māui	dirge
Pele	lament	Kamapua'a
snared	*menehune*	immortality

■ **Current Happenings or Trends of Significance to this Unit**

1. The first attempt by a Hawaiian governmental agency to popularize folklore was in 1923 when the Commission of Myth and Folk-Lore brought the famous author Padraic Colum to Hawai'i to study and re-tell its stories, primarily for the children of the Islands. See the Reading List for the three books which resulted from this study.

2. Mrs. Mary Kawena Puku'i and Miss Caroline Curtis re-told legends for the elementary school children. Their three volumes are given in the Reading List.

3. The books of legends written by Westervelt and published 1915-16 and long out-of-print were re-issued in 1963 at popular prices. See Reading List.

4. Bernice P. Irwin was one of several authors to write a book of modern tales in the style of the old legends.

5. The floats in the 1963 Aloha Week parade were required to have a theme which illustrated a Hawaiian legend. Research on legends began months in advance and many of the floats depicted scenes from legends of great interest to the spectators.

6. Dramatic clubs and groups with puppets and marionettes have dramatized legends for adults and children.

7. Bishop Museum continues to search for legends which have not been recorded. In 1956 an elderly resident of Kohala recorded on tape in Hawaiian "The Knee-Cap Fish Hook," an interesting story not known to the public. Perhaps many more stories are awaiting sympathetic listeners.

8. Local incidents of a dramatic nature are the subjects of stories which are developing into folk tales. Among these are the story of the collapse of the Pearl Harbor dry dock in 1914 because the shark goddess was not appeased, and the account of the death of the flyers who bombed the Mauna Loa lava flow and incurred the wrath of Pele. Tour drivers seem to be the most active groups in originating tales in Hawai'i today.

■ **Reading List**

Apple, Russell A., and Margaret Apple. *Tales of Old Hawaii.* Vol. I. Norfolk Island, Aus.: Island Heritage, 1977.

Armitage, George, and Henry Judd. *Ghost Dog and Other Legends.* Honolulu: Hawaiian Service, 1944.

Ashdown, Inez M. *Ke Alaloa o Maui.* The broad highway of Maui. Wailuku, Maui: Ace Printing Company, 1971.

Barrère, Dorothy B. *The Kumuhonua Legends.* A study of late 19th century Hawaiian stories of creation and origins. Pacific Anthropological Records No. 3. Honolulu: Bishop Museum Press, 1969.

Beamer, Winona. *Nā Hula o Hawai'i.* Songs and dances of five generations of the Beamer family. Island Heritage Bicentennial Library. Norfolk Island, Aus.: Island Heritage, 1976.

Beckwith, Martha W. *Hawaiian Mythology.* 1940. With a new introduction by Katharine Luomala. Honolulu: University Press of Hawaii, 1970.

———. *The Hawaiian Romance of Laieikawai.* Washington, D.C.: U.S. Government Printing Office, 1919.

———. *Kepelino's Traditions of Hawaii.* 1932. Honolulu: Bishop Museum Bulletin No. 95, 1971.

———, trans. and ed. *The Kumulipo.* A Hawaiian creation chant. 1951. Honolulu: University Press of Hawaii, 1972.

Bennett, Wendell C. *Archaeology of Kauai.* Honolulu: Bishop Museum Bulletin No. 80, 1931.

Brown, Marcia. *Backbone of the King.* The story of Paka'a and his son Ku. 1966. Honolulu: University of Hawaii Press, 1984 (rev. ed.).

Bryan, E.H. Jr. "Poetry, Music and the Hula." Ch. 15 in *Ancient Hawaiian Life.* 1938. Honolulu: Books about Hawaii, 1950.

Charlot, John. *The Hawaiian Poetry of Religion and Politics.* Honolulu: University of Hawaii Press, 1985.

———. *The Kamapua'a Literature.* The classical traditions of the Hawaiian pig god as a body of literature. Honolulu: University of Hawaii Press, 1987.

Chickering, William H. *Within the Sound of these Waves.* 1956. Westport, CT: Glenwood Press, 1971.

Chun Fat, Joseph K. *The Mystery of Ku'ula Rock.* Hicksville, NY: Exposition Press, 1975.

Colum, Padraic. *At the Gateways of the Day.* New Haven, CT: Yale University Press, 1924.

———. *The Bright Islands.* New Haven, CT: Yale University Press, 1925.

———. *Legends of Hawaii.* 1937. New Haven, CT: Yale University Press, 1960 (paperback).

Davis, Eleanor H. *Abraham Fornander, a Sense of History.* A biography. Honolulu: University Press of Hawaii, 1979.

Day, A. Grove, and Carl Stroven. *A Hawaiian Reader.* New York: Appleton-Century-Crofts, 1959.

———. *The Spell of Hawaii.* Honolulu: Mutual, 1968.

Elbert, Samuel H. "Hawaiian Poetry." In *Hawaiian Music and Musicians.* Ed. George S. Kanahele. Honolulu: University Press of Hawaii, 1979. 298-305.

———, ed. *Selections from Fornander's Hawaiian Antiquities and Folk-lore.* Honolulu: University Press of Hawaii, 1959.

Emerson, Nathaniel B. *Pele and Hiiaka.* Rutland, VT and Japan: C.E. Tuttle, 1978.

———. *Unwritten Literature of Hawaii.* Rutland, VT and Japan: C.E. Tuttle, 1965.

Fornander, Abraham. *Hawaiian Antiquities and Folklore.* Honolulu: Bishop Museum Memoirs 4, 5 and 6, 1916-19.

Gay, Lawrence K. *Tales of the Forbidden Island of Niihau.* Honolulu: Topgallant Publishing Company, 1981.

———. *True Stories of the Island of Lanai.* Honolulu: Mission Press, 1965.

Gay, Mary H. *Tales of Old Lahaina.* Honolulu: Topgallant Publishing Company, 1981.

Goldsberry, Steven. *Maui, the Demigod: An Epic Novel of Mythical Hawai'i.* New York: Poseidon Press, 1984.

Green, Laura. *Folktales from Hawaii.* Honolulu: Hawaiian Board Book Rooms, 1928.

Grey, Sir George. *Polynesian Mythology.* Auckland, N.Z.: 1885.

Hoyt, Helen P. *The Night Marchers.* The Hawaiian Bicentennial Library, Vol. XII. Norfolk Island, Aus.: Island Heritage, 1976.

Ihara, Violet K., and 'Iliahi Johnson. *The Eight Rainbows of 'Umi.* Honolulu: Topgallant Publishing Company, 1976.

Janion, Aubrey P. *Olowalu and Other Hawaiian Tales.* Island Heritage Bicentennial Library. Norfolk Island, Aus.: Island Heritage, 1976.

Johnson, Rubellite K., ed. and trans. *Ka Nupepa Ku'oko'a.* A chronicle of entries, October 1861-September 1862. Honolulu: Topgallant Publishing Company, 1975.

———. *Kumulipo.* Vol. I (Chants 1 and 2). Honolulu: Topgallant Publishing Company, 1981.

Kalakaua, King David. *Legends and Myths of Hawaii.* 1888. Rutland, VT and Japan: C.E. Tuttle, 1979.

Kelly, Marion. *Pele and Hi'iaka Visit the Sites at Kē'ē, Hā'ena, Island of Kaua'i.* Honolulu: Bishop Museum Press, 1984.

Kirtley, Bacil P. *A Motif-Index of Traditional Polynesian Narratives.* Honolulu: University Press of Hawaii, 1971.

Knudsen, Eric A. *Teller of Hawaiian Tales.* Honolulu: W.H. Male Advertising, 1945-46.

Kumulipo. Hawaiian creation myth. Reprint of Queen Lili'uokalani's 1897 version. Kentfield, CA: Pueo Press, 1978.

Lawrence, Mary S. *Old Time Hawaiians and Their Work.* 1912. Honolulu, n.p., 1939.

Lieb, Amos P., and A. Grove Day. *Hawaiian Legends in English.* An annotated bibliography. 2nd ed. Honolulu: University Press of Hawaii, 1979.

Luomala, Katharine. *Hula Ki'i, Hawaiian Puppetry.* Honolulu: University of Hawaii Press, 1984.

———. *Maui of a Thousand Tricks.* Honolulu: Bishop Museum Bulletin No. 198, 1949.

———. *Menehune of Polynesia.* Honolulu: Bishop Museum Bulletin No. 203, 1951.

———. *Oceanic, American Indian and African Myths of Snaring the Sun.* Honolulu: Bishop Museum Bulletin No. 168, 1940.

———. *Voices on the Wind.* Honolulu: Bishop Museum Special Publication No. 75, 1986 (rev. ed.).

Maguire, Eliza D. *Kona Legends.* 1926. Hilo: Petroglyph Press, 1966.

Nakuina, Emma M. Beckley. *Hawaii, Its People, Their Legends.* Honolulu: T.H., 1904.

Ne, Harriet. *Legends of Molokai.* Told by a daughter of Moloka'i. Honolulu: Topgallant Publishing Company, 1981.

Paki, Pilahi. *Legends of Hawaii, Oahu's Yesterday.* Honolulu: Victoria Publishers, 1972.

Plews, Edith R. "Poetry." Ch. 17 in *Ancient Hawaiian Civilization.* A series of lectures delivered at the Kamehameha Schools by E.S.C. Handy [and others]. 1933. Rutland, VT and Japan: C.E. Tuttle, 1965 (rev. ed.).

Pope, Katherine. *Hawaii, the Rainbow Land.* New York: Thomas Y. Crowell Co., 1924.

Pratt, Helen G. *The Hawaiians: An Island People.* 1941. Rutland, VT and Japan: C.E. Tuttle, 1963.

Pukui, Mary K. *'Ōlelo No'eau: Hawaiian Proverbs and Poetical Sayings.* Honolulu: Bishop Museum Press, 1983. (Nearly 3,000 entries.)

Pukui, Mary K., and Caroline Curtis. *Pikoi.* 1949. Honolulu: Kamehameha Schools Press, 1983.

———. *Tales of the Menehune.* 2nd ed. Honolulu: Kamehameha Schools Press, 1983.

———. *Water of Kane.* 1951. Honolulu: Kamehameha Schools Press, 1976.

Pukui, Mary K., and Alfons L. Korn. *The Echo of*

Our Song. Chants and poems of the Hawaiians. Honolulu: University Press of Hawaii, 1973.

Rice, William H. *Hawaiian Legends.* 1923. Reprinted and enlarged. Honolulu: Bishop Museum Special Publication No. 63 (with photos by Boone Morrison), 1977.

Smith, Charlotte H. *Legends of the Wailuku.* Honolulu: Charles R. Frazier, 1920.

Sterling, Elspeth, and Catherine C. Summers. *Sites of Oahu.* Honolulu: Department of Anthropology, Bishop Museum, 1978.

Stroven, Carl, and A. Grove Day. *The Spell of the Pacific.* New York: Macmillan, 1949.

Summers, Catherine C. *Molokai: A Site Survey.* Pacific Anthropological Records No. 14. Honolulu: Department of Anthropology, Bishop Museum, 1971.

Tatar, Elizabeth. "Chant." In *Hawaiian Music and Musicians.* Ed. George S. Kanahele. Honolulu: University Press of Hawaii, 1979. (Carefully researched information on many phases of chants.)

Thompson, Vivian L. *Hawaiian Myths of Earth, Sea and Sky.* 1966. Honolulu: University of Hawaii Press, 1988, rev. ed. (juvenile).

———. *Hawaiian Tales of Heroes and Champions.* Honolulu: University of Hawaii Press, 1986.

Thrum, Thomas G. *Hawaiian Folk Tales.* 1907. New York: A.M.S. Press, 1978.

———. *More Hawaiian Folk Tales.* Chicago: A.C. McClurg & Co., 1923.

———. *Tributes of Hawaiian Tradition.* Honolulu: n.p., 1920. See index to Thrum's *Hawaiian Annual* for more listings.

Tune, Suelyn C. *How Maui Slowed the Sun.* Honolulu: University of Hawaii Press, 1988 (juvenile).

Westervelt, William D. *Around the Poi Bowl and Legend of Paao.* Honolulu: Paradise of the Pacific, 1913.

———. *Hawaiian Historical Legends.* 1923. Rutland, VT and Japan: C.E. Tuttle, 1977.

———. *Hawaiian Legends of Old Honolulu.* 1916. Rutland, VT and Japan: C.E. Tuttle, 1964.

———. *Hawaiian Legends of Volcanoes.* 1916. Rutland, VT and Japan: C.E. Tuttle, 1964.

———. *Legends of Maui, a Demigod of Polynesia and His Mother Hina.* 1910. New York: A.M.S. Press, 1979.

Wichman, Juliet R. *Hawaiian Planting Traditions.* Honolulu: T.H., Honolulu Star-Bulletin, 1930.

Williams, Julie S. *And the Birds Appeared.* Honolulu: University of Hawaii Press, 1988 (juvenile).

Winne, Jane L., and Mary K. Pukui. *'Olelo No'eau a ka Hawaii.* Folk sayings from the Hawaiian. Honolulu: Privately printed, 1961.

UNIT 7:
Religious
Beliefs
and
Practices

RELIGIOUS BELIEFS AND PRACTICES

The Polynesians believed that nature was pervaded by super-normal powers. These powers were personified into gods, who were given certain names and particular attributes. The gods were jealous gods and became inimical if neglected. Thus to insure success in any important enterprise, a particular god had to be placated by a ritualistic phrase or incantation, an offering, or even by an elaborate ritual.

Dr. Peter Buck, Thrum's Annual for 1933, p.64.

Every aspect of life was carried out in accordance with deeply implanted religious beliefs. Each significant undertaking began and culminated with appropriate rituals. Among these activities were house building, canoe making, and the tasks involved in fishing and farming. The gods were invoked by those engaged in the serious undertaking of warfare and by players attempting to win in sports tournaments.

Events in the life of an individual from birth to death were celebrated with prayers and feasts which honored the person and the family gods.

By breaking a *kapu* or failing to properly honor the gods, the people believed they had angered them. Thus, their dedication to these spirits was, in many instances, due to their feeling of awe and fear of the gods, rather than affection for them.

Communion with the gods took place casually in the house or field, or in elaborate rituals and sacrifices of valuable commodities by the chiefs.

The priests, in conjunction with the high chiefs, conducted religious observances in the *heiau* under an elaborate system of prohibitions (*kapu*), which were strictly enforced.

■ **The Kumulipo,** The Hawaiian Creation chant (Kalākaua version).

This was composed about AD 1700 and consists of 2,102 lines. It is a genealogical prayer chant linking the royal family for which it was composed to the primary gods, the deified chiefs, the stars in the heavens, and the useful plants and animals on earth.

King Kalākaua's translation of this chant was printed in 1889 and Queen Liliʻuokalani's in 1897. Beckwith's translation with extensive explanatory notes was reprinted in 1972 with a helpful foreword by Katharine Luomala. The latest interpretation of Vol. 1 of this epic chant is by the noted Hawaiian scholar, Rubellite Kawena Johnson, and published in 1981.

Kumulipo means the origin or the source of life. Since *lipo* means deep, blue-black, some translate this "the origin in the deep, blue-black past." The first eleven lines of the chant are given here to share with the reader the poetic feeling, even evident in the English translation:

At the time when the earth became hot
At the time when the heavens turned about

At the time when the sun was darkened
To cause the moon to shine
The time of the rise of the Pleiades
The slime, this was the source of the earth
The source of the darkness that made darkness
The source of the night that made night
The intense darkness, the deep darkness
Darkness of the sun, darkness of the night
Nothing but night.
    (Beckwith, *Kumulipo,* 1972, p. 58)

Kamakau relates the story, obviously suggested by the Biblical Adam and Eve, of the creation of the first man, Hulihonua (man made of earth) and the first woman, Keakahulilani (the shadow changed by heaven). He places this story 28 generations before Wākea.

Kamakau's story, written in 1869, tells us, in brief:

The three gods who made man were Kāne, Kū, and Lono. Kanaloa did not want man to be a master but to be of the earth and return to earth.

At Mōkapu, Windward Oʻahu, in the red and blackish soil, Kāne drew the form of a man in the likeness of the gods. Likewise Kanaloa drew the figure of a man but his dirt figure remained lying there and became stone.

Neither figure had come to life.

Kāne appealed to Kū and Lono for help and asked them to chant *"Ola, Ola,"* (Live, Live). Kāne's earth figure became a living man. They named him Kānehulihonua "earth changed to man." He was alone except for his shadow (*aka*).

The gods changed his shadow into a wife whom the husband called Keakahulilani, "shadow changed by the heavens." They are the progenitors of the Hawaiian people and are the first named in Kamakau's three-page genealogy ending with such notables as Kalaniʻōpuʻu, Kiwalaō, and Keōpūolani. See Kamakau, 1961, pp. 433-36; Barrere, 1969, pp. 3-6.

■ Ke Akua (The Gods)

In common with their Polynesian ancestors, the Hawaiian people recognized four major gods (*akua*): Kāne, Kū, Lono, and Kanaloa. Among the countless demigods and goddesses were some that were common to other Polynesians, such as Pele, Hina, and Māui. Many of these lesser gods were of local origin. Each was believed to be able to help the people in a particular profession or craft, or was associated with natural phenomena. Family gods (*ʻaumākua*) served as guardians to the family

groups (*ʻohana*), and were represented by commonly known animals, plants, or sometimes images.

The images of wood, stone, or feather-covered basketry were believed to be the dwelling place of the spirits of certain gods. A specific ritual (*ho-ʻomanamana*) was carried out to cause the spirit to enter the image.

A careful study of Polynesian religion suggests that most of the gods and goddesses were once chiefs and chiefesses. Some may have arisen from the citizenry. Most certainly they were people of unusual ability, power and reputation. They were deified after death and through the years the stories of their prowess have been exaggerated.

Milu and Kihawahine are said to have lived in Hawaiʻi in historic times. Others, such as Māui, lived before the days that the settlers migrated to the many islands. Māui, therefore, is known Pacific wide.

Dr. Peter Buck, director of Bishop Museum, while a visiting professor of anthropology at Yale University in 1939, gave a series of three lectures in which he explained his views of Polynesian religion. A brief summary of his lectures follows:

■ Man Creates His Gods

The people of Polynesia, realizing from dreams, perhaps, that there was a spiritual essence or soul that was not destroyed by death but merely freed from its material envelope, evolved the concept of immortality.

The souls of the Polynesian ancestors were believed to live on in the spirit land of Hawaiki. Their descendants called upon them for assistance in the problems of this life. They wished for a continuity of help and so deified specific ancestors by name as gods who could be consulted when occasion demanded. Those of earlier times became the great gods known to all. Family gods were the *aumākua*. Thus man created his gods.

Faith in their gods supplemented by innate courage and supreme daring enabled them to cross the thousands of leagues of the vast Pacific stretching between southeast Asia, Hawaiʻi and Easter Island to complete the most marvelous odyssey the world has ever known.

■ The Gods Create Man.

With the passing of years and the growth of an intellectual and imaginative priesthood some of the deified ancestors had their human parentage changed to those of supernatural origin. Human parents were replaced by the personification of the Sky-father (Wākea) and the Earth-mother (Papa). These gods were able to create man.

■ The Death of the Gods.

The introduction of foreign cultures including new religions brought about an end to most of the belief in and dependence on the Polynesian gods. The death of the gods led to the end of much of Polynesian culture.

■ The Four Major Gods and their Realms

1. Kāne, the procreator, the provider of sunlight, fresh water, and the life substances in nature. As Kānenuiākea he was the maker of heaven, earth, and the things that filled them. He was called the "leading god among the great gods" and "many gods in one god."

The Pukui-Elbert glossary of Hawaiian gods informs us that there are more than 70 forms of Kāne. Kamakau, 1964, pp. 57-58, gives the names for 36. Among these are Kānehoalani, ruler of the heavens, and the name of the topmost peak in the Kualoa ridge, Oʻahu. Kānehūnāmoku is the hidden land or island of Kāne. Kahekili, famed chief and ruler, claimed descent from Kānehekili, god of thunder. Kahekili had the right side of his body tattooed solid black from head to foot to resemble that of his ancestor Kānehekili.

Kāne allowed no human sacrifices at his worship services. The 27th night of the lunar month was sacred to him.

Kāne and his companion Kanaloa opened springs of fresh water in dry areas. Sugar cane (kō) and the ʻōhia lehua are kino lau or earthly forms of Kāne.

The name Kāne means male.

The Water of Kāne
A query, a question
I put to you:
Where is the water of Kāne
At the Eastern Gate
Where the Sun comes in at Haʻehaʻe;
There is the water of Kāne.

A question I ask of you:
Where is the water of Kāne?
Out there with the floating Sun,
Where cloud-forms rest on Ocean's breast,
Uplifting their forms at Nihoa,
This side the base of Lehua;
There is the water of Kāne.

These are the first two of the six stanzas of *He Mele no Kāne* given in Emerson, 1965, pages 257-59 in Hawaiian and in English. It is a tradition in some of the local schools for the students to commit one or more of the stanzas to memory.

2. Kū represents the male generating power. As the god of war, his *heiau* were the most elaborate. They were of the *luakini* or *poʻokanaka* class with *kāhuna* of *aliʻi* ancestry. He demanded human sacrifices for the important rituals.

Pukui-Elbert write of dozens of forms of Kū. Kamakau gives 29 by name. Among these are:

Kūkāʻilimoku, snatcher of land. The feathered war god of Kamehameha I, and of his ancestors for many generations. It is also the name of the huge wooden figure in Bishop Museum.

Kūʻula is the widely used name of the god of fishermen.

Kūnuiākea, Kū of the great expanse, was an unseen god living in the highest heavens, and head of all the Kū gods.

The rising sun is referred to Kū, the setting sun to Hina, a female known as the wife of Kū. *Kāhuna* who practice medicine offer prayers to these two healers. When in the mountains gathering medicinal herbs, the *kāhuna* and their helpers stand before a plant facing the north (ʻākau). They pluck a branch with the right hand (toward the east) and offer a prayer to Kū. With the left hand they gather a branch (toward the west) and acknowledge Hina. The prayer asks for permission to remove the plant material from the forest and also that it heal the patient for whom it is gathered.

Kino lau, or earthly forms of Kū, are the ʻōhiʻa tree and the ʻio or hawk.

The third through the sixth nights of the lunar month are sacred to Kū.

The name Kū means upright.

3. Lono is credited with being the god of peace, agriculture and fertility, and such natural phenomena as the winds, dark rain clouds, rain, the sounds of the winds and rain and the sea. It is evident that he shares some of these with the other major gods.

Lono is called the patron of the *makahiki* and of sports. The *makahiki* sports tournaments were played before his banner, often called Lonomakua. The banner consisted of a tall pole and cross bar. The pole was tipped with a human-like head, called Lono. The cross bar was decorated with large sheets of white *kapa,* leis of feathers and ferns, and few skins of the *ka'upu* bird which was one of the earthly forms of Lono. Some informants say the *ka'upu* is the gannet or booby bird, others believe it to be the albatross.

Each of the four major gods could assume the form of a man and enjoy life with the people. Most of them had one to many other forms called *kino lau* (many bodies).

Lono could assume the shape of a hog or a hog-man called Kamapua'a. Stories are told of Kamapua'a's exploits on windward O'ahu. In the Hilo area of the Big Island he was intimately and tempestuously associated with the volcano goddess, Pele. He could cross the channels between the islands in the form of the fish *humuhumu-nuku-nuku-a-pua'a.*

In keeping with his pig *kino lau,* Lono's tree form was the *kukui.* The leaves of this candlenut tree resemble the snout and ears of a pig. *Kukui* wood was carved into the form of a pig's head, painted with *'alaea* (red ochre) and placed on the *ahupua'a* (altar decorated with a pig) at the time of the *makahiki.* Another *kino lau* was the *'aholehole* fish which has a pig-like snout.

Other plant *kino lau* of Lono were the *'uala* (sweet potato), taro leaves shaped like pigs' ears and the *ipu* (gourd). His followers could sense his presence in the dark rain clouds of the autumn, the lightning, thunder, rains, rainbows, and gushing springs.

Heiau for Lono (*māpele*) were set up to pray for rain and abundant crops. The offerings were products of the gardens, as well as pigs, but never human sacrifices.

We are told in the Pukui-Elbert glossary that there are some 50 Lono gods. Kamakau lists six by name.

The 28th night of the lunar month is sacred to Lono.

Gourd Helmets. Most that is known of the gourd helmets has been gleaned from the sketches made by Webber and from the knowledge that Cook's party saw them in use during the *Makahiki,* the season which was devoted to festivities in honor of the god Lono. Students of Hawaiian religion suggest that the gourd helmets or masks were worn by the priests and the attendants of Lono.

Webber made a dramatic drawing of "A Man of the Sandwich Islands, in a Mask." The mask was formed from a gourd (*ipu*) with circular apertures cut for the eyes and nose. Strips of *kapa* hung from holes cut in the lower rim of the gourd. Foliage decorated the top and back of the mask, giving an effect similar to the crest of some of the feather helmets. Some persons are quite certain that the foliage is the sedge *'uki* (Cladium). This sketch has been reproduced in color in Murray-Oliver, 1975, plates 29 and 30, p. 122, and in Feher, p. 91.

Gourd Mask: Capt. Cook's artist John Webber sketched paddlers in canoes wearing gourd masks. They were decorated at the crest with foliage which seems to be the sedge *'uki.* Strips of *kapa* hung from holes cut in the lower rim. The masks may have been associated with festivities honoring the god Lono.

Webber also sketched "A Canoe of the Sandwich Islands, the Rowers Masked." Of the ten men visible, all are wearing gourd masks. The three without paddles are holding objects of interest, but not easily identified, except for one which is a feather image, probably representing Lono.

A number of the gourd masks are being made and worn in Hawai'i today, especially by young men involved in the Kaho'olawe movement, and during dances dedicated to Lono, as taught in some of the *hula* schools.

4. Kanaloa was called the lord of the ocean and of the ocean winds. He was credited with being the god of the *he'e* or octopus. This eight-legged sea creature is usually called squid in

Hawai'i. In the *Kumulipo*, Kanaloa is "Kahe'e-haunawela," the evil smelling octopus.

Kanaloa's *kino lau* were the *he'e* and a medicinal herb called *'ala'alapūloa*. The *'ala'ala* is the liver of the octopus. The common names for this plant are *'uhaloa* or *hi'aloa (Waltheria indica)*. The root is aspirin-like in effect when chewed and is used to treat sore throats.

His followers believed that Kanaloa could heal a person who was suffering from being under a sorcerer's spell.

The gods Kāne and Kanaloa traveled together in their human forms to many parts of the islands. When visiting dry areas, Kāne would thrust his *kauila* wood staff into the ground and open springs. A number of these are known today.

In Hawai'i Kanaloa was considered the fourth in order of importance of the major gods. As Tangaroa, in the islands to the south, he was held in much greater esteem. In early Christian times in Hawai'i Kanaloa was equated with Satan.

Three nights of the lunar calendar are sacred to Kanaloa. His name is spelled Kāloa in naming these nights. They are the 24th (*Kāloakūkahi*), the 25th (*Kāloa kūlua*), and the 26th (*Kāloakūpau*).

The word *kanaloa* means secure, firm, established.

■ Demigods, Goddesses, and Heroes

The number of minor gods and godesses were said by David Malo to be "countless." The names of many of the gods have been lost since the decline of these beliefs in the year 1819. Some of the gods were known in Hawai'i only, others were known in many of the islands of Polynesia and beyond. A few of the special deities and heroes known in Hawai'i are:

Māui - the supernatural hero, known in the legends of Hawai'i and in those of many other Pacific Islands. Colum wrote of his Seven Famous Deeds and a number of his lesser accomplishments. See Unit 6 for a list of these deeds. Read *Luomala, Maui of a Thousand Tricks*.

Pele - goddess of the volcanoes. Pele is believed, according to her followers, to be the spirit that causes the eruptions and flows of lava at Kīlauea, Moku'āweoweo (summit crater on Mauna Loa) and other craters and vents on the Big Island. She is credited with causing the eruptions which through the centuries formed the Hawaiian Islands.

There are a number of versions relating to Pele's origin and her activities dating from the dim past. It is generally agreed that she came to Hawai'i from the islands to the south (Kahiki) with several brothers and sisters. Pele was seeking a home for herself and her family. To be a satisfactory dwelling for a fire goddess, she would need to dig a pit deep enough for her fires and also one free from ground water.

It is interesting to note that Pele followed the same path in probing for a home that the geologists do in describing the steps in the formation of these islands. Pele dug first on Ni'ihau, then Kaua'i and on O'ahu. She continued to dig, then abandoned each island in turn until she found the ideal conditions at Kīlauea on Hawai'i Island. Here she continues to make her home in Halema'uma'u crater called *"Lua Pele."*

When she appears to her followers in human form Pele may be a beautiful young girl or she may be a wrinkled old woman. Stories are told at the present time of her appearance in the latter guise.

Pele's visible spirit form is a flame or a cloud seen during an eruption. A few photographers have captured her fiery features on film, to the delight of her followers if not to the volcanologists.

Pele's destructive form is the lava flow with its accompanying sulphurous gases. Although flows have destroyed forests, pastures and evacuated villages, rarely has there been loss of human life. The largest in the past two centuries occurred in late 1790 when an estimated 400 men, women and children of Keōua's army were killed by lava, ash and gases from an explosive eruption as they were crossing the Kīlauea volcano area from Hilo to Ka'ū. A few of the footprints in the dried clay-like mud are preserved under glass on the site.

Hi'iakaikapoliopele is the youngest and favorite sister of Pele. The story of the adventures of Hi'iaka in service to her sister are told in Emerson's *Pele and Hi'iaka*.

Kamohoali'i is Pele's best known brother. He may assume human form or that of a huge but friendly shark known as the King of the Sharks. Other brothers and sisters seem to have led uneventful lives and are not often mentioned in the legends.

Pele's associations with Kamapua'a, the hogman, were stormy. Read about them in Beckwith, 1970.

Pele's descendants and the descendants of the

Pele priests worshipped her as their ʻaumakua. They took the kapa-wrapped bodies of their dead to Kīlauea to be consumed in the fires. Families that lived far from Kīlauea placed the bodies of their deceased in lave tubes or caves since such structures were formed by Pele.

We frown on the present-day reference to the Hawaiian volcano goddess by the French name Madame Pele.

ʻAilāʻau (wood eater) was the fire god before the arrival of Pele.

Kihawahine was a Maui chiefess who after death became a lizard goddess. Her images placed in heiau on Maui and Hawaiʻi were dressed in yellow kapa. Kamehameha I gave her, as a goddess, the prostrating kapu and carried out his conquests in her name. Kihawahine's home was a fishpond at Haneoʻo, Hāna district of Maui.

Other moʻo goddesses were **Hauwahine** of Kawainui Pond (or Swamp), Koʻolaupoko and **Laniwahine** of ʻUkoʻa Pond, Waialua, Oʻahu. When these goddesses were at home in their ponds the leaves on the bordering trees and weeds turned yellow and foam gathered on the surface of the water.

Moʻoinanea was the matriarch of all moʻo gods and goddesses. (See Pukui-Elbert, p.394).

Kamakau wrote that the moʻo gods and goddesses were shaped like the little house lizards. But they were terrifying in appearance as they were black in color and from 12 to 30 feet long.

Male moʻo deities are apt to be unfriendly. Hiʻiaka overcame one at Kualoa. His tail is the cone-shaped islet Mokoliʻi (little lizard) in Kāneʻohe Bay. The moʻo Laniloa once killed travelers near Lāʻie. He was cut up into the five islets seen today off Laniloa Point.

Milu was the ruler of the underworld, the world of darkness and the place of the dead. It is said that Milu was a chief, succeeding Wākea. His place of residence was either Kahakuloa, Maui, or Waipiʻo, Hawaiʻi. Milu was disobedient to the gods, especially to Kāne, and was thrust down at the time of his death. Kanaloa may have had a part in this opposition to Kāne. In time Milu was referred to as Satan.

The "Lua-o-Milu," pit of Milu or the underworld, will be discussed under the "Soul After Death."

■ **Deities of the Crafts and Craft Materials:**

ʻAiʻai - a god of fishermen and son of Kūʻula the principal god of fishermen. He located koʻa, fishing areas and built kūʻula fishing shrines.

Haʻinakolo - goddess of kapa makers and bird catchers.

Haʻulili - Kauaʻi god of speech.

Hinapukaiʻa - goddess of fishermen, wife of Kūʻula and mother of ʻAiʻai.

Kapo - goddess with two personalities. She was a hula goddess associated with Laka or a fierce goddess of sorcery. Daughter of Haumea and sister of Pele.

Kuʻialua - god of the students of lua fighting.

Kūkaʻoʻo - god of farmers and his digging stick, ʻōʻō.

Kūpāʻaikeʻe - god of canoe makers and inventor of the adze (koʻi).

Kūpulupulu - god of the forest and canoe makers.

Kūʻula (Kūʻulakai) - god of fishermen. As a man he lived on east Maui and is credited with building the first fish pond, loko iʻa. All fishermen's stone images and heiau are named for him, kūʻula.

Laʻahana - goddess of kapa makers and daughter of Maikohā, god of kapa makers.

Laka - a name used by three personages:
1. Goddess of the hula and of the forest plants associated with the hula.
2. A young navigator whose canoe was built for him by the menehune (helpful little folk of Hawaiian legend).
3. A god worshipped by canoe makers, also called Kūʻōhiʻalaka.

Lea - goddess of canoe makers. She took the form of the ʻelepaio, a flycatcher bird, and tested the soundness of the log proposed for a canoe.

Maikohā - god of kapa makers. Residents of both Kaupō, Maui, and Nuʻuanu Valley, Oʻahu, claim that from his grave in their area grew the first wauke plant.

Maʻiola - god of healing. His spirit, occupying certain trees, would counteract poisons when the wood was used as a remedy.

Mauliola - a god of health.

■ **Deities Exercising Control over the Forces and Moods of Nature, and of Certain human Interests**

ʻAilāʻau - god of fire before Pele arrived. Name means wood eater.

Haumea - goddess of motherhood, presided over childbirth. The "earth-mother" goddess, also called Papa and La'ila'i. Wākea was the first of her many husbands. Mother of Pele and her many siblings.

Hina - widely known goddess or demigoddess of Polynesia. Associated with the moon, *mahina.* Four Hina of Hawai'i are:
1. Wife of Akalana, mother of Māui.
2. Mother of Kamapua'a.
3. Mother of the island of Moloka'i. Island song - *Moloka'i Nui a Hina.*
4. Goddess associated with Kū. In gathering medicinal plants or those for the altar in the *hālau hula,* people used the left hand and prayed to Hina. The right hand was used for Kū.

Hina'ea - goddess of the sunrise and sunset. Her name comes from her ability to cure the children's disease *'ea* or thrush. She was a skilled *kapa* maker and decorator of *kapa* with the *'ohekapala* or bamboo stamps.

Hinalaulimukala - this goddess, whose name means Hina of the leaves of the seaweed called *limu-kala,* was the patron of the *kāhuna* who prescribed medicines from the sea. She was the most beautiful of the many Hina.

Hina'ōpūhalako'a - goddess of corals and spiny sea creatures. From her coral reef Māui may have secured a shell to make his famous fishhook, *manaiakalani,* to fish these islands from the sea.

Hinaulu'ōhi'a - goddess of the *'ōhi'a lehua* forest. No one shall gather *lehua* flowers or leaves on his way into the forest. Only on his return, with proper invocations, may he pluck them. A rainstorm is the least of the inconveniences that may follow when one tampers with these trees.

Hōkeo - a god who assisted Lono in bringing the winds to Hawai'i. He could assume the form of a gourd, *hōkeo.*

Hulu - an image wrapped in *kapa, akua kā'ai,* who assisted at childbirth.

Ka'ahupāhau - chiefess of the shark gods of Pearl Harbor (Pu'uloa). She was born a human but was changed into a shark. She protects humans in Pearl Harbor from shark attacks. This chiefess is named in the song *Pūpū O 'Ewa.*

Ka'alaenuiahina - the great mudhen, *'alae* bird, of Hina. This sorcery goddess held the secret of making fire in the days before humans could do so. Māui, after a series of attempts, wrested the secret from her. This was one of Māui's seven deeds to help his fellow men.

Kaiona - a goddess of Pu'u Ka'ala and a plain at Wai'anae. She was believed to help those lost in the forest by sending a bird to guide them to a trail leading to the lowlands.

Bernice Pauahi Bishop was affectionately called *Kaiona.* See the Founder's Day song, *"He Inoa no Pauahi."*

Kamapua'a - as a pig demigod, he created valleys and opened springs by his rootings. He could take the form of a handsome man, any one of a half dozen or more plants, and at times the god Lono. Many stories are told of his adventures and love affairs, and an especially tempestuous affair with Pele. His fish form was the *humuhumunukunuku-a-pua'a.*

Kānehekili - this god of thunder was first worshipped on Maui. His human body was dark on the right side and light of color on the left. High chief Kahekili (natural father of Kamehameha I) had his body tattooed from head to foot on his right side to be like his ancestor and namesake.

Kauhi - a demigod who was tethered to a peak by Pele at Makaua near Kahana Bay on O'ahu. Hi'iaka, during her journey, was unable to free him but he rose to a crouching position. He is now called the Crouching Lion.

Kūhaimoana - a shark god, brother of Pele and husband of Ka'ahupāhau, the shark goddess of Pearl Harbor. He was said to be 30 fathoms long.

La'amaomao - a goddess of the winds. She gave her son Pāka'a a wind calabash containing the bones of her mother. He could control the winds, for navigational purposes, by chanting the names of the winds.

The Ipu Makani o La'amaomao, or Calabash of the Winds, once belonging to King Kalākaua, is the property of Bishop Museum. A color photo of it may be seen in *Hawai'i, The Royal Isles,* page 12.

Lilinoe - a goddess of the mists and younger sister of Poli'ahu, snow goddess of Mauna Kea.

Limaloa - a god of mirages on Kaua'i and guardian of the sea.

Mauliola - a god of health. The word means breath of life. When someone sneezes his companion may say, *"Kihe a mauliola!"* Sneeze and live!

Niolopua - god of sleep. The word means handsome.

Poli'ahu - beautiful snow goddess of Mauna Kea, Hawai'i. In spite of her beauty and powers, she lost her husband and lovers.

■ The 'Aumākua (Singular - 'aumakua)

The 'aumākua were family or ancestor gods in contrast to akua whose realm was so extensive that they might be called impersonal gods. Most 'aumākua had been humans during their respected life on earth, working, advising, helping, and serving as examples to others. After death their spirits dwelled in the 'aumākua realm where they were able to keep in communication with their descendants on earth.

Through dreams the 'aumākua were able to send messages, offer advice, caution or even scold their family members on earth. Some of the advice was in answer to the prayers directed to the 'aumākua for help.

The mother or a relative might be told in a dream the name that must be used for a newborn baby. This inoa pō, name given in the night, must be used or ill would come upon the child.

A medical kahuna would appeal to his 'aumākua for help. In a dream, hō'ike na ka pō, he was told in detail the treatment that he must administer to his patient.

The bond between humans and their personal, ancestral gods was very real. By the age of seven a child was expected to say his own prayers to his 'aumākua. His family and his 'aumākua expected him to refrain from breaking the laws of the many gods, to observe and obey the kapu pronounced by the chiefs and kāhuna and to be a helpful person and refrain from hurting his fellow men in any way.

Through the years as the elders passed on into the next world the 'aumākua became more numerous. Mary Kawena Pukui told, in her two-volume Nānā i Ke Kumu, that she learned the names of 50 of her family 'aumākua and was expectd to know which one would be of help in certain situations.

The most visible of the 'aumākua were those that appeared on earth to their followers as an animal, a plant, a mineral or as one of nature's forces such as volcanic fire, lightening, or phosphorescent lights. Some stone and wooden images were designated as 'aumākua.

Kamakau (1964) and others tell of the kākū'ai or transfiguration ritual by which the spirit of the deceased is offered sacrifices of food, is transformed and lives again as an 'aumākua. The ceremony is especially dramatic when the soul of the deceased is transformed into a shark, a large lizard or a volcanic fire.

Some of the more common animal 'aumākua are listed here alphabetically:

'alae bird - mudhen	manō - shark
'enuhe - caterpillar	mo'o - lizard
honu - turtle	'ōpelu - fish
kōlea - plover	pueo - owl
loli - sea cucumber	puhi - eel

Among the plant 'aumākua are 'iliahi (sandalwood), kō (sugar cane), mai'a (banana), niu (coconut) and many others.

Some 'aumākua were born in animal form from human mothers. Examples most often given here were sharks. The baby shark was placed in the sea, fed daily, and remained a friend and helper for years to come.

Shark 'aumākua protected their followers from man-eating sharks, rescued them when a canoe was capsized and, of special interest, guided their canoes on short and long voyages. A great guide shark, Kalahiki, piloted canoes around Hawaiian waters, and some say he guided the voyaging canoes of the settlers who discovered Hawai'i. (Kamakau, 1964, pp. 74-75)

'Aumākua were also called kumupa'a by Kamakau. Kumupa'a means descended from the source.

■ 'Unihipili - the spirit of a dead person.

The spirit of the deceased was secured and controlled by a living person who became its master. The spirit was deified, fed with 'awa, guided and developed by prayers and suggestions until it became strong and acquired mana or power.

A cruel, unscrupulous person could produce an 'unihipili with a cruel nature. The master could send the spirit on errands of destruction. A kindly, gentle person could groom the spirit to become a kindly messenger for him.

A keeper could create an 'unihipili by the kahukahu method. He kept a portion of the body of the deceased, such as bones or hair in his home. Each morning and evening by calling and by prayer he asked the spirit to come and partake of 'awa. The spirit, although retaining his ties with the spirit world, became strong and a servant to his keeper.

The more elaborate kākū'ai method was to take the entire body to the place associated with his 'aumakua. The followers of Pele went to the active Kīlauea volcano. Those who claimed the mo'o went to a stream or swamp. Shark worshippers took the corpse to the sea. Followers of the thunder god asked a priest of Kānehekili to call down lightening and thunder to gather up the body and take it to the spirit world. In each of these cases the family brought offerings and the body was accepted or rejected. It is not clear with the kākū'ai method whether the transfigured spirits were controlled by one person or were free to move about doing deeds of good or evil as became their nature.

Once a keeper created an 'unihipili he had to continue to feed and attend it the rest of his life. If he neglected it the spirit would turn on him and destroy him.

■ Kālaipāhoa

Images, called poison gods or goddesses, were made from wood considered deadly poisonous that grew only at Maunaloa, Moloka'i. The three trees, believed to be possessed by the gods, from which kālaipāhoa were carved are the nīoi, a'e, and 'ohe. The few images made were always in the possession of the ruling chiefs. Scrapings from the backs of the images were placed in an enemy's food to cause his death. Chips were saved during the carving to be used in sorcery also.

These trees grow in many places and are known to be harmless. Only when the spirits of the gods entered them and the people worshipped them did the wood become poisonous.

The spirit of Ma'iola, god of healing, entered certain trees. If the bark of these was touched to the lips of a person who had eaten scrapings from kālaipāhoa he would recover at once.

After consolidating the islands under his rule, Kamehameha acquired all the kālaipāhoa images. Those in Bishop Museum have cavities in their backs. (Kamakau, 1964, pp. 128-31. Beckwith, 1970, pp. 111-13)

■ Feather Images or Gods

Feather images, peculiar to Hawai'i, were made by skilled craftsmen who used the technique employed in constructing the feather helmets. They extended the cap down to form a human-like head, face, and neck. As in the helmets, the 'ie'ie rootlets were twined into a framework and the entire structure was covered with fine netting decorated with small feathers. All of the images were made before the time of contact with foreigners.

Of the 19 known images, all have or have had a pair of pearl shell eyes with pupils formed by wooden pegs. Eight of the images have crests covered with feathers. Six of these are simple ones resembling the helmet crest. Bishop Museum's fine image, known to us as Kūkā'ilimoku, is an example of one with the simple crest. Webber sketched the only known image with a complicated double crest. The image may be seen in the British Museum. A color sketch appears on the cover and on p. 23 in Force and Force.

Eight images have head coverings of human hair. Bishop Museum's second image is of this type.

The mouths of all of the images except one were fitted with dog's teeth. This one exception grins fiercely with shark's teeth. An image in the British Museum has 144 canine teeth; Bishop Museum's Kūkā'ilimoku has 94.

Feather images range in height from ten and one-half to 41 inches high.

After a careful study of these images, Buck wrote: "Thus the Gods, as well as the chiefs, received the highest technical recognition that the craftsmen could provide." (Buck, 1957, p. 503)

■ Wooden Images

The wooden images are among the most dramatic of the achievements of the trained craftsmen. In the heiau the figures may be compared to theatrical stage settings which heightened the emotional impact of the impressive rituals conducted by robed priests and chiefs.

Experts have written that Hawaiian wood carving "appears to be the boldest and most vigorous of the independent but historically related sculptural traditions in Polynesia." (Cox and Davenport, 1974, p. 8)

A University of Hawaii art professor wrote, "If we were forced to choose a single specimen to represent the characteristic art of Polynesia, it might well be one of the extraordinary wooden gods of Hawaii." (Luquiens, 1931, p. 19)

The wooden images associated with religion represent human-like figures, as is true throughout most of Polynesia, but the craftsmen were free to express their ideas in oversize heads, horizontal figure-eight mouths, shortened limbs, and in some cases, a protruding jaw-tongue complex.

Three types of religious images are represented

in Bishop Museum by beautifully executed examples. The secular, utilitarian food bowls, including those supported by human figures, will be discussed under "Containers for Food and Drink."

■ **Temple images** that escaped the wholesale destruction in 1819 are superhuman in size. Cook wrote that the images were six feet tall on Hikiau heiau. Those sketched by L. Choris in 1816 and J. Arago in 1825, some years after iron tools were introduced, are larger.

Bishop Museum's fine example of a central or major temple image, captioned Kūkā'ilimoku, and on display in Hawaiian Hall, is 77 inches tall.

■ **Stick images** (akua kā'ai) are smaller, portable images, mounted on a shaft which varies from a few inches to two feet long. This shaft or stick allowed the image to be held aloft or to be placed in the sand or between stones in a terrace or wall. Many of the kā'ai images are carved with a great deal of precision and imagination.

Among Bishop Museum's stick images is an unusually fine pair. Although not identical in all details, they were taken from a cave near Kawai-hae, Hawai'i, in 1904. They stand 42 and one-half and 44 inches high, respectively.

■ **'Aumākua**, usually represented as free standing images, are larger and heavier of body than the stick images. A number have, or have had, pearl shell eyes, human hair pegged in, and teeth. These may be actual human teeth or bone carved to resemble teeth. In this group are the sorcery images, called kālaipāhoa, which have hollow cavities in their backs.

In this class, the powerful-appearing female image, 14 and one-half inches high, is displayed in Hawaiian Hall, Case 8 (Bishop Museum) so that the cavity may be seen. Also study the taller (36 inch) 'aumakua in the same case, with lizards painted on the forehead, cheeks, and chin.

The most realistic of Bishop Museum's 'aumakua images is a female figure with human hair, pearl shell eyes, and a satin-polished surface.

■ **Making the Wooden Images**

Some 150 examples of wood sculpture embodying the human figure are known in museums and private collections today. Countless numbers were destroyed in 1819, especially the large images which could not be removed to caves for safe-keeping by the local supporters of the old religion.

Six artists visited Hawai'i between 1778 and 1825 and sketched about 110 images. Most of those recorded before 1819 were destroyed in 1819.

Most of the able males must have learned to work with wood. They would construct or help make houses, canoes, food bowls, weapons, game implements, and tools. Perhaps they made the support figures for food bowls and drums.

The carving of images was the privilege of the priest-craftsman, who was skilled in religious ritual as well as in wood working.

Lehua

The wood most frequently used for images was 'ōhi'a lehua, believed to be an earthly manifestation of the gods Kāne and Kū. Images made from this extremely hard wood resisted weathering when exposed in the heiau. 'Ōhi'a trees grew in the rain forests to sizes sufficient to make the largest images.

Kauila wood, straight-grained and tough, was used to carve portable images. Since the tree grew straight and tall, it was ideal for the Lono pole. The pole supporting the Makahiki banner in Webber's "Boxing Match" lithograph is a little over ten feet tall.

The unusually fine pair of portable images in Bishop Museum are said to be made of kou wood. Other materials used in the images are: mother-of-pearl for eyes, human hair, human teeth, and bone. Some figures wear a simple garment of kapa.

Tools used by the sculptor were those with cutting edges, such as adzes, gouges, chisels, shark teeth fitted in a haft, and flakes of basalt or obsidian. Sanding and smoothing the wood was done with porous lava, coral, sand, and the skin of the shark or ray. The pump drill was suited for drilling holes for the insertion of human hair.

It seems certain to us today that the large images, and some smaller ones with intricate carving, made between 1779 and 1819, are the products of the work of introduced iron tools.

■ **Kāhuna** (Singular, kahuna)

The kāhuna were experts in their professions or crafts. Religion figures prominently in all of the activities of the kāhuna. The temple priests were closely associated with their chiefs and advised them in all important matters. The medical kāhuna, representing more than a dozen specialties, relied upon the spiritual aspects of their profession as well as their knowledge of the human body and of herb remedies and massage. Other kāhuna, experts in crafts, supervised the construction of houses and canoes.

The dreaded kāhuna were those who prayed victims to death (kāhuna 'anā'anā).

Some kāhuna wore robes and turbans, kā'ei po'o, of white kapa. Others wore colors which designated their allegiance to a certain god or to a skill or specialty.

The priests of Pele wore red and black kapa and never trimmed their hair and beards. They braided their hair and beards and knotted the ends to keep them out of the way.

■ **Classes of Kāhuna**

The following names were selected from longer lists compiled by Kamakau, Fornander and others:

Kahuna nui - the high priest. He was one of the chief advisors to the ruling chief and consulted with him on matters of importance. One of these was the proper time to wage war.

Kahuna pule - selected from the chiefly class. Pule means prayer. He conducted the rituals in the heiau.

Kahuna kaula - a prophet. A man or woman who foretold coming events and the outcome of such events. The spirit of his god caused each kaula to speak out fearlessly, often revealing a turn of events that his chief did not want to hear. Examples are:

1. While Kamehameha was making preparations to invade and conquer Kaua'i, a kaula named Namaka uttered this prophecy:

   No chief over the island of Hawaii shall place his foot upon the sacred sand of Kahamalu-'ili, none of its war canoes shall have power to come to Kauai, without a truce having been made between the islands. (Kamakau, 1961, p. 112)

2. Near the end of Kamehameha's conquests, the prophet Kapihe announced:

   The islands will be united, the kapu of the gods overthrown, those of the heavens (the chiefs) will be brought low, and those of the earth (the common people) will be raised up. (Kamakau, 1964, p. 7)

3. Near the end of the 18th century Ka'opulupulu, a noted kaula, prophesied that white men would become rulers, the native population would live (landless) like fishes of the sea, the line of chiefs would come to an end, and a stubborn generation would succeed them who would cause the native race to dwindle. (Kamakau, 1961, p. 167)

Kahuna hulihonua - the land experts.

Kahuna kuhikuhilani - one who reads signs and omens in the sky.

Kahuna kuhikuhipu'uone - one who locates sites, especially for building heiau. He may also select sites for fishponds and houses.

Kahuna oneoneihonua - one who dedicates a heiau with prayers and special services.

Kahuna kilo hōkū - one who studies the stars.

Kahuna kilo honua - one who reads signs in the earth.

Kahuna nānā uli - a weather prophet.

Kahuna po'i 'uhane - one who captures the souls of the living or the dead.

Kahuna 'anā'anā - one who prayed people to death.

Kāhuna having to do with illness and medical practices, some 15 of them, are discussed in Unit 16 of this book.

Kamakau wrote that after Kamehameha consolidated the islands he chose craftsmen to make many of the articles needed in the kingdom. He called these men kāhuna. A few of the many things these kāhuna-craftsmen made were canoes, hōlua sleds, surf boards, wooden bowls of many kinds, fish hooks and articles from gourds. (Kamakau, 1961, pp. 176-77)

■ Heiau - Temples of Worship

Although the people related to their gods at work and at play, they provided a variety of places, simple and elaborate, for religious services or observances. Men set up a small shrine in one end of their eating house (hale mua) where prayers and offerings were made to the family gods ('aumākua).

Agricultural heiau, called waihau and unu, were the scene of rituals held to improve crops. The offerings were pigs, bananas, and coconuts, usually the first of the harvest.

Fishermen erected simple shrines along the coast, and on the stone platforms placed kū'ula, a fish god, credited with bringing success to fishermen and causing fish to increase in numbers. Bird catchers erected their own simple stone platforms called ko'a in the mountains and on islets frequented by sea birds. Ceremonies were conducted here to cause the birds to multiply.

Of great importance were the large temples (heiau) dedicated to certain purposes or to certain gods. A typical heiau was enclosed by sturdy walls of lava stone, the floor was covered with smooth rocks and small pebbles, and the entire complex was open to the sky. Interior structures or furnishings were raised platforms of stone, grass houses for the storage of useful and sacred articles, wooden images, usually with awesome features, altars for holding sacrifices, and in some, an oracle tower ('anu'u) covered, at least when in use, with white kapa.

■ Kinds of Heiau

Luakini or po'o kanaka heiau are the largest of the structures, built by the highest chiefs on selected sites, dedicated with human offerings and the scene of human sacrifices.

Heiau hō'ola or healing temples are unique to Hawai'i, and attest to a more advanced state of medical learning and practice here than among any other Pacific people. Keāiwa on 'Aiea Heights is the best known temple of this type on O'ahu, but before 1819 there was at least one in each district throughout the inhabited islands.

Pu'uhonua were places of refuge to which accused persons could flee, find sanctuary, and be forgiven by the kāhuna for their misdeeds. In time of war, those persons not involved could take refuge in one of these sanctuaries. The only reconstructed one today is the Pu'uhonua o Hōnaunau, a national historical park at Hōnaunau, island of Hawai'i.

See pu'uhonua, Unit 18, Warfare.

■ Kapu

Kapu is spoken of as the system of laws regulating the privileges and prohibitions of the people. Some kapu were the long-standing laws of the land. The best known of these, affecting all classes, was the one forbidding men and women to eat together ('ai kapu). The abolishment of this kapu was announced in 1819 at the time that Kamehameha II ate with his Queens. This act also officially abolished all other kapu and temple worship.

Kapu regulating the conservation of natural resources were usually far-sighted and just. Other prohibitions, formulated by the priests and the chiefs for some type of social control, were often severe and unjust. The penalty for breaking a kapu was often death.

Capt. Cook observed the power of the kapu when all canoes were forbidden to enter or leave Kealakekua Bay until the return of one of his boats. (The name of the Bay, we are told, was originally Kealaikeakua, the pathway of the god. It was believed that a god slid down a cliff here leaving an imprint.) Information on name given to Homer Hayes by Pilipo Ha'ae, born near Hikiau heiau, on the Bay, about 1856.

A few additional kapu were:

Women were forbidden to eat certain foods. Most of these were the kino lau, or in some way associated with the major gods. Some kapu foods were pork, bananas (except iholena, pōpō'ulu and kaualau varieties), coconuts, and certain fish.

War was kapu during the Makahiki and all unnecessary work was discouraged.

When a kapu chief passed through a village, the people knelt, sat, or fell prostrate according to the power of the kapu of the chief.

A chief, his possessions and the land around his dwellings were kapu.

During the dedication of a luakini type of heiau, no noise could be made within hearing of the ceremony. The penalty for breaking this and many other *kapu* was death.

■ Kapu Sticks and Wands

One insignia or visible sign of a *kapu* is the hardwood pole, some four or five feet long, topped with a ball of white *kapa*. This *pūloʻuloʻu*, or *kapu* stick, was carried before a chief by a member selected from his household while he was walking from place to place.

Before the chief's *Hale mua* a pair of *pūloʻuloʻu* would be placed upright to denote the presence of the *kapu* person. When the sticks were crossed before his doorway, the message was clear that no one was to enter.

In European museums are seven wands all collected on Captain Cook's voyage. These wooden

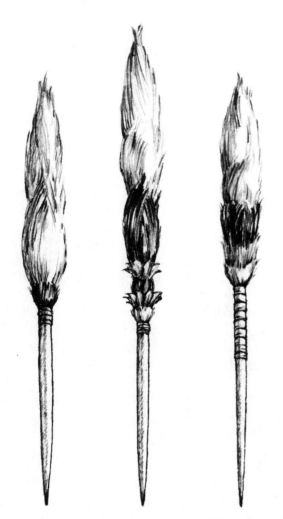

Tabooing Wands: Pointed wooden sticks decorated with dogs' hair and feathers were placed on fields, on walls and near buildings to indicate places that were *kapu*.

sticks, pointed at one end and decorated at the other with dog's hair and feathers are tabooing wands. They were placed around the perimeter of fields, on walls, or near dwellings or other buildings to indicate that the places were *kapu*.

■ Kānāwai

A decree or law pronounced by a ruler was a *kānāwai*. It could be a decree of life or one of death. A victorious high chief might pronounce this edict to save the lives of all of the chiefs and warriors who had been defeated by his forces and would otherwise be put to death. (Kamakau, 1964, p.11)

Edicts were classed as *kānāwai akua*, gods' laws, or *kānāwai kapu aliʻi*, chiefs, sacred laws. The difference between the two is slight because the chiefs claimed descent from the gods and the right to speak for them.

The *kānāwai*, decreed by rulers, usually affected many people, perhaps the entire kingdom. They usually referred to secular matters. The flow of water *(wai)*, so vital in taro farming, was controlled by regulations. This was probably the origin of the word *kānāwai* in early times.

Kapu differed from *kānāwai* in that they were more religious in nature.

Many *kānāwai* were decreed through the years. One of interest is that of Kualiʻi, ruler of Oʻahu, who proclaimed one that was fixed, constant and unchanging. It provided that old men and women could sleep along the highways in safety; that farmers and fishermen must welcome strangers and feed the hungry in the name of this *kānāwai*. It was decreed in the late 1600s as the *Kānāwai Niʻaupiʻo Kolowalu*.

Because of the righteousness of his decree, the gods gave Kualiʻi a long life. He died in Kailua, Oʻahu, in 1730 at the age of 175 years, wrote Kamakau (1964, pp. 14-15)

Best known today of these edicts is the Māmalahoa Kānāwai of Kamehameha I. This law commemorates the incident of the fisherman splintering a paddle over the head of Kamehameha at Pāpaʻi Bay, Puna, in 1783. The law was spoken by Kamehameha who was grateful for his deliverance and in memory of his steersman who lost his life as the result of this encounter. It was also a statement of forgiveness for the fisherman and his companions.

The decree was made at Kaipalaoa, Hilo, at

Kahale'iole'ole (the house without rat beams) sometime between the years 1796 and 1802.

This Law of the Splintered Paddle is called *Māmalahoe* (splintered paddle) or *Māmalahoa* from *hoa*, friend.

Māmalahoa (or *Māmalahoe*) *Kānāwai*:

E nā kānaka,
E mālama 'oukou i ke Akua,
A e mālamaho'i ke kānaka nui a me ke kānaka iki;
E hele ka 'elemakule, ka luahine, a me ke kama
A moe i ke ala,
'Aohe mea nānā e ho'opilikia,
Hewa no, make!

The Law of the Splintered Paddle:

O my people,
Honor thy God,
Respect alike (the rights of) men great and humble;
See to it that our aged, our women, and our children
Lay down to sleep by the roadside,
Without fear of harm,
Disobey, and die!

■ Heiau

A few of the more important and accessible *heiau* are listed here for the five larger islands. Except for five which have been restored to a greater or lesser extent, the rest are in disrepair. For many years people have been removing stones from *heiau* walls for building foundations and other forms of construction.

Hawaii:

Mo'okini - Kohala - *luakini* type

Pu'ukoholā and Mailekini - Kawaihae - *luakini*. These are in the National Park system.

Keikipu'ipu'i and 'Ahu'ena - Kailua - *luakini*.

Hikiau - Kealakekua - *luakini* type. Captain Cook and party conducted shore activities on this *heiau*.

Pu'uhonua o Hōnaunau - Hōnaunau, Kona - *pu'uhonua* or temple of refuge. This one has been more nearly restored than any other. It is now a National Historical Park with a visitors' center.

Waha'ula - Kalapana - *luakini*. Now part of the Hawai'i Volcanoes National Park with partial restoration and a visitors' center. The *heiau* model in Bishop Museum is Waha'ula as it might have looked before 1819.

Maui:

Pi'ilanihale - Hāna - *luakini*. Probably the largest *heiau* in the islands.

Ko'ihale - Waihe'e - unknown.

Lo'alo'a - Kaupō - *luakini*.

Pihanakalani or Haleki'i - Paukūkalo Ridge, Kahului - *luakini*.

Moloka'i:

'Ili'ili'ōpae - Mapulehu - *luakini*.

Kahakamalu and Kekui - Kalae - *unknown*.

O'ahu:

Pu'uomahuka - Pūpūkea - *luakini*. Largest on the island. Kaopulupulu was the priest.

Kūpolopolo - Waimea Bay - *luakini*.

Kawa'ewa'e - Kāne'ohe - *luakini*. Built by Olopana in the 12th century.

Ulupō - Kailua - type not certain. It is located in an agricultural area.

Kāne'ākī - Mākaha - Once an agricultural heiau, it was rebuilt into a *luakini*. It has been restored to the point of having two 'anu'u or oracle towers, a *lele* or sacrificial altar, a *hale pahu* or drum house, and a *hale mana* or house where divine messages are received.

Kū'īlioloa - Tip of Kāne'īlio Point, Wai'anae - class uncertain. Named for a legendary dog.

Keaīwa - 'Aiea - *heiau hō'ola,* or healing temple. Rededicated in 1951 and part of a state park.

Papa'ena'ena - Diamond Head Slope - *luakini*. Destroyed about 1856. Bishop Museum's *pahu heiau,* temple drum, is said to have come from this *heiau*.

Kaua'i:

Important *heiau* near the mouth of the Wailua river are;

Malae, the largest *heiau* on Kaua'i, some 324 by 273 feet with walls 10 feet thick. Queen Deborah Kapule converted it into cattle pens in 1830.

Poli'ahu, said to be a companion to Malae. Located on a ridge in a state park with a commanding view of the surrounding area. It is 242 by 165 feet in size with walls 5 to 6 feet thick.

Holoholokū was a *pu'uhonua* or temple of refuge and a sacred place for the birth of chiefly children. (It has the same function as Kūkaniloko, near Wahiawā, O'ahu.)

A saying has come down through the years about this birthplace:

Hānau ke 'li'i i loko o Holoholokū,
   He ali'i nui;
Hānau ke kanaka i loko o Holoholokū,
   He ali'i no;

Hānau ke aliʻi nui mawaho aʻe o Holoholokū,
'Aʻole aliʻi, he kanaka ia.

Which means:

A chief born within Holoholokū, is a high
chief;

A commoner born within Holoholokū, is a
chief indeed;

A high chief born outside Holoholokū, is not
a chief, he is a commoner.

Hikinaakalā, another heiau along the Wailua, is a
puʻuhonua.

Kēʻē at Hāʻena is the most famous heiau known in
Hawaiʻi devoted to the hula. Nearby are Kau-
luapāʻoa heiau, Keahuolaka and several impressive stones bearing names.

■ Mana

Mana is the power and authority of the gods
and the chiefs. It is found to some degree in all life.
The higher the rank of the chief or chiefess, the
higher is his or her mana.

A chief's inherent quality of leadership, ability
to command, his reservoir of physical and spiritual
strength, in fact his personal magnetism and
charisma, all emanate, at least in part, from mana.

"Worship was paid to the gods, because it was
firmly believed that the genius, power and inspira-
tion (mana) of a king was like that of a god." (Malo,
1976, p. 135).

The children of the high chiefs were married to
the children of other chiefs with high blood lines.
In this way the mana was not diluted.

By proper prayers, ceremonies and chants
(hoʻomana), images and other objects such as
stones could be caused to possess mana. The
kāhuna were trained to manipulate mana.

After death, the people believed, the greater
part of a person's mana went with him to the
'aumākua world unless he passed it on to a
descendant. However, some mana was thought to
linger in his name, name chants, bones, clothing,
hair and fingernails.

■ The Soul After Death

According to the learned people of ancient
times, Kamakau wrote, there was the worldly
realm in which we live, and there were three
realms for the spirits of the dead. They were:

1. Ao kuewa or ao ʻauwana - (ao means a realm,
world, or place; kuewa is a homeless, wandering
person. 'Auwana is to wander). When a soul had
not earned a rightful place in the 'aumākua world,
he wandered around on a treeless plain or strayed
in the underbrush. In this dreary existence he
would feed upon moths and spiders. A specific
place was known on each island where the spirits
wandered (Kamakau, 1964, p. 49).

If the person's earthly sins had been of great
magnitude, he might become a wandering spirit,
forever homeless and hungry. Eating was such a
delight to the people that to be forever hungry was
one of the greatest punishments.

To be abandoned or ignored by one's 'aumakua
and left to wander is the worst fate that can come
upon the deceased. Such friendless spirits were
thought to be evil and were avoided by humans.
Upon seeing a figure moving about at night it was
sometimes necessary to apply tests to separate the
lapu or ghost from a living person. If the figure in
question was really a spirit it would leave no trace
as it walked through grass or leaves, it showed no
reflection when looking into a pond or stream, and
if startled would vanish instantly.

Through their experiences with dreams, it was
easy for people to believe that the spirit of a sleeping
person leaves the body during sleep and may travel
far and have a wide variety of experiences.

There is an opening or duct at the inner corner
of each eye next to the nose. This is called lua-
'uhane, or soul-pit. People believed that the soul
left and re-entered the body of a sleeping person at
this point. The spirit must return from its dream
journey and slip back into the body in time for the
person to awaken normally. A sudden awakening,
such as caused by a loud noise, might cause one to
find he had been roused from sleep without his spirit.

If a person slipped from life before his work on
earth was accomplished, his 'aumakua would be
sure to find his spirit and conduct it back to his
body. It is said that some spirits were transported
in a closed coconut shell or a gourd to prevent them
from slipping away again. The 'aumakua skilled in
restoration to life (called kā-puku or kū-paku)
knew that he could slip the spirit under the nail of
the big toe and by proper massage and by uttering
the correct chants he would cause the spirit to
again fill the entire body. When life was restored
the person moved, opened his eyes, and vocalized
with sounds similar to the crow of a cock.

After the person had been fully restored to life he took a purifying bath. His 'ohana welcomed him from this experience which had a happy ending. The considerable number of people who died and returned to life were responsible for the stories told of visiting the several realms in the afterworld during this period that they were thought to be dead.

Leinaaka'uhane - place where the spirits leaped (leina) into the spirit ('uhane) world. There were spirit leaps on each island and were to be found on or near the fields where the spirits wandered (Kamakau, 1964, p. 49; Beckwith, 1970, pp. 155-56). One on O'ahu was on the Waialua side of Ka'ena Point. A more interesting one was called Lei Lono, located at Moanalua, O'ahu. Here grew the breadfruit tree of Leiwalo with "misleading" branches. On one side of the tree the branches were leafless and dry, but were actually alive. The branches on the other side were green and leafy, but were really dead.

A friendless and unattended soul as he approached the tree would be sure to grasp a green (but dead) branch which would break and allow him to be cast down into the darkness of Pō. (See the sketch of Leiwalo by Joseph Feher in Kamakau, 1964, p. 46.)

A faithful soul, attended by his 'aumakua, could by-pass the tree and be led to one of two places: He would be taken back to his body and be restored to life, if that was to be his destiny; or welcomed into the world of his ancestors, ao 'aumākua.

2. Ao 'aumākua - realm of the ancestors. This most desired of all places in the spirit world was created by Kānenuiākea, the god who created heaven, earth, and man. Family ties remained intact in this realm. One of the greatest joys was to have the family members united.

There were many dwelling places in the 'aumākua realm. If the family 'aumakua was manō the shark, the members knew that their kuleana, or rightful place, was in the deep ocean. Those who claimed Pele as an 'aumakua knew that their kuleana was in the volcanic crater.

Kamakau concludes his views of this realm by writing "So are gathered together those of the whole earth who belong to the 'aumākua realm; all are united in harmony." (Kamakau, 1964, p. 51)

3. Ao o Milu - the realm of Milu. As was the case of the other gods, Milu was once a chief on earth. But he disobeyed the gods and at his death was swept down into the underworld and became its ruler.

A soul, not forgiven by its 'aumakua for its transgressions on earth, might be sent to the realm of Milu which has been described as a land of twilight and shade, a barren, waterless waste without flowers or trees.

While some writers warn of fire, darkness, and cruelty in Milu's realm, others call it a shadowy place of drowsy existence. It is written that the gods can help the souls escape or aid in their rescue by their relatives still on earth.

■ **Huaka'i pō** - Marchers of the Night. From their experiences in relation to the spirits some people believe, even today, that the departed ones do return singly and in numbers to the scenes that they knew on earth.

The most dramatic and fearful of these are the Marchers of the Night. In these processions one sees, or senses, the gods, chiefs with their warriors, and chiefesses. These reappear usually in the form and wearing the apparel which distinguished them on earth. They may re-enact important events which they experienced while living. Perhaps their most common activity is to march along a trail which was well known to them in life. A number of these trails are known today. People living in the area may be disturbed by the fearful processions.

Sometimes the spirits march to heiau sites where the leaders may conduct a service. They have been known to visit the old playing fields and engage in their favorite games such as 'ulu maika and spear throwing.

When the marchers appear to conduct a dying relative to the 'aumākua realm, they are usually able to do this at night. Rarely must this be done in the daytime.

A procession of gods is distinguished by strong winds which may break down branches and shrubs to clear the path. Three gods and three goddesses traditionally lead, each carrying torches which burn with red flames. Members of their party chant.

The chiefs in procession are often accompanied by 'aumākua who are there to protect any of their living descendants who are so unfortunate as to be in the path of the marchers. The nose flute, pahu *drum,* and chanting accompanies this procession.

Persons confronted by the marchers must hide or they will be killed by the advance guard. An *'aumakua* in the ranks can save his descendants. Or a person might react as he would to a *kapu* chief. Some say that he must tear off his clothes and lie face down on the ground.

■ Understanding and Appreciations

1. Discuss the ability of the *kahuna 'anā'anā* to "pray" a person to death in the light of modern psychology or psycho-somatic medicine.

2. Try to imagine the fear that pervaded the lives of the people when you learn that the average family kept a small fire burning in the center of the house at night to keep away evil spirits. Imagine also the fear of breaking one of the many *kapu* or being the next victim marked for a human sacrifice.

3. From your reading try to find references to the *love* of the Polynesian gods as expressed by the worshippers. Note carefully any evidences of love as part of Hawaiian religion, or is it absent?

4. A broader understanding of Hawaiian religion may be gained by comparing it to other religions. Select certain elements in the Hawaiian religion and compare them to the Christian (Protestant and Catholic), Jewish, Hindu, Buddhist, or other faiths. For instance, some might compare the leaders (the priests, rabbis, preachers, and *kāhuna*) in each of the faiths in:

   a. The manner in which the leaders are selected.
   b. Their duties within the place of worship.
   c. Their duties outside the place of worship and their relation to their worshippers.
   d. The method of compensating these leaders.
   e. Their personal life, married or single, week-day activities.
   f. Training or schooling required.
   g. Other factors of interest or concern.

5. When the Hawaiian religion was abolished by the rulers under Kamehameha II the people were without a "way of life." Read about the arrival of the missionaries in 1820 and the spread of Christianity to the majority of the Hawaiian people. Titus Coan tells of the Great Awakening in 1838 and during the years to follow in his book *Life In Hawaii,* Ch. IV.

■ Student Activities

1. Read or scan the Kumulipo. Make comparisons with parts of the book of Genesis. (See Reading List - Beckwith 1951 or 1972, Barrere 1969, Beckwith-Kepelino 1932, Johnson, 1981)

2. Prepare a paper or talk on the concept of the Temples of Refuge. Is it right to forgive all transgressors of all crimes? Read Deuteronomy 19:1-13 and compare these Hebrew cities of refuge with the Hawaiian.

3. Sketch or carve from wood some of the temple images. Read about them in *Hawaiian Art,* Bishop Museum Special Publication No. 18. What is a tiki? The equivalent word in Hawaiian is *ki'i.*

4. Discuss the *'aumākua* with your older Hawaiian friends. Learn the name of their family *'aumakua* and whether or not it means anything to them at this time.

5. Visit Keaīwa Heiau on 'Aiea Heights. Read Dr. Nils Larsen's story of its function in early Hawai'i in the *Hawaiian Historical Society Report* for 1951 and of the rededication of this temple. Visit the herb garden nearby to learn the plants used by the *kahuna lapa'au.* List the *heiau* in your area and visit one of the sacrificial class. A list of *heiau* and sites is given in *Thrum's Annual* for 1938, pp. 121-142.

6. Make a list of *kapu* from your reading on this subject. Can you classify them as those helpful to society and those that seemed only to restrict the activities of the people?

7. Read the accounts of Kalākaua's attempts to revive the old religious practices in the 1880s.

8. List the *kāhuna* and their specialities as you read about the old religion. How many of them were helpful members of the community?

9. Read the story of Chiefess Kapi'olani defying Pele at Kīlauea in 1824. (Westervelt, *Legends of Volcanoes*)

10. Add to this list of Hawaiian gods and goddesses and in parallel columns name the Greek and Roman gods, if any:

Realm	Hawaiian	Greek	Roman
Great God	Kāne Kānenuiākea	Zeus	Jupiter
War	Kū Kūnuiākea	Ares	Mars
Love	Makanikeoe or Makanikau	Aphrodite	Venus
Ocean	Kanaloa	Poseidon	Neptune
Agriculture	Lono	Demeter	Ceres

■ **Audio-Visual Aids**

1. Bishop Museum - although Museum exhibits change from time to time, the following objects are usually on display:

   Heiau post image from Kaua'i with streamers of *kapa*. A colossal version of this image guards the Museum entrance at the Kalihi Street entrance.

   Large wooden image called Kūkā'ilimoku, one of a pair from a sacrificial altar.

   Kūkā'ilimoku, wickerwork image covered with feathers, the eyes are of pearl shell held in place with wooden pegs and the teeth are the canine teeth of dogs.

   Temple drum (*pahu heiau*) from a Diamond Head *heiau*. The drum head is of sharkskin.

   Model of Waha'ula *heiau*, a sacrificial temple (*po'o kanaka*) in Puna, island of Hawai'i.

   Wooden *akua* and *'aumākua* and also exhibits of stone *akua* and *kū'ula* or fishermen's gods.

   Stone *akua* and *'aumākua* have been placed among the courtyard plants. They are a *pueo* or owl *'aumakua,* a small shark and an eel *'aumakua.* Kapa'aheo is a large shark god of stone from Kohala, also in the Hawaiian courtyard or garden at Bishop Museum.

2. Students on the island of O'ahu should visit some of the remaining *heiau* such as Keaīwa on 'Aiea Heights, Pu'uomahuka at Waimea, or Ulupō near the Kailua Road. Many more are listed in McAllister's *Archaeology of Oahu,* Bishop Museum Bulletin 104, 1933, and in *The Sites of Oahu,* Bishop Museum, 1978. The remnants of *heiau* are to be found on all of the major islands and their locations may be learned from Bishop Museum publications or *kama-'āina* residents.

■ **Vocabulary**

Learn the significance or meaning of these words, some of which were not used earlier in this unit:

Kumulipo	kāhuna	kapu
Wākea	heiau	akualele
Papa	mana	huaka'i pō
Kāne	akua	pī kai
Kū	'aumakua	'imi ola
Lono	'uhane	'anā'anā
Kanaloa	pule	kū'ula
mū	ilāmuku	kauwā

■ **Current Happenings or Trends of Significance to this Unit**

1. The universal interest in religion causes the residents and visitors of the present time to be interested, or at least curious, about the old Hawaiian religion. *Heiau* sites are being cleared and marked and some temples are being restored if their original plans are known. The most important example is the City of Refuge National Historical Park at Hōnaunau, now called the Pu'uhonua o Hōnaunau.

2. Images are being copied in jewelry, statuettes for home decoration, and large, so-called "tiki" for garden use.

3. Hawaiian religious practices that might be judged "positive" and "negative" are used as themes or incidents in story telling, pageants, dramas, and novels.

4. Practices that purport to suggest early religious rituals are used today in some ground-breaking ceremonies for buildings and in dedicating completed projects.

5. Certain Hawaiian families remember the *'aumakua* of their ancestors but seem to expect no help or guidance from them as was once the custom.

6. A knowledge of psychology helps the present day thinker to understand the power of the *kahuna 'anā'anā* over his victim, or the mental lift that a fisherman received from his *kū'ula.*

7. Perhaps the most persistent belief is that of the existence of Pele, goddess of the volcanoes. Students understand the geological forces which cause an eruption yet are fascinated with the story that Pele was actually seen in the form of an old woman or an attractive girl just before or during an eruption.

8. Read about the many religions in Hawai'i today. (Mulholland, 1961. Also *Atlas of Hawaii*, 1973, pp. 124-25)

■ Evaluation

1. Test the students for word meaning and spelling by using the vocabulary list.
2. Check the student's understanding of some article or book assigned to him from the reading list and report by talk or essay.
3. Attempt to evaluate the students' intellectual and emotional maturity in a discussion of:
   a. Volcanic eruptions caused by Pele.
   b. Death predicted by an 'auku'u bird.
   c. The help that an 'aumakua is able to give a family.
   d. The collapse of the Pearl Harbor drydock because no ceremony was performed to appease the shark goddess Ka'ahupāhau. (Facts only in *Thrum's Annual*, 1914, p. 212, and 1920, pp. 39-41)

■ Reading List

Alexander, W.D. "The 'Hale o Keawe' at Honaunau, Hawaii." *Polynesian Society Journal*, 1894. 3:159-161.

Allen, Gwenfread E. *The Y.M.C.A. in Hawaii, 1869-1969*. Honolulu: The Young Men's Christian Association, 1969.

Barrère, Dorothy B. "Cosmogonic Genealogies of Hawaii." *Journal of the Polynesian Society*, December 1961. 70(4).

———. *The Kumuhonua Legends*. A study of late 19th century Hawaiian stories of creation and origins. Pacific Anthropological Records No. 3. Honolulu: Bishop Museum Press, 1969.

Beckwith, Martha W. *Hawaiian Mythology*. 1940. Honolulu: University Press of Hawaii, 1970.

———. *Kepelino's Traditions of Hawaii*. 1932. Honolulu: Bishop Museum Bulletin No. 95, 1971.

———. *The Kumulipo*. A Hawaiian creation chant. 1951. Honolulu: University Press of Hawaii, 1972.

Bicknell, James. "Hawaiian Kahunas and Their Practices." *The Friend*, September 1890.

Bobilin, Robert T. "Religions." *Atlas of Hawaii*. Ed. R. Warwick Armstrong. Developed and compiled by the Department of Geography, University of Hawaii. Honolulu: University Press of Hawaii, 1973.

Bryan, E.H. Jr. "Religion and Superstition." Ch. 17 in *Ancient Hawaiian Life*. 1938. Honolulu: Books About Hawaii, 1950. (Also good bibliography to 1950.)

Buck, Peter H. Ch. I, "Man Creates His Gods." Ch. II, "The Gods Create Man." Ch. III, "The Death of the Gods." In *Anthropology and Religion*. New Haven, CT: Yale University Press, 1939.

———. "Polynesian Religion." *Hawaiian Annual for 1933*. Honolulu: Thrum's Hawaiian Annual. 64-67. (Excellent short article.)

———. "Religion." In *Arts and Crafts of Hawaii*. Honolulu: Bishop Museum Special Publication No. 45, 1957. 465-532.

Coan, Titus. *Life in Hawaii, 1835-1881*. New York: Randolph & Company, 1882.

Colum, Padraic. *Legends of Hawaii*. 1937. New Haven, CT: Yale University Press, 1960 (paperback).

Cox, J. Halley, and William H. Davenport. *Hawaiian Sculpture*. Honolulu: University Press of Hawaii, 1974.

Daws, Alan G. "Evangelism in Hawaii: Titus Coan and the Great Revival of 1837." *Hawaiian Historical Society Annual Report*, 1960.

Dutton, Meiric K. *The Episcopal Church in Hawaii, Ninety Years of Service, 1862-1952*. The Missionary District of Honolulu, 1952. Reprinted in part, edited and illustrated by The Rev. John Paul Engelcke in *The Hawaiian Church Chronicle*. Honolulu, Queen Emma Square, 1979. (See issues for April, May, June and September, 1979.)

Emerson, Joseph S. "Kahunas and Kahunaism." *Mid-Pacific Magazine*, Jan.-June 1926.

———. *The Lesser Hawaiian Gods*. Hawaiian Historical Society Paper No. 2. Honolulu: Hawaiian Historical Society, 1892.

———. *Selections from a Kahuna's Book of Prayers*. Hawaiian Historical Society Report for 1917. Honolulu: Hawaiian Historical Society.

———. *Some Hawaiian Beliefs Regarding Spirits*.

Hawaiian Historical Society Report for 1901. Honolulu: Hawaiian Historical Society.

Emerson, Nathaniel B. *Pele and Hiiaka.* A myth from Hawaii. Rutland, VT and Japan: C.E. Tuttle, 1978.

Emory, Kenneth P. "Religion in Ancient Hawaii." In *Aspects of Hawaiian Life and Environment.* Honolulu: Kamehameha Schools Press, 1965.

Feher, Joseph. "Religion." In *Hawaii: A Pictorial History.* Honolulu: Bishop Museum Special Publication No. 58, 1969. 100-111.

Fornander, Abraham. *Hawaiian Antiquities and Folklore.* Honolulu: Bishop Museum Memoir, Vol. 6, No. 1, 1919. (Ancient religious ceremonies, Hawaiian priesthood.)

Gallagher, Charles F. *Hawaii and Its Gods.* New York, Tokyo, Honolulu: Weatherhill/Kapa, 1975.

Gutmanis, June. *Na Pule Kahiko: Ancient Hawaiian Prayers.* Honolulu: Editions Limited, 1983.

Handy, E.S.C. *Polynesian Religion.* Honolulu: Bishop Museum Bulletin No. 34, 1927.

———. "Religion and Education." Ch. 4 in *Ancient Hawaiian Civilization.* A series of lectures delivered at the Kamehameha Schools by E.S.C. Handy [and others]. 1933. Rutland, VT and Japan: C.E. Tuttle, 1965 (rev. ed.).

Handy, E.S.C., and Mary K. Pukui. *The Polynesian Family System in Ka'u, Hawai'i.* 1958. Rutland, VT and Japan: C.E. Tuttle, 1972.

Hayes, Homer A. "City of Refuge." *American Heritage,* Vol. II, No. 3, Spring 1951. 16-19.

Hoyt, Helen P. *The Night Marchers.* The Hawaiian Bicentennial Library, Vol. XII. Norfolk Island, Aus.: Island Heritage, 1976.

Johnson, Rubellite K. *Kumulipo.* Vol. I (Chants 1 and 2). Honolulu: Topgallant Publishing Company, 1981.

Kaeppler, Adrienne L. *Eleven Gods Assembled.* An exhibition of Hawaiian wooden images. Honolulu: Bishop Museum Press, 1979.

Kalakaua, King David. *Legends and Myths of Hawaii.* 1888. Rutland, VT and Japan: C.E. Tuttle, 1979. (See discussion of religion in the introduction.)

Kamakau, Samuel M. *Ka Po'e Kahiko.* The people of old. Honolulu: Bishop Museum Special Publication No. 51, 1964.

———. *Ruling Chiefs of Hawaii.* Honolulu: Kamehameha Schools Press, 1961. (See also *Index to Ruling Chiefs of Hawaii* by Elspeth Sterling, Bishop Museum, 1974.)

———. *The Works of the People of Old.* Honolulu: Bishop Museum Special Publication No. 61, 1976. (Articles on the kinds of *heiau* and the rituals performed.)

Larsen, Nils P. "Rededication of the Healing Heiau Keāiwa." *Hawaiian Historical Society Annual Report for 1951.* Honolulu: Hawaiian Historical Society.

Loomis, Albertine. *Grapes of Canaan.* Hawaii 1820. The true story of Hawaii's missionaries. 1951. Honolulu: Hawaiian Mission Children's Society, 1966 (paperback).

———. *To All People: A History of the Hawaii Conference of the United Church of Christ.* Honolulu: Hawaii Conference, 1970.

Luomala, Katharine. *Maui of a Thousand Tricks.* Honolulu: Bishop Museum Bulletin No. 198, 1949.

———. *Voices on the Wind.* Honolulu: Bishop Museum Special Publication No. 75, 1986 (rev. ed.).

Luquiens, Huc. *Hawaiian Art.* Honolulu: Bishop Museum Special Publication No. 18, 1931.

Malo, David. Chs. 35-37 in *Hawaiian Antiquities.* 1898. Honolulu: Bishop Museum Special Publication No. 2, 1976.

McBride, Leslie R. *The Kahuna.* Versatile mystics of old Hawaii. Hilo: Petroglyph Press, 1972.

Melville, Leinani. *Children of the Rainbow.* Religion, legends and gods of pre-Christian Hawaii. Wheaton, IL: The Theosophical Publishing House, 1969.

Mitchell, Donald D. Kilolani. *Hawaiian Treasures.* Religion, 47-58. Honolulu: Kamehameha Schools Press, 1978.

Morrill, Sibley S., ed. *The Kahunas.* The black and white magicians of Hawaii. Boston: Branden Press, 1968.

Mulholland, John F. *Hawaii's Religions.* Rutland, VT and Japan: C.E. Tuttle, 1970.

Nickerson, Thomas, comp. *Early Images of Hawaii.* Honolulu: University of Hawaii Press, 1986. (More than 150 prints, drawings and paintings of scenes and persons during the 100 years following Capt. Cook. Reproduced on microfiche with booklet of descriptions.)

Pratt, H. Douglas, et al. *A Field Guide to the Birds of Hawaii and the Tropical Pacific.* Princeton, NJ: Princeton University Press, 1987.

Pukui, Mary K., E.W. Haertig, and Catherine A. Lee. Nānā *i ke Kumu: Look to the Source.* Vol. I, 1972; Vol. II, 1979. Honolulu: Hui Hānai, Queen Liliʻuokalani Children's Center.

Rodman, Julius S. *The Kahuna Sorcerers of Hawaii, Past and Present.* Hicksville, NY: Exposition Press, 1979.

Rose, Roger G. *Hawaiʻi: The Royal Isles.* Honolulu: Bishop Museum Special Publication No. 67, 1980.

Schoofs, Robert. *Pioneers of the Faith.* History of the Catholic Mission in Hawaii (1827-1940). Honolulu: Hawaii Catholic Herald, 1973.

Shook, E. Victoria. *Hoʻoponopono.* Contemporary users of a Hawaiian problem-solving process. Honolulu: University of Hawaii, 1986.

Steiger, Brad. *Secrets of Kahuna Magic.* New York: Universal-Award House, 1971.

Sterling, Elspeth, and Catherine C. Summers. *Sites of Oahu.* Honolulu: Department of Anthropology, Bishop Museum, 1978.

Thrum, Thomas G. "The Gods of Ancient Times." *Hawaiian Annual for 1927.* Honolulu: Thrum's Hawaiian Annual.

———. "Heiaus: Their Kinds, Construction, Ceremonies." *Hawaiian Annual for 1910.* Honolulu: Thrum's Hawaiian Annual. 53-71. (See index to Thrum's *Hawaiian Annual* for more listings by Thrum and others on religion.)

Westervelt, William D. *Legends of Ghosts and Ghost-Gods.* Rutland, VT and Japan: C.E. Tuttle, 1963. (See especially "The Ghost of Wahaula Temple." This is the Puna temple represented by a model in Bishop Museum.)

———. *Hawaiian Legends of Volcanoes.* 1916. Rutland, VT and Japan: C.E. Tuttle, 1964.

Wilkerson, Clark. *Hawaiian Magic.* Honolulu: Clark Wilkerson, 1968.

Yzendoorn, Reginald. *History of the Catholic Mission in the Hawaiian Islands.* Honolulu: Honolulu Star-Bulletin Ltd., 1927.

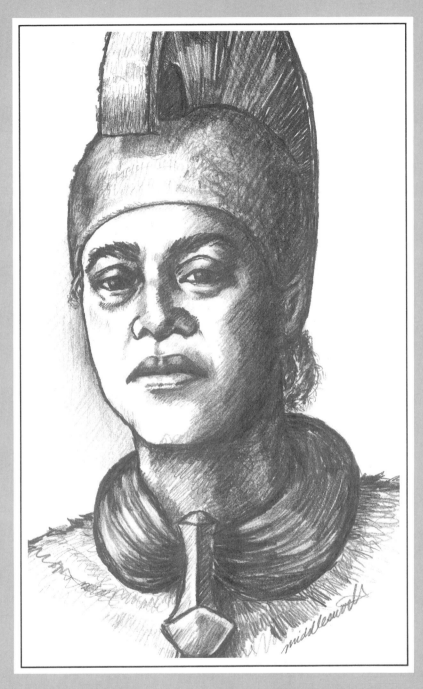

UNIT 8:
Symbols
of Royalty

SYMBOLS OF ROYALTY

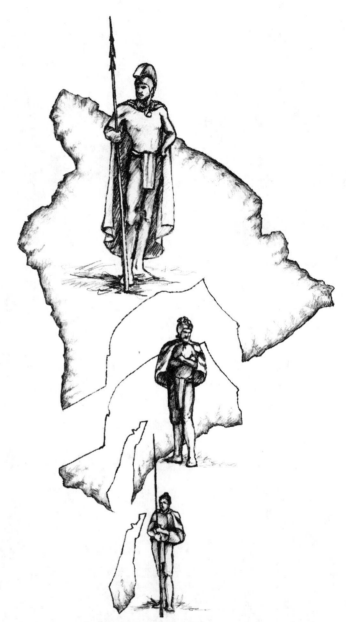

The royal personages were ranked from the very highest *kapu* chiefs down to those of minor importance. There are Hawaiian names for the various classes and ranks of rulers but they were called by the English titles, chiefs and chiefesses, by the early visitors to Hawai'i. The Kamehameha and Kalākaua dynasties favored British court customs and used the titles king and queen, prince and princess.

Hawaiian royalty by origin were from the same class of people as the working classes, although some writers have suggested that they might be from a different stock. Leadership gradually became the privilege of the strongest and the most intelligent. These leaders enjoyed the best food, frequent massage by experts, training in the performing arts, traditions, sports, and warfare. They came to believe that they were of divine origin and prepared genealogical chants which traced their ancestry to the gods. The genealogies on record trace the Hawaiian chiefs to their Tahitian ancestors of the 12th to 14th centuries. The names of the chiefs and chiefesses are known for this historic period. The genealogies may be traced back to the vague time of the culture heroes, and then to the mythical period of the creation of the islands and of men.

The *maka'āinana* are said to have fallen to their common status because they lost their genealogies. (Malo, 1976, p. 60)

The paramount chief, later called the king, was traditionally the ruler of an entire island, called a *mokupuni*. His domain might also include one or more of the smaller satellite islands, such as Ni'ihau to Kaua'i. Wars frequently caused changes

An Island and Two of its Subdivisions: An entire island, *Mokupuni*, was ruled by the paramount chief, the *ali'i nui*.

The larger islands were divided into districts, *Moku*, assigned to a chief called the *ali'i 'ai moku*.

An *Ahupua'a* within a *Moku* was under the direction of an *ali'i 'ai ahupua'a* or a *konohiki*. There were many subdivisions within a typical *Ahupua'a*.

in the boundaries of a chiefdom as will be shown in Unit 18.

The ruling chief delegated the supervision of each of the several large land sections of the island, called *moku*, to a chief of lesser rank. In this capacity he was called the *ali'i 'ai moku*. Smaller areas within the *moku*, called *ahupua'a*, were assigned to an *ali'i 'ai ahupua'a*. (See Unit 17)

The rulers were set apart from the general populace, the *maka'ainana*, by an elaborate, strickly enforced series of *kapu* or restrictions. The regalia or royal symbols of the chiefs differed somewhat according to their rank.

■ Feather Regalia for the Royal Men

The Hawaiian artisans surpassed all other Pacific Islanders in the variety and quality of their feather work. They were fortunate in being able to secure brilliant feathers from forest birds which were found nowhere else. They learned to tie these feathers to close-meshed, durable nets which they made from the strong fibers of the *olonā* plant, also endemic to Hawai'i. These craftsmen are to be commended for their patience in securing great numbers of the tiny feathers, for their ingenuity in creating garments not known elsewhere, and for their diligence in making such large numbers of the feathered articles.

Feathers from the small forest birds, although difficult to obtain in places far from the seaside homes of the people, were selected as being the most permanent, brilliantly-colored materials available with which to decorate the royal regalia.

Captain Cook admired the beauty and magnificence of the feather cloaks and helmets and wrote, ". . . the surface (of the garments) might be compared to the thickest velvet, which they resemble, both as to the feel, and the glossy appearance." (Cook, 1784, Vol. 2, p. 206)

"Feather cloaks, *'ahu'ula*, are the most spectacular of all objects of native Hawaiian manufacture and were the visual symbols of prestige and power in pre-European Hawaii." (Kaeppler, 1970, p. 92)

■ Snaring the Birds

Trained birdcatchers *(po'e hahai manu)* observed the feather birds in their native habitat and learned their feeding habits. Many of the birds sipped honey from the blossoms of the *lehua* or other trees or shrubs. A successful method of snaring birds was to place gum or the sticky fruits of the *pāpala kēpau* tree on a crosspiece fixed to the tip of a long pole. As the birdcatchers *(kia manu*, those who used gum on a pole) placed this on branches which the birds were known to frequent, they would imitate the call of the bird or intone a chant which they believed would attract the birds. The gum, which resembles our modern scotch tape in that it retained its adhesive qualities for a long time, held the bird's feet fast until it was lifted off by the hunter.

■ The Feather Birds

The most highly prized feathers came from the *mamo (Drepanis pacifica)* found only on the island of Hawai'i. This black bird, nearly eight inches in length, grew a few deep yellow feathers above and below the tail and on the thighs. It was snared by the bird catchers *(po'e hahai manu)*, the yellow plumage plucked, and the bird released to grow more feathers.

A species of *'ō'ō* was endemic to each island except Maui; all seem to be extinct now except the Kaua'i *'ō'ō'ā'ā (Moho braccatus)*. The largest *(Moho nobilis)*, 9 to 13 inches long, lived only on Hawai'i and were sought for their long, soft yellow feathers *('ō'ō'ē'ē)*, short yellow feathers *(pu'e)*, and glossy black body feathers. These were for leis, for garments, and occasionally for *kāhili*. The central pair of long black tail feathers *(puapua)* and the gray and white feathers under the tail, *(pīlali 'ō'ō)*, were prized for *kāhili*.

After plucking the desired yellow and black feathers from the *mamo* and *'ō'ō*, the birdcatchers removed the remaining gum from the bird's feet with *kukui* oil, then released it to grow more feathers. Despite the fact that but a few feathers were removed from the *mamo* and *'ō'ō*, and that they were not killed, these birds with the most highly prized of all feathers have become extinct. Changes in the habitat of the birds such as the destruction of some of their food plants by introduced animals, and the introduction of bird diseases by foreign birds, have caused these feather birds to die out. The remaining specie of *'ō'ō* on the island of Kaua'i does not have the bright yellow feathers prized by cloak makers.

The expert feather workers believed that feathers plucked from live birds retained their luster longer than those taken from dead birds.

Most of the red feathers came from the *'i'iwi (Vestiaria coccinea)* which was found on all the major islands. The birds' feathers are orange-red, wings and tail black, and the sharp, curved bill a pink-red. These birds are fairly common today on Kaua'i, Maui, and Hawai'i but rare or extinct on the other islands. (Berger, 1972, p. 182)

The 'i'iwi furnished the red feathers which ornament most of the existing articles of feather work. Since choice feathers covered most of their body, these small birds were killed and their skins removed and dried. The feathers could then be plucked and used later when needed. Though small as sparrows (about 5¾ inches in length), the bird catchers toasted them and used their flesh for food. Despite this treatment, the 'i'iwi are fairly common in certain forests.

The feathers of the 'apapane (Himatione sanguinea) are a deep crimson, the wings and tail black, and the slender beak is black. It is the most common of the honeycreeper birds, about 5½ inches in length, and may be seen in the forests on the six main islands today. 'Apapane feathers were seldom if ever used in regalia for the chiefs as the dark crimson feathers were inconspicuous at a distance (Brigham, 1899, p. 10). These feathers were made into leis for the chiefesses.

Olive green feathers from the 'ō'ū bird (6.3 inches in length) were used sparingly in capes, helmets and leis. The 'akialoa and the 'amakihi provided green feathers, but the extent of their use in feather work is difficult to determine.

The tropic or bos'n birds (koa'e) furnished both white and gray-and-white body feathers for capes. Both the red and the white quill-like tail feathers of these two species of koa'e ornamented kāhili.

The irridescent black body feathers and also the tail feathers of the frigate or man-of-war ('iwa) were used in kāhili and in some of the early capes, particularly those that were trapezoidal in shape.

The body and tail feathers of the domestic fowl (moa) were used in these early capes.

Although not identified on the labels of existing feather work, the following native birds are listed by Brigham as being sources of feathers: the crow ('alalā), black feathers; owl (pueo), and the hawk ('io), both having buff to brown and white feathers. They furnished the type of feathers usually used in kāhili.

David Samwell wrote in January 1779, while at Kealakekua, Hawai'i:

The woods are filled with birds of a most beautiful Plumage & some of a very sweet note, we bought many of them alive of the Indians [Hawaiians] who were employed in catching them with bird lime smeared on the end of a long rod which they thrust between the branches of the Trees. The bird

lime is made of breadfruit & milky juice of a small thorny tree which they call Kepaw [kēpau] (Beaglehole, p. 1167)

Diseases transmitted by some of the introduced birds, the aggressive behavior of others, mosquitoes which transmitted avian malaria, and the destruction of some of their natural habitats by man and grazing animals are believed to have been contributing factors to the death of most of the feather birds.

■ Olonā

The fine netting (nae) to which the feathers are attached was made from the fibers of the endemic shrub olonā (Touchardia latifolia), which thrived in the rain forests.

Olonā produces the strongest and finest plant fibers which man has been able to grow and make into cordage. This shrub, 8 to 10 feet in height, is a semi-cultivated plant of the greatest importance.

Planters go to forested areas and marshes, preferably about 2,000 feet in elevation, and clear away undergrowth, ferns, and vines. These are usually on the windward side of the island where the rainfall is some 180 inches a year and the streams flow continuously.

The workers plant stem cuttings and root shoots so thickly that a man cannot pass between them after they have sprouted and grown tall. This method of close planting produces straight stalks without branches.

A year after planting, the workers prepare for the harvest by building temporary shelters (hale kahi olonā) beside a stream and near the plants. Here the men and women are protected from the rains as they process the olonā.

When the olonā stems are the size of a man's finger and the leaves turn yellow they are broken off at the base. The bark is easily stripped off and the stems discarded.

The tools used are a narrow scraping board (papa'ololī) six to seven feet long and four to five inches wide. The scraper (uhi) is the bony plate from the back of a turtle (honu) some eight inches long and three inches wide with the scraping edge sharpened like an adze (ko'i).

A man or woman places a strip of bark on the board and scrapes (kahi) off the outer bark leaving long, clean, nearly-white fibers. These are dried in the sun or air.

To twist the fibers into cordage the worker,

Processing Olonā: The men scraped the outer layer from the *olonā* bark. Usually the women rolled the inner fibers on their thighs to form the strong cordage of various thicknesses.

usually a woman, selects a thin strip with but a few longitudinal fibers or perhaps, a thicker strip which will make a heavier cord. She holds one end of the strip in the left hand and with the right hand rolls the fibers on her thigh. More fibers are added at the end as needed until cords are produced that are hundreds of feet long, of uniform thickness, and without showing where the fibers are added and joined.

The fine nets to which the feathers were attached in making cloaks and capes and in covering helmets and images were made from two-ply *olonā* cord (Buck, 1957, p. 223). Slender netting gauges (*haha ka 'upena*) of wood, about one-third of an inch in diameter, or the even smaller coconut leaflet midribs (*nī'au*) were used to space the mesh of the netting. The cord was wound on a tiny shuttle (*hi'a*). A regular fisherman's netting knot secured the cords in forming the mesh. (Kamakau, 1976, p. 118)

■ The Netting

The rectangular or trapezoidal capes could be made from a single piece of netting, usually the larger-meshed *'upena* or fishnet, but sections of fine net (*nae*) were cut and fitted together for the foundation of the circular cloaks and capes. These sections were joined along the edges by a thread of *olonā* held in a bone needle, which passed in and out of the mesh and was knotted. The net maker attached a heavy four-ply cord to the neckline of the cloak or cape and provided foot-long cords for tying the garment to the wearer.

The natural strength and stiffness of the *olonā* fibers made it unnecessary for the workers to stretch the net on a frame while they tied on the feathers. They draped the net over a horizontal pole suspended from the rafters of the house or fastened it to a pole supported by two upright poles.

■ Tying the Feathers to the Netting

The cloak makers outlined the design on the netting to guide them in placing the feathers in the desired pattern of shapes and colors. The feathers were separated according to size and color, gathered into bunches containing a few larger ones or as many as 18 small ones. These were secured by the quills with a wisp of *olonā* and stored in gourd containers ready to use. (Buck, 1957, p. 224)

In bunching the yellow feathers, especially those from the *mamo,* the worker placed short red feathers (*'i'iwi pā'ū*) over the dark-colored quills. This task increased the time and work needed to bunch the feathers, but the artist-craftsman had learned that by covering the dark quills with red, he could obtain a warm, golden-yellow effect in the finished garment.

In making a cloak, the craftsman sat before the mesh foundation of the garment with the containers of feathers before him. He began tying the bunches of feathers, working from left to right along the bottom border, using two-ply *olonā* thread. He tied a second row above the first so that the upper row covered the quills of the feathers under it. The tying of the feathers continued upward in this manner. The last two rows were tied at the neckline sideways, with the last bunch of feathers fastened to the top right-hand corner.

The technique of tying on the fine net required that each bunch of feathers be placed so that the quills extended over two or more knots on the mesh, with the colored part of the feathers extending downward on the upper or outside of the net. One end of a thread was secured to the net, then the free end passed around the quills and the lower mesh knot at the base of the feathers. An overhand knot in the thread secured the quills and was then carried higher on the quills. Here the thread passed behind the knot in the mesh, around the quill tips, then was secured by a knot. This process was continued from left to right until the entire row of bunches of feathers had been secured to the net by knots tied around their quills. Feathers with long quills required three knots. (See Buck, 1957, p. 225, for sketches of tying techniques.)

A variety of designs add to the striking appearance of the cloaks and capes. The rectangular or trapezoidal capes, with feathers from sea birds and the jungle fowl, are seen in Sara Stone's sketches in a great number of colors and designs. The netting is generally coarse and many of the feathers are large. The circular garments, with fine netting, are largely yellow and red with some black and a very few with green feathers. (Stone, 1968 - see Reading List)

The designs are crescents, half-crescents, triangles, circles, squares, diamonds or lozenges, horizontal stripes, and others not easy to describe.

Nothing has been recorded about the meaning of the designs on feather garments. Since there are no two cloaks or capes alike, it is possible that a chief was recognized at a distance by the pattern of his garment.

David Samwell wrote at Kealakekua in 1779:

The Cloaks are made of fine Netting with red and yellow feathers curiously worked upon them; these they have of various Lengths, some coming no lower than the Waist & others trailing the Ground. A more rich and elegant Dress than this, perhaps the Arts of Europe, have not yet been able to supply. Inferior Chiefs have Cloaks made of Cock's Tail feathers with a collar of red & yellow, others of white bordered with Cocks feathers with a collar of red and yellow. . . . Some again wear yellow Cloth [kapa] in imitation of these Cloaks, which being of a very bright Colour appears very well at a distance. (Beaglehole, p. 1179)

■ 'Ahu'ula (red garment) Feather Cloaks

Of the 54 long cloaks believed to be preserved today, perhaps 21 are in the British Isles and 12 in other European countries. Four are in New Zealand museums, and one in Brazil. Of the 16 in the United States, 12 are in Bishop Museum and two in private collections in Honolulu. Fortunately for Hawai'i the 12 cloaks in Bishop Museum include those of great historic interest and unusual size or beauty.

Here are descriptions of five cloaks now in Bishop Museum:

The Mamo Cloak: The rich yellow cloak of *mamo* feathers which belonged to Kamehameha the Great is generally considered the most precious of the 'ahu'ula. It is in superb condition and the only all-yellow cloak known. Museum curator E.H. Bryan, Jr., estimated that 80,000 *mamo* birds were needed to furnish the nearly half million choice feathers in this royal robe. Kamehameha secured these *mamo* feathers from chiefly families who had been collecting them for some eight generations, or about 200 years.

. . . the value of the cloak would equal that of purest diamonds in the several European regalia, and including the price of the feathers, not less than a million dollars worth of labor was expended upon it, at the present rate of computing wages. (Jarves, 1839, p. 364)

Tiny red *'i'iwi* feathers were tied to the dark quills of the *mamo* feathers to mask this color. The red feathers formed a skirt or *pā'ū* for the base of

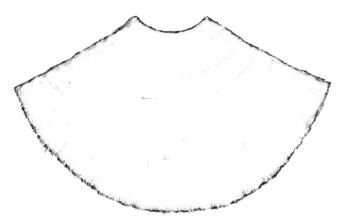

The Kamehameha cloak of choice *mamo* feathers is the only all-yellow cloak known today.

the *mamo* feathers. They are visible only upon close examination and attest to the effort and skill of the artist-craftsmen in securing a warm golden-yellow effect in the finished garment. This cloak is 56 inches in length, the front edges are 46 inches and the width at the base is 148 inches.

Kiwalaʻō Cloak: The yellow and red Kiwalaʻō cloak is of special historic interest. It was won by Kamehameha I when he and his forces defeated his cousin, Kiwalaʻō in the battle of Mokuʻōhai at Keʻei, Kona in 1782. Kiwalaʻō was wearing this cloak when he was killed in the battle.

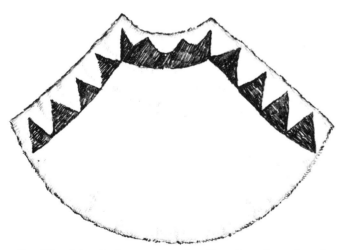

The Kiwalaʻō cloak was won by Kamehameha when he defeated the ruling chief Kiwalaʻō in battle in 1782. The cloak is made from ʻōʻō feathers ornamented with triangles of ʻiʻiwi.

This robe was named the "Queen's Cloak" in the years it was placed over Liliʻuokalani's throne during festivities in ʻIolani Palace, 1891-93. The Queen never wore the cloak. Yellow ʻōʻō and a few *mamo* feathers cover the cloak except for triangles of red ʻiʻiwi feathers at the neck and sides. This

garment is 60 inches in length, the front edges are 50 inches and the width at the base is 144 inches.

Joy Cloak: This striking cloak, named for the Joy family of Boston, Massachusetts, who owned it for some time, is the largest known. Its length is 66 inches, the width at the base is 156 inches. The velvety ʻiʻiwi red robe is ornamented with 22 large circles of yellow ʻōʻō, some interspersed with a few *mamo* feathers. Three yellow half-circles decorate the neckline. A yellow border and three yellow triangles on each front edge complete the pattern. The Joy family, we are told, lined the cloak with a woolen fabric (now removed) and used it as a sleigh robe.

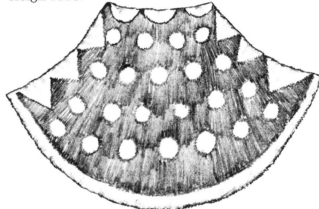

The Joy cloak is of rich red ʻiʻiwi with circles and triangles of yellow, largely ʻōʻō but some of *mamo*. The border is of ʻōʻō.

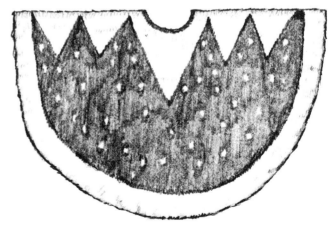

The Elgin cloak, red with a yellow border and triangles, is unique because of the flecks of yellow (ʻula kīnaʻu) dotted among the red feathers.

Elgin Cloak: This cloak of unusual beauty was purchased from the Elgin family of Scotland by the members of the Bishop Museum Association in 1968. It had belonged to the Earls of Elgin since 1792. (Kaeppler, 1970, p. 96-97) Kalaniʻōpuʻu, ruler of the island of Hawai'i at the time of Captain Cook's visit, is believed to have been the owner of this cloak. The body of the robe is of red 'i'iwi feathers, flecked with yellow ones, a design known as 'ula kīna'u. A wide yellow border and rich yellow triangles at the neck and sides are a pleasing contrast to the plush-like red. The length is 59 inches and the width of the cloak at the base is 108 inches.

Kintore Cloak: The latest cloak to return to Hawai'i is this well-preserved garment with horizontal red, yellow, and black stripes. The Countess of Kintore of Keith Hall, Aberdeenshire, Scotland, presented the cloak to Bishop Museum on the occasion of its 80th anniversary in 1969. This is the only one known today with horizontal stripes. It is also unique because of the large number of black feathers in the body of the garment. Its olonā network is the best preserved of all known cloaks. The Kintore robe is 58 inches long and 88 inches wide.

The Kintore cloak differs from others with its horizontal stripes and the large number of black feathers.

A red and yellow cloak given by Kalani'ōpu'u to Captain Cook on January 26, 1779, on the occasion of their first visit together is now the property of the National Museum, Wellington, New Zealand. This 60-inch cloak is pictured on page 41 in Force and Force. (See Reading List)

> Kalani'ōpu'u got up & threw in a graceful manner over the Captns Shoulders the Cloak he himself wore, & put a featherd Cap upon his head, & a very handsome fly flap [kāhili] in his hand: besides which he laid down at the Captains feet 5 or 6 Cloaks more, all very beautiful, & to them of the greatest Value. . . . (Beaglehole, p. 512)

■ **Kīpuka**, Shoulder Capes

After a detailed study of feather garments, Dr. Peter Buck wrote:

> The rectangular feather cape, an easy transition from the ti-leaf rain cape, was made by attaching large feathers instead of ti leaves to a foundation of coarse netting. (Buck, 1957, p. 218)

King, who accompanied Captain Cook, noted that the inferior chiefs wore the capes made with coarse feathers.

Several rectangular or trapezoidal capes have been preserved in which the fine mesh (nae) replaced the coarse in order that they could be decorated with the small, colorful feathers.

The next improvement was to change from the ill-fitting trapezoidal shape to the circular ones made with the netting of small mesh. These have a concave neck border, longer convex lower border, and edges which meet in front. These circular capes and cloaks were the prized possessions of the chiefs. Those in Bishop Museum range from 12 inches to 28 inches in depth.

Five trapezoidal capes are in museums in Europe. Bishop Museum now has one.

A cape, 15 inches in depth, was purchased for Bishop Museum from the Hooper Collection in 1977 by Honolulu resident Thurston Twigg-Smith. Colorful feathers at the neckline are 'i'iwi and 'ō'ō. Slender brown feathers of the jungle fowl (moa) cover the body of the cape with coarser blue-black feathers at the base. The netting is olonā nae. This is Bishop Museum's first and only cape with cock feathers. (Pictured in Force and Force, p. 61)

Inventories account for some 116 circular capes of which 20 are in Bishop Museum and seven in other collections in Hawai'i. Some 22 are known on the mainland of the United States, 39 in the British Isles, and 24 in other European countries. There are three of these capes in New Zealand and one in Australia. Two of Bishop Museum's finest circular capes are described here:

The Lady Franklin Cape: This is the most brilliant and best preserved cape in the museum. In 1861 Kamehameha IV presented this prized mantle to Lady Jane Franklin who had come to Hawai'i in search of her husband, the Arctic explorer, believed to be missing in the Pacific.

In the center of this rich yellow cape are large red and black crescents. Along the front edges are a pair of half-crescents of black with half-crescents of yellow in their centers, and a pair of red half-crescents decorated with yellow half-crescents in their centers. When worn the half-crescents meet along the front edge of the cape to form complete crescents. Small black and red squares add color to the neckline. The red feathers were once identified as 'apapane, but are actually 'i'iwi. The yellow and black are from the 'ō'ō bird. The Museum purchased this cape from the heir in 1909.

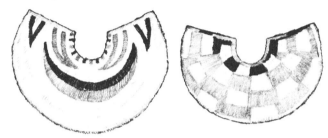

(Left) The Lady Franklin cape is prized for its bright yellow, red and black feathers fashioned into a pleasing design. *(Right)* The Starbuck cape is known for its checker-board pattern of yellow and black feathers.

The Starbuck Cape: This is the only one which is ornamented with large checker-board squares. These are yellow and black 'ō'ō on a background of 'i'iwi red. Captain Valentine Starbuck acquired this cape from Kamehameha II when he transported the royal party to England in 1824. The heirs returned the cape to the people of Hawai'i in May 1927. Of average size for a circular cape, its measurements in inches are: length at back 16.5, front 14.5, neckline 21.5, and base or border 85.

■ **Mahiole,** Feather Helmets

A feather-covered helmet *(mahiole)* and a long cloak were worn by a high chief on ceremonial occasions and on the battlefield. Helmets, unique to Hawai'i, were completely covered with feathers or with human hair, or were of basketry with mushroom-like ornaments at the crest. The latter two were the headdresses of lesser chiefs.

The foundation for the cap and crest is plaited from the long, slender aerial rootlets of the 'ie'ie vine.

'Ie'ie Vines and Rootlets: The rootlets of the 'ie'ie compare somewhat to the cane used in basket-making in other cultures, but these are superior in strength and durability to most others.

'Ie'ie vines, which climb upon trees in the rain

'Ie'ie Climber: This vine with pink-red flowers was sought in the mountains for its strong, slender aerial rootlets which formed the framework for helmets, baskets and other useful articles. The rootlets were twisted into cordage for lashing the posts of a house together.

forests on all of the islands, are known for their thin, *hala*-like leaves and pink-red flowers. Thin rootlets grow down toward the soil, reaching ten feet or more in length. The rootlets are ready to harvest when they are light brown in color and the outer skin-covering falls away when rolled between the hands.

The rootlets must be stored in a dry place for about a month and then are ready to be split into the required thickness for plaiting. Finely split rootlets are pliable, but larger sections must be softened in salt water before plaiting. The technique used in making the framework for feather images is similar to that employed in constructing the helmets.

The helmet consists of a cap which fits snugly to the wearer's head, and a crest. Buck divides the feather helmets into low-crested, wide-crested, and crescent-crested. The crest added height to the appearance of the warrior-chief and served to cushion blows which he might receive on the head in battle. A custom among the men was to cut their hair close at the side and leave a mane-like ridge, called a *mahiole,* on top. The helmet repeats these lines.

Covering the Helmet with Feathers: Most of the helmets are covered with feathers, which were tied to the fine netting as was done for the capes. The netting was fitted to the helmet framework and tied closely to it with *olonā* threads.

Another method of ornamenting the helmet consisted of tying feathers to a braid and fastening lengths of the braid so closely to the foundation that it was completely covered.

From King's journal:

The feather'd Cloaks and Caps [*mahiole*] we supposed [were] Ornaments which they wore only on particular Occasions, they set a great value & were unwilling to part with them; the Cap is a basket work coverd with short red feathers, & streaks of Yellow, black or green intermix'd; it is made to fit close to the head, a small semicircular space left for the Ear; on the middle of the Cap is a protuberance 3 Inches in height & breadth, extending the whole length, the upper part forming a larger curve and bends in the fore part, like a bill, this is often covered with red feathers somewhat longer than the other parts, & gives the Cap a strong resemblance of our ancient helmets; it has a rich and magnificent look; the Crest and protuberant part is differently shapd in height & breadth. (Beaglehole, p. 1392)

About 67 feather helmets are known to be in museums and private collections. Bishop Museum's helmets include three low-crested and one of the wide-crested type. There are eight helmets in museums on the U.S. mainland, 20 in England and Scotland, and 32 in collections in other European countries. There are two helmets in New Zealand.

■ **Hair and Mushroom Ornamented Helmets**

Bishop Museum possesses the only two hair-covered helmets known. Made without crests they resemble hair caps or wigs. The Museum has one of the five recorded mushroom-ornamented helmets. Since none now has feathers, Buck believed that these were made to be worn without feather ornamentation. (Buck, 1957, p. 245-48)

■ **Feathered Helmet Bands**

While on Kaua'i in 1779, Samwell wrote:

These people wear thick feathered rolls . . . round their feathered Caps which gives the whole head dress the appearance of a rich and elegant Turband, none of thes(e) Rolls at Ouwhaiee [Hawai'i]. (Beaglehole, p. 1231)

Helmet Band: This band, one of five known, was made from small red and yellow feathers. Other bands included black and green. Feathers of one color were tied closely to ten or so separate strands of *olonā* cordage. The red strands were placed beside an equal number of yellow ones, the band twisted slightly and the ends tied. This was a colorful addition to the base of the feather helmet.

Bishop Museum has a tinted-wash drawing of a chief, by Cook's artist John Webber, showing a feathered band worn at the base of his helmet. Only five of these bands are known; Bishop Museum has none. Drawings of these in color appear in Force and Force, pp. 35 and 37, and a separate band on p. 39. They measure some 30 inches long.

■ Gourd Helmets or Masks

These are discussed in Unit 7 as they are believed to be religious objects associated with the worship of the god Lono.

■ Feathered Aprons

The use of the feathered aprons has not been satisfactorily explained since no data was recorded with the specimens collected. Captain Cook's party returned to Europe with the two which are pictured in Force and Force, p. 63. These have been lost, but there are two in the British Museum and one each in museums in Dublin, Ireland, and in Leningrad. They were once labeled "feather mats."

The aprons are of matting, covered with feathers in patterns and provided with loops and lacings by which they could be tied to the body.

Cook's officers wrote that the warriors tied mats across the front of their bodies to protect them in battle. These feathered aprons were possibly worn by the chiefs across their stomachs, an area that the feather cloaks did not cover.

■ Kā'ei Kapu ō Liloa, the Sacred Cordon of Liloa

The highest symbol of Hawaiian rank and authority known today is the sacred cordon or sash (kā'ei kapu ō Liloa), now in Bishop Museum. Known also as a baldric this symbol was made from a finely woven olonā net 11 feet 10 inches long and 4½ inches wide. Red velvety 'i'iwi feathers completely covered both sides and a lei of yellow 'ō'ō feathers was tied closely to each border. The leis increase the width to six inches. This kā'ei was probably made before any of the cloaks in the Museum.

The end, which hung from the waist of the chiefly wearer like a loin cloth, is a heavy cuff of 'ō'ō feathers ornamented and weighted the full width with three rows of human teeth, each row separated by molar-size rosettes of fish teeth. A band of 'ō'ō feathers and teeth crosses the cordon 17 inches from the front end and another similar band is 33 inches from the front end.

The ruling chief wore the cordon over his kapa malo by placing the ornamented end in front, passing the other end over his left shoulder and bringing it down to his waist. He passed this free end twice around his waist, belt-like, and secured the free end under the bands of the belt at the rear. The Kamehameha statues show the correct position of the cordon as it should be worn at the front. (Unfortunately, the tooth ornaments and bands of feathers crossing it were not known to the sculptor, Thomas R. Gould.) The shoulder portion should be under, not over the cloak as shown in the statues. The length of the cordon requires the wearer to make two turns of the cordon at the belt line.

According to tradition this cordon was made by order of King Liloa for his son 'Umi and used to invest him when he became ruler of the island of Hawai'i, in the temple of Pāka'alana in Waipi'o valley, about 1475 A.D. It was conferred on each succeeding monarch of the island of Hawai'i from 'Umi to Kamehameha II. Presumably this investment took place at the time Kamehameha II was proclaimed heir in 1802 at five years of age.

Kaumuali'i, ruler of Kaua'i, received the cordon, capes, and a helmet from Kamehameha I in 1810 when he ceded his island to the conqueror. Early in his reign (1874-91) King Kalākaua brought the cordon from Kaua'i and his sister, Lili'uokalani, presented it to Bishop Museum on May 23, 1910. (Brigham, 1918, p. 30-33. See also R. Rose, 1978)

■ Malo, Loin Cloth

In addition to their feather-covered symbols of sovereignty just discussed, the chiefs, in common with all other men, wore a loin cloth or malo as their principal garment. These were usually of kapa, about nine inches wide and nine or more feet long depending upon the waistline of the wearer.

The kapa malo were white, of solid colors, or dyed with a pattern. When decorated with a different color on each surface it was a malo kapeke because the under side would be exposed (kapeke) when the wind blew.

Other symbols reserved exclusively for the chiefs, in addition to the ones discussed, are taken up in detail in other units. A few of them are:

Pūlo'ulo'u or kapu sticks; specially knotted kōkō or net slings to hold and carry food containers; *ipu kuha* or spittoons; and *pana'iole* or bows and arrows for rat shooting. Royal treatment for the high chiefs continued into death and some were buried in *kā'ai* or sennit caskets, plaited in a unique way, from coconut husk fiber.

■ Symbols and Garments for Royal Women

Feather Leis (*Nā Lei Hulu Manu*): Feather *leis*, the prized adornment of women of rank, were the only ornaments of feathers they were permitted to make or wear in the days of the *kapu*. *Lei* feathers were from the same birds that provided them for the choicest capes, but often smaller feathers were used. A typical feather *lei* is cylindrical, 17 to 25 inches long, and from three-quarters of an inch to three inches in diameter. Among the most highly prized were the all-yellow *leis* from the *mamo* or *'ō'ō* bird feathers. More often they were of two or more colors. The *paukū* style was made of bands of solid colors of varying widths following alternately the length of the *lei*. In the *mo'oni* style, the colored feathers were arranged spirally.

Bishop Museum's oldest feather *lei*, acquired in 1977 from the Hooper Collection, shows that the feathers were once tied in small bunches by their quills to a central foundation of *olonā*. More recently the *lei* feathers are twined on foreign cordage, such as yarn, by winding a thread over the quills of the feathers. In most *leis* the feathers are affixed with the tips curving outward to produce a fluffy appearance. Sometimes the feathers were reversed with the tips curving inward toward the foundation cord to make a thinner rope-like *lei*, (*lei kāmoe*).

After the introduction of hats (*pāpale*), both men and women have worn flat hat-band *leis* (*lei papa*). Modern hat *leis* are made from the feathers of peacocks, pheasants, and chickens, and of the feathers of ducks and geese dyed to the desired colors. The quills of these feathers are stitched securely to cloth bands of the desired width to make hat *leis*. With the revival of interest in Hawaiian culture today, both men and women are making attractive feather *leis*. Careful examination is necessary to distinguish the best of the modern round *leis* from museum specimens.

David Samwell wrote:

Their Ornaments are the Ereis [*He lei* or a *lei*] or feathered ruffs which they wear on their Heads & round their Necks; they are proud of these & wear

sometimes 4 or 5 on their Heads & one or two about their necks & they have a very beautiful appearance, being made of red and yellow feathers, black, white and green variously disposed, they are about an inch in thickness & long enough to go round their necks. . . . (Beaglehole, p. 1180)

Bracelets and Rings: Chiefesses wore bracelets made of plates of turtle shell interspersed with sections of bone or ivory. (See the sketch in Force and Force, p. 89) The plates of the turtle shell are so thin that it requires 20 or more to form an inch of the length of an average bracelet. The plates or pieces are cut to size, pierced in two places with a drill, then strung on *olonā* cords. When tied the

Ornaments for a Chiefess: (left to right) Bracelet or *kūpe'e* of many pieces of turtle shell with dividers of whale tooth ivory.

Wrist ornament of whale ivory carved as a realistic turtle. A cord passes through the body of the turtle to hold it to the wrist.

Lei of *'ō'ō* feathers (*'ō'ō 'ē'ē*) dotted with *'i'iwi* feathers.

Small limpet or *'opihi* shells with seeds from the *wiliwili* tree form this lei.

bracelet (kūpeʻe ʻea) completely encircles the wrist.

Realistic turtles, carved from bone or ivory, were strung on a fiber cord. Larger ones were worn as bracelets, the smaller ones as finger rings.

Sarah Stone sketched two; judging from their sizes in her picture, one must have been a ring, the other a bracelet (Force and Force, p. 95).

Samwell wrote in February 1779 about the dress and ornaments of the chiefesses of Kauaʻi: "They wear little images of turtle made of bone on their fingers like we do Seals, and some wear them on their wrists." (Beaglehole, p. 1180)

Pāʻū - Skirt: The sarong-like skirt of the women of all classes was a pāʻū of kapa which was worn from the waist to the knees. It might consist of a large number of folds around the body. The royal women wore pāʻū of finer texture with more elaborate or more colorful decoration.

Pāʻū of Nahiʻenaʻena: After the abolition of the kapu in 1819 chiefly women would not be restricted from wearing feather garments if they chose to do so. While Kamehameha II was in England in 1823-24 a feather pāʻū was made for his sister, Nahiʻenaʻena, to wear at the reception planned to celebrate his expected return. A great deal of time and work was expended in making this first and only feather garment for a chiefess.

Fine olonā netting, 20 feet and 8 inches long and 30 inches wide, was covered closely with rich yellow ʻōʻō feathers and ornamented at the ends with small triangles of red ʻiʻiwi and black ʻōʻō feathers.

In May, 1825, Lord Byron brought back to Hawaiʻi the bodies of the King and Queen who had died in London from measles. He was invited to meet the 11-year-old Kamehameha III and his sister, Nahiʻenaʻena, then 10 years of age. The Princess, influenced by foreign teaching, refused to wear the feather pāʻū in traditional style. Except for leis this would have been her only garment, covering her from waist to ankles. Present at the audience was American missionary Charles S. Stewart, who wrote that the young King and Princess sat on a sofa wearing European garments.

> Between them, and partly round the princess, lay a splendid garment of yellow feathers, edged with the vandyke pattern, points alternate black and red, and lined with crimson satin. (Stewart, 1970, p. 343)

Later Nahiʻenaʻena wore the pāʻū on ceremonial occasions. After her death in 1836 it was cut in two, sewed together along the edges, and used as a pall to ornament the caskets of Hawaiian kings through Kalākaua in 1891. It came to Bishop Museum in 1893 with other treasures from ʻIolani Palace.

■ **Royal Symbols used by Both Chiefs and Chiefesses**

Feather Kāhili: The feather kāhili were symbols of royalty. They may have developed as a more permanent and colorful form of symbol which was first provided by ti leaves on their stem, or from the fly whisks of southern Polynesia. A kāhili consists of a pole or handle bearing a cylinder or cluster of feathers at one end.

Kāhili were held and carried by young noblemen (lawe kāhili) related to the chiefs and chiefesses whom they accompanied. Large kāhili surrounded the royal bier during funeral rituals and were carried in funeral processions during the 19th and 20th centuries. The smaller hand kāhili served as fans and fly whisks held or waved near chiefly persons while they sat, ate, or slept.

King Kalākaua was believed to have possessed some 150 kāhili, which he displayed in ʻIolani Palace or stored in a special room in the Palace basement. Some 45 large kāhili and 80 small ones were displayed or stored in Bishop Museum in the 1890s. (Brigham, 1899, pp. 15-17, 23, 25)

The poles (kumu kāhili) supporting the feathers in the large kāhili ranged from eight to 14 feet in length. The oldest handles are discs of tortoise shell and sections of human bone strung on cores of kauila wood. The most historic of these on display in Bishop Museum has as a base the left shin-bone of high chief Kāneoneo of Kauaʻi. Decorating the rest of the pole are sections of bone from 11 of his fellow chiefs killed with him in the battle of Nuʻuanu in 1795. Some handles are of kauila wood spears shortened to the desired lengths. More recent ones were made from imported wood.

The large kāhili are topped with a cylinder of feathers (hulu manu) which was formed by tying tufts of feathers to the tip of a branch of split ʻieʻie rootlets which had been bound together. These seven- to 15-inch-long branches (koʻo) were tied by their bases to the upper part of the kāhili handle. Hundreds were needed to form the large decorative cylinders. The largest hulu or top on a kāhili in Bishop Museum measures 30 inches in diameter and is four feet long.

Feathers in the older *kāhili* were from the native *'ō'ō, 'i'iwi, koa'e, 'iwa, pueo,* and *moa.* Later, feathers from the ostrich, peacock, and duck were used. In pageantry today, dyed feathers, flowers, and leaves form the colorful cylinders.

Clerke, on his return visit to Kaua'i in 1779, wrote of a hand *kāhili* being carried on board his ship by the daughter of Kamakahelei, wife of Ka'eo.

> Her daughter had a curious fan or fly flapper compos'd of a bunch of Feathers made to adhere to a Human Bone as a Handle; the feathers were very fine & the Handle curiously wrought with Tortoise shell, which made it a pretty piece of furniture enough. [The bone was said to have come from the arm of an O'ahu chief killed by Ka'eo in battle.] (Beaglehole, p. 577)

Samwell, while on shipboard off Kaua'i in 1779, wrote that Kalanikoa, brother of Keawe, "came on board the Ship this morning [March 7] with a man carrying an enormous fly flap before him on his Shoulder. . . ." This is the only reference in the journals of Cook and his officers to the large ceremonial *kāhili* which became so popular later. (Beaglehole, p. 1227)

The name ascribed to each *kāhili* referred specifically to the handle (Brigham, 1899, p. 15) "Eleeleualani" (black rain of heaven) is the name of a *kāhili* said to be the oldest in the Museum. Among other *kāhili* names are: "Kaleoaloha" (voice of love) and "Malulani" (heavenly peace). When not in use by the chiefs the feather branches were untied and removed from the pole. They were stored in covered calabashes until needed. When a *kāhili* was assembled, a set of feathers was not always tied to the staff from which it came.

Smaller hand *kāhili,* usually three to four feet long, were made on handles of wood or tortoise shell and bone. In some instances a riding quirt formed the handle. The feathers, largely the same as those decorating the large *kāhili,* were usually tied directly to the handle. Since hand *kāhili* were much easier to construct they were more numerous than the larger ones. There were about 150 in Bishop Museum at the time of an inventory and study in 1976.

Lei Niho Palaoa: These lei with a hook-shaped pendant made from a sperm whale tooth *(palaoa)* suspended from many strands of braided human hair were highly prized by both chiefs and chief-esses. A great deal of skill and effort was required to make them.

The ivory hooks or pendants are from one to six inches long. The largest of the *leis* is made up of over a thousand strands of eight-ply braided human hair, each some nine inches long. Bishop Museum has 50 well-preserved *lei niho palaoa.*

David Samwell observed at Kealakekua January 18, 1779:

> An old woman called Oheina [Kahena], who is an Eree [ali'i] . . . came on board of us in some State this morning. She had a great Quantity of new red and white striped Cloth [kapa] wrapped round her Waist, on each arm large bracelets made of boar's Tusks of an enormous Size, and round her neck a thick bunch of human hair plaited in fine strings with a bone ornament called Parawa [palaoa] depending from it. (Beaglehole, p. 1160)

Makaloa Mats *(Moena Makaloa):* The beds of the chiefs were raised above the floor level and covered with the finely plaited *makaloa* mats. Buck describes these as the "finest sleeping mats in Polynesia." (Buck, 1947, p. 132)

These soft, flexible mats, made largely on Ni'ihau, had as many as 20 to 25 wefts or strands to the inch. They were made from a pale brown sedge, not *lau hala,* and by employing different plaiting styles, patterns were introduced without the use of color. However, the most interesting mats had colored geometric motifs in a variety of designs. The red-brown colored wefts in the patterns are from sheaths which grow at the base of the *makaloa* sedge or perhaps from another species of sedge. The plaiting of *makaloa* mats ceased years ago.

By gift and exchange, *makaloa* mats seem to have come into the possession of the chiefs on all of the islands. Cook wrote of the mats he saw on Kaua'i in 1778, "Their mats are both strong and fine and some are neatly coloured." (Beaglehole, p. 283)

James King observed mats at Kealakekua in 1779:

> Their Matts are superiour to the other Islands [Southern islands], both in fineness, & from the Variety of patterns in them, by working in Streaks of different Colours. (Beaglehole, pp. 625-626)

David Samwell wrote of the *makaloa* and *lau hala* mats:

> They have a great Variety of Matts, some all white but most of them variegated with brown slips running the whole length of them and giving them

a very beautiful appearance, these are worn by the Chiefs sometimes, while the more coarse and thick ones are laid on the floors of their Houses and made into Sails for their Canoes. (Beaglehole, p. 1187)

A very fine mat in Bishop Museum with 25 wefts per inch was worn by Kamehameha I as a *kīhei* or shoulder wrap.

■ The Symbols of Royalty become "Artificial Curiosities"

The traditional court life of the Hawaiian chiefs was abandoned with the abolishing of the *kapu* in 1819. Kamehameha II adopted military uniforms for formal attire and his queen Kamāmalu is pictured in a European gown and ostrich-plume hat.

■ Understandings and Appreciations

1. Picture, in your mind or on paper, the Hawaiian royal court. How does it compare in color and splendor with those of two or three other monarchies that you read about? Compare also the time, skill, and patience needed to fashion the court costumes in the Hawaiian and other courts.

2. Why did the chiefs desire yellow feathers in their *'ahu'ula* (red cloak)? What does this tell you about "supply and demand?"

3. What materials other than feathers might the chiefs of Hawai'i have used for their royal garments? Can you name any as colorful and color-fast?

4. Note that the tastes and demands of the royalty caused the people to produce some of the finest things in the culture - royal symbols of many kinds, fine houses, superior canoes, *heiau*, and fish ponds.

■ Student Activities

1. Sketch in color a properly dressed chief and chiefess with *kāhili* and *kāhili* bearers.

2. Make a wearable cape or cloak from crepe paper or other materials that you can improvise. If there is an available fund for costumes make

the garment from colored felt, crushed plush, or polyester fabric.

3. Construct a helmet of cardboard or of buckram and cover it with the same material as the cloak.

4. As a class project construct in miniature a chief's household with seven or so houses made from grass on cardboard frames or other suitable materials. Populate the area with cut-out figures carrying on their daily activities. This is an excellent subject for a diorama.

5. Write a playlet centered round the activities of the court. Some of the events might be: the visit of another chief and his household, a games contest, *hula* and music, storytelling, riddles and guessing games, or experiences with *menehune* or with Pele.

6. Sketch a design using the Hawaiian king and queen for a float suitable for one of the city parades such as those held on Kamehameha Day or during Aloha Week.

■ Audio-Visual Aids

1. Exhibits:
   Bishop Museum - Emblems of Royalty and various displays in Hawaiian Hall.
   Honolulu Academy of Arts - feather capes, *leis,* and other symbols of royalty.
   Queen Emma Museum - Both pre-European and later royal objects.
   All of the neighbor island museums have some exhibits pertinent to this subject.

2. Movies:
   Hawaiian Featherwork - with Johanna Cluney.
   Coronation in Hawaii - Court scene - Aloha Week.
   These are films from Cine-pic, Hawaii.

3. Plan to attend one of the coronation pageants on Lei Day, sponsored by the Parks Board or by local schools.

■ Vocabulary

ali'i	ipu kuha	malo
mahiole	'ahu'ula	pā'ū
maka'āinana	hōlua	lei hulu
kōkō	moena	kāhili

■ Current Happenings or Trends of Significance to this Unit

1. Athough the use of the royal garments and symbols was discontinued with the passing of the old order, the splendor and color has been retained in pageantry. The principal display of royal emblems is in the island courts of the annual Aloha Week festivities. Modern materials, used to construct the garments and symbols, are quite authentic in appearance. Similar pageantry may be seen on Kamehameha Day and in some of the Lei Day programs.

2. *Leis* are now made of dyed feathers in imitation of those of the rare or extinct feather birds. Yellow *leis*, genuine or imitation, are part of the regalia of the women of the Ka'ahumanu Society. Shoulder capes of felt and feather head *leis* are worn by the Hale o nā Ali'i Society.

3. Feather hat bands are an adaptation of the feather *lei*. Pheasant, peacock, or dyed feathers are sewed on a flat band of cloth one or two inches wide. These are particularly popular with *kama'āina* men and women.

4. There is a continuing market for *leis* or necklaces of small shells and colorful seeds. The *kukui* nut necklace is highly regarded by local women and men. Some jewelry in Hawaiian design is made from ivory. The pendant or tooth of the *lei palaoa* is sometimes worn with a ribbon or ivory beads instead of braided hair.

5. Small *kāhili* of flowers are used for table decorations and large *kāhili* of leaves or flowers for a colorful part of local pageants with Hawaiian themes.

■ Evaluation

1. Use the vocabulary for word definitions and spelling.

2. Evaluate the garments or symbols for form and color as suitable for pageantry rather than exactness to detail.

3. Check students' concepts of life in the feudal order of early Hawai'i in contrast to present day democratic Hawai'i.

■ Reading List

Ball, Stanley C. *Bishop Museum Handbook, Part II, Clothing.* Honolulu: Bishop Museum Special Publication No. 9, 1929. (Discusses tapa and featherwork.)

Barrère, Dorothy B. *Documentary Studies.* "Kamakahonu: Kamehameha's Last Residence," "The Morning Star Alone Knows," "Search for the Bones of Kamehameha." Pacific Anthropological Records No. 23. Honolulu: Bishop Museum Press, 1975.

Berger, Andrew J. *The Exotic Birds of Hawaii.* Norfolk Island, Aus.: Island Heritage, 1977.

———. *Hawaiian Bird Life.* 2nd ed. Honolulu: University Press of Hawaii, 1981.

Brigham, William T. *Hawaiian Featherwork.* Honolulu: Bishop Museum Memoirs, Vol. I, No. 1, 1899; Vol. I, No. 5, 1903; Vol. VII, No. 1, 1918.

———. *Mats and Basket Weaving of the Ancient Hawaiians.* Honolulu: Bishop Museum Memoir, Vol. II, No. 1, 1906.

Bryan, E.H. Jr. *Ancient Hawaiian Life.* 1938. Honolulu: Books About Hawaii, 1950.

Buck, Peter H. *Arts and Crafts of Hawaii.* Honolulu: Bishop Museum Special Publication No. 45, 1957.

Chickering, William H. *Within the Sound of these Waves.* 1941. Westport, CT: Glenwood Press, 1971. (Stories of eight of the famous chiefs.)

Cox, J. Halley. "Lei Niho Palaoa." In *Polynesian Culture History.* Essays in honor of Kenneth P. Emory. Honolulu: Bishop Museum Special Publication No. 56, 1967.

Daws, Alan G. *The Illustrated Atlas of Hawaii.* Norfolk Island, Aus.: Island Heritage, 1970.

Degener, Otto. *Plants of the Hawaii National Park.* 1930. Ann Arbor, MI: Edwards Bros. Inc., 1945.

Dunmire, William H. *Birds of the National Parks in Hawaii.* Hilo: Hawaii Natural History Association, 1961.

Emerson, Nathaniel B. "The Bird Hunters of Ancient Hawaii." In *Hawaiian Annual for 1895.* Honolulu: Thrum's Hawaiian Annual. 101-111.

Feher, Joseph. *Hawaii: A Pictorial History.* Honolulu: Bishop Museum Special Publication No. 58, 1969.

Force, Roland W., and Maryanne Force. *Arts and Artifacts of the 18th Century.* Honolulu: Bishop Museum Press, 1968.

Goldman, Irving. *Ancient Polynesian Society.* Chicago: University of Chicago Press, 1970.

Holt, John D. *The Art of Featherwork in Old Hawaii.* Honolulu: Topgallant Publishing Company, 1985.

———. *Monarchy in Hawaii.* Honolulu: Hogarth Press, 1971.

Ihara, Violet K., and Lillian A. Lum. *The Kingdom of Hawai'i, 1810-1893.* Eight film strips and 8 cassettes, one for each ruler, and a user guide. Sold as a set. Honolulu: Kompa Kompa Kompany, 1981. (Distributed by Academics Hawaii.)

Kaeppler, Adrienne L. *Feather Cloaks, Ship Captains and Lords.* Honolulu: Bishop Museum Occasional Paper XXIV, No. 6, 1970.

———. "Artificial Curiosities." An exposition of native manufactures collected on the three Pacific voyages of Captain James Cook. Honolulu: Bishop Museum Special Publication No. 65, 1978.

Kamakau, Samuel M. *Ruling Chiefs of Hawaii.* Honolulu: Kamehameha Schools Press, 1961. (See also *Index to Ruling Chiefs of Hawaii* by Elspeth Sterling, Bishop Museum, 1974.)

———. *The Works of the People of Old.* Honolulu: Bishop Museum Special Publication No. 61, 1976.

Kekuewa, Mary L., and Paulette Kahalepuna. *Feather Leis as an Art.* (Written by Milly Singletary.) Honolulu: Na Lima Mili Hulu No'eau, 1976.

Malo, David. *Hawaiian Antiquities.* 1898. Honolulu: Bishop Museum Special Publication No. 2, 1976.

Manning, Anita. "James D. Mills, Hilo Bird Collector." *The Hawaiian Journal of History,* 1978. 12:84-98.

McDonald, Marie A. *Ka Lei.* The leis of Hawaii. Honolulu: Topgallant Publishing Company, 1978.

McKenzie, Edith, and Ishmael W. Stagner. *Hawaiian Genealogies.* Vol. I, 1983; Vol. II, 1986; Vol. III, in preparation. Honolulu: University of Hawaii Press.

Mitchell, Donald D. Kilolani. *Hawaiian Treasures.* Royalty, 23-45. Honolulu: Kamehameha Schools Press, 1978.

Moriarity, Linda P. *Ni'ihau Shell Leis.* Honolulu: University of Hawaii Press, 1986. (Color photographs.)

Munro, George. *Birds of Hawaii.* Rutland, VT and Japan: C.E. Tuttle, 1961.

Rose, Roger G. *Hawai'i: The Royal Isles.* Honolulu: Bishop Museum Special Publication No. 67, 1980.

———. *Symbols of Sovereignty.* Feather girdles of Tahiti and Hawai'i. Pacific Anthropological Records No. 28. Honolulu: Department of Anthropology, Bishop Museum, 1978.

Rothschild, L.W.I. *The Avifauna of Laysan and the Neighboring Islands with a complete history to date of the birds of the Hawaiian Possessions.* London: R.H. Porter, 1893-1900.

Shallenberger, Robert J. *Hawai'i's Birds.* 3rd ed., rev. Honolulu: Hawaii Audubon Society, 1986.

Silverman, Jane. *Ka'ahumanu: Molder of Change.* Honolulu: Friends of the Judiciary History Center of Hawaii, 1987.

Sinclair, Marjorie. *Nahi'ena'ena, Sacred Daughter of Hawaii.* Honolulu: University Press of Hawaii, 1976. (Relates the incident of Nahi'ena'ena wearing the special feather pa'u.)

Spoehr, Anne H. *The Royal Lineages of Hawai'i.* Honolulu: Bishop Museum Press, 1988.

Stokes, John F.G. *Hawaiian Nets and Netting.* Honolulu: Bishop Museum Memoir, Vol. II, No. 1, 1906.

Stone, Sarah. *Art and Artifacts of the 18th Century.* Honolulu: Bishop Museum Press, 1968.

Valeri, Valerio. *Kingship and Sacrifice.* Ritual and society in ancient Hawaii. Translated from the French. Chicago: University of Chicago Press, 1985.

Webb, Lahilahi. "Featherwork and Clothing." Ch. 13 in *Ancient Hawaiian Civilization.* 1933. A series of lectures delivered at the Kamehameha Schools by E.S.C. Handy [and others]. Rutland, VT and Japan: C.E. Tuttle, 1965 (rev. ed.).

Wilson, Scott B., and A. Evans. *Aves Hawaiiensis.* The birds of the Sandwich Islands. London: R.H. Porter, 1899.

UNIT 9:
Planters
and Their
Products

PLANTERS AND THEIR PRODUCTS

The Hawaiian planters, aided by the fishermen, were able to produce the food needed to keep a population of some 300,000 persons properly nourished (population estimate at Captain Cook's time). In contrast to the accomplishments of these skilled agriculturists, the people of Hawai'i now import much more food than they produce.

Receipts for the diversified agricultural products grown in Hawai'i in 1988 totaled $168 million. This includes all farm products and livestock that were largely consumed locally. Excluded are sugar and pineapple, which are grown primarily for export.

However, locally produced beef and veal furnished only 28 percent of the need. Poultry meat produced in the State provided 18 percent of local consumption, but 90 percent of all eggs consumed in Hawai'i were laid here.

Hawai'i-grown vegetables filled 33 percent of the need in local markets. Thirty-five percent of fresh market fruits consumed in the State in 1988 were grown in Hawai'i. A glance at the shelves in the markets will show that much of the food consumed in Hawai'i is imported.

(The above figures are from the 1989 *State of Hawaii Data Book*, compiled by the Department of Business and Economic Development.)

Hawai'i is by nature a favored spot for agriculture. Many areas have good soil and abundant water. The sunny, subtropical climate encourages plant growth throughout the year. However, the travelers' legend of provident gods pouring an abundance of tropical foods into the arms of singing, dancing, nonworking native peoples is far from the actual story in Hawai'i.

■ The Hawaiian settlers brought with them from the south their principal food crops and other useful plants and a knowledge of their proper cultivation. They also brought their only domestic food animals, the pig, dog and chicken.

Captain Cook and other early visitors wrote of the Hawaiians' intelligent and thrifty use of land and water, of the abundance of the food produced and their knowledge of the conservation of their resources. Visiting ships were furnished with vast quantitites of vegetable and animal food.

As stated in the introduction, the farmers and fishermen of Kaua'i, Ni'ihau and Kona, Hawai'i furnished the officers and men, a total of 182, on Capt. Cook's ships an amazing amount of food. Lieut. King wrote that they consumed at least 16.8 tons of food and that there was considerable waste.

The crews also salted 16.8 tons of pork, and placed it in casks for use on the return voyage. Some was uneaten but edible when they reached England a year and a half later.

The somewhat limited allotment of land for each family determined that the Hawaiian man would be a gardener or planter, not a large scale farmer. This allowed him a closeness wherein he could study, understand and venerate his plants. The planter's keen observation of his crops caused him to detect genetic differences (mutants) that appeared and encouraged him to separate these unusual ones to be cultivated and tested for whatever special qualities they might possess.

The Hawaiian men were by nature more peace loving than the rest of their Polynesian relatives. Although ambitious and restless chiefs conscripted them into battle, the maka'ainana, the citizens, were agriculturists at heart. Even fishing was a supplementary rather than a principal means of food getting. The myths, traditions and folk customs are more concerned with plant than marine life. Boys were dedicated to Lono, god of agriculture, not to Kū, god of war.

■ Water

Wai, fresh water, gave life to the food plants, especially the staff of life - taro. *Wai* implies life and wealth. *Waiwai,* the word reduplicated means property or anything costly.

An *'auwai,* a man-made water course, brought water to the taro ponds. Each planter used the water he needed, then closed the inlet so that the next grower would receive water. *Kānāwai,* a law or rule, originally pertained to the water rights. The planters shared equally without greed or selfishness. An abundance of water brought prosperity.

The planters strong hands and feet were their most useful tools. With their hands they weeded, raked, cleared the soil and planted their gardens. They pushed soil around the plants, built mounds for planting certain crops and trampled the soil in the bottom of the taro ponds with their feet.

The farmers constructed but one agricultural tool, the digging stick *('ō'ō).* These hardwood poles, from two to six feet in length, were pointed at both ends or bore a flat, spade-like blade on one end. They were simple, undecorated and made with a stone adze *(ko'i)* from *kauila, uhiuhi, alahe'e* and *'ulei* wood. The *'ō'ō* was used to loosen the soil, dig holes or trenches for planting and for harvesting root crops.

Another tool, provided by nature, was the heavy, smooth butt of the coconut frond *(kū'au)* with which the builders beat and firmed the banks or walls of the taro ponds.

Most of the plant foods were harvested by hand or with the use of the *'ō'ō.* A special tool *(lou)* was needed to pick breadfruit *('ulu)* which grew on the trees out of reach. A short stick lashed obliquely across the end of a long wooden pole formed a hook used to loosen the ripe fruit. A young person climbed the tree and used the picker to twist off the fruit which then fell into the hands of his helper below.

The planters grew most of their food in the rich soil of the valleys and on the lower slopes of the hills. These gardens were usually some distance from their dwellings which, by preference, they built near the sea.

Weeds were not removed after being pulled but

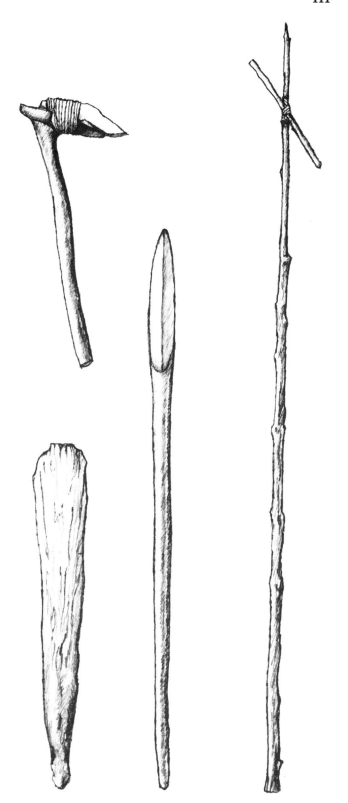

The Planters' Tools: The hafted adze *(ko'i)* was used to cut shrubs and trees and to make other tools of wood.

Long and short digging implements *('ō'ō)* served as spades and general gardening tools.

A long pole with a stick lashed across *(lou)* it twisted off the out-of-reach breadfruit and mountain apples.

were left to decay and add humus. Leafy materials, particularly *hau* leaves, were brought in as fertilizers.

The planters knew the type of soil in which each plant thrived and its preference to sun and moisture. Irrigation reached the status of engineering as the patches were designed for growing wet taro.

The religious aspect of farming was strictly observed. (Wichman, Ch. 10, pp. 109-117 and Traditions, pp. 1-40.) The proper time or season to plant certain crops is given in Taylor's *Hawaiian Almanac,* "Lunar Planting," pp. 38-40, and "Farmer's Calendar," pp. 41-44. Kepelino, Wichman and other writers stress the importance of ceremonials and timing in agriculture. The major gods and many demigods and goddesses were associated with various phases of agriculture.

The planters carried their garden products to their homes by hand or in gourds and calabashes. To handle these smooth, round containers filled with produce it was necessary to suspend them in nets *(kōkō)* and hang one from each end of a carrying pole *('auamo* or *māmaka).*

Carrying poles, fashioned from sturdy *kauila* or *'ūlei* wood, were from 40 to 92 inches in length and about an inch and one-half in thickness at the center. Most of them bore one or more flanges or knobs near the ends which held securely the cords of the suspended nets. These knobs were essential since the bearers climbed uphill and down and over rough terrain where it was impossible to hold the carrying pole horizontal. Large pigs, alive or killed for food or a sacrifice, were slung from the center of a pole which was carried by two men.

The poles made for carrying the chiefs' food and water were decorated. The knobs which secured the net loops were carved into the form of small human heads *('auamo ki'i).* Some poles bore a head at the very tip of each end as a decoration and simple knobs to hold the nets. On others, two pairs of heads served as the knobs. Although the heads faced upwards, one in each pair was carved to look forward and the other to look backward, as the pole was tilted up and down in use. This sentimental touch cheered the bearer as he journeyed to his gardens each morning. The two heads which were directed forward were planned to scan his path and to guide him safely on his way. The other heads looked back to watch over the members of his family whom he had left behind.

The craftsmen developed a variety of elaborate and complex forms of knots which were used to make some of the carrying nets supporting the vessels which were slung from the shoulder poles. The cordage in the nets was made from *olonā,* sennit *('aha), hau,* and *wauke* fibers.

Naturalist Menzies in Hawai'i with Captain Vancouver, 1792-94, observed:

> We could not indeed but admire the laudable ingenuity of these people in cultivating their soil with so much economy. The indefatigable labor in making these little fields in so rugged a situation, the care and industry with which they were transplanted, watered and kept in order, surpassed anything of the kind we had ever seen before. It showed in a conspicuous manner the ingenuity of the inhabitants in modifying their husbandry to different situations of soil and exposure, and with no small degree of pleasure we here beheld their labor rewarded with productive crops. (Menzies, 1920, p. 105)

The growing and harvesting of the food plants and the cooking of all foods was the work of the men. The belief that women were unclean because of menstruation forbade them from handling food that was to be consumed by others.

■ Plants Before the Arrival of Man

Scientists, who have made a study of the endemic plants, tell us that the first settlers to arrive found the land forested from the mountains down to the seashore. Certain plants had become adapted to the rainforests and the wet windward slopes of the islands. Others were able to grow on the leeward sides where the rainfall was scanty.

Since the islands were thrown up as hot masses of lava they were barren, for a time, of any forms of plant life. The ancestral forms, spores, seeds, roots or the living animals, had to come here by some means provided by nature.

It is certain that a limited number of ancestral immigrants found their way here, some by wind or wave, and gave rise to the plants that we call endemic. That is, they changed their forms enough during the long passage of time, that they are different from their ancestors and plants found anywhere else. Of the estimated 2,000 species of seed plants growing here at the time of the Polynesians' arrival all could have developed from 275 ancestors. The time span was so great that if one plant successfully established itself here every 20,000 to 30,000 years that feat would account for the 275 ancestors mentioned.

Seeds that blew to Hawai'i by way of great storms or arrived as stowaways on migratory birds may have sprouted in soil quite alien to their former habitat. These would need to adapt to new conditions or die. New forms developed in the varied environments until, in time, 95 percent of Hawai'i's plants (and also birds, insects and snails) were endemic, that is, kinds found nowhere else in the world. (Zimmerman, "Nature of the Land Biota.")

Of the 2,000 higher plants flourishing here at the time of the Polynesian colonists' arrival, very few were suitable food plants. They included species which furnished edible roots, stems, leaves or fruits. These edible portions were not very delicious in flavor or high in food value. A list of them is given in Unit 10, Foods. None required cultivation by man since they had been growing here unattended for countless centuries.

The plants that were brought here by the early settlers are listed in Unit 2 and repeated here in much greater detail. These include the plants used for food, building materials, clothing fibers, cordage, utensils and medicines. The emphasis in this unit is on agriculture, the cultivation and harvesting of these plants and the care of the animals. Their use as food is presented in Unit 10.

The order in discussing the plants here follows that established by Dr. Handy in "Native Planters of Old Hawai'i." The food plants are listed, as far as we know, in order of their importance in the Hawaiian diet.

The plants in the following list are called "Polynesian introductions."

1. Kalo or taro. *Colocasia esculenta.*

Nowhere else in the known world was taro cultivated so intensively or skillfully as it was in Hawai'i. Throughout the centuries of taro growing here the planters, through plant selection and recognition of mutants, developed more that 300 varieties. They also learned the climatic conditions under which each kind thrived and they ascribed certain useful qualities to each. Some were known to make excellent *poi,* others did not. Some kinds were grown especially for their large, tender leaves. Medical properties of some sort were a feature of others. A few possessed such flavor and color that they were reserved exclusively for the chiefly classes.

The planters of wet-land taro, who were also practicing engineers, built walls of earth, sometimes reinforced with stone, to enclose each taro pond *(lo'i kalo).* These varied greatly in size and shape and in some cases covered the rich bottom lands along both sides of a stream.

A ditch or watercourse *('auwai)* conducted cold water from a spring or from the upper levels of the principal stream to the top-most *lo'i kalo.* Openings were constructed in the walls of the ponds to allow the water to flow from the upper to the lower ponds and finally into the stream below. By closing the gates the water could be retained in the ponds.

Planting and cultivation methods for taro differed somewhat from one locality to another and with different families. Generally, a new pond, or one that had produced a crop and was to be replanted, was flooded with water, the soil trampled with the feet until the bottom was firm and then the *huli* were planted.

Kamakau wrote that the villagers, upon the invitation of the owner, would come to a newly constructed pond and make a festive occasion of treading and firming the bottom soil. This was done to form a firm bottom layer so that the water would not sink deeply into the soil.

Previous to the treading party the owner would prepare an ample supply of pork, *poi,* fish and other foods. He filled the pond with water and invited men, women and children who came in their usual brief *kapa* garments and also bedecked with leis of ferns and other greenery. Even *kapu* chiefs and chiefesses joined in the gaiety.

Each person treaded here and there, stirring up the mud with his feet, dancing, shouting, panting and generally having fun.

After a bath in the sea and a refreshing rinse in the stream nearby, the merrymakers feasted.

The mud settled to the pond bottom during the night and the taro *huli* were planted the next day. (Kamakau, 1976, p. 34)

The planting material or *huli* consisted of a half-inch thick slice taken from the very top of the taro root or corm. It was cut off with a knife-like stick made for that purpose or with a sharp shell. Some 6 to 10 inches of the bases of the leaf stems were left on the corm as part of the *huli.* These stems protruded above the water when planted.

Rootlets grew readily from the corm portion into the soft mud. The pond was kept flooded and weeded when necessary. Taro required a year, more or less, to grow to maturity.

Some taro was grown especially for the leaves (*lau kalo*). The tender ones could be cut off and cooked as soon as the plants were well established.

The banks between the taro ponds were planted with bananas, sugar cane, ti and *wauke*. Kinds of fish grown in the ponds were *'awa, 'ama'ama, o'opu,* and *āholehole.*

Varieties called dryland taro are grown in clearings in the lower forests where the soil is rich and the rainfall sufficient. Upland taro requires more weeding than the plants grown in ponds.

The taro plant has an important part in Hawaiian mythology and religion. According to one tradition, Hāloa, second son of Wākea, became the ancestor of the Hawaiian people. Haloa was named after the taro plant that grew over his brother's grave. King Kalākaua, who traced his lineage to Hāloa, used the taro leaf symbol in his crown which he placed on his head at his coronation in 1883.

Prayers were offered to Kāne, to Lono and to the family *'aumakua* at certain times during the growth and harvesting of the taro.

(Handy, 1972, pp. 71-118; Buck, p. 10, 13-14; Kamakau, 1976, pp. 31-37; Degener, pp. 79-85.)

2. 'Uala or Sweet Potato. *Ipomoea batatas.*

This member of the morning glory family produces a vigorous vine which spreads over the ground. From 200 to 400 bushels of tuberous roots may be produced from an acre of sweet potatoes. Plants are propagated from stem cuttings which root readily, never from the tubers. Some varieties of sweet potatoes will produce seed which may be used in plant experiments but never for commercial planting.

Sweet potatoes will grow in areas not suitable for taro such as gardens with poor soil and limited rainfall. Tubers may be ready for harvesting in 3 to 6 months, half of the time required for taro.

A favored method is to plant the stem cutting, usually 2 or 3, in a mound (*pu'e*) of earth some 6 to 10 inches high. They may be planted also in ridges or on flat ground. Less labor is required in planting and cultivating sweet potatoes than in taro.

Kamakau wrote of men and women, dressed colorfully in *kapa* garments and leis, working together planting sweet potatoes on the *palawai* or rich, moist bottom lands. If there were 20 or more men they were all dressed alike. They formed a line the width of the field and worked in perfect unison. They thrust their *'ō'ō* or digging sticks into the soil a first, second and third time, their arms rising and falling together, the women followed dropping two slips into each planting hole. (Kamakau, 1976, p. 24)

Sweet potato culture was the only major agricultural venture which involved women.

After a few months some of the sweet potato tubers were mature. The planter dug into the mound or the soil and pulled out the largest ones, leaving the smaller ones in the ground. In due time the entire crop of tubers was removed but some of the vines were left growing to furnish cuttings to propagate the next plants.

The sweet potato is the only food plant in Polynesia said to be of South American origin. After much study and discussion the details of the introduction of the sweet potato into the islands of Polynesia are still unclear. (Yen, D.E. *The Sweet Potato and Oceania.,* Barrau, J. *Plants and Migrations of Pacific Peoples.*) The sweet potato is not considered a sacred plant as is the taro. However, Kānepua'a (man hog) was considered god of the sweet potato, perhaps because he dug into the ground with his snout. Prayers were offered to the gods for rain, sunshine and favorable growing and harvesting conditions.

(Handy, 1972, pp. 118-149; Buck, p. 10; Kamakau, 1976, pp. 23-31.)

3. 'Ulu or breadfruit. *Artocarpus altilis.*

This attractive tree grows from 30 to 60 feet high with a trunk up to 2 feet in diameter. It is propagated from shoots sprouting up from roots that have grown some distance from the main trunk. The roots must be severed on each side of the shoot or sucker and a ball of earth formed around it. This new plant must be moved with great care to the hole into which it is to be planted. If pulled out of the earth and the roots freed from soil it will die. Breadfruit trees thrive in dark or red soil, never in sand or cinders.

In 1788 Captain William Bligh attempted to transport breadfruit plants from Tahiti to the Caribbean. The mutiny on his ship the Bounty caused the plants to be lost.

In 1792, on a second expedition, Bligh succeeded in taking 1,200 plants from Tahiti to Jamaica. They have spread throughout the Caribbean area.

Until recently Hawai'i has grown but a single variety of breadfruit. There are about 50 in the

Society Islands, fewer in Samoa but 200 varieties in the Marquesas Islands.

In Hawai'i the Puna area trees may bear 8 months of the year beginning in May. Elsewhere here the season is usually May through September. Breadfruit trees were once more common than they are now in Hawai'i.

The light-colored wood of the breadfruit is used to make surfboards, *poi* pounding boards, and dance drums *(pahu hula)*. Milky sap *(pīlali 'ulu)* from the tree furnishes glue for fastening gourds together in the *ipu heke* and for caulking seams in canoes.

The leaf sheath is used as fine sandpaper in polishing wooden bowls and *kukui* nuts. The gum or birdlime is used to trap and hold feather birds. (Handy, 1972, pp. 149-155; Buck, p. 8; Degener, pp. 124-130.)

4. Mai'a or bananas. *Musa* spp.

The banana plant *(mai'a)* is a succulent herb which grows from underground root stalks *(mole)* to heights of 20 feet or more in some varieties. Each plant bears one stalk of fruit *('ahui)*, then it is cut down or dies. More plants grow from root suckers *(pōhuli)* that come up from around the base of the original plant. Bananas grow best in moist areas protected from the wind.

Banana fruits *(hua mai'a)* are a nutritious food. Fibers *(hā mai'a)* are obtained from the trunk *(pū mai'a)*.

At least 50 varieties were known to the Hawaiian planters *(mahi'ai)*. Except in time of famine all but three kinds were reserved as food for the men. Those which women could eat were *iholena*, *pōpō'ulu* and *kaualau*.

Probably but a few varieties were brought to Hawai'i by the early colonists. The planters gave careful attention to the banana plants and fruit and selected for special propagation any that were unusual. In this way new varieties were detected and propagated. There is one Hawaiian strain growing in the wild that produces viable seed. By cross-pollinating these, new varieties may have been produced.

The gardeners planted bananas around their dwellings, on the banks between the wet taro ponds, in taro patches no longer flooded and used and in valleys and gulches protected from the winds. They were not grown in plantations.

In areas of considerable rainfall root suckers were planted any time of the year. In drier areas they were started at the beginning of the rainy season.

Hawaiian calendars give the favorable days and moon phase which are considered very important in planting bananas. (Handy, 1972, pp. 162-163). Noon is the time of day favored by most gardeners for planting the suckers although a few favor the evening or at night when the moon is directly overhead.

In some ceremonies *pū mai'a* is a substitute for the human body.

In spear practice, the wooden spear *(ihe)* is hurled into an upright *pū mai'a*.

Most of the bananas grown for the market today are introduced varieties. (Handy, 1972, pp. 155-167; Buck, p. 8; Neal, 1965, pp. 249-250; Degener, pp. 105-111.)

5. Niu or Coconut. *Cocos nucifera*.

The coconut tree *(lā'au niu)* probably has more uses than any other plant known to man.

The trunk is used for food bowls and for *hula* and temple drums; also for small canoes *(lolo niu)*. Children make toy canoes from the bloom sheath and call them *wa'a lolo niu*.

The heavy base or butt end of the frond *(kū'au)* is used to pound and firm taro pond walls. When used as a seat to slide down hillsides, this curved base of the frond is called *po'olau*.

Leaflets are plaited into fans *(pe'ahi)* and game balls *(kinipōpō)*.

Midribs *(ni'au)* are used for brooms *(pūlumi nī'au)*, shrimp snares *(pulu 'aha)*, needles for *lei* making, and a simple game *(panapana nī'au)*.

The husk covering the nut is used for fuel. Fibers from the husk *(pulu niu)* are braided or twisted into cordage *('aha)*.

Since Hawai'i is on the northern fringe of the coconut belt, the trees did not flourish here to the extent that they did and still do in the islands nearer the equator. Coconuts grow best near the beach, and in such localities the fruit sets on and matures while the trees are younger than on trees grown in the valleys or uplands.

A sprouted nut was planted in a hole in which an octopus *(he'e)* had been placed. The octopus, it was believed, gave the tree roots a firm grip and spread like its own arms and the nuts a round shape like the octopus head. Two varieties of coconuts were known in old Hawai'i, but several additional ones have been introduced.

(Handy, 1972, pp. 167-176; Buck, pp. 7-8; Degener, pp. 68-79.)

6. Uhi or yam. *Dioscorea alata.*

The *uhi* is not related to and must not be confused with the sweet potato which may also be called a yam.

Uhi are planted from pieces of the tuber which bear sprouts. Moist gulches and lower areas in the rain forest are favorable for the growth of yam vines. The vines must have support and this is usually supplied by trees. When grown in gardens, stakes are used to support the vines.

The vines grow during the summer, wither down in December, but the tubers in the ground continue to fill out. When new shoots appear at the beginning of the rainy season, the tubers are dug. They are cooked in the *imu* and eaten while hot. The flesh is too mealy to make *poi*.

Two other tuber-bearing vines, belonging to the same family as the *uhi*, were also called yams. They were not cultivated and were rarely for food.

Hoi, Dioscorea bulbifera, bore aerial tubers along the stem of the vine. These *kukui*-nut size tubers were poisonous but after sufficient washing could be eaten.

Pi'a, Dioscorea pentaphylla, bore small, edible underground tubers which were cooked and eaten while warm. Cold *pi'a* was pig food. This yam is not to be confused with *pia* or arrowroot.

(Handy, 1972, pp. 176-182; Buck, pp. 10-11.)

7. Pia or arrowroot. *Tacca leontopetalcides.*

Tubers, from which *pia* grows, are planted on the edge of moist woods or in areas suitable for upland taro. The plants grow without cultivation except for occasional weeding. The tubers mature in the summer, the leaves turn yellow and wither, indicating that the tubers are ready to harvest.

The leaves sprout on slender stems from the underground tubers and reach 2 to 3 feet in height. The much-divided leaves resemble somewhat those of the *papaia*. Greenish, fringy flowers appear on yard-long stems but no viable seeds result.

Pia is found in some home gardens at this time but is not grown commercially.

(Handy, 1972, p. 183; Buck p. 11, Neal p. 228)

8. Kō or sugar cane. *Saccharium officinarum.*

Sugar cane is a giant grass with stalks 15 to 20 feet and sometimes taller. Some 40 varieties have developed through the years that it has been cultivated.

Cane was planted in clumps where there was good soil and moisture. It was a favored and useful food plant around dwellings. Cane thrived along the banks of taro ponds. It served as hedges between fields and, when grown in thick clumps, was a good wind break.

The upper portion of a mature cane stalk was cut into sections and planted 6 to 8 inches deep. The stalks were laid flat in the hole and the plants sprouted from an eye or bud at each node.

In the lowlands the cane matured in 12 to 15 months but at higher elevations 18 to 24 months were required.

(Handy, 1972, pp. 183-188; Buck pp. 8-9; Kamakau, 1976, p. 39; Degener, pp. 56-66.)

9. 'Awa South Polynesia, Kava. *Piper methysticum.*

'Awa is a decorative shrub reaching 8 or more feet in height. The large, heart-shaped leaves emerge from stems which are swollen at the joints. The flowers are inconspicuous spikes.

The 'awa plant must have an abundance of moisture and prefers partial sun. Portions of the stalk of the 'awa which bore buds were planted in suitable moist areas. The plants grew from two to three years before they were large enough to use. 'Awa or kava is a ceremonial drink today in Samoa and other Pacific Islands but has fallen into disuse in Hawai'i.

The root of the mature plant contains a narcotic or tranquilizing substance which is soluable in water. Portions of the root are chewed or pounded, placed in a wooden bowl *(kānoa)* and water added. After mixing the 'awa and water the fibrous residue is removed with a strainer made from the stems of the 'ahu'awa sedge. 'Awa is drunk from cups *('apu'awa)* made from coconut shells cut lengthwise.

As a tranquilizer 'awa reduces or eliminates body pains, and is helpful for insomnia and anxiety. When drunk to excess over periods of time it causes scaliness of the skin and reddening of the eyes. It is a ceremonial drink among the chiefs, a pleasant relaxing potion for farmers and fishermen and an offering to the gods and the 'aumākua. (Handy, 1972, pp. 189-199.)

10. Hala or screwpine. *Pandanus odoratissimus.*

The *hala* or *pū hala*, planted by the Hawaiians near their houses, spread naturally from seeds to areas along the coast, lower valleys and the up-

Ready for a Day in the Mauka Garden: The planter, holding a piece of sugar cane, will transport the food packages and extra cane in the large gourd. He will suspend it and the water bottle on the ends of his carrying pole.

    He will wear the fiber sandles and carry or wear the ti leaf rain cape. He may return with taro and sweet potatoes in the large gourd.

lands where rainfall was sufficient. Nearly all parts of the pandanus plant were used for some purpose in the old culture.

The male tree, *hala hīnano*, bears the staminate flowering spike with powdery pollen and white bracts. The woody trunk *(kumu hala)* of the male is used for house posts and occasionally for bowls.

The female tree, *hala hua*, usually produces a number of fruit at a time. They resemble pineapples as they are composed of 50 or more wedge shaped drupes or seeds. These sprout readily when they fall to the moist earth. The wood of the female tree is soft.

Aerial prop roots grow from various parts of the trunk to the ground giving the appearance of a tree on stilts.

The leaves *(lau hala)* are plaited *(ulana)* into mats *(moena)*, baskets *(hīna'i)*, fans *(pe'ahi)*, pillows *(uluna)*, sandals *(kāma'a)* and canoe sails *(lā)*. The preparation of the *lau hala* and the *ulana* is women's work. Where *pili* is scarce and *lau hala* abundant the men thatch houses with the leaves.

(Handy, 1972, pp. 199-205.)

11. 'Ohe or bamboo. 'Ohe Hawai'i (Hawaiian bamboo) *Bambusa vulgaris*. 'Ohe Kahiki (Bamboo from Tahiti) *Schizostachyum glaucifolium*.

Bamboo sprouts are planted in moist areas where the plants grow to heights of 15 to 50 feet according to the variety.

The hollow stems, reaching four inches in diameter, are used for a variety of purposes. Nodes or joints divide the stems into sections.

Long bamboo poles are used for fishing rods and for thatching rafters in the house framework. Short sections are made into the musical instruments: split rattles *(pū'ili)*, nose flutes *('ohe hano ihu)* and stamping pipes *(kā'eke'eke/pahūpahū)*.

Strips of bamboo are cut into *kapa* stamps *('ohe kāpala)* and liners *(lapa)*. A sliver of green bamboo makes a very sharp knife *(pahi)*.

Most of the ornamental bamboo growing in Hawai'i today has been introduced, largely from Asia. (Handy, 1972, pp. 205-206.)

12. Wauke or Paper Mulberry. *Broussonetia papyrifera.*

Wauke was planted in patches throughout the islands where there was suitable soil, moisture, and protection from winds. Rich soil and considerable moisture are preferred. *Wauke* is propagated from the shoots that spring up from the roots of established plants or it is grown from cuttings. So many shoots spring up from the roots of the older plants that the *wauke* patch extends itself in all directions.

As the saplings grew the planter picked off the side branches *(lālā)* while they were buds. This resulted in a straight stalk which could be stripped into bark without holes along its length. Above the 8 or 9 foot level the branches and leaves were allowed to grow.

The walls of some taro ponds and the banks of streams were planted with *wauke.*

Some *wauke* is grown in home gardens today to provide the fibers for demonstrating the craft of *kapa* making. The bast or inner fibers of the *wauke* make the softest, finest and most durable *kapa* known.

When not harvested for its bark at 6 to 8 feet, it will become a tree up to 30 feet tall.

See Unit 15, Clothing, for more details (Handy, 1972, pp. 206-212).

13. Ipu or gourds. *Lagenaria siceraria.*

Hawaiians grew a larger variety and a greater number of gourds than did any of their fellow Pacific Islanders. The vines, grown from seeds, were carefully tended, and the gourds picked when mature. The gourds were carefully opened, cleaned and processed into a variety of containers. The largest gourds *(ipu nui)* were provided with lids and used to store *kapa,* feather regalia and other possessions.

When provided with carrying nets *(kōkō)* they were swung from shoulder poles *('auamo/māmaka)* and carried from place to place by bearers *(mea lawe).*

On sea voyages the gourd containers would float should the canoe overturn.

Fishermen carried their lines and hooks in gourds. Squat gourds formed rat guards by placing them on the posts of the offering platforms *(lele)* in certain *heiau.* Captain Cook's artist sketched paddlers wearing helmet-like masks of gourds. Most gourds for holding food and water were used with their natural color, but some were stained and decorated with geometric designs *(pāwehe).*

At least three introduced insects attack the gourd vines today with the result that gourd culture on a large scale has been discontinued. (Handy, 1972, pp. 212-222.)

14. Kī or ti. *Cordyline terminalis.*

Ti is a decorative and highly useful plant. It is grown especially for its shiny green leaves called *lā'ī,* a contraction of *lau* (leaf) and *kī.* It is easily propagated by cuttings from the stem. Ti thrives in deep, rich soil with an abundance of moisture.

Only the green ti is a Polynesian introduction. It grew in the villages, near the taro ponds and in the lower forests. Although the green ti blooms it does not produce viable seeds. Planting material must be carried from place to place by man. It does not require any form of cultivation.

Kī planted around dwellings is thought to ward off evil. Leaves worn around the neck and as wristlets and anklets are both decorative and serve as charms. A priest *(kahuna)* carried a stalk of *kī* into battle and to use as a flag of truce.

Lā'ī are tied to netting *('upena)* to make rain capes for bird catchers. Shelters in the forests are often thatched with *lā'ī* as are those in lowland areas where *pili* does not grow. Structures in the *heiau* sacred to the god Lono are thatched with *lā'ī.*

Sandals *(kāma'a lā'ī)* are braided from ti leaves to protect the feet when crossing rough lava.

Lā'ī are tied to the upper edge of a *hukilau* net to frighten the fish into staying in the net. A tuft of *lā'ī* is tied to an octopus lure *(lūhe'e)* to conceal the sharp bone hook.

Many varieties of colored ti have been introduced. Gardeners cross-pollinate the blossoms on these and from the resulting seeds more colorful plants have been produced. We are cautioned that the colored ti plants do not have the properties to ward off evil. (Handy, 1972, pp. 22-225.)

15. Olonā. *Touchardia latifolia.*

Olonā plants furnish the strongest fibers which man has been able to grow and make into cordage. This rain forest shrub was discussed in detail in Unit 8 as the plant which furnished the fibers to make the netting for feather garments. The people found many uses for the strong *olonā* fibers.

Olonā cordage is used to make fishlines *(aho),* fish nets with large mesh *('upena),* fine meshed nets *(nae)* onto which the feathers are tied in cloaks (ʻahuʻula), capes (kīpuka) and helmets (mahiole).

Olonā cords are knotted to make the carrying nets (kōkō) for food containers. Ti leaves are tied to an olonā net to make a rain cape (ʻahu lāʻī).

In warfare the cords in both the tripping weapon (pīkoi) and the strangling cord (kaʻane) are of olonā. Olonā cords are the core or foundation strand of the feather lei (lei hulu manu) and form the tying cords for the lei niho palaoa. Olonā mesh holds the dog teeth in the dance leglet (kūpeʻe niho ʻīlio).

No olonā is processed commercially today. (Handy, 1972, pp. 225-227.)

16. ʻŌlena or turmeric. *Curcuma domestica*

This semi-wild member of the ginger family is grown for its spicy yellow underground stems which are usually called roots. Leaf stalks come up in the spring, yellow and white flowers bloom, then the plant dies down in the autumn.

Ōlena

The pounded root is mixed with sea water in a calabash (ʻumeke lāʻau) and the solution sprinkled (pī kai) in places where there is a need to remove the restrictions of a kapu.

Juice from the crushed root is dropped into the ear to relieve earache, and into the nostrils and sinuses for sinusitis.

Juice from the raw root gives a yellow dye, and

from the cooked or steamed root a deep orange kapa dye.

ʻŌlena is grown today in gardens where it will receive sufficient moisture and preferably some shade. It continues to be used as a medicine by the older people. Students use the yellow ʻōlena juice as a dye in kapa making projects. (Handy, 1972, p. 228.)

17. Kukui or Candlenut tree. *Aleurites moluccana.*

The kukui trees, which grow to heights of 80 feet, form dense growths in the lower mountains and in the wet gulches. The silvery green of the mature leaves can be seen for many miles. The leaves on kukui seedlings are large and bright green.

The wood is used sparingly as it is soft and decays easily.

The inner bark is pounded, water added, making a stain for fish nets and a reddish-brown dye for kapa.

The gum (pīlali kukui) exuding from the trunk is chewed by children and also dissolved in water for a resin-like coating on kapa.

Children with thrush or coated tongue (ʻea) eat kukui blossoms mixed with cooked sweet potatoes (ʻuala) as a treatment for this ailment.

The sap exuding from a green nut at the point where it is broken from the stem is rubbed over the white coated area in the mouth of a child suffering from ʻea. Sap from a nut or leaf petiole, applied to punctures and wounds on the skin, forms a seal which hastens healing.

The hard shells of the nuts are polished and strung into leis. The flesh of the raw nut is a strong cathartic. The flesh of roasted nuts is pounded and salt is added to make the relish ʻinamona. Roasted kernels, chewed by fishermen on the reef or in canoes, are blown out over the small waves and ripples to form a film on the surface which increases visibility under the water.

Oil extracted from roasted nuts is burned, using one or more kapa wicks, in the stone lamps (poho kukui). Roasted kernels, strung on a coconut midrib (nīʻau) or bamboo splinter, form a type of candle (kōi, kālī, or ihoiho kukui). A torch (lamakū) consisting of a bamboo handle and a bundle of kōi kukui enclosed in a sheaf of ti leaves provides light for night activities.

Soot (paʻu) collected from burning roasted nuts gives a black dye for tattooing, for painting the hulls of canoes, and for dyeing.

If a family wanted a *kukui* tree near the house it was the belief that a stranger should plant it in the rear of the dwelling. One of the representations of the *kukui* tree was the human spirit. A *kukui* growing in front of the dwelling suggested that the home owner was exposing his soul to all who passed by. The silver glow eminating from this tree in the rear seemed to give the passing traveler or a visitor entering the garden modest glimpses of the homeowner's spirit.

(Handy, 1972, pp. 228-232.)

18. Kou. *Cordia subcordata.*

Kou is a quick-growing cultivated tree which may reach 30 feet in height. It provides shade around the houses *(hale)*, especially in the warm, leeward areas. The beauty of the wood and the ease with which it can be cut makes *kou* the most highly prized of all woods for food bowls *('umeke kou)* and platters *(pā kou).*

Images were carved from *kou.* A brown dye is obtained from the leaves. Leis are strung from the orange flowers. Read the legend to learn why no one wears a *kou* flower lei in one part of the 'Ewa district on O'ahu. (Handy, 1972, p. 232.)

19. Milo. *Thespesia populnea*

The *milo* is planted by man to shade his houses along the warm sunny beaches. The buoyant seeds fall and are carried by sea currents to other seaside locations. *Milo* is not found in the forests.

The trees reach heights of 40 feet with a trunk of 2 feet in diameter. The wood is rich brown with attractive grain and capable of taking a high polish. The wood is without unpleasant tasting sap so is made into food bowls *('umeke milo)* and platters *(pā milo). Milo* is second in popularity to *kou* as a wood for food containers.

Bell-shaped yellow flowers brighten the tree most of the year. The seeds are taken as a laxative. The young leaves may be eaten raw or cooked, perhaps only in time of necessity.

(Handy, 1972, p. 232.)

20. Kamani. *Calophyllum inophyllum.*

The red-brown wood from the trunk of the tree is made into food bowls *('umeke kamani)* and trays *(pā kamani).* There is no disagreeable sap in this wood. The kernels are removed from the spherical seeds, holes pierced in the shell and a yard long cord attached. The nut is whirled by the string producing a whistling sound *(oeoe).* Oil extracted

from the nut is useful in massage *(lomi)* and for oiling or waterproofing *kapa.* The small white flowers are prized for their odor. Kamani is propagated by seed.

(Neal, pp. 585-586.)

21. Hau. Hibiscus tiliaceus.

The *hau* is a spreading tree of the lowlands with tough, light-weight wood. Plantings are made from stem cuttings. Slightly curved branches are used for outrigger booms *('iako)* and for canoe floats *(ama)* if the lighter *wiliwili* wood is not available. Smaller branches were used for adze handles *('au ko'i),* for massage sticks *(lā'au lomi),* fire plows *('aunaki, 'aulima),* light-weight spears *(ihe)* for battle practice, fish net floats *(pīkoi)* and kite *(lupe)* framework.

The bark *('ili hau)* is twisted or braided into cordage. Although inferior to the strong fibers of the *'olonā* and to coconut-fiber sennit *('aha),* it has a number of uses. The slimy sap under the bark and the base of the flowers is a mild laxative.

(Handy, 1972, pp. 232-233.)

22. 'Ōhi'a 'ai or Mountain apple. *Eugenia malaccensis.*

This tree grows in the moist windward valleys to heights of 50 feet or more. It also thrives in parks and gardens near sea level where gardeners plant and care for it. The seeds may be carried to new areas in the valleys by pigs, rats or people who gather and eat juicy, crisp fruit and discard the seeds. The wood was used for houseposts, rafters and enclosures about the temples. The bark yielded a brown dye and an astringent medicine.

The Hawaiians recognized plant relationships as did the Swedish naturalist Linnaeus in 1773 when he devised the plan of giving each plant and animal two names. Earlier than this the Hawaiians named three related plants, the *'ōhi'a 'ai,* edible *'ōhia;* the *'ōhi'a lehua,* the lei flower of Hawai'i island; and *'ōhi'a hā,* a tree with edible red fruit about one-third inch in diameter.

This tree is also called *'ōhi'a leo,* a poetic way of saying that a person could talk *(leo)* while picking the fruit. Its cousin, *'ōhi'a lehua,* was called *'ōhi'a hāmau* or the silent *(hāmau)* one for it was *kapu* to talk while snaring feather birds among the *lehua* blossoms. (Neal, p. 636.)

■ There are a number of additional plants of some importance in Hawaiian life. Most of these grew wild and required no care from the planter. Those that are medicinal, dye or minor food plants are discussed in the appropriate units here.

A large number of fruits and vegetables have been introduced into Hawai'i. Some have been growing here so long that many people assume that they are native plants. Among these plants are the citrus fruits, coffee, guavas, lichee, macadamia nuts, mangoes, melons, papaya, passion fruit, pineapple and vegetables of many kinds.

Also introduced are non-Hawaiian varieties of plants which were established here prior to European times. Some of them are bamboo, bananas, berries, breadfruit, coconuts, sugar cane, sweet potatoes and taro.

■ Domesticated Animals

1. Pua'a or pig, hog. *Sus scrofa.*

Pigs were raised in great numbers for food and for religious and ceremonial purposes. They were free to roam about the village and its environs. Stone walls (*pā pōhaku*) and picket fences (*pā lā'au*) kept these animals from areas where they were not wanted. Mature hogs were penned in stone-walled enclosures and fattened. They were fed cooked taro (*kalo*), sweet potatoes (*'uala*), yams (*hoi*), bananas (*mai'a*) and breadfruit (*'ulu*). Some of these foods were the scraps and peelings not suitable for human consumption.

Some pigs escaped to the uplands and fed on *kukui* nuts, mountain apples (*'ōhi'a 'ai*) in season and the trunks of several kinds of ferns. From time to time these wild pigs came down from the forests and raided the gardens, particularly the sweet potato plots. In the wild the old boars developed long, curved ivory-like tusks (*ku'i pua'a*).

Some women and children took piglets as pets.

Mature hogs weighed a hundred pounds. They had lean bodies with long heads and small erect ears. The color of the bristles were all black (*hiwa*), striped (*olomea*), spotted (*pūko'a*) and combinations of these. Some pigs were hairless (*hulu 'ole*).

Ornamental and useful articles were fashioned from bones and tusks of the pig.

A small bunch of stiff black and white bristles formed the hackle (*hulu*) of the bonito (*aku*) fishhook. Shafts of the leg bones were shaped into fish hooks.

The most ornamental of the products from hogs were the pairs of long, curved ivory-like boars'

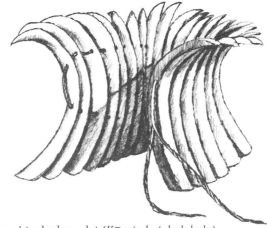

Boars' tusks bracelet (*Kūpe'e ho'okalakala*)

tusks (*ku'i pua'a*) or (*niho pua'a*). Bracelets (*kūpe'e ho'okalakala*) were made by drilling matching holes in two places in from 19 to 24 full length tusks, each 4 or 5 inches long. These holes accommodated the *olonā* cords which held the tusks lengthwise around the wrists. Each man might wear a pair of them while dancing.

Bracelets were also made by trimming the ends from the tusks to form wristlets about two inches wide.

Pigs were credited with the ability to recognize persons of rank (*ali'i*) who were living in exile and concealing their identity. These pigs were called "*pua'a 'imi ali'i.*" Pigs were also thought to be able to identify a sorcerer who had put a person to death.

Kamapua'a, the pig demigod or *kupua*, was credited with many accomplishments. He appeared as a handsome man, a pig or the fish *humuhumunukunukuapua'a*. He also appeared as any one of the following plants: the *'ama'u* or *hapu'u* ferns, *hala*, *kūkaepua'a* grass, taro leaf (*lau kalo*), *kukui*, *olomea* and *'uhaloa*. (Handy, 1972, pp. 250-253; Tomich, pp. 78-83; Malo, see index; Kramer, pp. 180-206.)

2. 'Īlio or dog. *Canis familiaris.*

'Īlio were raised in great numbers for food. They were offered to deities as gifts and to chiefs in form of gifts and taxes. Craftsmen made useful and ornamental articles from dog teeth, bones and hair.

'Īlio were small animals with long bodies, short legs, upstanding ears, and prominent eyes. In color the hair was all black, all white, dark-, light- or reddish-brown or brindled.

'Īlio always lived around the villages; often

they were kept in pens where they were fed and fattened on *poi*, cooked sweet potatoes (*'uala*) and broth (*kai*) made from cooked fish or pig. There was no suitable food for them in the wild.

Although they lived close to man the dogs were not really companions and they were not watch dogs. Some women suckled favorite puppies at their breasts and children took puppies as pets. These pets were casually used for human food when needed.

A few parts of the body of the dog were made into decorative objects. No use was made of the skin or pelt. However, a tuft of hair or a small piece of skin with the hair attached decorated the tip of the rod (*maile*) which the scorekeeper (*helu'ai*) used in directing the games *no'a* and *pūhenehene*.

Dog teeth (*niho 'īlio*) in numbers to a thousand were tied to each leg ornament (*kūpe'e niho'īlio*) worn by *hula* dancers. In making these the four canine teeth were removed from the dogs' jaws after they had been cooked and served at a meal. A hole was drilled through the root of each of the teeth, an *olonā* cord was strung through them and the teeth tied to a sturdy *olonā* net-like legging.

Canine teeth decorate the upper and lower jaws of the open mouths of the feather images (*kūkā'ilimoku*). From 74 to 144 teeth ornament the known images.

Dogs' teeth, filed to a uniform size, pierced with two holes in each and strung on two *olonā* cords made attractive bracelets (*kūpe'e*). Some 35 to 50 teeth were needed for a bracelet.

Of more practical use were the fishhooks and piercing instruments shaped from dog bones and teeth.

Small one-piece fishhooks were formed from the leg bones. Small unbarbed hooks were fashioned from molar teeth including the roots. Sharp canine teeth formed the points in some two-piece hooks.

Needles (*kui humuhumu*) and awls (*kui iwi*) for piercing *kapa* were made from the leg bones of dogs.

There are numerous references to dogs in myths and legends. Some mythical dogs assumed the shape of humans, ancestral guardians (*kupua*), water spirits (*mo'o*) and clouds. Petroglyphs may be attempts to immortalize some of these.

Read about these legendary dogs: Kū'īlioloa, Pa'e, Ka'upe, Hi-maka, and Puapua-lenalena. (Handy, 1972, pp. 242-250; Tomich, pp. 51-56;

Malo, see index; Kramer, pp. 101-114; Titcomb, Dog and Man.)

3. Moa or chickens. *Gallus gallus gallus.*

The Polynesian chicken, of Malaysian origin, was already domesticated when brought into the islands of the Pacific. The wild chickens found in Hawai'i or elsewhere were those that had reverted to the wild.

The domesticated chickens ran about the village and environs and largely foraged for themselves. They were fed scraps of food such as the inner skin scraped from the taro and the gratings from the coconut after the cream (*wai o ka niu*) had been expressed.

Wild chickens found sufficient food in the lower forests to live a healthy life. The cocks were heard crowing lustily in the early morning.

Chickens were of importance as offerings to temple gods and to family gods (*'aumākua*). The roosters were highly prized in the sport of cock fighting (*ho'ohākāmoa*). The shiny black tail feathers of the rooster were used in *kāhili*. These and selected body feathers covered coarse nets in the early form of trapezoid-shaped capes (*kīpuka*) and also covered *kapa* disks to form the head (*heke*) of the gourd rattle (*'ulī'ulī*). (Handy, 1972, pp. 254-257; Ball, Jungle Fowls.)

■ **Introduced Animals**

The larger animals introduced in 1778 and during the years to follow were those to be used for food, draft animals for agricultural work, some for pets and game animals for hunting.

The dogs and hogs have interbred with the native dogs and hogs until the local strains have completely lost their identity.

Antelope	'Anekelopa	Goats	Kao
Cattle	Pipi (beef)	Hogs	Pua'a
Cats	Pōpoki	Horses	Lio
Deer	Kia	Rabbits	'Iole lapaki
Dogs	'Īlio	Sheep	Hipa
Donkey	Kēkake	Water Buffalo	Pipi pākē
Game birds	Manu	Wallaby or	
		Kangaroo	Kanakalū

■ **Captain Cook Introduced Goats, Pigs and Plant Seeds**

Captain Cook left livestock and seeds in Hawai'i with the hope that these introduced animals and plants would thrive here and be a useful supple-

Animals Brought by the Early Settlers: On the voyaging canoes came the pigs, dogs and chickens for human food and for use in religious ceremonies. The rats, perhaps as stowaways, provided the chiefs with the game of rat-shooting with bow and arrows.

ment to the diet of the Hawaiian people. He also expressed an interest in encouraging the people to propagate these foreign animals and plants and make the resulting food available to British ships which would stop in Hawai'i for provisions in the years to come.

While off Ni'ihau, February 1, 1778, Cook wrote:

> I went [ashore] myself with the Pinnace and Launch . . . taking with me a Ram goat and two Ewes, a Boar and Sow pig of the English breed, the seeds of Millions [melons], Pumpkins and onions . . . I should have left these things at the other island [Kaua'i] had we not been so unexpectedly driven from it [by winds and currents]. (Beaglehole, p. 276)

Over a year later Samwell recorded in his journal on March 3, 1779, while off Kaua'i:

> We learnt from the Indians of Nehaw [Ni'ihau] about the two Goats that were left by Captain Cook and that in the Conflict the poor Goats were both killed. (Beaglehole, p. 1224)

Clerke wrote on March 7, 1779, that Chief Kāneoneo of Kaua'i had cared for the goats which Captain Cook had left 13 months earlier, and that the number had increased to seven. A dispute arose over their ownership, and all of the goats were killed on February 28, 1779.

Kramer (1971, p. 284) wrote that Vancouver left a male and a female goat on Hawai'i, another pair on Kaua'i, and several on Maui in 1793-94. Descendants of these goats found their way to all of the islands, where they have become destructive pests.

We know less of the fate of the seeds of the useful plants left by Cook. King wrote in March 1779, summarizing their experiences:

> The Captain took a deal of pains to rear some Melons at Owhyhee, and they promised to succeed very well, but they were so placed, that when the Village was burnt, his little garden must also have gone to ruin. (Beaglehole, p. 617)

Understandings and Appreciations

1. Discuss the food situation with someone who was concerned with this problem in Hawai'i in 1942, the first year of World War II. Except for sugar and pineapple, Hawai'i was producing a small percent of the food needed by its people. Note how the people looked forward to the "Convoys" of ships that brought the needed food from the mainland.

2. Read about the work of the Agricultural Department of the University of Hawaii in their endeavors to increase the production of many food crops. The agriculturists have developed varieties of small crops which are adapted to local conditions and are resistant to certain local diseases.

3. With No. 1 and 2 in mind, note that the Hawaiian farmer of old was able to help feed the 300,000 residents with no help from imported food. It is true, however, that he did not have to combat the many plant diseases, insects and weeds of foreign origin that are a problem to the farmers of today.

Student Activities

1. List the plants in your home gardens and in your school grounds and determine how many were here before the time of Captain Cook.

2. What use is being made of any of the native plants in these gardens — food, shade or ornamental?

3. Secure if possible Hawaiian sugar cane stalks and some from a commercial plantation. Note the thinner rind and tender fibers of the native cane. Though more pleasant to eat, it does not resist the insect pests and diseases. In a like manner, compare Hawaiian bananas and the introduced varieties.

4. From a list of the native Hawaiian food plants, note those that were propagated by seeds and by another means. Sprout a coconut in the classroom and note the growth of rootlets and fronds. Visit a park or garden with breadfruit trees or *wauke* and see the young plants growing from the roots of the mature tree or shrub.

5. Make an '*ō'ō* from a sapling an inch and one-half or two inches in diameter. It could be cut and sharpened with a hatchet. With this tool dig a hole to plant a shrub or small tree.

6. Make the simple form of *kōkō* or net to suspend a large coconut bowl, a gourd or wooden bowl.

Peter Buck, 1957, pp. 64-66, describes the making of what he calls a simple net container. Personal help might be needed here.

7. Place stem cuttings of ti in a shallow dish of water and watch them grow. Note that these stems are for sale in some gift shops frequented by visitors in Hawai'i.

Audio-Visual Aids and Field Trips

1. Check the film catalogs for movies on agriculture. Plan to see *Taro Tales* which is scheduled for the DOE instructional television in-school broadcasting series. An excellent illustrated Teacher's Guide accompanies this 20 minute film. A dozen suggestions are given in this Guide for field trips or other resources where classes may learn more about taro and poi. See also *A Trip to the Taro Patch*, a colorfully illustrated booklet for children. Text by Joyce Hanohano. Read the illustrated booklet, *Taro in Hawai'i*, by Bryan W. Begley.

2. The following parks and gardens feature a number of Hawaiian plants as well as introduced ones of interest. All welcome visitors. Phone the office listed in the telephone book to learn if a permit or reservation is required, if there is an admission charge and the hours that the facility is open for visitors.

O'ahu

1. Honolulu Botanic Gardens, City and County of Honolulu, Foster Botanic Garden, Vineyard Blvd.

Ho'omaluhia - Windward O'ahu. A new garden with some Hawaiian plants.

Hawaii Nature Center - Makiki Heights Drive. Sponsors nature walks to identify native Hawaiian plants and birds.

Wahiawā Botanic Garden. Excellent collection of native plants.

2. Keaīwa Heiau State Park, 'Aiea Heights, a number of Hawaiian plants of interest.

3. Kualoa Regional Park, City and County. Hawaiian plants of the windward beach zone.

4. Lyon Arboretum - Mānoa Road, many native plants. Taro a specialty.

5. Moanalua Valley, native plants in natural habitat.

6. Waimea Falls Park and Arboretum. Excellent collection of Hawaiian plants with informative labels.

7. Bishop Museum Courtyard and Grounds. Good collection of native plants. Courtyard plants are labelled.

Hawai'i Island

The Hawai'i Volcanoes National Park offers excellent opportunities to study native plants. Books and pamphlets are available to help in identifying the plants and learning their uses.

1. Mauna Loa - Kīlauea Area - Plants of the high altitudes and the rain forests.

2. Waha'ula Heiau Center - Plants of the windward beach areas.

3. Pu'uhonua o Hōnaunau - formerly the City of Refuge National Historical Park. Plants of the leeward or Kona coast.

Maui

1. Haleakala National Park. Native plants growing and labelled at the visitors' center upon entering the park. Silversword Garden at the summit.

2. Kahanu Gardens, Hāna. A branch of the Pacific Tropical Botanical Gardens of Lāwa'i, Kaua'i.

3. Maui County Zoological and Botanical Garden, near Kahului. Excellent collection of native plants with labels.

4. Ke'anae Arboretum, State Division of Forestry, Maui Division. Fine gardens of taro and other native plants.

5. Kapalua Botanical Garden, Kapalua Land Company, West Maui. Native plants.

Kaua'i

1. Pacific Tropical Botanical Garden, Lawa'i. Established by the Federal Government to propagate and study plants of the Pacific tropical regions.

■ **Current Happenings of Significance to this Unit**

1. Learn the story of taro production as it passed from the Hawaiian planters to the Chinese. Only the heavy producing varieties were retained, and many of the special types of taro have been lost. Why has taro production continued to decline?

2. Waimānalo and Wai'anae sugar plantations were discontinued and small farms have taken over the lands. What ethnic group of people are the farmers? What crops are they growing? Are any of the crops native food plants?

3. Kahuku Plantation on O'ahu discontinued growing and refining sugar. Note how the large sugar mill was converted to another use. Diversified farming and aquaculture have taken over at least a part of the plantation lands. Are these enterprises as profitable to the owners as sugar production?

4. Note the continued popularity of the lū'au among local people and the tourists. This stimulates the continued production of pigs, taro and poi, sweet potatoes and coconuts.

5. In 1988 some 3,700 field workers were employed to tend the 176,500 acres planted to sugar cane. Cane and its by-products brought in about $210 million. The pineapple plantations employed 1,750 field workers in 1988. A total of 659,000 tons of pineapples (fresh equivalent) were sold. Income from pineapple was $107.4 million. (The above figures are from the 1989 *State of Hawaii Data Book,* compiled by the State Department of Business and Economic Development.)

■ **Reading List**

Ball, Stanley C. *Jungle Fowls from Pacific Islands.* Honolulu: Bishop Museum Bulletin No. 108, 1933.

Barrau, Jacques. *Plants and Migrations of Pacific Peoples.* Honolulu: Bishop Museum Press, 1963. (Three articles on sweet potatoes.)

Beckwith, Martha W. *Kepelino's Traditions of Hawaii.* 1932. Honolulu: Bishop Museum Bulletin No. 95, 1971.

Begley, Brian W. *Taro in Hawaii.* Honolulu: Oriental Publishing Company, 1979. (Attractive color photos.)

Berger, Andrew J. *Hawaiian Birdlife.* 2nd ed. Honolulu: University Press of Hawaii, 1981.

Brennan, Joseph. *The Parker Ranch of Hawaii.* The saga of a ranch and a dynasty. New York: John Day, 1974.

Bryan, E.H. Jr. "Agriculture." Ch. 4 in *Ancient Hawaiian Life.* 1938. Honolulu: Books About Hawaii, 1950.

Buck, Peter H. *Arts and Crafts of Hawaii.* Honolulu: Bishop Museum Special Publication No. 45, 1957.

PLANTERS AND THEIR PRODUCTS

126

Degener, Otto. *Plants of the Hawaii National Park.* 1930. Ann Arbor, MI: Edwards Bros., Inc., 1945.

Dodge, Ernest S. *Hawaiian and Other Polynesian Gourds.* Honolulu: Topgallant Publishing Company, 1978.

Fornander, Abraham. *Hawaiian Antiquities and Folklore.* Honolulu: Bishop Museum Memoir, Vol. 6, No. 1, 1919. (Agriculture.)

Fosberg, F.R., ed. *Man's Place in the Island Ecosystem.* A Tenth Pacific Science Congress symposium. 1963. Honolulu: Bishop Museum Press, 1970.

Handy, E.S.C. *The Hawaiian Planter.* Vol. I. Honolulu: Bishop Museum Bulletin No. 161, 1940.

Handy, E.S.C., Elizabeth G. Handy, and Mary K. Pukui. *Native Planters in Old Hawaii. Their Life, Lore and Environment.* Honolulu: Bishop Museum Bulletin No. 233, 1972.

Handy, E.S.C., and Mary K. Pukui. *The Polynesian Family System in Ka'u.* 1958. Rutland, VT and Japan: C.E. Tuttle, 1972.

Hartt, Constance. *Harold Lloyd Lyon, Hawaii Sugar Botanist.* Honolulu: Lyon Arboretum, University Press of Hawaii, 1980.

Hobbs, Jean. *Hawaii, A Pageant of the Soil.* Stanford, CA: Stanford University Press, 1935.

Kennedy, T.F. *Farmers of the Pacific Islands.* Farming in Tonga, Samoa, Gilbert Islands (Kiribati) and Nauru. Wellington, Auckland, Sydney, Aus.: A.H. and A.W. Reed, 1968.

Krauss, Beatrice H. *Creating a Hawaiian Ethnobotanical Garden.* Honolulu: Lyon Arboretum, University of Hawaii, 1980.

———. *Ethnobotany of Hawai'i.* Honolulu: Department of Botany, University of Hawaii, 1974.

———. *Ethnobotany of the Hawaiians.* Lyon Arboretum Lecture No.5. Honolulu: Lynn Arboretum, University of Hawaii, 1975.

———. *Native Plants Used as Medicine in Hawaii.* Honolulu: Lyon Arboretum, University of Hawaii, 1979.

Kuck, Loraine E., and Richard Tongg. *The Modern Tropical Garden.* Honolulu: Tongg Publishing Company, 1955.

Malo, David. *Hawaiian Antiquities.* 1898. Honolulu: Bishop Museum Special Publication No. 2, 1976.

Neal, Marie C. *In Gardens of Hawaii.* 1948. Honolulu: Bishop Museum Special Publication No. 50, 1965 (rev. ed.).

Newman, T. Stell. *Hawaiian Fishing and Farming on the Island of Hawaii in A.D. 1778.* Honolulu: Department of Land and Natural Resources, 1970.

Taylor, Clarice B. *Hawaiian Almanac.* 1957. Honolulu: Tongg Publishing Company, 1965.

Taylor, Frank J., Earl M. Welty, and David W. Eyre. *From Land and Sea.* The story of Castle and Cooke of Hawaii. San Francisco: Chronicle Books, 1976.

Teho, Fortunato. *Plants of Hawaii.* How to grow them. Hilo: Petroglyph Press, 1971.

Titcomb, Margaret. *Dog and Man in the Ancient Pacific.* With special attention to Hawaii. Honolulu: Bishop Museum Special Publication No. 59, 1969.

———. "Kava in Hawaii." *Journal of the Polynesian Society,* 1948. 57(2).

Tuggle, H. David, and P. Bion Griffin. *Lapakahi Hawaii.* Archaeological studies of an area in North Kohala. Asian and Pacific Archaeology Series No. 5. Honolulu: Social Science Research Institute, University of Hawaii, 1973.

Whitney, Leo D., F.A.I. Bowers, and M. Takahashi. *Taro Varieties in Hawaii.* Honolulu: Hawaii Agricultural Experiment Station Bulletin No. 84, 1939. (86-page booklet with historical and botanical information on taro. 84 varieties described in detail.)

Wichman, Juliet R. *Hawaiian Planting Traditions.* Honolulu: T.H., Honolulu Star-Bulletin, 1930.

———. "Agriculture." Ch. 10 in *Ancient Hawaiian Civilization.* A series of lectures delivered at the Kamehameha Schools by E.S.C. Handy [and others]. 1933. Rutland, VT and Japan: C.E. Tuttle, 1965 (rev. ed.).

Yen, Douglas E. *The Sweet Potato and Oceania.* An essay in ethnobotany. Honolulu: Bishop Museum Bulletin No. 236, 1974.

Zimmerman, Elwood C. "Nature of the Land Biota." In *Man's Place in the Island Ecosystem.* Ed. F.R. Fosberg. 3rd printing. Honolulu: Bishop Museum Press, 1970.

UNIT 10
Preparing and
Serving Foods

PREPARING AND SERVING FOODS

The pioneer groups of Polynesians to settle in Hawai'i had to depend, at first, upon the plants and animals which they found here for their food. In time they were able to harvest the crops that grew from the slips, roots and seeds which they had brought from their homeland. And the offspring of their domestic animals could be eaten when they became numerous.

In contrast to the diet to which these people were accustomed the vegetable food found here was not particularly palatable nor highly nutritious.

There was an abundance of sea food since they were the first humans to fish in Hawaiian waters. *Limu* or seaweed, especially abundant off these shores, was a welcome condiment.

■   Edible plants established in Hawai'i by natural means and available to the earliest settlers were:

'Aheahea or 'Aweoweo. *Chenopodium oahuense.* Endemic.

A shrub growing to 4 or 5 feet in height, usually in the dry lowlands. The young, thick gray-green leaves and the plant tips are wrapped in ti leaves and cooked over hot coals (*lāwalu*). These add greens and roughage to the diet.

'Akala. Raspberry, *Rubus hawaiiensis, Rubus Macraei.* Endemic.

The *'ākala* is a shrub with stems, usually thornless, from 5 to 15 feet long. These may trail or stand erect. *'Ākala* usually grows in the uplands. It is abundant in some areas of the island of Hawai'i.

The reddish edible fruit is from 1 to 2 inches in length. It is crushed to make a pink (*'ākala*) dye.

'Ama'u (plural 'Āma'uma'u). Small tree fern. *Sadleria* spp. Endemic.

The *'ama'u*, a small tree fern, may reach 5 to 15 feet in height with fronds 2 to 3 feet long, reddish while young and green in maturity. It thrives in the rain forest and also grows on new lava flows.

The tasteless, starchy pith of the trunk is steamed and eaten by man in times of famine or fed to pigs.

Hala. Pandanus or screw pine. *Pandanus odoratissimus.*

Six species or varieties are endemic to the Hawaiian Islands.

The tender tip of the aerial root, although bitter in taste, is eaten raw or cooked. It is said to be rich in vitamin B. Children broke open (*kīkē hala*) the mature keys and ate the nut-like centers.

Hāpu'u. Tree fern, *Cibotium* spp. Endemic.

The *hāpu'u* are the giant tree ferns of the cool shady rain forest. The fronds rise to 30 feet or more, often growing under tall *'ōhi'a lehua* trees.

The trunks are cooked in the *imu* or in steam vents at the volcano for the starchy centers. This is a food for pigs (*pua'a*) and for humans in time of famine.

Handy wrote that one trunk may contain from 50 to 70 pounds of almost pure starch. (Handy, 1940, p. 214.)

The young curled fronds (*pepe'e*) are fed to *pua'a* or peeled and cooked for human food.

Hō'i'o-kula. *Dryopteris, (Cyclosorus) sandwiciensis.* Endemic.

A lowland fern which grows in moist, protected areas in thick stands to 6 feet in height. It is prized for its succulent young fronds (*pepe'e*) which are eaten raw and added to raw fish or shrimp. They are cooked with meat and other vegetables.

Lama. *Diospyros* spp. Endemic.

Lama trees grow from 20 to 40 feet in height in either wet or dry lower elevations. In thick stands of trees the trunks grow straight and reach a foot in diameter.

Immature fruits are green, then yellow and finally dark red. The fruit, (pi'oi) a relative of the persimmon, is food for man and birds when ripe.

Loulu. Fan palm, *Pritchardia* spp. Endemic.

Over 35 species and varieties of the *loulu* are endemic to *Hawai'i*. All palms except the *loulu* were brought here by man. Most *loulu* grow naturally at elevations of 2,000 to 3,000 feet in the rainforests. They may be grown from seed, domestically, at lower elevations.

The trees, 10 to 30 feet high, are topped with a cluster of large, fan-shaped leaves.

The small, unripe seeds (*hāwane*) are edible. The flesh resembles the immature coconut meat.

Māmaki. *Pipturus* spp. Endemic.

Māmaki, a large shrub or small tree, grows to 15 feet in height, in open wooded areas or on the outskirts of forests. It thrives without cultivation at altitudes of 1,500 to 4,000 feet.

The white, fleshy mulberry-like fruits are borne on the young stems. Though rather tasteless the fruit is eaten by people and by birds.

'Ōhelo. *Vaccinium* spp. Endemic.

The *'ōhelo* is a branched shrub, from 1 to 2 feet high, growing in the mountains of the four largest islands. It is a member of the cranberry family. The small, rounded berries, yellow, orange or red, are eaten raw or cooked.

The dried leaves are brewed into a tea for a general tonic.

'Ōhelo is considered sacred to the volcano goddess *Pele.* Visitors to the *Kīlauea* volcano area, where the plants grow in profusion, gather and throw fruiting branches into the firepit before eating any berries themselves.

'Ōhelo-papa. Strawberry, *Fragaria chiloensis* var. *sandwicensis.* Endemic.

The native strawberry grows in the mountains on Hawai'i and Maui at altitudes of 3,500 to 6,000 feet. The red, juicy fruit ripens between June and September. A white-fruited form which grows wild in the *Kīlauea* Volcano region is an introduced species, *Fragaria vesca.*

Pōpolo. *Solanum nigrum.* Indigenous.

Pōpolo, an erect herb 1 to 3 feet high, is common almost everywhere in the lowlands. The small white flowers develop into juicy berries (*hua pōpolo*) which are relished as eaten from the plant. The young shoots and tender leaves are steamed

in ti leaf packages (*laulau*) in the *imu*. They are a healthful pot herb or green food.

Another method of steaming food, called *pūholo,* requires a calabash (*'umeke lā'au*) with a tight fitting lid. Place a layer of ti leaves in the bottom, then add flesh food such as pork, fish or wild birds properly dressed. Add hot stones and a quantity of *pōpolo* leaves. Place the cover on tightly and steam for several hours.

'Ūlei. *Osteomeles anthyllidifolia.* Endemic.

'Ūlei is a rambling much branched shrub that spreads over the ground forming thickets not more than two feet high. It prefers dry areas from sea level to 4,000 feet in elevation. In some places *'ūlei* has been known to grow into a 12 foot high shrub.

The compound leaves are a shiny green, the rose-like flowers are white and the globular white fruits contain a sweet purple pulp. The flavor of these edible berries is similar to that of rose petals.

I'a - Flesh food

Flesh foods available were the native birds, *nene* or goose, *kōloa* or duck and the *ae'o* or stilt. A number of kinds of forest birds, although quite small were eaten.

Migratory birds favored for food were the *kōlea* or plover and the *kioea* or curlew. Malo lists many more small birds used for food in the 1951 edition, pp. 37-40.

■ **Hawaiian Breakfast, 1779.**

An introduction to Hawaiian food and table service will be David Samwell's account of a breakfast served on January 23, 1779. Surgeon's mate Samwell and Charles Clarke, second in command of the Cook expedition were guests of Chief *Palea* (Parea) at Kealakekua, Kona.

> [Parea] . . . ordered a matt to be spread for Us to sit on and he then withdrew, having left orders with his Servts to kill two pigs and roast them for our breakfast. . . . While the Pigs were roasting Parea himself spread a Table for us, he laid on the floor two rows of plantain [banana] leaves and another row across them which had a neat and clean appearance, before these and next to us was laid a piece of white Cloth [kapa] doubled, and behind all 5 Cocoa nuts stripped of the rind; he then brought some Ava root and asked us if we would drink any of the Liquor, this we declined but he ordered some to be prepared for himself and another Chief who was present. In a little time the Hogs were brought and placed upon the leaves in two wooden Dishes, and two other platters were

brought with sweet potatoes cold. Parea himself stood Carver, if disjointing the Meat with his Hands may entitle him to that Appellation, he divided it with his fingers into small bits, and having, as a mark of his peculiar Politeness and attention to strangers, put a piece into his Mouth and just sucked it, offered to feed us with it but we chose rather to help ourselves than put him to that Trouble. We made a hearty breakfast and finished it with Cocoa nut milk. (Beaglehole, pp. 1165-1166)

Foods in the Hawaiian diet would be classified today as carbohydrates (starches and sugars) fats and proteins.

The planters' crops which made up the bulk of the diet were the starches. The banana, a starch food actually changed to sugar when ripe. Sugar cane, and the root of the kī were the principal foods rich in sugar.

Protein came from the domestic animals and the fish and smaller sea animals. Grains which furnish protein elsewhere did not grow in Hawai'i.

The scientific names of the following plants were given in the previous unit.

■ Kalo or taro

The Hawaiian people were unique among Polynesians in preferring *poi* to the unpounded taro corm as their staple food. To satisfy this taste they were required to make a number of containers to store the semiliquid *poi* while it was fermenting and acquiring the desired flavor.

When mature taro plants were pulled by hand from the pond and garden, the leafy tops were cut off with a wooden taro cutter (*pālau kōhi*) (Buck, 1957, pp. 13-14) or a sharp shell. The washed, unpeeled corms were steamed in the *imu* until tender, (from two to six hours). The peeling was scraped off with an *opihi* shell, a piece of cowrie shell (*leho*) or a sharp stone, usually while the corm was hot. (Pukui, 1967, p. 426.) Implements for making *poi* from taro were: a *poi* pounding board, a stone pounder, wooden bowls or gourds to hold the water used while pounding and to store the *poi*.

■ Poi Boards and Pounders

Poi was pounded on heavy, slightly hollowed wooden boards (*papa ku'i poi*). Men hewed these with stone adzes from close-grained woods such as 'ōhi'a and 'ahakea. Boards for use by one man were circular or oval in shape and usually less than a

yard in diameter or length. Boards on which a man pounded at each end were rectangular, five or six feet long, about 16 inches wide with the bottom thickness from two to five inches. When in use, usually in a shady spot out-of-doors, the boards were placed on clean *lau hala* mats to prevent dust from getting into the *poi*.

The knobbed pounders (*pōhaku ku'i poi*) were used on all of the islands except Kaua'i. They are shaped somewhat like an inverted mushroom with a flaring convex pounding surface, a central neck or grip and a rounded knob at the top. Pounders were chipped from close-grained basalt and smoothed for ease in handling and in cleaning. They vary in size from small pounders five inches high and weighing two and one-half pounds to large ones over eight inches high and weighing over nine pounds.

■ Kaua'i Poi Pounding Stones

The men of Kaua'i made unique pounders which may have been used by the women more often than by the men to pound or grind taro into *poi*. They are named descriptively as stirrup and ring pounders. The former resembles somewhat in size and shape a rider's stirrup with a concave depression in the center but without the aperture which admits a foot into the stirrup. The ring pounder (*pōhaku ku'i 'ai puka*) is similar to the stirrup form except that the hole extends through the center to form a ring-shaped handle.

■ Wooden Food Containers

The Hawaiian craftsmen made the most attractive wooden bowls ('*umeke lā'au*) in Polynesia. These beautiful containers excelled in form, variety, size and in finish or polish. No surface carving marred the natural growth patterns in the wood. They were the most numerous of all wooden domestic utensils because they were needed to hold the semi-liquid *poi*, other foods and water.

Woods selected to make '*umeke* were determined by their ease in cutting, durability, attractive wood grain and freedom from resins which would impart unpleasant flavors to the food. The largest number of calabashes and those of the greatest size were made from *kou*, a wood admired for its contrasting light and dark tones. Smaller bowls were hewn from the rich-grained *milo* wood which was next in favor to *kou*. *Kamani* wood, a warm rose-brown in color, was made into smaller food bowls and platters. Occasionally 'ōhi'a and coconut wood were carved into food containers.

At the time of Dr. Brigham's study the largest 'umeke kou in Bishop Museum measured 28 and one-half inches in diameter and 19 and one-half inches high. Another was 23 and one-half by 20 inches. (Brigham, 1908, p. 161.) There were 36 'umeke more than 15 inches in diameter and 21 over 10 inches high in the Museum collections (Brigham, 1908, pp. 178-182). A great many of the hand-made bowls studied by Brigham were six to ten inches in diameter and four to seven inches high.

The craftsman in making wooden food vessels, selected a tree of the proper kind and size and felled it with a heavy stone adze. He cut the trunk into blocks and seasoned them for many months in a stream or taro pond. With a sharp adze he first shaped the outside of the vessel, without the use of measuring instruments, into a circular or symmetrical container. Next the worker, with adze and stone chisel, cut the wood from within the bowl. In order to work within the confined space of a tall bowl of small diameter the artisan lashed a length of hard wood directly to the base end of a stone chisel or gouge. This attached handle extended the cutting edge of the tool to the bottom of the bowl. He tapped the tip of the handle with a hammer stone to flake off pieces of wood. A stone

Adze Sharpening: A worker is sharpening a stone adze blade (ko'i) on a grindstone (hoana). Sand and water were added to the stone to hasten the sharpening.

chisel, usually on view in Bishop Museum, with a half-inch cutting edge and a length of 6.8 inches was the kind used without a handle in some types of carving. (Brigham, 1902, p. 91)

■ Shaping the Interior of a Bowl

A special adze (ko'i 'āwili), with the stone blade set in a rotating socket on the wooden handle was also used "axe-like" in confined spaces where a regular adze could not be swung.

In the process of hollowing some bowls kukui oil was rubbed into the core and small pieces of wood burned there until the wood of the bowl charred. The char was removed with a chisel or a coarse sanding stone. The interior surface of a wooden bowl was ground to a final finish with coarse and fine polishing stones to make it perfectly smooth for ease in keeping it clean.

■ Seasoning the Wooden Bowl

The completed container was treated to remove any bitterness remaining in the wood. This was done by soaking the bowl in the sea for several days, drying it, then filling it with taro and sweet potato peelings and salt water to soak for an additional time. This process was repeated, if necessary, until the wood was free from flavors.

■ Bowl Covers

Bowls for holding poi were often fitted with covers to keep out insects and to prevent a crust from forming on the surface of the poi. The easiest to make were covers cut from the bottom of a gourd of the proper size. Circular covers were carved from kou wood with a flange around the inner edge to hold them firmly on the bowls for which they were made. Covers were also used for food plates.

■ Support for the Wooden Bowl

The added thickness and weight of the bottoms of many of the bowls caused them to sit firmly on a mat even though the bottom was slightly rounded. Some families twisted ti leaves or lau hala into a ring and bound them with a cord forming a pō'aha. This was placed on the mat to hold the bowls with rounded bottoms.

■ Repairing Calabashes

Alternate filling with liquids and drying during

years of use caused some wooden bowls to crack. Repairing was so expertly done that patched vessels were considered especially valuable. Some patches were hourglass or wedge-shaped pieces of the same kind of wood as the calabash being repaired. Depressions were cut into the area of the crack and the patches inserted firmly. Some cracks were closed by boring small holes along each side with a bone awl and inserting wooden pegs at a slant. These pegs gave the appearance of lacing the edges together. Breadfruit sap or other vegetable gums were forced while warm into cracks or holes. When hard the gum held the patches in place or actually patched small cracks.

■ **Platters and Trays**

Some of the shallow wooden meat dishes were elongated platters (ke pā lā'au), usually about two feet in length. A few platters were carved with simple supporting runners. Circular plates, from five to 18 inches in diameter, were ordinarily used to hold food for one person.

The most elaborate of the wooden platters and bowls were those supported by human figures. Of the 14 known today four are supported by one figure, eight by two and two bowls are held high each by three human forms. Several of the supporting figures have or have had pearl shell eyes, teeth made from sections of bone or human teeth encircling wide open mouths. One has pegged-in human hair.

> The support figures are informal, suggesting the buffoon, the acrobat, or the playful imp. They exhibit neither noble bearing, pride, nor manifestations of mana. Instead, they are eternally committed to humble work, which they do lightly and with a cooperative and playful spirit. (Cox and Davenport, 1974, p. 51)

The largest carved platter in Bishop Museum is 45½ inches long including the figures at the ends, 10¾ inches wide and 10 inches high. It was said to have been made at the request of the great Maui Chief Kahekili to commemorate his victory over chief Kahahana of O'ahu. The figures supporting his meat platter represent the defeated Kahahana and his wife, Chiefess Kekuapo'i. Kahekili's scorn for the defeated, whom he had portrayed as servants holding his food, was further expressed by having their wide open mouths so placed that he could dip from them pa'akai (salt), 'inamona (kukuinut relish) or limu (seaweed).

■ **Finger Bowls**

Finger bowls (ipu holoi lima), not used elsewhere in Polynesia, testified to the Hawaiians' desire to keep their fingers clean while they were dining. Many of the bowls had a flange projecting upward from the inside of the bowl which permitted food to be scraped from between the fingers while they were being rinsed. Some had a compartment for water and another for fern leaves which were used as napkins.

■ **Dining**

Eating was a time of special pleasure rather than merely taking nourishment, especially for the ali'i. Usually, containers of food were placed on a long narrow mat (pākaukau) on the ground out-of-

Food Service: The fresh banana leaf in front of the chiefess will serve as a place-mat for the bowl of poi which her attendant is receiving from a young man. The platter, supported by runners, holds fish or dog's flesh. The circular wooden bowl is filled with the condiment seaweed and the low tray contains sweet potatoes from the imu. Near the finger-bowl is a freshly-opened drinking coconut supported by a ring twisted from ti leaves. The food vessels are made from kou, milo or kamani which are woods free from unpleasant tasting resins.

doors in good weather or on a floor mat indoors when necessary. Before 1819 the *'ai kapu* required that men, if dining indoors, eat in the *hale mua* and the women in the *hale 'aina*. Except for the *kapu ali'i* who ate from their personal dishes, *poi* was served in bowls and meat and other food in trays, (placed along the mat), which several persons shared.

Men sat at meals cross legged, their knees serving as arm rests and their feet tucked under their legs. Women sat with their knees together and their feet to one side and extending backwards. But one hand was used by both men and women to pick up morsels of food and convey them deliberately to their mouths. *Poi* was eaten with one or two fingers; only the greedy used three. The diner never gave the impression that he must hurry to consume his share of the food. Eating leisurely prolonged the meal and encouraged eating generously, especially among the chiefly class. The *ali'i* might pause for a massage *(lomi)*, then continue the repast. Finger bowls were one of the symbols of elegance in dining.

■ **Scrap Bowls**

Scrap bowls *(ipu 'aina)*, sometimes called spittoons *(ipu kuha)*, were unique to the chiefs of Hawai'i. These circular bowls, usually of *kou* wood, were from five to nine inches in diameter. Some were decorated with human teeth and variously shaped pieces of bone from enemies slain by the chiefs who used the bowls. One vessel was studded with 289 molar teeth; insults to many slain foes.

A chief gave the care of his scrap bowl to a trusted attendant *(kahu)*, usually a close relative, who guarded it continuously as he accompanied his chief. At meals the chief placed discarded scraps, bones and inedible fragments in the bowl. All of these materials *(maunu)* and, in addition, finger nail parings, locks of hair and spittle, could be used by a *kahuna 'anā'anā* to "pray" a chief to death. At the end of each day the attendant disposed of the contents of the bowl by burning, secret burying or by pouring them into the sea.

■ **Gourd Food Bowls**

The planters of Hawai'i grew a greater variety in shape and size and a greater quantity of gourds than did other Polynesians. They gave more care and attention to the vines and developing gourds

Pā'ina: The young chief has taken a bite of *poi* from the larger circular bowl. Meat, such as pork, dog or fish is served in the special platter supported by carved human figures. The small container is his finger-bowl. As the meal progresses other foods and condiments will be brought to the young man by his attendants.

than to any other cultivated crop. The Hawaiian fondness for the semi-liquid *poi* required them to make gourd bowls *('umeke pōhue)* in addition to the wooden food bowls. Gourds served also as light-weight water bottles and containers in which to store and transport food and if of a large size, personal possessions.

The general types of gourds grown were known as bitter, sweet and giant. The flesh of the bitter gourd *(ipu 'awa'awa)* was poisonous although small pieces were added to medicines of mixed herbs. The tough flesh was removed and the rind made into containers.

The pulp of the sweet gourd *(ipu mānalo)* was eaten while still immature. The ripe gourds were dried and made into food vessels for immediate use without the necessity of soaking and scraping to eliminate the unpleasant taste found in the bitter gourds.

The planters developed an extremely large gourd *(ipu nui)*, not known outside Hawai'i, which grew to several feet in diameter. It became extinct after being replaced by foreign food vessels. The *ipu nui* had a hard, durable rind and was often fitted with a lid (po'i) from another gourd of about the same size or by the careful cutting of its own top.

Gourd vines, grown from seeds, flourished in the same sunny areas where sweet potatoes were cultivated. The developing gourds were carefully tended to insure properly shaped fruit. After about six months of growth the gourds were picked, the tops removed and the shell processed for use.

Although gourds grew into a variety of shapes they may be classed as the squat forms which are greater in diameter than in height and the deep gourds which are of greater height than diameter.

Large squat gourds, fitted with lids, were used to store food and such personal possessions as kapa clothing, feather cloaks and capes. These articles were transported in gourds placed in carrying nets and suspended from shoulder poles. Covered gourds were ideal for carrying possessions by water since they floated if a canoe was swamped. Smaller gourds of the squat type were made into bowls and cups for serving food and water.

Hourglass-shaped gourds and those with long, slender necks became water bottles (hue wai). The stem end of these gourds was cut off, the seeds removed, and a cone shell used as a stopper.

■ Pāwehe Patterns on Gourds

Most gourd containers were used in their undecorated form but on Kaua'i, Ni'ihau and occasionally on O'ahu gourds were decorated with attractive geometric patterns ('umeke pāwehe or hue wai pāwehe). A design was incised into the outer skin of the rind and the skin on the area of the intended pattern was scraped off. The gourd was buried in a taro pond, immersed in vegetable dye, or both. In this way the scraped, exposed areas were colored black and the parts remaining covered by the skin retained their natural yellow-brown hue.

■ Twined Baskets

The Hawaiian women surpassed all other Polynesians in making twined baskets from 'ie'ie rootlets. These were so satisfactory that containers were not made from coconut leaves and very few were plaited from lau hala. Color was added by dyeing some of the rootlets black and brown.

Tightly made baskets usually enclosed large elongated gourds to protect them from breaking and to make them easier to carry. Twined baskets

also enclosed elongated wooden bowls. Gourds not enclosed cracked with use. Skillful artisans mended them by boring pairs of holes along the sides of the crack with a bone awl and closing the space with a lacing of olonā cordage.

■ Implements for Preparing Special Foods

The Hawaiian cooks needed the counterparts of the modern chefs' knives, peelers, stirring spoons and strainers.

Vegetable and flesh foods were cut with knives made from stone, shark teeth and bamboo. Few examples remain today since they were discarded after steel tools were introduced.

Pieces of stone with sharp edges, split off by weathering of close-grained basaltic rocks, were the simplest knives. During adze-making thin flat pieces of basalt were flaked off. Sharp pieces that could be held in the hand securely were satisfactory knives.

The serrated teeth of the larger sharks were very sharp and when lashed or pegged onto wooden handles were excellent knives.

The edge of a split piece of mature bamboo is exceedingly sharp. The flesh of hogs and dogs was cut with bamboo knives in preparing it for the imu and in carving the cooked meat.

Cylindrical pestles and dish-like mortars, simple and adequate for pounding various materials, were most frequently used in preparing medicines, dyes and vegetable oils. Among the few used for food preparation were small mullers and stone dishes used to crush roasted kukui nuts to make the relish 'inamona, and to grind rock salt crystals.

Nearly all of the attractive and useful implements and containers for processing and serving food in early Hawai'i have been replaced by articles of foreign make. A variety of hand and power tools have supplanted the simple 'ō'ō, although a few iron ones are in use today. The craftsmen began to use steel tools and power lathes to make great numbers of ornamental bowls from local and introduced woods. Foreign insects destroyed most of the kou trees and also the gourd vines. Machinery in today's poi factories, which grinds the taro, replaces the poi pounders and boards.

■ Cooking Implements and Utensils

The prohibitions of the early times required that the food for men and women be cooked and served separately. The men who prepared the food devised several effective methods of cooking despite the lack of clay or metal for fireproof utensils.

The commonest method of cooking was to steam or bake (kālua) in the ground oven (imu). Two or more men often worked together in preparing food. They dug a hole of suitable size and depth for the amount of food to be cooked. It might be four to eight feet across and one to two feet deep. They used an 'ō'ō to dig the hole and in this imu the workers placed a quantity of small and large pieces of firewood (wahie). They covered the wood with two to three dozen moderately porous lava stones each about the size of a double fist. These imu stones could be heated red hot and would hold the heat for hours.

■ Fire Making

Fire (ahi) for the imu was started by a fire plow which consisted of two pieces of dry wood, usually hau. The larger flat stick ('aunaki) was held in place on the ground or mat by the feet of the fire maker who sat before it. He held firmly in his hands a slender stick ('aulima) which he moved (heahi'a, a contraction of he ahi hi'a) by firm forward strokes over the lower one. This plowing motion produced a groove in the lower stick and caused wood dust (hāhā) to accumulate at the forward end. In about a minute heat from the friction caused the wood to smoke and sparks to appear in the wood dust. The lower stick was then lifted, turned over, and the sparks poured onto the fibers (pulu) of a dry coconut husk, or sometimes on kapa. The sparks burst into flame when the kindling material was blown upon by mouth, with a bamboo blower ('ohe-puhi-ahi), or waved vigorously in the air. The wood in the imu was lighted by fire secured in this way.

■ Placing Food in the Imu

After the imu stones were heated a pole was used to spread them out into a fairly smooth bed. Ti leaves and the moist fibers from a banana trunk were placed directly on the stones to insulate the contents from the intense heat, and to furnish moisture for steaming the food. After the food was in place more leaves were added to cover it and to help retain the heat. Upon this was placed a heavy lau hala mat, plaited especially for this purpose. Discarded mats or those which had served as floor

mats were never used to cover food.

The steamed food was removed after several hours. The time varied with the amount of food being cooked and the number and temperature of the stones.

Pork, fish, and fowls were steamed in calabashes with tight-fitting lids. These were usually heavy wooden bowls made especially for this type of cooking. The vessels were lined with ti leaves. Upon them were placed the flesh foods, taro leaves and perhaps other greens such as tender sweet potato leaves (palula) or pōpolo leaves. Hot stones surrounded the food and water was added as needed to form steam. When small birds were steamed special cylindrical stones ('eho) were heated and placed in their body cavities. After several hours in the closed calabash the food was tender. These "fireless cookers" were sometimes filled and carried on journeys and the food was consumed at the destination.

■ 'Uala or Sweet Potatoes

The root of the sweet potato is second in importance to taro as a staple starch food. Over 200 varieties were known to the Hawaiian planters. This plant can be grown in a variety of localities, it matures in three to six months and requires less work in planting and cultivation than does taro.

Sweet potatoes are eaten after being cooked in the imu. They are mashed and water added to make poi 'uala. The harvested roots may be kept for some time in the storehouse. Or the roots are cooked, placed in loosely woven baskets in the wind and dried.

Raw sweet potatoes are peeled, grated on a rough stone and mixed with coconut cream (wai o ka niu). This mixture is placed in ti-leaf bundles (laulau) and steamed in the imu to make a pudding called piele 'uala.

Sweet potatoes ('uala), cooked and peeled, were placed in a calabash and mashed with special wooden paddles (lā'au ho'owali 'ai) while adding water. This esteemed food was sweet potato poi. When coconut cream was added the dish was kō'elepālau.

The paddles were from one to two feet long with stirring blades from half an inch to two inches wide. Sweet potato poi was eaten with spoons (kī'o'e pālau) since it would not cling to the fingers as does taro poi. The spoons were made from elliptical-shaped sections of coconut shell three to four inches long and two to three and one-half inches wide.

The green leaves at the tips of the vines are steamed in the *imu* and eaten as a green food (*palula*).

Cooked tubers and fresh vines of the *'uala* are fed to pigs (*pua'a*).

■ 'Ulu or Breadfruit

Breadfruit as a starch is of secondary importance since the principal crop ripens from May through September with small numbers at other seasons. The mature fruit is broiled over coals (*pūlehu*) or cooked in the *imu* (*kālua*). It is eaten in this form or may be pounded into *poi 'ulu*. Ripe uncooked fruit is mashed, mixed with coconut cream, wrapped in ti-leaf bundles, and steamed in the *imu* to make the food *pepeie'e 'ulu*. This may be sliced when cold and dried in the sun until an oily film forms. If sunned occasionally to prevent mildew, this food will last from one breadfruit season until the next.

■ Mai'a or Bananas

The fruit of the banana (*hua mai'a*) was eaten raw or cooked according to the variety. The fruit was considered more of a delicacy than a staple starch food. During the times of the eating prohibitions (*'ai kapu*) all but three of the some 50 varieties were forbidden to women. Those not *kapu* to women were:

Iholena (also called *hilahila*). These common, small, thin-skinned bananas have salmon pink flesh which may be eaten raw or cooked.

Pōpō'ulu. The salmon pink flesh may be eaten raw but it is preferred baked.

Kaualau (meaning many raindrops). It is so named because the dark green fruits bear light green spots resembling raindrops. It is eaten only when cooked.

Mai'a kālua are bananas steamed in the *imu* in their skins and eaten hot or cold.

Mai'a pūlehu are bananas roasted in their skins over embers or hot ashes.

Poi mai'a is a *poi* of mashed cooked bananas made and eaten when *poi kalo* was not available. Water was added to thin this form of poi in Hawai'i but coconut cream (*wai o ka niu*) is used in Samoa.

After drinking *'awa* (kava) an unpleasant bitter taste remained in the mouth. Among several condiments (*pūpū*) eaten to remove this taste were sweet bananas.

■ Niu or Coconut

In preparing coconuts for food the husk is removed from the mature nut (*niu*) by forcing it onto the flattened point of a stout stick (*'ō* or *'ōniu*), about a yard long, the base end of which has been driven securely into the ground. The pointed end of a garden pick, which is usually used today to husk a coconut, is not as suitable as the husking stick as it causes the worker to perform his task while stooping almost to the ground.

The husk is pried off the shell in several sections. The husk (*'ili niu*) and the enclosed fibers (*pulu*) are saved for fuel or the *pulu niu* to make sennit (*'aha*).

The husked nut is tapped sharply with a stone in one or more places along its circumference to break it into halves. The coconut water (*wai niu*) is collected in a bowl. In the early days the flesh (*'i'o niu*) was scraped out with an *'opihi* shell or a grater made from a section of a cone shell. Today metal graters, meat grinders or food blenders are used to reduce the meat to fine particles so that the cream (*wai o ka niu*) can be expressed.

The inventive, resourceful Hawaiian men (who were the ones to grate the coconut flesh) would certainly have made a sturdy, effective grating tool if coconut had been an important part of their daily food. (The Samoans and other Pacific Islanders who use coconut regularly fix their grater to a stool for easy, efficient work.)

The grated flesh is mixed with the coconut water which was saved and kneaded with the hands or stirred with a large spoon to release the oil. Hot water is usually added to the gratings today. In earlier days a strainer made from the stems of the *'ahu'awa* sedge was dredged through the liquid to remove the gratings and retain the rich coconut cream. Today the liquid is poured through a cheese cloth or a cotton *poi* strainer to separate the gratings from the cream. The discarded coconut gratings (*oka niu*) are fed to the domestic animals.

■ Coconut Cream Dishes

The dishes prepared from coconut cream were all in the nature of desserts or special foods. This is an example to substantiate the belief that coconut was not a part of the staple everyday foods in the Hawaiian diet. These foods, all types of puddings

Kōʻelepālau - a pudding made of cooked sweet potatoes, peeled and mashed, to which coconut cream is added. The thick mixture was placed in ti-leaf bundles *(laulau)* and steamed in the *imu.*

Haupia - a pudding of coconut cream thickened with arrowroot starch *(pia).* Today sugar is added. Years ago this mixture was placed in a calabash and hot stones added until the pudding was thick. It was also cooked in ti-leaf bundles. A recipe, using today's cooking methods, is given at the end of this unit.

Kūlolo - is made from grated raw taro corms to which coconut cream is added. (Today brown sugar or honey are a modern touch.) The mixture was steamed in the *imu* in ti-leaf bundles for 10 hours or so. Long cooking was necessary because of the raw taro. A recipe for *kūlolo* is given at the end of this unit.

Piʻepiʻe ʻulu - is a pudding made from raw ripe breadfruit and coconut cream. The mixture was placed in ti-leaf bundles and cooked for a short time over hot coals.

Piele is a general name for puddings made from grated yams, crushed ripe bananas or mashed breadfruit mixed with coconut cream and steamed in the *imu.*

When a coconut tree of any age fell or was cut down out of necessity the growing tip was chopped out and eaten raw as the crisp, delicious "heart-of-palm."

■ Two Varieties of Coconuts

Niu hiwa was the coconut used for ceremonial and medicinal purposes and also as a food. The mature husk is dark green and the shell *(iwi niu)* is black *(hiwa)* when ripe.

Niu lelo was used only for food. The mature husk is reddish and the shell is yellow *(lelo)* before ripening to a brown.

■ Stages of Maturity in the Coconut

Niu ʻōʻio, the very young, unripe nut with jelly-like or "spoon-meat flesh." At this stage the shell is soft and white.

Niu haohao, the thin white shell has become firm and the flesh is soft and white.

Niu ʻilikole, called the half-ripe nut. The flabby flesh is eaten with red salt and *poi.* The firm shell has turned dark and the water *(wai niu)* is excellent for drinking. On some Pacific atolls which have no potable water some 3 to 5 nuts in this stage are provided for each person per day. Since the coconut water is sterile and the same density as human body fluids, doctors have used it in transfusions.

Niu oʻo, the flesh of the nut has matured but the husk has not yet dried.

Niu maloʻo, at this stage the husk has dried and the flesh matured. When one shakes the nut he hears water within. This is the best stage for grating the flesh to secure coconut cream and extracting the meat to be sold as copra. The nuts are planted at this point of ripeness.

Niu ʻōkaʻa, an old nut. The water has dried up and the flesh has separated from the shell and shrunk into a ball *(ʻōkaʻa).* Coconut oil *(manoʻi)* may be extracted from the dry meat.

Niu iho, the sprouting coconut with a ball of spongy white pulp within the shell. It is a delicacy, especially if the film that surrounds the sponge (which tastes like soap) is washed off.

■ Uhi or Yam

The vines of this yam grow during the summer, wither down in December, but the tubers in the ground continue to fill out. When new shoots appear at the beginning of the rainy season the tubers are dug. They are cooked in the *imu* and eaten while hot. The flesh is too mealy to make *poi.*

Captain Charles Clerke, in command of the expedition after Cook's death, wrote in his journal in February, 1779 as they were leaving Hawaiʻi that his principal aim was to secure a stock of yams. Niʻihau produced them in great abundance. They are the only roots that will keep on a voyage and are a substitute for bread.

■ Pia or Arrowroot

In the late summer the leaves of the arrowroot plants turn yellow, wither and die down. This indicates that the starch-bearing tubers are ready to harvest.

In earlier times the tubers were dug from the ground with an *ʻōʻō* but today a spade is used. The large tubers, weighing up to 3 or 4 pounds are set aside for food. The smaller ones, marble-size and smaller *(māʻili)* are planted for the next year's crop.

To prepare the starch, wash the tubers and peel off the thin brown skin. Grate them on a coarse stone and place the material in a bowl of fresh water. Grated *pia* is bitter so the water must be

Pia

changed a number of times. The starch and fibers settle to the bottom of a bowl of water so it is easy to pour off the water. Continue this until the starch is no longer bitter. It is possible to pick up handfulls of the starch, squeeze out the moisture and if the bitter flavor has gone one may dry the balls of *pia* in the sun.

When dry the *pia* is a starchy powder. The *haupia* recipe at the end of this unit calls for corn starch. If *pia* is substituted for corn starch the resulting pudding will be delicate, not stiff, and to be eaten with a spoon and not with the fingers.

In earlier days the *haupia* mixture was wrapped in ti-leaves and steamed in the *imu*.

As a medicine the raw starch is stirred in water and drunk as a treatment for diarrhea. It is also mixed with *'alaea* (red clay) and water and taken for dysentery.

■ Kō or Sugar Cane

Sugar cane stalks or stems are carried on journeys and chewed for quick energy. They are also chewed throughout the year by adults and children as one of the few sweet foods. The fibers cleanse the teeth and strengthen the gums.

The rind or skin is peeled from the stalk; the pulp is crushed, and the juice extracted by squeezing with the hands. The juice is fed to babies and used to sweeten such foods as starch and coconut milk pudding *(haupia)* and grated taro and coconut milk pudding *(kūlolo)*.

The juices of certain varieties are thought to have curative properties. Bitter tasting herb remedies are made more palatable with the addition of cane juice.

■ Kī or Ti (Only the green leafed plant.)

No other plant provided leaves which were needed in preparing foods, thatching houses, fishing, sports, clothing, medicine, religious rituals and warding off evil.

Kī refers to the plant and *mole kī* or *kī* to the root. Ti has become the common name. The name *lā'ī* for ti-leaf is a contraction of *lau* (leaf) and *kī*.

Raw foods are wrapped *(laulau)* in *lā'ī* and cooked in the *imu (kālua)* or broiled over coals *(lāwalu)*. Leaves in the *imu* insulate food from the hot stones and impart a flavor. Food is wrapped in *lā'ī* and stored or transported in bundles *(pū'olo)*.

Split dried ti leaves are tied to a net *('upena)* to make a rain cape. They are fashioned into sandals *(kāma'a)* to protect the feet when crossing rough terrain. In some areas dwellings were thatched with ti as were some temple structures dedicated to the god Lono.

Ti, grown in a favorable location for many years, may have a root weighing 200 to 300 pounds. Roots on the ordinary garden ti may weigh 50 to 60 pounds. A favorite confection years ago was *kī* baked in the *imu* for about 24 hours or until it became a sweet, brown, candy-like food.

A famous oven for *kī* root gave the district of Ka-imu-kī its name. Some say the menehune baked *kī* in this oven *(imu)*.

The root is dug, washed and preferably cut into pieces small enough to cook readily. The sugar in ti root is levulose which also occurs in honey and many ripe fruits. (Cane sugar is sucrose.)

Missionary William Ellis wrote of the ti root in 1823:

After baking, it appears like a different substance altogether, being of a yellowish brown colour, soft, though fibrous and saturated with a highly saccharine juice. It is sweet and pleasant to the taste, and much of it is eaten in this state, but the greater part is employed in making an intoxicating liquor (ʻōkolehao) much used by the natives.

Kī is baked today in the kitchen oven. Cut the root into small pieces, bake in a covered dish for 10 to 12 hours at 225 degrees, adding water as necessary to keep it from burning. When eaten in large quantities baked kī acts as a laxative.

Lieut. James Burney and Astronomer William Bayly, while anchored off Kauaʻi in 1779 with the Cook expedition wrote:

> . . . the natives came off with hogs and sweet potatoes in plenty, and a Root that appears like a Rotten Root of a tree, and as large as a man's thigh. It is very much like brown Sugar in tast but Rather Sweeter—the natives call it Tee [ti or kī]. . . . The Natives eat it sometimes Raw and other times Roasted. We made exceeding good Beer, by boiling it in Water, then let it ferment, so as to purge itself. (Beaglehole, p. 573)

After the introduction of the still into Hawaiʻi a liquor, called ʻōkolehao, was distilled from the ti root. The once popular confection of baked kī is rarely seen today.

■ **Domestic Animals as Food**

Puaʻa, Pig or Hog

Although pigs were raised in large numbers they were used chiefly in important feasts (ʻaha-ʻaina) or as offerings in religious ceremonies.

Taboos in eating (ʻai kapu) required that pork be restricted to men and to boys of 10 or 11 years who were old enough to eat in the men's eating house (hale mua).

Pigs to be cooked for food and for ceremonial offerings were killed by strangling. Most of the hair and bristles were singed off by dragging the carcass over rough hot stones. Any remaining hair was removed by scraping the skin with a rough lava stone (pōhaku ʻānai puaʻa).

Small pigs were cooked in the imu. After removing the entrails the body cavities were filled with hot stones, the flesh was salted and the carcass placed on ti or banana leaves which had been laid over the hot stones.

Large hogs were dressed, salted and the body cavity filled with hot stones. The hog was wrapped in coarse kapa and mats which were especially made for and used only for this purpose. (Kapa and mats which have been slept on or walked on were never used for covering food.) The hog was left until the stones had cooled, then the wrappings were removed. The cooked meat on the inside was cut away and eaten. The outer, under-done parts were cut into pieces and placed in the imu for re-cooking.

Pigs were highly prized as gifts to the gods and to humans. When the people took growing things from the forest they observed ceremonies to thank the gods for the bounty which they had received and to free themselves from harm. Pigs were important offerings in these ceremonies.

Canoe builders (kālaiwaʻa) would go into the koa forest (wao koa) and select a tree suitable for a canoe. Before cutting it they killed a pig, then cooked and ate it, along with other appropriate foods, at the base of the chosen tree. After this ceremony they were free to fell the tree, partly hollow the trunk and drag it down to the village for completion.

In a similar fashion the image carvers killed and consumed a pig with special ceremonies before felling and carving an ʻōhia tree into an image for a sacrificial temple (heiau luakini).

Pigs were cooked and offered in large numbers at the dedication of important temples (heiau). The gods which were honored or propitiated at these ceremonies were believed to accept the essence of the pork and, in most cases, the flesh was eaten by the chiefs and priests when the ritual was over. In some instances the animal body was placed on the sacrificial stand (lele) in the heiau and left there until the flesh decayed.

Live or cooked pigs were received by the tax collector in payment for the use of land or as tribute to a chief.

The likeness of the head of a pig was carved from kukui wood and placed on the stone altar (ahupuaʻa) at the time of the Makahiki.

Charles Clerke, Commander of the Cook expedition wrote while off Kauaʻi, February 2, 1779:

> This is the most extraordinary Hog Island we ever met with, take them for Number and size—in the course of this fore Noon my People have purchas'd on board here 70 head weighing upon an average at least a 100 lb apiece. (Beaglehole, p. 575)

Using salt obtained on Kauaʻi, this pork was salted for future use. The next day Clerke wrote:

> The Natives bring onboard so many Hogs we know not what to do with them, so are oblig'd to

give up that trade for the present. (Beaglehole, p. 575)

■ 'Īlio or Dog

Since dogs are now loved as pets and watch dogs, it is difficult for children and some adults to realize that in Hawai'i they were once raised for food.

All ranks of people ate the flesh of dogs, but tenant farmers seldom tasted them as they were taken from them by the chiefs for feasts throughout the year and as annual taxes. Dog flesh was more highly esteemed than pig or chicken.

In preparing a dog for food it was suffocated by binding the mouth and nostrils with a cord or by holding the mouth and nostrils until the animal expired. It was then singed by rubbing the carcass over red-hot stones until most of the hair was burned away. Any remaining hair was rubbed off with a coarse lava stone. After washing, the body cavity was opened and the entrails removed. Hot stones were placed in the cavity, the legs tied together and it was placed on ti or banana leaves in the hot imu and cooked until tender.

A variation in cooking dog was to cut the carcass into pieces, wrap them in bundles (laulau) and cook (kālua) these in the imu. Dog flesh was also placed on a bed of ti leaves in a calabash ('umeke lā'au), hot rocks added, the lid placed firmly on the vessel and the contents cooked (pūholo) until tender.

A special delicacy was fattened puppies which, after killing and cleaning, were flattened out whole and broiled (pālaha) over hot coals.

Roast dogs were appropriate offerings for female dieties and for the mo'o gods and goddesses that dwelled in the water.

■ Moa or Chicken

Of secondary importance was the flesh of the chicken for food. After the chicken was killed and cleaned it was wrapped in ti leaves and steamed in the imu. It had less flavor than the other flesh foods when eaten with poi.

"The eggs are not eaten," said an informant, "because it would be like eating a hen's unborn baby."

The moa of old Hawai'i resembled somewhat those used in cock fights today.

■ Sea Foods and Game Birds

Flesh foods in addition to the domestic animals were:

I'a or fish. Many kinds of fish were eaten both raw and cooked. (See Titcomb, Native Use of Fish in Hawaii.)

He'e or octopus. It is usually referred to as squid in Hawai'i. The fishermen often killed the he'e by biting the head. The flesh was pounded to break the muscle fibers and eaten raw or cooked, or the pounded squid was dried for future use.

'Opae or shrimp and ula or lobsters were caught in season and prized as food. Small shrimp were often salted and dried.

Manu. Wild birds such as the kōlea (plover), nēnē (goose), kioea (curlew), koloa (duck) and other birds were delicacies. All are protected by law now.

Other sea animals such as the 'opihi (limpet), loli (sea cucumber), (kūpe'e (nerita shell), pipipi (small mollusk) and pūpū (the general name for shellfish) were often secured by the women. Those might be eaten raw or cooked.

■ Pa'akai or Salt

Salt of excellent quality was gathered along rocky shores or produced in vessels or ponds by evaporation. The Hawaiians were the only Polynesians to use salt in its crystal form in their diet. The ponds at Hanapēpē, Kaua'i are the best remaining examples which show the method of producing quantities of salt by evaporation.

White salt was used in preparing dry fish and was eaten with certain foods. Meats were salted before cooking; vegetables usually not. The red-brown iron-bearing earth ('alaea), was added to white salt to make pa'akai 'ula'ula, the attractive red salt served at a lū'au. Poi was never salted. Pepper was not grown or used in old Hawai'i.

Commander Charles Clerke wrote of provisions secured at Ni'ihau:

> . . . the Natives supplied us . . . with such Quantities of Salt, that at leaving this Isle I had more on board than when I left England, nearly all of which was expended. (Beaglehole, p. 1322)

David Samwell recorded that salt was packaged in banana sheaths:

> . . . their chief Trade now being Salt, which they have wrapt in large rolls made from the rind of the plantain Tree. (Beaglehole, p. 1157)

Clerke reported at Kaua'i:

... here is likewise plenty of Salt so that an immense quantity of Meat might be purchas'd and cur'd among these islands. Iron is the current cash on our side, if you have plenty of it you may abound in the good things of this Country to what profusion you please. As to the idea of Pork not taking Salt in a Hot Country, that is truly fallacious, we have kept it a twelvemonth and then found it as perfectly free from any kind of putrefaction as on the day it was kill'd. (Beaglehole, p. 575)

■ Summary of the Methods of Cooking Food

Kālua - baking and steaming in the *imu* or ground oven.

Kō'ala - broiling unwrapped food over hot coals.

Kunu - broiling with special care as food prepared for a chief.

Pūlehu - cooking food in embers and hot ashes. Sweet potatoes, breadfruit and bananas were cooked in this manner.

Pālaha - meat is flattened out or spread out and broiled over coals.

Lāwalu - food is wrapped in ti leaves and broiled over coals.

Hākui - is boiling and *pūholo* is steaming food in a closed calabash using hot stones.

(See Titcomb, pp. 24-25, Buck, pp. 17-21 and Wise, pp. 93-96)

■ Feasts in Pre-European Times

Feasts were planned for the enjoyment of the participants, and to seek the fellowship, help or pardon of the gods. *'Aha'aina*, meaning gathering *('aha)* for a meal *('aina)* were usually large feasts commemorating special occasions or honoring certain persons.

Pā'ina, a small party, did not have the significance of an *'aha'aina*.

Lū'au, means young edible taro leaves. It is now used as the name for a feast in which Hawaiian foods, including *lū'au*, are served. The name *lū'au* for a Hawaiian meal and party is believed to date from 1856. (Pukui-Elbert Dictionary, 1971.)

Among the more significant pre-Cook *'aha'aina* are the following:

'Aha'aina kahukahu. A feast honoring a craftsman at the completion of his or her first work, such as a fish-net *('upena)*, wooden bowl *('umeke lā'au)*,

lau hala mat or *kapa*. The appropriate gods and the *'aumakua* were asked to grant greater skill and knowledge to the worker. The object on display was dedicated to the worker's *'aumakua*, never given away, and might eventually be buried with the worker. Although the attention was on the craftsman, some say that his product was dedicated at this feast also.

'Aha'aina ho'ola'a. At this feast, not the craftsman, but the finished product, such as a house, canoe or fish-net, was consecrated or dedicated to the *'aumakua* and the proper gods.

'Aha'aina maka luhi, (feast for the weary-eyed). After the guests had returned home from a large feast the host would provide the food for a party for the many workers who prepared and served the food for the host's guests, but had not had time to eat with them.

'Aha'aina ho'okipa. Feast of welcome *(kipa)*. The family *('ohana)* gathered, welcomed and honored one or more relatives who had returned from long absence. In this feast of welcome wailing chants *(uwē helu)* were an accustomed part of the joyful welcome. This was one of the happiest of the feasts.

'Aha'aina laulima. This feast honored the work of the many hands *(laulima)* which were involved in labor expended in the many phases of raising food. This work entailed clearing land, constructing irrigation ditches *('auwai)*, taro patches *(lo'i kalo)*, and fishponds *(loko i'a)*. Those who harvested the crops also enjoyed the feast which followed the completion of these tasks.

'Aha'aina māwaewae. A feast given shortly after the birth of a first child. Prayers and supplications were voiced to clear the way for this child and all siblings to follow.

'Aha'aina kala hala. Those present at this feast asked for pardon and forgiveness *(kala)* of the gods for their sins *(hala)*.

'Aha'aina 'ūniki. A feast for the graduates from the *hālau hula* (school of the dance) and the *hālau lua* (school of *lua* fighting).

'Aha'aina kahe. A feast given for the boy and his friends at the time of his circumcision (subincision or *kahe*).

'Aha'aina waimaka. A feast of tears *(waimaka)* observed by the *'ohana* on the first anniversary of the death of a family member.

David Malo wrote of a prayer service which was a part of the consecration of a sacrificial *heiau* (*luakini*). Called *kuili,* it was of unusual interest because of the number of baked hogs served to the worshippers. Fortunately for the farmer some years lapsed between the building and dedicating of these important *luakini.*

On the first night 800 hogs were baked for the priests and their men. They ate the pork and continued their prayers until morning.

The *kuili* service continued all day during which time 400 more pigs were baked and served. During the service which continued all night 240 more pigs were baked and eaten.

During the next and last day 400 more baked pigs were served to the priests but not to the chiefs.

A total of 1840 hogs were used in dedicating and freeing the *luakini* from *kapu.*

The following day another feast, with an unspecified number of pigs, was served to celebrate the ceremony of girding a *malo* on the *haku 'ōhi'a* image.

After this feast the high chief offered his gods 400 pigs, 400 bushels of bananas, 400 coconuts, 400 red fish and 400 pieces of *'oloa kapa.* (Malo, 1976, pp. 171-74.)

■ Understandings and Appreciations

1. Much credit should be given to the Polynesian settlers who brought the food plants and animals from the islands to the south and established them in their new home in Hawai'i. The first two or more years must have been "lean" years while the crops were maturing. Compare their problems to those of the Pilgrims (1620-22).

2. Discuss the problems that had to be solved by the Hawaiian people who developed a taste for *poi.* While other Polynesians were content with baked taro the Hawaiians made *poi*

pounders of several types, *poi* pounding boards and a variety of large vessels to hold this semi-liquid food.

3. Discuss the problem of cooking without utensils of metal or clay that could be placed over a fire.

4. Dietitians urge people today to plan their meals to include the foods containing carbohydrates, fats, proteins, vitamins and minerals. Did the Hawaiian diet contain adequate amounts of these?

5. Explain the Hawaiian method of putting the heat inside, not outside the container to cook food.

■ Student Activities

Individual and group activities are almost unlimited in a unit concerning food.

1. List the foods served at a typical *lū'au* at the present time. Check the foods known to be introduced such as *lomi* salmon, cake, soda water, pineapple and others. Then list the foods that might have been served at a *lū'au* before Captain Cook's time.

2. Prepare as a treat for the class whatever Hawaiian foods might be served with the equipment available. Coconuts can be grated in the classroom and *haupia* made in the school cafeteria. If taro can be grated *kūlolo* can be made. (Both recipes are attached.)
    Other simple food projects are:
    a. Adding *'alaea* earth to white rock salt to make red salt; and
    b. pounding and salting roasted *kukui* nuts to make *'inamona.*

3. Construct a diorama showing a Hawaiian household with the family at work preparing for a *lū'au.*

4. Trace the development of the methods of cooking. This would include the early use of open fires, then a variety of stoves using different types of fuels. Many types of cooking utensils were developed. The latest development known at this time is the microwave oven which roasts meats in a comparative short time.

■ Audio-Visual Aids

1. The Kapingamarangi Film, Bishop Museum and perhaps other sources, shows scenes of

preparing taro, breadfruit, coconut and *hala* for food in a natural setting on a Polynesian atoll.

2. From time to time there are free demonstrations of Hawaiian crafts and activities at school or neighborhood fairs. Watch for *poi* pounding and other kinds of food preparation.

3. Bishop Museum: Exhibit of various utensils used in preparing and serving food. A number of food plants grow in the Museum gardens.

4. Visit a *poi* factory, there are just a few left.

5. Take a field trip to the Fish Market to see and perhaps purchase foods at the Hawaiian booths.

6. Visit a wood working shop which specializes in making food dishes.

■ **Vocabulary**

kalo	'inamona	he'e	pa'akai
'ulu	kālua	'īlio	pā, ke pā
'uala	pūlehu	pua'a	'umeke
pia	lāwalu	moa	hue wai
kī	i'a		

■ **Current Happenings of Significance to This Unit**

1. Although many Hawaiian customs have been dropped, the popularity of Hawaiian food has increased. Island families of various ethnic groups celebrate birthdays, weddings, housewarmings and other occasions with a *lū'au*. Several of the Waikīkī hotels and dining spots serve a big *lū'au* each week for the tourists who wish to experience Hawaiian food. *Hula* dancing and singing are perpetuated by the *lū'au*.

2. The *imu* is prepared today much as it was in pre-European times. The men continue to do this form of cooking although the women have the responsibility of the daily food preparations in most Hawaiian homes.

3. A great change in the preparation of Hawaiian food has been the introduction of the *poi* factory where the taro is steamed, peeled, ground, strained and packaged in plastic bags. Despite the saving in labor the cost of *poi* has increased greatly. A few labor saving devices are being developed for growing taro in ponds.

4. The popularity of Hawaiian wooden dishes has increased. Local and introduced woods are used to make bowls, trays and platters, some of traditional Hawaiian designs and others of newly created shapes.

5. Canned *poi, laulau,* and *kūlolo* are shipped to certain fancy food stores on the mainland. *Poi* has been rated an excellent food for babies and invalids by local and mainland doctors. *Poi* would be used more extensively if it could be produced as cheaply as the cereal foods which are its chief competitors.

■ **Evaluation**

1. Use the vocabulary for a test of spelling and of word meaning.

2. If the pupils were permitted to prepare Hawaiian foods, check their skills in this area.

■ **Two Recipes**

HAUPIA

Quantity Recipe	Home Recipe
For each gallon	1 cup coconut cream
of coconut cream use:	1½ Tbsp. sugar
1½ cups of corn starch	1½ Tbsp. corn starch
1½ cups of sugar	Few drops vanilla
2 tsp. vanilla (optional)	(optional)
Makes 35 servings	*Makes 4 servings*

Add a cup of hot water to the grated meat of each mature coconut. Squeeze through a *poi* cloth or cheese cloth to secure the coconut cream.

Boil the coconut cream in a heavy, thick bottomed pot or kettle. An institutional steam kettle, such as those in school kitchens, is excellent. A double boiler is good but very slow. An electric roaster is excellent for cooking *haupia*.

Mix the starch and sugar with some of the coconut cream until the mixture is quite thick. When the coconut cream comes to a rolling boil, add the corn starch sugar mixture, stirring constantly. This should boil for 10 minutes or more. If a candy thermometer is used, the mixture should be heated to 160 degrees F. One indication that the *haupia* is done is that the mixture tends to free itself from the sides of the kettle when stirred. The vanilla is added after the fire has been turned off.

A convenient scheme is to line cardboard candy boxes with wax paper. Pour in the slightly cooled *haupia* and chill. Then place the lid on the boxes. These can be stored in the refrigerator much more easily than pans of various sizes. Cut the chilled *haupia* into squares and serve on a portion of a ti leaf.

CAUTION: Do not use coconut cream that is too rich. Thin with water or milk.

KŪLOLO
Taro-Coconut Pudding

Quantity Recipe	Home Recipe
25 lb. raw taro	2 medium taro
cream from about 20 coconuts	cream from 3 coconuts with the coconut water
4 boxes brown sugar *or* 2 boxs brown sugar and 2 cups of honey	3 Tbsp. brown sugar 2 Tbsp. honey
2 to 6 cups finely grated coconut meat may be added if desired.	½ cup finely grated coconut meat may be added if desired.
Serves 100 persons	*Serves 10 persons*

Quantity Recipe
Cooked in an Imu

Mix the grated taro, sugar, honey and part of the coconut cream. Add more coconut cream as needed until the mixture is as thin as pancake batter. Most people must rely on the proportions in the recipe as this mixture cannot be tasted for sweetness without real danger of the calcium oxalate in the raw taro causing painful itching (*mane'o*) in the mouth and throat. Persons with tender skin may be irritated on the hands and arms by the grated taro also. This mixture is poured into five gallon tins which have been lined with ti leaves. The tins, two-thirds full, are placed in a hot *imu* and baked all night. When removed, the *kūlolo* is cooled, sliced and served on a piece of ti leaf.

Home Recipe
Cooked in an Oven

Mix the finely grated taro, sugar and honey and add coconut cream until mixture is as thin as pancake batter. Do not taste! Place in greased baking pans, cover with ti leaves and aluminum foil and bake in a 325 degree oven for 2½ hours. Cool, slice and serve on a piece of ti leaf.

■ **Reading List**

Abbott, Isabella A., and Eleanor Williamson. *Limu.* An ethnobotanical study of some edible Hawaiian seaweeds. 1974. Lawa'i, Kaua'i: Pacific Tropical Botanical Garden, 1984.

Ahuna, Eleanor. *Hawaiian Shores and Foods.* Hilo: Hilo Printers, 1977. (Describes 15 foods, where found, how to harvest, prepare and serve.)

Allen, O.N., and Ethel K. Allen. *Manufacture of Poi from Taro in Hawaii.* With special emphasis on its fermentation. Hawaii Agricultural Experiment Station Bulletin No. 70. Honolulu: University of Hawaii Press, 1933.

Ball, Stanley C. *Jungle Fowls from Pacific Islands.* Honolulu: Bishop Museum Bulletin No. 108, 1933.

Bazore, Katherine. *Hawaiian and Pacific Foods.* New York: Gramercy Publishing Company, 1971.

Beckwith, Martha W. *Kepelino's Traditions of Hawaii.* 1932. Honolulu: Bishop Museum Bulletin No. 95, 1971.

Bryan, E.H. Jr. *Ancient Hawaiian Life.* 1938. Honolulu: Books About Hawaii, 1950.

Buck, Peter H. *Arts and Crafts of Hawaii.* Honolulu: Bishop Museum Special Publication No. 45, 1957.

Cox, J. Halley, and William H. Davenport. *Hawaiian Sculpture.* Honolulu: University Press of Hawaii, 1974. (Photos and descriptions of food bowls, platters and carrying poles decorated with human figures.)

Daws, Alan G. *The Illustrated Atlas of Hawaii.* Norfolk Island, Aus.: Island Heritage, 1970. (Color illustrations of island fish, fruits and vegetables.)

Degener, Otto. *Ferns and Flowering Plants of Hawaii National Park.* Honolulu: Honolulu Star-Bulletin, Ltd., 1930.

Edmondson, Charles H. "Animal Life." Ch. 27 in *Ancient Hawaiian Civilization.* A series of lectures delivered at Kamehameha Schools by E.S.C. Handy [and others]. 1933. Rutland, VT and Japan: C.E. Tuttle, 1965 (rev. ed.).

Fortner, Heather J. *The Limu Eater: A Cookbook of Hawaiian Seaweed.* Honolulu: Sea Grant Program, University of Hawaii, 1979. (Sketches and descriptions useful in identifying edible *limu*. A variety of recipes using *limu*.)

Handy, E.S.C. *The Hawaiian Planter.* Vol. I. Honolulu: Bishop Museum Bulletin No. 161, 1940.

Handy, E.S.C., Elizabeth G. Handy, and Mary K. Pukui. *Native Planters in Old Hawaii: Their Life, Lore and Environment.* Honolulu: Bishop Museum Bulletin No. 233, 1972.

Handy, E.S.C., and Mary K. Pukui. *The Polynesian Family System in Ka'u.* 1958. Rutland, VT and Japan: C.E. Tuttle, 1972.

Judd, Albert F. "Trees and Plants." Ch. 26 in *Ancient Hawaiian Civilization.* A series of lectures delivered at the Kamehameha Schools by E.S.C. Handy [and others]. 1933. Rutland, VT and Japan: C.E. Tuttle, 1965 (rev. ed.).

Kamakau, Samuel M. *The Works of the People of Old.* Honolulu: Bishop Museum Special Publication No. 61, 1976. (Articles on how fire was obtained, on food plants and on fish.)

Kennedy, Joseph, ed. "Ho'okupu Kalo (The gift of kalo)." *Native Planters,* 1982. I(1).

Kramer, Raymond J. *Hawaiian Land Mammals.* Rutland, VT and Japan: C.E. Tuttle, 1971. (Information on 23 species of native and introduced land mammals.)

Magruder, William H., and Jeffrey W. Hunt. *Seaweeds of Hawaii.* A photographic identification guide. Honolulu: Oriental Publishing Company, 1979.

Malo, David. *Hawaiian Antiquities.* 1898. Honolulu: Bishop Museum Special Publication No. 2, 1976.

Miller, Carey D. *Food Values of Poi, Taro and Limu.* Honolulu: Bishop Museum Bulletin No. 37, 1927.

———. *Food Values of Breadfruit, Taro Leaves, Coconut and Sugar Cane.* Honolulu: Bishop Museum Bulletin No. 64, 1929.

Miller, Carey D., Katherine Bazore, and Mary Bartow. *Fruits of Hawaii.* 4th ed. Honolulu: University Press of Hawaii, 1976.

Mitchell, Donald D. Kilolani. *Hawaiian Treasures.* Food and drink, 88-100. Honolulu: Kamehameha Schools Press, 1978.

Murai, Mary, Florence Pen, and Carey D. Miller. *Some Tropical South Pacific Island Foods.* Honolulu: University of Hawaii Press, 1958.

Na Lima Kokua. *Breadfruit (Ulu),* uses and recipes, 1976; *Taro (Kalo),* uses and recipes, 1977; *Coconut (Niu),* uses and recipes, 1980; *Sweet Potato ('Uala),* uses and recipes, 1983. Lawa'i, Kaua'i: Pacific Tropical Botanical Garden.

Neal, Marie C. *In Gardens of Hawaii.* 1948. Honolulu: Bishop Museum Special Publication No. 50, 1965 (rev. ed.).

Pukui, Mary K. "Poi Making." In *Polynesian Culture History.* Essays in honor of Kenneth P. Emory. Honolulu: Bishop Museum Special Publication No. 56, 1967.

Thrum, Thomas G. "Hawaiian Salt Making." *Hawaiian Annual for 1924.* Honolulu: Thrum's Hawaiian Annual.

Tinker, Spencer. *Animals of Hawaii.* Honolulu: Tongg Publishing Company, 1941. (See "The Hawaiian Dog," p. 86, and "The Pig," p. 118.)

Titcomb, Margaret. *Dog and Man in the Ancient Pacific.* With special attention to Hawaii. Honolulu: Bishop Museum Special Publication No. 59, 1969.

———. *Native use of Fish in Hawaii.* Honolulu: University Press of Hawaii, 1972 (reprint).

———. *Native Use of Marine Invertebrates in Old Hawaii.* Honolulu: University Press of Hawaii, 1979.

Tomich, P. Quentin. *Mammals in Hawaii.* Honolulu: Bishop Museum Special Publication No. 57, 1969.

Wang, Jaw-Kai, ed. *A Review of Colocasia esculenta and Its Potentials.* Honolulu: University of Hawaii Press, 1983. (Twenty investigators present in-depth studies of taro.)

Whitney, Leo D., F.A.I. Bowers, and M. Takahashi. *Taro Varieties in Hawaii.* Honolulu: Hawaii Agricultural Experiment Station Bulletin No. 85, University of Hawaii, 1939.

Wise, John H. "Food and Its Preparation." Ch. 8 in *Ancient Hawaiian Civilization.* A series of lectures delivered at the Kamehameha Schools by E.S.C. Handy [and others]. 1933. Rutland, VT and Japan: C.E. Tuttle, 1965 (rev. ed.).

UNIT 11:
Fish and
Fishing

FISH AND FISHING

The fishermen of old relied on their knowledge, skills and experience to help them secure the fish and other protein foods from the sea. They shared these foods with their 'ohana and members of the community.

The head fisherman (lawai'a po'o), and other successful fishermen were descended, in most cases, from a long line of fisherfolk. These men were in the possesssion of knowledge and secrets which had been handed down from those who made this form of food-getting their life work.

The equipment and the daily activities of the planter and the fisherman, both providers of food, are in interesting contrast.

The planter was in intimate contact with the soil. He could see, feel and manipulate the fertile earth. With his simple digging stick ('ō'ō), his knowledge, experience and diligence, he was able to provide quantities of food from his plants. He also fed and cared for his domestic animals which he kept near his house. He watched them mature into food animals for his use.

There were elements of the unknown and unpredictable in the activities of the fisherman. His domain usually extended from the shore seaward to the horizon. Sometimes he fished so far from land that he could see but the tops of the mountains of his home island.

Even with the aid of the film of kukui oil which he spat upon the surface of the water his vision into the ocean depths was limited. There was also a limit to the distance to which he could or should dive.

The fisherman's challenge was to catch a considerable number and variety of fish, which he had had no part in propagating. These fish, which travel singly or in schools, might or might not swim into his fishing grounds.

Despite these seeming uncertainties the fisher-men were eminently successful. Working singly or in groups they acquired, often by barter, one or more koa outrigger canoes (wa'a kaukahi) and olonā nets and lines of varying sizes from those craftsmen who worked with materials secured in the mountains.

By their own skills or by exchange they made or acquired fishhooks of a considerable number of sizes and designs. These were made from the bones of humans, dogs and birds. Some hooks were of pearl shell, whale ivory, bone and of wood. Many were one-piece hooks, the bonito hook was of two parts, and the squid lure consisted of five parts including the hackle or tail of ti leaves. These will be discussed later in this unit.

It is understandable that fishing was called the most varied and elaborate means of food getting in Hawai'i.

■　Methods of Fishing
1. Catching fish by hand.
Men and women reached under rocks and in holes to catch certain small fish, crayfish, loli and eels. A floating calabash or a net bag was tied to the waist by a line to hold the catch.

2. Spearing Fish.
Typical spears (kao) were slender hardwood poles 6 or 7 feet long with a single sharp point. Fishermen speared fish while swimming underwater, in shallow places as they walked along the reef, and by the light of kukui nut torches at night. (Buck, p. 288; Bryan, p. 15)

3. Fishing with a slip noose.
According to accounts from earlier days sharks were fed, stupified with 'awa, then caught with a slip noose and towed to shore alongside a canoe. (Buck, p. 289)

Fresh water shrimp ('ōpae) were snared by

patient, skillful men and women with a noose formed on the thread-like end of a coconut leaf midrib (ni'au).

4. Net fishing with gill nets ('upena ku'u).

A gill net with mesh (maka) as large as 2 to 2½ inches was set across a "fish run" or placed around a school of fish. The fish were removed by hand after they became enmeshed in the net. (Buck, pp. 296-97)

5. Fishing with seine nets ('upena pāloa).

These seines, 150 to 900 feet long, were made with a head or top rope studded with wooden floats and a foot or bottom rope containing stone sinkers. A favorite method of using the seine was to surround a school of fish on a sandy-bottomed fishing ground. The fishermen in the canoes set the net under the direction of a kilo or lookout in the prow of the canoe (Buck, p. 298) or by the kilo who stood on a promontory on shore high above the fishing area (Titcomb, 1972 pp. 5-6). These nets are used for the present day hukilau fishing.

6. Fishing with scoop nets.

(The Hawaiian name of the net designated the type of fish to be caught: 'upena pāo'o for rock fish or 'upena 'ōpae for shrimp.) A pliable wooden rod was bent into an oval with the two ends coming together to form a handle. A fine meshed net (nae) was fastened to the wooden loop and used by women to catch small fish and shrimp. Two parallel rods were joined at the tip end then pulled apart at the other end to form a triangular two-handed scoop net. (Buck, pp. 299-304)

7. Fishing with dip nets.

'Upena pāpa'i for crabs or 'upena uhu for uhu or parrot fish). Flexible rods supported a square or rectangular net which was dipped into the water with a piece of bait to attract crabs. Or a live uhu was tied through the gill and mouth by a cord which allowed it to swim naturally within the net. The fish served as a decoy and attracted other uhu into the net. (Buck, pp. 304-06)

8. Bag nets contain a bag or enclosure into which the fish were driven. These large nets with small mesh were used to catch flying fish (mālolo); 'ōhua, a small, highly prized fish; sharks, and many other fish that swam or were driven into them. (Buck, pp. 306-312)

For detailed information on net making, netting twine (olonā, hau, wauke, 'ahu'awa), gauges (haha),

needles (hi'a), menders (kī'o'e), and floats (pīkoi), see Buck, pp. 289-298.

9. Fishing with traps (hīna'i made of native fibers).

Traps, used in both fresh and salt water, were usually made of the aerial rootlets of the 'ie'ie vine.

Low circular traps were basket-like with an entrance on top. A stone sinker held the trap in place and bait such as crushed shrimp, crabs, wana, or sweet potatoes attracted the fish into the funnel-like opening.

Long cylindrical traps were set without bait in fresh water streams. The 'o'opu swam into the trap which was then lifted from the water, usually by women.

Funnel-shaped traps were used by women to catch shrimp in fresh water streams. The Museum has 22 traps of these three types, a reminder of the ingenuity of the Hawaiian fishermen of years ago. (Buck, pp. 312-323)

10. Fishing with fish hook and line.

For the latest classification and photographs of fishhooks see Emory, Fishhooks, pp. 7-13. An earlier classification with descriptions and sketches is used by Buck, pp. 324-342.

Simple one-piece fishhooks were made from pearl shell (uhi), human bone (makau iwi kanaka), dog bone (makau iwi 'īlio), dog teeth (niho 'īlio), bird bone (makau iwi manu), whale ivory (palaoa), whale bone (makau iwi koholā), turtle shell (makau 'ea), and occasionally wood. These hooks were barbless (kaiānoa), with an inside barb (kohe), an outside barb (hulu), an inside and outside barb (hui kala) or with two barbs (hululua). Eel hooks (maka pūhi) had two opposite barbs.

Two piece hooks were made from wood with bone points or two pieces of bone lashed together.

Composite fishhooks such as the bonito (aku) lure have a pearl shell shank (pā) with a bone point (lālā) and a tuft of pig bristles. The octopus (called squid in Hawai'i) lure hooks (makau lūhe'e) were made with a stone sinker (pōhaku lūhe'e), one or two cowrie shells (leho), a connecting stick, and a bone or wooden point (lālā) partly concealed by wisps of ti leaves.

Many kinds of fish were caught with the hook and line. Fishlines, as well as most of the nets, were made from the strong cordage fashioned from the inner bark of the olonā. (Kamakau, Thrum's Annual for 1919, pp. 69-74, Kamakau, 1976, pp. 44-45, 52-55.)

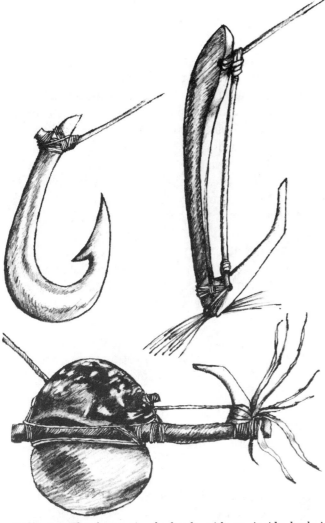

Fishhooks: The large simple hook with an inside barb is probably of whalebone. Smaller hooks of this type may be made of whale ivory or human bone.

A feature of the bonito or *aku* hook is its shank *(pā hīaku)* of pearl oyster shell. This flat, colorful part resembles a small food fish as it skips along the waves among the *aku* in a school. The point or hook is of bone, the hackle of black or white pig bristles and the ties and lines of *olonā*.

Cowrie squid lures *(leho heʻe)* were lowered by a line over the side of the canoe to attract and hook squid which feed upon the flesh of the cowrie *(leho)*. A cowrie shell and a stone sinker are tied to a wooden rod to which a hook is firmly lashed. A hackle or tail of ti leaves helps to hide the hook.

A good example of pole and line fishing is that of *aku* or bonito trolling, a popular sport with the chiefs as well as a means of securing food. The fishermen paddled their canoes beyond the reef and located schools of *aku* by watching for flocks of sea birds, particularly the *noio* or terns, which were feeding on small fish driven to the surface by the *aku*. Bait fish, *nehu,* were thrown to the *aku* as the canoes were paddled swiftly into the school.

The fishermen trolled the pearl-shell lure with an unbarbed hook which was attached to a stout fishing pole by a short line. The *aku* took the hook, were pulled into the canoe quickly and released. The hook was returned again and again as long as the canoe moved with the school of fish.

11. Throw net.

The throw net, a favorite of some fishermen and of local photographers, is said to have been introduced from Japan about 1890. (Bryan, p. 15)

12. Hola method of stupefying fish.

ʻAuhuhu and ʻākia are two native plants with narcotic juices. The pounded twigs and bark of one or the other were placed in tidal pools to stupefy fish and cause them to float or die. They were gathered into baskets and taken home. Fish obtained in this way were suitable for eating raw or cooked. (Bryan, 1933, pp. 104-107.)

■ **Properties and accessories needed by fishermen.**

In addition to the fishing apparatus discussed here the fishermen needed:

(1) Well made canoes with trained paddlers.

(2) Gourds or calabashes with close-fitting lids to transport the fishing implements. These would float if the canoe capsized. Gourds with stoppers were used for fresh drinking water. (Buck, pp. 346-351 and pp. 55-66.)

(3) Bait consisted of small fish and shrimp placed whole on hooks; live bait such as *nehu* to attract and excite the *aku; palu* or fish ground or mashed into soft bait for attracting fish; and squid liver bait *(pilipili heʻe)*. Heavy bait sticks *(lāʻau melomelo)* were smeared with bait and lowered into the water to attract fish. (Buck, pp. 351-356)

■ **Kapu and conservation of fish.**

Kapu protected the fish and other sea life during the spawning season. Malo, page 209, states that *ʻōpelu* were eaten during the summer while *aku* were *kapu,* then *aku* were used for food during the winter while *ʻōpelu* were *kapu.* Reports from writers of earlier times indicate that most kinds of fish were much more abundant then than now.

■   As in other phases of life, religion played an important part in fishing. Kūʻula or Kūʻulakai was a highly successful fisherman who lived at Alea-

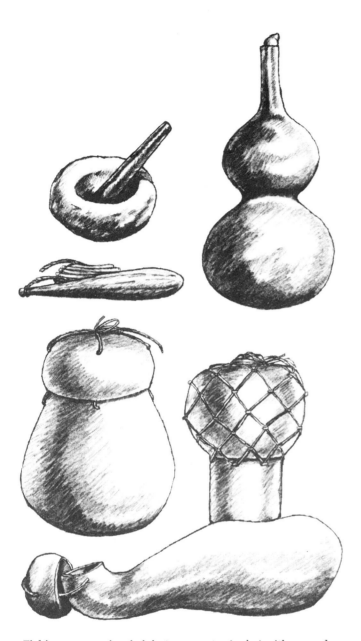

mai in the Hāna district of Maui many years ago. He is credited with building the first fishpond. His son 'Ai'ai, also a devoted fisherman, went about the islands building *kū'ula* and establishing fishing stations *(ko'a)* at favorable places in the sea where an abundance of fish might be caught. Fishermen were taught to locate the *ko'a* in the sea by taking sites on large or prominent objects on the shore.

In time Kū'ula, long after his death, became the principal god or *'aumakua* of fishermen. The name *kū'ula* refers to the god, and to carved or natural stone, whose functions were (or are) to attract fish and to cause fish to multiply. Large *kū'ula* were set up on promontories along the sea shores, or near streams and ponds. Small *kū'ula* were carried to sea in the fishing canoes to attract fish.

Fishermens' Shrine: A flat stone surrounded by pieces of water-worn coral provides a *kū'ula* for the fishermen to offer to their gods the first fish of the day's catch.

Fishing accessories: (a.) A stone mortar *(poho)* with a wooden pestle *(lā'au ku'i palu)* was used for grinding bait as small pieces of fish, ink sacs of squid *('ala'ala he'e)* and roasted coconut and kukui nuts.

(b.) Hour-glass shaped gourds *(hue wai pueo)* were suitable for carrying water. Fiber nets were knotted around the larger ones for ease in carrying and in hanging. A conical shell formed the stopper.

(c) Heavy wooden sticks *(lā'au melomelo)* were smeared with bait and lowered into the sea by a cord. Fish which were attracted to the bait were caught in a net.

(d) The elongated gourd at the bottom of the sketch is a water container with a coconut shell cover. The remaining containers, if small *(ipu lē'i)* would be used for carrying or storing fishhooks. If large *(poho aho)* they would be for fish lines. The one on the left was made from two gourds, the other has a wooden base with a gourd cover enclosed in a net *(kōkō)*. These gourds would float and the contents be saved should the fishing canoe overturn.

The larger, permanently located *kū'ula* were set in circular enclosures, nearly always built of limestone or coral. The altar, a platform of stone placed before *kū'ula*, and on which the offerings were placed, was called the *ko'a*. *(Ko'a* were also placed on bird islands to cause the birds to multiply.)

Within the enclosure of the large shrine, sometimes called a *heiau ko'a,* an *imu* was kept. Here pigs were cooked and eaten, along with other feast foods, as part of the ceremony of dedicating a new fishnet. Also within the area was a *lele* altar where bananas were offered. These may be a tribute to Kanaloa who is associated with bananas. (These fruit were never carried to sea by fishermen.)

The customs seem to have differed among the fishermen as to the number of fish that would be left on the fishing shrine when they returned from a successful catch. This is understandable since the fishermen prayed to and respected their own family 'aumakua as well as Kū'ula.

Upon returning from the sea some fishermen went to the ko'a with two fish in their right hand for the male 'aumākua and two in their left hand for the female 'aumākua. They addressed the gods and placed the fish on the altar. After the gods had received the "essence" (aka) of the offering the fishermen were free to take the fish away and add them to the catch for distribution and use. (Kamakakau, 1976, p. 64)

Maunupau wrote that the first fish caught was marked by cutting off its tail. It was placed in the bow of the canoe and was kapu. When ashore the fisherman placed this fish on the kū'ula for his 'aumakua.

Concerning offerings to the great god, Kānenuiākea, Kamakau wrote (1964, p. 63) that men made sacrifices and offerings of the first things that they obtained. This included the first-born of their animals, the first fruits of the earth and the first fishes caught. The god was pleased with the offerings of men.

■ Fishing knowledge.

The vast knowledge known to the expert fishermen was handed down from the informed and experienced elders to the interested youths. The head fisherman (po'o lawai'a) knew a great deal about the gods, the weather, the stars, the fish, fishing implements, canoes, birds and his fellow fishermen. (Titcomb, 1972, p. 5; Maunupau, pp. 101-107; Bryan, p. 17)

■ Fishponds

The early Hawaiians built a greater number and a larger variety of fishponds than did any other Pacific islanders. Their cultivation of food animals and plants in ponds was true aquaculture. About the year 1800 there were some 300 royal fish ponds producing food for the chiefs and kāhuna.

Loko was any type of a pond. Kuapā or pā was the man-made wall which enclosed the pond or separated it from the waters of the sea or a stream. Makahā were the sluice gates through which water (and perhaps small fish and nutritive sediments) flowed into the pond from the sea or stream, and out again, usually according to the tides. Hale kia'i was the guard house on the wall, usually near the makahā. The keeper of the pond who spent some of his time in the guard house was the kia'i loko. Waihau, 'aoa and ko'a were types of shrines, usually of stones and coral, built near the ponds and used in ceremonies to cause the fish to multiply or to express thanks for fish taken from the pond. 'Aoa were built near royal ponds. (Apple and Kikuchi, 1975). Waihau is also the name of an agricultural heiau. Menehune were the mythical dwarfs who were credited with building the walls (kuapā) of ponds which were so ancient that the actual builders had been forgotten.

Most of the large fishponds are believed to have been royal ponds. They were built for the high chiefs by their subjects and managed by keepers appointed by them. The products of the ponds were enjoyed by the high chiefs and priests (kāhuna). Since the chiefly needs were satisfied, in part, by the ponds, the general populace had greater use of the fish taken from the sea.

The chiefs controlled some small ponds and also small plots of land, both called kō'ele or hakuone. These royal ponds and royal gardens were tended by subjects appointed by the chiefs.

Apple and Kikuchi, in their study "Ancient Hawaii Shore Fishponds," give a list of the fish and other sea life raised in the fish ponds. Numbers 1 and 2 were said to be extremely sacred in Hawaiian culture. Numbers 3 and 4 were most frequently stocked in the ponds. The openings in the makahā and porous nature of the rock walls allowed some aquatic life to come into the ponds that might not have been the choice of the owners or keepers.

■ Aquatic Life in Fishponds

1. Ulua, called pāpio when young.
2. Āhole, called āholehole when young.
3. 'Ama'ama, mullet called 'anae when 1 foot long.
4. Awa, milkfish
5. Kākū, barracuda
6. Nehu, anchovy
7. 'O'opu, goby fish
8. Puhi, eel
9. Kamanu, amberfish
10. Kāhala, amberjack
11. Kūmū, goat fish
12. Kala, surgeonfish
13. Manini, reef surgeonfish
14. Palani, surgeonfish
15. pualu, surgeonfish
16. Uhu, parrotfish
17. 'Ō'io, bonefish

Loko I'a, a shoreline fishpond: He'eia fishpond on Kāne'ohe Bay is enclosed by a wall some 5,000 feet long and covers 88 acres. The Ko'olau Mountains are in the background and Kealohi Point extends into the Bay.

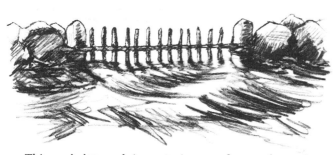

This *makahā* or sluice gate is one of several openings through the walls of the pond. The spaces between the sturdy wooden poles allow water, nutrients and small fish to pass in and out of the pond.

18. *Honu*, turtles, lived in ponds built especially for them. Pāhonu, Waimānalo, is an offshore turtle pond, 500 feet long and 50 feet wide, and visible at low tide. *Honu* or green turtles were kept here for the chiefs.

19. *'Opae*, shrimp, especially the transparent *'opaehuna* and the spiked *'opaekākala* would thrive in ponds. Among the crabs, *pāpa'i* and *'alamihi* are pond dwellers.

20. *Pupu* (mollusks). The bivalves, oysters and clams (*'olepe*) lived in the mud on the bottom. Univalve shellfish, which lived on the rock walls, were *'opihi, pipipi* and *kūpe'e*.

21. In addition to the pond algae (*limu*) eaten by the fish, Apple and Kikuchi name *limukalawai, limu'īlio* and *hulu'īlio* as pond seaweeds eaten by man.

22. *Lepo'aii'a* is the name of an edible mud found in the fishpond Kawainui, Kailua, O'ahu.

Fish confined in the ponds thrived in water 2 to 3 feet deep. Sunlight could penetrate water of this depth and promote the growth of algae on the bottom which was food for the plant-eating fish. Carnivorous fish ate smaller ones in the pond.

■ Apple and Kikuchi recommended 56 fishponds on the seven major islands in 1975 that should qualify for nomination to the National Register of Historic Places and they suggest that these ponds be restored as working fishponds. See their text for photographs of the fishponds and pages 136-148 for maps of the islands giving the location of the ponds.

The highest rated ponds for each island are given in order of preference:

Hawai'i

1. Lahuipua'a, Kalahuipua'a, Kohala
Private pond of some 10 acres with five associated ponds connected to it. Owned and maintained by *ali'i* continuously through 1974.

2. Kahapapa, 'Anaeho'omalu, Kona
Private pond of some 7 acres. Connected to the larger Ku'uali'i pond.

3. 'Aiopi'o, Honokōhau, Kona
Private pond of some 2 acres.

Eleven additional Big Island ponds are pictured and described in this study.

Maui

1. Lokonui, Hāna
Private pond of some 11 acres. Kamehameha I rebuilt the pond. It was inundated by the 1946 tsunami.

2. Lokoiki, Hāna
Private pond of some 2 acres. Inundated by the 1946 tsunami.

No additional ponds are listed for Maui.

O'ahu

1. Mōli'i on the border of *Hakipu'u* and *Kualoa ahupua'a, Ko'olaupoko*
Owned by City and County of Honolulu, some 124 acres. Wall is 4,000 feet long, 3 *makahā*.

2. Kalouwai, Waiale'e, Ko'olauloa
Owned by the State of Hawai'i, about one acre.

3. He'eia'uli, He'eia, Ko'olaupoko
Owned by the State of Hawai'i, some 88 acres. Wall 5,000 feet long, 12 feet wide, 5 *makahā*.

Ten additional O'ahu ponds are pictured and described in this study.

Kaua'i

1. Nōmilu, Kalāheokai
Private pond of some 4 acres. The *mo'o* was named Nōmilu.

2. 'Alekoko, Nāwiliwili
Private pond of some 32 acres, built by *menehune*. Guardian named Puhiula, shark *'aumakua* named 'Alekoko.

3. Kānoa, Hanalei
Private pond of some 4 acres.

Four additional ponds are pictured and described for Kaua'i.

Moloka'i

1. Kaina'ohe, Ka'amola
Private pond of some 17 acres. Coral wall 1770 feet long, 5 feet high, 2 *makahā*.

2. 'Ualapu'e, 'Ualapu'e
Owned by the State of Hawai'i, some 22 acres, coral wall, basalt fill, 1575 feet long, 8 to 19 feet wide, 4 feet high, 2 *makahā*.

3. Kaloko'eli, Kamiloloa
Owned by the State of Hawai'i, some 28 acres. Wall was 2800 feet long, 2 *makahā*.

Fifteen additional Moloka'i ponds are pictured and described in this study.

Lāna'i

On Lāna'i one pond without a recorded name is listed for Lopā, Kaohai. It is one acre is size, privately owned.

Ni'ihau

On Ni'ihau a nameless private pond of some 371 acres is located at Halulu Lake.

Kaho'olawe

We have no listing of ponds for Kaho'olawe.

■ Kinds of food from the sea

The people gathered and ate nearly all of the kinds of sea creatures that were suitable for human food. Some were eaten raw, others cooked or salted and dried. Some were given greater preference as food as they were more palatable than others.

A brief review, listed here beginning with the lower orders, will show how varied the sea food proved to be.

1. Mollusks - *pūpū*
a. Gastropods - with one shell. Fresh water forms were *hīhīwai* or *wī*; marine forms were *'opihi, pipipi, kūpe'e, leho, pū* and others.
b. Pelecypods - with two shells. *'ōlepe*, clams and oysters of a number of kinds.
c. Cephalopods - Squid and octopus. *He'e*, octopus and *mūhe'e*, squid.
2. Crustaceans, fresh water and marine.
'Ōpae or shrimp, 15 or more kinds.
Ula or lobsters, 9 or so kinds.
Pāpa'i or crabs, 60 or more kinds.
3. Echinoids - sea urchins.
'Ina, small, spiny urchins of several kinds.
Wana, large urchins with long poisonous spines.
Hāwa'e, pincushion urchins.
Hā'uke'uke, short flattened spines or slate-pencil spines.
4. Holothuroids, sea cucumbers.
Loli, several kinds, some edible.

For more information on these see Titcomb, 1979.

The highest animals, in order of development, which interested the fishermen were the many species of fish including the more primitive sharks and rays. Next were the turtles, and finally the marine mammals, the dolphins and whales. These animals are far too numerous to list here. We refer our readers to the books named in the Reading List at the end of this unit. See Daws, 1970; Gosline and Brock, 1960; Titcomb, 1972 and Tinker, 1973 and 1978.

■ Sea Foods Kapu to Women Before 1819

The *'ai kapu* which forbade, under penalty of death, certain foods to women included sea foods as well as the oft-quoted items - pork, bananas, and coconuts.

The chiefs and the priests had reasons for declaring certain foods *kapu*. The following are some of the sea foods *kapu* to women and the reasons for declaring them so if it is known.

Kūmū, a goatfish. It was one of the "sea pigs." This fish was the usual offering to the gods when the priests ask for a red fish. It was *kapu* to women because of its red color which suggested the menstrual period.

Moano, a goatfish. The old folks believed that this fish was red in color from eating *lehua* blossoms. No reason has been recorded of its *kapu* status except, like the *kūmū,* it is red in color.

Pualu, a surgeon fish. Has strong disagreeable smell like the *palani* fish. No recorded reason for it being *kapu.*

Ulua, a highly prized food fish. This fish was offered to the god Kū in his war ritual as a substitute for a human victim. Since an *ulua* replaces a man, the word means "man" or "sweetheart" in love songs.

Niuhi, the man-eating shark. It was the symbol of a high chief or a powerful warrior.

Hihimanu or *hāhālua,* the sting ray or manta ray is also called *lupe* or kite. *Kapu* because it is probably a form of the sea god Kanaloa. In the old days the flesh was rarely if ever used for food.

Nai'a or *Nu'ao,* the porpoise. *Kapu* as a form of Kanaloa.

Honu and *'ea,* sea turtles. *Kapu* as a form of Kanaloa. There were no land turtles in old Hawai'i.

Koholā or *palaoa,* whales. Although the terms interchange, *koholā* means whale and *palaoa* usually refers to the teeth, which from the sperm whale were used for the chiefly pendants *(lei palaoa)* and for fish hooks *(makau palaoa).* Flesh rarely eaten but *kapu* to women because of its being a form of Kanaloa.

■ Special Fish for the Chiefs

In earlier years certain chiefs developed tastes for fish that grew only in special ponds. Often these waters were far from the dwelling place of the chiefs. Runners *(kūkini)* who were trained to carry messages were, at times, instructed to bring fish to their chief. Here are three stories about the runners:

Mākoko was a celebrated runner of Kamehameha I on Hawai'i. He could carry a fish from the pond at Waiākea in Hilo and reach Kailua, Kona while it was still alive. The distance is a little over 100 miles.

Kaohele, son of Kumukoa, a ruler of Moloka'i who was a contemporary with Alapa'i nui of Hawai'i, was a celebrated *kūkini* or runner. He could run from Kalua'aha as far as Hālawa and return before a fish put on a fire at the time of his starting had time to be roasted.

Uluanui of O'ahu, a rival and friend of Kaohele, was a celebrated runner. He could carry a fish from Ka'elepulu pond, (now called Enchanted Lake) in Kailua around O'ahu by way of Waialua and bring it to Waikīkī while it was still alive and wriggling.

N.B. Emerson, author of the notes in Malo's "Hawaiian Antiquities," recorded these stories and then suggested that they are "impossible." They do remind us that the *kūkini* were trained to run long distances quite speedily.

■ Captain Cook and Officers Experience Hawaiian Fish

On the historic day, Monday, January 19, 1778, when Cook's ships became the first known foreign vessels to arrive at Kaua'i, the captain recorded in his journal that canoes, with three or four men in each, came alongside but would not come on board.

> [Cook was] . . . agreeably surprised to find them of the same Nation as the people of Otaheite and the other islands we had lately visited. . . . they exchanged a few fish they had in the Canoes for any thing we offered them, but valued nails, or iron above every other thing. . . . (Beaglehole, pp. 263-264)

Through this journal entry, we learn that fish were the first island products to be furnished Cook's party by barter.

Nearly two weeks later (February 1) Cook recorded that he purchased salted fish on Ni'ihau (Beaglehole, p. 277).

Upon returning from Alaska, Cook's ships reached the Maui Coast on November 26, 1778. Samwell wrote, "Several Canoes came off to us, the Indians behaved very friendly & sold us some Fish & other things for Iron Tois *(ko'i)* or Adzes. . . ." (Beaglehole, p. 1150)

On the same day Cook recorded, "We got from these people in exchange for Nails and pieces of iron a quantity of Cuttlefish. . . ." (Beaglehole, pp. 474-475)

The next day King recorded that people in canoes . . . brought some fish and taro, sweet potatoes, and breadfruit (Beaglehole, p. 497).

While Cook's ships were cruising off Hawai'i searching for an anchorage on January 8, 1779, the crew traded with the people and Samwell wrote, ". . . we bought a Turtle of them to day of that kind called ye Loggerhead." (Beaglehole, p. 1157)

In summarizing his observations about the

activities of the Kona people in February 1779, Samwell wrote:

> They catch fish with Nets and Hooks of different sizes made of Mother of pearl, bone & wood pointed with bone, the latter are of a great size with which they catch Sharks and other large fish. (Beaglehole, p. 1184)

Samwell wrote of gourds used by fishermen, ". . . others are long & just wide enough at the Mouth to admit a man's hand—in these they keep fish hooks & lines and various other things." (Beaglehole, p. 1183)

Also from Samwell:

> Before we left Keragegooa [Kealakekua], we saw many small fishhooks which they had made with the nails they got from us, & having daily Opportunity of seeing the Armourers work at the forge they learnt the necessity of heating iron before they attempted to beat it out. (Beaglehole, p. 1186)

■ Understandings and Appreciations

1. Discuss the problems involved in providing enough fish to furnish the chief protein food for 300,000 persons in old Hawai'i.

2. Study the system for dividing a large catch of fish among the villagers. (Titcomb, 1972, p. 8-11)

3. Even though fish were abundant in the old days the chiefs and advisors wisely conserved them through *kapu*. Discuss both the abundance and conservation. (Titcomb, 1972, p. 11-18)

4. In Emory's "Fishhooks," study the six plates showing photographs of nearly a hundred fishhooks and about 180 parts of hooks or of tools used in making them. This should help give one an appreciation of the ingenuity and industriousness of the fishermen and the makers of hooks.

■ Student Activities

1. Make a list of fishing implements which could be made in replica form. The list should include fishhooks of bone, shell or wood, small fish nets, net gauges and needles, net floats and sinkers and bait mortars. Make some of these replicas as individual or class projects.

2. Visit the fish market and learn the names of local food fish. How was each kind caught? Which fish are the most common? Which are the most popular with the customers?

3. Read one of the legends about the men who could change themselves into sharks, then back to men again. Read about the shark *'aumākua* who were believed to have had human mothers. Note that Kamapua'a could change himself into *humuhumu-nukunuku-a-pua'a* and swim from island to island.

4. Make a *lamakū* or torch for fishing. Roasted *kukui* nuts are enclosed in a cylindrical sheaf of ti leaves affixed to a bamboo handle.

■ Audio-Visual Aids

Bishop Museum
Exhibits of *kū'ula* or fish gods, *'aumākua* of a shark and an eel in the courtyard. Extensive collections of fishhooks and related material are in storage in the archaeological department.

Waikīkī Aquarium
Live fish in the display tanks, properly labeled, and also preserved and mounted specimens. The new educational exhibit shows the relationship between the products of the land and sea.

Kewalo Basin and Tuna Cannery
Sampans frequently unload large catches of tuna and a few other fish at the wharf.

■ Vocabulary

1. Learn the meaning of the following words that apply to fishing.

'upena	maka	makau
hīna'i	olonā	kilo
hi'a	kuapā	lama'kū
kukui	hukilau	kū'ula

2. Learn to identify the following sea animals.

i'a	aku	'ōpelu
uhu	mālolo	manō
nehu	'o'opu	'ōpae
he'e	wana	loli

■ Current Happenings of Significance to this Unit

1. Study the commercial fishing activities. Note that most of the fishing is carried on by men of Japanese ancestry in specially designed sampans. The fish are marketed by both Japanese

and Chinese dealers. The Hawaiian fishermen, once supreme, are represented by a small number who fish with nets or gather *'opihi* or crabs.

2. Note how the Hawaiian taste for fish has changed through the years. At a present day *lū'au* the host may serve *lomi* salmon made from salt salmon from the Pacific Northwest and butterfish, in the *laulau,* which is black cod, also from the mainland.

3. In an attempt to eradicate mosquitoes the following fish have been introduced into taro ponds and streams:
    mosquito fish *(gambusia)*
    moon fish *(platypoecilius)*
    guppys *(lebistes)*
    sword tails *(xiphophorus)*
    sail fins or mollies *(mollienesia)*
    a few others.

4. To add to the food supply, to increase sport fishing or to provide ornamental fish, the following have been introduced; Carp, Trout, Bass, Tilapia, and Goldfish.

5. Ta'ape, a marine food fish introduced into Hawaiian waters, has increased rapidly. The commercial catch in 1970 was more than 1,100 pounds; in 1988 it was almost 43,000 pounds, and had a cash value of more than $45,000. It is a bargain food fish with white, flaky meat.

    For a free copy of the brochures, "Ta'ape in Hawai'i" and "Taste Ta'ape," write the U.H. Sea Grant Publications, Spalding Hall 253, 2540 Maile Way, Honolulu, 96822.

6. The figures for the commercial fish catch for Hawai'i for the year ending June 30, 1988 were provided by the *State of Hawaii Data Book* for 1989, published annually by the Department of Business and Economic Development, Honolulu, Hawai'i.

    A word of caution regarding fish catch figures. The official totals do not include recreational catches or unreported commercial catches. The latter may greatly exceed reported totals.

    Of the many different species and subspecies of fish, only those with a total catch in 1988 of more than 100,000 pounds, or a cash value of more than $100,000, are listed separately.

Sea Catch by Species	Pounds Caught	Value
All species	11,042,507	$20,536,007
1. Aku (Skipjack)	3,877,692	3,947,685
2. 'Ahi (Yellowfin)	3,091,460	4,815,253
3. 'Ahi (Bigeye)	184,522	743,733
4. Striped marlin	206,243	246,206
5. Pacific blue marlin	487,140	365,449
6. Mahimahi	349,664	962,728
7. Ono	341,037	942,717
8. Hapu'upu'u	57,019	116,930
9. 'Ōpakapaka	355,315	1,215,539
10. Uku	180,444	477,223
11. Ehu	52,255	162,265
12. Onaga	170,279	775,450
13. Ulua	71,737	106,538
14. Akule	185,750	346,870
15. Lehi	36,444	108,346
16. 'Ōpelu	226,866	391,539
17. Lobster (Spiny)	233,986	2,301,571
18. Lobster (Slipper)	116,236	1,178,549

Thus 11 million pounds of fish and shellfish brought in nearly 21 million dollars.

Despite the neglect and destruction of Hawaiian fish ponds during this century (see pages 152-54), nearly 26,000 pounds of fish and crabs valued at $61,603 were marketed in the fiscal year ending June 30, 1988.

Much more information may be obtained from the State Division of Aquatic Resources under the Department of Land and Natural Resources, with offices at 1151 Punchbowl Street, Honolulu.

7. The Hawaiian Tuna Packers at Kewalo Basin, Honolulu, are able to can 15,000 tons of tuna per year, which is about one million cases of 48 cans each. About ninety percent of the output is shipped to the mainland; the remaining ten percent is sold in Hawai'i under the Coral Tuna label. The cans for packing the tuna are furnished by the Dole Company. Local fishermen cannot catch enough tuna to keep the local cannery running so they import fish from several sources.

8. Read the following illustrated newsletters for interesting information on the sea and its plants and animals:
    Hawai'i Coastal Zone News
    Beginning in May, 1976, the Coastal Zone

Management Program published many issues of this informative newsletter, and distributed them mainly to local residents. Publication of the *Hawai'i Coastal Zone News* ceased in 1982. Those interested should find back copies in the libraries.

> *Makai* "Toward the Sea"
> Sea Grant College Program
> 2540 Maile Way, Spalding Hall 252B
> Honolulu 96822

> *Aquaculture in Hawaii*
> Aquaculture Development Program
> 335 Merchant Street, Suite 359
> Honolulu 96813

> *Kilo i'a*

"A newsletter published bi-monthly by the Friends of the Waikiki Aquarium and dedicated to increasing the community's knowledge of the Waikiki Aquarium and Hawaii's marine life."

■ Evaluation

1. Use the vocabulary as a test for word meaning and spelling.
2. Assign and give an essay type quiz on several types of fishing such as:
   a) shark fishing using a slip noose
   b) *aku* fishing with live bait and the lure
   c) fishing with traps
   d) *hukilau* net fishing
3. Grade the craft projects such as the construction of replicas of fishhooks and nets.

■ Reading List

Apple, Russell A., and William K. Kikuchi. *Ancient Hawaiian Shore Zone Fishponds.* Honolulu: Office of the State Director, National Park Service, U.S. Department of the Interior, 1975.

Bryan, E.H. Jr. "Fish Poisoning." In *Hawaiian Nature Notes.* 1932-33. Honolulu: Honolulu Star-Bulletin, 1935.

Buck, Peter H. *Arts and Crafts of Hawaii.* Honolulu: Bishop Museum Special Publication No. 45, 1957.

Daws, Alan G. *The Illustrated Atlas of Hawaii.* Norfolk Island, Aus.: Island Heritage, 1970. (Eighteen excellent color pictures of island reef fish.)

Edmondson, Charles H. *Reef and Shore Fauna of Hawaii.* Honolulu: Bishop Museum Special Publication No. 22, 1946.

Emory, Kenneth P., William J. Bonk, and Yosohiko H. Sinoto. *Fishhooks.* 1959. Honolulu: Bishop Museum Special Publication No. 47, 1968.

Feher, Joseph. *Hawaii: A Pictorial History.* Honolulu: Bishop Museum Special Publication No. 58, 1969.

Fielding, Ann. *Hawaiian Reefs and Tidepools.* A guide to Hawai'i's shallow-water invertebrates. Honolulu: Oriental Publishing Company, 1979.

Gosline, William A., and Vernon E. Brock. *Handbook of Hawaiian Fishes.* Honolulu: University Press of Hawaii, 1960.

Hobson, Edmund S., and E.F. Chave. *Hawaiian Reef Animals.* Honolulu: University of Hawaii Press, 1972.

Hosaka, Edward. *Sport Fishing in Hawaii.* Honolulu: Bond's, 1944.

Jordan and Everman. *Bulletin of the U.S. Fish Commission.* 3 vols. Washington, D.C.: GPO, 1903-1905.

———. *The Shore Fishes of Hawaii.* Abridgment of Part 1, 1903. Rutland, VT and Japan: C.E. Tuttle, 1973.

Kamakau, Samuel M. "Olona, Its Cultivation and Uses." In *Hawaiian Annual for 1919.* Honolulu: Thrum's Hawaiian Annual. 69-74.

———. *The Works of the People of Old.* Olona, 44-46; Methods of Fishing, 59-88; Cultivation of Fish in Ponds, 47-50. Honolulu: Bishop Museum Special Publication No. 61, 1976.

Kay, E. Alison. *Hawaiian Marine Shells: Reef and Shore Fauna of Hawaii*. Sec. 4: Mollusca. Honolulu: Bishop Museum Special Publication No. 64, 1979.

Kelly, Marion. "Loko I'a O He'eia: He'eia Fishpond." Honolulu: Bishop Museum, Department of Anthropology Report No. 75-2, 1975.

Mackellar, Jean S. *Hawaii Goes Fishing*. 1956. Rutland, VT and Japan: C.E. Tuttle, 1968.

Malo, David. *Hawaiian Antiquities*. 1898. Honolulu: Bishop Museum Special Publication No. 2, 1976.

Maunupau, Thomas. "Aku and Ahi Fishing." Ch. 9 in *Ancient Hawaiian Civilization*. A series of lectures delivered at the Kamehameha Schools by E.S.C. Handy [and others]. 1933. Rutland, VT and Japan: C.E. Tuttle, 1965 (rev. ed.).

Mitchell, Donald D. Kilolani. *Hawaiian Treasures*. Fishing, 108-110. Honolulu: Kamehameha Schools Press, 1978.

Newman, T. Stell. *Hawaiian Fishing and Farming on the Island of Hawaii in A.D. 1778*. Honolulu: Department of Land and Natural Resources, 1970.

———. "Man in the Prehistoric Hawaiian Ecosystem." In *A Natural History of the Hawaiian Islands*. Honolulu: University Press of Hawaii, 1976. 559-603. (A discussion of fishing and farming methods.)

Pavloff, Nick, photographer. *Dillingham 1982 Tide Calendar*. Fishing tools of Old Hawaii. Tools and text provided by Bishop Museum, Honolulu.

Quirk, Stephen, and Betsy Harrison. *Hawaiian Seashells*. Honolulu: Robert Boom Company, 1972.

Randall, John E. *Underwater Guide to Hawaiian Reef Fishes*. Waterproof edition. Newton Square, PA: Harrowood Books, 1981.

Rizzuto, Jim. *Modern Hawaiian Gamefishing*. Honolulu: University Press of Hawaii, 1977.

Sakamoto, Michael R. *Pacific Shore Fishing*. Honolulu: University of Hawaii Press, 1985.

Stokes, John F.G. *Fish Poisoning in the Hawaiian Islands*. Honolulu: Bishop Museum Occasional Paper No. 7:10, 1921.

Summers, Catherine C. *Hawaiian Fishponds*. Honolulu: Bishop Museum Special Publication No. 52, 1964.

Thrum, Thomas G., ed. "Hawaiian Fish Stories and Superstitions," "Ku'ula, the Fish God of Hawaii." In *Hawaiian Annual for 1901*. Honolulu: Thrum's Hawaiian Annual.

Tinker, Spencer. *Fishes of Hawaii*. Honolulu: Hawaiian Services, Inc., 1978.

———. *Hawaiian Fishes*. Honolulu: Tongg Publishing Company, 1944.

———. *Pacific Crustacea*. Rutland, VT and Japan: C.E. Tuttle, 1965.

———. *Pacific Sea Shells*. Rutland, VT and Japan: C.E. Tuttle, 1958.

Tinker, Spencer W., and Charles J. DeLuca. *Sharks and Rays*. A handbook of the sharks and rays of Hawaii and the central Pacific Ocean. Rutland, VT and Japan: C.E. Tuttle, 1973.

Titcomb, Margaret. *Native Use of Fish in Hawaii*. Honolulu: University Press of Hawaii, 1972 (reprint).

———. *Native Use of Marine Invertebrates in Old Hawaii*. Honolulu: University Press of Hawaii, 1979.

UNIT 12:
Transportation, with Special Reference to Canoes

TRANSPORTATION
With Special Reference
to Canoes

Transportation in old Hawai'i was principally by water. The outrigger canoe could be paddled or sailed from one seaside village to another, often within the protection of a fringing coral reef. The passengers served as paddlers and the cargo of food and craft articles was stored in the hull.

The Hawaiian canoe (kaukahi) with a single outrigger (ama) on the port or left side to steady it was constructed to carry one person, (ko'okahi), two persons, (ko'olua) or an increasingly larger number until it provided room for eight persons (ko'owalu). The long narrow racing outrigger was called kialoa or a kioloa. The general name for canoe, wa'a, also applied to the hull which was usually hewn from a single koa log.

The double canoe (kaulua) had two hulls of nearly equal size and often had a platform (pola) secured to the cross booms ('iako) between the canoes. Large double canoes, built to carry colonists to distant Pacific islands (Tahiti to Hawai'i, for instance), had structures resembling grass houses built on the platforms to shelter the passengers and their plants and animals. The double war canoes, built as a war fleet for Kamehameha I, were called peleleu (Malo, pp. 131-135, Holmes, 1981, pp. 115-117). The catamaran is the modern double canoe.

The lack of roadways and the absence of beasts of burden in early Hawai'i made canoes the principal medium of transportation. Canoes were the ideal crafts for Pacific navigation since the shallow-draft hulls could clear the coral reefs in certain places around an island. The light-weight canoes could be carried above high-tide or into canoe sheds (hālau). Beached canoes were safe from shipworms and storms. Protected harbors with piers which are needed for ships today were not known in earlier times.

Strong paddlers propelled the canoes with sturdy koa paddles (hoe) along the shores, on fishing trips and even in the open sea when there was no wind. Triangular lau hala sails (lā) supported by a mast (kia) were used on both double and outrigger canoes. They are described by Buck, 1957, pp. 281-282, Holmes, 1981, pp. 52-54 and Hornell, Canoes of Oceania, Vol. 1, p. 18. Sailing canoes might average 120-140 miles a day. (On July 12, 1976, the Hōkūle'a sailed 170 nautical miles in 24 hours.) At this speed the journey from Nukuhiva in the Marquesas to Hawai'i would require 13-14 days. The voyage from Tahiti to Hawai'i might be made in 16 days (Golson, Polynesian Navigation, p. 72). Actually the Hōkūle'a required 22, 24, 31 and 35 days for the trips one way to and from Tahiti.

From the viewpoint of modern functional design the Hawaiian canoes were the finest in the Pacific. They were simple, sturdy, efficient and not burdened with surface ornamentation.

■ Hōkūle'a, Star of Joy

Discussions of canoes, especially double canoes, in this unit will contain numerous references to the now famous double-hulled canoe, the Hōkūle'a.

Our readers are urged to secure a copy of Lindo and Mower's book "Polynesian Seafaring Heritage," 1980, for a detailed story of the Hōkūle'a. This 184 page volume discusses many phases of canoe building, navigation and related subjects. Featured are maps, charts, photographs and many helps for teachers to use in sharing this subject with young people.

Also refer to Holmes, "The Hawaiian Canoe" for a profusely illustrated study of canoes. One learns in detail the story of the canoe from the koa tree in the forest to the finished craft. The author, a crew member on the Hōkūle'a, has been a canoeing and surfing enthusiast for years.

The Polynesian Voyaging Society, organized in 1973, planned and funded the building of the *Hōkūle'a* which was launched at Kualoa Park, O'ahu, in March 1974.

After training a crew the *Hōkūle'a* sailed for Tahiti on May 1, 1976 and arrived June 4. After a tumultuous welcome and reception the vessel made the return voyage to Honolulu July 4 to July 26, a round trip voyage of some 6,000 miles.

A second successful voyage was made to Tahiti March 16 to April 17, 1980 and the return May 13 to June 6.

This revival of interest and the search for knowledge concerning canoes and navigation has promoted a renewed respect for and pride in many of the earlier Hawaiian skills and accomplishments.

■ Canoe Making Tools and Materials

The principle tools used by the canoe builders (*kālai wa'a*) were:

Hafted adzes (*ko'i*) for felling the trees and removing excess wood.

Swivel adzes (*ko'i'āwili*) in which the stone blade could be turned to any angle. Also called *kūpā*, to dig or hew. Named for a god of canoe makers - Kūpā'aike'e.

Stone polishers (*pōhaku 'ānai wa'a*)

Stone chisels (*pōhaku pao*) used to make the lashing holes in the *wa'a* and *mo'o*.

Stone hammers (*pōhaku kāpili wa'a*) used to tap the chisels.

Pump drills (*nao wili*) used by some craftsmen to drill holes in the *wa'a* and *mo'o* for lashing the two together with sennit (*'aha*).

Wooden clamps (*pūki'i wa'a*)

Caulking Tools

(For descriptions and sketches see Buck, 1957, pp. 255-267, Holmes, 1981, pp. 25-29, and Lindo and Mower, 1980, pp. 41-42, 61-67.)

Materials needed to make a canoe were a large sound log, preferably *koa*, for the hull (*wa'a*), strips of wood, usually *'ahakea* or *'ulu*, for the gunwale strakes (*mo'o*) and the forward end piece (*lā'au ihu*), and the aft piece (*lā'au hope*). A pair of sturdy *hau* booms (*'iako*) connected the outrigger (*ama*) of *wiliwili* wood to the canoe. The parts were lashed together with sennit, or cordage from coconut husk fibers. Fishing canoes might be fitted with a fish spear rack (*haka*) of wood fastened to the fore boom. The other end of the

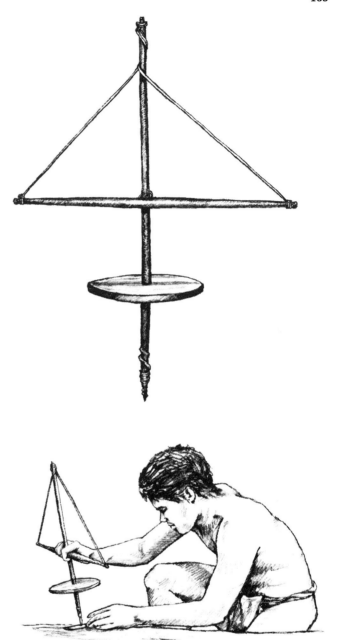

Pump Drill: The sea shell point of the pump drill was generally replaced with a nail after the introduction of iron. This tool drilled small holes in wood, shells, bones and the teeth of dogs and sharks for a variety of uses.

spears rested on the aft boom (*'iako*). (For descriptions and photographs see Buck, 1957, pp. 269-271, Feher, pp. 52-55, and Holmes, 1981, pp. 43-52.)

Accessories and furnishings for the canoe usually included a mat cover (*pā'ū*) to keep out the spray and water, paddles (*hoe*) of *koa*, bailers (*kā*

A Canoe Pāʻū: To keep water out when paddling in stormy seas the opening of the canoe could be covered the full length with a *pāʻū* of *lau hala* matting. Holes *(holo)* were drilled in the gunwale to hold small cords which secured a line *(ʻalihi paʻu)* stretching the length of the outside of the canoe. A sturdy rope *(hāunu)* passed through loops in the *ʻalihi* and criss-crossed from one side to the other to hold the *pāʻū* in place. Openings were provided in the *pāʻū* for the paddlers.

waʻa) of gourd, canoe anchors of stone *(pōhaku hekau)* and in time of war, stone canoe breakers *(pōhaku kuʻi waʻa).* The larger canoes were fitted with a mast *(kia)* and a triangular sail *(lā)* of *lau hala* matting.

■ Constructing a Canoe

The selecting and cutting of a forest tree for the canoe hull by the *kāhuna kālaiwaʻa* and his craftsmen was carried out with traditional religious rites. A feast was held on the spot and the *ʻelepaio* bird hopefully avoided the tree which indicated the soundness of the log for a canoe hull. Read Malo, pp. 126-128, and Buck, 1957, pp. 254-55. Buck in

Vikings of the Pacific (or *Sunrise*) describes this as a Polynesian undertaking (See Feher, pp. 50-53).

The roughly hollowed hull was prepared for the long haul from the rain forest to the beach for finishing. After more feasting and prayers for a safe journey, lines were fixed to the prow and stern of the unfinished canoe. The precarious journey was accomplished without mishap if the gods had been asked properly for assistance. Chants encouraged workers along the way. A triplet from one of these chants was used for some years by The Kamehameha Schools cheering section at football games:

Kīauau, Kīauau, Kīauau

Holo auau, holo auau, holo auau
Ho‘okahi ka umauma.
Hasten, hasten, hasten
Run quick, run quick, run quick
Keep your chests together (work in unity).

Another version of the above is:

Kīauau, Kīauau	Haul, Haul
Hukiauau, hukiauau	Pull on, pull on
Kōauau, kōauau	Draw on, draw on
Ho‘omālō ke kaula	Keep the rope taut
Mōkū a ke kaula	Keep the rope in position

(See Malo, p. 128; Buck, 1957, p. 256; Pukui, *Canoe Making Profession*, p. 157; Emory, *Conch Shell*, Vol. II, No. 4, pp. 44-45, Bishop Museum Association; Feher, pp. 50-51, for excellent information or sketches of shaping the hull and the hauling of the log to the shore.)

The unfinished canoe was placed in a canoe shed (*hālau wa‘a*) a large, airy structure with roof of thatch but open at the sides and ends. After a feast a *kapu* was placed on the *hālau* and only the *kāhuna kālaiwa‘a* and his craftsmen were allowed to enter to complete the canoe. (See Buck, 1957, pp. 256-264; Emory, *Flying Spray*, pp. 44-45; Pukui, *Canoe Making Profession*, pp. 157-159 and Malo, pp. 129-131.)

■ Dedicating the Canoe

Before the *kahuna kālaiwa‘a* released the canoe as sea worthy and ready for the owner he tested it on a trial trip and held a final feast of consecration (*lolo-wa‘a*) with offerings of pig, red fish and coconuts. (Bryan, p. 42, Malo, pp. 129-130, Buck, *Vikings of the Pacific*, pp. 33-34, tells of the christening of the vessel with sea water. *Inu kai* would be the Hawaiian equivalent and more appropriate than a champagne ceremony.)

Pule from Emerson for launching the canoe, *Hokule‘a*, of the Polynesian Voyaging Society, at Kualoa Regional Park, March 8, 1975, chanted by Kaupena Wong.

Ia wa‘a nui	That large canoe
Ia wa‘a kiolea	That long canoe
Ia wa‘a peleleu	That broad canoe
A lele māmala	Let chips fly
A manu o uka	The bird of the upland
A manu o kai	The bird of the lowland
‘Iwi pōlena	The *‘iwi pōlena* bird
A kau ka hōkū	The stars appear
A kau i ka mālama	The day light arrives
A pae i kula	Land ashore
‘Āmama ua noa	*‘Āmama*, the *kapu* is freed

Translated by Mary Kawena Pukui

■ Navigation

Polynesian navigation was "an enterprise that properly should rank among the great achievements of human history, and one that must have been flooded with human drama." (Emory, *Ancient Hawaiian Civilization*, p. 237.) "... the lack of nautical instruments makes the successful voyages all the more remarkable, for the navigational problems were solved with the naked eye and the exercise of human judgment." (Buck, 1957, p. 284.)

In coastal or inter-island canoe voyages in Hawaiian waters some portion of at least one island was nearly always visible in clear weather. Canoes were sailed or paddled in these waters, often at a speed of 5 to 7 or more knots an hour. (Golson, pp. 64-65.) Hornell quotes an informant who saw Hawaiian canoes paddled at the rate of 11 or 12 miles an hour. (Hornell, pp. 16-17.) The methods of paddling and steering are described by Hornell, page 16.

On the long voyage between islands or island groups the Polynesians proved to be skilled navigators for they visited, in pre-European times, every island in Polynesia. They colonized the habitable ones and used the smaller ones as "stepping stone" islets. Andrew Sharp, in *Ancient Voyagers in the Pacific*, wrote that the discovery and settling of the Pacific islands was due largely to accidental voyaging. Several scientists and seafaring men report that they disagree with him in *Polynesian Navigation* edited by Jack Golson.

The expert Hawaiian navigators (*kilolani*) proved their skill by their:

Knowledge of the stars, sun and moon.
Knowledge of the prevailing winds and sensitivity in quickly detecting changes in wind direction.
Knowledge of the ocean swells caused by the prevailing winds.
Ability to perceive slight changes in color of sky and water, such as the greenish reflection on the clouds above lagoon waters many miles away.
Knowledge of the flight of birds and their

general proximity to land.

The Hawaiians did not use a "magic" or "sacred" calabash as a sextant. (See Buck, 1957, p. 284, Bryan, *Stars over Hawaii*, pp. 44-45, Golson, p. 68 and 70, Lindo and Mower, pp. 94-96, 102-121.)

Polynesians were fearless seamen because they:

were expert swimmers.

were able to right a canoe after it swamped at sea.

had confidence in their seamanship and their guardian gods.

were able to carry food and water for the voyage which seldom exceeded 4 to 6 weeks.

were able to supplement their stores of food by catching fish and birds and to replenish their water by catching rain water in their matting sails. (See Bryan, p. 43, Buck, 1957, pp. 283-284, Golson, pp. 64-97, Emory, 1933 or 1965, pp. 242-45.)

■ Arcturus (Hōkūleʻa) and Sirius (ʻAʻā)

The bright star Arcturus, called *Hōkūleʻa* by the Hawaiian astronomers and navigators, passes directly over the island of Hawaiʻi. Navigators bringing their canoes from Tahiti knew that they were in the latitude of Hawaiʻi by the position of *Hōkūleʻa*.

When sailing south to Tahiti the navigators knew that the brightest of stars, Sirius, called ʻAʻā, passes directly over Tahiti. *Hōkūleʻawaʻa* was a common alternate name for ʻAʻā.

■ Captain Cook's Artists Sketch Canoes, 1778-79

Artist John Webber and Surgeon Wm. Ellis sketched five scenes of canoes and the people.

1. *Hawaiian Canoe with Masked Rowers,* Webber. A closeup of a double sailing canoe with ten masked paddlers. Clear details of the canoe, paddles, sail, and lines (Beaglehole, Plate 60b, pp. 624-625; Feher, p. 54).

2. *View of Kealakekua Bay,* Webber. The Resolution and the Discovery, two double canoes with sails and paddlers, some six outrigger canoes with sails, and at least 20 with paddlers only. A man on a surfboard is in the forefront of the picture (Feher, p. 136).

3. *Kalaniʻopuʻu Bringing Presents to Captain Cook on January 27, 1779,* Webber. The king's canoe is propelled by a large sail and some 20 paddlers. Two accompanying canoes use 18 to 20 paddlers each (Feher, p. 55; Beaglehole, Plate 56, pp. 528-529). The watercolor of this by Webber shows the chiefs' regalia in color (Murray-Oliver, 1969, p. 135, Plate 125).

4. *Outrigger Under Sail,* Webber. Shows details of canoe, sail, and paddles, also method of holding paddles, (Buck, 1957, p. 271; Feher, p. 53).

5. *Kealakekua Bay with Ships at Anchor,* Wm. Ellis. Two outrigger canoes with sails carrying three persons each. Other canoes in the distance (Beaglehole, pp. 528-529, Plate 57).

■ Captain Cook and Officers Wrote About Canoes

Cook and his men were well qualified to judge the canoes which they observed in great numbers in Hawaiian waters. By the time they reached Hawaiʻi they had seen and described in their journals the highly-ornamented Tahitian vessels, the elaborately-carved prows and sterns of the large Maori canoes, and the Tongan craft built of planks expertly joined together.

In Hawaiʻi the party was impressed with the vast number of canoes, which were expertly handled under sail or with paddles. In comparison to other Pacific Island craft, the Hawaiian canoes were functional in design and free from unnecessary ornamentation.

Cook described the canoes which he examined off Kauaʻi in 1778, and concluded his study of them with high praise:

As they are not more than fifteen or eighteen inches broad, those that go single have outriggers, which are shaped and fitted with more judgment than any I had before seen. They are rowed by paddles and some have a light triangular sail, like those of the Friendly Islands, [Tonga] extended to a mast and boom. (Beaglehole, pp. 282-283.)

Surgeon Wm. Ellis wrote:

[The Hawaiian canoes] . . . are the neatest we ever saw, and composed of two different coloured woods, the bottom being dark, the upper part light and furnished with an outrigger. (Beaglehole, p.283.)

John Ledyard, an American serving as Sergeant of the Marines on board the Resolution, wrote in his journal on January 17, 1779:

> While we were entering the bay which they called Kirekakooa [Kealakekua] . . . we were surrounded by so great a number of canoes that Cook ordered two officers into each top to number them with as much exactness as they could, and as they both exceeded 3000 in their amounts I shall with safety say there was 2500 and as there were an average of 6 persons at least in each canoe it will follow that there was at least 15,000 men, women and children in the canoes, besides those that were on floats [surfboards], swimming without floats, and actually on board and hanging round the outside of the ships.
>
> The crowds on shore were still more numerous. The beach, surrounding rocks, the tops of houses, the branches of trees and the adjacent hills were all covered, the shouts of joy, the admiration proceeding from the sonorous voices of the men confused with the shriller exclamations of the women dancing and clapping their hands, the overseting of canoes, cries of the children, goods on float, and hogs that were brought to market squealing formed one of the most tumultous and most curious prospects that can be imagined. (J.K. Munford, p. 103.)

On January 24, 1779, Samwell and two companions asked their friend Kanekoa to guide them into the forest above Kealakekua. They saw plantations of breadfruit, bananas, upland taro, sweet potatoes, ginger, and sugar cane.

> There are various Sorts of Trees here, the principal & largest of which is that called by the Indians Koa; it is a red wood like Mahogony, of this they build their canoes. . . . After following the path four [or] five miles in the forest we came to a place where we found three Men building Canoes with temporary Sheds for their Residence. . . . (Beaglehole, pp. 1166-67.)

Clerke, in summarizing his observations at the time of sailing from Hawai'i, wrote:

> Their Canoes are exceeding well built and some very large; we saw among them a vessel seventy-feet long, something more than three feet deep and about the same measurement in breadth, and there were many among them nearly of the same dimensions; the bottom of this was formed out of one tree, with a plank about a foot broad firmly secured by lashing to the Top to compleat the side and form the Gunwale. Some of our Explorers in the woods measured a tree of 19 feet in girth and rising very proportionably in its bulk to a great height, nor did this far, if at all, exceed in stateliness many of its neighbours; we never before met with this kind of wood, in its appear-

ance when cut it mostly resembles coarse Mahogany [koa]. (Beaglehole, p. 598.)

■ Canoes on Exhibit in Bishop Museum

Three excellent examples of outrigger canoes belong to the Museum and are often on display in Hawaiian Hall. A study of them will show that the design of canoes has remained much the same since Captain Cook's time. Unfortunately, there is not sufficient space in this hall to display these canoes with their outriggers and connecting booms lashed in place.

The largest canoe on exhibit bears this caption:

> Racing Canoe of Prince Jonah Kūhiō Kalaniana-'ole. This canoe was used for racing in Waikiki in the 19th and 20th centuries. It has the personal name 'A'a (to challenge). Gift of Elizabeth Kalaniana'ole Woods in 1923 in memory of Prince Jonah Kalaniana'ole and his aunt Queen Kapi'olani. In 1952 the canoe was completely restored and raced by the late Herbert M. Dowsett. It was returned to Bishop Museum in 1969 by Mrs. Herbert M. Dowsett.

The Museum's oldest canoe is 35 and one-half feet long, 20 inches wide, and 26 inches deep. It bears this label:

> A full size canoe made from a single koa log. The mo'o (gunwale strakes) are of 'ulu (breadfruit). The ama (outrigger) was of wiliwili wood and the 'iako (connecting bars) of hau, but they have been removed due to termite damage. This was considered a 'fast' canoe. It was the favorite deep sea fishing canoe of Kamehameha V. The Moanalua Racing Team always won when using this canoe. The canoe was named 'Nihoa' and was cared for by Keau. Gift of S.M. Damon, 19th century.

Canoes were light in weight, because the hulls were hewn to a thickness of not more than an inch and a half. A 24-foot outrigger canoe weighed less than 50 pounds.

■ Movement of People and Material on Land

The footpaths connecting the villages were narrow trails, following the shore where possible. Smooth, waterworn rocks were placed over rough lava flows or on terrain too rough for walking. When necessary the travelers wore sandals (kāma'a) made from wauke, hau, or lau hala fibers.

Examples of swift runners carrying fish considerable distances were given in the previous unit.

■ Containers on Carrying Poles

Food from the plantations and sea food from the beached canoe were carried to the village in wooden bowls ('umeke lā'au) and in large gourd vessels ('umeke pōhue). These were provided with lids which were used when it seemed advisable. Drinking water from springs upstream was carried in this way.

Since these containers were too large or too cumbersome to carry in the arms of the bearer they were hung in a carrying net (kōkō) made especially for this purpose. Two loops at the top of the kōkō

Carrying Poles: These sturdy poles served ideally in the tropics where back packs were used in cooler climates. On poles belonging to chiefs some of the knobs were carved into human heads with the faces looking upward.

were hooked over the end of the carrying pole and the loops were prevented from slipping off by knobs near the end of the pole.

The containers placed on each end of the pole were loaded, as nearly as possible, with produce of the same weight which caused the load to balance properly on the shoulder of the bearer.

The carrying poles, 'auamo or māmaka, were from 40 to 92 inches long and about an inch and a half thick in the middle. Kauila, a strong, durable wood was favored for the poles.

A few spears, ihe or pololū, had notches or fibers tied around the end opposite the point. These and the digging stick ('ō'ō) which was similiarly fixed could also be used as carrying poles.

Most of the food for the people was carried shorter or longer distances by these simple devices.

■ Mānele or Litter

A few persons were privileged to be carried from place to place by others. These were chiefesses whose kapu was so high that their feet should not touch the ground, and the infirm or the elderly.

They were carried on a mānele which has been variously translated as a litter, sedan chair, palanquin or stretcher. No pre-European mānele are known to this writer but the Mission House Museum has one so named from the missionary era. It is of finished lumber and built to carry one adult or an adult and child. Another longer mānele carried two adults with their backs to the bearers and their feet in contact. (See a sketch of each in Damon, 1927, pp. 96-97.)

At least one type of mānele used in the early days was made from two sturdy poles, similiar to the 'auamo but not necessarily with knobs at the ends. A series of short cross-pieces, each some 18 to 20 inches long were lashed to the poles which had been spaced about a foot apart. This would be the distance from one shoulder to the other on the sturdy men who would be the bearers. These crosspieces were lashed along the center of the poles to provide a platform for the person being carried. If in good health he would sit; otherwise, he would lie on the platform while a passenger.

For the mānele with two bearers the ends of the poles were placed on the shoulders of the fore and aft man. If the load was heavy four men were needed. Each bearer had a pole on one shoulder

Mānele: A chiefess being carried on a *mānele*. Her rank requires that her head be higher than those of her bearers.

and they were careful to walk in step.

In similiar fashion a net suspended between poles was used to carry a corpse to the burial site.

■ On Land the Men Bore the Loads

In studying the culture of a people who had no beasts of burden or wheeled vehicles it is astound-ing to note how much was carried in the hands or on the backs of sturdy men. In some instances the women carried lighter loads.

In house building the men carried the timbers for posts and rafters from the mountains to the house site. The women and older children carried bundles of *pili* grass for thatching the house.

In canoe building the men dragged the partly finished log from its home high in the mountains to the *hālau wa'a* along the beach. Poles for the outrigger and booms were also carried from some distance.

Building the larger *heiau* was a monumental task. Countless numbers of stones, some quite heavy, were carried from beaches, river beds and other sources in the hands or on the shoulders. House foundations, fishponds and water courses were constructed from stones, most of which were carried some distance. Some workmen stood side by side and formed a "menehune chain" up to several miles long. They passed the stones from man to man along the chain from their source to the site of the building project. The chain was said to have been 10 miles long in building the Mo'okini *heaiu* in Kohala, a feat requiring at least 15,000 sturdy men.

■ **Horses - Lio**

The first beasts of burden introduced into Hawai'i were horses brought from California on the merchant ship, a brig, the Lelia Byrd under Capt. William Shaler. Richard J. Cleveland, the supercargo, wrote the account of the voyage which was published in several editions. Cleveland is often credited with introducing the horses. In June, 1803, they landed a mare and a foal at Kawaihae, the residence of John Young. They left a horse and mare as a gift to Kamehameha I at Lahaina, Maui. To the disappointment of the donors the King showed no wonder or surprise upon receiving these large, useful animals. It was recorded that the king feared that these huge beasts would eat more than could be their worth.

The horse population reached a peak in Hawai'i in1884 with 30,640 animals. Automobiles and improved roads reduced the need for horses which numbered 12,073 in 1928.

Hawaiian men cut grass in the country districts and carried the bundles into town for horse feed. These hay vendors were a common sight in the 1880s when horses were highly popular. Each of the two bundles were taller than a man and some 18" in diameter. They were carried upright by a carrying pole which pierced each bundle a little above the center. These bundles of grass which sold for 25 cents each, must have been quite heavy and likely caused a callous to form on the shoulder of the vendor.

■ **Donkeys - Kēkake or 'ēkake**

Four donkeys arrived from England in 1825 and others were imported from time to time. They were used by bullock hunters to carry hides from the mountains, where the cattle were skinned, to the port towns. Taro growers used them to pack bags of taro up the steep trail from Waipi'o Valley. Donkeys that carried bags of coffee became known as Kona Nightingales. Jeeps are now doing much of the work once done by these sturdy little animals.

■ **Mules - hoki or piula**

Mules, hybrids between a jack and a mare, were probably shipped in and bred here after the importation of donkeys in 1825. Mule trains packed bags of taro from Waipi'o as recently as 1961. Mules were used extensively on sugar plantations until replaced by trucks and jeeps. A livestock count of 1900 indicated that there were 6,506 mules in Hawai'i and the 1920 estimate was 10,542. It is doubtful that there are any wild mules or horses in Hawai'i today. There are wild donkeys on Hawai'i island.

■ **Water Buffalo or Carabao**

The water buffalo had an important role in the developing economy of Hawai'i. These slow, docile-looking animals plowed taro ponds and rice paddies. They were domesticated in Southeast Asia some 5,000 years ago and have been used to pull two-wheeled carts and tread grain on the threshing floor. Also called the carabao in the Philippines, these animals with large feet are suited to work in mud. Since they have no sweat glands they must have water in which to wallow and cool off.

The first water buffalo recorded for Hawai'i were imported in the early 1880s from southern China by Walter Hill, at that time publisher of the Honolulu Bulletin. They were for a Chinese rice grower, Ah In, who had rice land both *mauka* and *makai* of North King Street not far from Pālama Settlement. Mr. C.R. Bishop helped pay the cost of $1,000 for the first pair.

Eventually more water buffalo were imported, they increased in numbers, and were shipped to all the major islands. A report made in 1903 listed 80 animals for the entire territory. In 1910 there were 399 carabao and in 1928 but 150.

Very few water buffalo remain in Hawai'i

today. The Kam Min Wong family of Ahilama Road, Kahalu'u, O'ahu have seven. Of the five adults, one black male is still used for plowing occasionally. While working, the animal has a wooden yoke across his neck and lines extend from this to the plow. He has a ring in his nose but he is guided by ropes on his yoke.

Occasionally a black bull and cow will have a white calf. The animals feed entirely on green grass. Perhaps we in Hawai'i will soon have to say, as did R.C. Wyllie, "this toiler in mud and water, this animal that plows, treads and hauls has become a relic of a past era."

■ Oxen

Several domestic animals are called oxen. Those in use in Hawai'i were cattle (Bostaurus). They were powerful work animals with heavy bodies, long tails and smooth curved horns.

In 1828 a group of foreign residents planted a hundred acres of sugar cane in Mānoa Valley. They converted their sugar mill near the waterfront in Honolulu into a rum distillery. Ka'ahumanu and the missionaries, owners of all of the oxen and oxcarts, refused to transport the ripe cane to the distillery.

R.C. Wyllie, minister of Foreign Relations under Kamehameha IV, spoke of the oxen as draft animals in an address before the Royal Hawaiian Agricultural Society in 1850:

> Oxen — these noble animals were used by the missionaries, about 1825-26. Many excellent teams are now in daily use in the city. . . . Several plantations kept from 10 to 15 yoke of good working oxen. Good yokes and good teamsters are much wanted to complete well trained and experienced teams.

Oxen were used on some sugar plantations as late as 1900 when they were replaced by horses and mules. Molokai Ranch used oxen as late as 1908.

■ Carts and Carriages

The first wheeled vehicle was brought to Honolulu in 1824. Mrs. Elisha Loomis, wife of the first printer wrote in her journal that Captain Wilds brought a carriage to which a horse could be hitched. Ka'ahumanu, the Queen Regent, purchased this yellow, one-horse carriage and two hand carts which were pulled by men.

In 1838 Queen Regent Kīna'u rode in a light blue hand cart lined with red velvet and drawn by 20 men. She sat in the cart backwards with her feet hanging down behind.

In 1849 the Royal Family rode in Honolulu's first Coach, drawn by four horses. Queen Victoria had presented the coach to Queen Pomare of Tahiti who, in turn, sold it to the Hawaiian ruling family.

Kamehameha III observed the fourth anniversary of Restoration Day, July 21, 1847, by inviting a huge number of his subjects to a lū'au at his country palace high in Nu'uanu Valley. This secluded retreat in the forest was called Kaniaka-pūpū, the song of the land shells.

The Royal Family, in a carriage drawn by four iron grey horses, headed the mid-morning procession to the site of the party. Following them were the military officers, cabinet ministers and chiefs on horseback. Then came one thousand horsewomen in bright, holiday attire and two thousand five hundred horsemen. A man stationed for the express purpose of checking their numbers counted 4,000 horses going up the valley and 4,600 returning. Visitors on horseback who had come over the Pali from the Ko'olau side numbered 600.

The food steward listed the following provisions consumed at the King's feast:

> 271 hogs, 482 large calabashes of poi, 602 chickens, 3 whole oxen, 2 barrels of salt pork, 2 barrels of biscuit, 3,125 salt fish, 1,820 fresh fish, 12 barrels of lū'au and cabbage, 4 barrels of onions, 80 bunches of bananas, 55 pineapples, 10 barrels of potatoes, 55 ducks, 82 turkeys, 2,245 coconuts, 4,000 taro, 180 squid. Also there were oranges, limes, grapes and various fruits served. (See Thrum's Annual for 1930. Also Sterling and Summers, 1978, p. 308.)

■ Railroads

The Kahului Railroad Company of Maui built the first steam railroad in 1880. In 1881 the Hawai'i Railway Company began operation to haul sugar and other freight from the Kohala plantations to the port of Māhukona, island of Hawai'i.

O'ahu's first railroad began operation on September 4, 1889, the dream of Benjamin F. Dillingham. Organized as the Oahu Railway and Land Company the line eventually ran around Ka'ena Point to Kahuku with a branch to the pineapple fields of Wahiawā. Its passenger and freight service were eventually replaced by buses and trucks.

The Hilo Railroad Company, organized by Mr.

Dillingham in March, 1899, laid tracks, at great expense, along the rugged Hamākua Coast to haul raw sugar from the plantations. Improved roads allowed trucks to haul its freight cheaper so the company folded.

On Kaua'i, the Kauai Railway Company, organized in 1906, served the plantations in the Port Allen area. The Ahukini Terminal and Railway, 1920, hauled freight in the Līhu'e region. Both were eventually replaced by trucks.

After the plantation and commercial railroads had ceased to operate in the islands the Lahaina-Ka'anapali and Pacific Railroad was organized to please the tourists. The company built six miles of track from Lahaina to Ka'anapali. They secured two steam locomotives, genuine antiques with classic tall-stack design. These were similar to the sugar-haul locomotives that once were the backbone of the island sugar industry. The service started on May 9, 1970, but was forced to close in mid-October, 1972 for lack of business. On July 1, 1973 the railroad reopened under new management and has been running since.

■ Shipping to and from Hawai'i

Honolulu harbor was opened to sea going vessels by Captain William Brown on November 21, 1794 when he entered the protected bay (Honolulu) with his tender, Jackal, and his sloop Prince Lee Boo.

The first shipyard was established at Honolulu in 1823 by James Robinson and Robert Lawrence. (Among the Robinson descendants living in Hawai'i today are those bearing his name and members of the prominent Holt family.)

Hawai'i's harbors and anchorages were busy during the whaling days, 1820 to 1871. During the peak years, around 1858, some 526 vessels and 5,000 whaling men would winter in Hawai'i. Petroleum, first pumped commercially in 1859, reduced the world's need for whale oil.

The first semi-steamer, with sail and steam engine was the Cormorant, a side-wheeler which arrived May 22, 1846. The first steam powered propeller ship, the USS Massachusetts came to Honolulu on April 19, 1849.

The first regular coast to Hawai'i service began with the arrival in Honolulu of the SS Ajax on January 27, 1886, 14 days from San Francisco.

In 1882 Captain William Matson launched the 200 ton schooner, Emma Claudina and began a shipping line that has served Hawai'i faithfully to this day. (See Worden, "Cargoes, Matson's first Century" 1981.)

Among the Matson vessels of later years, on which many kama'āina of today have traveled, were the Wilhelmina, 1909; Matsonia and Manoa, 1913, Maui 1917 and their first luxury liner the Malolo, 1927. The latter was refurbished and named the Matsonia (No.2).

Through the years there were five vessels named Lurline. Lurline I was a barkentine with sails launched in 1887. Lurline II, 1908-1928, was a freighter. Lurline III, 1933-1963 and Lurline IV were combination freight and passenger steamers.

Lurline V arrived in Honolulu September 13, 1973 on its maiden voyage as the first "roll-on, roll off" cargo ship of its type in the Pacific. The 700 foot, 25,000 ton ship left Los Angeles terminal for Honolulu with the following cargo:

197 40-foot trailers and containers, 108 shorter containers, 175 automobiles, 40 pieces of rolling stock which included buses, cement mixers, trucks, portable cranes, and 30 trailer loads of steel for the Honolulu (Aloha) Stadium. Among the 67 refrigerated containers aboard was one from Iowa containing 40,000 pounds of meat.

A second such ship will be put into service. The cost of the two and the terminal equipment is $72 million.

Over 98 percent of the cargo to and from the islands is shipped by surface vessels. Matson Navigation Company is the largest carrier of containerized cargo between Hawai'i and the west coast.

During 1989, 2,024 overseas vessels docked in Honolulu. Incoming cargo totaled 9.8 million tons, and outgoing cargo amounted to 2.6 million tons.

■ Transportation to the Neighbor Islands

Outriggers and double canoes served satisfactorily for inter-island transportation during Hawaiian days. The canoes carried passengers and their personal possessions. There was no heavy cargo.

Sailing vessels were next in service between the islands. Although the distances are short some ships were at sea 10 days or more before reaching port. Elizabeth Kinau Wilder wrote in her journal, 1838, of a 10 day voyage to Hilo.

The first steamship to enter the inter-island

trade was the Constitution, 600 tons, brought from San Francisco, June 24, 1852. Business was poor so it returned to San Francisco after one 72 mile trip to Lahaina, Maui and back.

The first financially successful inter-island steamer was the Kilauea, 414 tons, built in Boston, in 1858. From 1860-71 it was not profitable but S.G. Wilder, founded the Wilder Steamship Company, and made money with this vessel.

The Inter-Island Steam Navigation Company, organized in 1883, put a fleet of six steamers into operation. Wilder added more and the two companies continued in friendly fashion and finally merged in 1904 and were called the Inter-Island Steam Navigation Company. The names of their steamers built since 1926 are familiar to many kama'āina today. They were the Haleakala, Waialeale, Hualalai, and the smaller cattle boat, the Humuula.

Passengers for Maui and Hilo boarded their steamer in Honolulu at 4 p.m., Maui bound travelers went ashore by small boats at Mala landing, Lahaina about 11:30 p.m. Hilo passengers had breakfast and landed about 7:20 a.m. Channel waters are notoriously choppy which caused considerable seasickness. The time had come for a speedier and more pleasant form of travel. That was soon to be by air.

Receipts of cargo in 1987 included 5 million tons in interisland cargo.

■ Automobiles in Hawai'i

The first auto, a Wood Electric, came to Hawai'i in 1898. In July 1904 a Rambler, the first gasoline engine car, was imported. A White Steamer, the first of a number of steam-propelled cars, also came in 1904.

Electric cars proved to be unsatisfactory. Steamers eventually lost favor with motorists. Imagine having the boiler under your seat with the steam gauge registering 800 pounds.

Some 100 cars, mostly gas propelled, were bumping and sloshing over Hawai'i's unpaved roads and lanes by 1906. The auto tax was $20 a year. To secure the $2 driver's license the examiner required the operator to know three things: How to start the car, how to keep it going and how to stop it. The most challenging problem was to keep it running.

The speed limit was 15 miles an hour in town.

There were no stop lines, traffic signs or devices to aid or to confuse the driver. Horses and ox carts had the right of way at all crossings. Presumably pedestrians were on their own.

The first Floral Parade was staged in 1906 with 30 gaily decorated cars starting the long six mile trek from downtown Honolulu to Kapi'olani Park. Records do not show the number of autos that reached the Park.

Of the 100 cars, representing 24 different makes, recorded in 1906 by name of owner, make of car and license number, only four of the kinds are sold in Hawai'i today. They are Buick, Cadillac, Ford and Oldsmobile.

Hawai'i's first automobile traffic fatality was recorded in 1906. The victim was the father of the late Lester Marks, husband of Elizabeth Loy McCandless Marks.

On June 4, 1906 Mr. and Mrs. Louis Marks and their friends Mr. and Mrs. Charles A. Bon, drove to 'Aiea for a visit in the Marks family Winton, License No. 38. In maneuvering to start the return trip Marks backed the car on to the rain-drenched roadway. It turned a complete somersault down a 20-foot embankment spilling the occupants. Bon suffered a broken arm and Marks was killed as one of the canopy supports pierced his neck.

Automobiles and other power driven land vehicles are classed today into two categories.

1. Non-taxable vehicles are those operated by non-resident military personnel, consulates, the federal government, police and fire departments, State of Hawai'i, City and County and the disabled veterans.

2. Taxable vehicles are those not in the above classification. This group is ten times larger than the above.

Motor vehicles are divided into seven types, but for general discussion they may be thought of as passenger vehicles, trucks of several kinds, buses, and motorcycles. Statistics on vehicle registration may be obtained from the State of Hawaii Data Book, published annually by the State Department of Business and Economic Development. The figures below are updated to 1988.

Taxable and non-taxable motor vehicles registered for the entire state totaled 817,609; of these 579,998 were in the County of Honolulu. Totals for the other counties were: County of Hawai'i, 96,360; County of Kaua'i, 47,235; and County of Maui,

94,016. There are some 4,092 miles of streets and highways on the six islands.

■ Bicycles and Motorcycles

A Columbia bicycle was brought to Honolulu in 1892. Rambler bicycles with cushion tires followed and in 1896 bikes with pneumatic tires came into use. Enthusiasts for this form of transportation say that the bicycle is the most economical, carries more weight for its weight and cost and uses less roadway than any other vehicle invented by man.

In 1988 there were 113,311 bicycles in the state, with 103,529 of them on O'ahu.

A Cleveland Motorcycle with a third wheel was brought to Honolulu in 1902. Later the popular American makes were imported. Today a large number of Japanese-made motorcycles are sold. By the end of 1988 there were 11,544 motorcycles in the state. O'ahu had 9,234.

■ Mass Transit in Honolulu

On May 19, 1888 ground was broken and track laying started for a street railway system.

The horse or mule drawn streetcars were popular although more cars were needed and the schedule was unreliable. By July 1889, the trams speeded at eight miles an hour along King Street from Kalihi to Waikīkī, Beretania from Nu'uanu to Punahou.

Honolulu Rapid Transit was organized to operate electrically powered buses on Honolulu streets. Power came from overhead wires. Ten new buses began service on August 31, 1901 replacing the horse and mule drawn cars which had in service 33 horse cars, 113 horses and 194 mules. Eventually more comfortable, speedy gasoline-powered buses replaced other means of mass transit for Honolulu and rural O'ahu. There are 3,370 buses on O'ahu. For the entire state the total was 4,215 as of December 1988.

■ Airplanes

"Bud" Mars brought the first airplane (make not recorded) to Hawai'i and on December 31, 1910 staged an exhibition flight at Moanalua Park. Some 3,000 persons paid a dollar each to watch the flight which cost the promoter, E.H. Lewis, some $5,000. Many were able to watch free from outside the park.

Mr. Lewis purchased two Ryan 4 passenger planes in 1927 and flew paying passengers over O'ahu. All planes came to Hawai'i aboard freighters in crates and were reassembled here.

The first on record to fly between the islands was Major Harold M. Clark who flew from Honolulu to Maui then to Hawai'i where he crashed on cloud-enshrouded Mauna Kea. Two days later he reached a highway on foot, unhurt. The plane was never found.

■ Inter Island Air Travel

Inter Island Steam Navigation organized Inter Island Airways and purchased two Sikorsky S-38 Amphibian planes. These were put into service in November, 1929. More planes were added to meet the demands of residents and especially of visitors. From the first, every possible safety device and precaution have given the air service a perfect safety record. Of unusual interest are the flights over the active volcanic eruptions at night.

Airmail service between the islands began on October 8, 1934. Considerable cargo is carried on special planes. Air service proved to be so satisfactory that the steamers faded into history.

At the present time the two major air lines serving the neighbor islands are Hawaiian Air and Aloha. A number of smaller companies offer daily service also.

■ Hawai'i - Mainland Airplane Flights

The first plane to fly successfully from the mainland to Hawai'i landed at Wheeler Field, O'ahu on June 29, 1927. Lieuts. Lester J. Maitland and Albert F. Hegenberger piloted their tri-motor Army Air Corps Fokker C-2 called the Bird of Paradise from Oakland, California to O'ahu in 25 hours and 52 minutes. They carried at take-off 1,134 gallons of fuel and flew at top speed of 105 miles an hour.

Two years earlier a seaplane commanded by John Rogers had left San Francisco for O'ahu but ran out of fuel 250 miles short of Honolulu. Captain Rogers and his crew of four floated for nine days and were near starvation when rescued.

■ Smith and Bronte

On July 16, 1927, about a month before the Dole Derby was to begin Ernest Smith, pilot and Emory Bronte, navigator left the Oakland, California, airport for Wheeler Field, O'ahu. During the flight they were in touch with ships at sea and shore radio stations. At dawn they sent out a S O S call and then there was silence. Later a wireless message announced that they had landed unhurt in a *kiawe* tree on Moloka'i. Army planes flew them to Wheeler Field where they were honored as the first civilians to fly to Hawai'i from the mainland.

■ **The Dole Derby**

James D. Dole, president and manager of the Hawaiian Pineapple Company announced, just four days after Charles Lindberg flew solo across the Atlantic, that he would sponsor an airplane derby from the mainland to Hawai'i. The first prize was to be $25,000 and the second $10,000.

The Honolulu chapter of the National Aeronautic Association was responsible for the rules and details of the flight which was scheduled for August 12, 1927.

Eight entrants at Oakland on the eve of the flight agreed to postpone it to August 16. On that Tuesday morning four planes took off for O'ahu. One piloted by Auggie Peddler and another by Jack Frost were never heard from after flying into the horizon.

Before a throng of some 30,000 persons at Wheeler Field Arthur C. Goebel landed at 12:24 p.m. on August 17. He won $25,000 for his 26 hour, 17 minute race flight.

One hour and 56 minutes later Martin Jensen arrived in his yellow monoplane to win $10,000.

The navy conducted an exhaustive search for the missing fliers but no trace was found.

■ **Amelia Earhart**

On Friday afternoon, January 11, 1935, a crimson, single-engine Lockheed Vega monoplane left Wheeler Field, O'ahu. Alone in the plane was Amelia Earhart, already famous as the first woman to cross the Atlantic by air as a passenger and first woman to fly it alone. She was also the first woman to fly across the United States alone in both directions.

Amelia arrived in Oakland the next day and became the first person to fly solo from Hawai'i to the mainland. A bronze plaque on Diamond Head Road reminds us of this accomplishment.

Amelia Earhart returned to O'ahu with a crew of three which included pilot Fred Noonan, on March 17, 1937. Her plane this time was a twin-engine Lockheed Electra which was to take her, according to plans, around the world flying west from Hawai'i. On March 20 the plane was damaged in the take-off from Ford Island, Pearl Harbor and had to be shipped back to Lockheed in Burbank, California, to be repaired.

On May 20, 1937, Amelia Earhart and her navigator Fred Noonan left Oakland in the repaired Lockheed Electra for a trip around the world flying eastward. They touched down at airports along the way and reached Lae, New Guinea, from which they were to fly to tiny Howland Island and thence to Hawai'i.

Howland was one of five islets that had been occupied by young, Kamehameha School graduates for several years. The boys recorded weather conditions which would be valuable to flyers and their presence insured U.S. ownership of the islands. The air strip on Howland was named Kamakaiwi Field.

On July 2, Amelia and her pilot flew from Lae with 1,250 gallons of gasoline. U.S. Coast Guard vessels at Howland heard the Electra's radio signals for a time. Among the last messages were that the plane was running out of gas, and they believed that they were but 100 miles from Howland.

President Roosevelt ordered a massive search in which a carrier, several destroyers, a battleship, minesweeper and countless hundreds of planes took part. No trace was found of the plane or its occupants.

Amelia's sister, Mrs. Muriel Earhart Morrissey, on a visit to Honolulu in 1980 told this writer that she discounts the rumors that the Earhart plane landed on one of the Japanese Mandated Islands to the north. She more readily accepts the report by an airforce captain who has salvaged planes along the California coast. He made a detailed study of the flight of the Electra from Lae toward Howland Island. He concluded that there was condensation and loss of fuel from the gasoline drums that were stored for some time in tropical New Guinea. The result was that the aviators ran out of fuel shortly before reaching Howland Island. Mrs. Morrissey's sensitively written biography of her sister is listed at the end of this unit.

■ **Transpacific Air Service**

The first regularly scheduled air passenger service from Hawai'i to the mainland began in October, 1936. Air routes were awarded to three airlines, two of which flew to the Orient and the Antipodes also.

In 1969 a new ruling allowed five more airlines to fly in and out of Hawai'i. A number of foreign carriers serve Hawai'i on a regular schedule.

All airports are under government control. The first military airport, Luke Field, was dedicated April 29, 1919. John Rodgers, now the Honolulu International Airport, was the first territorial airport, dedicated March 21, 1927.

In addition to the 16 state and six military airports there are a number of privately owned ones. Heliports have been established where needed for helicopter landings.

Honolulu International Airport, the sixteenth busiest in the United States, recorded 377,919 total arrivals and departures in 1988.

Understandings and Appreciations

1. Review briefly the steps in the construction of a canoe in order to understand the tremendous amount of hand work needed. Note that at least four classes of artisans were involved.

    Workers in wood.

    Workers in stone to fashion and sharpen adzes.

    Experts in making sennit ('aha), the cordage from coconut husk fibers.

    Experts in lashing the mo'o to the wa'a and lashing the 'iako and the 'ama to the canoe.

2. Observe canoes or pictures of canoes which were made by joining strips of wood together as was done on the low islands (Tuamotu) which were without large forest trees. One can appreciate the huge koa trees of Hawai'i as material for dugout canoes.

3. Study the photographs, sketches or models of any Pacific Island canoes. Then one will appreciate the neat, trim, functional appearance of the Hawaiian canoes.

4. See the Dillingham Corporation Tide Chart Calendar for 1972 entitled canoes of Polynesia. Color paintings and detailed sketches of the construction of six Polynesian canoes by

Herbert Kawainui Kane. The canoes are Tuamotuan, Samoan, Tahitian traveling canoe, Atiu canoe, Tahitian war canoe and a double canoe of Hawai'i.

5. See the Dillingham Corporation Calendar for 1973 color paintings and detailed sketches by Herbert K. Kane of: Hawaiian double canoe, Hawaiian outrigger canoe, Marquesan, Maori, Fijian, Tongan, Manahiki and Rakahanga canoes.

6. The Dillingham Corporation Calendar for 1975 reproduces 13 paintings in color of ships that helped make "Hawai'i's Maritime History." Joseph Feher painted ships from the era of 1400 A.D. to 1975.

7. Scan the literature for figures on the sizes of Hawaiian canoes. A maximum length of 108 feet has been recorded although the average is less than 50 feet. Discuss the task involved in making and in navigating the large canoes.

8. Recall that transportation in old Hawai'i was largely by canoe, even from village to village. Compare this situation to the present day conditions where land transportation is over a network of highways for motor vehicles and sidewalks for pedestrians. Compare inter-island transportation by planes, barges and freighters to the canoes of old.

Student Activities

1. In the encyclopedia or other reference work read about the sextant, chronometer and other navigational aids not known to the early Polynesians.

2. Make model canoes of wood, then float or sail them. If a craft shop is not available make sketches of canoes.

3. Organize a hike into the rain forest and look for koa trees suitable for canoes. Ask a forest ranger about the cause or causes for the death of many koa trees. If you locate a "canoe tree" note the terrain over which it must be dragged to haul it to the nearest beach.

4. Try to cut wood with a stone adze by using firm, short chopping strokes. Use a hafted adze, not the stone blade alone.

5. Write an account of the launching of a canoe with sea water. Compare this to the champagne launching of a modern ship.

6. Look at old paddles for the midrib called 'upe or io. Tell why it is there by comparing it to other

Poynesian paddles. (Buck, 1957, pp. 278-280)

7. Read about the 'elepaio bird hopping along the trunk of a koa tree. What was the bird looking for? Degener writes, p. 177, that the crow or alalā visited the log also.

8. If the canoes could travel 7 miles an hour, how long would the voyage be from Honolulu to Nawiliwili? To Kahului? To Hilo? To Tahiti?

9. Learn the names of some of the principal stars in Hawaiian. See Bryan's Stars over Hawaii, pp. 45-48. Also books by R. Johnson, C. Lindo and W. Kyselka.

10. Read about the method of cooking at sea on a fireplace of stones with wood brought for that purpose.

11. Read the story of the remarkable aviatrix Amelia Earhart who three times focused attention on Hawai'i. Her biography was written by her sister Muriel Morrissey.

■ **Audio-Visual Aids**

Bishop Museum usually keeps outrigger canoes and one model of a double canoe on exhibit. Scores of model canoes and a number of full size canoes are in the study collection. A full size sail of lau hala matting from Kapingamarangi may be the only one of this type preserved in Hawai'i. A steam locomotive and railroad cars are on the museum grounds.

The Falls of Clyde, a four-masted bark, may be visited at Pier 5, Honolulu Harbor.

■ **Vocabulary**

1. Kinds of canoes: kaukahi, pukolu, peleleu, kaulua.
2. Parts of a canoe: wa'a, mo'o, 'iako, 'aha, ama, kia, lā.
3. Canoe accessories: hoe, kā wa'a, hālau, 'alihi pā'ū, pōhaku hekau, hue wai.
4. Navigation: kilolani, Hōkū-pa'a, Na-hiku, Mahina, Newe, hōkū-hele

■ **Current Happenings of Significance to this Unit**

1. The outrigger canoe is one of the few Hawaiian culture materials that persists today in a relatively unmodified form. A few canoes have been made in the past few years in the traditional design but the tools used were modern, and bolts or screws were used to hold the parts of the canoe together. The drastic change has been to make outrigger canoes of fiber glass or

some similar synthetic product.

2. Many double canoes in the Pacific today are not Hawaiian but catamarans — the Tamil, Indian word for double-hull vessel.

■ **Reading List**

Apo, Peter, and Bob Nagatani. No Ka Heihei Wa'a. Some thoughts and ideas about Hawaiian outrigger canoe racing. Honolulu: Hui Wa'a and Surfing Association, 1981.

Apple, Russell A. Trails: From Stepping Stones to Kerbstones. Honolulu: Bishop Museum Special Publication No. 53, 1965.

Best, Gerald M. Railroads of Hawaii. Narrow and standard gauge common carriers. San Marino, CA: Golden West Books, 1978.

Blackman, Maralyn. Hōkūle'a. Honolulu: Polynesian Voyaging Society, 1976. (Book 4 in a series for children on sea voyaging.)

Bryan, E.H. Jr. Ancient Hawaiian Life. 1938. Honolulu: Books About Hawaii, 1950.

———. Panala'au Memoirs. Colonizing the equatorial islands. Honolulu: Pacific Scientific Information Center, Bishop Museum, 1974.

———. Stars over Hawaii. Honolulu: Books about Hawaii, 1955.

Buck, Peter H. Arts and Crafts of Hawaii. Honolulu: Bishop Museum Special Publication No. 45, 1957.

———. Vikings of the Pacific. Chicago: University of Chicago Press, 1959. (First published in 1938 as Vikings of the Sunrise. New York: Frederick A. Stokes.)

Chun, Naomi. Hawaiian Canoe-Building Traditions. Honolulu: Kamehameha Schools/Bernice P. Bishop Estate, 1988.

Conde, Jessie C. Sugar Trains Pictorial. Felton, CA: Glenwood Publishers, 1975.

Conde, Jessie C., and Gerald M. Best. Sugar Trains. Narrow gauge rails of Hawaii. Felton, CA: Glenwood Publishers, 1973.

Damon, Ethel M. Father Bond of Kohala. Honolulu: The Friend, 1927.

Emory, Kenneth P. "Navigation." Ch. 22 in Ancient Hawaiian Civilization. A series of lectures delivered at the Kamehameha Schools by E.S.C. Handy [and others]. 1933. Rutland, VT and Japan: C.E. Tuttle, 1965 (rev. ed.).

———. "The Flying Spray." *Conch Shell*, Vols. I-III, 1963-1965. Honolulu: Bishop Museum Association.

Finney, Ben R., comp. *Pacific Navigation and Voyaging.* Wellington, N.Z.: Polynesian Society Memoir No. 39, 1976.

———. *Hōkūle'a: The Way to Tahiti.* New York: Dodd, Mead and Company, 1979.

Golson, Jack, ed. *Polynesian Navigation.* A symposium on Andrew Sharp's theory of Accidental Voyages. Wellington, N.Z.: Polynesian Society Memoir No. 34, 1963.

Haddon, A.C., and James Hornell. *Canoes of Oceania.* Vol. I, Hawaii. 1936. Honolulu: Bishop Museum Special Publication No. 27, 1975.

Haraguchi, Paul. *Weather in Hawaiian Waters.* Honolulu: Pacific Weather, Inc., 1979.

Henriques, Edgar. "Hawaiian Canoes." *Hawaiian Historical Society Annual Report,* Vol. 34. Honolulu: Hawaiian Historical Society, 1925.

Holmes, Tommy. *The Hawaiian Canoe.* Hanalei, Kaua'i: Editions Ltd., Gaylord Wilcox, Publisher, 1981. (An in-depth study of the canoe and its parts. Profusely illustrated. Special edition with covers of curly *koa* wood.)

Ihara, Violet K. DOE Liaison Teacher at Bishop Museum. *Life in Ancient Hawaii: Tools,* 1977. *Falls of Clyde, a Merchant Ship of the Past,* 1978. *The Folklore of the Zodiac,* 1981. Honolulu: Bishop Museum School Bulletins.

Johnson, Rubellite K., and John K. Mahelona. *Na Inoa Hoku.* A catalog of Hawaiian and Pacific star names. Honolulu: Topgallant Publishing Company, 1975.

Kamakau, Samuel M. *The Works of the People of Old.* Honolulu: Bishop Museum Special Publication No. 61, 1976. (Article on canoemaking.)

Krauss, Bob, et al. *Historic Waianae.* A place of kings. Norfolk Island, Aus.: Island Heritage, 1973.

Kyselka, Will, and George Bunton. *Polynesian Stars and Men.* The puzzle of the ancient navigation of the Polynesians. Honolulu: Bishop Museum Press, 1969.

Lewis, David. *The Voyaging Stars.* Secrets of the Pacific Island navigators. New York: W.W. Norton & Company, 1978.

———. *We, the Navigators.* The ancient art of land finding in the Pacific. Honolulu: University Press of Hawaii, 1975.

Lindo, Cecelia K., and Nancy A. Mower, eds. *Polynesian Seafaring Heritage.* Honolulu: Kamehameha Schools and the Polynesian Voyaging Society, 1980.

Malo, David. *Hawaiian Antiquities.* 1898. Honolulu: Bishop Museum Special Publication No. 2, 1976.

Mitchell, Donald D. Kilolani. *Hawaiian Treasures.* Canoes, 101-107. Honolulu: Kamehameha Schools Press, 1978.

Morrissey, Muriel E. *Courage is the Price.* The life of Amelia Earhart written by her sister. Wichita, Kansas: McCormack-Armstrong Publishing Division, 1963.

Munford, James K., ed. *John Ledyard's Journal of Captain Cook's Last Voyage.* Corvallis: Oregon State University Press, 1963.

Oahu Railway and Land Company. *A Brief History of Benjamin Franklin Dillingham and the Beginning of the O.R. and L.* Ten-page illustrated booklet. Honolulu: O.R. and L., Privately printed, 1961.

Pukui, Mary K., trans. "The Canoe Making Profession of Ancient Times." Honolulu: Bishop Museum Occasional Papers, Vol. 15, No. 13, 1939.

Sharp, Andrew. *Ancient Voyagers in the Pacific.* Wellington, N.Z.: Polynesian Society Memoir No. 32, 1956.

Stindt, Fred A. *Matson's Century of Ships.* Photos and descriptions of every Matson vessel during its 100-year history. 1982. Available from the author at 3363 Riviera West Drive, Kelseyville, CA 95451.

Worden, William L. *Cargoes, Matson's First Century in the Pacific.* Honolulu: University Press of Hawaii, 1981. (The story of Hawaiian shipping, with emphasis on the Matson Navigation Company but also discussing rival lines.)

Yardley, Paul T. *Millstones and Milestones: The Career of B.F. Dillingham, 1844-1918.* Honolulu: University Press of Hawaii for The B.F. Dillingham Company, Ltd., 1981.

Yost, Arthur H. *The Outrigger.* A history of the Outrigger Canoe Club, 1908-71. Honolulu: The Outrigger Canoe Club, 1972.

UNIT 13:
Games
and Pastimes

GAMES AND PASTIMES

The Hawaiian people devoted a vast amount of time to games, amusements, and relaxing pastimes before their way of life was changed by foreigners.

The names of over a hundred of the old games (*pā'ani kahiko*) are known, but the directions for playing a number of them are lost. The wide variety of games is a credit to the fun-loving people, since they developed many of them in Hawai'i.

The chiefs set aside large fields (*kahua*) for the tournaments, and constructed special courses for rolling the game stones. They built slides for racing downhill on sturdy, sleek sleds (*papa hōlua*). The chiefs and the people built large thatched structures or walled enclosures where they played games far into the night by torch light.

The sea was constantly alive with people swimming, diving, surfing and riding in canoes. Its beaches were a meeting place for relaxation and a variety of pastimes.

The *Makahiki*, the annual festive season of some four months' duration, was dedicated to the god Lono, patron of sports. During this time, approximately mid-October through mid-February, all unnecessary work ceased, war was *kapu*, and the temple services were suspended. The people paid their taxes to their chiefs in the form of handicrafts and garden products and were then free to play and dance.

■ Sports Champions

Very few of the Hawaiian sports required the players to be organized into teams. Exceptions were tug-of-war, canoe racing and some of the adult pastimes enjoyed at night. In men's sports the emphasis was upon training young warriors for the hand-to-hand fighting practiced in warfare.

Individuals became champions in boxing, wrestling, foot racing, spear throwing and other competitive sports.

The wholehearted participation in the games helped the people maintain the magnificent physique and graceful carriage which won the admiration of the early travelers to Hawai'i. These visitors praised the Hawaiian sportsmen for their vigor, bravery, dexterity and good humor. Games were a release from the oppression of the laws and restrictions of the times. Those played by the people of the working class provided relaxation from the toil of furnishing the necessities of life for themselves and for their chiefs.

■ The Decline of Hawaiian Games

Although the Hawaiian games were suited to the environment and to the temperament of the people, most of them were replaced by European sports within comparatively few years after the arrival of foreigners. Exceptions were the water sports, chiefly surfing and canoeing, which declined for a long period of time and were then revived. The loss of the native sports was the result of a number of factors.

The religious practices of the times permeated the conduct of the games.

The overthrow of the *kapu* system in 1819 swept away the gods, *kāhuna*, temples and consequently the religious ceremonies associated with the games.

Peace prevailed after Kamehameha I consolidated the islands. The chiefs no longer trained young men to be warriors through the promotion of sports as they had done in earlier times.

The Hawaiian people received with enthusiasm the new culture introduced by foreigners. They neglected the games to earn money to buy articles of foreign make. They readily accepted foreign games, not because they thought them superior but because they were new.

The chiefs and the people spent long hours learning to read and write. As they learned from their missionary teachers about the complex culture elsewhere, they were led to believe that their own way of life was inferior.

The betting that accompanied the Hawaiian games and the inevitable losses caused hardship and suffering among the unfortunate gamblers and their families. The missionaries recognized these conditions and sought to abolish the games in order to stamp out gambling.

The serious and industrious men and women of the mission were critical of all adults who used their time and energy in play during daytime "working" hours. The Hawaiians answered missionary William Ellis concerning this charge by explaining that "they built houses and cultivated their gardens from necessity, but followed their amusements because their hearts were fond of them."

The enthusiastic revival of interest in Hawaiian culture in the Islands at this time is especially noticeable in the area of Hawaiian games. These pastimes are becoming increasingly popular with people on school playgrounds, in public parks and in summer fun programs. Playground directors, club leaders and teachers ask for additional games to share with their young people. These pastimes are also fun at home, the vigorous ones in the back yard and the quiet ones in the living room or play room.

Groups organized to promote Hawaiian culture schedule workshops to give adults and youngsters the opportunity of making and using games implements. Commercial craft shops are marketing games kits. Spectators at pageants and festivals express keen interest in Hawaiian games demonstrations and contests.

Dress for the Players in Old Hawai'i

The principle garment for the men was a loin cloth or *malo* made from *kapa* which was pounded from plant fibers into an off-white fabric. It was worn white or dyed in solid colors and was sometimes decorated with geometric designs.

The women of old Hawai'i wore a waist-to-knee *pā'ū* of *kapa* which proved to be too scant to meet the dress standards imposed by foreigners who settled here. The successor to the *pā'ū* is the *kīkepa*, a sarong-like garment which covered the body from a low neckline to a point below the knees. It was secured over one shoulder and was more richly decorated than the man's *malo*.

Today the contestants should wear their usual play clothes except in pageantry where they are staging a revival of the earlier Hawaiian customs.

The games described in this book are for today's players. The rules given for some of them are essentially the same as those in use in old Hawai'i. Directions for other games have been modified somewhat to adapt them to our modern way of life. An effort has been made to retain the spirit and flavor of the traditional Hawaiian games.

The amusements described here were grouped by the author according to their nature and their demands upon the physique and skill of the players. Complete directions are given for the games which have proved to be popular and practical today. Addiional pastimes, described more briefly are added to give the reader an idea of the great variety of Hawaiian amusements.

Not all Hawaiian recreational activities require games equipment. More than 25 different games implements are used in playing the games described here. A few of them, such as ti leaves for sliding, are gifts from nature and require little or no additional fashioning by man. Some 18 materials such as different kinds of wood, fibers, leaves, nuts and stones are used in constructing the apparatus for playing the rest of the games. Most of these implements can be duplicated satisfactorily today.

E Pā'ani Kākou *(Let's Play)*

The directions given for playing the following games are based on the information in the available literature and on instructions shared by elderly informants. It has been possible to adapt the rules to our present day playgrounds without losing the spirit and flavor of the old games.

Games are directed by a coach *(kumu)* and judged by a referee *('uao)* or a scorekeeper *(helu'ai)*. The referee starts a game by calling out, *"ho'omākaukau"* get ready. He starts the action with *'oia* or go ahead. The cheering section members should call out *"maika'i"* when they see a good play and *"auwē,"* too bad, as a consolation.

Games of Strength and Endurance
Group I

The most strenuous of the sports were the tournament games (ho'okūkū) conducted on special fields (kahua) before large crowds of enthusiastic spectators. These matches brought district champions in competition with one another, and betting on the outcome was part of the excitement. Most of these sports required no game implements.

The sports most enjoyed by Captain Cook and his party were the two boxing matches (mokomoko). These were exhibitions presented in honor of the English visitors and, as usual, they were attended by large crowds of supporters.

It was at this exhibition that Webber sketched the "Boxing Match before Capt. Cook at Owhyie (Hawai'i) Sandwich Islands, Thursday, January 28, 1779."

This is the first known sketch of a Hawaiian sport by a European artist.

This picture forms the end papers in Mitchell's *Hawaiian Games for Today*.

■ Hākōkō *Hawaiian Wrestling*

Suitable for boys of all ages. Outdoors or on a mat indoors.

The pair of players engage in "catch-as-catch-can" type of wrestling. This is done while standing but no other rules are prescribed.

A player scores when he forces any part of his opponent's body except the soles of his feet to touch the ground. If both players go down together the referee should note who touches the ground first. The scoring should be agreed upon before the match; for instance, two throws out of three will determine the winner.

Face your opponent. At the signal from the referee use your favorite wrestling hold to get a firm grip on him. When you force him to the ground, or any part of his body except the soles of his feet to touch the ground, you score a point. Continue until a winner is declared by the referee.

This is an excellent sport for exhibitions and pageants as it is easy for a large number of persons to watch the players struggle to win.

■ Hākōkō Noho *Wrestling While Seated*

Suitable for boys and girls of all ages. On a grassy play-field or on a mat indoors.

Sit on the mat or play field with your right leg extended in front of you and your left foot under your right knee.

Your opponent does likewise. Move close together so that you put your left hands on each other's right shoulders and your right hands on the left side of each other's waists. In this position your bent left knees are in contact.

Attempt to unseat your opponent by pushing him over sideways with your right hand, aided as much as possible by your left hand. A player is unseated when he is forced over on his side. He usually releases one hand from his opponent and uses it to break his fall.

Unseat him two out of three times and you are the victor.

Boys should strip to the waist for this game so that they will not cling to their opponents' clothing.

■ Uma *Hand Wrestling*

Suitable for boys over ten years of age and for men. Outdoors or indoors.

Kneel on a grassy play field or on a sturdy mat. Place your right elbow on the ground or mat and your left hand on your back.

When your opponent has done the same, take his right hand by clasping your four fingers firmly around his. (An alternate method of clasping hands is to grasp each others' thumbs with the fingers curving around to the back of the hands. This hold can be used if the contestants agree to do so, but they should understand that it allows a player to press his finger tips into the muscles and nerves of his opponent's hand in a painful grip.)

At the starting signal from the referee, attempt to force your opponent's right hand to the ground while keeping your own elbow firmly on the ground.

You score when you force the back of his hand to the ground or cause him to move his elbow. When neither seems possible because of evenly matched players, the referee will render a decision, either a draw or a point by the one who showed better technique.

Instead of kneeling, players may lie prone, clasp hands and play as directed here. Sometimes contestants sit at a table for hand wrestling. Use caution here to avoid an injury or broken bone by forcing a competitor's arm over the edge of the table. Children under ten years of age may suffer a "green stick fracture" if allowed to strain beyond their limit in this game.

Uma should be played before groups small enough for all of the spectators to see the participants' hands.

■ **Pā Uma** *Standing Hand Wrestling*

Suitable for boys and men. Girls may organize a cheering section. Outdoors or indoors.

Players stand facing each other and clasp right thumbs. Your right feet must be in contact.

Place your right foot next to his so that your little toes touch. (Hawaiian games are played barefoot.) Hold this position with your right foot as you stand and wrestle. Your left foot may be moved to any position you wish to help you keep your balance.

At the signal from the referee, try to overcome your opponent's thrust and push his hand or both your hand and his to his chest.

You score when you touch his chest and have kept your right foot in position. If you score two out of three times you are the champion.

A variation of this game is to force your opponent's hand to touch your chest. Thus pulling is substituted for pushing. Left-handed players use their left hands with each other, if they wish to do so, but each wrestles with but one hand at a time.

This game may be watched by a large number of spectators who should be able to see the players struggle to reach each other's chests.

■ **Loulou** *Pulling Hooked Fingers*

Suitable for boys and girls of all ages. Playfield or indoors.

Two players take a firm stand facing each other, lock index fingers, and pull until one lets go or is pulled so far out of position that the referee declares him the loser.

Face your opponent and on the signal from the referee lock index fingers of your right hands (of left hands if both players are left handed). Place your thumb against your palm and cover it with your remaining three fingers. Stand with your right feet in contact during the entire play.

Pull with a straight pull. Do not twist or jerk.

You score when your opponent releases his hold or you are able to pull him out of his standing position. Two out of three will make you the *loulou* victor.

A variation of this game would be for the

players to use other than the index fingers.

The referee should encourage the contestants by calling, *"Huki! Huki!"* (Pull! Pull!) as the players strain for victory. In time the finger of one of the players will straighten out and his opponent will win the point. If this does not happen the referee will call a draw. A player loses if he moves his right foot out of position.

This game may be used in exhibitions or in pageantry as a large number of people can watch the players standing and straining to win. The referee should add life to the contest by encouraging the participants with his voice and gestures.

Be sure to pronounce the name of this game correctly (with the u sound clearly following the o). Don't say *lōlō* which translates "stupid" or "feeble-minded."

■ **Kulaʻi Wāwae** *Foot Pushing*

Suitable for boys and girls of all ages. Outdoors or indoors.

Players pair off and sit on the grass or on a mat. Each attempts to unseat the other by pushing his feet against his opponent's feet. This game is not interesting unless the players in each pair are the same weight and strength.

Sit facing your opponent. Brace yourself by placing your hands flat on the ground behind you and keeping your arms stiff. Flex your knees slightly. Your opponent should be opposite you in a similar position, close enough to you so that you can place your toes against his.

Push with your feet using a steady thrust or shorter surprise drives.

Your spectators are more entertained by your victory if you are able to push your opponent over on his back with his feet high in the air, or cause him to whirl a quarter turn. You are most apt to score by pushing his feet and causing him to move, even a little, away from you on the ground or mat. The referee must be alert to this movement in declaring a winner.

■ **Kulakuaʻi** *Chest Pushing*

Suitable for boys of all ages. Girls form the cheering section. Outdoors or indoors.

Stand and face your opponent.

At the signal from the referee, slap or push his chest with your open palms. Of course, you must avoid his thrusts and maintain your balance.

A strong slap on his chest should send him back out of his standing position and score a point for you. Two wins out of three makes you the victor.

A variant of this game is to ask the players to stand with their right feet in contact as in the game pā uma. A contestant scores when he pushes his opponent vigorously enough to cause him to move his right foot out of position.

■ Hukihuki or Pā'ume'ume *Tug-of-War*

Suitable for boys and men. Girls may play if they wish to do so. On a grassy playfield.

One of the few Hawaiian games requiring teamwork.

The players, divided into two equal sides, form a line along the opposite ends of the stout rope which they are to pull. The middle of the rope should be marked with a bright cloth. When the game begins this cloth should be in position over a coconut which is fastened to the ground by a short stake. Ten feet on either side of the coconut place other coconuts so that the three are in a line underneath the rope. A team wins when it pulls the rope far enough to bring the cloth marker over the coconut on its side of center. The supporters of each team should yell "huki, "huki" ("pull," "pull").

Games of Skill
Group II

Warriors-in-training strengthened their muscles and developed dexterity and skills by engaging in vigorous sports which required the use of games implements, some of them similar to the weapons used in warfare. Most of these were tournament games which employed implements that were thrown, thrust, or rolled along a prepared field. Many of these activities were of great interest to the spectators, who came in large numbers to the tournaments.

■ 'Ulu Maika *Rolling Stone Disks*

For men only in old Hawai'i. Today children and adults of both sexes. Playfield with close-cut grass or smooth, firm soil.

'Ulu Maika or 'Olohū was one of the most popular sports in early Hawai'i. Hundreds of skillfully fashioned playing stones, which may be called 'ulu or maika, are now in museums and private collections. Many specially prepared courses

(kahua maika), on which the stones were rolled, were in use in earlier times. Most of them have been destroyed.

Kits containing 'ulu maika stones and a pair of stakes can be purchased in Hawai'i. Although the stones varied in size in early times the typical ones used today are about 3¾ inches in diameter, 1½ inches thick in the center and 1 inch thick at the rim. The perimeter and each side is convex to help the disk roll on course.

Stakes, about a foot long, can be cut from broomsticks or split from lumber and sharpened at one end. Cords, and reels to keep them from becoming entangled, can be purchased at stores which sell fishing supplies.

As a test of strength the players roll the stone discs or maika as far as possible down a smooth course on the playing field.

As a demonstration of skill or accuracy the contestants roll the maika between two stakes on a smooth, grassy playfield.

The stakes may be placed 8 to 10 inches apart. The players may stand from 15 to 20 feet from the stakes. These conditions should be varied according to the age and skill of the players. The set-up should be difficult enough to challenge the contestants but not made impossible.

A player takes his position behind the starting point which is marked by a long cord at each end of the 'ulu maika course. He tries to roll one stone between the stakes and then his opponent at the othe end of the course retrieves it and rolls it back. If four stones are available, it is advisable to let each player roll four times in succession. His chances for success are often better on the third or fourth attempts which makes the game more enjoyable. His opponent then rolls the four stones back.

Directions for rolling the maika for skill and accuracy:

Determine the number of stones that each player is to roll and the method of scoring as suggested below. The player steps up to the starting line. The stone is held firmly with the thumb and first two fingers around the circumference of the stone. The player stoops over and aims down the course between and beyond the stakes. A point is scored for each stone that is rolled between the stakes.

Directions for rolling the maika for distance:

Provide each player with one or more stones

and mark the starting point. Place the referees some distance down the playfield to note where the stones stop rolling. If there are not enough stones to allow them to remain on the field until all have rolled, their positions should be marked with ti leaves by referees and the *maika* returned to the starting point for others to use.

The player steps up to a point a few feet from the starting line with the stone held firmly between the thumb and first two fingers. He gives added force to his underhanded throw by taking a few short running steps to the starting line. The player who rolls his stone the greatest distance wins a point.

■ Ihe Pahe‘e *Spear Sliding*

Suitable for both sexes 10 years of age and older. Playfield with grass clipped short.

Contestants slide a spear, from four to six feet long, over a grassy playfield. As a test of skill they attempt to slide it between a pair of stakes placed from 8 to 10 inches apart. As a test of strength they slide the *ihe* as far as possible down a long play field.

Ihe may be made in the form of replicas of specimens in Bishop Museum. Or broomsticks, preferably the hardwood ones from push brooms, make satisfactory substitutes for *ihe*.

Directions for sliding the *ihe* between pairs of stakes:

Step up to the starting line, grasp your *ihe* near the middle and with an underhand thrust slide it along the surface of the grass with sufficient force to drive it between the stakes.

You are the winner if your *ihe* goes between and clear of the stakes a greater number of times than that of your opponent.

Directions for sliding the *ihe* for distance:

Step up to the starting line, grasp the *ihe* near the middle and slide it along the grassy course with your greatest possible strength. Mark the spot where it stopped before returning the *ihe* to the starting line for additional plays.

■ Moa Pahe‘e *Dart Sliding*

For boys and girls from age 10 and for adults. Grassy field or on smooth, firm earth.

Contestants slide a torpedo-shaped dart called

Games Implements: The disk-shaped *‘ulu maika* stones were rolled between a pair of stakes.
The dart (*moa pahe‘e*) and the spear (*ihe pahe‘e*) were slid between the stakes. The highly-polished dart might be carried in a *lau hala* sheath.

moa over a grassy play field as a test of skill or strength. Sliding the moa is a greater challenge than handling the ihe as the moa is much more difficult to control. Game darts should be made from the pattern of the original ones in museums. There is no satisfactory substitute for the moa.

The directions are the same as for the ihe pahe'e.

Our favorite moa, a replica from the Bishop Museum collection is 14 inches long and 2½ inches in diameter at its thickest part which is 4 inches from the blunt end. Museum darts vary in length from 10 to 22 inches. Most of them are about 14 inches long.

■   **'Ō'ō ihe** *Spear Throwing*

For boys and girls of 10 years and older and for adults. A large playfield.

Players use a hardwood spear, 5 to 6 feet long, which has one thick, rather blunt end and a sharp end. In the sport 'ō'ō ihe the players throw the spear with considerable force, sharp end first, into the stalk of a banana plant. In earlier days this sport trained the young men for war. The banana stalk, which represented the human body, was cut into four to six foot lengths and secured in an upright position. This is done by driving a long sturdy stake into the ground and tying the banana stalk to it.

Directions: Step up to the starting line, some 5 to 6 yards from the banana stalk. Grasp the spear, sharp end forward, and hurl it into the banana stalk at the command of the referee. You score a point when the spear pierces the banana stalk and remains in it. Twist the spear as you remove it and you will not break the banana stalk loose from its ties.

■   **Kākā Lā'au** *Fencing With Spears*

For teen age boys and men. On a grassy playfield.

Each contestant uses a blunt wooden spear, six or seven feet long to touch his opponent or to intercept his opponent's spear. Broom handles, preferably the hardwood ones from push brooms, may be substituted for spears. A player scores when he touches any part of his opponent's body, except his head, with his spear. The first player to score ten strikes against his challenger may be declared the winner.

The referee stands at the side facing both players. As the one on the right scores he holds up

fingers on his right hand. He uses his left hand for the player on the left and is able in this way to keep score easily.

Grasp your spear near the middle but keep your hands a foot or more apart so that you may use either end of the spear easily.

Approach your opponent at the referee's signal and press the center of your spear between your hands against the same point on your opponent's spear. Repeat this touching procedure three times, then spring back deftly from this contact and you are ready to fence.

Attempt to touch your opponent's leg with the lower part of your spear and his arms and shoulders with the side of the upper part of the spear. Do not thrust with the point. At the same time you ward off his blows as he attempts to touch you.

You score a point when you touch any part of his body, except his head, with your spear.

Water Sports
Group III

■   **Lele Kawa** or **Lele 'Opu** *Plunging Feet First with the Least Possible Splash*

For children and adults who can swim and dive. Swimming pool with diving board or natural pool suited to diving.

A sport of leaping feet first into the water making the least possible splash. This is done from the diving board (papa lele kawa) at a swimming pool. In earlier times the people dived from cliffs or stream banks or from trees that over hung the water.

The diver places the tip of a leaf (hau or other broad leaf) between his lips and allows the rest of the leaf to form a shield to keep the water from entering his nose.

Step out on the diving board with a leaf in your mouth and your hands close to your sides. Slip into the water toes first with the least possible splash. The referee determines the winner by listening to the splash made by each diver.

■   **Lele Pahū** *Plunging Feet First With A Great Splash*

For children and adults who can swim and dive. Swimming pool or natural pool suitable for diving.

A fun-filled form of diving, the opposite of lele

kawa. Here the winner is the diver who makes the greatest splash as he strikes the water.

Dive from the board in your own way attempting to strike the water with the greatest sound and trying to splash water in all directions. The referee awards the prize to the biggest splash.

■ Kaupua *Diving For a Half-Submerged Object*

For young people and adults who can dive and swim. Natural pool or swimming pool.

A game in which the players swim and dive for a specific object. In early times a small green gourd was used. Today we dive for small green coconuts, green guavas or similar objects which will half-float in the water.

The divers line up along the edge of the pool. The referee throws the object into the pool some ten or more yards beyond the line of divers. When they see the object hit the water they dive and swim for it. The one who retrieves it is the winner.

This sport developed into the interesting custom of coin-diving during the days when many passenger steamers sailed in and out of Honolulu Harbor. Passengers tossed coins into the water and agile Hawaiian boys retrieved most of them before the coins could sink to the bottom.

■ Aho Loa *Long Breath*

Teenage boys and girls and adults. Swimming pool with good visibility.

This is a contest which checks a swimmer's ability to remain under water.

This game is not without danger when used with children. It should be conducted in a clear pool where the divers can be watched. Winning should not be stressed to the point that it will tempt a diver to remain under water too long.

Line up along the edge of the deep part of the pool. At the signal from the referee dive into the water. Use your good judgement in exhaling and in deciding just how you can best remain under water. The winner is the last one to come to the surface, alive. He doesn't win if he has to be rescued and revived.

As the name suggests this is a sport that measures a person's ability to hold his breath.

In the early days Hawai'i's chanters as well as divers engaged in exercises that developed their ability to hold their breath or to expel it slowly.

In Kona, Hawai'i, young chanters would gather at the shore just before sunset. At the moment the

disk of the sun touched the horizon the chanters would begin to intone—"Na-'u" and continue the "ū" without taking a breath (if possible) until the sun had slipped into the sea. The performance, which required about two minutes as timed by the setting sun, made a game of testing one's breath control.

■ Other Water Sports

WINDSURFING or BOARDSAILING

Windsurfing is called the fastest growing water sport in Hawai'i in the early 1980s. Kailua, O'ahu is the mecca for windsurfers who come from Europe, Asia and Australia to enjoy the sun, warm water and near-constant winds.

Windsurfers sail by standing on a specially designed surfboard which has a skeg at the stern and a much larger daggerboard or center board near the middle of the board. A triangular sail is held by the mast and controlled by a boom in the hands of the windsurfer.

In this spectator sport the surfer is involved with the waves and may attain speeds up to 30 miles an hour even in light winds.

So much has been published on the popular sports of surfing, canoe surfing and canoe racing that they are not discussed here.

Captain Cook's officers, most of whom (including Cook) could not swim, described Hawaiians as skillful swimmers and surfers. They observed that water sports were the chief amusement for people who were "masters of themselves in the water."

David Samwell, surgeons mate, wrote in his journal on January 22, 1779, his impressions of the boys and girls surfing:

On their putting off shore if they meet with the Surf too near in to afford them a tolerable long Space to run before it they dive under it with greatest Ease & proceed further out to sea.

Sometimes they fail in trying to get before the surf, as it requires great dexterity & address, and after struggling awhile in such a tremendous wave that we should have judged it impossible for any human being to live in it, they rise on the other side laughing and shaking their Locks & push on to meet the next Surf when they generally succeed, hardly ever being foiled in more than one attempt.

Thus these People find one of their Chief amusements in that which to us presented nothing but Horror & Destruction, and we saw with astonishment young boys and Girls about 9 or ten years of age playing amid such tempestuous

Waves that the hardiest of our seamen would have trembled to face, as to be involved in them among the Rocks, on which they broke with a tremendous Noise, they could look upon as no other than certain death. So true it is that many seeming difficulties are easily overcome by dexterity & Perseverance. (Beaglehole, pp. 1164-65)

From various sources we learn about more water sports.

Swimming ('au) for fun was a pastime enjoyed by individuals, small groups and by an entire village. Some community swims were ceremonies of purification (hi'uwai) held between midnight and daybreak. The day was then spent by the villagers in feasting and games.

Children made toy canoes from coconut bloom sheaths and from folded ti leaves. They floated them downstream or in the sea for casual fun or in competition. They also skipped or skimmed flat stones across the surface of the water (pōhaku kele or pākākā).

Many chiefs were devoted to the sport of shark hunting. Wooden bait platters with holes in the bottom were fixed to the prow of the fishing canoe. Decaying flesh was placed in the platters and the bait drippings attracted sharks. The chiefs speared the sharks for sport and as a form of spear practice for war. They also caught sharks on large wooden hooks fitted with bone points. These largest of all Hawaiian fishhooks were made especially for shark fishing.

Fishermen attracted sharks to the canoe with bait drippings and slipped a noose over the head or middle of the body of the shark. They pulled the helpless creature to shore in triumph.

Men rode sharks as one might ride a horse. Some riders developed the skill of guiding their sharks to shore. This sport was considered safe in Pearl Harbor (Pu'uloa) because the shark goddess Ka'ahupāhau and her brother Kahi'ukā kept all man-eating sharks from this harbor, the people believed.

Games For Quiet Moods
Group IV

■ **Pūhenehene** *Finding A Pebble On A Person*

For boys and girls 10 years and older. Indoors.

The boys and girls comprising each team sit in two rows facing one another. Each team should be kept small enough, five or six, so that they may be hidden under a *kapa*, blanket or sheet. If the team is large, the *kapa* must be used as a curtain between the teams, not a cover.

Two helpers are needed to handle the *kapa*. One hands a small smooth stone, the *no'a* to a member of one team. Together they cover the entire team with the *kapa*. The player with the stone hides it on the person of a teammate. The one who has hidden the stone calls out "pūheoheo." The referees remove the *kapa*.

The team which is guessing studies the faces of the members of the team having the stone. It is permissible for the persons on this team to look down at the floor or mat so that one of them will not reveal by his expression that he has the stone.

The members of the guessing team confer, then touch the shoulder of one with a *ni'au*, a coconut leaf midrib, called in this game a *maile*. They score a point if they have indicated the person having the stone. The players agree beforehand that the team wins which first earns five or ten points.

■ **No'a** *Finding A Pebble Under A Kapa*

For both sexes, 10 years and older. Indoors on a mat or outdoors on a sandy beach.

This game is suitable for mixed groups. It is an indoor game when played with bundles of *kapa* or cloth. Out of doors, especially on the beach, it may be played with piles of sand.

Divide your group into two teams; five players on a side are most satisfactory. Sit in two rows facing one another with the five piles of *kapa* or sand between the teams.

Decide which side shall play first. This team selects the one who is to hide the *no'a*. He takes the *no'a* in his hand, with his thumb holding it against his palm and fingers. With the back of his hand up and the stone hidden beneath, he places his hand in turn under each pile of *kapa* or sand. He may even return to one or more of the piles but must not prolong this hiding scheme. Sometime during the process he releases and hides the stone.

The players on the guessing side watch the muscles and tendons of the hand and arm of the person hiding the stone. Even his face may give a clue as he releases the stone.

The guessing team members confer and their spokesman touches one of the piles with the *maile*, a ni'au or coconut leaf midrib. If he guesses right, they score a point. The *no'a* is retrieved and the guessing side proceeds to hide the stone. The game continues until a score agreed upon before the game, is reached.

■ **Kilu** *Hawaiian Quoits*

For teen age boys and girls. Indoors on a mat.

The Kamehameha students enjoy this present-day adaptation or the game of *kilu*, which was played far into the night by the chiefs and chiefesses.

Equipment: Eight to twelve coconut shells sawed or broken in half crosswise, with the flesh removed. These may be used in the rough, brushed, or polished and waxed. One coconut shell, known as the *kilu*, is an oval-shaped coconut cut lengthwise.

The game should be played on a *lau hala* mat or any smooth floor. Seat 4 to 6 boys on one side of the mat and place one of the half shells in front of each of them. Seat an equal number of girls on the other side of the mat, 10 to 15 feet away from the boys, and place a half coconut in front of each, open side down.

The referee, called *helu ʻai* in Hawaiian, asks a boy on one end to begin and hands him the *kilu*. He rises to his knees, braces himself with his left hand and slides the *kilu* across the mat, flat or open side down. He should aim to strike the coconut which is in front of the girl of his choice.

Another way of propelling the coconut shell *kilu* across the mat is to hold it by its rim with the thumb and first finger. With its rounded side down give it a twist and a toss which causes it to spin, open side up, toward its goal. Some chiefs years ago were greatly admired by their fellow players for the skill they had developed in spinning (*ʻōniu*) the *kilu* to its mark.

When younger children play this game, the referee keeps count of the strikes as the boys and girls alternately slide the *kilu* across the mat to touch the shell of a favorite.

The high school boys and girls know this as *kilu honi*, or kissing *kilu*. The boy or girl who strikes the shell of a favorite may rise from his or her position and claim a kiss. (An occasional shy one may ask if he may put his kiss in the bank and claim it at a more opportune time.)

■ **Kimo** *Jackstones*

Boys and girls of all ages. On a mat indoors or outdoors.

The word *kimo* refers to the bobbing of the head up and down. This describes the movement of the head of the player as he follows the stone which he tosses into the air and then looks down as he gathers a pebble from the mat in front of him.

A smooth, rounded, water worn pebble is selected as the *pōhaku kimo* or the special stone which is to be tossed into the air. Some 50 or 100 small *ʻiliʻili* or smooth pebbles which are used in scoring are called the *ʻai*.

Sit on a mat facing your opponent with the *ʻai* spread out between you. After tossing your *pōhaku kimo* into the air, quickly pick up one *ʻai* with the same hand, then catch your *kimo* stone in the same hand as it comes down. Lay the *ʻai* stone aside and continue to toss the *kimo* and gain points by picking up *ʻai* one at a time. You continue until you fail to catch the *kimo* or failed to pick up a stone. The turn then goes to your opponent.

Your opponent follows the same procedure of amassing *ʻai* from the general pile until he misses. You alternate in this way until the *ʻai* are exhausted. The game may be declared finished and the *ʻai* counted to declare a winner.

However, if the players have agreed to do so before the game, they may prolong it by allowing the one who picks up the last pebble in the pile and is still eligible to play to move to his opponent's pile of winnings and play for them. This can continue until one player has earned all of his opponent's *ʻai*.

Dignified chiefs played *kimo* in old Hawaiʻi.

■ **Palaʻie** *Loop and Ball Game*

Boys and girls 9 years and older. Indoors and outdoors.

Palaʻie provides young people with an absorbing pastime and a craft activity demanding skill. Youngsters from the age of nine years and older enjoy making their own loop and ball and then using it.

The *palaʻie* implement consists of a flexible handle which ends in a loop and a ball, slightly larger than the loop. The ball is attached to the handle by a cord long enough to allow it to swing onto the loop. The handle is held horizontally and moved in such a way as to cause the ball to describe a complete circle as it swings and strikes the loop from above and from below.

The pleasure of this game is enhanced when a group of players sets the tempo for swinging the ball by chanting in unison.

Palaʻie becomes a competitive game if several

players set the ball in motion at the command of a referee. The swinging continues until all have missed except one.

The object of this game is not merely to catch the ball in the loop, although this may provide enjoyment for younger children. The real challenge comes from holding the handle horizontally and swinging the ball from the bottom of the loop to the top by describing a complete circle with the ball. With practice this may be done 50 or 100 times without missing.

To make the game implement:

Select 12 mature, firm, freshly cut nīʻau or coconut leaf midribs from leaflets 28 inches or longer if possible. If nīʻau are slender and pliable, use 15 or more to make the implement firm.

Gather these into a tight bundle and wind a strong cord firmly around the base at least 12 times and knot it securely.

Braid the nīʻau from the base to the tip in a 3-ply braid which will produce a flat, firm handle for the palaʻie.

Make a loop from the braided tip, using the portion far enough from the tip to form a firm loop which will not bend under the weight of the ball. The loop will be oval, some 3 by 4 inches. Tie the tip to the handle with a dozen or more turns of cord and trim off the free ends of nīʻau.

Make a ball of palm cloth, called ʻaʻa. This forms at the base of the coconut leaf (ʻaʻa niu). A superior cloth comes from the loulu or fan palm (ʻaʻa loulu). To make the ball, take a sheet of ʻaʻa or at least a square foot, place a very few fragments of the same material in the center as stuffing, then lift up the edges to form a ball about 3 or 4 inches in diameter. It must be slightly larger than the loop of the palaʻie and light in weight.

Close the ball by tying it with one end of a cord about a yard long. Use a heavy needle to draw the free end of the cord through the center of the ball and out the side opposite the tie. This allows the ball to swing with proper balance. Make a needle from a sliver of bamboo, or use an upholsterer's needle.

Attach the free end of the cord to the handle of the palaʻie. Note that the loop of the palaʻie is not centered but curves to one side. A right-handed player holds the handle so that the loop is toward the left. The string which carries the ball should be so secured that it emanates from the left side of the handle and is just long enough to allow the ball to reach the center of the loop.

Play palaʻie to the rhythm of this chant:

E kau, e kau e ʻio e	Perch, perch, o ʻio bird
E piʻi i wai no kāua	Go to the upland to get us some water
Ihea ka wai e kiʻi ai?	Where shall I find the water?
I uka wale o Niniʻole	In the far upland of Niniʻole.
He aha ka lāʻau e kau ai?	On what trees shall I perch?
He ʻōhiʻa la a he lama	On the ʻōhiʻa and the lama
O hele ka hōkū, ka malama.	The stars set, the night lights shine
Kau pū me ka māhina-hina.	And the dim moon above.
Nā wai ke ahi kau ʻui ʻuiki?	Whose light is blinking yonder?
Nā Pele mā i Kīlauea.	It belongs to Pele's family at Kīlauea.

Translation by Mary Kawena Pukui.

■ **Kōnane** *Hawaiian Checkers*

For children 10 years of age and older and for adults. Indoors or outdoors.

The kōnane board or stone, called papamū, is constructed with rows of slight depressions to mark the positions of the playing stones. The number of positions varies greatly on the papamū, but boards made with rows of 8 by 8 or 10 by 10 indentations are popular with present day players. For the papamū with 8 rows of 8 positions, the players would need 64 small stones called ʻiliʻili.

The 32 black ʻiliʻili, usually beach-worn lava pebbles, may be referred to as ʻeleʻele or ʻele, (black). The 32 white pebbles, beach-worn coral bits, may be called keʻokeʻo or kea (white).

The two players sit opposite each other and place the stones on the papamū which is on the floor or table between them. All of the positions are filled alternately with the dark and light pebbles.

The players agree that one of them shall pick up a dark and a light stone from near the center of the papamū, then hold them behind his back while he places one in each hand. He then presents his hands to his opponent with one stone concealed in each. His opponent touches one hand and in this manner selects the color of the stone with which he shall play. The two stones are not returned to the board but placed beside the papamū in a convenient place which will become the discard pile for all stones removed.

As the game begins, note that the object of kōnane, according to these rules, is to maneuver one's opponent into a position where he is unable to complete a play. The winner is not the one who

Kōnane - Checkers: Flat stones near bathing beaches were, at times, pitted with depressions to form a *papamū* on which to move the black and white playing stones.

has removed the most stones or has the smaller number remaining after jumping has ceased. However, these may be considered variations of the game if such rules are agreed upon at the beginning.

The player who is to play with the black stone moves first. Since there are two empty positions on the board, he moves a black stone over a white one into an empty place and removes the white stone. All moves are made by jumping over one or more of the rival's stones, providing that there is a vacant position to move to and that the stones are separated by just one vacant position. However, a player may jump over one stone and decline to move over a second even though the play is possible but probably not to his advantage.

Jumping must be towards or away from the players, or to the right or to the left. A player can never move in two directions in one play and never diagonally. As the game proceeds, there will be fewer stones and fewer chances to move. When, at last, a player is unable to jump in turn, the game is ended and blocked player loses.

For a second game, the player who used the black stones plays with the white ones, and they continue to alternate the color of playing stones with each game in a series.

■ **Hū** *Kukui Nut Tops*

Children 6 to 12 years. Indoors or out on a smooth surface.

Spinning *kukui* tops has proved to be an absorbing pastime for the younger pupils. The tops are easily assembled and make very acceptable gifts.

To Make: Drill a hole in the top of a mature *kukui* nut. We suggest a 11/64" drill bit. The drilling is easier if the top ridge is filed flat and the nut meat is esposed in the center. Make a stem from a sliver of bamboo some 2" long and wide enough to wedge tightly into the hole, or a disposable wooden chopstick may be used.

To Play: A twirl between the finger and thumb sets the top spinning on its tip. A number of schemes may be devised for making this into a competitive game.

Four pupils may form a group, spin their tops on the tips, and declare as the winner the one whose top spins longest. Or a series of ten spins may be scheduled in order to crown a winner. This same procedure may be followed, but this time spin the tops on their stems.

■ **Hei** *String Figures or Cat's Cradles*

For all ages. Indoors or out-of-doors.

Many island children know how to make a number of string figures. A few of them may know the name of a figure or its story.

Directions for making a great many *hei* are given in Dickey's "String Figures from Hawaii," Bishop Museum Bulletin No. 54, 1928. See pp. 23-24 in this bulletin and the film "Sports of Old Hawaii" for the following figure and chant:

Pāpiomakanui

'Auhea 'oe e pāpiomakanui e
    'ike mai 'oe ia'u.
Mai waiho 'oe a hala ka manawa
    alaila 'oe mana'o mai ia'u e
    pāpiomakali'ili'i

Listen, look at me like a
    large-eyed *pāpio* (friendly).
Don't delay, or my feelings may change,
    and you'll find me
    a small eyed *pāpio* (unfriendly).

The chant sequence used here was composed by Mrs. Violet-Marie Mahela Rosehill of The Kamehameha Schools.

In the book "Hawaiian Games for Today" by Mitchell, read about the following games and pastimes not discussed here:

1. *Kūkini* - foot racing.
2. *Lua* - a dangerous form of wrestling.
3. *Ku'iku'i* - boxing.
4. *He'e hōlua* - sledding down hill on a prepared slide.
5. *Hōlua kī* - sliding downhill on ti leaves.
6. *Āe'o* - stilt walking.
7. *Kū pololū* - pole vaulting.
8. *Pāhi'uhi'u* - throwing darts.
9. *Ke'a pua* - sliding sugar cane flower stalks.
10. *Pana 'iole* - shooting rats with bow and arrow.
11. *Moa nahele* - "cock-fighting" with plant stems.
12. *Lele koali* - swinging on morning glory vines.
13. *Kūwala po'o* - somersaults.
14. *Ho'okaka'a* - turning cart wheels.
15. *Pahipahi* - slapping hands and thighs.
16. *Pe'epe'ekua* - hide and seek.
17. *Hākā moa* - cock fighting.
18. *Makani 'ōahi* - hurling fire brands.

■ **Understandings and Appreciations**

1. Although people the world over are known to enjoy some types of games there were few who spent as much time or seemed to have more fun playing games than the Hawaiian people. Some games were brought from their ancestral homeland, others were developed locally.

2. The Hawaiian people utilized the sea, the streams and pools near waterfalls for aquatic sports, field for tournaments and sloping hills for sliding. Games implements were fashioned from stone, hard wood, seeds and leaves. The shark, cock, rat and perhaps the bat were the animals involved in sports. Hunting as it is practiced today was not known in Hawai'i and fishing, though fun, was considered foodgetting.

3. Since the more vigorous games were a method of training for war it is understandable that more sports were developed for men than for women and children. Very few sports were restricted to the chiefs. Among these were *pana'iole, hōlua,* and *kilu.* Some surfing areas were restricted.

4. The referee, *'uao,* checked fair play. He or the score keeper *helu 'ai,* announced the winners in contests.

5. Some ethnologists believe that betting may have been introduced into Hawai'i or to have developed shortly before European contact. It had become the most objectionable feature of sports at the time the first European observers noted that, in the excitement of contests, some persons gambled and lost all of their possessions and finally their bones.

6. Additional study of the games should show how many can be revived and introduced into island homes, school play yards and public playgrounds. Some games should be played for casual enjoyment and others for inter-class, inter-school or inter-playground competition.

7. Games and pastimes introduced from the United States and Europe:

   a. Football, considered the most popular game in Hawai'i this century, was probably first played at Punahou School about 1875. By the early 1890s there were several teams in Honolulu playing among themselves and eager to challenge visiting football teams. Competition is especially high among the high school football teams today. The best teams play before capacity crowds in the championship games at Aloha Stadium.

   b. Baseball was originated either by Abner Doubleday of Cooperstown, New York or by Alexander J. Cartwright. The honor of inventing the game which we now know as baseball belongs to Cartwright according to baseball historian Will Irwin. Cartwright came to Honolulu to live in 1849, four years after he marked out the first baseball diamond in New York City. The first game played here, shortly after Cartwright's arrival, was on a vacant lot next to the Fort at the foot of Fort Street. In the 1870s Punahou School boasted of its winning baseball teams. The game continues to flourish in Hawai'i with commercial, school, sandlot and Little League teams.

   c. Polo, believed to be the oldest game played with a ball, came to O'ahu in time for a local team to be prepared to play the first match in 1880. They met the officers of the H.M.S. Gannet on a field near Honolulu. The sport spread to the neighbor islands. In 1902 the Inter-Island Polo Association was formed.

d. Additional sports with a large number of enthusiastic participants among the adults are: auto and motorcycle racing, bowling, boxing, golf, sport fishing, tennis, wrestling and yachting.

e. Competitive sports, in addition to those listed above, which are of special interest to the students are: basketball, riflery, soccer, swimming, track and volleyball.

8. Sports of Oriental origin which are popular in Hawai'i with most of the ethnic groups are: aikido, jiu jitsu, judo, karate and sumo.

■ **Student Activities**

1. In a unit on games there are many possibilities for student activities. Elementary school children enter into the games with enthusiasm. In our experience the secondary school students enjoy the games suggested for them if they are not inhibited by numerous spectators. Since many of the games call for one player in contest with another, the supervisor should plan to have many such pairs on the field at one time. A number of the games may be played without the need of apparatus.

2. Certain games implements can be made in small workshops in the form of replicas of the genuine specimens. In other cases very satisfactory substitutes can be made. All pupils can learn to make *pala'ie,* tops, *kōnane* boards and a variety of other implements.

3. Students may write a play or pageant which includes a series of games. Secondary students might, in their play, award the winning athlete the hand of the chief's daughter in marriage.

4. At present Hawaiian games lessons are offered at some of the City and County Parks and Playgrounds under the Mayor's Summer Youth Program.

■ **Audio-Visual Aids**

1. Bishop Museum - on exhibit or in storage, most of the games implements, including a *hōlua* sled, the most perfect one known.

2. For several years the Moanalua Gardens Foundation has staged Hawaiian games during the Prince Lot Hula Festival in July. From time to time games demonstrations are a part of the Aloha Week festivities.

3. Color-sound film by Cine-pic, Sports of old Hawaii, 11 min.

■ **Vocabulary**

Review the names of the popular games with their English equivalents. Also learn:

helu 'ai	makahiki
'oia	Lono
pā'ani	kahua
'ālapa	lōkū
hoa paio	maoli
lamakū	lupe

■ **Current Happenings or Trends of Significance to this Unit**

1. Surf riding, which had ceased to be a sport early in this century, has become popular again in Hawai'i and has been introduced into nearly every country which has suitable surf. Improvements have been made in the designs and materials of surfboards. Several surfing magazines bring the latest news to enthusiasts. Meets or tournaments of international interest are held at certain O'ahu surfing sites each year.

Read Valerie Noble's book "Hawaiian Prophet," Alexander Hume Ford. This is the biography of the man credited with founding the Outrigger Canoe Club at Waikīkī and reviving the sport of surfing.

2. Outrigger canoes are again being made from *koa* or more recently from newer materials such as fiber glass. Annual races are staged. A popular one, from Moloka'i to Waikīkī, is held during Aloha Week.

3. Ti leaf sliding continues to be popular. String figures are a pastime for children but few people know the chants that once accompanied them.

■ **Evaluation**

1. The most practical check on the students' understanding of the games would be a play period during which they coached, refereed and played Hawaiian games.

2. Older students could do research on games of many lands and determine how Hawaiian games compared to and differed from sports elsewhere.

3. Students from families with Hawaiian backgrounds should attempt to learn games not on the present list.

4. The names of the games provide an interesting basis for studying pronunciation, meanings and spellings.

5. Games implements made in the craft shop should be tested on the playfield.

■ **Reading List**

Alexander, Mary C., and Charlotte P. Dodge. *Punahou, 1841-1941.* Berkeley and Los Angeles: University of California Press, 1941.

Beckwith, Martha W. *Hawaiian Mythology.* 1940. Honolulu: University Press of Hawaii, 1970. (See index for references to games.)

Blake, Tom. *Hawaiian Surfboard.* 1935. Honolulu: Paradise of the Pacific Press, 1963 (rev. ed., paperback).

Boulton, H.C. "Some Hawaiian Pastimes." *Journal of American Folklore,* 1890. 4(12):21-26.

Brennan, Joseph. *Duke Kahanamoku, Hawaii's Golden Man.* Honolulu: Hogarth Press, 1974. (See also the cover of the Hawaiian Telephone Directory for Dec. 1, 1979, to Jan. 30, 1981, with a watercolor of the Duke and a montage of old Hawaiian sports.)

Bryan, E.H. Jr. "Sports and Games." Ch. 14 in *Ancient Hawaiian Life.* 1938. Honolulu: Books About Hawaii, 1950.

Buck, Peter H. "Games and Recreation." In *Arts and Crafts of Hawaii.* Honolulu: Bishop Museum Special Publication No. 45, 1957.

Clark, John R.K. *The Beaches of O'ahu,* 1977. *The Beaches of Maui County,* 1989 (rev. ed.). *Beaches of the Big Island,* 1985. *Beaches of Kaua'i and Ni'ihau,* 1990. Honolulu: University of Hawaii Press.

Culin, Stewart. "Hawaiian Games." *American Anthropologist,* 1899. I(2):201-247.

Dickey, Lyle A. *String Figures from Hawaii.* Honolulu: Bishop Museum Bulletin No. 54, 1928.

Ellis, William. *Journal of William Ellis. Narrative of a Tour of Hawaii. . . .* 1826. Rutland, VT and Japan: C.E. Tuttle, 1979.

Emerson, Joseph S. "The Bow and Arrow in Hawaii." *Hawaiian Historical Society Report for 1915.* Honolulu: Hawaiian Historical Society.

Emory, Kenneth P. "Sports, Games and Amusements." Ch. 14 in *Ancient Hawaiian Civilization.* A series of lectures delivered at Kamehameha Schools by E.S.C. Handy [and others]. 1933. Rutland, VT and Japan: C.E. Tuttle, 1965 (rev. ed.).

Fast, Arlo, and George Seberg, eds. *Cruising Guide for the Hawaiian Islands.* Honolulu: Pacific Writers Corp., 1980.

Feher, Joseph. *Hawaii: A Pictorial History.* Honolulu: Bishop Museum Special Publication No. 58, 1969.

Finney, Ben R. "Surfing in Ancient Hawaii." *Journal of the Polynesian Society,* December 1959.

Fitzpatrick, James T. "The Ancient Art of the Bodyguards of Hawaiian Kings." *Black Belt* magazine, November 1966.

Fornander, Abraham. *Hawaiian Antiquities and Folklore.* Honolulu: Bishop Museum Memoirs, Vol. 6, Part 1, 1919.

Hemmings, Fred. *Surfing, Hawaii's Gift to the World of Sports.* Tokyo: Zokeisha Publishing Company, 1977.

Ii, John Papa. *Fragments of Hawaiian History.* Trans. Mary K. Pukui. 1959. Honolulu: Bishop Museum Press, 1963. (This edition has an extensive index.)

Kamakau, Samuel M. *Ruling Chiefs of Hawaii.* Honolulu: Kamehameha Schools Press, 1961. (See also *Index to Ruling Chiefs of Hawaii* by Elspeth P. Sterling, Bishop Museum, 1974.)

Kenn, Charles W. "Ancient Hawaiian Sports and Pastimes." *Mid-Pacific Magazine,* 1935. 48:308-316.

King, Samuel W. "Ancient Hawaiian Sports and Amusements." *Hawaii Educational Review,* September 1924.

Kuhns, Grant W. *On Surfing.* Rutland, VT and Japan: C.E. Tuttle, 1963.

Malo, David. Chs. 41, 57 in *Hawaiian Antiquities.* 1898. Honolulu: Bishop Museum Special Publication No. 2, 1976.

Mellen, George, ed. *The Sales Builder,* August 1936 and September 1938.

Mitchell, Donald D. Kilolani. *Hawaiian Games for Today*. 1975. Honolulu: Kamehameha Schools Press, 1980. (Cassette tape available with Hawaiian words and chants used in the book.)

———. *Hawaiian Treasures*. Games, 129-142. Honolulu: Kamehameha Schools Press, 1978.

Morgan, Frank, and Ben R. Finney. *A Pictorial History of Surfing*. Sydney, Aus.: Paul Hamlyn, 1970. (More than 600 illustrations, color and black and white.)

Muirhead, Desmond. *Surfing in Hawaii*. Flagstaff, AR: Northland Press, 1962.

O'Neill, James H. *Pocket Guide to the Gamefishes of Hawaii*. Honolulu: Hawaii Pocket Guides, 1978. (Vendor is Mid-Pacific Book Distributors, Honolulu.)

Osmun, Mark. *Honolulu Marathon*. New York: J.B. Lippincott, 1979.

Peterson, Harold. *The Man Who Invented Baseball: Alexander Joy Cartwright*. New York: Chas. Scribner's Sons, 1973.

Pukui, Mary K. "Games of My Hawaiian Childhood." *California Folklore Quarterly*, July 1943. II(3).

Rathbun, Linda M. *Bicycler's Guide to Hawaii*. Hilo: Petroglyph Press, 1976.

Rizzuto, Jim. *Modern Hawaiian Gamefishing*. Honolulu: University Press of Hawaii, 1977.

Smith, Robert. *Hiking Hawaii*, 1977; *Hiking Kauai*, 1979; *Hiking Maui*, 1977; *Hiking Oahu*, 1978. Berkeley: Wilderness Press.

Squire, James L. Jr., and Susan E. Smith. *Sport Fishing in Hawaii, Guam and American Samoa*. Rutland, VT and Japan: C.E. Tuttle, 1979.

Westervelt, William D. "Old Hawaiian Games." *Mid-Pacific Magazine*, October 1916.

UNIT 14:
Thatched Houses
and Other
Structures

THATCHED HOUSES AND OTHER STRUCTURES

The Hawaiian house (hale noho) was constructed to protect its occupants from the rain, the sun, and from the winds during the colder months of the year. Here the people kept their possessions and felt the security of belonging to a certain place in common with their 'ohana or family group. Since the climate was mild along the shores where most of the people lived, the houses were comparatively simple in construction. The framework of posts was lashed together with strong cordage and made waterproof by a covering of thatch. The small doorway was the only opening. Persons who recognize the resourcefulness and labor needed to construct one of these dwellings confer upon them the dignified name "house," never "shack" or "hut."

Life was said to have been pleasant in these houses in the pre-European days before the introduction of mosquitoes, flies, cockroaches, centipedes, scorpions, fleas, ants, termites and other small pests.

Not only did these small pests (mea kolo) affect the comfort and happiness of the grass house dwellers but the larger introduced animals became a nuisance also. The cattle (pipi) horses (lio) and goats (kao) were introduced, supposedly for the benefit of Hawaiian and foreign residents. But these animals fed upon the pili grass and ti leaves that grew in the lowlands and fringes of the forests. The leaves of these plants furnished the thatch for most of the houses. These same animals came into the unfenced yards and ate the thatch off the exterior of the houses. Another nuisance, at least to some of the occupants of these small dwellings, was the smoke from tobacco (paka). The grass house, designed long before tobacco and the tobacco pipe (ipu paka) were introduced, did not allow the smoke to escape readily.

As foreign building material became available and affordable the grass house was replaced with a frame house often with a corrugated iron roof.

The population in general (maka'āinana) usually lived in single one-room houses (hale noho).

Families often joined others of their kin into a related group ('ohana) whose houses formed a kauhale. A large grouping of family houses became a kūlana-kauhale or a village. (Handy-Pukui, 1972, pp. 5-7.)

■ A chief's household consisted of a number of houses, each serving a special purpose. A high chief might have most, but not necessarily all, of the following houses:

a. Hale noa or hale moe, the sleeping house for his entire family. A sleeping platform raised the chief and chiefess above the others. Noa implied that the house was free from the kapu which kept men and women apart. Moe is to sleep.

Food was not brought into the sleeping house. Here the family and their friends could visit, play quiet games and tell stories. The hale noa was usually the largest dwelling house in the compound.

b. Hale mua, the men's eating house, kapu to women. An altar (kuahu) was erected at one end and here the chief gave prayers and offerings each day to the family god or gods ('aumākua). These were represented by wooden or stone images. For an example of the prayer (pule ho'ola) see Handy, 1972, p. 297. The principal offering was 'awa but food selected from the men's fare might be added. After a lapse of time, during which the gods accepted the essence (aka) of the food, it was withdrawn and consumed by those present. Kapu sticks (pulo'ulo'u) were placed crossed before the door to indicate *kapu.*

c. *Hale ʻaina,* the women's eating house, *kapu* to men. Here the women and young boys ate the food prepared for them by the men.

d. *Hale peʻa,* a small house, some distance away from the others. The women remained here during their menstrual period. Food was brought to them by women in the family.

e. *Hale papaʻa* or *hale hoʻahu,* one or more storehouses, usually elevated two feet or more above the ground and fitted with floors of planks. Webber sketched a storehouse in his view of Waimea, Kauaʻi, January, 1778. Food crops were harvested, brought here and stored until needed. The perishable foods were cooked within a few days. Sweet potatoes (*ʻuala*), dried and salted foods such as fish, could be kept for some time. Tools (*ʻōʻō*) and items collected as taxes such as mats (*moena*), *kapa* and utensils (*ʻumeke*) were stored until needed. Malo wrote that storehouses were designed to keep the people contented. They could not desert a chief while they thought there was food in his storehouse.

f. *Hale kuku* or *hale kua,* a house where the *kapa*-making tools were kept and where the *kapa* was pounded and decorated, especially during inclement weather. Sometimes a second *hale* was constructed to hold the dye-making materials. It was the *hale hoʻoluʻu.* The *hale* were surrounded by a stone wall (*pā pōhaku*) to provide a drying yard. Here the *kapa* was spread out to dry and bleach, safe from the muddy feet of the village dogs and pigs. Men made the ribbed *kapa* (*hamo ʻula* or *kuaʻula*) in a work yard (*kahua hana*) and a drying yard (*kahua kaulaʻi*) which might cover two acres or more. The surrounding fence was of wooden palings and dried banana leaves.

g. *Hālau waʻa* was a large canoe house with a thatched roof but open on the sides and ends. Here were kept the canoes, paddles, fishnets and articles used in canoeing and fishing. The *auolo,* a canoe house smaller than the *hālau waʻa* housed the canoes of the *makaʻāinana.* The *hālau hula,* the house in which the *hula* was taught and the *hālau lua* in which the *lua* (a form of wrestling) was taught, evolved from the large airy *hālau waʻa.*

h. *Hale imu, hale umu* or *hale kāhumu* were names for the shelters for the outdoor ovens (*imu* or *umu*). Since they were used the year around in all kinds of weather it was necessary to have protection from the wind and the rain. A low,

crescent stone wall was built on the side of the *imu* from which the prevailing winds came. A roof was placed over this, often of *loulu* or fan palm leaves. Two such structures and their ovens were needed to cook the men's and the women's food. For convenience they were usually built near the *hale mua.* Firewood (*wahie*) was stored and kept dry here.

■   Some of the important houses, not a part of the chief's household, were those in the *heiau* or places of worship. In the large temples of sacrifice (*heiau luakini* or *poʻo kanaka*) would be built the drum house (*hale pahu*), the house of divine power (*hale mana*), a house for the bones of the departed chiefs, as was once the function of Hale o Keawe, (*hale poki*), and a small structure where the coconut cord (*ʻaha*) was stretched in a ceremony conducted by the chiefs (*hale wai ea*). See Ii, 1959, for sketches of these houses.

A small house (*hale lanalana*) was placed on the platform (*pola*) of a double canoe. Here persons and articles of special value could be free from the wind and sea spray. For photos and sketches of the *hale* on the Hokuleʻa see Lindo, 1980, pp. 54, 59 and 77.

Houses were distinquished by the kind of wood used in their framework such as *hale lama, hale kauila* or *hale hau.* A *hale pili* was thatched with *pili* grass, a *hale lau* with leaves from the *hala,* ti or sugar cane. Houses were called *hale pōhaku* (stone house) or *hale lāʻau* (frame house) when these building materials became popular.

The Pukui-Elbert Hawaiian-English Dictionary lists some 32 kinds or classes of houses of the pre-European period. Examples of the 36 peculiar to the post-European culture would be *hale kaʻa* (garage) or *hale inu kī* (tea house). The chiefs named both the house and the plot of ground upon which it stood. Princess Ruth Keʻelikōlani's house, Hale Keōua, was located on the tract known as Kaʻakopua. It is now the location of the Central Intermediate School in Honolulu.

■   **Constructing the Hawaiian House**

The processes involved in constructing the house are described by Bryan, 1950, Chapter 6, and by Buck, 1957, pp. 75-106.

The steps involved were, in brief, selecting a site for the house, procuring all the necessary materials, setting up and lashing the framework, and tying on the thatch. Most of this was done by the householder and his family with the help of his neighbors and friends in the village. The processes were too well known to require the services of an expert, except possibly the closing of the thatch over the ridgepole which prevented leaks.

The men cut the timbers in the mountain forests, carried them to the housesite and cut them into the desired lengths. The tool was the stone adze. The bark was removed from the timbers used in the better houses. Holes were dug with the ʻōʻō (digging stick) and the posts set in place after the upper ends had been cut to a point to receive the notch of the rafters. The entire framework was lashed together securely with coarse fibers such as ʻieʻie rootlets, ʻukiʻuki or sennit. A stone platform (paepae) raised the house floor above the damp earth. The large foundation stones which formed the floor of the house were covered with small pebbles (ʻiliʻili). These were strewn over and between the larger rocks in the foundation. The pebbly floor was often covered with dry grass. The people added floor mats of sturdy lau hala. Fine makaloa mats were used on the floors in some of the chiefs' houses.

Women and children helped gather large quantities of pili grass and men worked in pairs to tie it on to the thatch purlins. For thatching details, see Buck, 1957, pp. 102-106.

A wisp of grass (piko) was left uncut over the doorway to be featured later in the dedication of the house.

■ **Dedicating the house**

Religious rituals were observed in the entire process of housebuilding, but the most interesting one is the ceremonial cutting of the navel cord (piko) of the house. This is described in Malo, 1951, pp. 123-25. Pratt, 1963, gives a simpler version, pp. 118-19, and a chant, "Of the House," p. 148. Handy, in *Ancient Hawaiian Civilization*, pp. 69-72, records three chants in Hawaiian with English translations. A shorter chant, quoted by Handy, called a pule kūwa, was used in dedicating a house built for a man named Mea.

Kū lalani ka pule a ke olowalu i ke akua.
O kuwā wāhia i ka piko o ka hale o Mea.
A kū! A wā! A moku ka piko!
A moku, a moku iho la!
Orderly and harmonious is the prayer of the

multitude to god.
With an uttered (prayer) he severs now the piko of the house of Mea.
He stands! He cuts! The naval string is cut!
It is cut, lo it is cut!

Dr. Buck while Director of Bishop Museum made a detailed study of houses, and wrote:

In view of the fact that the hipped roof is not shown in sketches made on Kauai, Niihau and Hawaii during Cook's visit, it appears that this type of roof was not in vogue until after European contact. (Buck, 1957, p. 96.)

The hale pili in Bishop Museum, brought from Kauaʻi and reassembled in Hawaiian Hall in 1901, has a hipped roof. "It is probably the only house with authentic details that has survived." (Buck, 1957, p. 82.)

The hale pili in the Lyman House Memorial Museum, Hilo, was built recently using ʻōhia timbers, 4,000 feet of hau bark for cordage and pili grass for thatch.

Captain Cook and his officers wrote about houses.

David Samwell noted that there were six towns around the shores of Kealakekua Bay, where Cook's ships were anchored.

. . . the largest of these Towns which is Kawaroa [Kaʻawaloa] may contain about 70 or 80 Houses and the others abt 60 Each. . . . These Towns, tho' the Houses are close together, are not built regular so as to form any thing like streets but have paths running through them in a zig zag manner; most of the Houses have courts before them railed in, some have large squares walled in near them, covered with small Pebbles on which they dry and stain their Cloth [kapa].

Their houses in general are but small, being not above 6 or 7 yards long and abt 4 abroad, some few are 12 or 15 in length and 7 or 8 in breadth and they may be about as high as they are long; the entrance to them is just like the mouth of an oven & very little bigger, so that everyone is obliged to creep into them; this entrance is made out of a board cut in the proper form and placed in the wall, & they have a slider on the inside to draw across it occasionally.

As they have no light but what comes in at the door their Houses are very dark. The Sides of the Houses are low, the roof almost reaching to the ground; it approaches nearer the perpendicular than our Houses in England, which is probably intended for the more ready carrying off Rain; most of them are thatched with the leaves of the Sugar Cane. (Beaglehole, p.1176)

Captain Cook noted that strands of thatch could be pushed aside to let in light. This was done at night also to let a breeze come in near the head of a person on his sleeping mat.

> The door is so low that a man can hardly get in without going upon his hands and knees, and they have no other light except what may come through the crevices in the wall; some of our gentlemen observed that when they wanted light they made a hole in the wall and closed it again when they had done with it. The floor is covered with dry hay and upon this they spread Mats to sleep upon. (Beaglehole, p. 283.)

■ Grass Houses are Combustible

James King observed that a number of dwellings along the shores of Kealakekua Bay had been destroyed by fire within a period of a few days. He wrote, ". . . these accidents must I suppose often happen, from the Construction of their houses, & their being built very close together." (Beaglehole, p. 520.)

■ Household Furnishings

The houses occupied by families of the working people would contain the few items needed to prepare and serve their food and to clothe the occupants and keep them warm at night. The farmers would store here their digging sticks and carrying poles. Fishermen would keep their hooks, lines, nets, and other articles needed in their work.

In contrast, the houses of the chiefs might contain an extensive array of furnishings of excellent workmanship and great beauty. The articles described in the following sketches were used in the home, although no single family would be apt to possess all of them. Some of these furnishings may be seen in Bishop Museum. Photographs and sketches of many of them may be studied in Buck's *Arts and Crafts of Hawaii,* 1957.

■ Furnishings Used for Relaxing and Sleeping

Coarsely plaited *lau hala* mats covered the small stones on a portion of the floor. In the sleeping house *(hale noa* or *moe)* a small, stone-walled fireplace *(kapuahi)* was built in the center of the floor. Floor mats were laid along the walls away from any danger from the fire.

In cool areas of the islands and during the winter season, the fireplace provided pleasant warmth. Its chief function, however, was to keep away the spirits which were thought to roam about at night. The preferred fuel was charcoal saved from the *imu,* since it burned without smoke. Sandalwood *('iliahi)* and false sandalwood *(naio)* gave off a fragrance when burned. *Kukui* nut shells smouldered for a long time in the *kapuahi.* Usually someone awakened during the night and replenished this small fire when necessary.

After Samwell and two companions in Captain Cook's party were entertained in the house of the priest Kaimiki'i at Ke'ei on Kealakekua Bay, he wrote:

> In large Houses such as this Chiefs is they make the fire in the middle of the floor in a square place inclosed with thick pieces of wood. (Beaglehole, p. 1163.)

The bed *(hikie'e)* was a deep pile of mats across the end of the house. (The *pūne'e* is a modern, movable couch.) The chief's *hale noa* or sleeping house had a deep *hikie'e,* the upper coverings were the fine *makaloa* mats. Buck describes these as the "finest sleeping mats in Polynesia." (Buck, 1957, p. 132.)

These soft, flexible mats, made largely on Ni'ihau, have as many as 20 to 25 wefts or strands to the inch. They were made from a pale brown sedge, not *lau hala,* and by employing different plaiting styles, patterns were introduced without the use of color. However, the most interesting mats had colored geometric motifs in a variety of designs. The brown colored wefts in the pattern are from sheaths which grow at the base of the *makaloa* sedge or perhaps from another species of sedge. The plaiting of *makaloa* mats ceased years ago.

By gift and exchange, *makaloa* mats seem to have come into the possession of the chiefs on all the islands.

Cook wrote of the mats he saw on Kaua'i in 1778, "Their mats are both strong and fine and some are neatly coloured." (Beaglehole, p. 283.)

King observed mats at Kealakekua in 1779:

> Their Matts are superiour to the other Islands [islands ot the south], both in fineness, & from the Variety of patterns in them, by working in Streaks of different Colours. (Beaglehole, pp. 625-626.)

Samwell wrote of the *makaloa* and *lau hala* mats:

> They have a great Variety of Matts, some all white but most of them variegated with brown slips running the whole length of them and giving them

Hale Noa: Within the sleeping house the bed of the chief and chiefess was raised higher than the mats on which other members of the family slept. A small fire burned in the fireplace. Other furnishings on the mats are a kukui nut lamp, a massage stick and a nĭʻau broom. A gourd container in a net hangs from a rafter post.

a very beautiful appearance, these are worn by the Chiefs sometimes, while the more coarse and thick ones are laid on the floors of their Houses and made into Sails for their Canoes. (Beaglehole, p. 1187.)

A very fine mat in Bishop Museum with 25 wefts per inch was worn by Kamehameha I as a kīhei.

Bishop Museum has a total of 98 *makaloa* mats, samplers, and pieces (Buck, 1957, pp. 132-135).

The pillows *(uluna)* were plaited from *lau hala* and filled with folded *lau hala*. (Buck, pp. 135-136.)

When a person lay down to sleep he might cover himself with a bed *kapa (kapa moe)* or he might roll up his own bed *kapa*.

During the day the sleeping mats and *kapa* were rolled and placed on racks affixed to the rafters.

■ **Furnishings for Food and Drink:**

Food was prepared out-of-doors or in the *hale imu* and also served out-of-doors whenever the weather permitted. The smaller utensils concerned with food and drink were stored in the house. Important utensils were described and discussed in Unit 10, "Preparing and Serving Daily and Feast Food," but are mentioned here by name only as they are vessels, utensils and tools having to do with food and drink and would be kept in the house.

A post and crosspiece *(oleole kau ipu)* was erected outside the house to serve as a rack from which to suspend gourds or calabashes of food and water. (See photo of Bishop Museum's grass house in Buck, 1957, p. 83.)

In 1779 David Samwell wrote of a shelf and rack inside a house at Kealakekua Bay, Hawaii:

In one Corner of the House are two long pieces of wood stuck in the ground with a board between them forming kind of a shelf; on this they put their Bowls & other household furniture & hang their Calibashes of water &c to the Poles. (Beaglehole, p. 1176.)

Many of the following utensils and accesssories used in preparing and serving food are described in

Buck, 1957, pp. 22-73. Examples of most of them are on exhibit in Bishop Museum.

1. food scrapers of 'opihi and cowrie shells
2. hand shredders of stone or shell for grating coconuts
3. knives and cutters of stone, shark teeth and bamboo
4. breadfruit splitters of stone
5. pig scrapers of rough lava
6. sweet potato poi mixers of wood (lā'au ho'owali poi)
7. poi pounding boards of wood (papa ku'i poi)
8. stone food pounders (pōhaku ku'i poi or pōhaku ku'i 'ai), knobbed, ring or stirrup types
9. stone mortars and pestles
10. gourd food bowls ('umeke pōhue), decorated gourd bowls ('umeke pāwehe). The larger gourd and wooden bowls were carried by suspending them in nets (kōkō) which hung from the ends of a carrying pole ('auamo or māmaka).
11. wooden food bowls ('umeke lā'au). Those with rounded bases would rest on a ring-like support (pō'aha) made of lau hala or ti leaves bound with a cord.
12. platters (pā) of wood, some supported by wooden runners or human figures.
13. cups of wood, gourds or coconut shells (ipu or 'apu)
14. spoons, scoop-like of coconut shells (ki'o'e)
15. finger bowls (ipu holoi lima)
16. scrap bowls (ipu 'aina) and spittoons (ipu kuha)
17. gourd water containers (huewai). They were filled with liquid by using gourd or coconut shell funnels (kānuku).
18. 'awa bowls (kānoa), strainers (ahu 'awa) and cups ('apu 'awa).
19. salt evaporating pans of stone, (poho kaha pa'akai), outside the house in the sunshine and breeze to hasten evaporation of water.

■ Furnishings for light and heat

Since Hawaiian homes were highly inflammable, great care was needed in handling candles, lamps and torches. The two imu were located some distance from the houses for greater safety.

1. kukui nut candles (ihoiho kukui). Roasted, shelled kukui nuts were strung on a coconut leaf midrib (nī'au) or a sliver of bamboo ('ohe). When the top nut was lighted, it burned for two or three minutes giving off a yellow light with some smoke. An attendant inverted the candle to light the second nut before the first burned out. The base of the candle was placed in a stone receptacle to hold it upright. Large numbers of these candles were needed for an evening of story-telling.

2. torches (lama-kū). Roasted kukui nuts were enclosed in a sheaf of ti leaves which were secured to a bamboo handle. The torch, often three feet long, furnished light for out-of-doors events and during fishing (lamalama).

3. stone lamps (poho kukui). These lamps varied in size and shape but were usually cylindrical stones with a cavity in the top to hold the oil. Kukui or kamani nut oil was preferred, but sometimes animal fat was used. A wick of twisted kapa conducted the oil up to its tip near the rim of the lamp where it burned with a yellow flame.

4. Fire making. Fire (ahi) was made by rubbing (hi'a or heahi'a, a contraction of he ahi hi'a) a pointed stick of wood ('aulima) usually held in both hands, along a groove in a large piece of wood ('aunaki). While seated the fire maker held the 'aunaki firmly between his feet. The rubbing motion (also called kuolo) plowed up wood fibers (hānā) which became hot and glowed due to the friction. The glowing sparks were transferred to the fibers (pulu) of a mature dry coconut or to kapa fibers and blown until the material ignited. Dry hau wood was, and is today, preferred for both pieces of the fire maker. Fire can be made in less than a minute by persons familiar with the process.

■ Furnishings for Cleanliness and Health

Captain Cook wrote that cleanliness and neatness prevailed in the houses and villages which he visited.

A platform (paepae) of large stones raised the floor of the house above the earth. These stones were covered with pebbles ('ili'ili) which were in turn covered with dry grass and lau hala mats. The mats were small enough to be easily carried through the doorway for sunning and airing.

Unpleasant housing conditions were reported by some Europeans who visited houses of the poorer types or by those who made their observations after foreign insects and vermin were introduced.

1. *pūpū niʻau* or *pūlumi niʻau* were a broom-like bundle of coconut leaflet midribs used to sweep the mats, the *paepae* and the pathways near the house.

2. articles stored in the house that contributed to personal cleanliness were the bath rubbers of cellular lava (Brigham, p. 17), finger bowls (Buck, pp. 52-53) and scrap and refuse bowls (Buck, pp. 53-55). The *lomi* or massage stick (*lāʻau lomi*) is noted here among the items promoting health and also in the unit on medical practices.

3. Hawaiian combs *(kahi lauoho)*, constructed with teeth of coconut leaflet midribs *(niʻau)* secured by *olonā* cords to bands of bamboo, were used in the care of the hair by both men and women. Stone mirrors *(kilo pōhaku)*, highly polished discs of close-grained black lava, gave a satisfactory reflection when the surface was oiled or placed in a calabash of water. (Brigham, 1902, pp. 66-67.)

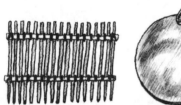

Personal Grooming: (left to right) A comb for the hair was made from coconut leaflet midribs lashed to bamboo strips.

Fine-grained basalt was polished to make a stone mirror. It gave a reflection when the surface was oiled or the stone was placed in a bowl of water.

Cellular lava stones that fit the hand easily served as bath stones. They were rubbed over the skin while bathing.

Sanitary regulations imposed by *kapu* controlled the disposal of garbage and human wastes. The paths in the village were swept clean with *niʻau* broom. Owners of pigs, dogs and chickens observed rules concerning the control and cleanliness of these animals.

Structures in Post-European Times

■ Palaces of Thatch

The men's house *(hale mua)* was a structure of importance to a chief and especially to the ruling chief of an island. Here he met with his fellow chiefs, advisers and the *kāhuna*. In this sanctuary for men only they dined, discussed the affairs of state and paid tribute to their gods. In most of the *hale mua*, unless the chief had a special *hale heiau*, an altar occupied a place of prominence in one end. Here the chief made daily offerings to special gods and to his family *ʻaumākua*.

When foreign vessels began to visit in Hawaiian waters, harbors had not been developed so the ships anchored at any one of many favorable spots. The captain would come ashore, seek out the ranking chief and make plans to trade for such supplies as water, firewood and food.

The only suitable place indoors to confer with a male visitor would be in the *hale mua*.

After consolidating the islands, Kamehameha preferred to be the one in authority to deal with the visiting officers. He invited them into his *hale mua* for a social time and to discuss their needs. They referred to this structure as Kamehameha's palace. Since the king moved his court a number of times between 1795 and 1819 he built a number of palaces.

■ Halehui was the First

Kamehameha decided to remain on Oʻahu for some time after winning the battle of Nuʻuanu in May, 1795, and adding this island to his kingdom. As Oʻahu rulers had done before him Kamehameha established his first residence at Waikīkī, and made his headquarters here from 1795 to 1809. Honolulu harbor was opened in November 1794 and Kamehamaha, a shrewd trader, chose to be on hand to personally conduct business. In 1809, near the waterfront Kamehameha had built the usual compound of structures needed by a ruling chief. He named his *hale mua*, the largest of the thatched houses, Halehui. Of special note was one storehouse within the compound and two large stone storehouses nearby for the foreign goods which he acquired. Halehui served as Kamehameha's palace until he departed in 1812 to take up his residence in

Kona. Kamehameha built and maintained a two-story brick "palace" at Lahaina in which he lived when in residence there. It was built about 1800 and served as a warehouse more than a dwelling.

■ Kamakahonu (the eye of the turtle), the palace in Kona.

With his family and attendants Kamehameha left Honolulu (then called Kou) in 1812 and sailed to Kona in three American ships. He lived temporarily on the site now occupied by Hulihee Palace. But he had a strong desire to make his permanent home at Kamakahonu.

Although Kamehameha, as ruler, owned all of the land, this parcel had been assigned to his chiefly adviser, the late Keaweaheulu. His son, Naihe, now residing on the site, readily gave it to Kamehameha. (The bodies of Keaweaheulu and Naihe are in the Kalākaua crypt, Royal Mausoleum, Nu'uanu.)

The hale mua, which they called Kamakahonu, was Kamehameha's palace until his death in 1819. In the compound were houses for his wives, and storehouses of foreign construction to hold the wealth he acquired from visiting ships.

During a period of drought Kamehameha joined his men in cultivating their own food crops at his farm called Kuahewa. He built a special house, Hale nānā mahina 'ai, which name explained that from it he watched his farm lands, (nānā - to watch, mahina'ai, the same as mahi'ai - farm).

Kamehameha restored Ahu'ena Heiau near Kamakahonu, a temple dedicated to Lono at certain seasons and, it is said, to human sacrifices at other times. He died at Kamakahonu on May 8, 1819. His bones were prepared for burial according to the ancient custom. Two dear friends secreted them so carefully that they have not been found. (See Barrere, 1975, pp. 1-57.)

■ Pākākā (to skim stones over the water)

The palace of Kamehameha II, Liholiho, on Honolulu Harbor at a favorite canoe landing place called Pākākā, was a large thatched building. It was the executive building from 1821 to 1824.

A visitor, in 1823, the Rev. Charles Stewart, described the structure as perhaps 50 feet long, 30 feet wide, eight feet high at the sides and 30 feet at the peak of the roof.

The timbers were all straight, substantial and beautifully hewn. They were lashed together with sennit. Two large doors opened at each end and on the sides were windows with venetian shutters but no glass. The floor was covered with mats.

Palace furnishings included a variety of tables, chairs, sofas, mirrors and two full length paintings of Liholiho.

This palace was no longer the expansion of the hale mua of Kamehameha I's time. Liholiho had helped abolish the kapu traditions, some of which restricted women's privileges. Here he held court with his five wives at or near his side.

■ Haleuluhe (House of the Uluhe ferns)

The thatched palace of Kamehameha III, built by O'ahu's governor, Boki, was near the site of the present St. Andrew's Cathedral on Beretania Street, Honolulu.

In a walled compound of several acres stood the palace and a number of separate buildings used by the king's family and his household for sleeping, dining and as offices.

Haleuluhe, according to the Rev. Charles Stewart, who visited it in 1839, was a large, single-room structure some 100 or more feet long, 50 or 60 feet wide and 40 or so feet high. It was beautifully thatched with pili grass and the exterior ornamented with edging of dark brown uluhe ferns fronds at the corners, and from the ground to the peak and along the ridge pole of the roof.

The supporting timbers of Haleuluhe were straight, substantial and of a dark wood. Of special notice were the bands and patterns of sennit cordage which had been bleached white, then used to lash the posts together in regular, attractive patterns.

The floor was a pavement of stone and mortar, spread with a cement of lime which produced a smoothness resembling marble. Makaloa mats covered the floor.

At each end of the large room were folding glass doors and the large windows on the sides were hung with crimson damask draperies. The furnishings were foreign made tables, chairs, mirrors, glass chandeliers and portraits in oil of Liholiho and Kamāmalu painted in London.

When receiving guests the young king sat in an arm chair over which was spread a yellow feather cloak. He would wear a dress uniform with gold epaulettes, silk stockings and pumps. With him would be Ka'ahumanu, Kīna'u and Kekāuluohi.

R.J. Baker's "Early Hawaiian Prints" reproduces in black and white a copy of the water color of Haleuluhe Palace, 1826.

Joseph Feher, 1969, pp. 147, 177, 288 shows thatched houses with the decorative edging of *uluhe* ferns.

■ Halekauwila (House of kauila wood)

This large structure was built near the Honolulu Fort in the early 1830s and replaced Haleuluhe as the official seat of government for Kamehameha III about 1836. Timbers which Ka'ahumanu had brought from the sacred Hale-o-Keawe at Hōnaunau, Kona, Hawai'i were used in its construction.

Commander Charles Wilkes visited the king at this palace on September 30, 1840. He estimated the building to be 40 by 60 feet with movable screens which could divide the one room into several.

The interior is shown in some detail in a sketch called a cartoon by Masselot. It shows Kamehameha III, his chiefs and visiting naval officers at Halekauwila in July, 1837. This sketch appears in a number of publications. See Judd, 1975, p. 36 and Gast, 1973 following page 84; Feher, 1969, p. 189.

■ Hale Piula (House of the Tin Roof)

The next palace to be built in Lahaina, following the brick structure of Kamehameha I, was Hale Piula. Work on it commenced about 1838 when coral blocks were used to make the structure some 40 by 120 feet. The two story building, with a surrounding lanai for each floor, was outstanding because of its metal roof which was painted red.

Kamehameha III and his consort, Kalama, lived in a compound of thatched cottages on an islet some distance to the rear of Hale Piula.

The king moved his government to Honolulu in 1845. Hale Piula was so badly damaged in a wind storm in 1858 that it was not rebuilt.

■ The First 'Iolani Palace ('Iolani - bird of heaven)

This one-story structure, with a high basement, an encircling wide lanai and a cupola or look-out room on top, was built of coral blocks. The building was some 50 by 75 feet with a lanai 10 feet wide. It occupied a site on or near that of the present 'Iolani Palace.

The furnishings in this palace prove that Hawai-

Koa

ian royalty were living in a style much like European monarchs.

The rooms were richly carpeted. *Koa* furniture, made by a German cabinet maker of Honolulu, consisted of sofas, chairs, bedsteads and tables.

Possessions on display indicating Hawaiian royalty were tall *kāhili* and two feather cloaks of Kamehameha I.

Table service consisted of both gold plated and silver knives, forks and spoons. There were sets of tea and of coffee pots, fine glassware and the best imported china.

See Allen, 1978, for information on the oil paintings and art objects.

The first 'Iolani Palace was the government house for Kamehameha III, IV, V, Lunalilo and for the first part of King Kalākaua's reign. The monarchs and their families lived in cottages on the grounds and used the palace for receptions and government business.

Time and termites eventually weakened this structure and it was torn down in 1879 and plans made for the new 'Iolani Palace.

■ The Present 'Iolani Palace

The corner stone of 'Iolani Palace was laid using a Masonic Ceremony on December 31, 1879. This was Queen Kapiolani's 45th birthday.

In December of 1882 the construction was complete enough for the Royal Family to use the

Palace as their residence. Actually they preferred to live in the comfortable two story wooden bungalow (Hale 'Akala) on the grounds close by.

The first formal function was a banquet given by the King for fellow Masons on December 27, 1882.

The coronation of the King and Queen on February 12, 1883 was the incentive for many festivities in the Palace and on the lawn.

'Iolani Palace is described as of American Florentine architecture. The four story building, including the basement and attic, is of brick and iron with a facing of cement and concrete block trimmings. It is 140 by 120 feet in size.

The Palace has been completely renovated and restored recently. So much has been and is being written about this "only royal palace in the United States" that no more will be said here. We refer our readers to Allen, 1978; and Judd, 1975.

Other Structures Associated With Royalty

■ **Ali'iōlani Hale**
(a chief known unto the heavens)

Originally designed in 1869 to house Hawai'i's rulers, Kamehameha V asked that it be built to accommodate the legislature, courts and some of the ministries.

■ **Hānaiakamalama**
Queen Emma's Summer Palace

The name means Foster Child of the god Kamalama. He was one of the ancestral gods of Mary Kaoanaeha, wife of the Englishman John Young. They were grandparents of Queen Emma. John Young II purchased this frame house and land for $6000. The house was built sometime between 1843 and 1849. Young willed the property to Queen Emma. This family summer home is now a museum.

■ **Foreign Style Houses in Hawai'i**

The only foreigners in residence in Hawai'i before 1820 were men. They seem to have accepted the living conditions afforded by the thatched houses. At least we have no record of their building other types of dwellings.

The mission families were welcomed by the chiefs and given quarters in some of the best existing houses or, in some cases, dwellings were built for them. The women in the mission were unhappy in the thatched houses and recorded their dislikes in their journals or in letters to relatives in New England. Slowly they erected living quarters of a type that they had known and liked.

The first frame house to be set up in Hawai'i came from Boston around Cape Horn in 1821. It was ready-cut so this two-story structure was assembled in the missionary compound when the King gave permission. In 1823 the mission built a coral-in-mortar structure to house the mission press which was brought on the Brig Thaddeus in 1820. It still stands at this time near the frame house.

In 1831 the mission constructed the two-story Chamberlain house of coral blocks taken from the Kaka'ako reef not far away. Its architectual style resembles somewhat that of the frame mission house and both have been called "bleakly Puritan."

Present day architects, with the accumulated knowledge of the varying moods that make up Hawai'i's climatic conditions, are able to design what has been called the environmental house or home. Properly planned dwellings can be cooled by the prevailing winds, be built with eaves having the proper wide overhang that carry away the water from tropical showers and feature wide doors that lead out to a broad lanai which in turn seem to flow out into the garden.

The mission houses in Honolulu, of New England design, do not have the features which were later called Hawaiian. But it is of interest that the Rev. William P. Alexander, in 1841 designed the Waioli Mission Church on windward Kaua'i. It stands today proudly exhibiting its Hawaiian style roof, and wide eaves sheltering a spacious lanai that encircles the structure.

■ **Keoua Hale, Princess Ruth's Mansion**

Princess Ruth Ke'elikōlani built the huge, ornate structure, referred to as her palace, out of envy of King Kalākaua's 'Iolani Palace which was under construction at the same time.

The mansion, Keōua Hale, built on 4.31 acres of land called Ka'akopua at 21 Emma Street, was completed in 1882. A lū'au dedicating the building was held on February 9 and a grand ball the next night.

The princess became ill after the festivities, retired to her grass house in Kona, and died May

24, 1883.

Before her death Princess Ruth had willed Keōua Hale, said to have cost $89,000., and a great deal of property to her cousin Princess Pauahi Bishop. The Bishops lived at Keōua Hale until Pauahi's death in 1884, Mr. Bishop continued to occupy the mansion until he moved to California in 1894.

Mr. Bishop returned Keōua Hale to the Bernice Pauahi Bishop Estate. The Trustees sold it in 1895 to the Board of Education of the Republic of Hawaii for $30,000. It housed Honolulu High School until 1908 when Central Grammar School moved into the premises. After serving as a school for 30 years it was razed in 1925. Central Intermediate School now occupies the site. (See Zambucka, 1977, for photographs and descriptions of Keōua Hale and its builder.)

■ Hulihe'e Palace, Kailua, Kona

John Adams Kuakini built this palace of lava rock cemented with mortar made from coral. The interior woodwork is of *koa* and *'ōhi'a*. The walls are three feet thick. The structure was built during the years 1837-38 and has been occupied as a residence or used as a historic house museum since. Kuakini, who served as governor of Hawai'i Island, was a brother of Ka'ahumanu.

■ Haleakalā, House of the Sun

High Chief Abner Pākī and his wife Konia built this two story dwelling about 1851. Mrs. Bishop inherited the home after the death of her parents. There were cottages in the rear for servants and also stables. The Bishops, noted for their hospitality, entertained frequently. The house and extensive gardens were on the *mauka* side of King Street including Bishop which had not been opened as a street. Bernice Pauahi Bishop was born on this site in 1831 in a house called Aikupika.

■ Washington Place

Captain John Dominis built this splendid mansion during the years 1842 to 1846 on three acres of land which he purchased on Beretania Street. This two story residence has 17 rooms, an extensive lanai and is called Greek Revival architecture.

Captain Dominis sailed for China to purchase furniture for the new home and was never seen again. Mrs. Dominis and son John Owen continued to live in the residence which was named Washing-ton Place by the U.S. Commissioner to Hawai'i who rented a part of the building as the Legation. In 1862 John Owen Dominis married Kalākaua's sister Lydia who became Princess, then Queen Lili'uokalani. Upon the death of her husband the Queen inherited Washington Place and lived there until her death in 1917. Since 1922 it has been the Executive Mansion for Hawai'i's governors.

■ Other Mansions

The Honorable A.S. Cleghorn, governor of O'ahu under King Kalākaua, built a mid-Victorian mansion on Queen Emma Street in the early 1870s. Cleghorn was married to the Princess Likelike, sister of the King. The Princess Ka'iulani was born to the Cleghorns here in 1875. In 1878 the ornate frame mansion was sold to industrialist James and Mrs. (Maipinepine) Campbell and here Abigail (later Princess Kawānanakoa) and two of her sisters were born. In 1926 the members of the Pacific Club purchased the home and later replaced it with a clubhouse of modern design. (The Cleghorns moved to Waikīkī to their spacious home 'Āinahau set in extensive, well-landscaped gardens.)

In the 1880s Claus Spreckels, wealthy business man of San Francisco and Hawai'i and intimate of King Kalākaua, built a lavish, ornate mansion at Punahou and Wilder Streets. This frame building, two stories with cupola, frescoed ceilings and stained glass windows, was later purchased by Jonah Kumalae, remodeled and moved to Isenberg Street. It served as the St. Louis Alumni Clubhouse until it accidentally burned in 1954.

On each of the larger islands visitors may see historic houses that are architecturally interesting.

The following are but a few former dwellings now open to the public.

In Hilo, Hawai'i the missionary Lyman family built a two story frame house in 1839, now the Lyman House Memorial Museum.

The Rev. William Richards built a spacious frame house in Lahaina, Maui, which was occupied by Dr. Dwight Baldwin and family in 1835. It now welcomes visitors as the Baldwin Home Missionary Museum.

The Rev. Edward T. Bailey, in 1840, built a home of coral blocks in Wailuku, Maui. It is now a museum called Hale Hō'ike'ike.

At Hanalei, Kaua'i, the Waioli Mission House, 1836, may be visited on application to the caretaker. Grove Farm Homestead in Līhu'e is now open to visitors.

———————

■ **Understanding and Appreciations**

1. Discuss the meanings of the words house and home. Consider the feeling of security that the members of a family develop concerning their own home.

2. List the housebuilding materials that were found in old Hawai'i. Did the people make good use of the available materials? Note the short life of certain of these products.

3. List the building materials that are brought in from afar to construct houses and business buildings. Judge these materials for durability, resistance to fire, to decay and to termites.

4. Note the harmony in the shades of brown in the Hawaiian house and its principal furnishings. The *pili* grass was fragrant when fresh. The burning *kukui* nuts and the oil give a yellow glow and a pleasant odor.

5. Discuss the architect as a professional man in Hawai'i today. If you were an architect tell how you would plan a house for the enjoyment of outdoor-indoor living, for the easy access from rooms to lanai to garden.

6. Attend the ceremonies of dedication for a house or public building. What part of the ritual has been retained from pre-European practices?

7. After studying the web of the spider, the hive of bees, the nests of certain birds and the dam of beavers a person wrote, "Of all creatures who fabricate their dwellings man is the only one still trying to learn how." What do you think?

■ **Student Activities**

Craft activities for the school or home workshop in this unit of learning would include one or more of the following:

1. Construct a model of a grass house using small branches or wooden disposable chopsticks for posts and framework. Or make the sides and roof of the model from cardboard. Thatch or cover with grass. Dedicate the house by cutting the *piko* and reciting a chant.

2. Make a *pūlumi ni'au* by tying 30 to 40 coconut leaflet midribs at their bases to form a bundle-like broom. Use it.

3. Make a *kahi lauoho* or comb of *ni'au* cut to 2½ lengths and lashed securely to strips of bamboo about 4" long. (See Feher, p. 63.)

4. String the kernels from six to eight roasted *kukui* nuts on a sliver of bamboo to form a candle, *kō'i* or *ihoiho kukui*. Light the nut at the top and note its yellow flame and distinctive odor.

5. From seasoned *hau* wood cut the larger *'aunaki* and the pointed *'aulima* to make a fire plow. (Feher, p. 36.) Try to make fire.

6. Learn to plait *lau hala*. If a teacher is not available refer to the booklet, "The Story of Lauhala" by Stall.

■ **Research Activities**

1. Study the six views of Honolulu in 1853 by the artist Paul Emmert. Note the type of architecture used in the houses and public buildings of that era. These views are reproduced in Thrum's Annual for 1899, pp. 86-103 and Thrum's for 1915, pp. 45-60.

2. Read about Princess Ruth's house, Hale Keōua, built on Emma Street in 1778-79. This huge frame mansion housed Honolulu's first public high school. See Feher, p. 288 for a photograph of Hale Keoua and, in great contrast, one of her grass house in Kona.

3. Learn more about the Adobe Schoolhouse, built in 1835, off Mission Lane, near the Mission Children's Library. It is the only adobe building still standing in Honolulu. Wooden studs support the roof while the adobe bricks fill in the spaces. Read Bob Krauss, The Honolulu Advertiser, May 7, 1981, A 10, for story and photos.

Audio-Visual Activities

Movie: Bishop Museum's film Kapingama-rangi shows the steps in constructing a dwelling and a meeting house on this Polynesian atoll.

Field Trips: Go to Bishop Museum to see the most authentic of all Hawaiian grass houses. Study the houses constructed more recently at the Polynesian Culture Center. Visitors and residents on the neighbor islands will see grass houses on Kaua'i and in Kona.

Visit or read about some of the historic homes or buildings in Honolulu:

The Mission Houses on King Street - 1821, 1823, 1828.

Washington Place, 1846 (usually open to the public on New Year's Day)

Old School Hall, Punahou 1852

Ali'iōlani Hale, 1874

'Iolani Palace, 1879-1882

Hānaiakamalama, Queen Emma's Summer Palace, about 1850

Kawaiaha'o Church, 1841-1842

On the island of Hawai'i visit these historic buildings:

Kona - Hulihe'e Palace, home of Governor Kuakini, 1837

Moku'aikaua Church, 1823, 1825, 1837

Hilo - Lyman House Memorial, 1839

On Maui visit:

Lahaina - Baldwin House, 1834

Lahainaluna - Hale Pa'i the first print shop, 1835

Wailuku - Bailey House, Hale Hō'ike'ike, 1840

On Kaua'i visit:

Wai'oli Mission House, 1841

Vocabulary

Learn the difference in meaning in these pairs of words:

house	home
weave	plait
cement	concrete
hikie'e	pūne'e
architect	contractor
dedicate	consecrate
thatch	shingle

Current Happenings and Trends

During the century following the construction of the missionaries' first frame house in Honolulu, the Hawaiian *hale* disappeared completely. For a time grass houses were modified by building the walls of foreign materials and retaining the roof of thatch. Wooden doors and small-paned windows became fashionable. A few frame houses were built in the style of the gable roof grass house.

The dominant type of dwelling built in Hawai'i's urban areas during the nineteenth century was in the style of the New England house which was not suited to comfortable tropical living.

At the present time architects are designing houses to take advantage of the charms of the Hawaiian environment. These structures open on to wide lanais which extend into the garden. Relative freedom from insects and other forms of animal life, so agressive in other tropical areas, makes this type of living a delightful experience. Unfortunately, many of the low-priced houses now being built are box-like structures which shut the occupants from their gardens.

The rapid increase in population and the relative scarcity of land in Hawai'i has caused many people to seek apartments and condominiums. The condominium became a desirable investment as well as a convenient and luxurious dwelling when an enabling law, passed in 1961, provided for individual ownership of a single unit within a multiunit structure. Since that time thousands of condominium units have been completed, most of them classed "Luxury high rise."

Air conditioning is being installed in single family dwellings as well as in apartments and condominiums. This trend is changing the style of new construction in Hawai'i. The earlier pattern of large airy rooms with high ceilings and many windows is giving way to artificially cooled rooms walled off from the gardens and the trade winds.

Building permits issued in 1988 totaled 24,032, only slightly higher than the number issued in the previous year. The value of these building permits is estimated at $1.8 billion.

In 1988 some 2,287 employers engaged in mining and contract construction employed 23,292 persons, giving them the average annual wage of $31,703 per worker, a total payroll of $738.4 million. The *State of Hawaii Data Book* has more information on the construction industry.

■ Evaluation

Check the students' concept of the house as a home.

Have the pupils express feelings which show that they were able, figuratively, to enter into the model houses or sketches of houses and gain a feeling of security and belonging?

Evaluate such skills as making fire or constructing some of the items suggested as craft projects.

Review the terms used in this unit to check word understandings.

■ Reading List

Abernathy, Jane F., and Suelyn C. Tune. *Made in Hawai'i.* Honolulu: University of Hawaii Press, 1983.

Allen, Gwenfread E. *Hawaii's Iolani Palace and Its Kings and Queens.* Honolulu: Aloha Graphics, 1978.

Apple, Russell A. *The Hawaiian Thatched House.* 1971. Norfolk Island, Aus.: Island Heritage, 1973.

———. *Pahu-kahi-lua.* Homestead of John Young, Kawaihae, Hawaii. Honolulu: Pu'ukohola Heiau National Historical Site, National Park Service, 1978.

Barrère, Dorothy B. *Kamehameha in Kona.* Two documentary studies. Pacific Anthropological Records No. 23. Honolulu: Bishop Museum Press, 1975.

Beckwith, Martha W. *Kepelino's Traditions of Hawaii.* 1932. Honolulu: Bishop Museum Bulletin No. 95, 1971.

Bird, Arden J., Steven Goldsberry, and J. Puninani Kanekoa Bird. *The Craft of Hawaiian Lauhala Weaving (Plaiting).* Honolulu: University of Hawaii Press, 1983.

Brigham, William T. *The Ancient Hawaiian House.* Honolulu: Bishop Museum Memoir, Vol. II, No. 3, 1908.

———. *Stone Implements of the Ancient Hawaiians.* Honolulu: Bishop Museum Memoir, Vol. I, No. 4, 1902.

Bryan, E.H. Jr. *Ancient Hawaiian Life.* 1938. Honolulu: Books About Hawaii, 1950.

Buck, Peter H. *Arts and Crafts of Hawaii.* Honolulu: Bishop Museum Special Publication No. 45, 1957.

Bushnell, Oswald A. *A Walk Through Old Honolulu.* Honolulu: Kapa Associates, [1975].

Degener, Otto. *Plants of the Hawaii National Park.* 1930. Ann Arbor, MI: Edwards Bros., Inc., 1945.

Ellis, William. *Journal William Ellis. A Narrative of a Tour of Hawaii. . . .* 1826. Honolulu: Rutland, VT and Japan: C.E. Tuttle, 1979.

Fairfax, Geoffrey W. *The Architecture of Honolulu.* Norfolk Island, Aus.: Island Heritage, 1972.

Farrell, Andrew. *The Story of Iolani Palace.* Honolulu: Board of Commissioners of Public Archives, 1936.

Feher, Joseph. *Hawaii: A Pictorial History.* Honolulu: Bishop Museum Special Publication No. 58, 1969.

Gast, Ross H. *Don Francisco de Paula Marin.* Honolulu: University Press of Hawaii, 1973.

Handy, E.S.C. "Houses and Villages." Ch. 6 in *Ancient Hawaiian Civilization.* A series of lectures delivered at the Kamehameha Schools by E.S.C. Handy [and others]. 1933. Rutland, VT and Japan: C.E. Tuttle, 1965 (rev. ed.).

Handy, E.S.C., and Mary K. Pukui. *The Polynesian Family System in Ka'u, Hawai'i.* 1958. Rutland, VT and Japan: C.E. Tuttle, 1972.

Hazama, Dorothy. *The Ancient Hawaiians.* Who were they? How did they live? Honolulu: Hogarth Press, 1974. (Information on constructing, dedicating and furnishing the Hawaiian house.)

Ii, John Papa. *Fragments of Hawaiian History.* Trans. Mary K. Pukui. 1959. Honolulu: Bishop Museum Press, 1963.

Judd, Walter F. *Palaces and Forts of the Hawaiian Kingdom.* From thatch to American Florentine. Palo Alto, CA: Pacific Books, 1975.

Kamakau, Samuel M. *Ka Po'e Kahiko.* The people of old. Honolulu: Bishop Museum Special Publication No. 51, 1964.

———. *Ruling Chiefs of Hawaii.* Honolulu: Kamehameha Schools Press, 1961.

———. *The Works of the People of Old.* Honolulu: Bishop Museum Special Publication No. 61, 1976. (House building, 95-108.)

Lydecker, Robert C. *History of Washington Place.* Honolulu: Honolulu Star-Bulletin, 1931 (reprint).

Malo, David. *Hawaiian Antiquities.* 1898. Honolulu: Bishop Museum Special Publication No. 2, 1976.

Mellen, George, ed. *The Sales Builder,* October 1938.

Mitchell, Donald D. Kilolani. *Hawaiian Treasures. Houses,* 81-100. Honolulu: Kamehameha Schools Press, 1978.

Morrison, Boone. *Journal of a Pioneer Builder.* William H. Lentz, Kilauea, Hawaii, 1877-78. Kīlauea: Hawaii Natural History Association, 1977.

Olson, Gunder E., comp. *The Story of the Volcano House.* Hilo: Petroglyph Press, 1974.

Pratt, Helen G. *The Hawaiians: An Island People.* 1941. Rutland, VT and Japan: C.E. Tuttle, 1963.

Seckel, Harry W. *Hawaiian Residential Architecture.* Honolulu: Bishop Museum Miscellaneous Publication, 1954.

Stall, Edna W. *Historic Homes of Hawaii.* Privately printed, 1937.

———. *The Story of Lauhala. 1953. Hilo: Petroglyph Press, 1974.*

Summers, Catherine C. The Hawaiian Grass House in Bishop Museum. Honolulu: Bishop Museum Press, 1988.

Taylor, Clarice B. "Hawaiian House." *Tales About Hawaii.* Honolulu Star-Bulletin clippings, January 27-March 3, 1953.

Zambucka, Kristin. *The High Chiefess Ruth Keelikolani.* Honolulu: Mana Publishing Company, 1977.

UNIT 15:
Clothing, with Special Reference to Making, Decorating and Using Kapa

CLOTHING
with Special Reference to
Making, Decorating and Using Kapa

When the Hawaiian people migrated from the islands to the south they brought with them the plants and the skills needed to make and decorate bark cloth fabrics. Although the Hawaiian climate was mild, they needed clothing to protect them from the rain, wind, chilly temperatures of the cooler season and the cold of the higher altitudes.

The people could express their desire for color and style through designing, decorating and wearing their kapa garments. Their simple form of modesty called for persons above the age of eight years or so to wear the malo or pāʻū during the day. Water sports were enjoyed without the burden of clothing. Warriors skilled in certain types of fighting went into combat wearing but a coating of coconut oil.

The principal materials used in the Pacific Islands for making clothing were the fibers from the inner bark of certain plants. The product made from these fibers is called "bark cloth" in English although the widely-known Polynesian word tapa appears in the larger English dictionaries. The Hawaiian equivalent, kapa, which means "the beaten thing," is used in this unit to designate specifically the Hawaiian-made product.

People in many parts of the world make, or have made for as long as 2,000 years, cloth-like or paper-like materials from plant fibers. (See Reading List, Ling, Shun-Sheng, "Bark Cloth Culture and the Invention of Paper-Making in Ancient China.") The kapa makers improved their tools and techniques so markedly after arriving in Hawaiʻi that Hawaiian kapa is considered unique by ethnologists. It is the finest in the Pacific and probably in the world when judged for the variety and quality of its workmanship, the numbers of colors and designs used in its decoration and the great selection of tools and implements employed in producing it.

The account of the origin of kapa and tales involving the tools, dyes or the finished material, have been handed down to us by the story-tellers of old Hawaiʻi. One legend tells us that the first wauke plant to furnish the soft bark for garments grew from the grave of an elderly man named Maikohā who was buried in Nuʻuanu Valley on Oʻahu. In time he became the ancestor-god of kapa makers. One of his daughters, Lauhuki, became the patron of kapa pounders. (Westervelt spells her name Lauhuiki.) Her sister, Laʻahana, was the ʻaumakua of those who created kapa designs, both watermarks in the fibers and patterns on the finished material. A man, Ehu, discovered the colors in the plant juices and so became the patron of those engaged in the dyeing processes. Hai is named also as a god of the kapa beaters. (Westervelt, 1963, p. 59. Brigham, Bishop Museum Catalogue, part I, p. 23, 1892.)

Hina, mother of the demi-god Māui, was the great legendary kapa maker. Her famous son accomplished one of his notable deeds, that of snaring the sun and causing him to travel more slowly, in order that Hina might have more daylight hours in which to dry her kapa. "The clouds of many colors are Hina's kapa spread out in the sky. Sometimes they lie in sheets, sometimes they are in fluffy piles." (Colum, 1960, p. 47; Buck, 1957, pp. 167-68.)

The more durable cotton and linen fabrics from Europe and America and colorful silks from the Orient gradually replaced kapa. At the present time, however, "bark cloth" is made on several Pacific islands. Some of it is used by the older people for ceremonial garments but the greater part is sold to tourists or exported as a native handicraft. Most of the tapa on sale in Honolulu gift shops is Samoan (siapo), Tongan (hiapo) or Fijian (masi).

■ Making Kapa

In brief, the process of *kapa* making consists of securing the proper bast fibers, soaking them until they are soft, beating them to the desired texture, joining as many strips as necessary to secure a *kapa* of the size needed, then drying and bleaching it in the sun.

"Well-made tapa must be clearer than moonlight; clearer than snow on the mountains." (Kamakau, 1976, p. 113.)

Actually, this process requires a great deal of knowledge, skill and practice as well as the proper raw materials and tools. Individuals who are practicing this art gave brief demonstrations from time to time of pounding and softening the *wauke* bast fibers at workshops or fairs. Lack of time prevents them from carrying this process to completion in the presence of those watching. With all that has been written about *kapa* making, it is surprising to learn that only a few persons have made the large sheets of fine-textured Hawaiian *kapa* since sometime in the past century.

Descriptions of the *kapa* making process are given in greater or lesser detail by the following authors:

Bishop, Marsha B. *Hawaiian Life of the Pre-European Period.*
Brigham, William T. *Ka Hana Kapa.*
Bryan, E.H. Jr. *Ancient Hawaiian Life.*
Bryan, William A. *Natural History of Hawaii.*
Buck, Peter H. *Arts and Crafts of Hawaii.*
Curtis, Caroline. *Manu, Girl of Old Hawaii.*
Kamakau, S.M. *The Works of the People of Old.*
Kooijman, Simon. *Tapa in Polynesia.*
Pratt, Helen G. *The Hawaiians: An Island People.*

Persons planning to engage in a project of *kapa* making should read several of the articles suggested here and talk with informed persons to get a clearer picture of the steps in this complicated process.

Manuscripts describing details of *kapa* making and dyeing, and revealing hither-to unpublished processes in this art are being written for eventual publication by practicing *kapa* makers Malia Solomon and Wesley Sen of Honolulu and Puanani Van Dorpe of Lahaina, Maui. Other skilled artists

in this field who share their knowledge in workshops and in their writings are Carla Freitas, Dennis Kanaʻe Keawe and Ann Kimura.

■ Materials Used

The inner bark or bast fibers of the *wauke*, *(Broussonetia papyrifera),* a plant which was cultivated near the villages, or in small plantations located in moist, sheltered valleys, made the best *kapa*. *Wauke* saplings were cut when they had reached the height of six to ten feet and were about an inch in diameter. Known as the paper mulberry, this plant grows in China, Japan, the Pacific Islands and the eastern and western sections of the U.S. Sunset Magazine for September, 1963, pictured a row of paper mulberry trees growing in Southern California where they had reached a height of 50 feet with branches spreading to 40 feet.

Wauke

In Hawaiʻi *wauke* grows best in rich soil with considerable moisture and protection from the winds. It is propagated from the shoots that spring up from the roots of established plants. If these shoots are not removed a few *wauke* plants can develop into a patch ever increasing in size. When grown in close proximity to one another the plants are not as apt to sprout branches on the sides of the stems. If side shoots develop they should be removed in order to produce stems with unbroken bark. *Wauke* can be propagated from stem cuttings.

Botanists recognize but one specie (*papyrifera*) of *wauke* but *kapa* makers speak of a number of varieties. Their relative merits in *kapa* making were not recorded but are being rediscovered. One variety has heart-shaped leaves that are usually one to three lobed (*lau manamana*). Another variety called *pō'aha* or *po'a'aha* has somewhat smaller, rounded leaves (*lau poepoe*) that are not lobed. The latter variety seems to have been used to make the fine bed *kapa* by the fermentation process. Young succulent fibers are easier to process and make the softest *kapa*.

Māmaki (*Pipturus* spp.), a large shrub or small tree, grows to 15 feet in height in open wooded areas or on the outskirts of the forests. It thrives without cultivation at altitudes of 1,500 to 4,000 feet. *Māmaki* fibers make a firm, heavy *kapa*, not as soft and white as *wauke*. Some 19 species and varieties of *māmaki* are endemic to the Hawaiian Islands. Sometimes *māmaki* and *wauke* fibers were pounded together.

Some ten percent of the *kapa* in Bishop Museum is from *māmaki*.

Even though *māmaki kapa* was secondary to that made from *wauke* it was valuable in exchange for other goods.

In 1840 Kawaiaha'o Church was under construction and the builders needed 100,000 wooden shingles for the roof. Dr. G.P. Judd wrote in his diary:

> July 8th, 1840. Having received the promise of a *mano* or two (a *mano* is 10 X 400, equal to 4,000) of *māmaki kapa* and 200 cattle from the king (to be exhanged for shingles for the church). I started to Waialua to hire the 100,000 shinges made.
>
> July 18. Received the *māmaki*, & *lau* - 2800 - not counted. (Ethel Damon, "The Stone Church at Kawaiahao." pp. 52-53)

The fibers of other plants were occasionally used for *kapa* in Hawai'i. Among them were the young shoots of the breadfruit (*pō'ulu*), the *'oloa* (*ma'aloa* or *mā'oloa*) *Neraudia melastomaefolia*, a relative of the *māmaki*, the *hau*, and the strong bark of the *'ākia*, *Wikstroemia* spp. The fibers of the Hawaiian raspberry (*'ākala*) have been listed as a source of *kapa*. Kamakau wrote that *'ākala* was a kind of *kapa* made from long, young shoots of *wauke*. With the *wauke* plant so choice and abundant the *kapa* makers had no need to resort to inferior

fibers.

■ Tools in Kapa Making

The women made the *kapa* with tools which were fashioned for them by the men. Most of the implements were of wood or bamboo. The men, skilled in the use of the adze and a few carving tools, made the greatest number and variety of implements for pounding and decorating *kapa* used anywhere in the Pacific.

The adze (*ko'i*), a stone blade lashed to a wooden handle, or a stone knife was used by the men to cut the plants which furnished the fibers. These were cut close to the ground and the roots were left to produce new shoots for the next year.

A clam or similar shell, an adze blade or the thumb nail was used to split the bark the full length of the plant stem. The split bark was removed in one piece from the stem by peeling if off with the thumbs and fingers or preferably by securing one end of the bark between the first and second fingers and twirling the entire stem around and around the hand. This wound the bark in a tight roll with the bast fibers on the outside.

A shell or turtle bone scraper was used to scrape off the outer brown and green bark (*epidermis*) from the strip after it was unrolled and placed on a flat surface. The scraping was done on the *kapa* log (*kua kuku*) or on the *olonā* scraping board (*lā'au kahi olonā*). These boards were 65 to 89 inches long and 2½ to 10 inches wide.

Some *kapa* makers cut and loosen the epidermis at the base or wide end of the strip. After separating the two layers they pull off the outer bark in one piece. Much less time and work is required by this process.

After proper scraping, only the white bast fibers remained. If of *wauke* they were soaked 7 to 10 days, usually in sea water. *Māmaki* strips were soaked for 10 days in fresh water.

The bast fibers may be dried and stored for processing at some future time. Or, after being soaked, they are ready for the first beating.

A large smooth stone (*kua pōhaku*) was the first anvil on which the soaked strips were pounded. This was done with a round, smooth beater (*hohoa*).

The flat-topped wooden anvil (*kua kuku* or *kua lā'au*) provided the smooth surface for the final beating and implanting of a watermark. The anvils were hewn from *nānū* (*gardenia*) or *kāwa'u* wood because they gave a pleasant sound when struck with the beaters. Other woods such as *kauila*, *'ōhi'a* and *māmane* were used but must have been heavy for the women to handle.

The anvil was nearly two yards long, quadrangular in cross section with a longitudinal groove on the underside cut deep enough to reduce the weight of the implement. When in use, a stone was usually placed on the ground under each end to raise the *kua* to a convenient height. Some women used a *lau hala* pillow (*uluna*) under each end of the log. The anvil gave off a resonant sound when struck with the beaters. A code, invented by the women, permitted them to convey messages for great distances. This "kapa talk," not shared with the men, has been lost with much of the rest of the art of *kapa* making.

The wooden beaters were made by the men using their stone adzes. Heavy woods such as *kauila*, *uhiuhi*, *'ōhi'a*, *koai'a* and a few others were used. Grooves and longitudinal lines on the early beaters were incised with shark tooth implements, bone tools and the blades of adzes. The more intricate post-Cook designs were cut in with metal tools.

The round beaters (*hohoa*), 14 to 15 inches long and about two inches in diameter, were used in the first process of softening the bast fibers. Most of them were made with a smooth surface but some were incised with parallel grooves and ridges running the length of the beater. The only one known today which was collected by Capt. Cook's party is of this grooved type. After the introduction of cotton cloth the women were taught to launder their clothes by pounding them on smooth stones along the streams using the *hohoa*. Many beaters were worn out by this usage.

The square or four-surfaced beaters (*i'e kuku*) were approximately the size of the *hohoa* and were used for the final beating of the sheets of *kapa*. Their special function was implanting the watermark into the thin *kapa* by striking it while wet on the smooth surface of the *kua kuku*.

Each of the four surfaces of a beater, which were about two inches wide, had, in most instances, a different design. When a surface was left without markings it was to smooth the *kapa* at the end of the beating. Many of the *i'e kuku* had one or two sides with fine to coarse ridges and grooves. These softened the bark fibers and left a watermark.

The designs on the beaters represent a great many geometric figures and ideas from nature. Brigham (1911, pp. 80-95) studied the patterns on 340 beaters and recorded the names for many of them. They are the most varied of the tapa beaters in all Polynesia. Some of the names of the patterns are:

mole - smooth	lau ma'u - fern leaf
hālua - shallow grooves	iwi pūhi - eel bone
pepehi - deep grooves	maka 'upena - net meshes
ho'opa'i - sharp ridges	'upena pūpū - net with
niho manō - shark teeth	dots
	lei hala - pandanus lei

■ Making Kapa

A study of the literature, examination of existing examples and discussions with people now experimenting with *kapa* show that at least two different processes were employed in making Hawai'i's bark cloth.

The method called *paku* was used in manufacturing the sturdy product used for clothing and for use out-of-doors where it would be exposed to the elements.

The second method entailed soaking the cleaned bark for many days, allowing it to ferment or ripen, beating it into a pulp and finally pounding it into sheets and adding the watermark. This fine, soft *kapa* was used for bedding and for the clothing of chiefs. It is this *kapa* that is admired in museum collections today.

■ Kapa by the paku method

The *paku* process of *kapa* making was the simple, common method of furnishing clothing for the multitude of working people. It required no long soaking of fibers and no need for beaters with the watermark designs.

In this process the bark was stripped from the stem of the plant and the outer epidermal layer scraped or stripped from the inner fibers. The moist bast was beaten at once on the *kua kuku* with the *hohoa* using its natural juices. Additional strips, laid along the first ones, were overlapped and pounded. The width of the sheet increased as more strips were added. It is said that little or no water need be added during the beating.

More strips might be laid over the top of the partly beaten lengths. When pounded into the existing fibers a form of felting resulted.

When dried and held up to the light the longitudinal fibers could be seen running the length of the material. These fibers and its thickness contributed to the strength and wearing quality of this type of *kapa*.

From this product was made the *malo*, *pā'ū* and *kīhei* as clothing for the working people. The ribbed *kapa (kua'ula)*, which was made by men, according to Kamakau, was produced in large quantities from this sturdy product.

Data for the *paku* process and the following one concerning fermented fibers are abridged from unpublished manuscripts by Puanani Van Dorpe, Wesley Sen and from notes in Bishop Museum taken by J.F.G. Stokes from informants Wahineaea, Kaahaaina and Kalokuokamaile.

■ Making Kapa from Fermented Fibers

Tall young *wauke* of the type called *po'aha* are cut to make this choice type of *kapa*. The bark is stripped off, the outer epidermis scraped or peeled away, and the white inner bast fibers placed in a ti leaf bundle and soaked in the sea for 10 days or more. The strips, now soft, are removed from the salt water and rinsed. Five strips are placed, one on top of the other, and tied at intervals with fibers from the *po'aha*. This bundle is placed lengthwise on the *kapa* log and beaten with a smooth *hohoa*.

The mass widens, becomes felted, and the tie fibers break and are pounded in with the rest. This product is called *mo'omo'o* and is usually dried and bleached in the sun. It may be stored away until needed. One *mo'omo'o* is sufficient to make one sheet of *kapa*.

When the *kapa* making is to continue the *mo'omo'o* are rolled into coils, soaked in fresh water, then wrapped in ti leaves and placed in a covered bowl. After ten days or more the water is squeezed from the coils and the fibers are soft (*palahē*) or ripe.

Each *mo'omo'o* is left rolled like a mass of pulp or a round cake, any remaining slimy water is squeezed from it, and it is kneaded until it becomes tough as dough. The ball is then laid on the *kapa* log and beaten to thoroughly mix the fibers.

As the pulpy material spreads in all directions from the beating, the edges are folded back from each side toward the center. Water is sprinkled on the expanding fibers and care is taken to see that the sheet is beaten so that it is even in thickness throughout.

As the mass spreads the finished part moves toward the woman who is beating the *kapa* and she rolls it up. When the entire sheet is finished she folds it in two and beats it again. A second, third and fourth beating may be done, depending upon the thinness that the worker desires.

When, at last, there are no thick places to be beaten again, no thin places to be filled and nothing else to be done, the beating of the *kapa* is finished. This final stage is termed *holua* and the watermark is beaten in at this time.

The finished damp sheet of *kapa* is laid on the small, clean pebbles in the drying yard and weighted down with stones along the edges. As the *kapa* dries the stones are moved to make sure that the shrinkage is even.

Five such sheets are needed to make a *kapa moe* or *ku'inakapa* (bed covering). The four inner sheets *(iho)* remain white and the outer or top sheet *(kilohana)* is decorated. These are sewed together along one side using a bone awl to pierce the material and a thread of twisted *kapa*. Newly made *kapa* is folded and made fragrant with such plants as sandalwood chips, *maile* leaves, *mokihana* berries and the powdered root of the mountain ginger.

■ Watermarking Kapa

A finished strip or sheet of *kapa* was placed on the smooth, flat surface of the anvil while wet and struck with one of the patterned surfaces of the *i'e kuku*. The ridges of the beater design struck deeply into the wet *kapa* while the spaces between left no mark. This process was repeated again and again until the entire surface was marked. After drying, the *kapa* must be held up to the light to appreciate the watermarks. *Kapa* was made softer by beating portions of the fibers thinner in this way.

■ Kua'ula

A ribbed finish *(kua'ula)* is apparent on many of the early thick *kapa*. The ribbing was done on a grooving board *(papa hole)* with a sharp-edged grooving tool *(ko'i hole)*. Dampened *kapa* was placed on the board, and a bamboo ruler held parallel to the grooves. The tip of the grooving tool, guided by the ruler, pressed the *kapa* into each succeeding groove, causing the ribbed effect. One type of grooving tool was made from a thin slice of wood, 8 to 10 inches long at the lower or grooving edge. The ends curved upward. The upper short, thick edge provided a handle. (Buck, p. 185.)

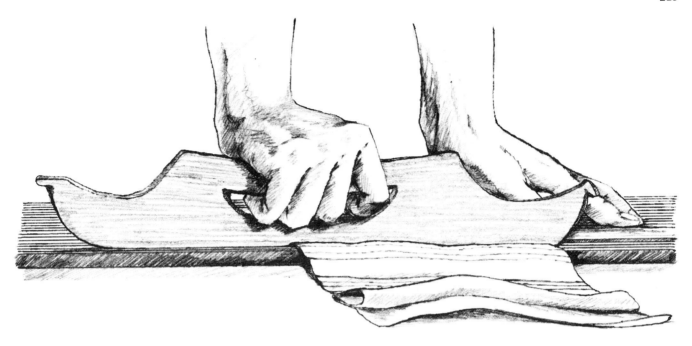

Ribbed Kapa Clothing: Men ribbed or grooved the heavier *kapa (kua'ula)* used for clothing. The wet fabric was placed on a grooved board and the worker pressed the sharp edge of the ribbing tool *(ko'i hole)* into the grooves of the board. His tool was guided by a bamboo ruler held firmly in his left hand.

Kamakau (1976, p. 112) described a grooving tool made from a pig's jawbone trimmed to fit into the grooves in the board. Unfortunately no such instrument is known today.

The boards, usually 30 to 50 inches long and 4 to 10 inches wide were grooved on both sides. The grooves, coarse to fine, were 11 to 15 per inch. Two grooved anvils are known. (Buck, 1957, p. 184-85.)

Skilled *kapa* makers, VanDorpe and Sen, have found it extremely difficult to produce ribbed *kapa* when following the directions recorded in the literature. Some phase of the process may have been omitted by the writers who were not themselves *kapa* makers.

Kua'ula was the one kind of *kapa* regularly made by the men. They made ribbed *kapa* in great quantities, since it was preferred for the men's *malo* and the women's *pā'ū* (Kamakau, 1976, pp. 112-113; Kooijman, 1972, pp. 116-117). This is an exception to the statement made by a number of writers that *kapa* making was exclusively women's work.

■ Large *kapa* were made by pounding out a mass of fibers of considerable size. Very large sheets consisted of smaller sheets, overlapped at the edges and felted into one piece so completely that there was no sign of the joined edges.

Two or more pieces of *kapa* were sometimes sewn together. The edges to be joined were pierced with needles *(kui)* of bone or wood. Cordage of finely twisted *kapa* was drawn through the holes in a neat and sturdy fashion.

■ Hale Kuku and Pā

The most skilled of the women *kapa* makers in the village was called the *loea*. Quite often she was a chiefess who took pride in directing her women into the *kapa* making skills. She had a *hale kuku*, a *kapa* beating house, in which she stored the tools and dyes needed in her work. The actual beating would be done out-of-doors during good weather. Application of dyes was done in this house or another house built especially for this skill. The area was surrounded by a stone wall *(pā pōhaku)* which kept out domestic animals that might walk on the *kapa* that were spread out to dry.

■ Dyeing Hawaiian Kapa

The finished, bleached *kapa* was used in its undecorated state for a number of purposes. Four of the five sheets *(iho)* of the large bed *kapa, (kapa moe)*, were white while the outer or top sheet *(kilohana)* was decorated. Clothing might be worn undecorated although the upper classes preferred color. Traditionally white were the garment and turban of certain classes of *kāhuna* and the pieces of *kapa* used on kites *(lupe), kapu* sticks *(pūlo-ʻuloʻu),* lamp wicks, streamers on gourd helmets and bands tied around trees to indicate that the fruit or nuts were *kapu.*

The love of color and design, and probably a spirit of rivalry, caused the *kapa* makers to develop a larger number of dyes and a greater number of unique implements to apply the color to *kapa* than is found in any other part of the Pacific.

■ Dyes

The available literature on the subject gives lists of Hawaiian plants which furnish color from their roots, bark, leaves, fruits or flowers. Also mentioned are animal products and colored earth. Very few directions have been recorded telling how specific colors may be obtained from these raw materials. Almost nothing has been written about mixing the pure colors from dye sources to obtain blends or shades of color.

In recent years local teachers and playground directors, in carrying out experiments with their pupils, have obtained some attractive dyes from indigenous plants and also from introduced ones.

Refer to the Reading List for the published material on dyes by the following persons:

Blitman, Elaine. *Na Hoʻoluʻu o Hawaiʻi.* Punahou School.
Krauss, Beatrice H. *Ethnobotany of the Hawaiians.* Lyon Arboretum.
McDonald, Marie. "Native Dyes." Kamuela, Hawaiʻi.

Others who have not as yet published the results of their experiments are:

Solomon, Malia, formerly of Ulu Mau Village.
Van Dorpe, Puanani, of Lahaina, Maui.
Yamasaki, Joanne, Kamehameha School graduate.
Sen, Wesley, of Honolulu.

The procedures that many of the dye makers follow in processing their dyes are:

To obtain dyes from leaves, petals and berries, soak them from a few hours to several days in fresh or salt water. Some plant tissues may begin to mold or decay in fresh water after 18 hours at room temperature. Plan to crush and process these before they deteriorate. Add cold or hot water to the crushed tissues. Simmer if the color is too pale. Add salt to a sample of the dye to see if it improves

A‘ali‘i

the color.

To obtain dye from root or stem bark, scrape off the outer bark, pound or crush and soak the inner color-bearing layer in fresh or salt water. Simmer to deepen the color. Add salt if it improves the color.

Strain through a cloth to remove all plant particles.

Use swatches of real *kapa,* pelon, white cotton or linen to test the color of the dye. Wet the swatches before placing them in the dye. Soak them in hot or cold dye for many hours.

Plant juices that are acid may be made alkaline by adding burned coral lime (calcium carbonate). This sometimes produces an attractive color change.

Often a problem arises in correctly naming the color of the dye produced. Some colors change or fade in time. Art supply stores sell color books, charts and compasses which display an array of shades of color by name and some by number. This writer has not found an inexpensive and easy-to-use one.

In pre-European times the color was released

from some of the plant fibers by stone boiling. Enough hot stones were placed in a calabash or gourd containing the dye materials to bring the solution to a simmer. A close fitting lid retained the heat and held the steam. Today an enamel kettle is used over a stove for simmering dye-producing substances and for boiling cloth in the dye. Colors may be deepened by boiling away some of the water.

■   The following is a brief list of dye plants and other dye substances with suggestions for obtaining the colors. See Neal, *In Gardens of Hawaii*, for the scientific names and descriptions of the plants. The page numbers are for the 1965 edition of the book.

1. *'A'ali'i*, Neal p. 536. Simmer the ripe seed capsules in a little water for a red-brown dye. Cloth placed in this dye should be boiled for greater permanence of color.

2. *'Ākala*, raspberry, Neal p. 390. The pink, edible fruit was crushed to make a pink (*'ākala*) dye. The color may vary from candy pink to deep burgundy according to the dilution of the dye. Although listed as a plant furnishing fibers for *kapa*, the designation *'ākala* may refer to the dye, not the fibers.

3. *'Ala'alawainui*, Neal 293. The juicy leaves and stems of this small, native forest herb were crushed and the resulting juices gave a gray dye. More experiments are needed to learn if the juices should be applied to fabric hot or cold and with or without salt.

4. *'Ama'u* (plural *'Āma'uma'u*), Neal p. 22. The outer rind of the trunk of this mountain fern was crushed and used for a reddish brown dye.

5. *Koki'o* or *aloalo*, hibiscus, Neal p. 560. Although the native red hibiscus was originally used for a dye one may now use the hardy garden varieties. Pound the root or stem bark and add water. This will produce a brown stain in cold water or a deeper brown if simmered. Today the red flowers are simmered in water and a lavender dye is produced. With lime added the color becomes silver gray.

6. *Kou*, Neal p. 714. Crush mature leaves and add cold water for a brown stain. When simmered they produce a yellow brown dye.

7. *Kukui*, Neal p. 504. Pound root or stem bark and add water for a brown dye. Simmer for a darker shade. A considerable amount of bark may be cut or scraped from forest trees without harm to them. Cut off the bark in vertical strips. Do not remove bark from around the trees by making circular cuts. This is called girdling a tree and will kill it if the cut is deep. It is unlawful to mutilate trees along our streets or in our parks.

The soot (*pa'u*) from the *kukui* nut gives an excellent black dye. To collect the soot, support a smooth flat stone at least a foot square upon a pair of stones tall enough to allow room to hold a *kukui* nut candle underneath the smooth stone. String whole or pieces of roasted *kukui* nuts on a wire, coconut leaflet midrib (*nī'au*) or a sliver of bamboo. Hold the burning nuts so close to the underside of the smooth stone that the soot gathers on it. Scrape this into a coconut dye dish and add oil. *Kukui* or *kamani* oils were used but cooking oils may be substituted today. This dye was favored as the pigment in tattooing and in waterproofing the hull of the canoes.

For a water soluble black dye pound the fleshy green rinds of mature *kukui* nuts and add water. Fishermen prepared a dye for their nets in this way using salt water.

When the bark of the *kukui* tree is cut a gum or resin (*pīlali*) exudes. When this thick sap is dissolved in fresh water for a couple of days the resulting solution can be painted on *kapa* to give it a resin-like coating. This finish protected the dyes and made the *kapa* stronger and waterproof. Kamakau wrote that the varnish used to make *kapa* shiny was made of eggs of the hen and the spider mixed with other things. (Kamakau, 1976, p. 113.)

8. *Ma'o* or *huluhulu*, Neal p. 566. The leaves from this native cotton are pounded and fresh water is added to give a chartreuse which changes to brown-red. Ma'o blossoms in cold water give an olive-green color.

9. *Nānū* or *nā'ū*, Neal p. 800. This native gardenia may grow into a tree 18 feet high. The yellow pulp of the fruit, which grows to one inch in diameter, is used to dye *kapa* an attractive yellow color. The seed capsule of the introduced gardenia also produces a yellow dye.

10. *Noni*, Neal p. 804. Pound the inner root bark and add water for a yellow dye. Add coral lime

to the yellow infusion and it will change to brick red. This color change makes a dramatic demonstration. Coral heads or coral fragments picked up from the beach may be placed in an *imu* or on the glowing coals in the charcoal grill and burned, then crushed or pounded into powder. Any lime, calcium carbonate, may be used. The principle involved is changing the acid solution to alkaline.

Writers who were misinformed about *noni* dyes have stated that the root bark produces yellow and stem bark gives a red dye.

Kapa dyed a *noni* yellow may, preferably while still wet from the dye bath, become red when dipped into the sea.

11. *'Ōhi'a 'ai*, mountain apple, Neal p. 636. Neither the abundant cerise tufts on the flowers nor the crimson skin on the apple-like fruit was used to produce a dye although this has been suggested. Water is added to the pounded inner bark of the trunk to give a brown dye.

12. *'Ōlena* or turmeric, Neal p. 255. Peel and crush the rhizome, add water, strain and the result is a yellow dye. Young rhizomes or underground stems yield a light yellow dye; the older ones a deep orange. *'Ōlena, noni* and *nānū* were the chief sources of yellow dye for *kapa*.

13. *Pala'ā, palapala'ā*, lace fern, Neal p. 15. A red-brown dye was extracted from the fronds or from the stems and the fronds. It seems logical that the firm, wirey stems, the only part of the frond that is red-brown, would have to be simmered to extract the color.

14. *'Uki'uki*, Neal p. 191. There are three species of this native mountain lily. *Dianella sandwicensis*, found on all of the larger islands except Hawai'i, bears blue berries with a deep blue pulp when mature. When crushed these produce a dye which will color *kapa* an attractive blue-lavender.

The berries on the other species of *'uki'uki* give a yellow-brown stain.

Bishop Museum has no documented examples of *'uki'uki* dyed *kapa*.

Kapa made in post-European times may have been dyed blue with laundry bluing or from a dye made from the indigo plant which was introduced about 1850 to produce blue dye commercially. (Neal, p. 447.)

15. *'Ulei*, Neal p. 387. Boil the ripe seeds to obtain a lavender dye. The fleshy seeds are nearly white in appearance but the pulp is lavender. These seeds are edible.

16. *'Alaea lepo*, an iron bearing clay, also called an ocherous earth. When stirred in water the reddish particles remain in suspension for some time, then settle. Since *'alaea* does not dissolve in water it can be painted on *kapa* or wood but it is slow to penetrate the fibers. This is the *'alaea* that is pounded with white salt to make the red salt served at a *lū'au*.

There is a yellow form of the clay that is occasionally used in the same way.

17. *'Alaea lā'au* or lipstick plant, Neal p. 589. The mature seeds of this introduced plant are covered with an orange-red pigment which may be dissolved in water or oil to make a bright dye.

■ **Summary of the Common Dyes by Color**

Blue	'Uki'uki berries
Brown	Kokio stem and root bark
	Kou leaves
	Kukui trunk and root bark
	'Ōhi'a 'ai trunk and root bark
Black	Black mud in the old taro ponds
	Kukui nut meat burned to soot
	Kukui nut shell and meat burned and ground
	Kukui fleshy green nut rinds in salt water
Gray	'Ala'alawainui leaves and stems
	Gray taro pond mud
	Red hibiscus blossoms with lime
Green	Ma'o blossoms
Lavendar	Hibiscus blossoms
	'Ulei berries
	Wana, ina, hā'uke'uke, sea urchins
Pink	'Ākala fruit
Red Brown	'A'ali'i capsules
	'Alaea lā'au and 'alaea lepo
	'Amau fern bark
	Ma'o leaves, boiled
	Noni root bark with lime or salt
	Pala'ā fern fronds and stems
Yellow	Hōlei trunk and root bark
	Nānū fruit capsules
	Noni root bark
	'Ōlena root or rhizome
	Yellow ocherous earth
Yellow Brown	Kou leaves

Two dozen or more additional dye materials are mentioned in the literature but are not listed here either because the materials are too difficult to obtain or because they have failed to give a satisfactory dye in experiments at The Kamehameha Schools. Much more work remains to be done to rediscover the techniques of producing the native dyes.

■ Tools and Implements for Dyeing and Decorating Kapa

A large calabash ('umeke lā'au) or gourd ('umeke pōhue) held a quantity of dye for dipping (ho'olu'u) and coloring an entire piece of kapa.

A dye bag of kapa was used as a swab to apply dye to one side of a sheet of kapa only. Brushes made from the fibrous ends of the seeds or keys of pandanus (hala) were used as paint brushes.

A tightly twisted cord (kaula kākau) was dipped in the dye, held firmly by each end over the fabric and snapped onto it. The imprints of the twists in the cord made a segmented line on the kapa. This could be repeated in different colors and in different directions.

Bamboo stamps ('ohe kāpala) on which designs were carved in a variety of geometric patterns were used for a form of block printing. (Buck, 1957, pp. 191-202.) The carved end of the stamp was dipped into a container of liquid dye, then the excess was removed by tapping the stamp against the rim of the dye bowl. The carved end bearing the film of dye was pressed against the kapa, dipped and pressed again and again until a continuous line or an intricate pattern had been stamped on the kapa. This unique and highly effective method of designing kapa was confined to Hawai'i. These are believed to be post-European and were made with metal tools.

Bamboo liners (lapa) were used in a decorating process almost identical to that of the stamps. (Buck, p. 203.) The prongs, ranging from one to nine on a liner, resemble somewhat the tines of a table fork. These were dipped into dye and pressed against the kapa to form single or parallel lines in a variety of combinations. The lapa were not used like an ink pen where color flows from the tip as some writers have indicated. (Buck, p. 209.)

Other implements identified with the dyeing process were stone dye mortars (poho pōhaku) and stone pestles (pōhaku ku'i) for crushing dye materials. (Buck, p. 204.) Gathering the dye materials

and compounding the dyes was men's work.

■ Division of Work Between the Sexes

Kapa making is generally considered the finest craft of the Hawaiian women. They accepted the huge task of furnishing the people (about 300,000 at the time of Captain Cook) with clothing and bedding of kapa and accomplished it with creative artistry.

The men helped the women by cutting, with sturdy adzes, the wauke saplings which were cultivated near the villages and by cutting the māmaki and transporting it from the mountains. Their greatest contribution was to fashion the wooden, stone and bamboo tools for the women to use.

From hardwood logs the men cut the smooth-topped anvils (kua kuku). These were sturdy enough for hard wear, yet made light enough for easy transport by means of a deep v-shaped groove cut on the under side. They shaped smooth, round beaters (hohoa) from hard wood, usually koai'a (koai'e) or kauila. With great skill they fashioned the square beaters and, using shark-tooth tools, incised the four surfaces with a wealth of original designs. Great variety also occurs in the bamboo stamps ('ohe kāpala) and to a lesser extent in the liners (lapa) which were the contributions of the men to this craft. The shark-tooth carving tools were made by anchoring the sharp, serrated shark-teeth in the tip or along the side of hardwood handles. Chisels with good cutting blades were made from bone and from basalt. The records are not clear concerning the exact use of each of these tools in wood carving before they were replaced by steel cutting implements.

■ Uses of Kapa in Hawaii

The most extensive use of kapa was for garments and bed clothing. The style of dress was essentially the same for all classes, except that the chiefs and chiefesses were provided with better made and more attractively decorated garments. The working classes could not wear or even handle the clothing of the chiefs.

The women's skirt (pā'ū) was two or more yards long and a yard or less wide. It was worn around the waist and extended below the knees. In putting on this garment a women held one corner of the upper border to her waist, wrapped the free end around and tucked the corner in at the waist line. In the upper corner of the outer end she might tie or roll a *kukui* nut or pebble. When this weighted corner was tucked into the waist fold of the *pā'ū*, the garment was held securely. The visible portion of the *pā'ū* was usually decorated. For some garments five *wauke pā'ū* were stitched into one skirt. A bone needle was used to pierce the fabrics along one end and the thread was twisted from *kapa*.

The men and women wore a similar garment, the *pā'ū hula* when dancing. (See lithographs by Choris and other artists of the early days, Feher, pp. 122, 123, 124.) The *pā'ū* with a bow in front is being worn by *hula* dancers today.

The men's garment was a loin cloth (*malo*) about nine inches wide and nine or more feet long. Some were dyed in solid colors, others were decorated with elaborate designs. To put on a *malo* the man holds the end that is to be the front flap under

Malo: Using his chin and his hands each male was able to tie on his own *malo* or loin cloth.

his chin. He passes the free end between his legs and holds it with one hand against his back while he wraps the remaining portion around his waist until it meets the fold in back and can be slipped underneath it. The front end is released from the chin and falls to form a flap in front. A similar flap may be made in the back by spreading out the end piece and securing it over the waist band.

A shawl (*kīhei*), rectangular in shape, was worn by men and women when it was needed for warmth. Sketches and writings from earlier days inform us that the *kīhei* was worn in two or more ways. It might be centered over the left shoulder and the upper corners tied over the right shoulder thus giving protection to both arms. Or it was centered over one shoulder and the corners knotted under the opposite arm. Often it was thrown over the shoulders and tied in front. *Kīhei* were usually decorated with attractive designs.

The feather garments are not considered clothing in this study but are discussed in Unit 8 - Symbols of Royalty.

The bed *kapa* (*ku'ina kapa* or *kapa moe*) usually consisted of a decorated cover sheet (*kilohana*) and four under sheets of the same size of white *kapa* (*iho*). The five sheets were sewn together along one edge with thread made of twisted strips of *kapa*. Needles (*kui humu*) were of hardwood or bone. An ivory or bone awl (*kui humuhumu kapa*) was used to pierce holes in the sheets before sewing.

In the old culture there were many other uses for *kapa*. The tall oracle tower ('*anu'u*) in the *heiau* was covered with a durable grade of white or light colored *kapa*. The kapu sticks (*pūlo'ulo'u*) consisted of stout *kauila* wood poles topped with balls of white *kapa*. A twist of *kapa* served as a wick (*kaula ahi*) in the *kukui* oil lamp. The *hau* wood or bamboo frames of the kites (*lupe*) *were covered with white kapa*. When a ball of twisted *kapa* cord was lighted the end smouldered for some time, thus providing a means of carrying fire. Soft white *kapa* served as bandages.

Certain images in the *heiau* were dressed in *kapa* during seasonal ceremonies. The dead were wrapped in burial sheets of black or brown *kapa*.

A sheet of *kapa* was placed over the bride and bridegroom at the marriage ceremony (*ho'āo*) of young *ali'i*. Sheer *kapa* was beaten to serve as nets after mosquitoes were introduced.

Kapa was waterproofed and strengthened by

saturating it in *kukui, kamani,* and perhaps, coconut oil. Oiled *kapa* was used for the fisherman's *malo* and, after the introduction of horses, for the riding *pā'ū. Kapa* was perfumed by placing among the folds the leaves of the *maile* vine, berries of the *mokihana* or powdered heartwood of the sandalwood tree *('iliahi).*

Sandals *(kāma'a)* were braided from ti leaves, *lau hala, hau* bark or partly beaten *wauke* fibers. People wore them in crossing rough terrain such as coarse lava and coral but otherwise they went barefoot.

■ Washing Kapa

Soiled garments were placed in a stream of clear flowing water and weighted with stones. When the water-soluble dirt was washed away the *kapa* was squeezed, spread out and dried. It could not be rubbed as is done today with the cotton clothing. There was no soap nor any satisfactory substitute. Since washing caused the water-soluble dyes to fade the *kapa* was either dyed again or added to *kapa* which was being made.

■ Captain Cook's Officers wrote about Kapa

Cook and his men were the first Europeans to see and write about *kapa.* It is significant to read their comments about this fabric before it had been influenced by foreign ideas. Cook's ships were here during the *Makahiki,* at which time all work, including *kapa* making had stopped. But the women with whom the Englishmen were on intimate terms demonstrated the making and decorating processes.

David Samwell, surgeon's mate, wrote of the dress of the men and women and of the *kapa:*

> The Dress of the Men in general consists of a piece of Cloth called maro [malo] about 2 hands broad, tyed round the waist; this is universal among them & they wear nothing else except on some particular occasions. (Beaglehole, p. 1179.)

> And the women: They have in general less cloathing than any women we have seen in the South Sea Islands, the lower sort among them frequently going with only a narrow slip of Cloth round their Waist forming a small apron before; the better sort have large Pieces of Cloth brought several times round their middle, which comes as low as the Knee & makes them very bulky but does not cover the Breasts. The generality of the young women have a piece of Cloth which they call Paw [pā'ū] round their Waist which descends something lower than the Knee, it is lapt four or 5 times

round them and tucked in behind, and . . . certain it is that we thought this Paw [pā'ū] had a very becoming and not an inelegant appearance. In the Evening they generally go more clad, having large pieces of white fine cloth [kīhei] thrown all over them like the Otaheite Girls. (Beaglehole, p. 1180.)

> They have a great many sort of Cloths [kapa] of different thickness & colour. It is made of the bark of . . . I-outa [wauke]. They have some White, black, red, yellow, green and gray & some of them exceedingly beautiful, bearing a very great resemblance to the printed Cottons in England; this is all thick Cloth & the most common being in universal Use among them. When a piece of cloth is prepared it is spread out in the Sun to dry, after which it is painted or striped by the women which they do with a small brush made from the stem of a plant [key or seed of the hala], & at this work they are all very expert; they call it "cappara" [kāpala] & always give the same appellation to our writing . . . (Beaglehole, pp. 1186-1187.)

Charles Clerke, second in command, wrote:

> Their Cloathe [kapa] is composed of the same Materials, as at the Friendly [Tonga] and Society Islands, but differently manufactured; it is here much stronger and firmer, than I ever saw it: but these People excell most, in the art of dying; they dye in a variety of fashions, some of them in my Opinion beautifull; their colours are clear and good, and the being wet takes no effect upon them. (Beaglehole, p. 1320.)

> They dye their Cloth in a variety of fashions, and with such a degree of exactitude that we made no doubt but they must have contrived some method of printing it, however we several times saw them, during our stay, lay on the different colours by hand with an Instrument resembling a Pen made with a Reed [bamboo], and found that constant practice had brought them to this degree of excellence, for that they had no idea of any other method; their colours are mostly superior and stand the water infinitely better than anything of the kind we have ever met with among Indians before. (Beaglehole, p. 594.)

■ Revival of Kapa Making

A number of men and women known to this writer are now spending a great deal of time growing the best varieties of plants for use in *kapa* making, searching the literature for more and more information, then practicing and improving their techniques in processing the fibers into very creditable *kapa.* Most of them are recording their results for eventual publication.

One of these skilled and devoted *kapa* makers has expressed her feelings in these words:

The more I am able to retrieve of this ancient art, the more I admire the intelligence and artistry of the women of old Hawai'i, who thought, beyond the pain in their arms, to create with the most modest material resources, an art form of infinite variety, subtlety and beauty. (Puanani Van Dorpe)

■ Introduced Clothing

The desire for garments of woven materials began, at least for the men, with the visits of Captain Cook in 1778-79. As vessels continued to stop in Hawai'i the crews exchanged European style clothing for island products. A king or high chief who had extensive goods to barter might trade for an outfit consisting of coat, trousers and shoes, or a military uniform resplendent with braid and buttons. The common man often secured but one foreign garment which he would wear in combination with his native garb, to the amusement of European visitors.

The chiefesses admired the dresses worn by the missionary women on their arrival in 1820 and asked to have some made for them at once. They were able to provide bolts of cloth which had been received from China in exchange for sandalwood. As the generous size of the chiefesses made it impractical to copy the Boston fashions of 1820 the missionary women designed a simple garment, not for style, but merely to cover the scantily clad chiefesses. Their basic patterns proved to be so practical and so comfortable that now, a century and a half later, these styles are gaining in popularity and challenging the designers to create many variations of the originals.

Informants differ concerning the origin and definition of the names of these early garments. The Pukui-Elbert Dictionary defines the holokū as the loose, seamed dress with a train and usually a yoke, patterned after the Mother Hubbard of the missionaries.

The mu'umu'u, which means "cut off" or "shortened," was originally a loose gown with the yoke omitted and the sleeves sometimes cut short.

Traditionally, the holokū, made of rich silk or brocade, had a yoke, sometimes a high neck, long sleeves and a long train. It was worn on formal occasions. The mu'umu'u in the early days was a dress for home wear. It was made full and unfitted with high or low neck and long or short sleeves. It is the more comfortable mu'umu'u that has challenged the present day designers to create many

variations for home, street and party wear.

The transition garment between the scant pā'ū and the dress is the kīkepa. The pā'ū, a waist to knee wrap-around skirt, was widened to form the kīkepa, which covered the body from neckline to ankles. It is a sleeveless sarong-type garment with a corner brought over one shoulder and secured. Kīkepa of a variety of colors are worn in pageantry and by hula dancers today.

■ Hawaiian Quilts

The Hawaiian house, thatched with grass, was gradually replaced in post-European times by the frame cottage. The low pile of sleeping mats gave way to beds. The finest bedsteads were four-posters, often king size, turned from the red-brown koa wood. Sheets and blankets purchased at the store replaced the colorful bed kapa.

The creative energy that the Hawaiian women spent in making the sleeping kapa was transferred to designing and sewing the unique quilts which they called kapa kuiki. The women learned from the missionaries to make clothing and patchwork quilts. They created designs to utilize two quilt-size pieces of new material to make the quilt top. There were no "scrap bags" in the Hawaiian home and the women were reluctant to cut new materials into patchwork pieces.

Hundreds of quilt patterns have been designed during the century and more following their origin. Some have a border (lei) and a central (piko) of a gay color which is appliqued on a background of white or less often a contrasting solid color. In others the design radiates (ku) out from the center to fill loosely the entire background.

To make the design a piece of paper the size of the quilt is folded into quarters. On the top quarter one-fourth of the design is drawn, then cut through the four layers. When unfolded the design is ready for inspection and approval. If it pleases its creator it is folded again and laid over the cloth, preferably imperial broadcloth, also folded into quarters, and cut to form the decorative portion of the quilt top.

This colored, openwork design is appliqued to a sheet, usually of white imperial broadcloth, but it may be a solid color or a fine print. Over the backing or bottom sheet of the quilt, of unbleached cotton or a calico print, is laid a padding of polyester dacron, one-fourth inch in thickness. When the upper sheet and its design is stitched to the lower one it is ready to be placed in the frames to be quilted.

Hawaiian quilting is uniquely attractive since the quilting stitches usually follow the outline of the design (kuiki lau). On some quilts, however, the more traditional stitches are used for variety.

The originator of the quilt design usually gave it a Hawaiian name suggested by the motif depicted. It was a matter of pride in the Hawaiian family to provide each child with at least one quilt which he would eventually take to his own home.

Hawaiian quilts are recognized as a unique and intricate form of needle work, a colorful addition to America's folk arts and crafts.

■ Current Trends in Dress

American and European styles are standard dress for most of the people of Hawai'i today. Jet travel to Hollywood, New York and Paris keeps the women in touch with the recognized fashion centers. Clothing designers in Honolulu, however, are creating styles that are in demand by local and visiting shoppers. Distinctive features of the local styles are the addition of designs from the Hawaiians, Chinese, Japanese and Filipinos. The emphasis in this subtropical resort area is on casual dress, sportswear and bathing suits. Although many women prefer flowers in their hair, a few wear locally made lau hala hats. Some sports shoes and sandals are made in Hawai'i, most of them with a thong between the toes.

Tradition, which has allowed men a minimum of color and variety in clothing, was disregarded in Hawai'i with the designing of the aloha shirt. These colorful garments have long or short sleeves and the tails may be worn in or out. They may match a man's swim trunks or may be made of the same pattern as his wife's mu'umu'u.

The annual festivities with pageants or parades such as Lei Day on May 1, Kamehameha Day on June 11 and Aloha Week in October are stimulating the wearing of Hawai'i's colorful garments.

Women participants in the pageants or parades wear, according to the era they are portraying, a kīkepa, or a riding pā'ū, holokū or mu'umu'u. With these they wear appropriate leis and jewelry to fit the costume. Men participants wear a malo, or a white shirt and trousers with a red sash, or an aloha shirt and slacks.

Spectators at these festivities are encouraged to wear mu'umu'u and aloha shirts. The 1965 Aloha Week Committee promoted the policy of asking business men and women to wear aloha shirts and mu'umu'u each Friday for a three month period or from Kamehameha Day through Aloha Week. The idea proved to be so popular that it has now been extended to Hawaiian dress every Friday throughout the year.

In 1986 4,200 persons were employed in the textile and garment manufacturing industry, and were paid $43.1 million in wages. Hawai'i's garment industry accounted for $164.6 million in wholesale sales. The Hawaiian Fashion Guild made up of local garment makers, plans to make Hawai'i the resort fashion capital of the world. (The 1989 State of Hawaii Data Book.)

■ Understanding and Appreciation Kapa and Clothing

Consider the topic of clothing in relation to man and his developing civilization. What has motivated man to design and wear clothes? Modesty, comfort or to satisfy his love of adornment?

Why did the Hawaiian people make a great effort to secure and wear European clothes when their own were better suited to the climate?

Note the features of Hawaiian kapa making which are not characteristic of bark cloth elsewhere: beaters with incised designs which produced distinctive watermarks in the fibers; bamboo stamps with a large variety of designs; and dye colors, especially blue and green, which were superior to the colors elsewhere. Note also the special implements which produced ribbed kapa, and the greatest variety in texture from coarse to sheer, almost transparent material.

The quality of kapa was influenced by the specific contributions of the women and the men. The men made the tools and the women pounded and decorated the kapa. Did the women demand beater and stamp patterns different from those of all other kapa makers, or was there a spirited competition among the men to create new and original motifs?

Try to imagine the work necessary to clothe the adults in Hawai'i's early population estimated at some 300,000 persons.

Compare *kapa* with other Polynesian bark cloth. Since Samoan tapa is easy to obtain, note its coarse fibers which are not felted, the absence of watermarks and the cruder application of designs. What is Samoan tapa used for today?

List the colors found in Hawaiian *kapa*. This may be done by observing the specimens on display in Bishop Museum or studying the color plates in the book *Ka Hana Kapa*. What colors are missing? Do the shades of color in the *kapa* clothing seem to be appropriate for the Hawaiian skin, eye and hair color?

Were any *kapa* designs suggested by plant or animal forms?

Kapa makers invoked several gods as they prepared for their work. Name some of them. Do you think that this ceremony created a more sincere attitude in the mind of the worker for his work?

Why were the styles in Hawai'i of the 1800s copied from those in vogue in the cities of the east coast of the United States? For women this usually meant heavy fabrics, many undergarments, long sleeves and high collars. The men's suits, including vests, were of wool and the hats of felt. At the same time the Englishmen who lived and worked in their colonies in the tropics wore walking shorts, light-weight shirts with open collars, and pith helmets.

Although the Polynesians never invented a loom they did plait fibers by hand as fine as 20 or more strands to the inch in the best mats. The Polynesian inhabitants of Kapingamarangi learned to use the loom skillfully when it was introduced to their atoll by visitors from neighboring Micronesia. Weaving was taught to the Hawaiian girls in the mission schools where they learned to card and spin wool and cotton for thread. Why is there no weaving industry in Hawai'i today?

■ **Student Activities**

The activity of first importance would be to attempt to make *kapa* from suitable plant fibers. *Wauke* grows in some local parks and gardens. *Māmaki* thrives in some rain forest areas which are not in the Forest or Water Reserve. Bark from breadfruit saplings may be used. Beaters are available in some family or school collections or a substitute is easily made. A finished piece of lumber such as a "four by six" may be used for an anvil.

A substitute for *kapa* may be made as follows: Crumple wrapping paper in water. Spread this out to dry then smooth it with a regular or steam iron. Apply designs to this with a *hala* brush, a taut string or a stamp dipped in native dye or in paint. The imitation *kapa* may be improved by spraying it lightly with plastic starch before decorating.

Dyes may be made from the plants listed in this unit or from introduced plants such as the mulberry fruit, yellow onion skins or Java plums. The Children's Center, Department of Parks and Recreation, has carried on successful experiments with native and introduced plants for dyes. See their leaflet.

Learn to put on a *malo, kīkepa* and a *kīhei*.

Where there is a school gardening project grow *wauke* for its fibers and the dye plants that will thrive in the locality. *Noni* should grow on almost any school campus. The hardy lipstick plant (*'alaea*) is one of the most satisfactory of the introduced dye plants.

Secure a shark tooth, mount it in a handle and use it as a carving tool to cut a design in a strip of bamboo for a bamboo stamp (*'ohekāpala*).

Make a study of the uses of *kapa* designs in modern Hawai'i. Bring to class examples of sportswear with *kapa* designs. Are these Hawaiian, Samoan or Fijian? Bring samples of gift wrapping paper, cardboard boxes, book covers and ceramics that are decorated with *kapa* designs.

Cut an original pattern the size of a pillow top to learn the technique of designing a Hawaiian quilt.

Trace the history of the development of the *holokū* and the *mu'umu'u*. Illustrate the changing styles with sketches.

Study the fabrics woven by members of the local weaving clubs as they are displayed from time to time at art galleries or hobby fairs. Make a list of the fibers used, especially those native to Hawai'i.

■ **Audio-Visual Aids**

Field Trips:

Bishop Museum. Exhibits show *kapa* and tools for *kapa* making. Hawaiian culture exhibits show the use of *kapa* in the *heiau,* on certain images, on the canoe paddler's gourd helmet and as clothing. The *wauke* shrubs and several dye plants are growing in the Museum courtyard.

Honolulu Academy of Arts. Some fine *kapa* is

usually on display. Watch for special exhibits.

See Unit 9 for a list of some of the Botanical Gardens that feature Hawaiian plants.

Movies:

Check the film lists from your favorite distributors for films illustrating this unit of study.

"Life in Samoa" and "Children of Samoa" show tapa making. George Tahara, Cine-Pic Hawaii, Honolulu. "Kapingamarangi," filmed during the 1947 Bishop Museum expedition to this Polynesian atoll shows the steps in making a tapa *malo* from breadfruit bark. Men weave on the loom using local fibers.

■ **Vocabulary**

fabric	*kapu*	barter
felting	indigenous	fashion
watermark	pigment	casual dress
water soluble	*hoʻāo*	rice paper

■ **Evaluation**

Check the craft projects completed by the students such as the pounding of *kapa* samples, making and using dyes, making *kapa* tools and any needlework activities.

Evaluate such skills as learning to put on a *malo, pāʻū, kīkepa,* and a *kīhei.*

Grade the students' sketches of *kapa* designs, figures wearing the different styles of clothing or the development of the *muʻumuʻu* or *holokū.*

Review the pertinent terms used in class to check word understanding.

■ **Reading List**

Ball, Stanley C. *Bishop Museum Handbook, Part II, Clothing.* 1924. Honolulu: Bishop Museum Special Publication No. 9, 1929.

Barrère, Dorothy B. "Hawaiian Quilting: A Way of Life." *The Conch Shell,* Vol. III, No. 2. Honolulu: Bishop Museum Association, 1965.

Bishop, Marsha B. *Hawaiian Life of the Pre-European Period.* Salem: Peabody Museum, 1940.

Blitman, Elaine. *Na Hoʻoluʻu o Hawaiʻi.* Dyes of Hawaiʻi. Honolulu: Privately printed, 1972.

Brigham, William T. *Ka Hana Kapa: The making of bark cloth in Hawaiʻi.* Honolulu: Bishop Museum Press, 1911. (Includes portfolio of 27 color plates.)

———. "Hawaiian Kapa Making." *Hawaiian Annual for 1896.* Honolulu: Thrum's Hawaiian Annual. 76-86.

Bryan, E.H. Jr. "Fiberwork." Ch. 12 in *Ancient Hawaiian Civilization.* A series of lectures delivered at the Kamehameha Schools by E.S.C. Handy [and others]. 1933. Rutland, VT and Japan: C.E. Tuttle, 1965 (rev. ed.).

———. "Clothing and Ornaments." Ch. 8 in *Ancient Hawaiian Life.* 1938. Honolulu: Books About Hawaii, 1950.

———. "Cloth and Cord from Nettle Plants." Ch. 20 in *Hawaiian Nature Notes.* 1932-33. Honolulu: Honolulu Star-Bulletin, Ltd., 1935.

Bryan, W.A. *Natural History of Hawaii.* Honolulu: The Hawaiian Gazette, 1915. 69-72.

Buck, Peter H. *Arts and Crafts of Hawaii.* Honolulu: Bishop Museum Special Publication No. 45, 1957. 165-213.

Charlot, Jean. *Choris and Kamehameha.* Honolulu: Bishop Museum Press, 1958.

Colum, Padriac. *Legends of Hawaii.* 1937. New Haven, CT: Yale University Press, 1960 (paperback).

Curtis, Caroline. *Manu, A Girl of Old Hawaii.* Honolulu: Tongg Publishing Company, 1958.

Degener, Otto. *Plants of the Hawaii National Park.* 1930. Ann Arbor, MI: Edwards Bros., Inc., 1945. (See index for *kapa* and dye plants.)

Delpech, Frances R. "A Century of Hawaiian Fashions." *Paradise of the Pacific,* Nov. 1950. 14-17.

Ellis, William. *Journal of William Ellis.* A Narrative of a Tour of Hawaii. . . . 1826. Rutland, VT and Japan: C.E. Tuttle, 1979. (See index for clothing and *kapa.*)

Greiner, Ruth. *Polynesian Decorative Design.* Honolulu: Bishop Museum Press Bulletin No. 7, 1923.

Ihara, Violet K. "Hawaiian Bark Cloth or Kapa." Honolulu: Hawaii State Department of Education Research Bulletin No. 1, Bishop Museum, 1979.

Inns, Helen. *Your Hawaiian Quilt, "How To Make It."* Honolulu: Hawaii Home Demonstration Council, 1957. (16 pages, 15 photos, 4 sketches.)

Inns, Helen, and Mary Lee. "Your Own Hawaiian Quilt—How-to-Make-It." U.E. Club Series,

H-15-4/56. Honolulu: University of Hawaii Agricultural Extension Service Leaflet [1956?]. (5 pages, 4 illustrations.)

Jones, Stella. *Hawaiian Quilts.* 1930. Honolulu: Daughters of Hawaii, The Honolulu Academy of Arts, and the Mission Houses Museum, 1973 (rev. ed.). (Revised edition has 53 pages, 20 black and white photos.)

Judd, Albert F. "Trees and Plants." Ch. 26 in *Ancient Hawaiian Civilization.* 1933. Rutland, VT and Japan: C.E. Tuttle, 1965 (rev. ed.).

Kaeppler, Adrienne L. *The Fabrics of Hawaii.* Bark cloth. Leigh-on-Sea, Eng.: F. Lewis, 1975.

Kamakau, Samuel M. *The Works of the People of Old. Kapa* making and kinds of *kapa*, 108-116, *Wauke*, 39-41. Honolulu: Bishop Museum Special Publication No. 61, 1976.

Kooijman, Simon. *Tapa in Polynesia.* Honolulu: Bishop Museum Bulletin No. 234, 1972.

Krauss, Beatrice H. *Ethnobotany of Hawai'i.* Honolulu: Department of Botany, University of Hawaii, 1974.

———. *Ethnobotany of the Hawaiians.* Lyon Arboretum Lecture No. 5. Honolulu: Lyon Arboretum, University of Hawaii, 1975.

Krohn, Val F. *Hawaii Dye Plants and Dye Recipes.* Ed. Suzie Jacobs. 1878. Honolulu: n.p., 1980.

Lamoureux, Charles H. *Trailside Plants of Hawai'i's National Parks.* Hawaii Volcanoes National Park: Hawaii Natural History Association, 1976.

Lane, Rose W. "Hawaiian Quilts." *Woman's Day,* May 1963, p. 54. (8 color illustrations.)

Ling, Shun-Sheng. "Bark Cloth Culture and the Invention of Paper-Making in Ancient China." Honolulu: Tenth Pacific Science Congress, 1961. Mimeo. 26 pages. (The Director of the Institute of Ethnology, Taiwan, wrote of the connection between tapa and paper of the Orient and the Pacific Islands.)

Luquiens, M.H. *Hawaiian Art.* Honolulu: Bishop Museum Special Publication No. 18, 1931.

Malo, David. *Hawaiian Antiquities.* 1898. Honolulu: Bishop Museum Special Publication No. 2, 1976. (See index under tapa.)

McDonald, Marie A. "Native Dyes." Honolulu: Children's Center, Department of Parks and Recreation, March 16, 1964. Mimeo.

Mellen, George, ed. *The Sales Builder,* July 1940.

Mitchell, Donald D. Kilolani. *Hawaiian Treasures.* Clothing, 71-79. Honolulu: Kamehameha Schools Press, 1978.

Neal, Marie C. *In Gardens of Hawaii.* 1948. Honolulu: Bishop Museum Special Publication No. 50, 1965 (rev. ed.). (See index for *kapa* and dye plants.)

Pratt, Helen G. Ch. 26 in *The Hawaiians: An Island People.* Rutland, VT and Japan: C.E. Tuttle, 1963.

Pritchard, Mary J. *Siapo.* Bark cloth art of Samoa. Honolulu: University of Hawaii Press, 1985. (Profusely illustrated. Hawaiian craftsmen will note the almost identical techniques of making Samoan *siapo* and Hawaiian *kapa* in the early stages.)

Pukui, Mary K., and Caroline Curtis. *Tales of the Menehune.* 2nd ed. Honolulu: Kamehameha Schools Press, 1983.

———. *Water of Kane.* 1951. Honolulu: Kamehameha Schools Press, 1976.

Rose, Roger G., comp. *Na Kapa Hawaii.* Honolulu: Artmobile Hawaii No'onani, Department of Education, State of Hawaii, 1971-72.

Shaw, Alexander. *A Collection of Various Specimens of Cloth Obtained in the Three Voyages of Captain Cook, 1768-1779.* (A large amount of tapa was collected, cut into pieces and bound or pasted into books. The Bishop Museum Library has more than one of these books.)

Titcomb, Margaret. *The Ancient Hawaiians.* How they clothed themselves. Honolulu: Hogarth Press, 1974.

Thurston, Lucy G. *Life and Times of Mrs. Lucy G. Thurston.* 1882. Ann Arbor, MI: S.C. Andrews, 1934. (See index under clothing and *kapa*.)

Webb, Lahilahi. "Feather Work and Clothing." Ch. 13 in *Ancient Hawaiian Civilization.* A series of lectures delivered at the Kamehameha Schools by E.S.C. Handy [and others]. 1933. Rutland, VT and Japan: C.E. Tuttle, 1965 (rev. ed.).

Westervelt, William D. *Hawaiian Legends of Old Honolulu.* 1916. Rutland, VT and Japan: C.E. Tuttle, 1964.

UNIT 16:
Maintaining
Physical and
Mental
Health

MAINTAINING PHYSICAL AND MENTAL HEALTH

The Hawaiian people, in pre-European times, were healthy, hardy and remarkably free from disease. Proper diet, exercise through work and play, outdoor living and a belief in their gods and *kāhuna* of healing kept the people healthy.

They were tall and well-developed with splendidly shaped torsos and fine muscular limbs of excellent proportions.

The average height of the working class was about five feet ten inches; many of the chiefs were over six feet. A skeleton from one of the burial caves measured six feet seven and three-quarters inches and there is evidence that men of larger stature were not unusual.

Mature chiefs often weighed as much as three hundred pounds. The chiefesses were looked upon with great favor if they exceeded their chiefs in weight. The Hawaiian word *mōmona* means both corpulent and sweet.

Through the centuries the chiefly classes enjoyed choice food, healthful exercise and careful grooming. Their superior physique was the result of excellent physical care and the choice of mates from the families of the *ali'i*. The close intermarriage of the nobility in pre-European times seemed to have had no ill effects on the physical and mental health of the progeny.

The color of the average Hawaiian was olive-brown or rich brown, never black. The fishermen and taro planters were darker through long exposure to the sun. Chiefs and chiefesses, whose *kapu* caused them to remain indoors during the day, had lighter than average complexions.

The people kept their skin in excellent condition by bathing, often two or three times a day, in salt, then in fresh water. A massage using coconut oil usually followed the bath. Since the people ate with their fingers it was their practice to wash their hands regularly before meals. The chiefs used specially designed finger bowls of polished wood.

The early explorers admired the even, white teeth of the Hawaiian people. Their sound, attractive teeth were the result of proper diet rather than dental hygiene as it is practiced today.

As the people chewed sugar cane for its sweet juice the coarse fibers cleaned their teeth and massaged their gums. Their toothpicks were of wood and bone, while salt and charcoal were their tooth powders.

The heads of the Hawaiian people were well formed and resembled those of their Caucasian ancestors. Their jaws were of good proportions as were their chins and cheeks. Since a flattened nose was admired, some parents resorted to pressure and massage in infancy to shape it.

Hawaiian hair was black or dark brown and was straight, wavy or curly, but never kinky. Coconut oil replaced the natural oils after the frequent shampoos. Hair styles varied with rank and sex. Girls allowed their hair to grow long until they reached the age of fourteen or fifteen years when it was cut quite short. Mature women wore their hair cropped short. The most distinctive hair style of the men consisted of a crest of hair from front to back across the crown in contrast to the close-cropped hair over the ears. This style resembled the crest on the feather helmet. Hair was cut with a knife of split bamboo or a cutting tool with one or more shark teeth fixed to a wooden handle. In some instances the "barber" placed a small plate of turtle shell in his left hand, with his thumb he held a lock of hair on it and cut the hair against the shell.

A distinctive physical characteristic of the Hawaiian people admired by the early visitors from the West was their ease and grace of movement. Walking was unhurried, smooth and dignified. Specifically noted by early writers were the expressive hand gestures of a chief in oratory, a citizen in conversation and a dancer interpreting a *hula*.

The people lived in villages usually located along the shore near the mouths of streams. Fresh water bathing was in the stream near the village while drinking water was collected in gourds or calabashes farther upstream.

Areas of wooded or unused land behind the village were set aside for persons to deposit personal wastes. The ever-present fear that anything intimately associated with a person might be secured and taken to a *kahuna 'anā'anā* motivated the people to hide wastes, discarded clothing, hair and nail parings. These materials became the "bait" *(maunu)* for the *kahuna* to use in praying his victim to death.

■ The Hawaiian medical *kāhuna* administered enemas, performed autopsies, and employed massage, steam baths, diet and rest. The general practitioner, the herb doctor, was supported by more than a dozen specialists who were highly trained in their specific fields of healing.

"Thus the Hawaiians had stepped over the border of ignorance and were on the threshold of the scientific investigation of disease." Sir Peter Buck, M.D. quoted by Larsen, Rededication, pp. 8-9.

The Hawaiian doctor was eminently successful in treating his patients in pre-European times. Since this isolated group of islands was practically free from bacteria and viruses harmful to man, the chief physical conditions that confronted the doctor were constipation, and injuries caused in wars and accidents. He was quite naturally unable to apply Hawaiian remedies to the score of introduced diseases that came in with foreigners. Even the European and American physicians at that time were unsuccessful in coping with many of these diseases of the 19th and early 20th centuries. Long isolation from the rest of the world and its infectious germs prevented the Hawaiian people from developing immunity to these diseases. Illnesses which caused very few fatalities among Western and Oriental people took a high death toll among the Polynesians. The young, robust monarchs, Kamehameha II and his queen Kamāmalu died of measles in London in 1824.

■ In pre-European times the serious ailments were thought to be caused by evil influences which might emanate from the outside *(ma waho)*.
1. by professional sorcerers *(kāhuna 'anā'anā)*,
2. by spite, hate or jealousy expressed by unfriendly persons, or
3. by one or more of the many evil spirits pervading the land.

Or the cause of an ailment might be within *(ma loko)* the patient himself such as his own hate or jealousy. Or he may have broken or failed to observe one or more of the many *kapu*. The cause of the ailment had to be determined before the proper treatment could be administered.

Ailments that were diagnosed as physical in nature were treated by massage, steam baths, or herbs in the form of remedies for internal or external use. The religious phase continued to play an important part in the physical treatments. Herbs were gathered, prepared and administered according to well-defined rituals including the propitiation of the proper dieties.

Before the patient was treated the *kahuna lapa'au* performed the ritual of mental cleansing or *ho'oponopono*. In this counseling type of service the patient and all the members of the household were helped to clear their minds of hatred, jealousy and bitterness. Under the guidance of the *kahuna* those present talked over their problems and resolved their differences. The unburdening continued until all obstacles were cleared away and all offenders were forgiven.

The *ho'oponopono* technique cleared and prepared the mind of the patient and the minds and thoughts of those attending or near him so that all of them could take part in the prayers offered with the medication. It was understood that the body could not be healed until the spirit was cured.

■ **The Gods in Medicine**

The *kāhuna* and the people addressed the primary gods *(akua)*, the family guardians *('aumākua)*, and the special gods of medicine in diagnosing and treating illnesses.

Some of the *kāhuna* of the primary gods Kū, Kāne, and Lono practiced medicine as a part of their duties. Many special *heiau (heiau ho'ōla)* were devoted to the art of healing.

Mauliola is recognized as a god of health, Haumea is the goddess of motherhood and Kānepua'a is a god of fertility. The *kālaipāhoa* gods were represented as human figures hewn from wood that was thought to be poisonous. (Kamakau, 1964, pp. 128-131.) The god Ma'iola is referred to today as an important god of medicine and the healing arts.

■ The Medical Kāhuna

The kāhuna were the experts, the professionals who had acquired great knowledge and skill through long and careful instruction. They began their training while quite young as apprentices to their skilled elders. In the medical field this training period would last for many years. Nearly every trade and profession was directed by a kahuna. The following list includes only those concerned with phases of medicine and healing. They are arranged alphabetically, not in any order of importance.

Kāhuna a ka 'alawa maka - diagnosed by insight and by critical observation.

Kāhuna aloha - were the love inducing specialists.

Kāhuna 'anā'anā - were best known for their ability to pray victims to death. Some of them were also skilled in the art of saving the life of a victim who was "being prayed against." (Kamakau, 1964)

Kāhuna 'ea - treated the ailments of children.

Kāhuna hāhā - diagnosed conditions by feeling with the fingers. A table of pebbles (papa 'ili'ili) was arranged in the form of a man (See Kamakau, 1964, p. 94 for a sketch). Some 480 red, black and white pebbles of various sizes, texture and density represented the parts of the body from head to foot. During at least part of the instruction pupils learning to be kāhuna hāhā were blindfolded. The trainees gained knowledge, under an experienced teacher, of the parts of the body. They developed a very keen sense of touch. These kāhuna belonged to the order of the god Lonopūhā who guided them in making a diagnosis of a disease.

Kāhuna ha'iha'i iwi - were skilled in setting broken bones.

Kāhuna ho'ohāpai keiki - induced pregnancy.

Kāhuna ho'ohānau keiki - delivered the babies.

Kāhuna ho'opi'opi'o - could inflict illness by gesture. By indicating a part of his body he could cause an illness or injury in the same part of his victim's body. He could also counteract the harm caused by another kahuna.

Kāhuna kāhea - healed through the power of suggestion.

Kāhuna kuni - performed life-giving (kuni ola) and death causing (kuni make) rituals. They are not associated with the kāhuna 'anā'anā.

Kāhuna lā'au lapa'au - were the herb doctors. They may be compared to the general practitioners of today. Lā'au in this instance refers to herbs, lapa'au is medical practice. The largest number of practicing medical kāhuna belonged to this group. In many cases they gave a patient a purgative to induce vomiting, then an enema. He was then ready to take the herbs that the kahuna would prescribe. Most of the Hawaiian elders who administer herbal remedies to their families today belong to this group.

Kāhuna lena - diagnosed illnesses by sight.

Kāhuna lomilomi were skilled in massage. They treated the patient by manipulation and massage, by heat and herbal steam baths (pūholo) and by vocal and mental suggestion. One treatment was to roll or scrape a scoriaceous or bubbly spherical lava stone, (pōhaku kuai kua) over the back and the soles of the feet. Some of these stones in collections today have been mis-called spherical ('ulu maika).

Kāhuna makani - could induce spirits to enter the patient.

Kāhuna 'ō'ō - healed children who had boils or lumps by lancing the infected parts. He was also an abortionist who pierced ('ō'ō) the fetus.

Kāhuna pā'ao'ao - diagnosed and treated disorders in infants.

■ Herbs and Herb Remedies

Several writers have recorded that more than 300 plants and minerals were used in preparing Hawaiian medicines. For many centuries the Hawaiians conducted careful research in order to learn what specific effects the properties in these plants had upon the human body. In some prescriptions a part of but one plant, such as the bud or bark, would be the only medicine prescribed. For other treatments the medicine would be compounded from two or three or even ten or more herbs and sometimes minerals and animal products would be added.

When the kāhuna lapa'au needed medicinal plants he first asked the permission of the gods to go into the forest. Then he had to specify the names of the plants he wished to gather.

"In picking branches and leaves, the person must use his right hand first on the right side of the plant, addressing the god Kū. Then he must use his left hand on the left side of the plant, addressing the goddess Hina. Prayers to the god Kū and the goddess Hina were applied to all medicinal plants." (Larsen, Rededication, p. 4)

The thirty plants listed here were selected as those most often called for in the herb remedies and those easy to identify and secure today. Nearly all are native plants, known to have flourished in Hawai'i before the arrival of Captain Cook in 1778. The medicinal properties of most of these plants are not known but studies are being conducted at the University of Hawaii to determine the chemical nature of the most important ones.

The juice of the sugar cane was included in an herb potion to sweeten it and make it more palatable. Cane juice and the edible portions of the banana, breadfruit and taro were prescribed to nourish and strengthen the patient. The 'āweoweo, pōpolo, young sweet potato leaves (palula), and taro leaves are pot herbs known to be rich in vitamins and minerals. These formed a part of some of the medicines that were cooked before administering. A few herbs, such as the bright orange root of the 'ōlena gave an attractive color to the potion. Patients who take Hawaiian medicines today agree that some of the plant products which are prescribed frequently, such as the ripe fruit of the noni, are vile to the taste. Perhaps the patient recovers through sheer determination to avoid taking more of the noni juice.

■ **Medicinal Plants**

The medicinal plants are listed alphabetically by their Hawaiian name. The number following the name gives the page on which the plant is discussed in Neal, *In Gardens of Hawaii*, 1965 edition. In this list the medical reference is often but one of several listed by the various kāhuna. These are not prescriptions or recipes for herb medicines. Although the plants listed here are largely native the disorders mentioned are introduced if they are caused by a bacterium or virus.

'A'ali'i, 536. A shrub with reddish to yellowish seed capsules. Tea brewed from the leaves was a treatment for rash, itch and insomnia. Leaf tips were chewed fresh or dried and also smoked to treat asthma.

'Ahu'awa, 86. A sedge. The stem fibers were used to strain liquids. The dried stems were crushed into a powder to treat skin diseases.

'Ākia, 615. Shrub to small tree. The leaves and tips of stems were pounded and used as a narcotic to stupefy fish in tidal pools. Not an internal poison to humans but the sap will cause a rash on the skin of some persons. Tea from leaves and stems was a relaxant.

'Akoko, 516. Shrubs and trees. The name means "blood colored." Milky sap is taken by mothers who are nursing infants to increase the flow of milk. Buds and leaves were chewed for debility.

'Ala'alawainui, 293. Small succulent herb. The leaves were crushed and the juice added to other herbs to treat for asthma and general debility.

The following prescription, using 'ala'alawainui, is from an old herbal, translated from the Hawaiian by Akaiko Akana, page 13 (See Reading List). It is given here to show the variety of plant materials included in one 'apu and the casual method of measuring the quantity used:

For wasting away of the body and for general weakness, take a hatful of the stems of the herb 'ala'alawai'nuipehu; one young shoot of the tree fern; eight shoots of hala root; two pieces (the size of the palm of the hand) of mountain apple bark; three segments of white sugar cane; two fully matured noni fruit.

Pound these together thoroughly and then have the juice of the mixture strained and cleaned. Put into the liquid thus prepared one red-hot stone. Stir as it cooks and then allow it to cool. At the right temperature, the patient drinks the whole of it. After which he eats two iholena bananas and then takes a drink of water.

This remedy is taken morning and evening for five consecutive days. White flesh fish, broiled on charcoal, and kukui nut, together with young taro leaf that is thoroughly cooked, should be taken for food. Boiled pure salt water from the ocean should be taken as a laxative after the treatment.

'Auhuhu, 448. Slender herb. The leaves were pounded and used to stupefy fish. A narcotic for patients, added to the juice of other herbs.

'Awa, 291. Shrub with narcotic properties in the roots. An infusion was made from the pounded root. A small quantity is relaxing, larger amounts induce sleep. This was the most effective sedative prescribed by the kahuna. Used as a poultice for toothache. More on 'awa under comments by Capt. Cook's officers.

'Awapuhi kuahiwi, 257. The mountain ginger. The spicy underground stems were thought to have healing properties, especially for abdominal distress. A small piece was forced into a hollow aching tooth. Ginger and ʻawa roots were pounded together and applied to sprains and bruises.

ʻĀweoweo or ʻĀheahea, 331. Sturdy shrubs which grew in the drier areas. The leaves were steamed as a pot herb. The vitamins in the leaves added to its food and "strengthening" value. The chlorophyll-containing leaves had a healing effect when pounded and applied to wounds. The flower buds were chewed thoroughly and fed to infants.

ʻĒkaha, 21. The bird's-nest fern. Tea steeped from the leaves was recommended for general weakness.

Hala, 51. The pandanus tree. The tender young tips of the aerial roots were eaten for their vitalizing effect which we know now to be due to their vitamin content. The soft portions of the seed sections were chewed and fed to constipated children. The powdery pollen from the male blossoms (hīnano) was thought to have medicinal value.

Hāpuʻu. 10. Tree fern. The silky pulu was used to pad bandages. Center of starchy trunk was cooked for animal and human food.

Hau, 559. A common spreading tree belonging to the hibiscus family. The slimy juice from the bark was given to women before childbirth and to children as a gentle laxative. The juices of hau bark and noni were stone boiled and given as an enema. The young leaf buds were chewed twice a day for a dry throat.

Hōʻiʻo. 21. The tender fronds of this fern were used for food and medicine. Green fronds were crushed and applied to boils.

ʻIlima, 552. A common native shrub. The yellow blossoms were chewed and fed to infants as a tonic and a mild laxative. Both asthma and general debility were treated by drinking an infusion prepared from ʻilima flowers and leaf shoots to which a variety of other herbs were added.

Ipu ʻawaʻawa, 815. The bitter gourd. The bitter pulp was thought to be poisonous. The young shoots and leaves were chewed to induce sleep. The pounded gourd pulp and ripe noni were diluted with water for an enema. The mature gourd was made into a calabash for compounding and storing medicines. Some gourds grew or were trained to grow in the proper shapes for funnels and for implements used to administer an enema.

Kalo, 157. Wet- or Dry-land taro plants with starchy tubers. The root was made into poi which was mixed with coconut juice and served as a "strengthening medicine." The cooked green leaves were rich in vitamins and minerals. The raw juice was applied to the skin as a medicine but the presence of calcium oxalate crystals makes it unpleasant or even painfully irritating. The raw scraped pulp was mixed with sugar cane juice, and noni fruit and administered as a laxative.

Kaunaʻoa, 364. A dodder with orange slender stems; lei of Lānaʻi. Plant boiled and solution applied while hot to skin rash.

Kī or Ti, 203. Slender plant with starchy root and useful leaves. It was grown outside the dwelling and around the heiau to keep away evil influences. The fresh green leaves cooled the brow and relieved a headache. The leaves were dipped into water containing salt and ʻōlena and used to sprinkle both people and places to purify them. This ceremony was called pī kai or kuikala. The young ti leaf, not yet unfolded, was a sterile bandage for a wound.

Koa, 408. Leaves and bark pounded, salt added and applied to sprains.

Koali or kowali, 703. The morning glory vines with pink to blue blossoms. The juice of the plant is a purgative. The root and stem bark was crushed, salted, and bound over a fracture until it healed.

The koali was used after battles for spear wounds and broken bones. Koali root and salt

Hau

were pounded together and bound by bandage to arthritic joints.

Kō, 77. Sugar cane. At least 40 varieties were developed and some were named to indicate their magical qualities. Certain canes formed an important ingredient in the medicines. *Kōkea,* white cane, is mentioned most often. *Kōpilimai* had the power to unite lovers. For bad cuts an effective medicine was made from the young shoots of the cane, sweet potato vines and salt. This was baked in ti leaves over charcoal and the juice squeezed out for the healing medicine. Akana explains the powerful effects of this medicine:

> If any member of the body is entirely severed, the same could be restored to its place by placing it over where it has come off and, after having it fastened to its proper place with the aid of the dried banana stalk, this furnishing a groove in which the injured part lies with the severed portion held in place by fibers, by pouring the liquid from the medicine over and around the cut. It is claimed that the strength of the remedy not only hastens the knitting of the severed parts but eliminates the scar from where the injury has occurred. (Akana, p. 53.)

Comment, if the above is not clear: Translator Akana means that the severed arm or leg, after fastening it on to the body again, was placed in the trough-shaped banana trunk sheath and flooded with the healing liquid.

Kokiʻo or aloalo, 556. Hibiscus of several varieties and colors were used medicinally, the properties of the introduced plants are as effective as those of the native species. The leaves and buds were chewed and fed to small children or eaten by the adults for constipation. A treatment popular in times past known as "purifying" the blood could be done with an infusion of hibiscus roots and the addition of some ten other herbs. The liquid strained from these pounded plant tissues was drunk three times a day for five days. Just how the patient or his *kahuna* determined that the treatment had "purified" the blood is not recorded.

Koʻokoʻolau, 844. About 45 kinds of this Bidens are native to Hawaiʻi. The leaves, either fresh or dried, are brewed into a tea which is used to the present time as a tonic for fever and heartburn. The introduced Bidens, the beggar's tick which is a common weed, is a substitute for the native varieties.

Kūkae puaʻa, 72. This common grass is used for "general weakness" or a "run down condition."

Three times a day the young leaves are chewed and swallowed. As a "cure" for cataract the leaves are chewed until the mass becomes a thick liquid. This is blown into the eye to cover the cataract. The treatment is repeated morning and evening for five days, after which the patient washes his eyes each morning with clean water for five days. An alternative treatment, according to some informants, is to scrape the cataract with a blade of this grass. As an offering to the gods this grass is a substitute for a pig *(puaʻa).*

Kukui, 504. All parts of this candlenut tree are useful. The raw nut is prized as the most effective of the cathartics and the easiest to obtain. If its action is too free it may be slowed or stopped by eating starch *(pia)* or *poi.* One or more raw nuts would be somewhat poisonous to the average person. One-half of a raw nut should be sufficient for a laxative. Roasting changes this quality and improves the flavor of the nut. When pounded and salted the roasted nuts become the condiment called *ʻinamona.* It is a mild laxative. The juice which exudes when a leaf or green nut is broken from the stem is applied to form a seal over a cut or puncture. The disease called *ʻea* or thrush that produces white patches in the mouth and on the tongue is treated with *kukui* sap. *Kukui* blossoms, bark and the charcoal from the burned nuts are added to certain medicines.

Laukahi, 792. Introduced species are now used in place of the native plantain which provided leaves for a poultice for sores and boils. The juice of *laukahi* will stop the flow of blood from a wound. Tea brewed from fresh or dried leaves will help cure a persistent cold.

Limu. Various sea weeds were added to the herb remedies. The *kāhuna* used liverworts and mosses which he also called *limu.*

Maiʻa, 245. In addition to its value as a food the fruit of the ripe banana was eaten to counteract the unpleasant taste of certain medicines. Some 13 varieties of bananas are listed in the herbals as having medicinal values. The juice from the flower buds was used as a treatment for *ʻea* or thrush and also added to a number of herb mixtures.

Māmaki, 318. Dried leaves are steeped for a tea to treat general debility. Fruit is eaten for a mild laxative; crushed and applied to wounds; and fed to children for *ʻea* or thrush.

Moa, moanahele, page 1. A green, leafless plant which thrives in moist places. One form, growing upright is called *moa*. A similar form with slender branches hanging down is *pipi*. A cathartic tea is brewed from the stems. The dust-like yellow spores released from fruiting capsules are used like talcum powder.

Naupakakahakai, 820, *Naupakakuahiwi*, 819. Crushed leaves and bark of root applied to cuts and to skin ailments

Niu, 119. The coconut palm provided a number of products for the medical *kāhuna*. Liquids were strained through the cloth-like fiber (*'a'a niu*) from the base of the frond. A number of prescriptions called for the sterile coconut water from within the shell. The flesh of the nut was nourishing and its oil (*mano'i*) was used in treating the hair and the skin. Coconut shells were cut in half lengthwise and polished to provide cups (*'apu*) for drinking *'awa* and medicines.

Noni, 804. A shrub or small tree of great importance in Hawaiian medicine. The ripe fruit was used as a poultice to bring boils to a head. The fruit, although unpleasant to the taste, was a common ingredient in internal medicines. A chemical study and clinical experiments now under way may show that the fruit is effective in treating kidney diseases. The leaves and stem bark were stone-boiled and the liquid drunk as a tonic.

'Ōhi'a 'ai, 636. The mountain apple, a deep green tree of the rain-drenched valleys, is best known for its pink-red edible fruit. No medical properties are listed for the fruit. The bark of the tree was chewed or added to other herbs to make a rinse as a remedy for sores in the mouth. The bark, leaves and young buds were pounded with herbs and the strained juice drunk as a body building tonic. Deep cuts were treated with juice from the bark which had been pounded with salt.

'Ōhi'a lehua, 637. A common tree of the rain forests. A favorite tea, which served as a tonic, was brewed from the reddish juvenile leaves (*liko lehua*). The scarlet stamens forming the blossoms were added to the slimy *hau* bark and given to a woman at the time of childbirth.

'Ōlena, 255. The turmeric of the spice industry is grown for its orange underground stems. These root-like stems were used either raw or cooked. The raw juice was dropped into the ear for earache and applied to the nostrils or throat for disorders there. A ball of tree fern silk (*pulu*) was saturated with *'ōlena* juice and given to a patient with a disorder of the nostrils. He was instructed to

inhale the ginger-like fumes ten times a day. After a treatment of five days the patient must refrain from using *'ōlena* for three or four days. He may then resume the treatment if he was not cured. *'Ōlena* juice in sea water was sprinkled on persons or places (*pī kai 'ōlena*) to purify them or to remove a *kapu*.

Pia, 228. The arrowroot starch was prepared by grating the tubers and washing the starch in fresh water to remove the bitter flavor. The smooth starch was stirred in fresh water and drunk as a cure for diarrhea and dysentery. As a food *pia* was a "strengthening medicine." The silky starch was used on the skin like talcum powder.

Pōhinahina, 728. Tea brewed from the seeds and leaves was applied to relieve pain in the back and to treat swollen feet.

Pōhuehue, 709. The beach morning glory. The seeds were administered as a cathartic. The stems and leaves were pounded and added to a mixture of herbs, probably for their laxative value. Although considered poisonous in large quantity, the roots and leaves were cooked and eaten in times of scarcity of food.

Pōpolo, 744. This common herb in the nightshade family features prominently in Hawaiian medicine. The bruised leaves with salt added, were used to heal wounds, an action that we might

Pōpolo

explain today as the healing effect of the chlorophyll. The ripe, pleasant-tasting berries were a mild laxative, often eaten by children. Juice crushed from the green plant was said to "tone up" the digestive tract. The young shoots and leaves were steamed and eaten as a pot herb.

Puakala, 367. The prickly poppy furnished a pain-relieving sap which would alleviate toothache. It also removed warts.

'Uala or *'uwala*, 706. At least a dozen varieties of the sweet potato were believed to have medicinal value. The cooked root and the tender leaves (*palula*) were served as healthful and strengthening foods. Some varieties were eaten to induce vomiting which was aided by tickling the throat with a feather. Nursing mothers wore a sweet potato vine and leaves as a *lei* to increase the flow of milk.

'Uhaloa, hi'aloa, 'ala'alapuloa or *kanakaloa*, 575. A wide-spread herb. The bark of the root is chewed to relieve sore throat. The effect is similar to aspirin which gives it the name of Hawaiian aspirin today. The macerated leaves are applied as a poultice.

Uhike'oke'o, 230. The starchy tuber of the white yam, when eaten warm, was credited with healing effects.

'Ulei, 387. Leaves and roots brewed into a tonic for general debility.

'Ulu, 302. The cooked breadfruit is a source of important vitamins and readily digested starch. The milky sap which exudes freely is applied to skin eruptions, boils and wounds.

Wauke, 301. Sap is a mild laxative and a tonic for expectant mothers. Fibers pounded into a fine *kapa* and used for bandages. Children chewed fresh bast fibers to strengthen their teeth.

Wāwae'iole, 2. Rat's foot. The yellow spores are used for talcum powder. The plant was boiled to make a bath for rheumatic patients.

■ The following plants, according to the botanists, have been introduced into Hawai'i, some of them in the early days of European contact. All have acquired Hawaiian names and many *kama-'āina* believe that certain ones are native.

'Aloe, pānini'awa'awa, 196. Ornamental succulent plants of several species. The thick leaves contain a slimy juice which is applied to cuts and burns. The juice is taken as a laxative. Although the Latin name for this genus of plants is "aloe," (*'aloe*) has been added to the Hawaiian dictionary.

Ha'uoi, 721. Also spelled *ha'uōwī, owi, oi* and *joee*. An introduced verbena or vervain. The leaves and stems are pounded, the juice extracted and applied externally for skin ailments. The affected area is then powdered with *pia* starch. The juices are also applied to an injured area of the body which includes muscle and bone damage, supposing that the juices have a penetrating effect.

'Ihi, 473. This oxalis or yellow wood sorrel was introduced from Europe. The clover-like leaves are pleasantly tart due to oxalic acid. Juice from the leaves is added to sugar cane juice and *'alaea lepo* for a tonic.

'Ilie'e or *hilie'e*, 667. This wild plumbago is mildly poisonous. A juice is extracted from the root as a treatment for dry mouth. *Hili* means to stain brown. The juice from this plant will deepen the color of tattoo marks.

'Inikō, 447. An indigo blue dye is made from this common wild shrub after it has fermented in water. Salt is added to the juice of the *'inikō* and *puakala* to make a solution to treat backache.

Kuawa, guava, 632. The leaf and flower buds are eaten to control diarrhea. A tea is brewed from the leaf buds to provide the same treatment.

Lapine or *lukini*, lemon grass, 79. A tea is brewed from the lemon scented leaves and drunk as a general tonic. When the leaves are added to a tub of hot bath water they give off a fragrant oil which is thought to be medicinal.

Lēkō, watercress, 372. The peppery leaves and tender stems are eaten raw or cooked. A weedy species called *pā'ihi* and the larger cultivated form are used medicinally.

Nīoi, chili pepper, 742. The ripe, red peppers are pounded with salt and applied to aching muscles and to areas of the body afflicted with rheumatism.

Palepīwa, nuhōlani, 640. The name *palepīwa* means to ward off fever. *Nuhōlani* is New Holland, Australia, the home of the eucalytus trees. The leaves, especially from the lemon-scented variety were used in a steam or sweat bath (*pūlo'ulo'u*). Leaves were boiled in water and the patient breathed the steam which contained eucalyptus oil vapors.

■ Minerals in Hawaiian medicines were salt (*pa'akai*), red clay (*lepo 'alaea*), gray clay (*lepo pālolo*), charcoal (*lānahu*), and ashes (*lehu*). Water was secured from the sea (*kai*), springs (*wai puna*), rain (*wai lani*) and dew caught in the taro leaf since it represented water which had not touched the earth (wai 'apo, wai hua). Animal products in medicine were urine, fish, and the smaller sea creatures.

■ Materials Used by the Kāhuna in Medical Practice

The kāhuna lapaʻau kept large and small wooden calabashes ('umeke) and gourds (ipu) to hold and to mix the liquid ingredients for their medicines. Coconut shells ('apu) were cut and polished to be used for smaller vessels and for dippers. Selected stones were heated in the imu and dropped into calabashes containing liquids to boil the contents.

Stone pounders (pōhaku kuʻi lāʻau) were used to crush plant tissues, seeds and minerals. Adzes and knives of stone or shell were needed in gathering the bark from trees and shrubs and for cutting it into sections of the proper size.

The knife for simple surgery was the split bamboo. For the patient who must massage his own back and neck muscles a curved stick (lāʻau lomi) was devised. A tapered gourd was cut to form a funnel. When the neck of the funnel was stuffed with plant fibers, such as the ʻahuʻawa, it was a useful strainer.

Large sheets of kapa or lau hala mats were used to cover the patient for steam baths. Smaller pieces of kapa were cut or torn to serve as bandages.

Kukui nuts, coconuts and the dried stems and leaves of some herbs were kept by the kāhuna lapaʻau at the heiau hoʻōla at all times. However, most of the medicines were compounded from fresh herbs. In an herb garden near the heiau the kāhuna grew the plants that would thrive in this particular locality. The garden near Keāiwa Heiau on ʻAiea Heights is an example of this practice. The kahuna made regular trips before dawn to the rain forest or to the beach to secure fresh plant materials for medicines.

■ The Pani or Closing the Medical Treatment

When the patient had taken the prescribed medicine for a given number of days and had recovered from his illness, he was instructed to terminate the treatment by eating a certain food or a selection of foods. These were called the pani or closing foods. The particular pani was usually determined by referring to the Kumulipo chant of creation. (See Beckwith, 1972, and Handy, 1934, p. 25.) This traditional chant recognizes an affilia-

tion between the living things on the land and in the sea and enumerates them in pairs. The pani would be the marine counterpart of the principal land-grown herb in the medicine. Note the rhyming in the pairs of names of land-grown herbs and their marine affiliates.

'akiʻaki (rush grass)	- puakī (eel)
alaheʻe (shrub)	- heʻe (squid)
'awa (shrub)	- 'aʻawa (fish)
hau (tree)	- pāhau (fish)

■ Medicinal Plants from Other Parts of the World

In the world's earlier civilizations man searched for tonics, balms and cures among the plants in his fields and forests. Names of plants and the ailments for which they were used are found in the early records from China, India, Babylon, Egypt and Greece. These plants became widespread as the seeds or cuttings were transported to many parts of the world.

The medical properties extracted from a number of these plants are important medicines today. Of greater importance is the fact that chemists have been able to extract and isolate the healing elements from the plants, then produce them synthetically in the laboratory in great quantity at reasonable prices.

A cure for malaria comes from the bark of the chinchona tree. It was synthesized as atabrin and then later refined and called daraprin.

Digitalis from the foxglove plant has long been a valuable heart stimulant.

Ephedrine, originally from the plant ephedra, is effective in treating asthma and hay fever.

Opium, the sap from the seed-case of the poppy, was refined into morphine, an important pain-killing drug. Since it is habit-forming it must be administered by a doctor. Cocaine, from the leaves of the coca (not the cacao from which we get cocoa) is a pain-killer but is also habit-forming. Novocain, synthesized since 1904, does not have habit-forming properties.

The sap from the 'aloe is used internally as a laxative and applied to the skin to heal cuts and burns.

Cortisone, for the treatment of arthritis, is extracted from Mexican yams, agaves, yuccas, and sisal plants.

From Rauwolfia, a plant from the mountains of India, an extract was prepared to reduce high blood pressure. It is now produced chemically as reserpine, a tranquilizer. This drug, and several others related to it, reduces nervous tensions in patients in mental hospitals.

Tonics, pleasant to the taste but of uncertain medicinal value, are made from sassafras and sarsparilla.

Laxatives are prepared from the leaves of the senna, the roots of Chinese rhubarb, the seeds of the castor bean and psyllium and the bark of the cascara tree. Dysentery is treated with an extract from the roots of the ipecac or its chemical derivative known as emetine.

Plants with poisons deadly to man include strychnine, henbane, hemlock, certain mushrooms, ergot and curare. Some of these, when administered in small quantities, are useful medicines.

■ Captain Cook's Officers Wrote About 'Awa

There are numerous references in the Cook journals to the use of the drink 'awa by the chiefs. At this time, and for some years to follow, the Europeans believed that 'awa was an intoxicating beverage. Actually, this infusion made from the root of a pepper plant *(Piper methysticum)* is a narcotic drink, a tranquilizer, and not an intoxicant. 'Awa was an offering to the gods, a ceremonial and hospitable drink for the chiefs, and a relaxing beverage for the hard-working farmers and fishermen who seem to have used it in moderation without ill effects. Historians agree that the Hawaiians had no alcoholic liquors until they

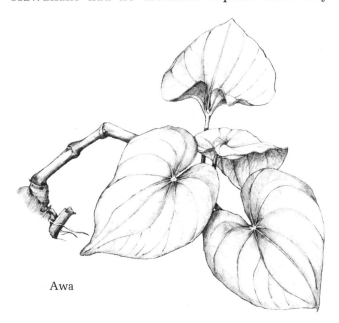

Awa

were introduced after Captain Cook's time.

The 'awa or kava drunk today in the Pacific is diluted considerably with fresh water, compared to the beverage described in Cook's journals. There is no longer the need to rinse the bitter potion from the mouth immediately nor to counteract a bitter taste with a bite of food.

Samwell wrote of the method of preparing and drinking 'awa at the house of Chief Palea:

> Parea before he eat any meat drank a cup of Ava, but this he did as if he had been taking a dose of Physic, his Servant immediately supplying him with water to wash his mouth & a piece of Sugar Cane to take the Taste off.
>
> In preparing the Ava they mix no water with it except one mouthful, which he who chews it takes to wash his Mouth, & this he spits into the bowl among the chewed root. (Beaglehole, p. 1166)

Samwell wrote of an 'awa ceremony in a double canoe:

> A Chief in one large double Canoe drank his Morning Dose of the intoxicating Liquor called Kava with his attendants along side the Ship; they prepare it by chewing the root in their Mouths like they do at all the South Sea Islands; while this Operation was going forward the Chief himself began a Song or gave out the Stave & was joined by all his people in the Canoe, when the Liquor was ready the man who had prepared it gave some in Cups to those around him who were allowed to drink it, being inferior to Chiefs and dependents on the other, they held their Cups in their Hands without offering to drink till the Song was concluded, then they all gave a shout together & emptied their Cups; after this a Cup of Liquor was given to the Chief himself, who repeated some words in a Chanting manner by himself & was answered by the rest, he repeated them three times & was answered as often, upon which he emptied his Cup. Then he dipped his fingers into a wooden Bowl containing some thin pudding [poi] & what stuck to them he sucked off one by one, & this method rendered the use of spoon unnecessary. (Beaglehole, pp. 1160-1161)

In this ceremony *poi* was the *pūpū* which took the bitter taste of the 'awa from the chief's mouth.

The following statement by King is one of several in which the visitors note the sore eyes and scaly skin of the 'awa drinkers, even among the young men not yet forty years of age.

> The Excess with which the Chief(s) drink the Kava, destroys their Strength & makes them sad objects of Debauchery; they far outdo in the use of this pernicious root all the other Indians [Poly-

nesians] we have visit'd; the more Scaly their bodies are, the honourable it is with them.

. . . I believe in a short time by disusing this liquor the soreness of the Eyes goes away; at least we made some of our friends refrain & they recovered amaz'ingly. The immediate effects of the Kava is making them stupid & heavy. (Beaglehole, p. 612.)

Samwell wrote of the 'awa bowls:

Some of them are with images to them and these are their Ava bowls, the feet of the Images are made to support the bowls & a hole is made for the liquor to flow out of their Mouths, & in some of them out of their back sides; these Ava bowls are very scarce being only in the Possession of their Kings . . . (Beaglehole, pp. 1182-1183.)

Hawaiian historian, Samuel Kamakau, expressed his views of 'awa in 1869:

At the time when the gods mingled with men and they talked to each other, the gods fetched this food down from Ho-aniani-kū, a realm of the gods, and gave it to man to plant and to drink.

'Awa was a refuge and an absolution. Over the 'awa cup were handed down the tabus and laws of the chiefs, the tabus of the gods, and the laws of the gods governing solemn vows and here the wrongdoer received absolution from his wrongdoing. That was the way, and the priestly practice, of ka po'e kahiko [the people of old]. (Kamakau, 1976, p. 43.)

■ **Important Events Concerning Sickness and Health in Hawai'i**

The impact of introduced diseases on the Hawaiian people and their attempts to alleviate them is shown, in part, by the following chart of significant events. The figures concerning cases of illness and death during the epidemics vary according to the source consulted. This information is based on Halford, *9 Doctors and God*, Thrum's *Annual for 1897*, *Hawaii Historical Review* and newspaper accounts.

500- From the time of their arrival from the
750 Polynesian islands to the southeast until the
A.D. coming of the Europeans, the Hawaiian people lived in healthful isolation from the infections and epidemics of the rest of the world.

1778 Veneral diseases were introduced by Captain Cook's sailors and spread to all of the islands causing much suffering and many deaths.

1804 Epidemic of ma'i 'ōku'u, probably cholera, killed thousands and thwarted Kamehameha's second attempt to conquer Kaua'i.

1819 Overthrow of the *kapu* following the death of Kamehameha I. *Heiau* destroyed or neglected and the *kāhuna* lost their powers. Medical *kāhuna* were forced to adapt to a new political and social order. Alcohol and tobacco, hitherto unknown to Hawai'i, were introduced during these years. Don Marin, a Spaniard, served as a foreign physician to Kamehameha I in addition to the king's native medical *kāhuna*. Colds and pneumonia were introduced. The Hawaiian people had little resistence to introduced contagious diseases.

1820 Dr. Thomas Holman, the first missionary physician, arrived and served one and a half years.

1826 Mosquitoes introduced from the ship Wellington at Lahaina. They were more pestiferous than disease carrying. Influenza reported.

1828 Dr. G.P. Judd, missionary doctor, arrived for a lifetime of service in Hawai'i. Office in Honolulu.

1831 Dr. Dwight Baldwin, missionary doctor, arrived for service on Maui.

1832 Whooping cough epidemic killed thousands.

1836 Kuhina nui Kīna'u ordered Honolulu harbor pilots check crews and passengers of incoming vessels for small pox.

1837 Hospital for United States seamen established at Waikīkī.

1838 The Lahainaluna Press published Dr. Judd's *Anatomia*, the first medical book in Hawaiian.

1839 Vital statistics and quarantine laws established.

1840 First case of leprosy in a Hawaiian detected by Dr. Baldwin. It is estimated that 4,000 died of leprosy in the 30 years to follow.

1841 Hospital for English seamen established in Honolulu.

1843 U.S. hospital established at Lahaina.

1845 Hospital for French seamen built in Honolulu.

1847 Dr. Robert W. Wood opened the first public pharmacy in Honolulu.

1848- Diarrhea epidemic. Long and severe influ-
1849 enza epidemic. Measles from Mexico said to have killed from 10 to 25 per cent of the Hawaiian people. Whooping cough from California. Nearly every child born during this period died. Over 10,000 died in these epidmics.

1849 Model vital statistics act passed. French government forced Hawai'i to purchase alcoholic beverages.

1850 Health care began on the sugar plantations. First Board of Health appointed. None in any state in the U.S. at this time. Native population was 82,035.

1853- First small pox epidemic, estimated 10,000
1854 cases and 7,000 deaths in a population of 70,000. Leprosy diagnosed on O'ahu by Dr. William Hillebrand.

1854 Small pox vaccination made compulsory.

1856 Dr. Charles H. Wetmore, missionary doctor, opened the first drug store in Hilo. Hawaii Medical Society chartered by Kamehameha IV.

1860 Epidemic of measles and whooping cough. Queen's Hospital opened, sponsored by Kamehameha IV and Queen Emma.

1861 Second small pox epidemic.

1862 First insane asylum established.

1866 First lepers sent to Moloka'i. Settlement located on the peninsula at Kalawao.

1868 Hawaiian Board of Health licensed native medical practitioners, (kāhuna lapa'au).

1870 Scarlet fever introduced.

1871 Dr. G.P. Judd opened a medical school of haole medicine for young Hawaiian men.

1873 Another small pox epidemic, called the third.

1874 Father Damien began service to the lepers at Kalaupapa.

1878 Garbage and refuse disposal and street cleaning began in Honolulu.

1879 Whooping cough and measles epidemics through 1881.

1880 First cases of mumps.

1882 Fourth small pox epidemic, 780 cases, 282 deaths.

1883 First mention of beriberi.

1886 First plantation hospital, Makaweli, Kaua'i.

1888 Mother Marianne (1836-1918) Third Order of St. Francis, began work with the lepers on Moloka'i.

1889 Severe cases of whooping cough. Father Damien died, age 49.

1890 Diphtheria epidemic. Kapi'olani Maternity Hospital opened.

1891 Legislature established drug and food laws.

1892 Serious bronchitis and pneumonia.

1895 Asiatic cholera epidemic, 91 cases, 65 deaths. Hawai'i Medical Association changes name to Hawaii Medical Society.

1899 Bubonic plague in Honolulu. (Now believed to be restricted to the Hāmākua coast, Hawai'i, with no case reported since 1949.)

1900 Kuakini Hospital founded by the Japanese for all races.

1901 Lē'ahi Hospital established in Honolulu for tuberculosis patients.

1903 Hawai'i Dental Society organized.

1907 Tripler Army Hospital opened. Now an Armed Forces facility.

1909 Kauikeōlani Children's Hospital opened.

1910 Board of Health established a Tuberculosis Bureau.

1911 Yellow fever threatened. Citizens destroyed mosquito breeding places. Dr. Homer Hayes, first intern at Queen's Hospital.

1912 Animal quarantine laws passed. Hawai'i remained free from rabies. Pu'umaile Hospital for tuberculosis patients opened in Hilo.

1913 Hawai'i Medical Library started.

1916 First Nursing School started at Queen's Hospital.

1917 Mahelona Hospital on Kaua'i opened for tuberculosis patients.

1927 St. Francis Hospital opened in Honolulu.

1929 Diphtheria immunization campaign began.

1930 State Hospital relocated in Kāne'ohe on O'ahu. It was then called the Territorial Hospital, earlier the O'ahu Insane Asylum. Shriner's Hospital for Crippled Children moved to Punahou Street.

1938 Hawaii Medical Service Association formed.

1943 Dengue, a war-time introduction, was stamped out by mosquito control.

1947 First Mental Health clinics organized.

1953 Hawaii Medical Society became Hawaii Medical Association.

1955 Alcoholism Clinic opened. First Salk polio vaccine received.

1959 Hawai'i became the 50th state.

The State Office of Health Education at this time gave an encouraging report. Highlights are: the threat of T.B. is controlled though not conquered; plague and typhus under control; no case of small pox in 44 years, no typhoid death in 11 years; Hansen's disease patients released each year are double the number of new cases reported; diphtheria and whooping cough are non-existent. Hawai'i is not plagued with the tropical diseases such as malaria, dengue, filariasis, or yellow fever.

At this time Hawai'i had 30 hospitals (Kaiser Hospital opened this year) with a capacity of 4,500 beds. These up-to-date hospitals on the six major islands are staffed with well trained doctors and nurses. There are 85 pharmacies and 228 registered pharmacists. The Hawai'i Dental Society has 350 member dentists.

1978 Dental health was only fair: the average number of decayed, missing or filled teeth was 6.85 for intermediate school students and 10.61 for those in high school.

1988 Vital indices generally reflect the high health standards of Hawai'i. Expectation of life at birth in 1984-86 was 75.37 years for males and 80.92 years for females. The crude death rate in 1988 was only 5.4 per 1,000 resident population. Deaths under one year of age per 1,000 live births numbered 10.8 in 1988. Diseases of the heart have accounted for almost one third of all deaths in recent years; cancer, for one-fourth.

Fully 98.6 percent of all babies were born in hospitals in 1988. The most common communicable disease reported to authorities was scarlet fever with 3,620 cases.

State mental health facilities served 8,389 patients in 1988, but the number of in-patients at the end of the year was only 260.

Marriages numbered 17,281, with about 44 percent accounted for by nonresidents. Divorces reached a total of 5,020.

1989. The state had 22 acute care civilian hospitals (with 2,855 beds), 38 long-term care facilities (with 3,191 beds), and nine specialty care facilities (with 808 beds).

As of March 1989, there were 2,425 physicians and surgeons, 882 dentists, 8,218 professional nurses, and 516 pharmacists licensed and living in Hawai'i.

(The above statistics 1978-1989, are from the *State of Hawaii Data Book*, which is published annually as a statistical abstract by the Department of Business and Economic Development in Honolulu.)

■ School of Medicine

The University of Hawaii School of Medicine graduated its first class on May 29, 1969, in the Sinclair Auditorium, Lē'ahi Hospital, Honolulu. The 24 men and one woman who completed the two-year course received awards of promotion and have been accepted by high-ranking medical schools on the mainland.

The School opened in 1967 with Dr. Windsor C. Cutting as dean and an outstanding faculty. The size of the first class was to be limited to 25 but 27 highly qualified students were selected from 500 applicants.

In 1973 the School, now called the John A. Burns School of Medicine, became a full four-year institution granting M.D. degrees.

■ Rabies

Rabies, an acute infectious disease fatal to man and certain animals, was unknown in Hawai'i because of strictly enforced animal quarantine. What became known as the Great O'ahu Rabies Scare started October 5, 1967, when a boy at Schofield Barracks was bitten by a rat that was diagnosed as being rabid. Some 27 persons were treated for bites from animals declared to be rabid and 81 more received antirabies shots after they were bitten or scratched by animals considered suspicious.

Since dogs and cats transmit rabies many persons had their pets vaccinated. An estimated 2,500 dogs and cats were destroyed. On December 21 the National Communicable Disease Center in Atlanta, Georgia, reported, on the basis of specimens sent to them, that Oʻahu was free from rabies as the cases were not diagnosed correctly. The state continues to require dogs and cats coming from the mainland and from most foreign countries to be quarantined for 120 days.

■ Hawaiian Attitude toward Medicines Today

Exposure of over a century and a half to Western medicine has not converted all of the Hawaiian people to full acceptance of modern medical practices. Illness, especially when serious, is a deep-seated emotional experience for the patient and for the members of his family. Many Hawaiian people observe that modern doctors prescribe treatment for the physical body and neglect the psychological and the emotional.

The grandparent in the Hawaiian family today is usually able to provide treatments that have been handed down through the years. They may tell with pride about cures that border on miracles after the haole doctor had failed. On the other hand there are cases where the herb treatment was unsuccessful and the haole doctor was called in too late.

As long as the older practitioners wish to use herbs for the physical ills and *hoʻoponopono* for mental cleansing, Hawaiian medicine will most surely be practiced. The question to be answered in this regard is: "When does one use Hawaiian medicine?" A physician of Hawaiian ancestry has suggested: If the illness is an introduced disease caused by bacteria or virus it should be treated with modern medicines prescribed by a licensed physician. Minor illnesses may respond to the herb remedies.

■ Understandings and Appreciations

1. Why are we ill? Discuss physical ills and mental disorders. In a happier mood - why are we well so much of the time? Shall we add the word "wellness" to the dictionary?

2. Think about man's great desire to be in good health. He visits doctors, dentists and patronizes hospitals. He may purchase medicines, vitamin tablets and drugs of uncertain value. Some persons visit healing stones (at Wahiawā), or travel to resorts to drink healing waters. Some persons use stimulants to stir up their feelings or tranquilizers to calm their reactions.

3. Decide upon a general policy for using Hawaiian herbs or other folk or home remedies.

4. Read about the government agencies that maintain a staff of specialists who help to insure that we have properly prepared and inspected food, potable water and pure drugs. Other public servants attend to rubbish and garbage disposal, sewage disposal and cleaning the streets and highways.

5. Read "Current Hawaiiana," a bibliography of publications on Hawaiian subjects compiled by the staff of the Hawaiian and Pacific section of the University of Hawaii Library. This quarterly lists the reports of the State Board of Health, the Hawaii Medical Association and the many organizations or societies that are concerned with a specific health problem such as cancer, tuberculosis, heart, mental health and others. See these publications in the local library or ask for copies from the organizations publishing them.

6. Some new residents who have brought dogs and cats criticize our law which requires that they be quarantined for 120 days. What do you think about this?

■ Student Activities

1. Read about Hawaiʻi's first Medical School founded in 1870. Dr. G.P. Judd instructed ten young Hawaiian men in the medical practices of that period. He attempted to substitute scientific medicine for some of the *kāhuna* methods that were medically unwise.

2. Make a *lāʻau lomi* or massage stick (Feher, p. 121). Search for a properly curved limb on a *hau* or guava tree. Talk to someone who can demonstrate *lomilomi* as it was done with the hands, also with the elbows and even by walking on the patient's back.

3. Collect the medicinal plants growing in your neighborhood and divide the native from the

introduced. Plant a garden of medicinal plants at your home or, if permitted, on your school grounds. Select hardy ones that you might use.

4. Learn to recognize the poisonous plants of our islands. Learn what part or parts of the plant contain poisons. How do these affect the different parts of the human body?

   Example: Oleander. All parts of the plant contain poisons. When handled these produce a rash on the skin of some persons. When eaten these affect most of the systems of the body in that they may cause vomiting, dizziness, irregular heart action and respiratory paralysis.

■ **Audio-Visual Aids**

Field trips will offer opportunities for seeing and hearing about the subject matter in this unit.

1. Bishop Museum. Visit the grounds and garden court to see the following plants which are medicinal or are associated with medicine:

ʻākia	ʻalaʻalawainui	ʻawa
hala	hāpuʻu	hau
hōʻiʻo	ʻilima	kalo
kī	kō	kokiʻo
kou	kukui	niu
noni	ʻōhiʻa ʻai	ʻōhiʻa lehua
ʻōlena	pia	ʻuala
wauke		

2. Keaīwa Heiau, ʻAiea Heights. A *heiau hoʻōla* or healing temple. A number of plants associated with healing grow in a garden nearby. This area is maintained as a state park with facilities for picknicking. If a group of 25 or more wishes to visit the *heiau* and park it is necessary for someone to apply in person for a permit from the Department of State Parks, Room 310, Kalanimokū Building, 1151 Punchbowl Street, Honolulu.

3. Visit a Chinese druggist's shop. Ask the druggist to show you some of the plant and animal products that he uses to compound Chinese medicines. Perhaps he can show you acupuncture needles.

■ **Vocabulary**

herb remedies	narcotic	plague
pharmacy	stimulant	epidemic
adequate diet	sedative	infection
sorcery	quarantine	immunity
bacteria	isolation	massage
virus	Hygeia	wellness

■ **Evaluation**

1. Check carefully to determine that the pupils understand the nature of folk medicine in contrast to modern medicine and medical practices.

2. Evaluate the student projects such as collecting medicinal or poisonous plants, planting a garden of healing herbs, making a massage stick or collecting stories about Hawaiian medical practices.

3. Review the vocabulary words in this unit.

4. Give credit for pertinent news clippings brought in or for books read on this subject.

■ **Reading List**

Akana, Akaiko, trans. *Hawaiian Herbs of Medicinal Value.* Comp. D.M. Kaaiakamanu and K.K. Akina. 1922. Honolulu: Pacific Books, 1968. (One of the few herbals to be translated and printed. 119 plants listed and prescriptions given for their uses.)

Arnold, Harry L., M.D. *Poisonous Plants of Hawaii.* Honolulu: Tongg Publishing Company, 1944.

Arrigoni, Ed. *A Nature Walk to Kaʻena, Oʻahu.* 1977. Honolulu: Topgallant Publishing Company, 1978.

Baldwin, Roger E. *Hawaii's Poisonous Plants.* Hilo: Petroglyph Press, 1979.

Beaglehole, Ernest. *Some Modern Hawaiians.* Medical references, 89-91. Research Publication No. 19. Honolulu: University of Hawaii Press, 1937.

Beckwith, Martha W. *The Kumulipo.* A Hawaiian creation chant. 1951. Honolulu: University Press of Hawaii, 1972.

Blaisdell, Richard K., M.D. Articles in *Health.*

Briggs, Vernon. *Experiences of a Medical Student, 1881.* Boston: David Nickerson, 1926. (Informative account of a 17-year-old young man commissioned to vaccinate 800 persons in rural Oʻahu.)

Bryan, E.H. Jr. *Ancient Hawaiian Life.* 1938. Honolulu: Books About Hawaii, 1950.

Buck, Peter H. *Arts and Crafts of Hawaii.* Honolulu: Bishop Museum Special Publication No. 45, 1957.

Bushnell, Oswald A. "Hygiene and Sanitation Among the Ancient Hawaiians." *Hawaii Historical Review,* October 1966.

———. "Ka 'Oihana Lapa'au o Hawaii Kahiko." *Malamalama,* Vol. VIII, No. 2, Dec. 1966. Honolulu: University of Hawaii.

———. *Molokai.* Honolulu: University Press of Hawaii, 1975 (reprint). (A novel with much about leprosy.)

———. "Dr. Edward Arning, the first microbiologist in Hawaii." *The Hawaiian Journal of History,* 1967, Vol. I.

Bushnell, Oswald A., and Sister Mary Laurence Hanley, OSF. *A Song of Pilgrimage and Exile.* The life and spirit of Mother Marianne of Molokai. Chicago: Franciscan Herald Press, 1982.

Chun, Malcolm N., trans. *Hawaiian Medicine Book; He Buke Laau Lapaau.* 1858-59. Honolulu: Bess Press, 1986.

Daws, Alan G. *Holy Man: Father Damien of Molokai.* New York: Harper and Row, 1973. (A biography of the priest who served the lepers.)

Degener, Otto. *Ferns and Flowering Plants of the Hawaii National Park.* Honolulu: Honolulu Star-Bulletin, 1930. (See index for the medicinal plants and their uses.)

Ellis, William. *Journal of William Ellis. Narrative of a Tour of Hawaii.* . . . 1826. Rutland, VT and Japan: C.E. Tuttle, 1979.

Emerson, Joseph S. "Kahunas and Kahunaism." *Mid-Pacific Magazine,* Jan.-June 1926.

Feher, Joseph. *Hawaii: A Pictorial History.* Honolulu: Bishop Museum Special Publication No. 58, 1969.

Force, Roland W. "Medical Lore in Ancient Hawaii." *The Conch Shell,* Vol. III, No. 4. Honolulu: Bishop Museum Association, 1966.

Greer, Richard A. "In the Shadow of Death." *Hawaii Historical Review,* July 1966. (Smallpox epidemic of 1853.)

———. "Oahu's Ordeal: The Smallpox Epidemic of 1853." Pt. II. *Hawaii Historical Review,* Oct. 1965.

Gugelyk, Ted, and Milton Bloomsbaum. *Ma'i Ho'oka'awale, The Separating Sickness.* Honolulu: Leprosy Research Project, Social Science Research Institute, University of Hawaii, 1979.

Gutmanis, June. *Kahuna La'au Lapa'au.* The practice of Hawaiian herbal medicine. Norfolk island, Aus.: Island Heritage, 1979.

Halford, Francis J. *Nine Doctors and God.* Honolulu: University Press of Hawaii, 1955.

Handy, E.S.C., Elizabeth G. Handy, and Mary K. Pukui. *Native Planters in Old Hawaii. Their Life, Lore, and Environment.* Honolulu: Bishop Museum Bulletin No. 233, 1972.

Handy, E.S.C., Mary K. Pukui, and Katherine Livermore. *Outline of Hawaiian Therapeutics.* Honolulu: Bishop Museum Bulletin No. 126, 1934.

Hawaii State Department of Health. "Common Poisonous Plants of Hawaii." Honolulu, 1966.

Holman, Lucia R. *Journal of Lucia R. Holman.* Honolulu: Bishop Museum Special Publication 17, 1931.

Honolulu Advertiser. "Hawaii's Health." Statehood edition, Section VIII, June 23, 1959.

Ii, John Papa. *Fragments of Hawaiian History.* Trans. Mary K. Pukui. 1959. Honolulu: Bishop Museum Press, 1963.

Johnson, Harold M. "The Kahuna, Hawaiian Sorcerer." *Archives of Dermatology,* Nov. 1964. 90:530-535.

Judd, Dr. G.P. "Remarks on the climate of the Sandwich Islands, and its probable effects on man." *Hawaiian Spectator,* 1838. 1(2):18-27.

Judd, Garrett IV. *Dr. Judd, Hawaii's Friend.* Honolulu: University Press of Hawaii, 1960.

Judd, Laura F. *Honolulu Sketches of Life, Social, Political and Religious—1828-1861.* Honolulu: n.p., 1928.

Kamakau, Samuel M. *Ka Po'e Kahiko.* The people of old. Honolulu: Bishop Museum Special Publication No. 51, 1964. (One of the best published explanations of the *kahuna,* medical practices, magic and sorcery.)

Kimura, Larry. "Kahuna Lapa'au." *Hawaii Historical Review,* Jan. 1966. 273-75.

Krauss, Beatrice H. *Native Plants Used as Medicine in Hawaii.* Honolulu: Lyon Arboretum Association, University of Hawaii, 1979.

HEALTH

248

Lamoureux, Charles H. *Trailside Plants of Hawai'i's National Parks.* Hilo: Hawaii Natural History Association, 1976.

Larsen, Nils P. "Ancient Hawaiian Medical Practices Viewed by a Doctor." Ch. 4, part 2, in *Ancient Hawaiian Civilization.* A series of lectures delivered at the Kamehameha Schools by E.S.C. Handy [and others]. 1933. Rutland, VT and Japan: C.E. Tuttle, 1965 (rev. ed.).

———. "Medical Art in Ancient Hawaii." *Hawaiian Historical Society Report for 1944.* Honolulu: Hawaiian Historical Society.

———. "Rededication of the Healing Heiau Keaiwa." *Hawaiian Historical Society Report for 1951.* Honolulu: Hawaiian Historical Society.

Lewis, Frances. *History of Nursing in Hawaii.* Node, WY: Germann-Kilmer, 1969.

MacCaughey, Vaughn. "Ancient Hawaiians." *Mid-Pacific Magazine,* Sept. 1918.

Malo, David. Chs. 25, 26 and 32 in *Hawaiian Antiquities.* 1898. Honolulu: Bishop Museum Special Publication No. 2, 1976.

———. "On the Decrease of the Population on the Hawaiian Islands." *Hawaiian Spectator,* 1839. II(2):122-130.

McBride, Leslie R. *Practical Folk Medicine of Hawaii.* Hilo: Petroglyph Press, 1975.

Mellen, George, ed. "Healthy Hawaii and Why." *The Sales Builder,* October 1936. 9(10):2-15.

Merlin, Mark D. *Hawaiian Coastal Plants.* Honolulu: Oriental Publishing Company, n.d.

———. *Hawaiian Forest Plants.* Honolulu: Oriental Publishing Company, 1976.

Middleton, Elizabeth. "Hawaiian Medicine." Waimea, Kaua'i: Hui o Laka, Kōke'e Natural History Museum, n.d. (4 pages, mimeo.)

Morris, Aldyth. *Damien.* Honolulu: University Press of Hawaii, 1980. (A drama with references to leprosy.)

Neal, Marie C. *In Gardens of Hawaii.* 1948. Honolulu: Bishop Museum Special Publication No. 50, 1965 (rev. ed.). (Medicinal plants listed by page number in this unit are found in this publication.)

Pope, Willis T. *Manual of Wayside Plants of Hawaii.* 1929. Rutland, VT and Japan: C.E. Tuttle, 1968.

Pukui, Mary K. *Hawaiian Beliefs and Customs during Birth, Infancy and Childhood.* Honolulu: Bishop Museum Occasional Paper XVI, No. 17, 1942.

Pukui, Mary K., E.W. Haertig, and Catherine A. Lee. *Nānā i ke Kumu: Look to the Source.* Vol. I, 1972; Vol. II, 1979. Honolulu: Hui Hānai, Queen Lili'uokalani Children's Center.

Rock, Joseph I. *The Indigenous Trees of the Hawaiian Islands.* Lāwa'i, Kaua'i: Pacific Tropical Botanical Garden, 1974 (reprint).

Snow, Charles E. *Early Hawaiians.* An initial study of skeletal remains from Mokapu, Oahu. Lexington: University Press of Kentucky, 1974.

Stone, Robert B., and Lola Stone. *Hawaiian and Polynesian Miracle Health Secrets.* West Nyack, NY: Parker Publishing Company, 1980.

Taylor, Clarice B. "Hawaiian Medicine." *Hawaiian Almanac.* Honolulu: Tongg Publishing Company, 1965 (4th printing). 47.

Thrum, Thomas G. "Hawaiian Epidemics." *Hawaiian Annual for 1897.* Honolulu: Thrum's Hawaiian Annual. 95-101.

Uilamakamakane, Kili Luika. *The Art of Hawaiian Lomilomi Massage.* An ancient system of body therapy and healing practiced throughout Polynesia. Captain Cook, Hawaii: Hawaiian Islands Publishing Company, 1982.

Wise, John H. "Medicine." Ch. 24, part 1, in *Ancient Hawaiian Civilization.* A series of lectures delivered at the Kamehameha Schools by E.S.C. Handy [and others]. 1933. Rutland, VT and Japan: C.E. Tuttle, 1965 (rev. ed.).

Zschokke, Theo. C. "Poisonous Plants Now Found in the Hawaiian Islands." Agricultural Notes No. 49. Honolulu: University of Hawaii Agriculture Extension Service, May 3, 1933.

UNIT 17:
The Land
and the People

THE LAND AND THE PEOPLE

■ **Nohona** - The Mode of life

"Polynesian social evolution reached its greatest development in the Hawaiian Islands, where all changes in direction or further elaborations of traditional forms under way elsewhere finally came to fruition." (Goldman, 1970, p. 200.)

The Hawaiian people were described by the first European visitors as radiantly healthy and of near physical perfection. They were genial, affectionate and generous. A highly developed agricultural system and skillful and intensive fishing methods provided the food needed for a relatively large population. Their shelter and clothing were suited to the subtropical climate.

The people were under the supervision of ruling chiefs who directed the activities of their industrious followers. Education was direct and effective. Artists expressed their ideas in the religious objects of wood, stone and feathers; in the symbols associated with royalty and in restrained decoration of useful household objects, tools and implements. Dances, usually accompanied by musical instruments, were dedicated to the gods, the chiefs or expressed love of family and nature. Exploits of the gods and heroes were recited by trained storytellers or chanted in poetical language.

Isolation from the populous continents protected the people from contagious diseases. Work and play kept them in good physical condition. The production of food, the construction of their shelters and the making of clothing were more than routine tasks of providing necessities. These were carried out with the belief that their gods were pleased with the results of their labors and their gods and 'aumākua were providing divine guidance in their pursuits.

Many of the most significant and interesting features of the traditional culture of Hawai'i were abandoned by the people at a time when there were no trained observers to record and evaluate them. These losses can never be regained.

Ka 'Āina - The Land

■ **Hawai'i Pae 'āina.** (pae - group, cluster; 'āina - land)

This term refers to all the Hawaiian Islands. Until Kamehameha I consolidated the archipelago under one rule the people thought and spoke of them as individual island chiefdoms since they were separated politically. The inhabitants were of common ancestry, however, and there was considerable travel between the islands.

The term pae 'aina is used today as "Aha Pae 'āina," a meeting or assembly of delegates representing the people from all of the inhabited islands.

■ **Mokupuni.** (moku - island; puni - surrounded)

Mokupuni refers to an entire island as a political land division which was ruled by a high chief, the ali'i nui. Moku 'āina or simply moku is an island in a geographical sense. The ruler of a mokupuni might be called the ali'i 'ai aupuni (ali'i - chief; 'ai - to rule; aupuni - kingdom) or the ali'i mokupuni. His kingdom might include more than one island or just a part of one of the largest islands. Politically Ni'ihau usually belonged to Kaua'i, and the islands of Moloka'i, Lāna'i, and Kaho'olawe were often satellites of Maui. The ruling chief of Kona and Kohala held, at times, Hāna and Kipahulu, on Maui. Wars of conquest caused political re-grouping of the islands.

At the time of Captain Cook's visit (1778-79) the Hawaiian islands were divided into four "kingdoms."

1. The entire island of Hawai'i and the Hāna district of Maui were ruled by Kalani'ōpu'u.
2. Maui (except Hāna), Moloka'i, Lāna'i and Kaho'olawe were under the rule of Kahekili.
3. O'ahu was ruled by Peleioholani.
4. Kaua'i and Ni'ihau were ruled by Kaneoneo in 1778 and were under the young Keawe in 1779.

Moku

A *moku*, a large district within the *mokupuni* or island, was ruled by the *ali'i 'ai moku* (chief who rules the district). He was appointed by the *ali'i nui*.

Moku are usually called districts today and the boundaries of most of them are about the same as they were in Kamehameha's time.

In usage, *moku* meaning district should not be confused with *moku* meaning island. Since Captain Cook's time *moku* has also meant ship since his vessels appeared to be floating islands.

Moku on Hawai'i

Ancient and present names are the same. The use of north and south are modern

Hilo- Now North and South Hilo

Puna

Ka'ū

Kona - Now North and South Kona

Kohala - Now North and South Kohala

Hāmākua

Moku on O'ahu

Kona (now Honolulu)

'Ewa

Wai'anae

Waialua

Ko'olau Loa

Ko'olau Poko

Wahiawā was created in 1913 as the 7th district

Island of Lāna'i

The entire island is a *mokupuni*, now attached to the *moku* of Lahaina, Maui.

Island of Kaho'olawe

A *mokupuni* attached to the Makāwao district of Maui.

Moku on Maui

Ancient names of divisions

Hāmākua Poko

Hāmākua Loa

Ko'olau

Hāna

Kīpahulu

Kaupō

Kahikinui

Honua'ula

Kula

Lāhainā

Kā'anapali

Modern names for Maui

Lahaina, includes Lāna'i

Wailuku

Makāwao, includes Kaho'olawe

Hāna

Moku on Moloka'i

Kona has been, since 1859, Moloka'i district, a part of Maui County.

Ko'olau, since 1909, has been Kalawao district consisting of Kalaupapa, Kalawao and Waikolu. Politically it is separate from Moloka'i and has the status of Kalawao County. It is governed for the most part by the State Board of Health.

Moku on Kaua'i

Ancient names of divisions

Puna

Kona

Nā pali

Halele'a

Ko'olau

Waimea (large part of Kona and Ni'ihau)

Hanalei (all of Nā pali, Halele'a and half of Ko'olau)

Modern names for Kaua'i

Līhu'e (half of Puna)

Kawaihau (half of Puna and half of Ko'olau)

Kōloa (small part of Kona)

Island of Ni'ihau

The entire island is a *mokupuni*. It is now attached to the Waimea *moku* or district of Kaua'i.

Ahupua'a.
(Ahu - altar; *pua'a* - pig) A pig's head carved of *kukui* wood was placed on an altar of stones to mark the boundary line. At least from the time of 'Umi the *moku* have been divided into *ahupua'a*, the most important of the land divisions in pre-Cook Hawai'i. The *ahupua'a* on the windward sides of the islands were usually entire valleys with the ridges between them as their boundaries. All of the *ahupua'a* were given names and their boundaries carefully defined. The names were descriptive or derived from legendary or historical sources. The boundaries were known to the residents more often by their natural features than by man-made markers.

Nearly every *ahupua'a* was a tract of land extending from the summit of the mountain to the sea and on to the outer edge of the reef. If there was no reef the boundary extended into the sea a distance that would be a mile and a half by our present-day measurement. These tracts varied in size from 100 acres to over 100,000 acres. Kahuku on Hawai'i included over 184,000 acres.

The *ahupua'a*, with its varied plant zones from the rain forest down to the beach, provided most of the needs of the dwellers within it. From the forests the people secured trees for canoes, house-posts and temple images. Here grew the hardwood saplings for spears, *olonā* for the strongest cordage, *māmaki* for *kapa* and a number of medicinal plants. Birds living in the rain forest provided feathers for the royal cloaks, helmets and leis.

Plants growing unattended somewhat lower were the *kukui*, bamboo, ti and *pili* grass. Farmers planted bananas, yams, *pia*, *'awa* and gourds in this zone.

The rich lands along the streams produced taro,

Current Names of the Moku or Districts

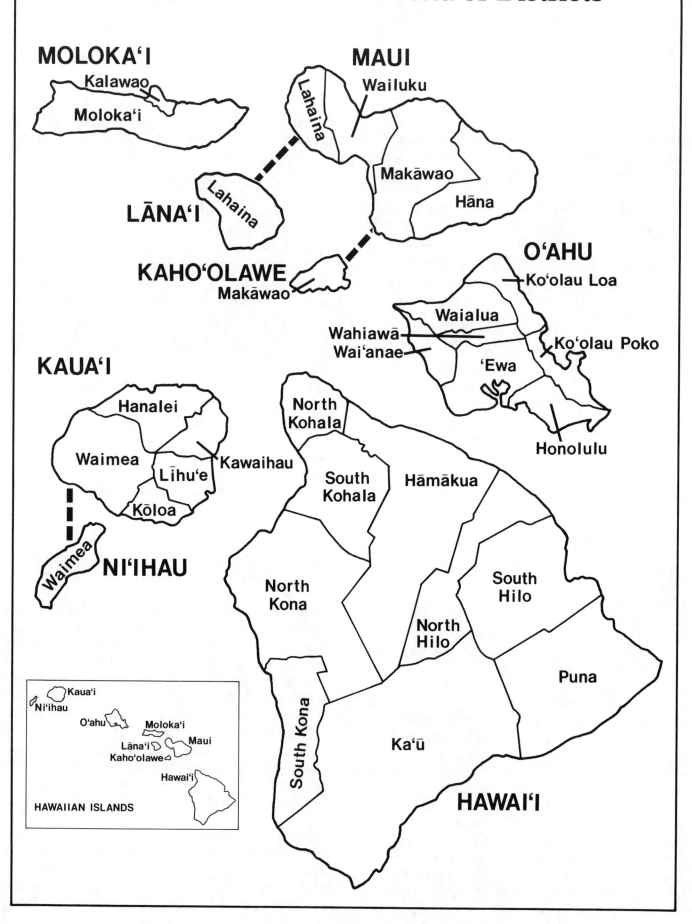

MOLOKA‘I
Kalawao
Moloka‘i

MAUI
Lahaina
Wailuku
Makāwao
Hāna

LĀNA‘I
Lahaina

KAHO‘OLAWE
Makāwao

O‘AHU
Ko‘olau Loa
Waialua
Wahiawā
Wai‘anae
Ko‘olau Poko
‘Ewa
Honolulu

KAUA‘I
Hanalei
Waimea
Līhu‘e
Kawaihau
Kōloa

Waimea
NI‘IHAU

North Kohala
South Kohala
Hāmākua
South Hilo
North Kona
North Hilo
Puna
South Kona
Ka‘ū
HAWAI‘I

Kaua‘i
Ni‘ihau
O‘ahu
Moloka‘i
Lāna‘i
Maui
Kaho‘olawe
Hawai‘i
HAWAIIAN ISLANDS

sweet potatoes and sugar cane.

Thriving near the sea were coconut, *kou* and *milo* trees. The grass houses were most numerous in this zone and the people planted ti and sugar cane near their dwellings.

The sea furnished much of the protein food.

Early European and American visitors to Hawai'i were impressed with the extensive plantings and the wise use of the tillable soil. The cleanliness of the houses of both chiefs and commoners received special praise. (Vermin that caused harsh criticism a few years later were introduced.) Archibald Campbell wrote in the early 1800s of the "natural ingenuity and unwearied industry" of the Hawaiian people.

The activities of the people within the *ahupua'a* were under the direction of an appointed chief, the *ali'i 'ai ahupua'a*, or of the *konohiki*. Families (*'ohana*) occupied areas within the valley for their use. Each family might have a plot near the beach, not far from the fresh water stream, as a site for one or several houses. Another plot would be taro land in the rich valley floor. Lands higher in the valley might be assigned, or such areas might be used in common by the villagers under the direction of the *konohiki*.

Some families were primarily planters, others were principally fishermen. Some engaged in both activities. A few lived some of the time in the upper valleys or on the higher slopes called the *kula* land where they cultivated plants adapted to these zones.

There was a constant sharing of food and useful products between the families. Traditionally, the families lived on their *ahupua'a* lands for many generations. The extended family or *'ohana* might consist of many related households. When these families worked on communal projects they were under the direction of their *haku*, the eldest male of the senior branch. Such group activities would be housebuilding, *hukilau* fishing and preparing feasts.

The families paid taxes to their *ali'i 'ai ahupua'a* or *konohiki* in the form of their handcrafts and the products of the land and the sea. This chief kept a part, then passed the rest to the *ali'i 'ai moku* who retained a part and gave the rest to the high chief.

■ **'Ili** (strip of land). An *'ili* is a strip of land within an *ahupua'a*. If it was one continuous strip, running from *makai* to *mauka*, it was an *'ili pa'a* (a

Ahupua'a: The tax collectors walked around the island with the ocean on their left. At the point where they entered a land section called an *ahupua'a* they would see a pig's head carved from *kukui* wood on an altar of stones. This was the *ahupua'a* monument which marked the boundary line of this land section.

fixed or complete land section). If it was composed of detached pieces of land it was an *'ili lele* or a *lele*. The word *lele*, meaning fly or jump, indicates that one section might be on the beach, another in the valley and a third section in the *mauka* area. These were all "'*ili* of the *ahu-pua'a*" and subject to the chief or *konohiki* of the *ahupua'a*.

'Ili kūpono (land of special merit), or shortened to *'ili kū*, were within an *ahupua'a* yet independent of it and its chief. Tribute from the *'ili kū* went directly to the *ali'i nui*. A change of chiefs governing the *ahupua'a* did not affect the status of the *'ili kūpono*. This was the only form of land in old Hawai'i that carried a permanent title. Waikoloa, in the *ahupua'a* of Waimea, Hawai'i, is an *'ili kū* of extensive acreage.

Land sections of decreasing size and importance were the *mo'o, paukū, kīhāpai* and *kō'ele* (later called *Pō'alima*). These terms are rarely used today. Thrum's Annual for 1925 lists 130 Hawaiian land terms which were compiled and explained by Curtis J. Lyons.

■ Kuleana (right, title, ownership, interest).

One of the commonest land terms in use today is *kuleana*. Technically this refers to the small tracts on which the working people lived and which they cultivated and improved for their own use before the *Māhele*. The term *kuleana* was applied to these plots of land when they were awarded to the tenants in fee simple (total right of ownership) by the Land Commission. Most of the *kuleana* were valuable taro or farm lands.

When not using *kuleana* as a land term it refers to a person's fields of interest, his rights or his responsibilities. Families inherited the right (*kuleana*) to be buried in the sea, in Pele's crater or any place that was the realm of their *'aumakua* or guardian (Kamakau 1964, p. 50). Today we may say, "His *kuleana* is fishing."

■ Konohiki (chief's agent in charge of a tract of land).

In the days before the *Māhele* the *konohiki* represented his chief as the land supervisor or agent over an *ahupua'a* or other large tract of land. Later the landlords came to be known as *konohiki*.

Konohiki lands were those which were awarded to the chiefs and *konohiki* as *Māhele* Awards or Land Commission Awards.

Konohiki Fishing Rights were the rights which gave exclusive privilege to the owners of an *ahupua'a* or *'ili kūpono* to catch fish in the waters off-shore from their lands. Tenants on these lands, however, enjoyed certain fishing privileges that were granted them by the owners. Some land owners reserved one kind of fish for themselves exclusively. Others took one-third of the fish caught by their tenants.

Water Rights. The *konohiki* served as *luna wai* (water boss) under his chief as he supervised the distribution of irrigation water flowing from the mountain streams and springs into the taro ponds (*lo'i kalo*) and other gardens. (Handy, 1972, pp. 57-67.)

Water rights and fishing rights are respected in Hawai'i today. The Honolulu Star-Bulletin, January 11, 1973, reported a State Supreme Court decision concerning the water rights of two sugar plantations, other land owners, and the State in Hanapēpē Valley, Kaua'i. The decision was based on "historic rights dating back to the *Māhele* and the Hawaiian practices and customs that preceded it."

■ Ka Po'e - The People

According to tradition as recorded by Kamakau (1964, p. 3) the first man and woman were created in the "very ancient past" at Mōkapu, on O'ahu. For 53 generations the people lived and spread over all Hawai'i before the first ruling chief emerged (Chief Kapawa of Waialua, O'ahu). The people gradually separated into orders or degrees of chiefs, the *kāhuna* or priests, the working class (*maka'āinana*), and the outcasts (*kauwā*).

■ Ali'i 'ai aupuni

The supreme ruler (*ali'i 'ai aupuni*) was called the *ali'i nui*, and much later the *mō'ī* or king. In pre-European times his kingdom was an island (*mokupuni*), a part of one of the largest islands, or several islands. Kamehameha I was the first *ali'i* to rule the entire group of islands (*pae 'āina*). He was called "*Ka Na'i Aupuni*," the conqueror of the nation.

The rank of the supreme ruler was determined by his ancestry, which should be the highest in the kingdom; and by his power to establish himself through military prowess and political talent as the ruler over all other or competing chiefs. His subjects recognized the claim of the *ali'i 'ai aupuni* that he was a descendent of the gods. This gave him the highest *kapu* in the kingdom and with it, protection, authority and prestige. Because of high rank and *kapu* he possessed *mana*, or divine power. His subjects accredited him with the ability to commune with and to intercede with the gods.

Those who became high chiefs had been trained from boyhood by capable and carefully selected *kahu* or guardians to lead their people in peace and in war. By rigorous training a chief developed proficiency in personal combat and in manly sports. He acquired knowledge and skill in organized warfare and in conducting or participating in the highest religious ceremonies in the *heiau*.

The title *mō'ī*, meaning king or ruler, is in general use today. It is probably of post-European origin since it first appeared in print in 1832 (Pukui-Elbert, 1971, p. 231). King Kalākaua (1836-

1891), author (1874) of the words of "Hawai'i Pono'ī," now our State song, wrote "Nānā i kou Mō'ī," Look to your King. In this song *ali'i* is translated "chief." (See Resource Unit 4, for Hawai'i Pono'ī, Hawaiian and English words.)

The *ali'i 'ai aupuni* maintained a large household which might occupy or make use of seven or more houses. (See Resource Unit 14 for the names and functions of the houses.) An important structure was his storehouse *(hale papa'a* or *hale ho'āhu)* filled with materials, including food, needed by his family and his subjects. The citizens, although generally free to live where they chose, would not desert a chief with a full storehouse.

In times of peace the ruler was, to his subjects, "Father Lono," an earthly representative of Lono, god of rain, agriculture and patron of sports. In time of war he was identified with Kū, the powerful god of war. (Handy, 1931, pp. 12-13.)

David Malo, (1951, p. 187) compared the government under a high chief to the human body.

The head is the king or *ali'i 'ai aupuni.*

The shoulders and chest are the chiefs, the *ali'i 'ai moku* and the *ali'i 'ai ahupua'a.*

The right hand is the high priest *(kahuna nui),* keeper of the king's idol and advisor to him in religious matters.

The left hand is the prime minister *(kālaimoku)* who looks after the interests of the king and the people.

The right foot represents the soldiers *(koa).*

The left foot represents the farmers *(mahi'ai)* and the fishermen *(lawai'a).*

The fingers and toes are the other working people *(maka'āinana).*

(See sketch called Government under the Ali'i 'Ai Aupuni.)

Malo (1951, p. 191) also compares the king to a house.

Handy (1972, p. 326) speaks of the ruling *ali'i* as one "in most instances more like a father to his people than a despot." Taxes paid to him were "an investment, for giving calls for return in kind."

■ **Nā Kāhuna,** experts in religion, the professions and the crafts.

The ruling chief was guided in making important decisions by a powerful priesthood of highly trained experts. Only the temple priests were traditionally of *ali'i* ancestry and their positions were hereditary.

The chiefly priests of the great war god Kū were the highest ranking *kāhuna* in the kingdom. The chiefs always consulted these *kāhuna* before making any preparations for war.

The *kāhuna* of the peaceful deity Lono, though highly respected chiefs, were lower in rank than the priests of Kū.

Kāhuna who were experts in the professions and crafts were highly skilled citizens. Kamakau (1964, p.98) lists eight classes of medical *kāhuna* and experts in many fields. (See Kamakau index, pp. 154-55.)

The only dreaded members of the priesthood were the the *kāhuna 'anā'anā* and the *kāhuna kuni* who prayed people to death.

The chiefs sought the advice of the *kāhuna* before engaging in any undertaking of importance. This dependence of the chiefs upon their services gave the *kāhuna* an influential and powerful position in the government.

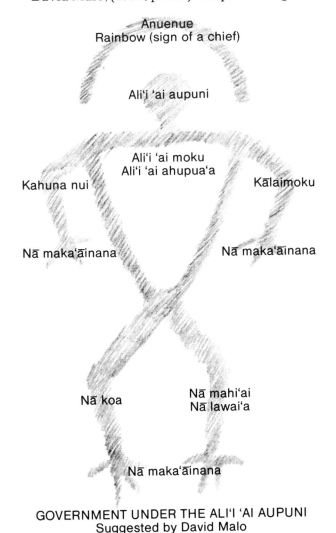

GOVERNMENT UNDER THE ALI'I 'AI AUPUNI
Suggested by David Malo

An example of a ruling chief seeking a *kahuna*'s advice during historical times is one told of the ambitious Kamehameha. In 1790 he controlled but half of the island of Hawai'i but his burning desire was to consolidate all of the islands under his rule. Kamehameha sought the help of Kapoukahi, a prophet and temple builder of the island of Kaua'i. This *kahuna* advised Kamehameha to rebuild the *heiau* Pu'u Koholā at Kawaihae on Hawai'i and to dedicate it to his war god Kūkā'ilimoku. After he completed this task, he was told, his plan would be fulfilled.

Kamehameha rebuilt and dedicated Pu'u Koholā under Kapoukahi's personal direction. He apparently gained spiritual strength and hope from this experience for by armed conflicts and strategy, he united the islands.

■ **Kālai-moku** (*Kālai* - to carve or shape. *moku* - island).

This officer, sometimes called the prime minister or counselor, advised his high chief in conducting the secular affairs of the kingdom. The *Kālaimoku* and the *kāhuna* were, next to the high chief, the most powerful men in the kingdom.

The title "*kālaimoku*" may be translated "island shaper." When a high chief replaced his predecessor through inheritance, selection or as a conquering warrior he asked his *kālaimoku* to devise a plan for redistributing the lands among the chiefs who were faithful to him.

The *kālaimoku* was responsible for the collection of taxes and for the management of the agricultural lands, irrigation, fishponds and fishing.

The *kālaimoku* lived apart from the chief's household. The two met at the request of either of them in the king's *Hale Manawa* (Malo, 1961, p. 196) and discussed matters of concern. The *kālaimoku* also attended all conferences between the ruler and his council of chiefs. The king listened to the advice given him by his chiefs and, says Malo, he accepted it only when it was in keeping with the advice of his *kālaimoku*.

Traditionally the prime minister was instructed during his years of training by the elder *kālaimoku* whom he would succeed. Often a *kālaimoku* advised a succession of rulers and learned much from each.

The *kālaimoku* was trained in all phases of warfare. He advised the ruler, the chiefs and the people on matters of diet and health. He managed the ruler's storehouses.

Malo wrote (p. 197) that the *kālaimoku* did not care for "luxury or display, nor distinction, wealth or land." He was intent on serving the king and his people.

■ **Konohiki** (Originally, the head man of an *ahupua'a*. By the time of the *Māhele*, 1848, the *konohiki* had become land owners and they sat with the chiefs in receiving *Māhele* lands).

The *konohiki,* usually a trusted relative of the *Ali'i-nui,* was a lesser chief who served as the general executive and tax collector over an *ahupua'a*. He was appointed by his ruler and served under the *kālaimoku*. In most cases he was not, when selected, a resident of the *ahupua'a* and was not related to its inhabitants. Unlike these leaders in other parts of Polynesia (or in Hawai'i today) he had not been chosen because of his ability as a leader among his own people, but had been placed over the residents of the *ahupua'a* by the high chief.

The *konohiki* directed the farming activities such as planting and harvesting, building irrigation ditches (*'auwai*), supervising the distribution of irrigation water, building taro ponds (*lo'i*) and clearing patches for dry land taro in the *mauka* areas.

The *konohiki* designated or re-affirmed certain reef and offshore areas as the fishing rights or privileges of certain families. Some of these are known and respected today as "*konohiki* rights." He enforced the fishing *kapu*, one of which allowed no *'ōpelu* to be caught from January through June (by our calendar) and no *aku* from July through December, a *kapu* which protected these fish during their breeding season. The *konohiki* supervised fishing enterprises in which many villagers participated, such as a *hukilau* or trolling for *aku*. When the catch was brought ashore the *konohiki* divided the fish by distributing some to the chief and his household, some to the *kahuna* and the rest to the families which participated in the venture.

The *konohiki* conscripted men from the working class as soldiers, and other men with specific skills, such as canoe builders, to be in the service of the ruling chief. His ability to furnish many willing soldiers or workers was evidence of his reputation as a just *konohiki*. When a man in his position was cruel and severe in his treatment of his people they often moved to another *ahupua'a* as was their privilege. Since farmers, fishermen and, at times, soldiers were essential to the life of the *ahupua'a*, a *konohiki* dared not be too harsh or unjust.

The *konohiki* collected the taxes from his people in the form of food which the high chief and his family needed throughout the year. At the time of the *makahiki* he collected such non-perishable products as *kapa*, mats, wooden utensils and such handicrafts as the people made for this form of gift-giving. Food was a part of the *makahiki* tax and, being perishable, it was distributed at once, presumably to the chiefs for whom it was intended.

■ **Kahu.** (Attendant, guardian, keeper)

A number of *kahu* lived in or near the chief's household. These honored and trusted attendants to the chief *(kahu ali'i)* were usually relatives. Some served as guardians and instructors to the chief's sons *(kahu keiki)*.

The chief's *kahu* were in charge of his *kāhili*, clothing, spittoon *(ipu kuha)* and all personal possessions. He guarded these against enemies who might take these personal articles and bring harm to the chief through sorcery. *Kahu akua* cared for the temple images and *kahu wai* guarded the irrigation water rights.

The *kahu* to the young *ali'i* were tutors and guardians, thoroughly familiar with the knowledge, lore and skills every chief should know and be able to practice. The *kahu* trained the *ali'i* from childhood in such physical activities as sports, and the art of personal combat in warfare. They schooled their young charges in folklore, navigation, genealogies and the rites and ceremonies which were performed by chiefs in their social, political and religious life.

At the present time the word *kahu* is used by the Hawaiian congregations in the Christian churches to refer to their pastor *(kahu* or *kahu hipa*, keeper of the sheep).

■ **Haku** (director, functioning head of an *'ōhana*)

The *haku* was the elder male of the senior branch of the entire *'ōhana*. He was the head of the council of the extended family and presided over the meetings. He had authority over the individuals and the household in supervising the work, worship and the various activities planned by the families. The *haku* listened to the advice and opinions of the householders but he had the deciding word.

■ **Maka'āinana** - people on the land. (Handy, 1972, p. 20, wrote, "The *maka'āinana* were the planters and fishers who lived on *(ma)* the *(ka)* land *('āina)*; the final *na* is a plural substantive.")

The *maka'āinana* made up the largest segment of the population. In addition to their work as the planters and the fishermen they were the craftsmen and the soldiers. They were the major source of manpower. Although from the same basic stock and genetic inheritance as the *ali'i*, a gradual separation of the two groups had come about through the years.

The *ali'i* emerged as individuals of high intellect and of superior physique which improved with proper diet, exercise and good grooming. The *ali'i* selected their mates from the best blood lines and preserved their genealogies which they believed linked them to the gods.

Historians have written that the *maka'āinana* became commoners through the loss of their genealogies. Malo wrote "Perhaps in the earliest time all people were *ali'i* . . ." (Malo, 1976, p. 60) He suggests that some became commoners because they wandered off in pursuit of pleasure, and others were banished by fellow chiefs because of misconduct. The loss of their genealogies, however, caused them to become common, and this group became the most numerous in the kingdoms. They accepted the time-consuming physical tasks and were unable to devote much time to intellectual pursuits.

When a prominent chief was defeated and killed in battle the remaining members of his family might disperse and retire into the country districts. They could change their names and live as *maka'āinana*. Although the elders in these families knew their ancestry it became a policy not to discuss their family line with the children as they grew into maturity.

The young people were certain to ask questions about their forebears but they would be told that it was a subject not to be discussed. This is said to have been the fate of his remaining relatives in Ka'ū after their ruler, Keōuaku'ahu'ula, was sacrificed by the forces of Kamehameha at Pu'ukoholā in 1791.

Kamakau wrote (1964, p. 8), "of the *maka'āinana* it was said that, in the end, the well-being (pono) of the kingdom was in their hands."

The material necessities and the luxuries of the people of old Hawai'i were produced by these skilled workers. The culture materials which we admire in the museums and private collections today as the unique arts and crafts of Hawai'i are from the hands and minds of these "commoners who were not common."

Some of the work was done by the people at the request of or at the command of the chiefs. Certain chiefs and chiefesses personally directed their people in their work. Campbell, after living with the people for 13 months, wrote of them, "They are distinguished by great ingenuity in all their arts and manufactures, as well as by a most persevering industry." (Campbell, 1822/1967, p. 121.)

The maka'āinana lived on the lands assigned to them by the chiefs as long as they worked acceptably and paid adequate taxes. They could be removed from their lands by the konohiki or any chief with authority in the ahupua'a. If they were unhappy under a chief they were free to move to another ahupua'a.

In answer to questions asked about the rank and status of the Hawaiian people living today we have an answer from Dr. Handy: "With the principle of caste (classes of people) gone, there commenced the process of levelling through miscellaneous marriage, which has made all Hawaiians of the present time maka'āinana." (Handy, 1931 p. 28.)

■ **Kauwā** (Servant, outcast, untouchable). (This word is spelled kauwā in the literature but there is a trend toward deleting the W in the UW words. The spelling would be kauā and the pronunciation remains the same.)

In a more modern use of this word a person of high birth might humble himself in the presence of others by calling himself a kauwā, as one might say "your humble servant."

Translators of the Bible used the word kauwā as servant. "Kauwā a ke Akua." Servant of God.

The motto used in the early days of the Honolulu Rotary Club, given we are told by Dr. William Westervelt, was:

"E ho'okauwā 'a'ole no ka uku."

Do not enslave yourself to your business.

Among those who served a chief would be his kauwā kua kāhili, his kāhili bearers and his kauwā lawelawe, those who carried his belongings. These were all highly respected people. Some in the service of a chief were ali'i, often relatives of lower rank than the ruling family.

The kauwā as a class of people lived a pitiful existence in Hawai'i before the kapu were discontinued in 1819. They were the outcasts who lived apart from the chiefs and the people on lands assigned to them and kapu to all others. The kauwā were dreaded and abhorred. Any contact with them defiled a free person and would cause him to be put to shame.

The origin of the kauwā as a class is not clear. Some scholars believe that their segregation and exclusion from the society of others was due to a kapu of defilement from some early period in Hawaiian life. Although Malo wrote (1961, p. 69) that the kauwā were descended from Ha'akauilana and Papa they seem to have suffered a complete loss of their genealogies in early times.

A settlement of these outcasts occupied one of the least fertile and favorable areas in each district or moku. Should one of them wish to see the ruling chief he would cover his head with kapa and approach his master with great humility. The chief would grant him audience and consider his request. The kauwā farmed, fished and provided for their own needs. They were not slaves in the service of their chief despite the fact that the word kauwā is sometimes translated "slave."

Kepelino (1932, p. 142) wrote that there were a thousand or more kauwā in Hawai'i. This was his estimate during the latter days of the old culture which Kepelino describes so vividly but not always in agreement with other Hawaiian historians.

The chief function of the kauwā in Hawaiian society was that of furnishing victims for human sacrifices in the heiau. When a temple ceremony that required a sacrifice was to be performed, the chief sent a kahuna or a messenger to the boundary of the kauwā lands where he called out for a victim. The men among the kauwā decided who should be the one to be sacrificed. This unfortunate person said farewell to his family and friends and accompanied the messenger to certain death. It is said that the kauwā victim would lie down in the ocean and let himself be drowned. Drowning was the usual method of killing the man to be sacrificed.

Chiefs or chiefesses were known to have taken kauwā as mates. The men were said to have been strong and fine looking and the women were attractive. An ali'i or maka'āinana might form an alliance with a kauwā because the individual was attractive or perhaps he did not know that the person was an outcast. If children were born to this union and their ancestry became known the children were put to death.

Some children lived, their "tainted" kauwā blood undiscovered, and they matured and were known to have married into ali'i families. This union, of course, without the knowledge of the members of the chiefly families. This is a prime reason for the ali'i families making all efforts to study their genealogies carefully. When mates were being selected for their offspring the chiefs wanted to rule out the presence of any dreaded kauwā ancestors in the family lines.

After the kapu were abolished in 1819 the distinctions between the people gradually became less important. The kauwā left their reservations, slowly merged with the common people, and fortunately for them, their identity was lost.

■ Nā Kapu - The Rules or Restrictions

The social and political behavior of all of the people was regulated in the strictest sense by an elaborate set of rules and prohibitions called kapu or to historians "The Kapu System." These evolved through the years as an effective, though rigid and severe means of regulating the relationships between the chiefs and the people, and between men and women, in nearly every phase of their lives. The kapu also controlled man's use of the riches of his natural environment and were the bases of a very effective system of conservation. Kapu were decreed by the chiefs and the kāhuna who pronounced them, in some cases at least, as being the will of the gods.

The great body of kapu were rigid rules of conduct, supposedly known to everyone and observed or obeyed faithfully. Offenders were apprehended and punished, the most common penalty being death. At any time a temporary kapu could be placed on a person, place or object by the high chief or his kahuna. When this was announced the people attempted to inform others as quickly as possible about the new edict to prevent the innocent from being punished.

The gods and all things associated with them were sacred, therefore kapu. The kapu extended to the chiefs, god-like themselves because of their descent from the gods. Kapu safeguarded the mana of the chiefs by protecting them from the people.

Since mana was inherited the highest chief held the greatest degree of divine power.

Both Malo and Kamakau wrote about the degrees of rank among the members of the chiefly classes. They recorded the nature of the kapu or respect that each rank required of its subjects.

The ali'i with the highest rank were the ni'aupi'o which translates "coconut leaflet midrib bent back upon itself." This is a figurative way of referring to a brother-sister marriage. These mates must have a mother and father both of ni'aupi'o rank. This highest degree of royalty could also be maintained by the marriage of a ni'aupi'o chief and chiefess, even though they were not brother and sister.

The ni'aupi'o were recognized by their subjects with the prostrating kapu or kapu moe. While kneeling the people touched their foreheads to the earth and did not look up until the royal personages had passed by. Ali'i of lesser rank required the kapu noho or sitting kapu.

In descending order from the ni'aupi'o Kamakau (1964, pp. 4-6) describes ten more classes of chiefs. The elements involved in determining the rank of the royal personages, although involved and somewhat difficult to follow, gives insight into the importance of bloodlines among the Hawaiian ali'i.

Among the ali'i of historic times who held high rank were Kamehamehanui, Kalolanui, Kalani-'ōpu'u, Kīwala'ō, Keōpūolani and her two sons who became Kamehameha II and III and their sister Nahi'ena'ena.

The presence of the high chiefs in the village and the fields completely halted all activities. The kapu chiefs went out from their houses at night, when possible, for at this time their shadows fell on no person and the shadows of the commoners were not cast upon them.

■ Examples of Kapu

The most widely known kapu is the one which required men and women to eat separately ('ai kapu). Since the men prepared and served the food they were forced to make separate ovens (imu) for the men's and women's food. The poi was pounded separately.

Men performed the rites of worshipping the gods, which included offering portions of food to the gods. This took place in the Hale mua or men's eating house where the images of the gods occupied a place of honor. Women were not permitted to enter the *Hale mua* or to participate in these religious rites as they were believed to be "periodically unclean."

Handy and Pukui (1958, p. 177) list the important foods which were *kapu* to women and show the relationship of these foods to the gods. Some examples are:

Pork, a feast food for the gods, chiefs and priests; related to the god Lono in his form Kamapua'a (pua'a - pig).

Bananas, the tree was the earthly form of the god Kanaloa. Women were permitted to eat at all times the *iholena, pōpō'ulu* and *kaualau* bananas.

Coconuts, the tree was a form of the body of the god Kū.

Whale, porpoise, turtle, spotted sting ray were probably a form of the god Kanaloa whose chief realm was the sea.

Many of the *'aumākua* or family gods were thought of as spirits which took animal or plant forms. Members of a family were strictly forbidden to eat these, their family *'aumākua*.

The list of *kapu* is long and, like the Ten Commandments, many are stated in the negative, at least as they have been made known to us in English. There were 72 regularly designated *kapu* days in the year. The chiefs and priests declared special ones. Fear of punishment and death caused the people to obey these rules strictly. Public executioners called *mū* killed the offenders by strangling, decapitation, clubbing, burning or drowning. The *kapu* system gave the authorities power and control over the political, social and economic life of the people.

Pūlo'ulo'u, poles capped with balls of white *kapa,* were the "kapu sticks" which, when placed before a chief's compound, warned all unauthorized persons to keep out. (This *kapu* did not, of course, extend to the members of the chief's family or his attendants.)

A few other signs, such as *kapa* streamers or knotted coconut leaves, marked a place as *kapu*.

Captain Cook observed the power of a *kapu* placed on Kealakekua Bay by Kalani'ōpu'u during which time all canoes were forbidden to go in or out of the bay until a boat taken from Cook was returned to him.

Cook asked for a field along the bay shore to use in setting up astronomical instruments. Pointed wooden sticks decorated at one end with dogs' hair and feathers were the "tabooing wands" that kept all others from the area.

Foreigners in Hawai'i (only men before 1820) completely ignored even the most sacred of the *kapu*. The people observed that no punishment came to them, either from the authorities or from the gods. But as long as Kamehameha I lived the *kapu* of the land continued to be the way of life for the Hawaiian people.

During the ceremonies observing the death of the great Kamehameha the *kapu* were disregarded by chiefs and the people alike as was the custom at the passing of a beloved ruler. As part of the widespread laxity, men and women ate together and the women ate *kapu* foods. Liholiho, as the new king, would have, by tradition, declared the *kapu* in force again after a given number of days of mourning, cleansing and purification. But he was persuaded to do otherwise by his mother, the highest *kapu* chiefess Keōpūolani and by his aunt, the newly appointed Kuhina-nui Ka'ahumanu and perhaps by his favorite wife and half-sister Kamāmalu.

Liholiho ate with these chiefesses publically, thus announcing that this highly important *kapu* was abolished. Historian Kamakau wrote (1961, p. 318, 222-228) that not a month had passed after the death of Kamehameha before the eating *kapu* was ended. Liholiho and Ka'ahumanu gave orders to have all of the *kapu* abolished on all of the islands. This caused rejoicing on the part of most but not all of the people. It was the women who were especially happy to be freed from discriminations.

With the *kapu* ended, the *heiau* walls were torn down, wooden images and temple structures burned and the priests stripped of their power and influence. The people were without a religion and without laws to regulate their social and political life. However, the beliefs, customs and habits of a lifetime could not be erased swiftly and completely by the decree which abolished the *kapu* system.

Adherents to the old system hid images in caves and perhaps visited them regularly. Hale-o-Keawe at Hōnaunau which housed the remains of the royal dead remained sacred. Pele continued to be a powerful force and the gods of fishing and agriculture were visited as usual.

Highlands Intermediate School teachers compiled a list of 20 *kapu* of ancient Hawai'i which are printed in *Hawai'i, Our Cultural Heritage,* 1973, p. 703. An extensive list of *kapu* for Hawai'i and Polynesia, as revealed through myths and legends, are given in Kirtley, 1971, pp. 143-164.

■ Superstitions

Some restrictions or prohibitions were subtly imposed by the people themselves as a means of social control. These were not *kapu* decreed by the chiefs and the *kāhuna* which carried punishment if disobeyed. These might be called the codes of conduct of that time but are certain to be thought of as superstitions today. The penalty for failing to observe these was a calamity of some sort that came upon the offender such as bad luck, illness or the loss of property or a loved one.

A common example of this is the warning about picking *lehua* blossoms, which is often repeated incorrectly today. In the early version, young people, while on a day's outing in the mountains, were told not to pick *lehua* blossoms on their way to their destination. To do so would bring rain and spoil their fun. However, they could gather as many flowers as they wished on the way home. This warning seems to have been invented by the adults who learned that the young people got lost and had to be rescued (by the adults) when they left their trail on their way to the mountains to scurry here and there for *lehua*. This did not happen when the youngsters gathered flowers as they returned on the trails now familiar to them. (Today the warning is: if you pick *lehua* it will rain.)

Another superstition or restriction warns that it is "bad luck" to carry pig home from a *lūʻau* at night. Some Honolulu residents say that it is bad luck to carry pork over the Nuʻuanu Pali at night, a warning whispered in pre-tunnel days.

This seems to have originated in the days when pig was a rare delicacy for the working people. While the men were busy preparing to serve the food after opening the *imu* many of them yielded to the temptation of sending a *pūʻolo* of pig home by one of their sons. When, at last, the people gathered to eat (this is after 1819 when all ate together), "*Auwē*, little or no pig!" A situation of this nature was easier to correct by superstitious fear than by rule or decree. Hence the whispered warning: it is bad luck to carry pig after dark.

In modern times the bad luck has often been in the form of a tire blowout or some unexplainable failure of the car motor.

Most of the superstitions that place prohibitions or restrictions on people's actions or conduct can be analyzed to show that they were created to cause the people to regulate certain of their activities for their own good or for the benefit of others.

■ Ka Makahiki

The festival of the *makahiki* was one of the happiest of the ceremonies of the year. Its beginning was announced each year by the *kāhuna* when they first observed the rising of the Pleiades *(Makaliʻi)* over the eastern horizon at sunset. This was about the middle of October, or during the *kapu* days of Kū, month of ʻIkuwā by the lunar calendar in use in pre-European days on the island of Hawaiʻi. (Malo, 1951, p. 141 and note p. 151; also Handy, 1972, pp. 330-331.) Because of changes through the centuries these dates do not correspond to those in the Hawaiian Moon Calendar distributed annually by the Prince Kuhio Hawaiian Civic Club and other Hawaiian Calendars on the market.

During the *makahiki* a *kapu* was placed on war, ceremonies in the temples ceased and all unnecessary work stopped. The preparation and serving of food continued, of course, but such work as house and canoe building, making of *kapa* and *lau hala* products and the planting of crops was suspended for the four-month festival.

The people assembled the tributes which they were to present to their high chief as taxes when he or his representatives visited their district. Since the *Makahiki* was a harvest festival the products of the gardens and plantations were of special significance. The flesh foods offered were dogs, fowls, fish and other edible sea creatures. (Hogs, a form of Lono, were not suitable.) From the gardens came taro, sweet potatoes, bananas, breadfruit, yams, arrowroot, coconuts and sugar cane.

Since many of the foods were perishable they were received as a tribute to the high chief, then distributed to the members of the party which traveled with him, his court and his *kāhuna*. (Handy, 1972, p. 350). The workers who presented these gifts understood that they were to receive in return the blessings of the chief (and through him the blessings of the gods) which would assure them a year of good crops, sufficient rain and general prosperity and happiness.

Gifts of a more durable nature presented to the chief consisted of *kapa*, mats and many articles fashioned from wood. Some of these were taken to the chief's storehouse.

The details of the visit of the *Makahiki* god, *Lono-makua,* the tax collectors and *kāhuna* to each district is too long to be reviewed here. See Handy, 1972, pp. 327-389 and Malo, 1976, pp. 141-159.

After the taxes were paid the people relaxed, played games and danced. Some work was resumed before the four-month festival was over but this period afforded the workers much needed relief from their regular work and from the anxieties of life under the *kapu* system.

■ Land Ownership in the 1800s

After uniting the islands Kamehameha I made no marked changes in the traditional land system. As the supreme ruler of the Kingdom he owned all of the land and was priviledged to choose the tracts that he wanted for himself and to delegate the rest to the care of his loyal chiefs. These in turn appointed lesser chiefs as overseers of the land sections such as an *ahupua'a.* The last in line were the working class, most of whom were tenant farmers and fishermen who lived on plots of land at the pleasure of their chiefs. They paid as taxes a portion of the products of the land and sea and were required to give personal services as requested by those in authority.

Kamehameha II made no important changes in the distribution of the lands during his short reign. The chiefs by this time considered themselves secure on their lands.

The foreign population increased noticeably during the early years of the reign of Kamehameha III. Each estimate of the population showed a decline in the number of Hawaiian people due, not only to deaths from introduced diseases but also to adverse psychological conditions. The people were urged or required by their foreign teachers to accept Western ideals which they did not understand, and which, in some instances were physically harmful to them.

Traders settled in the port towns, particularly Honolulu, Lahaina and Hilo and built stores and warehouses. They asked the chiefs for land so that their business investments would be secure. The missionaries, now permanently established, needed land for their churches, their schools and for themselves. Foreigners began to demand the right to own land outright. Some of them saw the possibilities in types of agriculture, such as growing sugar cane, which would require large tracts of land in order to be economically feasible. Because of the heavy investments necessary to clear and cultivate large acreages, and to build a sugar mill, the prospective planters wanted to own the land in fee simple. (Note: The land could have been leased to the planters.)

The comparatively few foreigners who expressed themselves as being interested in the financial status of the Hawaiian people believed that the working class would be more secure on their land by owning it.

The Declaration of Rights of 1839, enacted by Kamehameha III and his chiefs, changed for all time the government and the land system of Hawai'i. Sometimes called Hawai'i's Magna Charta, this bill of rights granted protection to the land and property of the people as well as that of the chiefs. This guarantee extended to the property of the foreign residents also, much against the wishes of many of the Hawaiian people.

In 1840 Kamehameha III gave his people their first written constitution. This established in Hawai'i a constitutional monarchy replacing the absolute one. The constitution provided for a legislature consisting of a House of Nobles, appointed by the King, and a body of Representatives elected by the people. The King continued to be recognized as the owner of the land but the land was not to be considered his private property. Neither the chiefs, the people nor the foreigners could be removed from their land without cause.

■ Ka Māhele - The Great Māhele

The most revolutionary and far-reaching legislation ever enacted involving land ownership in Hawai'i was the Great Māhele. It was instituted to give the chiefs the title to the land which they claimed and to satisfy the foreigners' demands for outright ownership of land. It was an attempt to encourage the working class to continue cultivating the lands on which they were living but to which they had no real claim. A few persons in the government, at least, believed that the security of fee simple ownership of their lands would cause the native planters to remain in the country districts instead of flocking to the port towns in great numbers as they were doing.

Technically, the Great Māhele refers to the decisions made in the series of meetings held by Kamehameha III and more than 240 of his chiefs and *konohiki* from January 27 through March 7,

1848. During this time they settled their undivided interests in the lands of Hawai'i. The Māhele did not convey title to the lands. All recipients were required to present their claims to the Land Commission for their awards.

Popularly the Māhele is thought of, though incorrectly, as dividing (māhele) the lands of Hawai'i three ways, a third for the Crown and Government, a third for the chiefs and the remaining third as the kuleana lands for the tenants who were living on them.

■ The Land Commission

A Board of Commissioners to Quiet Land Titles was appointed by Kamehameha III through the Legislative Act of December 10, 1845. The Board of five members drew up the Principles to guide them in awarding lands to the many persons who would appear before them as claimants. This document, completed on August 20, 1846, and approved by the Legislative Council on October 26, 1846, gave the rules by which all claims were to be awarded. (See Bailey, Indices, p. 12)

The Land Commission, as the Board was generally called, took testimony for 12,000 individual claims during their visits to all of the islands. Officially, their work came to a close on March 31, 1855, after nearly ten years of diligent work and difficult decisions. The Land Commission Awards are recorded in 10 large volumes. Fifty smaller volumes hold the testimonies taken from claimants. These originals are carefully preserved in the Archives of Hawaii, Kekāuluohi, 'Iolani Palace grounds.

In 1929 the Land office published the "Indices of Land Commission Awards," a volume of over 1700 pages, in Hawaiian and English, giving an alphabetical list of awards by Awardees and also the awards by islands and by districts. This book, compiled and published by Charles T. Bailey, Commissioner of Public Lands, is readily available in libraries throughout Hawai'i.

When the Legislature approved the Principles to be followed by the Land Commission they could have instructed this body to grant land in fee simple to native Hawaiians only, as had been done in Samoa and other Pacific island countries. Unfortunately for the Hawaiian people they did not do so. A Legislative act of July 10, 1850 authorized the sale of lands in fee simple to resident aliens. Later, on August 6, 1850, a Legislative act authorized the awarding of kuleana lands to native tenants.

■ The Māhele and subsequent Legislative acts provided that lands be awarded in the following catagories:

1. Crown Lands (called King's Lands from 1848-1865).

Nearly one-third of the land in the Kingdom (about one million acres) was retained by the King as his own private property. This transaction was recorded in the Māhele Book on March 8, 1848. Kamehameha III and his successors, Kamehameha IV and V, were free to sell, lease or mortgage these lands. Considerable land was sold and more might have been lost to the Crown had not the Legislative act of January 3, 1865, early in the reign of Kamehameha V, made the King's Lands inalienable. Thereafter they were known as the Crown Lands.

At the overthrow of the Monarchy in 1893 the remaining Crown Lands were made a part of the public domain.

2. Government Lands

Kamehameha III, on March 8, 1848, set apart the larger part of the land granted to him by the Māhele (about one and one-half million acres) as Government Lands which were intended to produce revenue for the operation of the government.

Portions of these lands were sold from time to time for revenue to meet government expenses. Purchasers, largely foreigners or haole residents, were given Royal Patent Grants since it was not necessary to go before the Land Commission for an award or title to the land from this source.

The Minister of the Interior reported for the 1849-1850 fiscal year the sale of 27,292 acres and for the next fiscal year 31,518 acres of government land. Fuchs (1961, p. 16) wrote that by 1886 two-thirds of the Government Lands had been sold. Between 1850 and 1890 pasture lands sold for an average of twenty-five cents an acre while good taro land brought five dollars an acre.

3. Konohiki Lands

Early in the reign of Kamehameha III the chiefs and konohiki had only the illusion of ownership of their lands. During the meetings held from late January to early March, 1848, the King and some 240 chiefs and konohiki divided the lands, agreed upon tracts that each was to claim, and listed them in the Māhele Book.

Chiefs and *konohiki,* according to their rank, were given one or more of the large tracts, an *ahupua'a* or *'ili kūpono.* Those closest to the ruling line received more generous awards. (More than 90 are listed for Victoria Kamāmalu.) (Bailey, 1929, pp. 60-64) These grants retained the ancient land names and respected those early boundaries, without benefit of surveys at that time. It was not until 1870 that the Government began accurate surveys of the lands in Hawai'i.

The *Konohiki* Grants included about a million and a half acres. Although the Grant was listed in the Māhele Book the chief did not receive title to the land until he or his agent appeared before the Land Commission to substantiate his claim.

Awardees in most cases were required to pay the Government a fee (commutation) for the land amounting to about one-third of the value of the unimproved land. This was a very modest figure using 1848 land values. Many of the awardees returned to the Government one-third of the land in lieu of cash payment.

In order to accommodate chiefs who failed to claim the lands listed for them in the Māhele Book additional laws were passed in 1860 and 1892 to give them or their heirs an opportunity to claim the lands. Most of the *konohiki* lands were sold by their owners, the chiefs and *konohiki,* before the Monarchy came to an end in 1893. (Fuchs, 1961, p. 16.)

4. Fort Lands

Fifty-two *'ili* in Honolulu were set apart for the support of the Fort on the harbor front. These lands were cultivated for a time by the soldiers. When no longer required for this purpose the Fort Lands were sold at public auction except for a tract of fifty acres which was set aside for the Royal Hawaiian Agricultural Society (organized in 1850) to use in plant experiments.

The Fort, called Kekuanohu, was begun in 1816 and, after completion, served both military and peaceful purposes. It was demolished in 1857 and is remembered today through the name Fort Street.

5. School Lands

In 1840 the Legislature passed a law providing for government schools. In 1846 a school department was organized under a Minister of Public Instruction.

The Act of July 9, 1850 set apart "one-twentieth part of all the lands then belonging to the government . . . for the general purposes of education." (Hobbs, 1935, p. 56.)

The Minister of Public Instruction was authorized to sell, lease or otherwise dispose of the school lands to help finance the work of the school department. By 1881 much of the school land had been sold as indicated by the 3,312 sales recorded. Some of the land was used for school sites and some was leased out to provide an income. (Hobbs, 1935, p. 58.) To finance the expanding system of public schools the legislature also made appropriations from government general funds. (Wist, 1940, p. 60.)

6. Kuleana Lands

By authority of the Legislative Act of August 6, 1850 citizens were able to place their claims before the Land Commission to secure ownership of the lands on which they were living or which they were cultivating. No land was granted unless it was requested. Unfortunately, many tenant-farmers were under the impression that occupancy or use gave them the right to their land. Untold numbers of planters failed to appear before the Land Commission to secure fee simple title to their choice agricultural Lands.

About 30,000 acres were awarded to tenant-farmers and other claimants numbering 9,337 to 11,000 according to the varying figures on record. Although the size of the award averaged about three acres for each family this land was considered the most productive in the Kingdom. These *kuleana* were located within the Crown, Government or *konohiki* lands and were granted fee simple to native tenants who occupied, cultivated or had improved the land. The farmers were not required to pay commutation since this fee was paid by the chiefs who owned the larger tracts in which these *kuleana* were located.

Fee simple ownership of a small plot did not, in many cases, include all of the privileges that the planters had enjoyed as tenants under the chiefs. Many did not continue to have water and fishing rights or the use of other lands such as *mauka* plots for grazing and inland farming. When conditions were not suitable for making a living by cultivation of their lands, many of the farmers abandoned their *kuleana* and moved to the port towns. The title to their lands then reverted to the owners of the *ahuapu'a* or *'ili* in which they were located.

Some owners lost their newly-acquired *kuleana* lands because they were still exchanging, not selling, their products and had no cash with which to pay taxes.

It is of interest to read the names of the people awarded lands by the Commission. (See Bailey, Indices of Land Commission Awards, 1929.) The first three pages of the Numerical Index of Patents on Awards, Mahele Book 1, Oʻahu, (Bailey, pp. 1383-85) contain 80 names of which 23 are persons with Hawaiian names and 57 with foreign names, largely American and British.

House lots in Honolulu, Lahaina and Hilo were granted to the native tenants who occupied them. Since they were no longer considered a part of a large tract on which a chief had paid commutation, the grantees paid one-fourth of the value of the improved land.

After the *kuleana* lands were granted to the native tenants who requested them the ancient system of land tenure in Hawaiʻi came to an end (November 1, 1855). According to Fuchs (1961, p. 16) by 1936 about six percent of the original *kuleana* lands were in the possession of Hawaiians or part-Hawaiians. His reasoning is this; "most of the commoners lost their land because they valued other things more." Fuchs does not name the "other things" specifically but he writes of "efforts to recapture the past" and "*aloha* and *pilikia*." What did the Hawaiian people value more than land in pre-statehood days?

■ **Land Terms in use in Hawaiʻi Today**

Fee simple. Absolute right of ownership of the land which is registered on a deed. See Chinen, *Original Land Titles,* for explanation of types of fee simple ownership of land in Hawaiʻi such as Awards, Grants, Patents and Deeds.

Leasehold. A person or organization secures the right to use a parcel of land for a specific period of time and, in turn, agrees to pay for using it. Holders of leases in Hawaiʻi may be able, in some cases, to purchase their leased land if certain conditions are met.

Condominium. The owner has absolute rights to a specific unit of property within a "total package" which carries joint ownership rights. Most of Hawaiʻi's condominiums are apartment buildings on leased or fee simple land. After purchasing a unit each individual owner pays his share of the lease, taxes and other costs of main-

taining the total complex.

■ **Land Classified By Use**

The State Land Commission was established in 1961 to classify and regulate Hawaiʻi's limited land area. It is charged with preserving agricultural lands against urban encroachment and with protecting recreational, wild life and scenic areas. The four million acres of land in Hawaiʻi are classified in some charts as follows:

1. Plantation Agriculture. One-third million acres of prime agricultural lands are devoted to growing sugar and pineapple. Urbanization is claiming many acres of agricultural land each year.

2. Nonplantation Agriculture. Of the one million acres here the largest portion is grazing land, much of it making up the ranches of the Big Island and Maui. Other lands are devoted to growing coffee, macadamia nuts, vegetables and to raising dairy cattle, swine and poultry.

3. Forests and Forest Reserve, one and one-half million acres.

4. Recreation. Of the one-third million acres in this class the largest portion is in the National Parks on Hawaiʻi and Maui. Game management areas, recreational parks and playgrounds make up the rest.

5. Urban, 155,700 acres. This includes land already in civilian residential use, military housing and lands designated for future growth. These lands comprise but four percent of the total. Developers continue to exert pressure to have more land re-classified into urban.

6. Steep and barren lands, one-half million acres. The Big Island has the greatest amount of barren land. All islands have cliffs, steep slopes and areas that are not usable at this time. About twelve percent of the total land is in this class.

There is also a classification by land use districts, See Atlas of Hawaii, pp. 136-139 for maps of the islands showing the districts.

1. Urban districts consist of land now in urban use and a reserve for future growth. Land use here is administered by the Counties.

2. Rural districts are lands devoted to small farms and having low-density residential lots.

3. Agricultural districts include lands with capa-

city for intensive cultivation. For agricultural and rural districts the Land Use Commission establishes regulations and the Counties administer them.

4. Conservation districts - the land is administered solely by the State Department of Land and Natural Resources.

Land Classification By Ownership

The greatest portion of the four million acres of land in Hawai'i is owned by the Federal and State governments and by approximately 39 large landowners. The system of leasing land rather than selling it has allowed the large landowners to retain title to their holdings and to receive revenue by leasing it.

Lands owned by the State and counties, including Hawaiian Home Lands, comprised 29.8 percent of the total or 1,203,140 acres in 1988. A great amount of State land is in conservation and therefore does not provide revenue.

In 1988 the Federal government had title to 8.4 percent or 338,035 acres. This includes all of the Northwestern Hawaiian Islands (Nihoa to Kure), most of Kaho'olawe, large acreages of national parks on Hawai'i and Maui and the land occupied by extensive military installations on O'ahu.

Six private landowners controlled 22.6 percent of all land in Hawaii in 1988, or more than 912,853 acres of land. The six landowners with the largest holdings in Hawaii are as follows:

1. Bernice P. Bishop Estate   339,197 acres
2. Richard S. Smart (Parker Ranch)   139,301 acres
3. Castle and Cooke, Inc.   129,220 acres
4. Samuel M. Damon Estate   121,598 acres
5. C. Brewer and Company, Ltd.   90,689 acres
6. Alexander and Baldwin, Inc.   92,848 acres

Other major private landowners include the James Campbell Estate, Amfac, Inc., Molokai Ranch, Ltd., and Gay and Robinson.

(These figures were taken from the 1989 *State of Hawaii Data Book*, which warns: "Considerable caution is necessary in comparing statistics from different sources on land use, ownership, or tenure. Variations in definitions and survey dates seriously affect comparability in many instances. . . .")

Homesteading in Hawai'i

The Hawaiian homesteads of today are familiar to most island residents. But not many people realize that the kingdom, at the time of Kalākaua, and later the Territory of Hawai'i offered many acres of land to citizens of all ethnic groups. Homesteading is a plan to make land available at a minimum cost to residents who will live upon and cultivate it.

The Homestead Act of 1884, with amendments in 1888, 1890 and 1892, allowed some 557 claimants to acquire 8,491 acres of land between 1884 and 1895.

The Land Act of 1895, under the Republic of Hawai'i, offered more land until 90,000 acres of former crown lands were given as homesteads. Citizens who claimed homesteads were largely Hawaiian, Portuguese and American. Very few Orientals had gained citizenship at this time so were ineligible to claim land.

The Republic of Hawai'i took ownership of about 985,000 acres of crown land and some 828,000 acres of government land that had belonged to the Kingdom of Hawai'i and its rulers. (Hobbs, 1935, p. 108.)

Issuance of homestead leases did not stop until 1951 but few people seemed to be aware of this.

Most of those who took homesteads abandoned them. Large land holders purchased these parcels which became available on all the major islands. Only persons of Hawaiian ancestry are offered homesteads now.

The Department of Hawaiian Home Lands

Prince Jonah Kūhiō Kalaniana'ole is called the Father of the Hawaiian Homes Commission Act. In 1920, as Hawai'i's delegate to Congress he introduced a resolution creating the Hawaiian Homes Commission which was "to permit people of Hawaiian blood to again get possession of land in Hawai'i, which is their home." Though introduced in 1920 the act was not passed until July 9, 1921.

From the days of the Great Māhele the Hawaiian people have been rapidly losing possession of their lands. Many abandoned their healthful and productive life of farming and fishing and flocked to the towns where they lived in slums or below-standard conditions. Prince Kūhiō and other local leaders, seriously concerned about the social and economic plight of the Hawaiians, hoped that the people could be rehabilitated by returning them to the land. At the time the Homes Act was passed the Hawaiian population was estimated at 22,500 persons. Captain Cook had estimated the population at 300,000 in 1779. At the time of the Māhele there were approximately 80,000 Hawaiians.

The story of the Department of Hawaiian Home Lands, created by the Commission, is long, involved and very interesting. In addition to the brief sketch here the reader should refer to the bibliography appended to this unit.

Land granted to the Hawaiian Homes Commission was marginal land which had been rejected by the sugar planters and ranchers. The Act excluded all cultivated sugar lands, obviously the best agricultural tracts and all public lands under lease or agreement.

The Homes Commission Act called for some 200,000 acres but when the lands were surveyed, most of them for the first time in 1972, there were but 189,878 acres. Through the years the Commissioners have, as they are empowered to do, exchanged some lands which were needed for public purposes, for tracts of comparable value elsewhere.

The Commission is composed of eight members, appointed by the Governor for four year terms. At least four must be native Hawaiian. Each island with homestead lands is represented by one or more commissioners. The chairman's appointment must be confirmed by the Legislature.

From the first the commissioners have been devoted to their tasks. The first meeting of the newly appointed commission was on September 16, 1921. Within the first 15 months they held 63 regular and six special meetings. Their problem through the years has been that there is too little money available to open up new lands for leases. People on the long waiting list have blamed the commissioners for the limited availability of lands.

The Act allows prospective homesteaders to apply for:

1. Residential land of not more than one acre.
2. Farm land with residence or farm land only.
3. Ranch land with residence or ranch land only.

Leases for these lands are for a period of 99 years at one dollar a year regardless of the size. Applicants must be of one-half or more Hawaiian ancestry, be over 21 years of age and able to occupy and use the land within a year after it is granted. Homesteaders may borrow money to build a house or purchase livestock or farm equipment when money is available. Unfortunately money was not always to be had for these purposes.

The Commission is, from time to time, without sufficient money to develop new lands by constructing roads and bringing in utilities. Lands not devoted to homesteads may be leased to provide money for projects that the Commission is planning. At present, more than half of the land is leased to non-homesteaders.

By 1933 some 4,000 acres of Moloka'i farm lands were leased by homesteaders to the pineapple companies. They employed Filipino laborers to work on the land and sent monthly checks to the homesteaders. This defeated the original purpose of rehabilitation. Some families went into debt by purchasing luxury items on credit beyond the amount of their monthly checks.

One pineapple company has disposed of its Moloka'i venture and the other is said to be phasing out operations. This will cause unemployment and leave some 12,000 acres of land available for some type of farm use.

Some Moloka'i homesteaders did farm their land, raising alfalfa, tomatoes, and other vegetable crops. In many instances the land was poor; winds, dust and pests took their toll. Water was often not available in quantity that was needed. Transportation costs were high and transport slow in moving the crops to the markets in Honolulu.

In 1965 the State Legislature passed Act 4 which allowed income from homestead lands to be used for educational programs for pupils from the homesteads. The funds cannot be used for Hawaiian children other than those from homesteads. Act 4 also allows the commission to grant loans to allow qualified Hawaiians to purchase houses anywhere in the community.

As of June 30, 1989, more than 5,778 homestead leases have been awarded statewide for either residential, farm, or ranch homesteads.

The seven homestead areas on the island of Hawai'i have 1,017 residential lots and 530 farms and ranches with a total of 1,547.

On Maui the three homestead tracts have 492 residences.

There are five homestead tracts on Moloka'i, which include 319 residences and 476 farms and ranches for a total of 795.

There are 2,365 residential lots and 64 farms on O'ahu's five homestead areas.

The two homesteads on Kaua'i have 399 residences and 48 farms or ranches for a total of 447.

The statewide summary for homestead awards is 4,592 residences, 1,095 farms, and 93 ranches. The grand total is 5,778 homestead leases.

There were 18,766 applicants on the waiting list for homestead leases as of June 30, 1989. About 60 percent of these have applied for residential lands and nearly half want to reside on Oʻahu.

(See the latest annual report of the Department of Hawaiian Home Lands for more information.)

■ ʻĀpuka ʻĀina or Adverse Possession

A great many of the Hawaiian people became landless by failing to sign the proper documents to claim ownership or by selling, abandoning or losing the property through non-payment of taxes. This was the plight of many planters who had received private ownership through the Māhele to the lands on which they had long lived. As time passed many of these people became disheartened to realize that they were landless.

Some people, who had a deed to their property but were not living on or cultivating it, found others doing so.

This was a process known as quiet title action or adverse possession. It has been a legal way to gain ownership of land since 1870. If the "possessor" occupied the land in a continuous, open, "hostile" and "notorious" fashion for ten years the property could become his.

The "hostile" and "notorious" test is for the person to fence the land, allow no one else to occupy it and claim it as his alone. This is ʻāpuka ʻāina, a basically fraudulent (though technically legal) method of gaining ownership of another's land.

The purpose of adverse possession, since 1870, was to allow people to claim and make use of land that was lying fallow. The supposition was that there were no heirs or that no one cared for the land enough to develop it. A defense of adverse possession is that it is a means of clearing title to land when the ownership was in dispute.

To gain title through this process, a claim to the property must be published in the legal notice column of a newspaper. However, it is well known that these notices often go unread.

In 1973 the legislature changed the adverse possession law from 10 years to 20 years before the "possessor" could seek title. The 1978 Constitutional Convention drafted an amendment to limit adverse possession to claims on land up to five acres.

There is no record of the number of acres of land that the Hawaiian people have lost through ʻāpuka ʻāina. Nor is it known how many of the 30,000 acres of kuleana lands granted them in the Māhele are still owned by their descendants. Over forty years ago it was estimated that but six per cent of the original kuleana lands were owned by Hawaiians.

■ Charitable Trusts Funded by the Aliʻi

The ruling family received income from the Crown Lands which could not be sold. Other aliʻi families retained at least a part of the lands granted them by the Māhele and placed these in charitable land trusts for the benefit of their people. This, in a sense, caused their subjects to realize that they had rights in these bequests of land and that they were no longer impoverished.

King William Charles Lunalilo (1873-74) was granted considerable land in the Māhele. In addition to the ahupuaʻa of Kaʻalaea and Lāʻie on windward Oʻahu, he received a choice tract in Honolulu. This began at the top of Maunalani Heights, extended down through all of Kaimukī, part of Kapahulu and Waiʻalaeiki and included Diamond Head and Black Point. This grant of 2,200 acres was valued in 1850 at $2,315. (Sales Builder, July 1939.)

In his will Lunalilo instructed his trustees to sell land to build Lunalilo Home. They sold the district of Kaimuki to the government as unimproved property for $30,000. Most of his lands were sold after his death at the prevailing prices for those days.

Lunalilo asked his trustees to construct and maintain a home "for the use and accomodation of poor, destitute and infirm people of Hawaiian blood or extraction, giving preference to old people; . . ."

The Lunalilo Home was opened in 1883 on or near the site now occupied by Roosevelt High School. It could house 50 men and women and it provided quarters for the necessary attendants. After nearly 50 years this home was abandoned for a new home in the Koko Head area, built in 1927. This structure accommodates about the same number of persons. The land occupied by the first home and gardens was sold for residential lots.

Princess Ruth Keʻelikōlani, who died May 15, 1883, received land through the Māhele, and had inherited a considerable number of the Kamehameha family lands as a half-sister to Kamehameha IV and V and Victoria Kamāmalu. Ruth willed over a third of a million acres of these lands to her cousin Bernice Pauahi Bishop. They form a large part of the Bishop Estate today.

ʻĀinahau (hau tree land), in the heart of Waikīkī belonged to Princess Ruth. She gave 10 acres of land to her god-child the Princess Kaʻiulani at the time of her baptism in 1875.

Kaʻiulani's father, the Honorable A.S. Cleghorn, built a beautiful home and, with the aid of his wife, the Princess Likelike, landscaped the area into lush, tropical gardens.

Likelike died in 1887 and Kaʻiulani in 1899. In his will before his died in 1910, Mr. Cleghorn directed his trustees to offer to the government the beautiful home and gardens for a public park to be called Kaʻiulani Park. The Territorial Legislature rejected the offer saying the upkeep would be too expensive. ʻĀinahau was later subdivided into lots and sold.

Princess Bernice Pauahi Bishop inherited lands from her parents, Konia and Pākī, and from her Aunt ʻAkāhi which totaled some 25,000 acres. The largest part of her estate came from her cousin, Princess Ruth, a total of some 353,000 acres. After Pauahi's death in 1884 the Trustees began to make plans for The Kamehameha Schools for Hawaiian boys and girls. This story was told in detail by Dr. Frank E. Midkiff in his lecture "The Kamehameha Schools and the Bishop Estate" printed in *Some Aspects of Hawaiian Life and Environment,* 1971.

King Kamehameha IV and **Queen Emma** personally solicited funds from Honolulu citizens to build a hospital. The corner stone was laid in July, 1860 and the hospital named Queen's to honor Emma. After her death in 1885 her lands, some 13,000 acres, were placed in trust for the continued but partial support of this facility, now known as the Queen's Medical Center.

King Kalākaua and **Queen Kapiʻolani** were deeply moved at the high death and low birth rate among the Hawaiian people. The Queen headed a society called "Hooulu a Hoola Lahui" which was organized to "increase and preserve the nation," as the name translates.

The Queen and her aides collected $8,000 from the people to found the Kapiʻolani Maternity Home. On June 14, 1890 the Queen gave a large residence and the land at Beretania and Makiki to house the original Home. She had inherited this property from her sister, the Princess Kekaulike, mother of the Princes David Kawānanakoa and Jonah Kūhiō Kalanianaʻole.

The Queen willed a lifetime interest in her personal lands to her nephews but upon their passing the property reverted to the maternity home.

In 1929 the hospital moved to a three-story, 50 bed facility on Punahou Street called the Kapiolani Maternity and Gynecological Hospital. It has now combined with the Kauikeaolani Children's Hospital and is known as the Kapiolani Children's Medical Center.

Liliʻuokalani, the only ruling queen of Hawaiʻi, died November 11, 1917. Her will reads, in part, "From and after the death of the Grantor, all of the property of the trust estate, both principal and income, . . . shall be used by the Trustees for the benefit of orphan and other destitute children . . . in the Hawaiian Islands, the preference to be given to Hawaiian children of pure or part aboriginal blood."

The estate consisted of over 9,000 acres including the valuable Waikīkī property called Hamohamo.

The Honolulu offices and counseling rooms of the Queen Liliʻuokalani Children's Center are at 1300 Hālona Street. There are also rural Oʻahu and neighbor island centers.

■ **Understandings and Appreciations**

Explain what you think is meant by the statement: The land does not belong to you, you belong to the land.

Most of the 4,000 entries in the revised edition of *Place Names of Hawaii* are in Hawaiian. Many people take pleasure in learning the meanings and the stories concerning place names that are near their homes and places of work. The following example shows that it is not always possible to translate place names fully without learning their story.

Ko'olau (windward) and *Poko* (short) is translated "short Ko'olau" and *Ko'olau Loa,* "long Ko'olau." These district names actually refer to the Makahiki gods, *akua loa* which made a circuit of O'ahu traveling to the right and *akua poko* which formed a procession traveling to the left from Kalaeoka'ō'io. The two god-images met at Kalaeoka'ō'io (cape of the bonefish) between Kualoa and Ka'a'awa. This is the dividing line between the districts which were named for the short god and the long god. One district is not appreciably longer, or shorter, than the other. (Kamakau, 1964, p. 20.)

In his book "The Lands of Hawaii" Thomas Creighton has written on "The Worth of Hawaii's Lands" as a - Source of Pleasure, Source of Sustenance, Source of Shelter, Source of Wealth, Source of Power. An interesting exercise is to think about these "sources" and suggest answers or examples for each. Then read what author Creighton has written. Does it require personal ownership of land to realize these "sources?"

The motto of the Kingdom and now the State of Hawai'i is deeply rooted in love for the land. See Unit 4.

■ **Student Activities**

1. Kōlea, the plover, is a bird that gets fat feeding in Hawai'i, then goes elsewhere to lay its eggs. Why are some transient businessmen called kōlea?

2. How did the early Hawaiians describe the boundaries of a tract of land? What is the work of a modern surveyor? How does he determine land boundaries? (By the 1880s Hawai'i's survey department was as advanced as any in the world.)

3. Read the papers to keep in touch with the progress being made by residential leaseholders in being allowed to buy the property that they are now leasing from the larger land holders.

4. Make a list of superstitions known to you and your family. Do you observe any of them today?

5. Read about land in Samoa and Tonga where by law the native people own all of the land.

Could the Hawaiian government have restricted land ownership to the Hawaiian people only at the time of the Māhele?

6. Attempt to learn all you can about the land on which you and your family now lives. Name the *ahupua'a* and learn who received it in the Māhele. Does the street have a Hawaiian name? If so, what is its meaning and the *mo'olelo* (story) about it. What was the use of the land before it became residential? If your family is in possession of the land deed, study it for additional land names and earlier owners.

Most of the above can be researched for the school in which the students are in attendance.

■ **Audio-Visual Aids**

1. Walk or drive to a place where the mountains and the descending streams and ridges are visible. In many cases the extent of an *ahupua'a* can be seen. This is true on the green, windward side of the larger islands. Refer to Bailey, 1929, for maps naming the *moku* and *ahupua'a.*

2. Study "The Ahupua'a" a poster in color, 26x37 inches, picturing an *ahupua'a* in pre-Cook times. Quadrangles with numbers and a 62 page booklet help one in locating and learning about the 41 plants and 30 cultural activities pictured. See Reading List under Kamehameha Schools.

3. Listen to songs which express the Hawaiian love of the land—*aloha 'āina.* Often heard today is *Kaulana Nā Pua,* "Famous are the Flowers," written in 1893. It was also called *Mele 'Ai Pōhaku,* the stone-eating song and *Mele Aloha 'Āina,* the Patriots' Song. A number of recent compositions express love for the island of Kaho'olawe.

4. Learn to recognize the constellation called the Pleiades or Makali'i. It announced the beginning of the Makahiki. The astronomers at the Bishop Museum Planetarium (Kilolani) have informed us that this constellation will be visible on the eastern horizon beginning at 8:20 p.m. on November 1. We may date the beginning of our present-day Makahiki as of November 1 this year and at least during the decade of the 1980s. The change in the position of the stars and constellations in relation to the earth is so slow that we will not notice it during this ten year period.

■ **Vocabulary**

Define:

Nohona, lōkahi, kuleana, hale ʻauhau.

Land terms - fee simple and leased lands.

Who are these little people? Menehune, ʻeʻepa and kaʻaimaiʻa (Beckwith, 1970, pp. 321-22).

■ **Current Happenings or Trends of Significance to this Unit**

Beginning August 20, 1981, real property taxes are no longer collected by the state but by the county governments. Land and property values are assessed by the counties also. Assessment for tax purposes was formerly 70 percent of the market value. Now, however, the tax rate is fixed by the county councils.

According to the *State of Hawaii Data Book* for 1989, the resident population for the State of Hawaiʻi as of July 1, 1988 was:

Civilian	971,500
Military dependents	69,900
Armed Forces	56,800
Total	1,098,200

The assessor's gross valuation of real property as of January 1, 1989, for all Hawaiʻi was:

Land	42,778.9 billion
Improvements	34,147.8 billion
Total	76,926.7 billion

■ **Reading List**

Adler, Jacob. *Claus Spreckles: The Sugar King in Hawaii.* Honolulu: University of Hawaii Press, 1966.

Amundson, Ronald. *The Issue of Hawaiian Native Claims: A Sourcebook.* Hilo: Big Island Media Advisory Council, 1980.

Anderson, Robert N., et al. *Kauai.* Socio-economic profile. Departmental Paper No. 35. Honolulu: Hawaii Agricultural Experiment Station, May 1975.

———. *Molokai Issues and Options.* Honolulu: State Department of Business and Economic Development, 1983.

Apple, Russell A., and Peg Apple. *Land, Liliʻuokalani and Annexation.* Honolulu: Topgallant Publishing Company, 1979.

Armstrong, R. Warwick, ed. *Atlas of Hawaii.* 2nd ed. Developed and compiled by the Department of Geography, University of Hawaii. Honolulu: University Press of Hawaii, 1983.

Bailey, Charles T. *Indices of Awards.* Made by The Board of Commissioners to Quiet Land Titles in the Hawaiian Islands. Honolulu: Star-Bulletin Press, 1929.

Brennan, Joseph. *The Parker Ranch of Hawaiʻi.* The saga of a ranch and a dynasty. New York: John Day, 1974.

Callies, David L. *Regulating Paradise.* Land use controls in Hawaii. Honolulu: University of Hawaii Press, 1984.

Chinen, Jon J. *The Great Mahele.* Hawaii's land division of 1848. Honolulu: University of Hawaii Press, 1958.

———. *Original Land Titles in Hawaii.* Privately printed, 1961.

Clark, John R.K. *Beaches of the Big Island,* 1985. *Beaches of Kauaʻi and Niʻihau,* 1990. *Beaches of Maui County,* 1989 (rev. ed.). *The Beaches of Oʻahu,* 1977. Honolulu: University of Hawaii Press.

Cooke, George P. *Moolelo O Molokai.* A ranch story of Molokai. Honolulu: Honolulu Star-Bulletin, 1949.

Cooke, Sophie J. *Sincerely Sophie.* Honolulu: Tongg Publishing Company, 1964. (Concerns her experiences on Molokaʻi, rural Oʻahu and Honolulu.)

Creighton, Thomas H. *The Lands of Hawaii.* Their use and misuse. Honolulu: University Press of Hawaii, 1978.

Daws, Alan G. *Shoal of Time.* Honolulu: University Press of Hawaii, 1975.

Devaney, Dennis M. *Kaneʻohe: A History of Change.* 1976. Honolulu: Bess Press, 1982 (rev. ed.). Kaneʻohe's history over the last 200 years.

Emory, Kenneth P. *The Island of Lanai.* A survey of native culture. Honolulu: Bishop Museum Bulletin No. 12, 1969 (reprint).

Fuchs, Lawrence H. *Hawaii Pono: A Social History.* New York: Harcourt Brace Jovanovich, 1961.

Gay, Lawrence K. *True Stories of the Island of Lanai.* Honolulu: The Mission Press, 1965.

Goldman, Irving. *Ancient Polynesian Society.* Chicago: University of Chicago Press, 1970.

Handy, E.S.C. *Cultural Revolution in Hawaii.* Honolulu: American Council, Institute of Pacific Relations, 1931.

Hobbs, Jean. *Hawaii: A Pageant of the Soil.* Stanford, CA: Stanford University Press, 1935.

Horowitz, Robert H., and Norman Meller. *Land and Politics in Hawaii.* East Lansing, MI: Bureau of Social and Political Research, Michigan State University, 1963.

Joesting, Edward. *Kauai: The Separate Kingdom.* Honolulu: University of Hawaii Press, 1984.

Kamakau, Samuel M. *Ka Poʻe Kahiko.* The people of old. Honolulu: Bishop Museum Special Publication No. 51, 1964.

———. *The Works of the People of Old.* Honolulu: Bishop Museum Special Publication No. 61, 1976.

Kamehameha Schools, Extension Education Division, Hawaiian Studies Institute. *The Ahupuaʻa.* Honolulu: Kamehameha Schools Press, 1979. (A kit consisting of a color poster picturing an ideal *ahupuaʻa* in pre-Cook days, quadrangles that help identify life pictured in the valley, and a 62-page booklet.)

Kirtley, Bacil P. *A Motif Index of Traditional Polynesian Narratives.* Honolulu: University Press of Hawaii, 1971.

MacDonald, Gordon A., and Will Kyselka. *Anatomy of an Island.* A geological history of Oahu. Honolulu: Bishop Museum Special Publication No. 55, 1967.

Malo, David. *Hawaiian Antiquities.* 1898. Honolulu: Bishop Museum Special Publication No. 2, 1976.

Midkiff, Frank E. "The Kamehameha Schools and the Bishop Estate." In *Aspects of Hawaiian Life and Environment.* Commentaries on significant Hawaiian topics by fifteen recognized authorities. 2nd ed. Honolulu: Kamehameha Schools Press, 1971.

Nordyke, Eleanor C. *The Peopling of Hawaii.* Honolulu: University Press of Hawaii for the East-West Center Population Institute, 1977.

Parker, Linda S. *Native American Estate.* The struggle over Indian and Hawaiian lands. Honolulu: University of Hawaii Press, 1989.

Pukui, Mary K., Samuel H. Elbert, and Esther T. Mookini. *Place Names of Hawaii.* Revised and expanded edition. Honolulu: University Press of Hawaii, 1974. (Paperback edition 1976; *Pocket Place Names of Hawaii, 1989.*)

Pukui, Mary K., E.W. Haertig, M.D., and Catherine A. Lee. *Nana I Ke Kumu II: Look to the Source.* Vol. I, 1972; Vol. II, 1979. Honolulu: Hui Hanai.

Simonds, William A. *Kamaaina: A Century in Hawaii.* The one hundredth anniversary of American Factors, Ltd. [Honolulu?]: Privately printed, 1949.

Simpich, Frederick, Jr. *Dynasty in the Pacific.* The story of Amfac, Inc. New York: McGraw-Hill Book Company, 1974.

Speakman, Cummins E. *Mowee.* An informal history of the Hawaiian island (Maui). Salem, MA: Peabody Museum of Salem, 1978.

Sterling, Elspeth P., and Catherine C. Summers. *Sites of Oahu.* Honolulu: Department of Anthropology, Bishop Museum, 1978.

Taylor, Frank J., Earl M. Welty, and David W. Eyre. *From Land and Sea.* The story of Castle and Cooke of Hawaii. San Francisco: Chronicle Books, 1976.

Wise, John H. "The History of Land Ownership in Hawaii." In *Ancient Hawaiian Civilization.* A series of lectures delivered at the Kamehameha Schools by E.S.C. Handy [and others]. 1933. Rutland, VT and Japan: C.E. Tuttle, 1965 (rev. ed.).

Wist, Benjamin O. *A Century of Public Education in Hawaii. (1840-1940).* Honolulu: Hawaii Educational Review, 1940.

UNIT 18:
Warfare
and
Weapons

WARFARE AND WEAPONS

After the Polynesian settlers came to Hawai'i they were able to live peacefully for many generations in their spacious, fertile islands. Lands were in abundance for gardens, house sites, play fields, and temples. None needed to covet his neighbors' riches.

According to tradition, families governed themselves for 53 generations, during which time no man ... "was made chief over another. Kapawa was the first to be set up as a ruling chief. This was at Waialua, O'ahu; and from then on, the group of Hawaiian Islands became established as chief-ruled kingdoms ..." (Kamakau, 1964, p. 3.)

As the years passed the population grew, the choice lands were settled and the chiefs began to look with envy and greed upon their neighbors' possessions. Aggressive rulers fought to control more land and thus increase their wealth and prestige. Those attacked had to defend themselves. Some chiefs engaged in war as an exciting diversion from the otherwise routine life; others fought to avenge real or imaginary wrongs.

Priests became powerful and ordered larger and larger temples built to propitiate their gods and increase the prestige of their chiefs. The priests and chiefs promulgated laws with ever sterner demands, and eventually added human bodies to the sacrifices in the *heiau luakini*.

In the 13th century Kalaunuiohua became the first chief to attempt to unite the islands by force. Not content as the ruler of the island of Hawai'i, he sailed with his warriors and conquered Maui, Moloka'i and O'ahu. Kūkona, king of Kaua'i, destroyed his armies and his dream. (Fornander II, 1969, pp. 67-69.) Other ambitious chiefs continued to bring upon the people destruction of property, famine and death from frequent warfare, which a historian called ... often the object of highest ambition, the road to most envied distinction, and the source of most ardent delight.

Sheldon Dibble, in his *History of the Sandwich Islands*, 1843, p. 40, wrote:

Far back as memory goes, war was a principal occupation of both chiefs and people.

It does not appear that many of their wars were very destructive of human life. The evil of bloodshed in many cases did not appear so great as the destruction of food by the conquering party and the subsequent miseries of famine.

Handy, in the *Native Planter*, p. 17, wrote:

Actually the planters enjoyed precedence over the warrior, as is evidenced by the fact that a boy child, when he entered the company of men, was consecrated by ritual in honor of Lono, god of rain and agriculture. There was no rite dedicating a boy to Kū, the god of war.

Some great chiefs ruled with wisdom and foresight and provided periods of peace with the opportunity for their subjects to develop, practice and enjoy their skills in agriculture, fishing, and handcrafts. Lonoikamakahiki, grandson of 'Umi, is credited with introducing "... competitive annual games as a substitute for warfare." (Feher, 1969, p. 132)

Kamehameha, cognizant of the long history of war and its attendant evils, led his warriors in the final series of battles which ended Hawaiian warfare, except for one brief skirmish (at Kuamo'o in Kona) shortly after his death. Whether Kamehameha fought with the noble purpose of stamping out war or to satisfy his ambitions to be the first ruler of all Hawai'i, we may never know.

Men of the chiefly class were taught the tactics of war from boyhood. In battle the chiefs (ali'i) occupied the command positions; the citizens were the soldiers (koa). The chiefs in consultation with their counselors (kalaimoku) and priests (kāhuna) planned the strategy of the battles. Selected young men resided in the court of the ruling chief or in the households of the district chiefs to be trained as professional soldiers. Vigorous games, during which they wrestled, boxed, raced, and threw spears, were an important part of their instruction. The games and sham battles provided exercise in military tactics as well as entertainment for the members of the chief's court and his guests.

The working men trained themselves through sports and battle practice. They made their own weapons and kept them in their houses ready for immediate use. All able-bodied men were expected to be ready to fight at the call of their chief.

Women in general were not trained to fight but certain especially dedicated ones known as *koa wāhine* (brave women) or *wāhine kaua* (battle women) were taught by the men. They accompanied the warriors to the scene of battle. If the women had to fight they fought. When a woman saw that her husband was in real danger she would rush into the conflict and help him fight. Women were known to have taken the places of their husbands who had been killed.

Chiefesses traditionally accompanied their husbands to the scene of battle but remained some distance from the conflict. An account, perpetuated in chant and dance, tells of the chiefess Manono and her chiefly husband Kekuaokalani dying together in the battle of Kuamo'o, Kona, as they protested the overthrow of the *kapu*. (Kuykendall, 1938, p. 69.)

■ **Dress for Battle**

A large army in battle formation was truly a colorful and awesome spectacle. The king or highest chief, occupying the central command position, wore a full-length feather cloak (*'ahu'ula*), usually of yellow, red, and black feathers arranged in his own distinctive pattern. His crested helmet (*mahiole*) of firm basketry was covered with feathers; his loin cloth (*malo*) was of fine *kapa* and he often wore his neck lei of braided human hair with a whale-tooth pendant (*lei niho palaoa*). Lesser chiefs, surrounded by their troops in position along the flanks, wore shoulder capes (*kīpuka*) and were usually without helmets.

Captain Charles Clerke of the James Cook expedition gave his opinion of the protection that a chief might receive when wearing his helmet and cloak.

Their first onset [in battle] is always made by a Volley of Stones, now the Basket work of the Cap is so strong and compact as to render the head

perfectly secure from any assault of this sort, and the Cloak being loose about the body in a great measure destroys the force of any stone that may take place there . . . even when they come near enough to attack with their Spears these cloaks . . . must still be of service as they have not the true mark of a Man's body with those things about it, and many a good thrust must be foiled by them which might otherwise contribute something to the fate of the day. (Beaglehole, pp. 594-95)

Several rectangular feather-covered mats collected by the Cook expedition are now believed to have been worn by chiefs in battle. They could be tied to the body by the loops and lacings along their ends. "It is possible that they served as protective garments worn across the chest or stomach with the feather cloaks." (Kaeppler, 1978, pp. 59-60)

Cook's officers wrote nothing about these "protective garments" but they did record information about the warriors protecting their bodies during conflict by tying on coarse mats. (Mitchell, 1978, pp. 68-69)

The two garments or feathered aprons returned from Europe to Bishop Museum in 1978 for the Artificial Curiosities exhibit were: 21 inches long and one-third as wide, and 16 inches in length and one-half as wide.

The priests (*kāhuna*) wore robes and turbans (*kā'ei po'o*) of white *kapa*. One would carry his chief's feather-covered war god (*Kūkā'ilimoku*) elevated on a staff, another might carry a stalk of green ti leaves. Ti, a symbol of divine power and a charm against evil spirits, was also used as a flag of truce. (Degener, 1930, p. 97)

Warriors who hurled sling stones wore loin cloths (*malo*) which provided a waist-band over which they could slip their fiber sling and the tie-cords of a net-bag of sling stones. The net-bag of stones could be tied to the waist band on the right and thrown across the chest and over the left shoulder while running.

Some warriors went into battle with only a coating of coconut oil, since in hand-to-hand encounters an enemy could take advantage of an opponent by grasping him by the waistband of his loin cloth. (Degener, 1930, p. 140)

Captain Cook was told that the warriors wore sturdy mats about their bodies in battle. He and his officers saw these in use in the conflicts which resulted in Cook's death. Captain Clerke wrote, "The inferior people upon these occasions [war], to answer the purposes of these Cloaks wear mats which are just as good in the article of defense but vastly more awkward and cumbersome . . ." (Beaglehole, p. 595)

No specimens of the warriors' mats are known today, but they seem to have been plaited from *lau hala* and provided with loops and ties by which they could be secured to the body.

Just before Captain Cook was killed, surgeon's mate David Samwell wrote that the Hawaiians were arming in great numbers.

> . . . with spears, daggers, clubs and stones, and putting on their coarse thick matts which they use as armour to defend themselves from stones and the weapons used at these islands. (Beaglehole, p. 535)

■ War Gods

Kamehameha inherited Kūkaʻilimoku (Kū - snatcher of the land), the feathered god of the temples of Kū, from his uncle, Kalaniʻōpuʻu. For many generations it had been the war god of the line of Keawe kings of the island of Hawaiʻi. According to the traditions of the priesthood of Paʻao (a priest from Tahiti in the early times), sacrificial temples *(luakini)* were built for this image, which was one of the manifestations of the great god Kū. Within them a shelter house *(hale malu)* was built with posts of ʻōhiʻa wood (an earthly form of Kū) for the god Kūkaʻilimoku. Human sacrifices were performed here before an army ventured on any war-like endeavors. Kūkaʻilimoku was carried into battle by the high priest where the image was said to have uttered cries which could be heard above the din of the conflict.

The feathered Kūkaʻilimoku on display in Bishop Museum, Honolulu, is believed to have belonged to Kamehameha and the Keawe kings. It is formed from a framework of basketry 27 inches high and covered with an *olonā* net to which the red *ʻiʻiwi* feathers are attached. Above the large pearl-shell eyes are eyebrows of black feathers. The open mouth is lined with 94 eye-teeth of dogs. The crest of the helmet and the collar at the base of the neck are of yellow feathers, also attached to the netting.

Kamehameha, after uniting the islands, converted the lands of his war god Kūkaʻilimoku into places of refuge *(puʻuhonua)* so that all who entered them would be freed from whatever crime they had committed. This may have been in grati-

tude for the god's help. In a similar dual fashion, the great god Kū was the god of war and also of healing.

Other Kū gods were of wood, draped in *kapa* during the ceremonies in which they were involved, and with feathers attached to their heads. When the images were consulted concerning plans for warfare, it is written, the feathers stood up, whirled about, or flew from the god to the inquiring person as a sign that he would have success in the coming venture. (Beckwith, 1970, p. 28; Kamakau, 1961, p. 148.) On display in Bishop Museum is a wooden temple image over six tall labeled "Kūkaʻilimoku."

■ Weapons

Warriors made their weapons of wood, stone, and shark teeth and kept them in excellent condition for immediate use. Hawaiian warriors preferred the dense, heavy *kauila* wood spears and daggers as their principal weapons. Celebrated fighters named their favorite weapons and accredited them with magic powers. Palila, a soldier from Alanapo, Kauaʻi, slew the giant warrior Olomana of Koʻolau Poko, Oʻahu, with his war club named Huliāmahi (Huliāmahi means "strong"). (Fornander, 1918-19, Vol. V, p. 146)

The stone adze *(koʻi)* was the chief cutting tool of the craftsman. He selected adzes of varying sizes to fell trees and saplings and fashion them into spears and other weapons of wood. He used stone polishers *(pōhaku ʻānai)* in varying degrees of coarseness to smooth the wood. Polishers were of coarse lava, pumice, coral limestone, the sandpaper-like skin of sharks and rays, and finally the smooth, shiny surface of fine-grained basalt. Upon completion and during the life of the weapon the warrior rubbed *kukui* oil on the surface of the wood to polish and protect it.

Spears: *Pololū* were hardwood spears, 9 to 18 feet long, with smooth, blade-like points and knobs or grips at the base. The spear shaft was from 1.5 to 2 inches thick. A warrior held the *pololū* firmly against his right side, charged, and thrust the blade into his opponent or used it to trip him. This maneuver opened the ranks in the enemy column and caused the warriors to scatter. In rough terraine the soldier used this spear in vaulting *(kūpololū)* over streams or lava crevices.

Ihe: *Ihe* were the highly popular short spears, 6 to 8 feet long, with barbed points *(ihe laumeki)* or without barbs but tipped with a round or blade point. The warriors hurled these weapons at times with an underhand throw, although sometimes they held them firmly with the point forward and charged the enemy. In battle practice and in games the men threw the spears (ʻōʻō ihe) into the soft tissues of upright banana stalks. In battle, soldiers used their *ihe* to ward off spears thrown at them, or they caught the spears, when possible, and hurled them back at their opponents. A smooth-tipped spear could be pulled more readily from the body of a fallen warrior and used again than could one with rows of barbs pointing backward.

The use of spears is told in this eye-witness account of a battle in which two chiefs were attacking Kamehameha's forces near Panaʻewa, Hawaiʻi:

> The *pololu* and *ihe* spears rained down like bath-water; the blood flowed like water and soaked into the dry earth of that hill. The spears were entangled like a rainbow arched on both sides. In the thick of the fight between the two sides, Kahuʻena and Kahahawai showed their skill in handling and warding off *pololu* and *ihe* spears from descending upon their forces. As they brushed aside the weapons descending upon them from all sides, their own weapons waved in the air like the tail feathers of the bosun [sic] bird, waving in the wind. (Kamakau, 1961, p. 125)

Another account shows how a lone warrior won the battle for his entire army:

> Kekūhaupiʻo stepped out alone between the assembled armies of Hawaiʻi and Maui and challenged the entire Maui army. The Maui warriors hurled at him their javelins, long spears "and every kind of pain inflicting implement . . ." He was not hit. Since Maui was now without weapons, they lost the battle. (Fornander, Vol. V, p. 454)

Two useful combinations of weapons and tools were an *ihe* with notches at the base which allowed it to be used as a carrying pole (ʻauamo) and an *ihe* with a blade which converted the base into a farmer's digging stick (ʻōʻō). These allowed the worker to defend himself should he be attacked while engaged in his peaceful pursuits.

Daggers: *Pāhoa*, weapons not found elsewhere in Polynesia, were preferred by Hawaiian warriors. They were able to stab more quickly with a dagger than to swing and strike with a club. Most of the daggers were made from a single piece of hardwood, pointed at one end and pierced near the

middle for the insertion of a wrist-cord which prevented the warrior from dropping his weapon in combat. Cords were braided from *olonā* or sennit (ʻaha). Buck divides pāhoa into five types: (Buck, 1964, pp. 424-38)

1. Truncheon daggers resembled the sharpened end of a spear and averaged two to three feet long.
2. Bludgeon daggers, pointed at one end and club-like at the other, were effective in piercing or clubbing a victim.
3. Long-bladed daggers, one to three feet long, bore double-edged blades which tapered to a sharp point.
4. Curved-bladed daggers, known from three Kauaʻi island specimens, are one to two feet long. A warrior held the thick shaft and pierced with the curved blade or struck with the knobbed end.
5. Shark-tooth daggers, with flattened club-like heads, were edged with shark teeth. The handle

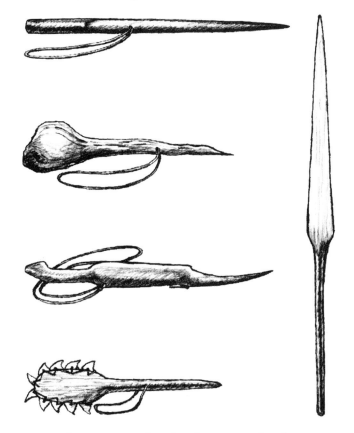

Pāhoa: The warrior preferred a dagger as a hand weapon realizing that it was quicker to stab with a single stroke than to lift and strike with a club. Daggers were pointed at one end, some at both ends and others were both a dagger and a sharktooth club.

ended in a sharp point below the wrist cord. Buck describes one with 10 shark teeth and another with 23 teeth lashed around the edge.

Other daggers were made from the beaks of swordfish. Armorers working at the forges on ships visiting Hawai'i in the early days made many iron daggers for use in the islands.

Captain Cook "was stabbed in the back with a pāhoa; a spear was at the same time driven through his body; he fell into the water, and spoke no more." (Ellis, 1917, p. 99) Captain Nathaniel Portlock, who accompanied Cook, refused to make daggers on a later visit to Hawai'i in his own vessel. He gave as his reason ". . . with one of the daggers given by us to the natives of Owhyhee my much lamented Commander Captain Cook was killed." (Portlock, 1789, p. 77)

Clubs: Clubs, called *newa* or *lā'au pālau,* were crude and undecorated in comparison to the attractive, decorated clubs made by other Pacific Islanders. The known clubs may be divided into smooth, rough, and stone-headed forms. (Buck, 1957, pp. 438-443)

1. Smooth-headed clubs vary from 10 to 18 inches in length and are of hard wood polished smooth. They resemble somewhat the *hohoa* or round *kapa* beater, also used as a club. Whale bone was made into smooth, baton-like clubs.

2. Rough-headed clubs were fashioned from natural root or limb enlargements. The branch from which the knot or root grew was smoothed to form the handle.

3. Stone-headed clubs were among the few weapons made from more than one piece of material. A head of basaltic lava, 3½ to 9 inches long, was grooved with longitudinal furrows to hold the sennit cord which lashed it to the tip of a wooden handle.

Adzes, which had sharp stone blades lashed to wooden hafts *(ko'i pāhoa),* were also effective club-like weapons and were used frequently in hand-to-hand fighting.

Shark-Tooth Weapons: The serrated edge of a shark tooth provided one of the sharpest cutting tools available in this culture without metal. One or two teeth pegged or lashed to a wooden handle served as a tool for carving wood or cutting flesh for food or bait. Weapons contained from one to 30 shark teeth firmly fastened to handles of wood, bone, or, rarely, fiber. One, two or three holes

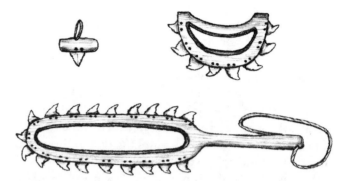

Shark-tooth Weapons: Shark teeth were pegged or lashed to wooden handles to form effective weapons. The larger ones are held in the hand, the cord loop on the smaller one slips over the middle finger.

were made in the base of the tooth and matching holes in the handles by pump drills or bone awls. Wooden pegs and strong *olonā* cords held the teeth firmly to the handles.

A shark-tooth weapon was highly effective in cutting the throat of an enemy or disemboweling him. Kamakau described the use of the *leiomano,* a single-tooth weapon, at the battle of Moku'ōhai, Kona, in 1782, during which Kamehameha I gained his first important victory with the death of his cousin and rival, the young ruler Kīwala'ō who was stunned from a sling stone. ". . . seeing Kīwala'ō lying prostrate, Ke'eaumoku crawled to him with his sharks-tooth weapon *(leiomano)* in his hand and cut his throat with it so that he died." (Kamakau, 1961, p. 121)

Buck, after a careful study of known specimens, divided shark-tooth implements into four main classes with a total of 16 types. He classified them according to the number of teeth and the method of their attachment to handles of various shapes and materials. (Buck, 1964, pp. 443-55)

■ **Tripping Weapons and Hand Clubs:** Pīkoi or tripping weapons were not used elsewhere in Polynesia. In Hawai'i a warrior ran towards his opponent whirling a weight of stone or wood by the long *olonā* cord to which it was attached. As he drew close enough for contact, he whirled the weight so that it and the rope wrapped around his enemy's legs or body. A firm jerk on the rope would throw him to the ground where he could be dispatched with a dagger, club, or shark-tooth weapon.

Wooden pīkoi in Bishop Museum are knobbed weapons with or without handles and bearing cords 18 to 42 feet long. Stone pīkoi are similar in

Pikoi: The whirling weight and its cord were wrapped around the legs of an enemy warrior to trip him.

Stone Hand Club: A warrior added weight to his blows by holding this club in his clenched fist.

Sling and Stone: Ovoid stones were hurled with great accuracy and force into the enemy ranks with the use of a fiber sling.

shape to those made of wood. They weigh from three to four and a half pounds. (Buck, 1964, pp. 455-59)

Stone hand clubs were cylindrical stones constricted in the center for ease in holding in the clenched fist. The flaring ends of these five-inch-long stones protruded on both sides beyond the palm of the hand and added weight to the blows that a warrior delivered to an opponent.

Slings and Sling Stones: A fiber sling (ma‘a) was used to hurl ovoid stones (‘alā a ka ma‘a or pōhaku ‘alā). The slings were plaited or braided from sennit (‘aha), hau bark (‘ili hau), fibers from the aerial roots of the hala (ule hala), or from human hair (lauoho). A cord, a yard or more long, was attached to each side of the pouch (‘eke‘eke ma‘a) of the sling.

Unfortunately, no slings made in pre-European times are known to exist in the collections today.

The warrior held the ends of the cords in his hand, whirled the sling above his head, and released one cord to free and hurl the stone to the desired mark.

Fornander recorded these accounts of the use of the sling which were told to him by Hawaiian informants:

Kemamo, a Kaua‘i warrior, in a contest hurled a sling stone more than six miles. (Fornander, 1918-19, Vol. V, page 224)

Kekūhaupi‘o stepped out in front of the Hawai‘i army as it faced the enemy forces of Maui. He challenged Maui's sling shot expert ‘Oulu to a contest which would be decided by the outcome of three stones hurled by ‘Oulu. As they stood 36 feet apart Kekūhaupi‘o raised his foot as ‘Oulu's first stone cut a deep furrow in the earth "and the spot was permeated with heat as if it were a fire." Kekūhaupi‘o quickly asked for aid from the god Lono and offered the second stone to him. He was thus able to dodge this stone. He confused ‘Oulu by an insulting shout of victory in which he claimed that the last stone was his. Again he won. The Hawai‘i army, through Kekūhaupi‘o, was successful that day. (Fornander, 1918-19, Vol. 5, pp. 454-56)

Field Stones: Nounou - the art of fighting with stones. The writers of the Captain Cook journals make a number of references to the use of field stones as weapons. Men paddling out to visit Cook's ships for the first time carried stones in their canoes as their only weapons of defense. (Beaglehole, pp. 264, 1150)

Captain Clerke, noting that stones of various sizes were handy and effective weapons wrote, ". . . and as to their Stones, Nature has furnished them most abundantly in every part of their Country." (Beaglehole, p. 538)

Stones and daggers were the principal weapons used against the English. Officers and men were bruised and knocked down by stones and parties fetching water were attacked by stones which were rolled downhill toward them. (Mitchell, 1978, pp. 66-68)

Strangling Cords: Strangling cords (ka‘ane) were not implements of war, but are included here since they were instruments used in executing law breakers, killing victims for sacrificial offerings and destroying persons at the request of the chiefs. Some forms of offerings required that the victims should not be mangled or bloody. Strangling satisfied this requisite.

Bishop Museum's collection contains nine cords, each of eight-ply olonā plaited in a square braid. The ends of the two- to three-yard-long cords are fixed to small, spindle-shaped wooden or ivory handles which are two to three inches long.

Public executioners (mū) dispatched some of the victims with these strangling cords.

Bows (pana) and arrows (pua pana) were used in the game of rat shooting (pana 'iole) but never against man.

Lua or ku'ialua: Most of the actual fighting was done with weapons, but certain young men selected for their physical prowess and ability to control their tempers were trained in the dangerous form of wrestling called the lua. Experts in this skill served as body guards to the chiefs. They were able to grapple with an opponent and break his limb bones, dislocate his bones at the joints, and inflict severe pain by pressing on nerve centers made known to them in their training. Very few men have knowledge of the lua today.

■ Declaring War

A chief would declare war only after determining that the gods considered conditions favorable. Learning the will of the gods depended to a large extent upon the interpretations revealed by the kahuna nui as he studied cloud formations, translated the meanings of his visions and dreams, and observed the appearance of the entrails of pigs and fowls which had been killed especially for this purpose.

An intelligent, well-informed priest was certainly influenced by his knowledge of the desires and capabilities of his chief and the known strength of the enemy. Ellis wrote ". . . it is probable the answer of the diviners was given with due regard to the previously known views of the king and chiefs." (Ellis, 1917, p. 112)

After the chief had received favorable answers from his kahuna nui, his counselors (kālaimoku), and his warrior-chiefs, a time was set to begin hostilities. If the conflict was to be one of great importance and magnitude, human sacrifices were offered to the gods. In the prayers accompanying the sacrifices the kahuna nui did not pray for the protection of his chiefs and warriors. Rather, he asked that the gods be present at the battle to destroy the power, courage, and strength of the enemy. (Ellis, 1917, p. 111)

The humans to be sacrificed were enemy captives, kapu breakers, kauwā (outcasts), or persons who had not shared in the necessary work and were therefore in disfavor with the chiefs. "The

number offered at one time," wrote Ellis, "varied according to circumstances, two, four, or seven, or ten, or even twenty, we have been informed, have been offered at once." (Ellis, 1917, p. 112) The victims were killed outside the heiau luakini and taken, unclothed, to the sacrificial altar. The bodies, along with those of hogs, which might be offered at the same time, were left on the altar to decay. Only in the heiau luakini or po'okanaka, which were dedicated to the god of war, Kū, were human sacrifices offered. These temples were usually large, prominently located, and housed the wooden and feather war gods. Some were built, or rebuilt, as a part of the necessary preparations for an important war maneuver. The famed kahuna, Kapoukahi, told Kamehameha that if he rebuilt the heiau Pu'ukoholā at Kawaihae he would succeed in conquering the islands. (Kamakau, 1961, p. 150)

■ Final Preparations for War

The high chief sent his messengers (lele) to the district chiefs to inform them of the number of warriors needed for the coming conflict. In a major engagement every able-bodied man was expected to respond promptly and without complaint. The few who attempted to avoid military services were disgraced by having an ear lobe split and being led by a rope into the presence of the assembled soldiers. These "slackers" might be used as sacrifices on the altar of the heiau po'okanaka.

Warriors reported to the designated place of rendezvous with their weapons, food, water in gourd bottles, and kukui nut torches. It was common practice for two warriors to go to camp with the ends of a pololū spear resting on their shoulders. Food in ti-leaf bundles and other provisions hung from the spear. (Brigham, 1908, p. 133) At the encampment the chief occupied a large, temporary structure and the warriors were housed in smaller shelters roofed with palm or ti leaves. Large clusters of C-shaped stone shelters still visible on lava flows on Hawai'i and Maui probably served as army shelters for soldiers. (Emory, Kenneth P. Pers. Comm. 1976) When the warriors were all assembled, they checked their weapons and listened to their chief as he outlined the plans for the coming battle.

The wives, children, and elderly persons who remained behind continued their activities to the best of their abilities. When the conflict was near villages, the people would flee to a temple of refuge (pu'uhonua) or move to the mountains. In some areas lava tubes and caves served as temporary dwellings. A cave in the Kona district could shelter a vast number of persons and be defended by two armed guards at its entryway. (Homer Hayes, Pers. Comm. 1976) To meet the need for food in these emergencies, the farmers, in peace times,planted taro, yams, bananas, and ti near their mountain shelters.

■ Pu'uhonua

Pu'uhonua, which gave lawbreakers refuge, safety, and forgiveness for their wrong-doings, took several forms. The most prominent were the walled temples of which the restored City of Refuge National Historical Park at Hōnaunau, Hawai'i, now re-named Pu'uhonua o Hōnaunau, is the remaining example. Coconut Island or Mokuola in Hilo Bay was a place of refuge.

To be freed it was necessary for the accused person to flee from the executioner (mū) and reach safety within the *pu'uhonua*. Of the three murderers who raced toward the refuge land of Paunau, Lahaina, Maui, the two fastest reached the *pu'uhonua* but the third and slowest was caught and killed. Another pu'uhonua on Maui was Kukuipuka at Waihe'e. (Kamakau, 1961, p. 313)

Ahupua'a or other tracts of land could be designated pu'uhonua. The best known on O'ahu were Kualoa and Waikāne. Kawiwi at Wai'anae was a place of refuge during time of war. (Thrum, 1911, p. 152)

After uniting the islands, Kamehameha dissolved the established places of refuge except those on Kaua'i. He and Ka'ahumanu were themselves deemed sanctuaries and pardoned wrongdoers who came to them. Kamehameha designated the lands of his god Kūkā'ilimoku as pu'uhonua.

■ Fortification or Pu'ukaua

The chiefs built few fortifications in the early days of Hawaiian warfare since the fighting was usually offensive and took place in the open country. Most of the known forts or strongholds were built on a hilltop and called "pu'ukaua," war hill.

The most famous of the known fortresses, Ka'uiki, which occupied a hilltop on the bay at Hāna, Maui, was the scene of numerous attacks through the years. It was ascended by a ladder made from the trunks of the 'ōhi'a tree lashed

A Cave Shelter: When it was known that a battle was to be fought near a village the women, children and the elderly sought shelter in a mountain cave. One warrior might be sufficient to guard the entrance to such a cave.

together with 'ie'ie vine roots. The fort was guarded at night, during one siege, by a huge image of a warrior named Kawalaki'i in war dress and club. The attacking party guessed that they were being deceived, destroyed the image, and took the fort at night. (Kamakau, 1961, p. 30) Kahekili captured Ka'uiki in 1782 by cutting off its water supply. (Kamakau, 1961, p. 116)

The fortified hill of Kāhili in the Lahaina Luna area of Maui was occupied by Kahekili and his troops in an indecisive battle against Kalani'ōpu'u from Hawai'i who had among his chiefly warriors Kekūhaupi'o and Kamehameha. Here Pua, the two-handed fighter, speared Kekūhaupi'o. (Kamakau, 1961, p. 89) Ke'eaumoku had a fort built on a hill between Pololū and Honoke'ā, island of Hawai'i. (Kamakau, 1961, p. 83) Hauola in the Waimea district of Kaua'i was a fort covering 20 acres on a plateau 800 feet in elevation. (Thrum's 1907, pp. 163-64)

The remains of a fort and place of refuge at Kailua, Kona, built years ago for the use of the populace were visible in 1823. The walls of lava rock, laid without cement, were 18 to 20 feet high and 14 feet thick at the base. The warriors fought the enemy from this fort with sling stones, spears, and clubs. (Ellis, 1917, pp. 76-77, 115)

The warriors in charge of the beacon fortress, Haipu, at Ahipu'u (hill of fire), Nu'uanu valley, maintained a large heap of firewood ready to ignite at a moment's notice. By means of this bonfire they warned the chiefs in the Honolulu district that a raiding party was coming over the Pali from the Ko'olau side of O'ahu. (Summers, 1978, p. 300)

Some natural places of safety served as refuges for women and children and also as forts from which warriors attacked the approaching enemy. Lava tube caves, some with flowing or seeping water, formed natural sanctuaries. Walls were built to block the access to hilltops or cliffs and shelter was provided for a time in these places. From cliffs above pathways the warriors rolled down stones and rocks on the enemy. (Ellis, 1917, pp. 114-15) The notches on the ridge at Nu'uanu Pali must have had this function. (McAllister, 1933, p. 88)

■ Battles

Battle formations differed according to the nature of the field and the size of the forces involved. The kahului or crescent formation was used on large, level fields and usually involved large numbers of warriors. The makawalu formation was necessary when the ground was broken by trees or lava boulders. Warriors moved in small groups toward the enemy. In the kūkula formation, used by consent of the opposing leaders, the soldiers formed solid lines facing each other. It was in this situation that a champion would step forward and challenge an opponent to a duel.

Most battles were fought in the daytime according to Hawaiian codes of warfare. War was kapu during the four months of the Makahiki, approximately from the end of October to the end of February. (Handy, 1972, pp. 329-346) Instead of surprise attacks, representatives from the opposing forces agreed upon the place, date of the battle, and the fighting methods. If enemy forces were to arrive in canoes, they were usually allowed to land unmolested and to set up their encampment.

An army might be positioned in a huge crescent, called the open plain (kahului) formation. The king, or his commanding chief, occupied the central position. He stood in the midst of his warriors with his wife, his priest with his god elevated on a staff, and his dearest friends. Lesser chiefs, each in charge of his warriors, were placed by the commander in the flanks to complete the crescent. Priests with war gods accompanied these chiefs also.

Warriors numbering into the thousands would make up the largest of these armies. Each soldier would be armed with his favorite weapon, such as a short or long spear or a sling, and, in addition, one of the hand weapons, a club or dagger.

Even after the forces were in formation the armies had to wait until the astrologer indicated that the signs and conditions were right. He might urge the chief to fight because the omens were unfavorable for the enemy. At times the astrologer warned the leader not to fight on a particular day.

As the armies were at ease near each other, priests from each side offered sacrifices to their respective chief's gods. Each built a fire in the space between the armies and placed upon it a pig which had been killed by strangling. The opposing chiefs offered prayers which ended the kapu and signaled that the time had arrived for the battle to begin. (Malo, 1951, p. 197)

The action might begin with a shower of sling stones, hurled from a distance, to harass the enemy. As the formations moved closer warriors hurled short spears, thus thinning the ranks on both sides. Soldiers able to dodge or ward off the spears recovered them and threw them back at the enemy. Men from the rear rushed in with their long spears held firmly at their sides to thrust and trip. Many now met their opponents in hand-to-hand conflict with clubs, daggers, and shark-tooth weapons. At times all of the troops would be engaged in the battle. Or, there might be a series of partial engagements among those in the center or in the flanks.

The bodies of the first, second, and third warriors to fall in battle were secured, if possible, by men from the opposing side, even at the risk of death to those sent in to accomplish this. When the warrior secured the fallen victim, he might cut or tear off a handful of hair (not scalp) and hold it aloft to encourage his fellow soldiers. If the victim were a chief or person of importance he would call out his name. He would remove his ornaments of rank if he were a chief. The bodies of these first to fall were dragged to a priest who offered them to the gods on the battlefield. (Ellis, 1917, p. 119)

Battles usually continued until one side admitted that it had lost the contest. A common cause of defeat was the death of the high chief and leader, or his flight from the scene. At the loss of the high chief the lesser chiefs and warriors were stricken with grief which destroyed their will to fight.

If, as the battle progressed, neither side was gaining the victory a truce (kāpae) would be called. The first side to desire peace sent a messenger into the enemy ranks to confer with the commander. He carried a stalk of green ti leaves and a young banana tree to assure his safe conduct. If he were favorably received the rival chief gave orders to cease fighting and a council of peace followed.

The chiefs in consultation agreed to a settlement and went to the heiau to confirm the terms. They killed a pig and poured its blood on the ground to signify that the side which broke the peace terms would shed blood. The high chiefs from both sides joined in braiding a maile lei and placing it in the heiau. The messengers announced "Ua pau ke kaua," the war is ended. The people rejoiced. (Ellis, 1917, p. 121)

When an army was defeated the victorious chiefs and their forces were unmerciful in their treatment of the enemy not slain in battle. The lands of the vanquished chiefs were claimed by the conqueror and divided among his chiefs according to the decisions made by him and his counselor. Some fortunate members of the defeated forces were sometimes able to take sanctuary in the temples of refuge. Those who escaped immediate death went into hiding or fled into the mountains. They were sure to be hunted by the victors for many months. When captured they were killed at once or led to the conquering chief to be dispatched in his presence or kept for a sacrifice in the heiau luakini at a later time. If a chief found it inadvisable for him to put another chief to death, he could resort to 'anā'anā. He would engage a kahuna 'anā'anā skilled in the practice of "praying" another person to death and compensate him for causing his victim to die by sorcery. (Fornander II, 1969, pp. 142-43)

Occasionally high-ranking chiefs among the defeated were pardoned and allowed to return home. Usually they were related to or on friendly terms with the victorious chief. High-ranking chiefs were usually sacrificed but not enslaved. Defeat or capture did not destroy the divine power (mana) or rank of a chief. (Goldman, 1970, p. 205)

The retainers of a chief killed in battle tied his wrists and ankles to his pololū and carried the body home for proper burial. A chief who returned home in victory set his pololū upright in front of his house.

Planters on the conquered lands might remain to cultivate the lands of their new ruler, or they might be driven away and replaced with followers of the victorious chief.

The fallen warriors on the victorious side were buried according to the wishes of their families. The defeated forces were usually driven from the area and not allowed to collect their dead. These bodies were allowed to decay in the sun or were devoured by pigs and dogs. Cairns might be formed later by stones heaped on the bones.

■ Naval Battles and War Canoes

Few battles were fought at sea since canoes loaded with warrior-paddlers and their weapons were at a disadvantage in the choppy, sometimes stormy waters around the islands. Seaborne troops were usually allowed by the enemy to land and engage in the traditional forms of land battles. However, fleets of as many as a hundred canoes on each side did sometimes meet in conflict. (Ellis, 1917, p. 115) While some distance from one another the warriors hurled sling stones and spears. Weapons that missed the canoes and paddlers were lost in the deep waters. Large stone canoe breakers (pōhaku ku'i wa'a) were hurled at enemy canoes when within striking distance, then hauled back by the sennit cord lashed to the stone. These breakers damaged canoes, their outriggers and supports, and killed or injured some of the occupants. At close quarters the paddler-warriors fought with spears, clubs, and daggers. (Kane, Dec. 1974, pp. 766-67)

The last battle fought by the great ruler Kahekili and his forces was in canoes off the Waimanu cliffs, island of Hawai'i, in 1791. His opponent, Kamehameha, used several double canoes and a sloop manned by John Young and Isaac Davis, whose principal weapon was a cannon (pū). Both sides lost men but neither won the conflict. In keeping with Hawaiian custom the battle was given a descriptive name: Kepūwaha'ula, the red-mouthed cannon. (Kamakau, 1961, p. 162)

Fleets of canoes transported forces from one part of an island to another and between the islands. After landing the warriors, the canoes anchored off-shore in the care of a token force to be ready to carry the remaining members of its army to safety in case of a defeat. In some instances canoes were dragged ashore and the outriggers removed so that the aggressors, under pressure of defeat, could not use the canoes to escape.

During the last decade of the 18th century Kamehameha commanded his canoe builders to construct a fleet of large war canoes, called peleleu. These were hewn from koa trees grown in the mountains of the island of Hawai'i. With these peleleu he transported his warriors and their equipment to O'ahu and planned to use them for the conquest of Kaua'i.

Kamehameha's victories brought Hawaiian warfare to an end and inaugurated an era of peaceful pursuits. The sketches of three of his decisive battles which follow give information about war during the time of the Conqueror.

Warfare, on a grand scale, ended with the battle of Nu'uanu in 1795. However, after Kamehameha II and his chiefesses abolished the kapu regulations in 1819, the disgruntled Chief Kekuaokalani and his wife Manono met the King's forces in battle at Kuamo'o and another in Hāmākua and these were the very last acts of Hawaiian warfare.

■ The Battle of Moku'ōhai

Kalani'ōpu'u, aging ruler of the island of Hawai'i, called his chiefs together in 1780 at his residence in Waipi'o Valley and announced the names of his successors. He proclaimed that his high-born son, Kiwala'ō, should be heir to his kingdom. He gave the custody of the war god, Kūkā'ilimoku, and the responsibility of maintaining its temples to his nephew, Kamehameha. No change in title was mentioned concerning Kamehameha's lands in Kohala which were his by inheritance.

To consolidate his chiefdom Kalani'opu'u marched into Puna, captured the rebel chief Imakakoloa, and prepared to have him sacrificed at the heiau of Pākini at Kamā'oa which Kalani'ōpu'u had built. Kiwala'ō, representing his father, began the sacrificial ceremony but Kamehameha, who had been entrusted with the services in these heiau, stepped in ahead of his cousin and completed the ritual by placing the body of the fallen chief on the altar. This action caused a rift between the cousins and prompted some of the chiefs to question Kamehameha's actions. At the urging of Kalani'ōpu'u, Kamehameha departed immediately for his lands in Kohala where he spent his time in sports and pleasurable activities.

Shortly afterwards, in April of 1782, Kalani'ōpu'u died and Kiwala'ō, with the proper rituals, deposited his bones in the royal mausoleum Hale-o-Keawe at Hōnaunau, Kona.

Kiwala'ō, without consulting Kamehameha and the landed Kona chiefs, decided, upon the advice of counselors, to redivide the lands of the island of Hawai'i. Kiwala'ō's uncle, the kapu chief, Keawema'uhili, assumed the role of chief counselor and pretending to carry out the wishes of Kalani'ōpu'u, influenced the young ruler to favor him with extensive grants of land in Hilo and in Kona. Kiwala'ō's half-brother, Keōua Kuahu'ula, received less land than should have been his share. Kamehameha and his fellow chiefs were deprived of lands, largely in Kona, that had been theirs previously. Their cry was heard, "Ua aho e kaua." "It is better to go to war." (Emerson, 1903, p.17)

The disgruntled Kona chiefs turned to Kamehameha to lead them in their struggle for the lands they deemed to be rightfully theirs. These influential men of high rank and extensive experience as warriors were: Keaweāheulu, uncle and counselor to Kamehameha; Keʻeaumoku, father of Kaʻahumanu; Kamanawa and Kameʻeiamoku, uncles of Kamehameha and the royal twins portrayed on the coat of arms of Hawaiʻi; Kekūhaupiʻo, great warrior who had instructed Kamehameha in military tactics; and Kamehameha's brothers or half-brothers, Kalaʻimamahū, Kawelookalani, and Keliʻimaikaʻi. The names of these chiefs appear again and again in the historical events of the years to follow.

Chiefs aligned with Kiwalaʻō were from Hilo, Puna, and Kaʻū. Since their cause proved to be a losing one their names, except for Keōua and Keawemaʻuhili, were largely lost with their defeat.

Among the events leading to the battle of Mokuʻōhai was an ʻawa drinking ceremony of significance. Kamehameha and Kekūhaupiʻo visited Kiwalaʻō in Hōnaunau and sat with his friends for the ceremony. Kekūhaupiʻo asked that Kamehameha be permitted to prepare ʻawa as a favor to Kiwalaʻō since Kamehameha ranked next to him in the kingdom. Kamehameha handed the finished drink to Kiwalaʻō who, thoughtlessly, or as an insult, passed it to a favorite rather than drinking it himself. Kekūhaupiʻo struck the ʻawa bowl from the favorite's hand and forced Kamehameha from the house to show contempt for this insulting treatment.

The real crisis was brought on by the rashness of Keōua who was infuriated at his treatment in the land division. He led his chiefs and warriors in cutting down coconut trees on Kamehameha's lands at Keomo, Kona, an act which signified his declaration of war against the land owner. He killed some of Kamehameha's retainers and took their bodies to Hōnaunau. There Kiwalaʻō further insulted his cousin by presiding at the sacrificial altar in the heiau.

For four days there were minor skirmishes during which the forces of Kiwalaʻō and Keōua irritated Kamehameha and his warriors. The decisive battle was fought on the fifth day on the dry, rocky plain of Keʻei, a field strewn with jagged lava and marked with mounds and holes.

While Kamehameha was conducting services, which were a prelude to war, in a heiau in Kealakekua, Holoae, a kahuna of this temple who had served Kalaniʻōpuʻu, told Kamehameha that his opponents would be defeated and that Kiwalaʻō would be killed. (Kamakau, 1961, p. 121) In the meantime, Kamehameha's chiefs and warriors went to the Keʻei battlefield and in the early encounters lost a number of their men.

When Kiwalaʻō had completed the ceremony at the altar a kahuna warned him saying, "The flood tide is yours in the morning, but it will ebb in the afternoon. Postpone the fighting until tomorrow." (Kamakau, 1961, p. 121) Kiwalaʻō did not heed these words but returned to the field of battle.

During the conflict Keʻeaumoku became entangled with his long spear and fell. The enemy chiefs Kahaʻi and Nuhi rushed to him and wounded him with their daggers. Kiwalaʻō was nearby and called to them to rescue Keʻeaumoku's lei palaoa before it should be soiled with blood. The fallen chief's half-brother, Kamanawa, hurried with his warriors and drove away the assailants. One of the rescuers, Ke-akua-wahine, saw that Kiwalaʻō was too absorbed in obtaining the lei palaoa to realize his own dangerous position. He felled Kiwalaʻō with a sling stone. Keʻeaumoku, although injured and bleeding, crawled to Kiwalaʻō and cut his throat with a shark-tooth weapon (leiomano). (Kamakau, 1961, p. 121)

Another historian wrote that Kiwalaʻō fell from stones which the warrior Pahia threw by hand. (Ii, 1963, p. 14)

Ellis, during a visit to the Keʻei battlefield in 1823, was told that Kiwalaʻō stooped to remove the lei palaoa from Keʻeaumoku who, though wounded, grasped Kiwalaʻō by his hair and pulled him down. Kamehameha and his warriors rushed in, speared and stabbed Kiwalaʻō causing him to fall and die on the body of the wounded Keʻeaumoku. (Ellis, 1917, p. 109)

Kamehameha's arrival on the battlefield instilled courage in his troops. He killed his first victim of the day, the rival chief Ke-ahia, a friend who had deserted him and had joined the enemy forces.

With the news of Kiwalaʻō's death his chiefs and warriors scattered. Keōua fled to his canoe which was waiting off shore and sailed to his district of Kaʻū. He became the ruler of this district and part of Puna.

Kapu chief Keawemaʻuhili, taken prisoner and intended as a sacrifice, was allowed to escape; the guards were in awe of his high rank. He became the ruler of Hilo and the parts of Hāmāmkua and Puna that bordered on his district.

Other defeated chiefs and warriors fled to safety within the puʻuhonua at Hōnaunau.

Kamehameha gained his first victory at the battle of Moku'ōhai. He interpreted this as a sign that the gods were on his side and that he had the right to rule. Through success in this battle he secured the districts of Kona, Kohala, and part of Hāmākua, but large parts of the island of Hawai'i were controlled by his rivals. His powerful Kona chiefs continued to advise and support him in his efforts to consolidate the island and, eventually, the entire kingdom.

"Between the death of Kiwala'ō at the battle of Moku'ōhai in 1782 and the sacrifice of Keōua Kuahuula at Pu'ukoholā there were some ten years of almost continuous warfare among the chiefs of Hawai'i, Maui and O'ahu." (Ii, 1963, p. 15)

■ The Battle of Kepaniwai

During the eight years following the battle of Moku'ōhai, July, 1782, Kamehameha had been unable to wrest the Hilo district from Keawema-'uhili or Ka'ū from Keōua. However, his relations with his rival Keawema'uhili had improved so that he was able to ask him for canoes, men, and feather capes to equip a war expedition to Maui. Keawema'uhili sent a large force of men, canoes, and arms under the command of his own sons. Keōua refused to aid Kamehameha and criticized Keawema'uhili for doing so. He reasoned that it was "wrong to fight against the sons of Kahekili." (Kamakau, 1961, p. 147)

Kamehameha's own well-trained and equipped warriors were strengthened by quantities of foreign weapons which he had secured by barter and by the skills of his capable English aides John Young and Isaac Davis. The summer of 1790 seemed to Kamehameha to be a strategic time to invade Maui, then under the rule of Kalanikupule, son of Kahekili, who had now established his court on O'ahu.

Kahekili had defeated the Hawai'i island forces of Kalani'ōpu'u a number of times during their frequent attempts to conquer Maui in the years from 1775 to 1786. Kamehameha had been a brave and skillful participant in these ill-fated expeditions. The most inglorious defeat came during the campaign in which Kalani'ōpu'u's famous 'Ālapa and Pi'ipi'i regiments took part. The 800 young nobles in these brigades were of rank so high that they were privileged to eat with their king (ali'i 'ai alo). Of all his warriors these were the bravest and most courageous. All were equal in height, bore spears of equal length, and were resplendent in feather capes and helmets.

Kalani'ōpu'u landed some six divisions of warriors near Mā'alaea, Maui, and directed the 'Ālapa to march at once toward Wailuku. In a fiercely contested battle, Kahekili's forces annihilated all but two of them. Grief-stricken and revengeful Kalani'ōpu'u marched his remaining army to Wailuku the following day to avenge the loss of his gallant 'Ālapa regiment. There was slaughter on both sides and the Hawai'i forces were again defeated and driven back to Mā'alaea.

With no hope for victory Kalani'ōpu'u sought favorable terms of peace from Kahekili by sending as his ambassador his son and heir, the chief Kiwala'ō. He was the son of Kahekili's sister, the kapu chiefess Kalola. Dressed in a feather cloak, helmet, and the symbols of his rank he was accompanied by the chiefly twins, Kame'eiamoku, carrying the ipu kuha (royal spitoon), and Kama-nawa carrying the chief's kāhili (feather standard). These chiefs were half-brothers of Kahekili. So high was Kiwala'ō's rank that all of the soldiers prostrated themselves as the royal party passed through their ranks. Kiwala'ō was graciously received by his uncle, peace terms were agreed upon, and the Hawai'i forces returned home in defeat.

Cognizant of but not discouraged by the series of defeats suffered by his uncle, Kalani'ōpu'u, Kamehameha sailed from Kohala for Maui with a large fleet of canoes bearing warriors with Hawaiian and foreign weapons. His Kona chiefs, counselors, and the principal chiefesses were in the party. The forces landed at Hāna and marched along the windward coast where they won a number of skirmishes. Kamehameha felt assured of success in the encounters to come since the feathers on the head of his war god, Kūkā'ilimoku, bristled and stood upright, a sign that encouraged him to fight. (Kamakau, 1961, p. 148)

At Kokomo, Maui's forces met the invaders in a desperate battle which was decided, not by the continued fighting of the massed armies, but by the prowess of their leaders. Maui's Kapakāhili stepped forward alone and met Kamehameha in combat while their armies watched the duel with great concern. The type of weapons used is not recorded, but Kapakāhili was killed and his forces dispersed. The victorious chief accompanied his warriors by sea to Kahului where their canoes filled the bay and the beaches nearby.

Kalanikupule, warned of Kamehameha's approaching armies, sent the aged, the women and children to seek refuge on the mountainous sides of Wailuku and ʻĪao valleys. Here they would be removed from the danger of spears and gun fire but, unhappily, could look down upon the slaughter and horror of the battle below. The fighting began in Wailuku (water of destruction) but the Maui warriors were forced to retreat into ʻĪao (cloud supreme) where the walls were precipitous and the head of the valley blocked by vertical cliffs.

There is a tradition that Kamehameha climbed to a promontory overlooking his troops, early in the battle, and shouted by way of encouragement and admonition:

Imua e nā pōkiʻi,
E inu i ka wai ʻawaʻawa
ʻAʻohe hope e hoʻi mai ai.

Forward my little brothers,
Drink of the bitter water
There is no retreat.

The Hawaiʻi invaders had superior guns and the cannon "Lopaka" (Robert) handled by Young and Davis. It was one of the most bitter battles ever fought on Hawaiian soil. (Fornander II, 1969, p. 237) The shouts of defiance among the warriors, the clashing of spears and clatter of musket and boom of cannon, and the wailing of the women who looked down on the carnage from the steep sides of the valley, were sounds which terrified all who heard them.

> In this battle, Kamehameha displayed much skill in his arrangements. His active mind turned every mistake of his enemy to his own advantage, and seized upon the most favorable moments for a charge or retreat. His prodigious strength, for which he was remarkable, joined with a stout person, and great personal courage, which had already established him a reputation for prowess throughout the group, availed his troops much. While his bodily exertions were not needed, he remained quiet, issuing orders with coolness and sagacity: if the line of battle wavered, he rushed forward, shouting with his deep-toned voice, and heading his guards, led them to victory. (Jarves, 1843, pp. 140-41)

The corpses of the slain from both armies were so numerous that they clogged (pani) the waters of the streams. The battle was named "Kepaniwai, the damming of the waters. Others referred to it as "Kaʻuwaʻupali" (clawed off the cliff) which describes the warriors being thrown or falling from the narrow trails on the cliffs. Kalanikupule and his fellow chiefs escaped over a narrow pass in the mountains and sailed to Oʻahu. The chiefesses were escorted over the pass and taken by canoe to Molokaʻi.

The story of this fiercely contested and bloody battle of Kepaniwai continues to be told. Each year countless numbers of island residents and visitors from afar view the lush, green ʻĪao valley and the Needle, a 2,250-foot vertical shaft of lava which dominates the scene. They visit Kepaniwai park with its clear stream and call to mind that these waters were dammed by the bodies of fallen warriors nearly two centuries ago.

By this victory Maui was added to Kamehameha's domain for he had destroyed its fighting forces and had driven its chiefs to Oʻahu. He sent his armies back to Hawaiʻi and sailed to Molokaʻi with his chiefly advisors on a mission of great significance. Now in residence on Molokaʻi was the ailing kapu chiefess Kalola, widow of Kalaniʻōpuʻu and sister of Kahekili. With her were her daughters Kekuʻiapoiwa Liliha, and Kalaniakua and her granddaughter, Keōpūolani, the highest in rank of the young chiefesses. Before Kalola died she promised her daughters and granddaughter to Kamehameha. (Fornander II, 1969, p. 238) He agreed to take these chiefesses to the island of Hawaiʻi where he would care for them in a style in keeping with their high rank. During the mourning rites for Kalola, Kamehameha was tattooed and had his eye teeth knocked out to show his respect for the memory of the departed chiefess. (Kamakau, 1961, p. 149) (Sometime after Kamehameha's victory in the Battle of Nuʻuanu, 1795, he married Keōpūolani at Waikīkī. She bore him the sons who became Kamehameha II and III.)

While on Molokaʻi Kamehameha sent two messengers to Oʻahu to get information intended to help him gain supremacy over the islands. One was Haʻaloʻu, grandmother of Kaʻahumanu, who consulted a Kauaʻi kahuna then in residence at Waikīkī. He was of the Hulihonua order, skilled in locating and building heiau. The wise man, Kapoukahi, answered, "If he makes this house (Puʻukoholā heiau at Kawaihae) for his god, he can gain the kingdom without a scratch to his own skin." (Kamakau, 1961, p. 150) The island of Hawaiʻi became Kamehameha's when he re-built Puʻukoholā in 1794 and sacrificed his rival Keōua Kuahuʻula on its altar.

The messenger Kikāne carried a black and a white game stone (ʻulu maika) to Kahekili at Waikīkī. The great chief remarked that the white stone represented peaceful pursuits and the black one, war. Kikāne informed him that Kamehameha planned to make war on Oʻahu and wanted to know the proper place for landing his warriors and the most suitable field for battle. Kahekili replied, "Go back and tell Kamehameha to return to Hawaii and watch, and when the black tapa covers Kahekili and the black pig rests his nose, then is the time to cast stones. Then, when light is snuffed out at Kahiki, that is the time to come and take the land." (Kahekili's figurative reference to his death and his advice to Kamehameha. Kamakau, 1961, p. 150.)

■ The Battle of Nuʻuanu

Kamehameha realized, early in 1795, the conditions were right for him to add the island of Oʻahu to his realm. Kahekili, who had died in July of the previous year, had told Kamehameha through his messenger, Kikāne, that after his death Kamehameha could take possession of Oʻahu. (Kamakau, 1961, p. 150)

For some twelve years Kamehameha's builders had been constructing large canoes and now there were about 960 in his fleet. (Fornander, 1918-19, Vol. V, p. 690) He was credited with having 20 foreign vessels weighing from 20 to 40 tons, all armed and manned by the year 1795. (Kenn, 1945, p. 1337)

The peleleu canoes were not a part of this fleet which invaded Oʻahu but were built after 1795 for the planned conquest of Kauaʻi. These war canoes were 5 to 6 feet deep and 3 to 4 feet wide, hewn from huge koa trees obtained from the forests above Hilo, Kaʻū and South Kona. They were double or single and were usually rigged with sails of western design.

There may have been 20 or fewer of these canoes although writers have stated that they numbered from 800 to 960. (Holmes, 1981, pp. 115-117)

The conqueror's quantity of arms and ammunition, which he had acquired by barter, was substantially increased from the stores of the two chiefs he was soon to meet in conflict. The officers George Lamport and William Bonallack of the English vessels Jackall and Prince Lee Boo called

on Kamehameha on the island of Hawaiʻi and gave him arms and ammunition which Kalanikupule of Oʻahu had placed on board in preparation for his invasion of Kamehameha's domain. The Oʻahu ruler had ordered the captains of these ships killed on January 1, 1795, and prepared to use the vessels for his conquest of Hawaiʻi. The officers and crew now in command had been able to force Kalanikupule and his party ashore on Oʻahu, then sail for Hawaiʻi. They informed Kamehameha of the conditions on Oʻahu, then departed for China. (Kuykendall, 1938, pp. 45-46)

In February, 1795, Kamehameha sailed from Kohala with his large fleet of ships, canoes and warriors, all well armed and organized. His strength may have numbered 16,000 men, including his faithful Kona chiefs who had supported him in other campaigns. (Jarves, 1843, p. 180) Sixteen foreigners were in the invasion force with John Young, Isaac Davis, and Peter Anderson in charge of the cannons. (Alexander, 1891, p. 143) As was the custom, the chiefesses and other women of rank accompanied their husbands and relatives.

The invasion fleet stopped at Lahaina where, in war-like tradition, they appropriated all of the available food to add to their provisions. They then destroyed the settlement and parts of west Maui. By this act Kamehameha reaffirmed his control of Maui which he had gained in the battle of Kepaniwai some five years earlier.

Sojourn on Molokaʻi: At Kaunakakai, Molokaʻi, Kamehameha and his forces rested and made final plans for the invasion of Oʻahu. The conqueror met frequently with his chiefs and counselors in secret sessions. Kaʻiana, who had joined Kamehameha with his own warriors and a large quantity of ammunition which he had brought from China, was not invited to the council of chiefs. In telling his younger brother, Nahiolea, of his being excluded from the planning sessions, Kaʻiana expressed fear that the chiefs were plotting to kill him. He reasoned that he faced death whether he followed Kamehameha or defected and joined the forces on Oʻahu. He became convinced that it would be better to die in battle facing the foe than to be killed secretly by Kamehameha's agents. Nahiolea reminded him that he had given all of his weapons to Kamehameha. (Kamakau, 1961, pp. 153, 172)

Kaʻiana, a descendant of the senior branch of the line of Keawe kings of Hawaiʻi, considered himself to be of higher rank than Kamehameha. He found it demeaning to pay allegiance to the conqueror whose position of leadership was, he reasoned, the result of the support of his Kona chiefs and good fortune in battle. The chiefs accused Ka'iana of presuming to be superior because of his knowledge of foreign ways through his travels in China and along the North American coast. Ka'iana speculated that his forces combined with those of Kalanikupule might defeat Kamehameha and that he, not the conqueror, might rule the islands.

Ka'iana Defects: About mid-April, 1795, Kamehameha sailed from Moloka'i for O'ahu with the largest fleet ever assembled for Hawaiian warfare. (Alexander, 1891, p. 143) At the beginning of the voyage Ka'iana kissed his wife, Kekupuohi, farewell and told her that he was defecting to join the forces of Kalanikupule. ". . . if I die, see that I am secretly buried," he said to Kekupuohi as he began this apparent "suicide journey." (Kamakau, 1961, p. 172) His wife, a chiefess of great beauty, remained with Kamehameha. Sometime during the passage Ka'iana, his brother Nahiolea, and a considerable number of friends, retainers, and warriors slipped away from the invasion fleet and landed on the Ko'olau shores of O'ahu. They crossed the mountains into Nu'uanu valley and joined Kalanikupule. Ka'iana's forces may have numbered 2,000 according to tradition, although the published accounts fail to give the number.

The Invaders Land on O'ahu: Kamehameha landed his forces on the beaches extending from Wai'alae to Waikīkī, covering the shoreline for a distance of seven miles. They spent several days organizing their troops before marching to meet the enemy.

O'ahu's defenders were led by their ruler, Kalanikupule, and by Ka'iana, neither of whom had been long identified with this island. The former, a Maui chief, was given the rule of O'ahu by his father, Kahekili, who in conquering it had killed or driven away all of the O'ahu chiefs. Kalanikupule had been defeated by Kamehameha at the battle of Kepaniwai five years earlier. Both defending chiefs had lost quantities of arms and ammunition to Kamehameha.

The Battle: Kalanikupule stationed his troops, believed to have been between 8 and 10 thousand men, at La'imi and Pū'iwa, and towards the mountains as far as Luakaha. He placed warriors on the steep slopes along the right side of Nu'uanu valley in full view of the plains below. Their elevation above the approaching invaders was planned to give them an advantage over the invaders.

Kamehameha's forces which had been beached at Wai'alae marched inland through the plains (Kaimukī) and joined the Waikīkī-based troops which were proceeding through Mō'ili'ili. They continued behind Punchbowl crater into Nu'uanu and met Kalanikupule's warriors at La'imi and Pū'iwa (now the site of Queen Emma's Summer Palace).

At first the opposing forces seemed to be evenly matched and the battle raged on several fronts without a decision. A division of O'ahu troops under Ka'iana fought with shoulder guns from behind a stone wall at La'imi. The wall gave them protection and a sense of security as did the steep slope below which slowed the movement of the approaching enemy.

John Young led the invaders at this point and fired his cannon toward the stone wall. A cannon ball knocked stones into the ranks of the O'ahu soldiers and caused such confusion that they began to disperse. This cannon ball killed chief Ka'iana. His death caused such consternation among his troops that they scattered and fled. (Jarves, 1843, p. 181) Ka'iana's brother Nahiolea was also killed early in the battle.

Kamehameha's forces continued to charge the enemy, many of whom were retreating higher into the valley. The slaughter was greater among the O'ahu ranks because they had lost their direction and spirit at the death of Ka'iana. Kamehameha's artillery was superior, his guns more numerous, and his troops more disciplined. A large number of O'ahu warriors escaped by climbing up the sides of the mountains that flanked Nu'uanu valley. A number fled to the head of the valley to the precipice, Nu'uanu Pali. The foot path that led down to the plains below was not wide enough for a retreating army, but it did permit a comparative few to escape. The rest were driven over the Pali by the pursuing forces and were killed as they fell on the rocks several hundred feet below.

It has been written that at this hour the mountain pass filled to the brink with a dense mist because the usually brisk winds stopped sweeping it into the valley below. Fortunately, the warriors as they leaped saw only the enveloping folds of the cloud-bank in front of them. Its mists shielded their eyes from the dizzying height and the rocks which meant certain death below. (Gowan, 1919, p. 248)

Kaolaulani, brother of the defeated ruler, escaped unharmed and sailed to Kaua'i. Kalanikupule fled into the Ko'olau mountains where he hid from his pursuers for several months. He led a miserable and precarious life until he was captured in upper Waipi'o, 'Ewa district, and was killed. His body was brought to Kamehameha who sacrificed it to his god Kūkā'ilimoku at Moanalua. (Alexander, 1891, p. 145)

The O'ahu chiefs, chiefesses and their followers who were taken prisoner were saved and pardoned by Ka'ahumanu. Her power as a person served in the same manner as a pu'uhonua or a place of refuge. (Kamakau, 1961, pp. 312-13)

The battle for the control of O'ahu was won by the invaders in one day of fighting. Kamehameha divided the O'ahu lands among the chiefs who had supported him. He left in their possession certain ahupua'a held by the kāhuna.

Notches at the Pali: Visitors approaching the Pali notice the two artificial-appearing notches on the right (Kōnāhuanui) side of the ridge. These are about 30 feet wide and 12 feet deep and are cut into the crest of the ridge which is but a few feet across. One informant wrote that these notches were dug at the request of Chief Ka'iana to be used as implacements for cannons, and that shots from two cannons placed here fell heavily on the chiefs and soldiers of Kamehameha. Armed soldiers from the invasion force were said to have captured the cannons by ascending the ridge on the Mānoa side of the valley. (Ka Nai Aupuni, 1906) This story places the actual fighting much higher in the valley than the traditional versions.

Another unlikely story is that the notches "were built for the guns of Kamehameha, and that later his canoes were drawn up through the notches, the body of the canoe through one and the outrigger through the other." (McAllister, 1933, p.88)

A more probable explanation is that they were used to store boulders by soldiers protecting the Pali trail in earlier times. The great stones were rolled down on the enemy using the path on either side. (McAllister, 1933, p. 88)

Through the years the beauty of Nu'uanu valley and the Pali have continued to attract great numbers of residents and visitors. As the story is told of the warriors being driven over the Pali, the numbers that perished have been exaggerated. In 1796 Broughton wrote that the O'ahu defenders lost 300. (Broughton, 1804, p. 41) The same year Charles Bishop was told that "not less than 500 of the enemy fell." Also that not more than 20 of the invaders were killed. (Bishop, mms. 1796) In 1823 Ellis was told that 400 had been driven over the Pali. (Ellis, 1917, p. 27)

In 1823 James Macrae, botanist, with Lord Byron, learned that the warriors "were found in the thousands, lifeless at the bottom of the cliff." (Wilson, 1922, p. 39) In 1843 Jarves wrote that 300 O'ahu men perished. (Jarves, 1843, p. 181) In 1854 Bates gave the Pali loss at 3,000. (Bates, 1854, p. 92)

In 1897 Whitehouse and Wilson, while improving the Pali road, found an estimated 800 skulls, along with other bones, at the foot of the precipice. They believed these to be the remains of O'ahu warriors defeated by Kamehameha a hundred years earlier. (*The Island Call*, Oct. 1953)

In 1914 the Pali loss was reported at 10,000 men (Historians discount this story completely.) (Lydgate, 1928, p. 28)

Fornander wrote concerning the battle of Nu'uanu: "It is the closing scene in the ancient history of the Hawaiian Islands." (Fornander II, 1969, p. 348) Feudal wars had now come to an end, a new era had begun. Within a few years Kamehameha consolidated the islands into a peaceful kingdom and his people enjoyed freedom from the oppression of warfare.

During the century of rule to follow by Hawaiian monarchs there were no armed conflicts of any consequence within the kingdom nor invasions that caused bloodshed by foreign forces.

However, there were, through the years, threats from the Russians, French, and British. The Russians built forts on Kaua'i which they were forced to abandon (Pierce, 1965, pp. 13-15). The French threatened for religious and economic reasons, Catholicism and wine. Britisher Lord George Paulet took control of the government from February through July, 1843, after which it was restored to Kamehameha III.

Kamehameha I maintained a guard of some 200 uniformed men and also reserves numbering perhaps 2,000. These men had muskets and hand guns acquired by barter from foreign ships. (Mellen, March 1937, p. 7)

After the death of Kamehameha the men under

arms served largely as police in Honolulu and around the Palace, although the governor of each island had charge of the forts, militia, and arms on his own island.

The kings, through the years, depended upon a certain "balance of powers" between the government forces of the United States, France, and Britain, who sent warships in and out of Honolulu harbor to "protect their investments and residents in Hawaii." The Hawaiian government had to depend upon diplomacy rather than armed forces to keep from being annexed by one of the foreign powers.

Through the first half of the 19th century the safety within the Hawaiian islands was entrusted to military organizations named Artillery Men, Native Infantry, and the Militia.

In 1852 some 50 foreign businessmen organized the first Hawaiian Guard in Honolulu to quell riots and keep peace in Honolulu. This company is considered the parent of the present Hawaii National Guard. During 1857 the Honolulu Rifles were organized for the purpose of defending life and property.

The Leleiohoku Guard consisted of some 100 Hawaiian men, excellent riders and equipped with arms and handsome uniforms. Other forces, some short lived, were the Prince's Own, and the Mamalahoa organized by King Kalākaua.

Household troops assigned to police the Palace grounds and protect the royal family were, from time to time, the King's Guard, King's Own, Ali'i Koa, and the Queen's Own.

After a long period of comparative peace in the kingdom, a series of incidents and "revolutions" clouded the last years of Hawaiian rule. The bloodless "revolution of 1887" resulted in the new Constitution of 1887. The Wilcox revolution of 1889, an attempt to proclaim a new constitution, resulted in seven deaths and a dozen wounded among the insurgents. Their leader, Robert W. Wilcox, was a Hawaiian who had been sent to Italy to study engineering and military tactics.

The revolution of 1893 was a swift take-over of Queen Lili'uokalani's government by the Committee of Safety, aided by troops landed from the United States cruiser, Boston. Members of the Committee of Safety established a Provisional Government and secured the surrender of the Queen, the Palace, the police, and the royal military force.

The Insurrection of 1895 was led by supporters of Queen Lili'uokalani who hoped to restore her to the throne. Arms and ammunition were brought in from San Francisco. A few skirmishes in Waikīkī, Pālolo, and Mānoa resulted in the death of several men and the wounding of others. The Provisional Government became the Republic of Hawaii and its leaders sought to become a state or territory of the United States. Congress declined to act on this request, but reconsidered in 1898 when the Spanish-American War focused attention on Hawai'i.

The Hawaiian government offered the United States the use of its harbors and other facilities that the troop ships and troops might need in sailing from San Francisco to Manila. The ladies of Honolulu organized well in advance of the arrival of American troops who were to make a one-day stop-over in Honolulu. On June 2, 1898, about 2,400 men came ashore and were fed, without charge, at tables on the Executive Building grounds. The Honolulu women prepared this quantity of food for the visiting "Boys in Blue:"

One ton of potato salad, 10,000 ham sandwiches, 2,500 pounds of roast beef, roast turkeys, roast chickens, 3,000 gallons of milk, 800 watermelons, 20,000 mangoes, 800 pineapples, 5,000 oranges; coffee, soda water, cigars, and candy. (Pratt, 1944, p. 25-28)

Annexation of Hawai'i to the United States became official on August 12, 1898, and Hawai'i became a Territory on June 14, 1900. The defense of Hawai'i then became the duty of the military forces of the United States government. A brief listing of the important military installations established, largely on O'ahu, indicate the United States government's recognition of Hawai'i as a strategic outpost in the Pacific. Dates given here are for the time of occupancy of the military installations. Some were established or planned earlier than the dates which follow:

1876 - Reciprocity Treaty. Hawaiian government agreed not to lease any port, harbor, or territory to any government but the United States.

1887 - Hawai'i granted the United States the right to make a harbor, at its own expense, in the Pearl River and have the exclusive use of it. The plan, though never carried out, was to establish a coaling and repair station for U.S. vessels at Pearl Harbor.

1898 - Camp McKinley at Kapi'olani Park, Honolulu, a tent encampment of infantry and engineers.

1898 - Dredging began at Pearl Harbor.

1900 - Members of the Republic of Hawai'i's National Guard took the oath of allegiance to the United States and became a part of the U.S. military system. Companies were organized in Hilo, Hawai'i, and Wailuku, Maui, bringing the Guard to a regiment of nine companies with some 525 men.

1907 - Fort Shafter and Tripler Hospital, near Honolulu. Fort Shafter became the headquarters for the Hawaiian Department.

1907 - Fort Armstrong, Honolulu harbor entrance.

1908 - The first ROTC unit in Hawai'i was established at The Kamehameha School for Boys. Punahou began military instruction in 1915. A Students' Army Training Corps (SATC) was established at the College of Hawai'i in 1918.

1909 - Schofield Barracks, Leilehua Plains, Wahiawā, one of the largest of the military posts in the United States.

1909 - Fort De Russy, Waikīkī, now recreational, not military.

1909 - Fort Ruger, inland slopes of Diamond Head and including Diamond Head crater.

1913 - Fort Kamehameha, protected entrance to Pearl Harbor.

1918 - Luke Field, Ford Island, Pearl Harbor. (Ford Island was known earlier as Moku 'Ume'ume.)

1919 - Drydock at Pearl Harbor completed. First drydock collapsed in 1913 as it was nearing completion.

1922 - Wheeler Field, established on the edge of the Schofield Barracks reservation. (Now Wheeler Air Force Base.)

1935 - Hickam Field. Between Pearl Harbor and Fort Kamehameha. (Now Hickam Air Force Base.)

■ Hawai'i and the First World War

The first World War was called the conflict that gave Hawai'i its first real opportunity to work with the country of which it was now a part. (Pratt, 1944, p. 210)

Although the war was fought in Europe, half the world away, it affected Hawaiian life in many ways:

Ships were diverted from Hawaiian service to the Atlantic.

Sugar profits increased, stockholders and plan-tation employees shared in the profits, and the plantations improved their accommodations for laborers.

Hackfeld and Company and its department store Ehlers, founded by Germans in Hawai'i, were reorganized and renamed American Factors and Liberty House.

The Hawai'i Chapter of the American Red Cross contributed money and also surgical dressings and hospital supplies worth more than a half-million dollars. (Sales Builder, March 1937, p. 12)

Volunteers and draftees through the Selective Service Law and members of the National Guard from Hawai'i served in the war, a total of nearly 10,000.

■ World War II

The attack on Pearl Harbor, December 7, 1941, plunged the United States into the throes of World War II. The initial attack caused the U.S. a total of 3,478 casualties in dead, wounded, and missing. American warships sunk or badly damaged numbered 19; more than 200 planes were lost.

Hawai'i's people lived under martial law, observed blackout restrictions, redoubled their efforts in wartime jobs, and maintained understanding if not cheerful attitudes through food and gasoline rationing and other inconveniences.

More than 40,000 residents of Hawai'i served actively in some military branch. The death toll reached 805, and 2,200 came home permanently disabled. Americans of Japanese ancestry (AJA) were among the most distinguished and most decorated officers and soldiers from Hawai'i. (Jabulka, Hawaii Book, 1961, pp. 50-52)

■ Korean War, June 25, 1950 - July 27, 1953

When Communist troops from North Korea invaded South Korea in 1950 the United Nations asked its member nations to help repulse the attacks. Of the 16 nations that responded the United States sent over 90% of the military help of all kinds.

At that time Hawai'i's Korean Community numbered about 7000 persons, the largest outside Korea and Japan. Most of these were U.S. citizens.

Thousands of unskilled workers were sent from Hawai'i to Guam and Okinawa to help with war-oriented activities at these outposts. Extensive construction and repairs at the Pearl Harbor Naval Shipyard prepared ships for duty in the Far

East.

Early in the conflict 17,000 men left Hawai'i for Korea, some were AJA's from the 100th and 442nd Divisions.

With a population of about a half million in 1950 Hawai'i supplied about two and a half times the national average of men sent into Korea. Island casualties were listed as 341 killed in action, 879 wounded, 79 missing in action and 40 prisoners of war.

Hostilities ended July 27, 1953, but a peace treaty has never been signed.

■ Vietnam War, 1957 - April 30, 1975

Communist dominated forces from North Vietnam invaded South Vietnam in 1957 against the demands of the free nations of the world. The United States never declared war against North Vietnam but sent forces and arms to aid South Vietnam until the number of American troops reached a peak of more than a half million by February, 1969.

Its mid-ocean location causes Hawai'i to have greater involvement than the other states during Pacific conflicts. Some 13,000 residents served in Vietnam and 221 died in battle.

Many of the Americans wounded in Vietnam were flown to the huge Tripler Army Medical Center on O'ahu for treatment. Some 2,500 servicemen flew to Hawai'i for a period of "Rest and Recreation."

This conflict, unpopular with many Americans, provoked fewer protests in Hawai'i than on the mainland.

The North Vietnam Communists claimed a complete victory over South Vietnam on April 30, 1975. The United States hurriedly evacuated, by a fleet of 81 helicopters, an estimated 1,373 Americans and 5,695 Vietnamese to U.S. Navy ships in the South China Sea. A large number of the Vietnamese refugees settled in Hawai'i.

■ Understandings and Appreciations

Do you think Kamehameha I fought long and hard to unite the islands and stop bloody warfare or did he want the honor of being the first supreme ruler?

It was the custom to give names to military campaigns. Read about the following battles with colorful names in Kamakau, 1961.

Bad Child Campaign, p. 124
Battle of the Bitter Rains, p. 125
The Red Mouth Cannon, p. 162
Pig-eating of Kukeawe, p. 142
Red Mantle, p. 143
Spilled Brains, p. 146

For many more see the Index to Kamakau 1961 by Sterling, pp. 81-82.

Kamehameha was supported in his campaigns to unite the islands by a number of capable and loyal chiefs. The first four listed here were his uncles.

Ke'eaumoku, father of Ka'ahumanu
Kamanawa and
Kame'eiamoku were called the Royal Twins. They are the chiefs pictured on the coat-of-arms.
Keaweaheulu escorted Keōua to his death at Pu'u Kohalā.
Kekūhaupi'o, Kamehameha's instructor in sports and war tactics.
Kalanimokū. After the kingdom was consolidated he was the treasurer and in charge of dividing the lands among the chiefs and people.

Consider seriously Fornander's statement concerning Kamehameha's victory at the battle of Nu'uanu, "It is the closing scene in the ancient history of the Hawaiian Islands."

Learn more about the four Hawaiian rulers of earlier times that are still remembered for their long reigns of peace and progress:

Liloa of Hawai'i
Pi'ilani of Maui
Kakuhihewa of O'ahu
Mano Kalanipo of Kaua'i

These monarchs have been remembered in the chants for centuries.

■ Student Activities

1. Make a sling (ma'a) from available fiber and chip out an ovoid sling stone (pōhaku 'alā) from soft stone. (Buck 1957, pp. 461-62) Use it in a large field with caution.

2. Secure a sturdy stick, a foot long or so, and use it as a club (lā'au) by drawing it back or lifting it, then strike an imaginary enemy. Secondly,

use it as a pointed dagger *(pāhoa)* by thrusting it into the body of your imaginary enemy. Which weapon could be used faster and be perhaps more deadly? Note that the Hawaiian warriors greatly preferred one over the other.

3. Sharpen the end of a discarded broom handle to make a simple spear *(ihe)*. Set up a banana trunk as suggested in the game *'ō'ō ihe* in Unit 13. Engage in preparation for war by hurling the spear into the banana (which represents the human body).

4. Check the actual sharpness of a shark tooth. Look at the pictures of a dozen or more *leiomano* or other shark tooth weapons and assess their effectiveness.

5. Readers on the Big Island locate the battlefield Moku'ōhai at Ke'ei. Review the story of the death of Kīwala'ō. On Maui visit 'Īao Valley and the scene of the battle of Kepaniwai. On O'ahu try to imagine scenes from the battle of Nu'uanu as you drive from Queen Emma's Summer Palace to the Pali. How many warriors jumped to their death below?

6. Learn in Hawaiian Kamehameha's battle cry at the Battle of Kepaniwai, Maui.

7. Read about the fort at the Honolulu Harbor entrance which gave Fort Street its name.

8. Also read about the Russian Fort Elizabeth at Waimea, Kaua'i.

9. Read about the young Kamehameha and the *naha* stone.

10. Learn the significance of the notches on the ridge at Nu'uanu Pali.

■ Audio-Visual Aids

1. Study the display of weapons in Hawaiian Hall, Bishop Museum.

2. The U.S. Army Museum of Hawai'i at Fort DeRussy on Kalia Road, Waikīkī displays "implements of destruction" from the American Revolution through the Vietnam War.

3. The Arizona Memorial Visitor Center is popular with visitors to Pearl Harbor. The telephone book lists Arizona Memorial Navy Boat Tours and Bus Shuttle.

■ Vocabulary

Learn the meanings of the words in these thoughts:

Greed made enemies of neighbor chiefs
Ambition made high chiefs yearn to be mightier
Powerful priests decreed stricter *kapu*
Powerful priests raised larger *heiau*
Powerful priests demanded greater sacrifices, not pigs or fish but men's bodies
Warriors were combatants, competitors, rivals, fighters, aggressors, assailants, Anymore?
Winners were the victorious, the conquerors.
Losers were the vanquished, the defeated.

■ Current Trends of Significance to this Unit

The "Artificial Curiosities" exhibit at Bishop Museum, 1978-79, renewed interest in the shark tooth weapons since a large number were on display. A review of Cook's journal brought out phases of warfare not often discussed by later writers. Examples: the large number of field stones used as weapons and the warriors use of plaited mats for armor-like protection.

The *lua* or *ku'ialua* a dangerous form of wrestling including bone-breaking, has been considered all but a lost art. Today certain *kumu hula* are teaching dances which include steps and motions of the *lua*. Actually the *hula* and *lua* have much in common. Both are taught by skilled *kumu* to selected students in groups. The steps and holds have names, much training is needed to perfect the art and the students graduate with a *'uniki*. The *lua* instructor is called an *'ōlohe*. Some women learned the *lua* as a means of self-defense.

■ Reading List

Alexander, W.D. *A Brief History of the Hawaiian People.* New York: American Book Company, 1899.

Bates, G. *Sandwich Island Notes by a Haole.* New York: Harper, 1854.

Beaglehole, J.C., ed. *The Journals of Captain James Cook.* Vol. III, Parts 1 and 2. Cambridge, UK: Hakluyt Society, Cambridge University Press, 1967.

Beckwith, Martha W. *Hawaiian Mythology*. 1940. Honolulu: University Press of Hawaii, 1970.

Bishop, Charles. *Commercial Journal*. 1894. 95 and 96. Honolulu: Mss. in Archives of Hawai'i.

Brigham, William T. *The Ancient Hawaiian House*. Honolulu: Bishop Museum Memoir, Vol. II, No. 3, 1908.

Broughton, W.R. *Voyage of Discovery to the North Pacific Ocean*. London, 1804.

Buck, Peter H. "War and Weapons." Section 10 in *Arts and Crafts of Hawaii*. 1957. Honolulu: Bishop Museum Special Publication No. 45, 1964.

Degener, Otto. *Plants of the Hawaii National Park*. 1930. Ann Arbor, MI: Edwards Bros., Inc., 1945.

Dibble, Sheldon. *History of the Sandwich Islands*. 1843. Honolulu: T.H., T.G. Thrum, 1909.

Ellis, William. *Journal of William Ellis. Narrative of a Tour of Hawaii. . . .* 1826. Rutland, VT and Japan: C.E. Tuttle, 1979.

Emerson, Nathaniel B. "Mamala-hoa." *Hawaiian Historical Society Report for 1903*. Honolulu: Hawaiian Historical Society, 1903.

Emory, Kenneth P. "Warfare." Ch. 21 in *Ancient Hawaiian Civilization*. A series of lectures delivered at the Kamehameha Schools by E.S.C. Handy [and others]. 1933. Rutland, VT and Japan: C.E. Tuttle, 1965 (rev. ed.).

Feher, Joseph. *Hawaii: A Pictorial History*. Honolulu: Bishop Museum Special Publication No. 58, 1969.

Force, Roland W., and Maryanne Force. *Arts and Artifacts of the 18th Century*. Honolulu: Bishop Museum Press, 1968.

Fornander, Abraham. *Hawaiian Antiquities and Folklore*. Honolulu: Bishop Museum Memoir, Vol. V, Part II, 1919.

———. *An Account of the Polynesian Race*. Vol. II. Rutland, VT and Japan: C.E. Tuttle, 1969.

Goldman, Irving. *Ancient Polynesian Society*. Chicago: University of Chicago Press, 1970.

Gowan, H. *The Napoleon of the Pacific*. New York: Fleming H. Revells Company, 1919.

Handy, E.S.C., Elizabeth G. Handy, and Mary K. Pukui. *Native Planters in Old Hawaii. Their Life, Lore and Environment*. Honolulu: Bishop Museum Bulletin No. 233, 1972.

Ii, John Papa. *Fragments of Hawaiian History*. Trans. Mary K. Pukui. 1959. Honolulu: Bishop Museum Press, 1963.

Jarves, James J. *History of the Hawaiian or Sandwich Islands*. Boston: Tappan and Dennet, 1843.

Kaeppler, Adrienne. "Artificial Curiosities." An exposition of native manufactures collected on the three Pacific voyages of Captain James Cook. Honolulu: Bishop Museum Special Publication No. 65, 1978.

Kamakau, Samuel M. *Ka Po'e Kahiko*. The people of old. Honolulu: Bishop Museum Special Publication No. 51, 1964.

———. *Ruling Chiefs of Hawai'i*. Honolulu: Kamehameha Schools Press, 1961.

———. *The Works of the People of Old*. Honolulu: Bishop Museum Special Publication No. 61, 1976.

Kane, Herbert K. "The Pathfinders." Seven paintings by Kane. *National Geographic Magazine*, December 1974.

Kenn, Charles W. "The Army and Navy of Kamehameha I." *U.S. Naval Institute Proceedings*. Washington, D.C., November 1945.

Kuykendall, Ralph S. *The Hawaiian Kingdom*. Vol. I: 1778-1854, Foundation and Transformation. Honolulu: University Press of Hawaii, 1938.

Lydgate, J. "The Defeat of Kamehameha, 1796." *Hawaiian Historical Society Annual Report* for 1928. Honolulu: Hawaiian Historical Society, 1928.

Malo, David. *Hawaiian Antiquities*. 1898. Honolulu: Bishop Museum Special Publication No. 2, 1976.

McAllister, J. Gilbert. *Archaeology of Oahu*. Honolulu: Bishop Museum Bulletin No. 104, 1933.

Mitchell, Donald D. Kilolani. *Hawaiian Treasures*. Warfare and Weapons, 59-69. Honolulu: Kamehameha Schools Press, 1978.

Pierce, Richard A. *Russia's Hawaiian Adventure, 1815-1817*. Berkeley and Los Angeles: University of California Press, 1965.

Portlock, Nathaniel. *A Voyage Round the World.* London, 1789.

Pratt, Helen G. *Hawaii, Off-shore Territory.* New York: Scribner's, 1944.

Sterling, Elspeth P., and Catherine C. Summers. *Sites of Oahu.* Honolulu: Department of Anthropology, Bishop Museum, 1978.

Warfield, Charles L. *History of the Hawaiian National Guard.* Feudal times to June 30, 1935. Honolulu: C.L. Warfield, 1935.

Wilson, William, ed. *With Lord Byron in the Sandwich Islands in 1825.* Extracts from the diary of James Macrae, botanist. Honolulu: J. Macrae, 1922.

READING LIST—GENERAL
Papa Heluhelu Laulaha

Chun, Malcolm N., ed. *Mo'olelo Hawai'i*. Honolulu: Kapiolani Community College, Folk Press, 1987. (Hawaiian antiquities.)

Day, A. Grove. *History Makers of Hawaii: A Biographical Dictionary*. Honolulu: Mutual Publishing, 1984.

Degener, Otto. *Ferns and Flowering Plants of Hawaii National Park*. Honolulu: Honolulu Star-Bulletin, 1930.

Fielding, Ann, and Ed Robinson. *An Underwater Guide to Hawaii*. Honolulu: University of Hawaii Press, 1987.

Foster, Nelson, et al. *Hawai'i, A Calendar of Natural Events*. Honolulu: Bishop Museum Press and Kamehameha Schools Press, 1988. (Profusely illustrated calendar with informative captions.)

Haselwood, E.L., et al. *Handbook of Hawaiian Weeds*. Indexed edition. Honolulu: University of Hawaii Press, 1983.

Hawaii Library Association. *Hawaiian Legends Index*. Honolulu, 1976.

Kanahele, George S. *Ku Kanaka—Stand Tall*. A search for Hawaiian values. Honolulu: University of Hawaii Press, 1986. (The author ponders the question, "Who and what is a Hawaiian and what is his or her importance in modern day society?")

Kaufman, Gregory D., and Paul H. Forestell. *Hawaii's Humpback Whales: A Complete Whalewatcher's Guide*. Maui, Hawaii: Pacific Whale Foundation Press, 1986.

Kepler, Angela K. *Hawaiian Heritage Plants*. Honolulu: Oriental Publishing Company, 1983.

Kirch, Patrick V. *Feathered Gods and Fishhooks*. An introduction to Hawaiian archeology and prehistory. Honolulu: University of Hawaii Press, 1985.

Kittleson, David J. *The Hawaiians, An Annotated Bibliography*. Honolulu: University of Hawaii Press, 1984.

Krauss, Bob. *Keneti, the South Seas Adventures of Kenneth Emory*. Honolulu: University of Hawaii Press, 1988.

Krauss, Bob, with William P. Alexander. *Grove Farm Plantation*. The biography of a Hawaiian sugar plantation. Palo Alto, CA: Pacific Books, 1965.

Kramer, Raymond J. *Hawaiian Land Mammals*. Rutland, VT and Japan: C.E. Tuttle, 1971.

Lamb, Samuel H. *Native Trees and Shrubs of the Hawaiian Islands*. Santa Fe, NM: Sunstone Press, 1981.

Luomala, Katharine. "The Native Dog in the Polynesian System of Values." In *Culture in History*. New York: Columbia University Press, 1960.

Mellen, George, ed. *The Sales Builder*. May 1937; April, June, 1938; June 1940.

Mill, Susan W., et al. *An Indexed Bibliography of the Flowering Plants of Hawaii*. Honolulu: University of Hawaii Press and Bishop Museum Press, 1989.

Nakanishi, Wendy. *Aquatic Birds of the Hawaiian Islands*. Printed text, film strips picturing the birds and a cassette tape-recording of the narration and the cries of the birds. Honolulu: Governor's Committee on Hawaiian Text Materials, 1973. (Distributed through the State Department of Education.)

Nakkim, Lynn K. *Mahele of Maui (Road to Hana)*. Honolulu: Seashore Press, 1984.

Peterson, Barbara B., ed. *Notable Women of Hawaii*. Honolulu: University of Hawaii Press, 1984.

Pukui, Mary K., and Samuel H. Elbert. *Hawaiian Dictionary*. Hawaiian-English and English-Hawaiian. Revised and enlarged. Honolulu: University of Hawaii Press, 1986.

Ronck, Ronn. *Ronck's Hawaii Almanac*. Honolulu: University of Hawaii Press, 1984.

Root, Eileen. *Hawaiian Names-English Names*. Kailua, Hawai'i: Press Pacifica, 1987.

Rotar, Peter P. *Grasses of Hawaii*. Honolulu: University of Hawaii Press, 1968.

Silva, Wendell and Alan Suemori, eds. *Nana I Na Loea Hula*. Look to the hula resources.

298

Honolulu: Kalihi-Palama Culture and Arts Society, 1984. (One hundred forty biographies and photos of hula resource experts.)

Spriggs, Matthew, and Patricia L. Tanaka. *Na Mea 'Imi I Ka Wa Kahiko.* An annotated bibliography of Hawaiian archeology. Honolulu: University of Hawaii Press, 1988.

Stone, Charles P. *Hawai'i's Terrestrial Ecosystems: Preservation and Management.* Honolulu: University of Hawaii, Cooperative National Park Resource Studies Unit, 1985.

Tinker, Spencer. *Animals of Hawaii.* Honolulu: Tongg Publishing Company, 1941.

Tomich, P. Quentin. *Mammals in Hawaii.* 1969. Honolulu: Bishop Museum Special Publication No. 57, 1986.

Valier, Kathy. *On the Na Pali Coast.* A guide for hikers and boaters. Honolulu: University of Hawaii Press, 1988.

Van Riper, Sandra, and Charles van Riper. *A Field Guide to the Mammals in Hawaii.* Honolulu: Oriental Publishing Company, 1982.

Vaughn, Palani. *Na Leo i ka Makani—Voices on the Wind.* Historic photographs of Hawaiians of yesteryear. Honolulu: Mutual Publishing Company, 1987.

INDEX
Papa Kuhikuhi